International Financial Reporting

PEARSON
Education

We work with leading authors to develop the strongest educational materials in accountancy, bringing cutting-edge thinking and best learning practice to a global market.

Under a range of well-known imprints, including Financial Times Prentice Hall, we craft high quality print and electronic publications which help readers to understand and apply their content, whether studying or at work.

To find out more about the complete range of our publishing, please visit us on the World Wide Web at: **www.pearsoned.co.uk**

Third Edition

International Financial Reporting
A Comparative Approach

CLARE ROBERTS

PAULINE WEETMAN

PAUL GORDON

FT Prentice Hall
FINANCIAL TIMES

An imprint of **Pearson Education**
Harlow, England • London • New York • Boston • San Francisco • Toronto • Sydney • Singapore • Hong Kong
Tokyo • Seoul • Taipei • New Delhi • Cape Town • Madrid • Mexico City • Amsterdam • Munich • Paris • Milan

Pearson Education Limited

Edinburgh Gate
Harlow
Essex CM20 2JE
England

and Associated Companies throughout the world

Visit us on the World Wide Web at:
www.pearsoned.co.uk

First published in Great Britain by Financial Times Professional Limited 1998

Second edition 2002
Third edition 2005

ISBN 0273-68118-4

British Library Cataloguing-in-Publication Data
A catalogue record for this book is available from the British Library.

Library of Congress Cataloging-in-Publication Data

10   9   8   7   6   5   4   3   2   1
07   06   05

Typeset by 68 in 9/12 Stone.
Printed by Ashford Colour Press Ltd., Gosport.

The publisher's policy is to use paper manufactured from sustainable forests.

Contents

Part 3 SIGNIFICANT INFLUENCES ON INTERNATIONAL ACCOUNTING PRACTICES

Part 4 FROM NATIONAL TO INTERNATIONAL STANDARDS

Part 5   INFORMING INTERNATIONAL EQUITY MARKETS

14   Investors and listed companies   575

15   Transparency and disclosure   611

Supporting resources

Visit **www.pearsoned.co.uk/roberts** to find valuable online resources

For instructors
- Complete, downloadable Learning Resources
- PowerPoint slides that can be downloaded and used as OHTs

For more information please contact your local Pearson Education sales representative or visit **www.pearsoned.co.uk/roberts**

Preface

Introduction

This third edition takes as its theme 'increasing harmonization in financial statements; mixed comparability and diversity in assurance and corporate reporting'.

January 2005 marked a significant stage in the move towards acceptance of international financial reporting standards (IFRS) as the basis for harmonizing financial statements. It was the date from which listed companies in member states of the European Union (EU) were required to apply IFRS in their consolidated financial statements, in place of the accounting standards of their home countries. Beyond Europe other countries have taken a range of attitudes. Some have adopted the IFRS in full; some have revised their national standards to incorporate the main aspects of IFRS with some local variation; others are still considering their options.

The third edition of this book reflects the contrasting forces of the focus on global harmonization, on the one hand, and the desire to retain some element of national identity control, on the other hand. The national identity remains most apparent in the regulation of assurance of the quality of financial statements and in the wider narrative reporting that accompanies the financial statements.

In an ideal world there would be no further scope for a comparative study of international financial reporting because harmonization would be complete. In reality, differences persist. Although the International Organization of Securities Commissions (IOSCO) endorsed IFRS in 2000, it left an option for individual securities commissions to scrutinize the IFRS and add further conditions to them. The IASB has faced the challenge of establishing confidence in its independence as a standard setter, while having no direct powers of enforcement or scrutiny. In the period from 2000 to 2005 we observed the legislators of two major economic groupings (the EU and the US) using the language of 'convergence' while preserving territorial positions. The European Commission retained its right of political control over the legal process across member states. The Securities and Exchange Commission of the United States awaited reassurance about mechanisms for enforcement of high-quality international accounting standards that would retain a level playing field for US companies.

The challenge to accounting standards took a new direction following the collapse of a major US company, Enron, which showed that even the US accounting standards were not immune from criticism. It seemed that the mechanisms of corporate governance and regulatory oversight were inadequate to protect stakeholders. Further corporate scandals indicated that problems of this kind could exist in large listed companies in countries beyond the US.

Corporate failures caused a major loss of confidence for investors in global markets. To restore confidence, the processes of corporate governance and assurance (including audit) have been revised significantly in many countries, although regulation remains primarily under national laws. We are now aware that the implementation of any system of financial reporting is critically dependent on the quality of the corporate governance and assurance mechanisms of the national regulator.

As a separate aspect of accountability for social and environmental matters, there has been increasing emphasis on corporate social reporting (CSR) to the point where high-quality CSR information is seen as essential by those evaluating investment possibilities. Information about responsibilities to employees, customers, communities and society in general is now a common feature of many annual reports. It is part of the wider focus on narrative reporting to explain the activities of the business.

In this third edition we aim to provide insight into the areas of comparability, and the persistence of diversity, in the corporate annual reports of listed companies across global markets. We also indicate how national diversity may continue to be significant for non-listed companies and for reporting in a national context. All the developments we have described in this introduction are fascinating to researchers and we have built into the third edition a wide range of examples of research studies in this area that will be of interest to students and may offer ideas for their own future research projects.

Aim of the book

This text aims to bring to undergraduate and postgraduate courses in accounting and finance an awareness of similarities and differences in accounting practices and an ability to analyze the causes and consequences of those similarities and differences. There is a strong emphasis placed on IASB Standards as the focus of comparison.

The book aims also to familiarize students with the growing body of research into international accounting practices, giving detailed explanation of research methods that may encourage students to apply such techniques in project work.

Structure of the book

The book is divided into five modules (Parts 1 to 5) each of which deals with a separate aspect of international corporate reporting. The full text is suitable for a full 15-week semester but the modular structure allows lecturers to plan selectively for shorter courses.

The third edition starts in Part 1 by describing in Chapter 1 the achievements of the IASB in establishing its position as an international standard setter and explaining in Chapter 2 how the IFRS have developed to be more rigorous in application. Chapter 3, entirely new to this edition, provides a new feature by exploring the complex framework of assurance mechanisms that have been established to give credibility to international and national reporting practices. It reflects the actions taken by a wide range of institutions, both statutory and voluntary, to restore confidence in financial reporting after the Asian economic crisis and the collapse of Enron in the US.

Part 2 presents the well-regarded analytical focus of the book by setting the analytical framework for the study of accounting practice and explaining the methods used in various types of comparative reporting study. The institutional framework is described in Chapter 4, covering in general terms the influence of the political system, the economic system, the legal system, the tax system, the financing system and the accounting profession. Cultural influences on accounting rules and practice are critically evaluated in Chapter 5 using well-known academic sources. Classification of accounting systems, as presented in Chapter 6, provides a framework indicating international similarities and differences. Practical approaches to measuring international differences in accounting rules and practices are presented in Chapter 7, drawing on methods established in the research literature that are suitable for student project applications.

Part 3 describes two powerful forces that are shaping the development of international standards: the US with its system of US GAAP and the EU with 25 member states committed to the application of IFRS from 2005. The accounting system in the US is a rival to the IFRS as a potential global accounting system. The approach taken by the EU in undertaking to require all listed companies to use IFRS from 2005 has given a major endorsement to IFRS.

Part 4 describes how a selection of countries have moved towards adoption of IFRS. We have included in our selection two countries with strongly established capital markets (UK and Japan), three countries with established capital markets in Europe (France, Germany and The Netherlands) and two countries that are still at relatively early stages of development of capital markets (Poland and China). In these country chapters we relate accounting developments to the institutional environment within which accounting practice operates. We recognize that whatever selection we make does not please everyone; to meet this concern there is further information on other countries in the Lecturer's Guide provided to accompany this edition.

Part 5 takes us to the international capital markets with a discussion in Chapter 14 of the motivations and strategies of investors and listed companies who operate across national boundaries in investing and in issuing shares. Chapter 15 is new to this edition and reflects the growing importance of narrative reporting in achieving transparency in financial reporting. The chapter explains and illustrates the range of approaches taken by companies to improve transparency through disclosure. Chapter 16 is also new to this edition and explains the significant achievements of IFRS in bringing harmonization to accounting regulation and practice in three areas: business combinations; segmental reporting; and foreign currency translation.

Particular features

We have retained from previous editions the features that students and lecturers have identified as particularly helpful:

- *there is a strong emphasis on IASB Standards* as a basis for convergence of accounting measurement and disclosure, with explanation of how the IASB is receiving careful and serious attention from standard-setting authorities in many countries;
- *experienced researchers* show how the methods used in research papers may be understood and applied in undergraduate honours and postgraduate courses;
- *linking themes across chapters* explain harmonized accounting and national reporting differences in the context of an institutional framework, a cultural perspective and a comparison with IFRS;
- *examples of accounting practices* drawn from published accounts;
- *names of major companies* in each country are given as a guide to students intending to investigate further;
- *case studies* are drawn from practice and from research studies to illustrate the general points of principle contained in early chapters;
- *end-of-chapter questions* encourage students to analyze and compare the information within and between chapters;
- *an accompanying Lecturer's Guide* assists students and lecturers in the practical exploration of the wealth of material available for study of aspects of international

accounting. This Guide is available free to lecturers adopting this text and can be accessed via a Supplement download site at www.pearsoned.co.uk/roberts

New features of this edition are:

- *focus on accountability in corporate reporting*;
- *description of corporate governance and assurance initiatives* that have developed out of Enron and other major corporate failures;
- *transparency and disclosure through narrative information* in annual reports, explaining the legislation and guidance available and giving examples of the range of practices that have emerged;
- *the development of financial reporting practices across Europe* is integrated in one chapter with particular reference to Poland as the largest economy entering the EU in the 2004 enlargement.

Flexible course design

The material in this book is sufficient for a full semester's course of study, in the typical half-year semester lasting around 15 weeks. For shorter periods the modular structure allows selection of relevant material. For a course focusing on the comparison of IASB and US GAAP as global influences on European accounting, Parts 1 and 3, with Chapter 10, would form a suitable basis. For a study of research methods in comparative financial reporting, Part 2 with Chapters 14 and 15 give methods of research and their application. To contrast the rate of implementation of IFRS in different regimes, Part 1 with Chapters 10 and 12 would provide an interesting comparison between Europe and Japan. For those wishing to establish a basis for comparative financial analysis, Part 1 with Chapters 14 and 16 give the basis for understanding and comparing consolidated financial statements.

Target readership

This book is targeted at final-year undergraduate students on degree courses in accounting or business studies. It is also appropriate for use in a core module of a specialist postgraduate MSc taught course or an MBA. It has an international perspective, in its basis of IFRS, and so is not restricted to study within a particular country. It is also a useful basis for research students in planning research projects in comparative financial reporting.

The book should also be of interest to professional readers and general management because it focuses on analysis of financial statements rather than techniques of preparation of accounts.

Support material: project work and tutorial guidance

For students learning about comparative accounting practices, it is essential to have first-hand experience of that practice. This means students must handle, read, observe and think about accounting information as it appears in practice. It may be in printed annual reports; increasingly it is also available on company websites.

As a first step in familiarization we have included selected Exhibits in the country chapters. In the student section of the Lecturer's Guide we suggest questions that will help students to think about the Exhibits and may help the tutor in guiding discussion. We also suggest tutorial question sheets for every chapter.

The next step for students is to carry out project work with company material. In this way they discover the practical problems of reading and understanding annual reports that we have all experienced as researchers and that equity analysts experience in practice. To make efficient use of class time we have provided project material in the Lecturer's Guide available via the Supplement download site. We also give the project assignment sheets and instructions for students. The projects and relevant materials cover:

- relating perceptions of culture to accounting values;
- comparisons of accounting policies and harmonization measures;
- disclosure and measurement practices, with the comparability index;
- assessment of voluntary disclosure;
- reconciliation statements; and
- the use of web-based materials.

Companion website

On the Companion website, **www.pearsoned.co.uk/roberts**, lecturers will find project material that can be downloaded, as well as tutorial notes and guidance on end-of-chapter questions. Lecturers will find overheads for lectures and ideas on how to plan and assess teaching.

Acknowledgements

The authors have used much of the material of this text in their respective teaching assignments with final-year and postgraduate students and are appreciative of feedback from students in several universities.

They are grateful to the following reviewers of the international chapters for the first edition:

Australia

Chris Kelly
Senior Lecturer
Deakin University
Geelong
Victoria 3217

China

Professor Zhengfei Lu
School of International Business
Nanjing University
22 Hankou Road
Nanjing
Jiangsu 210008

France

Professor Jean-Claude Scheid
Conservatoire National des Arts et Métiers
Institut National des Techniques Économiques et Comptables (INTEC)
292 Rue St Martin
Paris 75141

Germany

Professor Dr Wolfgang Ballwieser
Ludwig-Maximilians-Universität
Seminar für Rechnungswesen und Prüfung
Ludwigstrasse 28/RG
Munich 80539

Hungary

Professor Derek Bailey
Thames Valley University
St Mary's Road
London W5 5RF

Japan

Professor Kazuo Hiramatsu
School of Business Administration
Kwansei Gakuin University
1-1-155 Uegahara Nishinomiya
Hyogo 662

The Netherlands

D H van Offeren
Assistant Professor of Accounting
University of Amsterdam
Roetersstraat 11
1018 WB Amsterdam

US

Professor James A Schweikart
Dept of Accounting
E. Claiborn Robins School of Business
University of Richmond
Virginia 23173

In moving to the third edition the authors are grateful for helpful observations from Professor Steve Zeff; for suggestions in relation to Chapter 13 from Professor Simon Gao and Professor Jason Xiao; for a summary of a literature review in Chapter 7 from Dr Nazli Mohd Anum Ghazali; and for information in Chapter 10 from Dr Marek Schroeder.

Particular thanks for encouragement and support with the second edition must go to Richard Whitbread, Anna Herbert and Sadie McClelland at Pearson Education. For the third edition the authors are grateful for the support of Paula Harris and Paul Mitchell at Pearson Education.

Publisher's acknowledgements

We are grateful to the following for permission to reproduce copyright material:

Exhibit 1.8 from International Accounting Standards Committee Foundation, Annual Report (2003), Statement of Activities. Reproduced with permission © IASCF (www.iasb.org); Exhibit 3.6 from List of Auditing Standards at 2002: IASplus China Newsletter April 2002 © Deloitte Touche Tohmaiju; Exhibit 4.6 from International Share Ownership from Australian Stock Exchange (June 2003), permission of Australian Stock Exchange; Exhibit 5.1 from Gray, *Accounting Foundation* (1988). Published by Blackwell Publishing Ltd; Exhibit 6.6 reprinted from Accounting Organizations and Society, Vol 1, D'Arcy, *Accounting classification*, pp 327–349, (2001) with permission from Elsevier; Exhibit 6.9 from Gray *Two-Dimensional Classifications* (1988). Published by Blackwell Publishing Ltd; Exhibits 6.12 and 7.2 from Nobes's Proposed Hierarchical Classification of Accounting Systems (1998), *Abacus* Vol 34 p 181. Published by Blackwell Publishing Limited; Exhibit 7.1 extracted from Deloitte & Touche, VNO-NCW (2002) reprinted with permission of Deloitte Accountants BV; Exhibit 7.14 reprinted from The Conservatism Principle and the Asymmetric Timeliness of Earnings, in *Journal of Accounting and Economics*, Vol 24 p 3–37, with permission from Elsevier, (Basu, 1997); Appendix 7.2 from PhD thesis by Dr. Nazli Anum Mohd Ghazali, reprinted with kind permission; Exhibits 8.1, 10.1, 11.1, 12.2, 13.1 and 13.17 from *The Pocket World in Figures 2004* reprinted with permission Profile Books Limited; Exhibits 8.7 and 8.9 from Altria Group Inc. Annual Report (2003) pp 42–3 and 44; Exhibit 8.10 from Pfizer Annual Report (2003) p 23, reproduced with permission of Pfizer Inc. All rights reserved; Exhibit 10.3 from Accounting Standard Setting in Europe, FEE 2000, by permission of Fédération des Experts-Compatables Européens; Exhibit 10.14 from FEE survey of Enforcement Mechanisms in Europe (2001) p 12, by permission of Fédération des Experts-Compatables Européens; Exhibit 10.19 from Balance Sheet of Parent Company, Alcatel, reproduced with kind permission of Alcatel SA; Exhibit 11.5 from National Statistics www.statistics.gov.uk; Exhibit 12.7 from Organization of the Financial Accounting Standards Foundation, (2001). By permission of Financial Accounting Standards Foundation; Exhibit 12.8 from Organisation of the ASBJ (2004) by permission of Financial Accounting Standards Foundation; Exhibit 12.10 from Consolidated Accounts in *Journal of Accounting and Public Policy*, McKinnon and Harrison, p 209, (1985) with permission from Elsevier; Exhibit 15.2 from BT Annual Report (2004). © BT Plc; Exhibit 12.11 from Japanese Corporate Groupings and the Informativeness of Earnings in *Journal of International Financial Management and Accounting*, published by Blackwell Publishing Limited, Douthett E.B. and Jung K. (2001) 12(2) pp 133–159. www.blackwell-synergy.com; Exhibit 14.17 from Acceptance and Observance of International Accounting Standards in *International Journal of Accounting*, Elsevier, Street, D.L., Gray, S.J. and Bryant, S.M. Vol 34 pp 11–48, (1999); Exhibit 15.1 from Patel, S. Balic, A., Bwakira, L., Bradley, S. and Dallas, G., *Transparency and Disclosure Study – Europe*, (April 2003). Published by Standard & Poor's, a division of The McGraw-Hill Companies, Inc.; Exhibit 15.2 from BT Annual Report and Form 20-F (2004), p 154. © BT Plc; Exhibit 15.7 from Motorola Annual Report (2002) © Motorola Inc.; Exhibit 16.15 from Nestlé Annual Report (2003) pp 19–22, © Nestlé SA, Switzerland; Exhibit 16.16 from Unilever plc Annual Report and Accounts (2002) © Unilever plc and Unilever N.V.

We are grateful to the various companies whose annual reports we refer to in this book for permission to reproduce their copyright material.

We are grateful to the Financial Times Limited for permission to reprint the following material:

Exhibit 10.10, Europe 500 analysed by country, © *Financial Times*, 27 May 2004.

In some instances we have been unable to trace the owners of copyright material, and we would appreciate any information that would enable us to do so.

Plan of the book

Part 1 SETTING AND REGULATING INTERNATIONAL FINANCIAL REPORTING STANDARDS		
Chapter 1 Developing global accounting standards	Chapter 2 International financial reporting standards	Chapter 3 Confidence and assurance

Part 2 CONTRASTING HARMONIZATION AND DIVERSITY ACROSS FINANCIAL REPORTING SYSTEMS			
Chapter 4 Institutional and external influences	Chapter 5 Cultural influences	Chapter 6 Classification of accounting systems	Chapter 7 Measuring harmonization and diversity

Part 3 SIGNIFICANT INFLUENCES ON INTERNATIONAL ACCOUNTING PRACTICES	
Chapter 8 The United States	Chapter 9 The European Union

Part 4 FROM NATIONAL TO INTERNATIONAL STANDARDS			
Chapter 10 Europe	Chapter 11 United Kingdom	Chapter 12 Japan	Chapter 13 China

Part 5 INFORMING INTERNATIONAL EQUITY MARKETS		
Chapter 14 Investors and listed companies	Chapter 15 Transparency and disclosure	Chapter 16 Issues in multinational accounting

PART 1

Setting and regulating international financial reporting standards

Introduction to Part 1

In Chapters 1 and 2 we explain in detail the most ambitious and far-reaching influence for harmonization, represented by the work of the International Accounting Standards Board (IASB) and its predecessor the International Accounting Standards Committee (IASC). The IASB and IASC have not worked in isolation, as Chapter 1 shows in describing the multitude of bodies and groups which have worked towards particular aspects of harmonization across particular country groupings. However, the work of the IASB and IASC has provided a comprehensive set of IASB Standards, described in Chapter 2. To some extent, that work lay in the background of national accounting standard-setting for many years; it has now come to the fore in a very visible manner because of the desire to achieve a set of standards that are acceptable to stock exchange regulators in markets around the world.

Chapter 3 is new to this edition and reflects the enormity of changes in corporate governance and assurance across many countries. There have been events, particularly the Asian economic crisis of 1997 and the collapse of Enron in 2001, that have severely shaken confidence in accounting information. Restoring confidence and providing assurance in the integrity and reliability of financial reporting has posed a major challenge to regulators around the world. Chapter 3 leads with the Sarbanes–Oxley Act of 2002 in the US, described as the most significant legislation in the US since that of the 1930s, following the Wall Street crash. Chapter 3 explains the procedures taken in a range of countries in recent years to establish or reinforce confidence in the financial reporting systems of companies.

Purpose of Part 1

The chapters of Part 1 have two major aims. The first is to explain the workings of the IASB and the standards (IAS and IFRS) that it is controlling. The second is to explain the system of assurance and audit that surrounds the implementation of IFRS.

Part 1 forms a self-contained module that describes the system of reporting and assurance facing listed companies that have chosen, or are obliged, to use global standards. If they are using IFRS then they face the challenges of implementing the standards described in Chapter 2 and they will probably be drawn into the processes of consultation described in Chapter 1. If they are using US GAAP, either by choice or by compulsion, they may be closer to satisfying the US regulators but may be less comparable to the growing body of companies using IFRS. Chapter 1 described the convergence project that is removing some of the differences between IFRS and US GAAP. Whatever the global reporting system used, companies face the requirements of assurance demanded by the organizations described in Chapter 3.

Learning outcomes

Specific learning outcomes are set out at the start of each chapter but overall, on completion of Part 1, the student should be able to:

- explain and discuss the work of the IASB in setting a system of international reporting standards;
- explain and discuss the key features of each IAS and IFRS, knowing the main steps in development of each standard;
- explain and discuss the mechanisms for audit and assurance that have been formed in recent years in response to crises of confidence caused by major financial collapses.

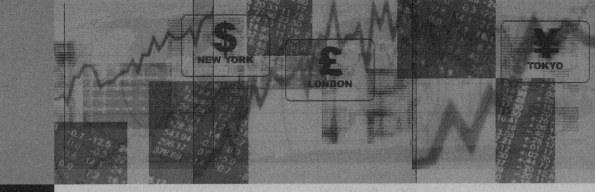

1 Developing global accounting standards

Learning outcomes

After reading this chapter you should be able to:

● Discuss the arguments for and against global accounting standards.

● Describe the main international organizations that are encouraging international cooperation.

● Explain the nature and operations of the IASB.

● Understand the challenges facing the IASB in its work.

● Understand the key stages of historical development of international accounting standards.

● Describe the main features of the Framework for the Preparation and Presentation of Financial Statements.

● Explain how multinational companies demonstrate their use of global accounting standards.

1.1 Introduction

The main purpose of this chapter is to establish a comprehensive knowledge and understanding of the nature and operation of the International Accounting Standards Board (IASB) and the development of International Financial Reporting Standards (IFRS) that are capable of achieving wide international acceptance. The work of the IASB is set in the context of other organizations supporting global harmonization. To maintain a critical understanding of the achievements of the IASB it is important to be able to weigh the benefits of global standards against the limitations of losing national identity. We begin with a summary of the support for, and opposition to, global accounting standards. We then explain the wider range of activities towards global and regional harmonization before explaining in detail the IASB and its operations. We summarize the conceptual framework underpinning IFRS and conclude with a description of the variety of ways in which multinational companies show their use of global standards.

1.2 Global accounting standards: support and opposition

1.2.1 The case for global accounting standards

Exhibit 1.1 sets out a simple statement of the argument for having global accounting standards that are accepted and applied in all countries for all companies. Read this statement and think about whether you agree with it.

We know that companies do find themselves reporting different measures of profit and net assets in different capital markets, solely because different accounting rules are applied.

| Exhibit 1.1 | An argument in favour of global accounting standards |

> Accounting is essentially concerned with measurement, so it would be reasonable to expect that principles of measurement should be the same in any country. The language used to add words of explanation may differ but the reported values should not be affected by barriers of language. Companies operating and reporting in more than one country should not experience different measures of financial outcomes solely because of the accounting principles of the country in which the head office is located.

Exhibit 1.2 gives examples based on companies' annual reports where these companies are required to report profits using two different sets of accounting rules. We know about these differences because the companies provide the information to stock market regulators in other countries. However, in many cases companies only report in their home stock market and so we never know how much the reported accounting profit or loss depends on the nature of the accounting rules.

We also know that even before the European Union made IFRS compulsory for listed companies in 2005, increasing numbers of companies were using IFRS or US GAAP in preference to their national standards in group accounts.[1] There was an increasing competition between the two systems as to which would take the international lead. So let us explore further the benefits to companies of having one set of accounting standards that can be applied anywhere in the world. There are benefits to the companies in

| Exhibit 1.2 | Reported differences in profit under different accounting rules |

Comparing US GAAP and UK GAAP

ScottishPower (2003/4 annual report p.114)

	£m
Profit for the year under UK GAAP	482.6
Profit for the year under US GAAP	789.3
Difference as a % of US GAAP	38.9%

Comparing US GAAP and Norwegian GAAP

Norsk Hydro (2003 annual report, Note 28)

	NOK million
Operating profit for the year under Norwegian GAAP	23,948
Operating profit for the year under US GAAP	24,358
Difference as a % of US GAAP	1.7%

Comparing Chinese (PRC) GAAP and IFRS

China Petroleum & Chemical Corporation (2003 Annual Report, p.160)

	RMB millions
Net profit under the PRC Accounting Rules and Regulations	19,011
Net profit under IFRS	21,593
Difference as a % of IFRS	12.0%

---

[1] Haller (2002), Tarca (2004).

preparing information, to investors and other stakeholders in using information, and to national governments and other regulators in ensuring that the business of a company operating in their country gives a fair benefit to the country.

For *multinational companies* the availability of one set of global accounting standards reduces the costs compared with dual reporting. At present stock exchange regulators, particularly the Securities and Exchange Commission (SEC) in the US, may require a foreign registrant company to prepare financial statements using a set of accounting standards familiar to the stock exchange. Even if the company does not have to produce a full set of financial statements, it may have to produce a 'reconciliation' statement explaining the differences between reported profit and reported net assets under two different sets of accounting standards. This dual reporting involves additional costs of preparation and may confuse readers who cannot understand why accounting numbers are different when the operations of the business are unchanged.

The benefits to multinational companies of having one set of global accounting standards are:

- reduction in costs;
- reduction in the risk of uncertainty and misunderstanding;
- more effective communication with investors;
- comparability within the group of parent and subsidiaries in different countries;
- comparability with other companies in the industry, nationally and internationally;
- comparability of contractual terms, such as lending contracts and management performance bonuses;
- reduction in excuses for non-disclosure based on national perceptions of secrecy;
- sharing and extending best practice.

For *investors*, the benefits of global accounting standards lie in having assurance about the comparability and the high standard of the accounting information provided. We know from research[2] that even professional fund managers do not fully understand the complexities of comparing accounting information prepared under different rules. One of the ways in which they cope with this uncertainty is to avoid investing in companies whose accounting they do not understand. This may well lead to missed opportunities for those whose investments are being managed. The benefits to investors of having one set of global accounting standards are:

- reduces the cost of obtaining information by reducing the need to learn different accounting systems;
- reduces the likelihood of making poor decisions by reducing the risk of misunderstanding different accounting systems;
- reduces the risk of missing investment opportunities through avoiding unfamiliar national accounting;[3]
- allows investors to focus on global comparability of activity across industries rather than being confined to investments within particular countries;
- helps investors whose attention is limited because of the amount of information available and the limits to information processing power.[4]

---

[2] Miles and Nobes (1998).

[3] Miles and Nobes (1998).

[4] Hirshleifer and Teoh (2003).

For *national governments*, accounting information gives a basis for taxation and for ensuring that companies operating in their country show sufficient care for the resources used in the country. Some national governments set accounting rules in legislation. Others allow independent standard-setting bodies to set national standards. In either case there is a cost of establishing and reviewing the accounting standards. Very often we see cases where the national accounting regulations of one country look much like those of another and it seems wasteful of time and effort to develop national rules that are almost identical to established rules that appear to work well elsewhere. There is also a need for those who regulate the national stock markets to ensure that there is a fair market for investors. So if the national government and national regulators can accept a set of global standards there are benefits in:

- reducing the cost of setting and monitoring national accounting regulation;
- avoiding duplication of effort across national boundaries;
- encouraging international flows of capital across national borders;
- giving greater confidence to international investors and lenders;
- developing countries having access to high quality standards;[5]
- reducing pressure on national governments from multinationals.[6]

1.2.2 Questioning the trend towards uniformity

For those who support the need for convergence on one set of global standards, the next question is 'which set to choose'? This is the first point of disagreement because some believe that generally accepted accounting principles in the US (US GAAP) provide a high quality set of standards that would be acceptable anywhere in the world. Others believe that a more neutral approach is to draw on the international financial reporting standards (IFRS) of the International Accounting Standards Board (IASB).[7] Some feel that IFRS are closely influenced by the Anglo-American model and have a homogeneity that does not recognize national diversity.[8] Mutual recognition of different approaches, with benchmarks to guide comparability, would be more respectful of different identities. The US regulators take the view that US standards are high quality and question anything that does not meet the detailed content of US GAAP. Other countries take the view that US rules are biased towards US needs and want to have a direct involvement in setting a truly international set of standards. This second view has been helped greatly by the European Commission recommending that, from 2005, all listed companies in EU member states will apply IFRS. Other countries have adopted, or adapted, IFRS in their national accounting regulations. The debate is not yet resolved and so this book will start with a detailed discussion of the work of the IASB and the IFRS it sets, but it will also give detail of the US system of financial reporting as a potential alternative global approach.

Among those who ask more fundamental questions about convergence on one set of global standards, some ask 'what creates true harmony?'. McLeay *et al.* (1999) argue that the level of harmony depends on adopting the same accounting method under the

---

[5] Chamisa (2000).

[6] Rahman (1998).

[7] Leuz (2003).

[8] Hoarau (1995).

same circumstances (such as across the same industry), rather than forcing uniformity on all companies regardless of circumstances.

Others question the suitability of either US GAAP or IFRS. Both are written for companies in highly developed capital markets. They are then used as a basis for an accounting system in developing economies that have little or no capital market transactions, and may not be appropriate to such economies.[9] There have been stages in the development of the IASB, and its predecessor IASC, when projects were begun with the intention of focusing on developing economies, but relatively little has emerged.

For *national companies* with little or no international need for support or financing, the benefit of international standards, rather than national standards, may be limited. Particular problems are:

- national companies have limited opportunities to influence an international standard setter;
- the company's business and economic circumstances may not be faithfully represented by the prescribed accounting procedures of the global standard.

For *investors* the use of global standards may appear intuitively appealing but the investors may not understand the basis on which the standards have been written, particularly the strong focus on serving the needs of developed capital markets. Limitations for investors are:

- using global standards gives an appearance of comparability but hides real differences in commercial activity;
- the use of global standards, particularly in the early years of changeover, can cause confusion nationally, especially if the global standards are seen as reducing precision.[10]

For *national governments* the attraction of saving costs may be outweighed by the loss of control over the nature and content of the accounting standards. Also the government still has the task of ensuring compliance with the standards. Limitations for national governments are:

- There is no reason to believe that 'one system fits all'.
- Harmonizing on full disclosure may be detrimental to developing countries by putting them at a competitive disadvantage.[11]
- Developing countries may not be able to influence global standards as much as developed countries.[12]
- Global standards are not essential for companies operating within a single country.
- Comparability of financial reporting standards needs comparability of compliance.
- Incentives for companies to avoid compliance may dominate, so that high-quality standards do not guarantee high-quality financial reporting.[13]
- Having a monopoly standard setter rather than competitive standards may lead to poorer standards.[14]

---

[9] Larson and Kenny (1995).

[10] Barth *et al.* (1999).

[11] Kirby (2001).

[12] Rahman (1998).

[13] Ball *et al.* (2003), Holthausen (2003).

[14] Sunder (2002).

1.2.3 Harmonization or standardization?

Even when there is agreement that the benefits of global accounting standards outweigh the limitations, there is still a question of 'What kind of standards?'. Do we want harmonization leading to harmony, or standardization leading to uniformity? **Harmonization** is a process by which accounting moves away from total diversity of practice. The end result is the state of **harmony** where all participants in the process cluster around one of the available methods of accounting, or around a limited number of very closely related methods. **Standardization** is a process by which all participants agree to follow the same or very similar accounting practices. Where this agreement is achieved, the end result is a state of **uniformity**.[15]

Those who support an aim of achieving **harmony** take a liberal view of what is meant by similarity of accounting method. It may be achieved as a result of natural forces such as changes in culture, growth of economic groupings, international trade, political dependency, or evolution of new securities markets. Such forces cause enterprises, accounting organizations or national regulators to learn from and imitate each other's practices. International organizations seeking to promote harmony are usually formed by groups of like-minded individuals or representatives of national organizations, who try to use powers of persuasion and argument to promote harmonization.

Those who support an aim of achieving **uniformity** take a much stricter view of what is meant by the same or very similar accounting practices. Achievement of uniformity within a defined period of time requires the intervention of a regulator or facilitator. The regulator may try to use powers of persuasion and argument to establish a body of support but eventually the powers of enforcement are used to ensure full compliance, with penalties being applied for non-compliance.

1.3 Organizations supporting international cooperation

Before we move into the detailed study of the work of the International Accounting Standards Board, we provide a flavour of the organizations around the world that are seeking to harmonize aspects of international accounting practice or at least to foster understanding. Some are private-sector federations of interested bodies, some are governmental or intergovernmental organizations, and some others rely on committed individuals for their continuity.

The following sections explain a variety of leading international accountancy organizations. Some operate at a regional level defined by geographic linking of more than one country or state. Others have a worldwide level of operation, although membership and geographical coverage may vary from one to the next.

1.3.1 Regional accountancy bodies

Regional accountancy bodies are in the main non-governmental organizations (NGOs). Although at the outset a number of these bodies had ambitions to develop accounting standards, little real success has been achieved. Most of these regional professional organizations have concentrated their energies on educational matters, organization of conferences and the general dissemination of information to their

---

[15] Tay and Parker (1990).

members and the wider business community. Some have acted as effective pressure groups at global level, ensuring that their distinctive regional voice is heard in the international accounting standard-setting process. The leading regional accountancy bodies are listed in Exhibit 1.3.

The lack of any significant progress in standard setting by regional bodies is partly due to the problem of enforcement. Non-governmental bodies generally lack the

Exhibit 1.3	The leading regional accountancy bodies

ECSAFA	**Eastern, Central and Southern African Federation of Accountants** This is a body which represents professional accountancy bodies in the region. www.ecsafa.org
ABWA	**Association of Accountancy Bodies in West Africa** Members are Nigeria, Ghana, Liberia, Sierra Leone and Senegal. www.ican-ngr.org/affiliates/affil.htm
AFA	**Association of Southeast Asian Nations (ASEAN) Federation of Accountants** The economic linkages fostered by ASEAN led naturally to the linking of professional accountants. Brunei, Indonesia, Malaysia, the Philippines, Singapore and Thailand are the member nations. www.afa-central.com
CAPA	**Confederation of Asian and Pacific Accountants** Established by professional accountancy bodies as a forum for discussion of accounting problems met by accountants in Asia and Pacific countries. www.capa.com.my
FEE	**Fédération des Experts Comptables Européens (Federation of European Accountants)** Brings together professional bodies from European countries, including but not restricted to the EU, to work towards enhancing European harmonization. www.fee.be
NRF	**Nordic Federation of Public Accountants** The NRF includes Denmark, Finland, Iceland, Norway and Sweden. www.nrfaccount.se
ASCA	**Arab Society of Certified Accountants** ASCA was established in London in 1984 as an Arab professional institution with an international character. It has members in Bahrain, Egypt, Emirates, Jordan, Kuwait, Libya, Oman, Palestine, Saudi Arabia, Syria, Tunisia, Yemen. www.ascasociety.org
IAA	**Interamerican Accounting Association** Membership covers accountancy bodies in countries of Central and South America. Activities include translation of International Accounting Standards. Works closely with IFAC.
ICAC	**Institute of Chartered Accountants of the Caribbean** Members are the chartered accountancy bodies of The Bahamas, Barbados, Belize, Guyana, Jamaica, St Kitts-Nevis, St Lucia, Trinidad and Tobago, Antigua and Barbuda. www.icac.org.jm

power to insist on compliance with their rules. For a regional accounting standard-setting body to be effective one of the following methods of enforcement would be required:

- the professional accountancy bodies or auditing authorities of each member state of the region agree to apply or approve the regional standards rather than national variations;
- those who govern companies (management or regulators) in each member state agree to apply or approve the regional standards rather than national variations;
- national legislators or standard setters agree on the use of common regional standards;
- national stock exchanges agree to accept the standards defined on a regional basis.

The first two of these conditions have not generally been achieved, probably because business which crosses national boundaries is international in nature rather than being contained to a specific region linking a group of companies or states. Standardization has required the intervention of wider groupings of accountancy bodies and interested persons, intergovernmental organizations, and action by securities markets at an international level.

1.3.2 Wider groupings of accountancy bodies and interested persons

There are organizations which have formed to link accountancy bodies and interested persons across national boundaries (see Exhibit 1.4). These have all formed as a result of various voluntary initiatives. They are not driven by national governments.

Central to international cooperation in accounting is the International Federation of Accountants (IFAC). Formed in 1977, its members are professional accountancy bodies in many countries. The mission of IFAC is to serve the public interest, strengthen the accountancy profession worldwide and contribute to the development of strong international economies by establishing and promoting adherence to high-quality professional standards, furthering the international convergence of such standards, and speaking out on public interest issues where the profession's expertise is most relevant. In relation to its members IFAC acts as leader, facilitator, collaborator and observer.[16]

The IFAC Council contains one representative from each member body. It meets once each year to elect the IFAC Board and to discuss changes to the Constitution. The IFAC Board contains 21 members from 17 countries. These members are elected for three-year terms and are responsible for setting policy and overseeing IFAC operations, the implementation of programmes, and the work of IFAC technical committees and task forces. The Board meets three times a year. Detailed work is carried out by the technical committees and task forces, supported by a full-time Secretariat headquartered in New York.

Each committee is given responsibility in particular technical areas of IFAC work covering auditing, education, ethics and the public sector. From the perspective of published financial information perhaps the most important work is that of the IAASB (see Chapter 3). International Standards on Auditing (ISAs) are intended for international acceptance.

---

[16] IFAC Constitution, revised (2003).

Exhibit 1.4	Organizations of accountancy bodies and interested persons linking across national boundaries

IFAC — **International Federation of Accountants**
Supports IASB as source of international accounting standards. Important work in the area of auditing is done by IAASB (see below). IFAC also has committees dealing with Education, Ethics, Financial and management accounting, and the Public sector. Organizes World Congress of Accountants every five years.
www.ifac.org

IFAD — **International Forum on Accountancy Development**
Brings together development banks, agencies and international accounting firms to discuss coordinating resources when assisting nations to develop the profession. Encouraged by IFAC.
www.ifad.net

IAASB — **International Auditing and Assurance Standards Board**
A committee of IFAC (see above). Issues International Standards on Auditing. Aims to establish high quality auditing, assurance, quality control and related services standards and to improve the uniformity of practice by professional accountants throughout the world.
www.ifac.org/IAASB

IASB — **International Accounting Standards Board**
Founded by private-sector professional accountancy bodies with the purpose of issuing International Financial Reporting Standards (section 1.4).
www.iasb.org

G4 — **Group of Four (G4)**
Accountancy bodies in the US, Canada, the UK, Australia and New Zealand worked together in the late 1990s to provide joint input to the development of the work of IASC and to influence international developments. (G4 + 1 was the name given to this group plus the IASC.) Dissolved at start of 2001 because of potential duplication with new IASB work.

EAA — **European Accounting Association**
International organization bringing together institutional and individual membership from around the world. Organizes annual conference and publishes an academic journal.
www.eaa-online.org/home/index.cfm

IAAER — **International Association for Accounting Education and Research**
Academic community members concerned with promoting excellence in education and research.
www.iaaer.org

IFAC encourages international accountancy cooperation on a sub-global basis. To this end it recognizes specific regional accountancy bodies (see Exhibit 1.5) whose views are actively sought by IFAC committees as representing the distinctive views and interests of their members.

Neither IFAC nor its recognized regional bodies have attempted directly to develop accounting standards at an international level. Instead IFAC accepts that the IASB is the major source of authoritative guidance on standardization of international accounting practices.

Exhibit 1.5	**Regional accountancy bodies recognized by IFAC**

CAPA	Confederation of Asian and Pacific Accountants
ECSAFA	Eastern, Central and Southern African Federation of Accountants
ABWA	Association of Accountancy Bodies in West Africa
FEE	Fédération des Experts Comptables Européens (Federation of European Accountants)
IAA	Interamerican Accounting Association

1.3.3 Intergovernmental organizations

IASB works closely with a number of intergovernmental bodies. These are shown in Exhibit 1.6. These bodies cooperate with each other and with IASB.

Chapter 9 considers the work of the European Commission in more detail.

1.3.4 Organizations of securities markets and analysts

Exhibit 1.7 lists some of the coordinating organizations for securities markets, analysts and fund managers.

Securities markets regulators are particularly interested in the presentation of accounting information as a means of ensuring an efficient market. They have the power to accept or refuse a company's access to the market. The regulators seek to apply strict accounting requirements but also want to avoid undue restrictions which will

Exhibit 1.6	**Intergovernmental organizations**

EU	**European Commission** European Commission issues Directives which form a basis for national law within each member country. Accounting Directives (Fourth and Seventh) are largely concerned with harmonization of presentation in financial statements. The Internal Market Directorate-General has the main responsibility. <http://europa.eu.int/comm/dgs/internal_market/index_en.htm>
OECD	**Organization for Economic Cooperation and Development** Established by 24 of the world's 'developed' countries to promote world trade and global economic growth. Is concerned with financial reporting by multinational companies. OECD has a Working Group on Accounting Standards, issues guidelines for multinational companies, carries out surveys and publishes reports. Work extends to Central and Eastern Europe, e.g. the Coordinating Council on Accounting Methodology in the CIS (Former Soviet Union). www.oecd.org/home
ISAR	**Intergovernmental Working Group of Experts on International Standards of Accounting and Reporting** Operates within the United Nations, with a particular interest in accounting and reporting issues of the developing countries. Carries out surveys and publishes reports. Makes recommendations with regard to transnational companies. www.unctad.org

Exhibit 1.7	Organizations of securities markets and analysts

IOSCO	**International Organization of Securities Commissions** Securities regulators around the world come together to promote high standards in the operation of securities markets. www.iosco.org
CFA Institute	**Chartered Financial Analysts Institute** (Formerly AIMR: Association for Investment Management and Research). A US body which educates and examines investment analysts, and carries out research. www.cfainstitute.org
EFFAS	**European Federation of Financial Analysts' Societies** Has developed the European method of financial analysis. This involves a standardized approach to the classification and presentation of financial statements. www.effas.com
CESR	**The Committee of European Securities Regulators** Established by a European Commission Decision of June 2001. www.europfesco.org
FEAS	**Federation of Euro-Asian Stock Exchanges** 25 members, all emerging stock exchanges in Eastern Europe, Central and South Asia and the Middle East. www.feas.org

inhibit growth of the market. They are able to enforce regulations on those companies which seek to raise finance through the stock market.

Analysts who are writing reports on companies need some reassurance about comparability and need to be aware of the usefulness of a standard approach to accounting practice when making international comparisons.

1.3.5 Preparers' organizations

Financial Executives International (FEI)[17] is a US-based association for corporate finance executives. It was founded in 1931 as the Controllers Institute of America and became the Financial Executives Institute in 1962. In November 2000 it opened membership to financial executives around the world and took the 'International' description into its title. One aspect of FEI's activity is lobbying standard setters as a representative of chief finance officers. Zeff (2002) suggests that the challenges given by the FEI to FASB on controversial issues give an indication of the type of political pressure that IASB may face in future.

1.4 The IASCF and the IASB

The International Accounting Standards Committee Foundation (IASCF) is an independent body, not controlled by any particular government or professional organization. Its main purpose is to oversee the IASB in setting the accounting principles which are used

---

[17] www.fei.org

by businesses and other organizations around the world concerned with financial reporting.

The objectives of the IASB as stated in its Constitution[18] are:

(a) to develop in the public interest, a single set of high-quality, understandable and enforceable global accounting standards that require high-quality, transparent and comparable information in financial statements and other financial reporting to help participants in the world's capital markets and other users make economic decisions;

(b) to promote the use and rigorous application of those standards; and

(c) to bring about convergence of national accounting standards and International Accounting Standards and International Financial Reporting Standards to high-quality solutions.

These objectives were seen as giving a more precise focus to the objectives originally written in 1973 (see section 1.7).

The updated wording reflects the growing emphasis on the world's capital markets and the move towards rigour in application. The term 'high-quality' is also emphasized; this reflects a strong US influence on the constitutional changes that formed the IASB (see section 1.7.5 and also Chapter 8).

1.4.1 The Trustees

The governance of the IASCF rests with the Trustees. There are 19 Trustees, initially appointed by a Nominating Committee but thereafter taking responsibility themselves for filling vacancies as these arise. Trustees are required to show a firm commitment to the IASB as a high-quality global standard-setter, to be financially knowledgeable, and to have the ability to meet the time commitment expected. Each Trustee must have an understanding of, and be sensitive to, international issues relevant to the success of an international organization responsible for the development of high-quality global accounting standards for use in the world's capital markets and by other users. To ensure an adequate geographic representation it is required that six Trustees be appointed from North America, six from Europe, four from the Asia/Pacific region and three from any area, subject to overall geographic balance. Other conditions are attached to the appointment of Trustees in order to ensure a broad spread of interests. The appointment is for a term of three years, renewable once.

The Trustees meet twice in each year and are responsible for fundraising. They appoint the members of the IASB, the members of the International Financial Reporting Interpretations Committee and the members of the Standards Advisory Council.

1.4.2 The International Accounting Standards Board (IASB)

The IASB comprises 14 members, appointed by the IASCF Trustees. Twelve of the Board members commit all their time in paid employment to IASB (described as 'full-time') and two are in part-time employment with IASB. The foremost qualification for membership of the Board is technical expertise. The people chosen represent the best available combination of technical skills and background experience of relevant international business and market conditions. The selection is not based on geographical representation.

---

[18] Issued 2000, revised 2002.

The idea of balance requires at least five to have a background as practising auditors, at least three a background in the preparation of financial statements, at least three a background as users of financial statements, and at least one an academic background.

Publication of an exposure draft, standard or interpretation requires approval by eight of the 14 members of the Board. Other matters require a simple majority of those present, subject to 60 per cent attendance either in person or by telecommunications link.

1.4.3 The International Financial Reporting Interpretations Committee (IFRIC)

The IFRIC emerged in 2002 as a revised version of the Standing Interpretations Committee (SIC). There are 12 members of IFRIC, appointed by the IASCF Trustees. One role of IFRIC is to interpret the application of standards, in the context of the IASB's framework, and to produce draft Interpretations for public comment, from which it prepares a final version of the Interpretation. A second role for IFRIC, added in 2002, is to address practice issues for which no relevant IFRSs exist. In these circumstances IFRIC must apply the principles of the IASB *Framework* (see section 1.8). Once a Draft Interpretation has been approved by IFRIC, the document is submitted to the Board. It is then released for public comment provided that no more than four Board members object to its publication. IFRIC reconsiders its proposals in the light of comments received and then submits the final Interpretation to the Board for approval. A simple majority of the Board is sufficient.[19]

1.4.4 The Standards Advisory Council

The Standards Advisory Council provides a forum for participation by organizations and individuals from a wide range of interests and geographic representation. The SAC advises the IASB on agenda decisions and the priorities of the IASB's work, informs the IASB of the views of organizations and individuals on the Council and gives other advice to the IASB or the Trustees. There are around 30 members of the SAC.

1.4.5 Financing the IASB

From its inception in 1973 the International Accounting Standards Committee described itself as a 'low budget organization', relying a great deal on help from persons around the world who were willing to give time to support its activities. Professional accountancy bodies made contributions. International organizations gave grants for specific projects. Sales of publications also made a contribution.

From 2000 the responsibility for fundraising has fallen on the IASCF Trustees. They have continued to raise funds from existing sources but have also explored others such as contributions from multinational companies and stock markets whose needs are served by the IASB. There is a challenge in being seen to raise funds in a balanced way from contributors in many countries so that different countries can be seen to be making fair contributions, especially where those countries find they are not represented on the IASB. There is also a challenge in balancing transparency of information on sources of finance against the desire of some donors to maintain confidentiality. It is important to know that the

---

[19] IASB Insight, January 2002, p. 2.

| Exhibit 1.8 | IASC Foundation, sources of operating revenues, 2003 |

| | 2003 | 2002 |
	(£000)	(£000)
Contributions	9,680	11,675
Other income	22	24
Publications and related revenues	2,957	2,303
Less direct cost of sales	(1,398)	(1,272)
	1,559	1,031
Total operating revenues	11,261	12,730

Source: International Accounting Standards Committee Foundation annual report (2003), Statement of Activities, p. 16.

independent standard-setter is not influenced by significant contributors. Hence there is a list of IASCF 'underwriters and supporters' at the end of the annual report. Categories of funders cover Accounting firms, Underwriter companies, Supporters, Central Banks and Government Entities, International Organizations, and Other Official Organizations and Associations.[20] Exhibit 1.8 sets out the operating revenues for 2003.

1.5 Operation of the IASB

The IASB issues International Financial Reporting Standards (IFRS). The generic term 'IFRS' is defined as including the new IFRS issued by the IASB, the existing IASs issued by the predecessor IASC, and the Interpretations issued by IFRIC (or its predecessor SIC).[21] This section explains the procedures by which a proposal eventually becomes a standard. It then continues by explaining the IASB's lack of direct powers of enforcement. Finally it discusses the consultation process that establishes acceptance of the IFRS.

1.5.1 Procedure for issuing a standard

First of all there has to be an idea. Ideas may come from IASB members, the Standards Advisory Council, other organizations and individuals and the IASB staff. Whatever the source, the first stage is a project proposal which is approved by the IASB.

The IASB in 2001 set an initial technical agenda with ambitious targets. Several topics were planned for simultaneous exposure and debate in several countries, with feedback to the IASB to achieve convergence. Before any Standard is issued the IASB publishes an Exposure Draft for comment by a specified date. Comments received on Exposure Drafts are available on the IASB website, unless respondents request confidentiality. However there is more consultation behind the scenes. Exhibit 1.9 sets out the due process described by the IASB in its revision of IAS 32 and IAS 39 published in December 2003.

---

[20] IASCF Annual Report 2003, p. 23.

[21] IAS 1 Presentation of Financial Statements, revised December 2003, para 11.

Exhibit 1.9	Due process in revising IAS 32 and IAS 39

- Published an exposure draft in June 2002; received over 170 comment letters.
- Conducted nine round-table discussions in March 2003, in which over 100 organizations and individuals took part.
- Discussions with the Standards Advisory Council and the IASB's partner standard-setters.
- Discussions about the issues raised on the exposure draft in every Board meeting from March to October 2003. The IASB considered 61 agenda papers about issues raised on the exposure draft, amounting to over 1,200 pages.
- Further exposure draft on 'macro hedging' published in August 2003. Received over 120 comment letters. Proposals continued to be reviewed but the revised standards were not delayed for this one issue to be completed. A further revision was envisaged.
- In March 2004 issued an Amendment to IAS 39 on *Fair Value Hedge Accounting for a Portfolio Hedge of Interest Rate Risk*.
- In April 2004 published an exposure draft on a proposed limited amendment to the *Fair Value Option*, in response to concerns of some supervisory bodies that the fair value option might be used inappropriately.

Source: based on IASB Insight, January 2004, p. 2; IASB Insight, April/May 2004, p. 1.

The IASB announced in 2004 that it would take steps to improve communication with its constituents and the transparency of the Board's deliberative processes. Observer Notes for IASB meetings are available on the website ahead of meetings. Webcasting is also envisaged.[22]

1.5.2 Power of enforcement

The power of enforcement has diminished over time. When the IASC was founded its members agreed to use their best endeavours and persuasive influence to ensure compliance with the standards. It was intended that each professional accounting association within the IASC would ensure that the external auditors would satisfy themselves as to observance of the standards and would disclose cases of non-compliance; appropriate action was to be taken against any auditor who did not follow these recommendations. Later, revised wording of the agreement among members acknowledged that IASC pronouncements would not override the standards followed by individual countries. By 1982, the agreement no longer contained the requirement that the auditors should disclose the extent of non-compliance. The failure of the agreement to make any mention of obligations placed on auditors continues; the route to enforcement has now moved in the direction of applying the powers of national stock exchanges which subscribe to the IOSCO agreement on the acceptance of core standards.

One of the key concerns of the US SEC relates to the rigour and enforceability of IASB Standards. Comments made by respondents indicate that effective enforcement

---

[22] IASB Insight, January 2004, p. 4.

will require the cooperation of many organizations. One view is that the SEC should not accept IASB Standards until all the arrangements are in place; the alternative view is that by accepting IASB Standards the major securities regulators will encourage such arrangements more quickly.

1.5.3 Consultation

The IASB has to gain acceptance of its standards by national regulators. It has no power to force acceptance, and so must rely on its powers of persuasion and the quality of its standards. It therefore liaises with national standard setters by having 'liaison members' of the Board whose particular remit includes maintaining liaisons with national standard setters in Australasia, Canada, France, Germany, Japan, the UK and the US. The IASB also holds meetings with other standard setters.[23]

An important liaison activity took place at a joint meeting in Norwalk, Connecticut, US, in September 2002, when the IASB and the Financial Accounting Standards Board (FASB) pledged to use their best efforts to make their existing financial reporting standards fully compatible as soon as was practical, and to coordinate their future work programmes to ensure that, once achieved, compatibility was maintained. To achieve this, they agreed a programme of short-term and longer-term actions to remove a variety of differences.[24] The intensification of this programme during 2004 was explained by the IASB chairman in terms of the window of opportunity given by support from senior business leaders and policymakers in the US. He also pointed out that no effort to develop truly global standards would be successful without the participation of the US.[25]

1.6 The IASB standards

As explained earlier, the IASB has responsibility for issuing new IFRSs, taking over and gradually updating the inherited IASs, issuing IFRICs as developed by IFRIC and taking over the inherited SICs. The IASB indicated that it would create a 'stable platform' of standards in preparation for the changeover to IFRS in Europe and elsewhere in 2005. This 'stable platform' was completed in March 2004.[26] Standards issued after that date would not take effect until 2006.

The standards in issue at March 2004 are shown in Exhibit 1.10. In each case the title of the standard is followed by the date of the most recent version and the history of previous revisions. There are notes indicating amendments brought about either by the Comparability Project (see section 1.7.3) or by the achievement of the core standards programme (see section 1.7.4).

---

[23] IASCF Annual Report 2002, p. 4.
[24] IASCF Annual Report 2002, p. 5.
[25] IASB Insight, April/May 2004, p. 8.
[26] IASB Insight, April/May 2004, p. 1.

Exhibit 1.10	IASB Standards in issue, March 2004	
IFRS 1	First-time Adoption of International Financial Reporting Standards	Issued 2003
IFRS 2	Share-based Payment	Issued 2004
IFRS 3	Business Combinations	Issued 2004
IFRS 4	Insurance Contracts	Issued 2004
IFRS 5	Non-current Assets held for Sale and Discontinued Operations	Issued 2004
IAS 1	Presentation of Financial Statements	Revised 2003, superseding 1997 version, which replaced former IAS 1, 5 and 13
IAS 2[1]	Inventories	Revised 2003, superseding 1993 version,[2] superseding 1975 version
IAS 3	Consolidated Financial Statements (withdrawn)	Superseded by IAS 27 and IAS 28
IAS 4	Depreciation Accounting (withdrawn)	Now in IAS 16, 22 and 38
IAS 5	Information to be Disclosed in Financial Statements (withdrawn)	Superseded by IAS 1 (1998)
IAS 6	Accounting Responses to Changing Prices (withdrawn)	Superseded by IAS 15
IAS 7[1]	Cash Flow Statements	Issued 1992, superseding 1977 version
IAS 8[1]	Accounting Policies, Changes in Accounting Estimates and Errors	Revised 2003, superseding 1993 version,[2] superseding 1978 version
IAS 9	Research and Development Costs (withdrawn)	Superseded by IAS 38
IAS 10	Events after the Balance Sheet Date	Revised 2003, superseding 1999 version, superseding 1978 version, reformatted 1995
IAS 11[1]	Construction Contracts	Issued 1993,[2] superseding 1979 version
IAS 12	Income Taxes	Issued 1996, superseding 1979 version, reformatted 1995
IAS 13	Presentation of Current Assets and Current Liabilities (withdrawn)	Superseded by IAS 1 (1998)
IAS 14	Segment Reporting	Issued 1997, superseding 1983 version, reformatted 1995
IAS 15	Information Reflecting the Effects of Changing Prices (withdrawn)	Withdrawn 2003
IAS 16	Property, Plant and Equipment	Revised 2003, superseding 1998 version; issued 1993,[2] superseding 1982 version
IAS 17	Leases	Revised 2003, superseding 1997 version, superseding 1982,[2] reformatted 1995
IAS 18	Revenue	Issued 1993,[2] superseding 1982 version
IAS 19	Employee Benefits	Amended 2002, 2000, issued 1998, superseding 1993 and 1982[2] versions
IAS 20	Accounting for Government Grants and Disclosure of Government Assistance	Issued 1983, reformatted 1995
IAS 21	The Effects of Changes in Foreign Exchange Rates	Revised 2003, superseding 1993 version,[2] superseding 1983 version

▶

IAS 22	Business Combinations (withdrawn)	Withdrawn March 2004, see IFRS 3
IAS 23	Borrowing Costs	Issued 1993,[2] superseding 1984 version
IAS 24	Related Party Disclosures	Revised 2003, superseding 1984 version, reformatted 1995
IAS 25	Accounting for Investments (withdrawn)	Now in IAS 32, 39 and 40
IAS 26	Accounting and Reporting by Retirement Benefit Plans	Issued 1987, reformatted 1995
IAS 27	Consolidated and Separate Financial Statements	Revised 2003, superseding 2000 version, superseding 1989 version, reformatted 1995
IAS 28	Investments in Associates	Revised 2003, superseding 2000 and 1998 revisions, superseding 1989 version, reformatted 1995
IAS 29[1]	Financial Reporting in Hyperinflationary Economies	Issued 1989, reformatted 1995
IAS 30	Disclosure in the Financial Statements of Banks and Similar Financial Institutions	Issued 1990, reformatted 1995
IAS 31	Interests in Joint Ventures	Revised 2003, superseding 2000 version, amended 1998, issued 1990, reformatted 1995
IAS 32	Financial Instruments: Disclosure and Presentation	Revised 2003, superseding 2000 version and 1998 version, issued 1995
IAS 33	Earnings per Share	Revised 2003, issued 1997
IAS 34	Interim Financial Reporting	Issued 1998
IAS 35	Discontinuing Operations (withdrawn)	Withdrawn 2004, see IFRS 5
IAS 36	Impairment of Assets	Revised 2004, superseding 1998 version
IAS 37	Provisions, Contingent Liabilities and Contingent Assets	Issued 1998, supersedes parts of IAS 10
IAS 38	Intangible Assets	Revised 2004, replaces 1998 version
IAS 39	Financial Instruments: Recognition and Measurement	Revised 2003, superseding 2000 version, issued 1998
IAS 40	Investment Property	Revised 2003, issued 2000
IAS 41	Agriculture	Issued 2001

[1] Indicates that the IAS was acceptable to IOSCO as a core standard without further revision.
[2] Indicates that the IAS was listed for attention in the Comparability Project exposure draft E 32.

Although it is useful to have the standards listed in numerical sequence, for purposes of considering the impact and relevance of the standards it is more convenient to rearrange them according to the accounting issues they address. This rearrangement is presented in Exhibit 1.11.

Chapter 2 contains summaries of the key aspects of each standard, explaining where there were controversial issues to settle in the Comparability Project. It gives an indication of the work that was undertaken in moving forward from the Comparability Project in meeting the IOSCO target.

The IFRICs and SICs are listed in Exhibit 1.12.

Exhibit 1.11 Classification of IASB standards, by accounting issue

Disclosure and presentation

General aspects
IFRS 1	First-time Adoption of International Financial Reporting Standards
IAS 1	Presentation of Financial Statements

Specific aspects
IAS 7	Cash Flow Statements
IAS 8	Accounting Policies, Changes in Accounting Estimates and Errors
IFRS 5	Non-current Assets Held for Sale and Discontinued Operations
IAS 14	Segment Reporting
IAS 24	Related Party Disclosures
IAS 33	Earnings per Share
IAS 34	Interim Financial Reporting

Asset recognition and measurement
IAS 2	Inventories
IAS 16	Property, Plant and Equipment
IAS 36	Impairment of Assets
IAS 23	Borrowing Costs
IAS 25	Accounting for Investments
IAS 38	Intangible Assets
IAS 40	Investment Property

Liability recognition and measurement
IAS 10	Events after the Balance Sheet Date
IAS 37	Provisions, Contingent Liabilities and Contingent Assets
IAS 12	Income Taxes
IAS 17	Leases
IAS 19	Employee Benefits

Financial instruments: Assets and Liabilities
IAS 32	Financial Instruments: Disclosure and Presentation
IAS 39	Financial Instruments: Recognition and Measurement

Recognition of economic activity
IAS 11	Construction Contracts
IAS 18	Revenue
IAS 20	Accounting for Government Grants and Disclosure of Government Assistance
IFRS 2	Share-based Payment

Measurement of inflation
IAS 29	Financial Reporting in Hyperinflationary Economies

Group accounting
IAS 21	The Effects of Changes in Foreign Exchange Rates
IFRS 3	Business Combinations
IAS 27	Consolidated and Separate Financial Statements
IAS 28	Investments in Associates
IAS 31	Interests in Joint Ventures

Specialist industries
IAS 26	Accounting and Reporting by Retirement Benefit Plans
IAS 30	Disclosure in the Financial Statements of Banks and Similar Financial Institutions
IAS 41	Agriculture
IFRS 4	Insurance Contracts

| Exhibit 1.12 | List of IFRICs and SICs, December 2004 |

There were no IFRICs in issue at March 2004. Many SICs had been taken into revisions of IAS or new IFRS and withdrawn, leaving the following list remaining:

SIC-7	Introduction of the Euro (IAS 21)
SIC-10	Government Assistance – No Specific Relation to Operating Activities (IAS 20)
SIC-12	Consolidation – Special Purpose Entities (IAS 27)
SIC-13	Jointly Controlled Entities – Non-Monetary Contributions by Venturers (IAS 31)
SIC-15	Operating Leases – Incentives (IAS 17)
SIC-21	Income Taxes – Recovery of Revalued Non-Depreciable Assets (IAS 12)
SIC-25	Income Taxes – Changes in the Tax Status of an Enterprise or its Shareholders (IAS 12)
SIC-27	Evaluating the Substance of Transactions involving the Legal Form of a Lease
SIC-29	Disclosure – Service Concession Arrangements
SIC-31	Revenue – Barter Transactions Involving Advertising Services
SIC-32	Intangible Assets – Web Site Costs

IFRICs issued later in 2004 were:

IFRIC 1	Changes in Existing Decommissioning, Restoration and Similar Liabilities
IFRIC	Amendment to SIC-12 Consolidation – Special Purpose Entities
IFRIC 2	Members' Shares in Co-operative Entities and Similar Instruments
IFRIC 3	Emission Rights
IFRIC 4	Determining Whether an Arrangement contains a Lease
IFRIC 5	Rights to Interests arising from Decommissioning, Restoration and Environmental Rehabilitation Funds

1.7 Changing styles of setting international standards

The IASC was formed in 1973 through an agreement made by professional accountancy bodies from Australia, Canada, France, Germany, Ireland, Japan, Mexico, The Netherlands, the UK and the US. Its objectives at that time were:

● to formulate and publish in the public interest accounting standards to be observed in the presentation of financial statements and to promote their worldwide acceptance and observance; and

● to work generally for the improvement and harmonization of regulations, accounting standards and procedures relating to the presentation of financial statements.

From 1983 the membership of IASC included all the professional accountancy bodies that were members of IFAC.[27] A joint meeting of all members took place every two and a half years. Although IASC is older than IFAC by four years, the creation of IFAC brought into being a global structure from which IASC could obtain wider authority.[28]

In May 2000 the IASC agreed a change in its Constitution to reflect the changing nature of the work of setting international accounting standards. IASC retained its independence by having its own constitution that, from 2000, could be altered only by a meeting of the Trustees. Under the 2000 Constitution the members ceased to have a formal role in the decisions of the IASC Foundation.

---

[27] For membership of IFAC, see website.

[28] A useful historical discussion of the operation of the IASC is provided by Cairns (2002), Ch. 1.

Various phases have been identified in the standard-setting process operated by the IASC as predecessor of the current IASB (see Exhibit 1.13). It issued International Accounting Standards (IASs). This section discusses those phases and the factors which have influenced a change of direction.

1.7.1 The early standards

The first standards from the IASC in the 1970s were basic, straightforward and largely non-controversial. They had a high level of generality and concentrated primarily on matters of presentation and disclosure rather than more controversial issues of measurement (Nair and Frank, 1981).

1.7.2 Increasing use of permitted alternatives

Standards issued during the 1980s dealt with more complex issues reflecting problematic subjects under active consideration in the leading accounting countries. This led to increasingly frequent use of options within which the prevailing accounting practices of most of the major accounting nations could be accommodated. In this way the IASs did not pose a threat to national differences. It had been noted that most IASs had two acceptable alternative treatments because of the necessity of ensuring that the required 75 per cent of the 14 voting members of the Board voted in favour (see comments of Arthur R. Wyatt, IASC, in Fleming, 1991).

Empirical research studies have from time to time been made on the effectiveness of IASC. A study of the application of accounting methods by major companies in a range of major accounting nations over the 1970s found that IASs had little impact on the accounting practices of the companies surveyed. Except for a few instances, companies which followed a particular accounting method prior to the promulgation of the standard continued to follow the same practice after the standard was issued (Evans and Taylor, 1982). Of the initial 16 standards issued, eight permitted alternative accounting treatments, and hence allowed flexibility (Choi and Bavishi, 1982). That flexibility was attributed to attempts to accommodate the variety of treatments that existed in reporting standards already adopted by developed countries.

By the mid-1980s other researchers were also observing that the IASs had not succeeded in changing existing national standards, or in establishing new standards. For example, studies showed that in eight of the 24 international standards issued up to 1984, alternative solutions were permitted (Most, 1984). This was perceived as being due to lack of enforceability. The programme of IASs was seen as having value insofar as it succeeded in

Exhibit 1.13	Phases in the development of the work of the IASC

Stage	
1 Issue of general standards	1973–79
2 Development of more detailed standards	1980–89
3 Reduction of flexibility – Comparability Project	1989–95
4 IOSCO core standards programme	1995–99
5 Convergence and Improvements	2000–05 and beyond

codifying generally accepted practice (McKinnon and Janell, 1984). However, by the end of the 1980s there was a high degree of flexibility within the standards.

Purvis *et al.* (1991), analyzing compliance with IASs as indicated in an IASC survey of 1988, found a high level of national conformity with those standards issued early in the life of the IASC but much lower levels of conformity for those issued closer to 1988. The authors observed that the results were not surprising since the nature of the earlier standards, addressing fundamental issues at a general level, meant that countries could comply with minimum need for change, especially in view of the permitted alternative treatments. Furthermore the passage of time permitted countries which initially had non-conforming standards to adopt new ones in line with IASs.

A reaction to the extent of choice in IASs began in 1989 with a project to reduce flexibility. A second phase began in 1995, intended to meet the demands of IOSCO for an acceptable set of core standards.

1.7.3 The Comparability Project

In 1989 the IASC launched a major initiative to bring greater comparability to financial statements.

1.7.3.1 Exposure draft E 32

The initiative was represented by an exposure draft, E 32, which contained proposals to reduce the number of alternative treatments allowed in the IASs issued to date. The exposure draft contained recommendations on matters of free choice that might have had a material effect on the definition, recognition, measurement and display of net income and assets and liabilities in the financial statements of an enterprise. E 32 was seen as the first stage in a continuing process of improvement; it acknowledged that free choice had been necessary in the past to gain acceptance of certain standards.

The IASC also decided to reformat all IASs in such a way as to highlight the significant points of principle in bold italic type. The document would also present, in normal type, explanations of each significant point of principle in the standard.

1.7.3.2 Need for change

The main impetus for these changes was the increase in cross-border financing. Wyatt (in Fleming, 1991) claimed that the American Institute of Certified Public Accountants (AICPA) along with other accounting bodies had agreed in writing to attempt to ensure that the standard-setting bodies in their countries moved towards international standards. IOSCO encouraged the IASC in its project and, according to Wyatt, intended to encourage securities regulators in member countries to require use of IASs, providing that the IASC could produce results of adequate quality.

1.7.3.3 Statement of intent

The initial proposals contained in E 32 were modified and explained further in a Statement of Intent issued in 1990. The Statement of Intent explained that, where it was not possible to gain agreement on a single recommended approach, there would be a 'benchmark treatment' and an 'allowed alternative treatment'. The word 'benchmark' had gained greater acceptance than the word 'preferred' used in the exposure draft E 32. The benchmark treatment was to be regarded as a point of reference for the Board when making its choice between alternatives.

Following on from the Comparability Project, the trend was to make IASs more prescriptive. Some national accounting traditions appear to be at variance with the resulting standards and removal of previously permitted options to focus on one method only has inevitably been a process of robust negotiation. In that process, some observers have identified increasing dominance of accounting principles originating in the US and the UK.

1.7.3.4 Potential for success

The potential for the Comparability Project to succeed depended on the level of conformity existing at the time of the project and the subsequent intentions of national standard setters with regard to the subsequent revision of IASs. Research has been undertaken assessing the extent to which the financial reporting practices of countries agreed with the accounting practices contained in the standards issued by the IASC following the Comparability Project. The results showed that there was substantial agreement (Salter *et al.*, 1996; Roberts *et al.*, 1996). Partners in major firms of accountants were asked to indicate the percentage of significant organizations in their country which already followed the recommended accounting treatments (benchmark or allowed alternative) contained in the IASs that were to take effect from January 1995. The average level of national agreement with the IASs was 68.4 per cent. The results for the US (75.96 per cent) and the UK (74.78 per cent), seen as countries with a strong influence on the development of IASs, were higher than the average but Australia, classed within the 'Anglo-Saxon' sphere of influence, was lower (64.75 per cent). Malaysia (70.80 per cent) has a tradition derived from British influence. Japan (63.86 per cent) and Germany (57.70 per cent) were lower but the flexibility of group accounting in France contributed to a higher score (71.69 per cent).

In no single country did corporate accounting practice exactly match the revised rules resulting from the Comparability Project. The countries with the least change required in bringing existing practice into line with the revised IASs tended to belong to the UK/US tradition. Countries with the greatest change required were typically those classified as 'code law' countries (see section 4.4.2) which are regarded as adopting a conservative approach to measurement of accounting income and assets.

1.7.3.5 Evaluation of the Comparability Project

Some of the more interesting debates resulting from the Comparability Project will be discussed in Chapter 2, in explaining the context of specific standards as they are operating in their revised form. The Comparability Project was a bold initiative to reduce options but there are views that it did not entirely succeed because of strong interest groups. It has been suggested that the standard setters of the member states of the EU did not give sufficient signs of unity on issues where the US influence was dominant (a detailed discussion has been provided by Gernon *et al.*, 1990). The Comparability Project did achieve some reduction of options compared with accounting practice in the UK and US but left a number of allowed alternatives in areas where UK and US practice differed, including amortization of goodwill, deferred taxation, valuation of property, plant and equipment, inventory valuation and accounting for fundamental errors (Weetman *et al.*, 1993).

1.7.4 The Core Standards programme

1.7.4.1 Relations with IOSCO

In its present form IOSCO dates from the mid-1980s. Its objectives include:

- the establishment of standards and effective surveillance of international securities transactions;

● provision of mutual assistance to ensure the integrity of the markets by a rigorous application of standards and by effective enforcement against offenders.

A working party was established to cooperate with the IASC with a view to identifying accounting standards which security regulators might be ready to accept in the case of multinational offerings. At its annual conference in 1987 a resolution was passed to promote the use of common standards in accounting and auditing practice. In that same year IOSCO became a member of the IASC Consultative Group. IOSCO gave active support to the E 32 Comparability Project, and in 1996 IOSCO accepted observer status on the IASC Board.

1.7.4.2 Identifying the Core standards

In 1995 the IASC made a significant agreement with IOSCO. The agreement stated that the goal of both IASC and IOSCO was that financial statements prepared in accordance with IASs can be used in cross-border offerings and listings as an alternative to national accounting standards. The achievement of this goal was made conditional on completion of the IASC Work Programme, scheduled for 1999. The Work Programme concentrates on a core set of standards and has come to be referred to more commonly as 'the core standards programme'. By March 1996 the Board had revised the target date to March 1998, in response to requests from international companies and from members of IOSCO. The revised target saved 15 months on the original plan.

The core standards programme was a very significant step towards helping companies which had a listing on stock exchanges outside their own country and were sometimes required to prepare their financial statements using the generally accepted accounting principles of that country. That condition was applied in particular by the US SEC, and the detail of the additional disclosures was perceived as deterring many companies from seeking a listing in US stock markets.

In effect, IASs were already acceptable for cross-border listings on most major stock exchanges before the core standards programme was put in place. The notable exceptions were the US, Canada and Japan. Japan and Canada indicated by various actions that they were favourably disposed to IASs and so the key factor for acceptability was the US SEC.

1.7.5 IOSCO acceptance and a 'stable platform'

On completion of the Core Standards programme at the end of 1998 the IASC had to turn its attention to making the standards effective, in competition with the influence of US GAAP. Companies in other countries, such as Germany, were looking for global listings, including US listings, and were exploring the relative attractions of US GAAP and IASC standards as the basis for consolidated financial statements.

The reaction to the IASC's initial exploration of the issues indicated that there would be no easy answer. For acceptance of IASC standards in the US, the SEC indicated that it would expect to see a standard-setting Board which had all the features of the FASB, particularly a relatively small number of full-time members and the choice of the best experts available, regardless of geographical origin. The European Commission wanted to see a broader-based Board with guaranteed geographical spread of representation. During the comment period it became apparent that, to have a credible future in the US capital market, the IASC would need to act in a way consistent with the expectations of the SEC.

Early in 2000 the IASC Board indicated that it approved of a structure based on a Board of experts and that it would not pursue the alternative of geographical representation on the Board. The geographical spread would come in a Standards Advisory Council which would not have direct standard-setting responsibilities. The SEC then indicated its approval of this direction by issuing a Concept Release as the first stage of the SEC's own consultative process. The Concept Release (February 2000) identified what the SEC regarded as the necessary components of a high-quality financial reporting framework and asked questions about the elements of such a framework. The questions asked were set under various headings:

- Are the core standards sufficiently comprehensive? (Q1–Q3)
- Are the IASC standards of sufficiently high quality? (Q4–Q7)
- Can the IASC standards be rigorously interpreted and applied? (Q8–Q26)

These questions were originally signalled in a press release published by the SEC in April 1996.[29]

The questions on 'high quality' are directed towards how closely the IASC standards resemble US GAAP. Overall the questions focus mainly on interpretation and enforcement, with relatively little enquiry into the intrinsic merits. High-quality standards are said to consist of a comprehensive set of neutral principles that require consistent, comparable, relevant and reliable information that is useful to those who make capital allocation decisions. There were 26 questions, supported by detail described as 'supplementary information' indicating areas where the SEC might have concerns. The problems were seen to lie as much in enforcement as in the standards themselves.

The phrase 'high-quality standards' has appeared in abundance in comments from the SEC, so that the appearance of this phrase in the revised Objectives of the Constitution was not a great surprise.

1.7.5.1 IOSCO acceptance

In May 2000 IOSCO announced completion of its assessment of the accounting standards issued by the IASC. The Presidents Committee of IOSCO referred to the 30 standards and related interpretations evaluated by them (described as 'the IASC 2000 standards'). It recommended that IOSCO members permit incoming multinational issuers to use the IASC 2000 standards to prepare their financial statements for cross-border offerings and listings, as supplemented where necessary by one or more of three supplemental treatments of reconciliation, disclosure and interpretation.

- *Reconciliation* means requiring reconciliation of certain items to show the effect of applying a different accounting method, in contrast with the method applied under IASC standards.
- *Disclosure* means requiring additional disclosures, either in the presentation of the financial statements or in the footnotes.
- *Interpretation* means specifying the use of a particular alternative provided in an IASC standard, or a particular interpretation in cases where the IASC standard is unclear or silent.

---

[29] The Press Release is not available electronically but is summarized in the *Report on Promoting Global Pre-eminence of American Securities Markets*, SEC, October 1997, www.sec.gov/news/studies/acctgsp.htm.

This resolution confirmed the good working relationship between IASC and IOSCO but left considerable discretion with the separate market regulators who were the members of IOSCO. It was for each securities commission or regulator to decide whether to accept the IOSCO recommendation and whether to apply supplemental treatments. In particular, if the SEC in the US were to continue requiring reconciliations to US GAAP there would be a risk that foreign registrants on US stock exchanges would regard this as too costly and troublesome and would apply US GAAP in preference to IASB Standards. Chapters 8 and 9 explain in more detail how the regulators in the US and the EU proceeded from this point.

1.7.5.2 A stable platform for 2005

When the IASB started to plan its work programme in 2001, an important focus was the intention of the European Commission to adopt IFRS for all listed companies in member states from 1 January 2005. It was clear that these countries would require time to prepare for the change to IFRS. The IASB decided that only those standards issued by March 2004 would apply from 1 January 2005. Any standards issued after March 2004 would apply from 2006 or later. This would give a 'stable platform' in March 2004 followed by 21 months without further changes.

To achieve the stable platform the IASB put in place an Improvements project to raise the quality and consistency of financial reporting generally. The general phase of improvements removed options in IASs that had caused uncertainty and reduced comparability. This general phase produced a set of revised standards issued in December 2003. Specific improvements were made to IAS 32 and IAS 39. New standards given priority for 2005 were developed in IFRS 2 (share-based payments), IFRS 3 (business combinations), IFRS 4 (insurance contracts) and IFRS 5 (non-current assets and discontinued operations).

1.7.5.3 Beyond the stable platform

The IASB continued to develop projects after March 2004. The subjects identified for attention were:

- Business combinations – phase II
- Exploration and evaluation assets
- Convergence with national standard setters
- Financial instruments and insurance
- Disclosures of risks arising from financial instruments
- Revenue recognition
- Measurement
- Accounting standards for small and medium-sized entities.

The Board also invited comments on its process of consultation, aware that there were views that it was too remote and not sufficiently accessible to its constituents. In response the website contains expanded notes for observers of the Board meetings.

1.7.6 IASB and developing countries

By 1989 research was observing that IASs were strongly influenced by the accounting practices of developed countries, and there appeared to be a potentially patronising assumption that the accounting standards of these countries should be adopted by others (Rivera, 1989). The author of the 1989 study identified problems as:

● lack of a structured theoretical accounting framework underlying the preparation of specific standards;

● a multiplicity of permitted reporting options introduced in the current standards;

● a tendency to address only those issues developed in or related to advanced economic environments where sophisticated markets and information prevail;

● lack of enforceability of international standards at local and international level.

During the 1990s attention was drawn to the apparent overrepresentation of the interests of developed nations on the Board of IASC. It was asked whether the views and evidence of the developing countries, as a majority of the membership by number, were being heard and considered (Wallace, 1990). It was suggested in the same study that the most critical issue concerning the adoption of the IASs was their relevance to developing countries. A study published at the same time (Hove, 1990) found that the US and the UK exerted very significant levels of influence on IASC standards. The reason suggested was that both countries had devoted considerable time and effort to developing extensive and well-codified sets of standards and would therefore have most to lose if any international standards were fundamentally different from their own. The study noted, however, that the influence of the UK and the US was unlikely to be directed towards the particular interests of less-developed countries.

The issue of developing countries has not been resolved in the changes implemented since 2000, which have focused on the accounting needs of developed capital markets and the long-term future of the IASC as an organization. When the IASB was formed as a group of experts, regardless of national representation, the Standards Advisory Council was offered as the representative forum. In the 2003 annual report of the IASC Foundation the SAC was afforded two paragraphs, mainly describing discussions of its constitutional role.[30]

In 2002 the IASB announced the start of a process for developing accounting standards for small and medium-sized entities (SMEs). The Board decided that the SME standards should be developed by extracting fundamental concepts and principles from the IASB Framework and from IFRS and interpretations. Any modifications would be based on the needs of users but would start from the position of assuming no change to the principles of recognition and measurement in IFRS. Developing countries are likely to have particular problems in taking IFRS to small companies but it seemed that the particular needs of entities in such countries would not receive special attention in this project. Emerging and transition economies were mentioned in passing in the 2003 report of the IASB chairman.[31]

1.8 IASB framework

In 1989 the IASC issued a framework which has been adopted by the IASB and may be regarded as a statement of key principles to be applied in accounting practices (IASC, 1989). The framework is not itself an accounting standard. The purpose of the framework document is to assist:

---

[30] IASCF Annual Report (2003) paras 59–60.
[31] IASCF Annual Report (2003) para 74.

- the Board in development and review of IASs;
- the Board in promotion of harmonization by providing a basis for reducing the number of alternative accounting treatments permitted by IASs;
- national standard-setting bodies in developing national standards;
- preparers of financial statements in applying IASs and dealing with topics on which IASs do not yet exist;
- auditors in forming an opinion as to whether financial statements conform to IASs;
- users in interpreting financial statements prepared in conformity with IASs;
- those interested in the formulation of IASs by providing information about the approach used by the IASC (now IASB).

The framework deals with:

- the objectives of financial statements;
- the qualitative characteristics that determine the usefulness of information in financial statements;
- the definition, recognition and measurement of the elements from which financial statements are constructed;
- concepts of capital and capital maintenance.

The framework document is concerned with general-purpose financial statements which normally include a balance sheet, an income statement, a statement of change in financial position, and those notes and other statements and explanatory material that are an integral part of the financial statements. 'Financial statements' does not include reports by directors, statements by the chairman, or discussion and analysis by management that may be included in an entity's financial or annual report.

The users of financial statements are identified as present and potential investors, employees, lenders, suppliers and other trade creditors, customers, government and their agents and the public. Although all of the information needs of these users cannot be met by financial statements, it is reasonable to think that providing the information needs of investors will ensure that most of the needs of other users can be satisfied.

1.8.1 Objective of financial statements

The objective of financial statements is to provide information about the *financial position, performance* and *changes in financial position* of an enterprise that is useful to a wide range of users in *making economic decisions*. They do not provide all the information users need since they largely portray the financial effects of past events and do not necessarily provide non-financial information. Financial statements also show the results of the stewardship of management or the accountability of management for the resources entrusted to it. In particular:

1 *Economic decisions* taken by users require an evaluation of the ability of an enterprise to generate cash and the timing and certainty of their generation.

2 The *financial position* of an entity is affected by the economic resources it controls, its financial structure, its liquidity and solvency, and its capacity to adapt to changes in the environment in which it operates. Information about financial structure is useful

in predicting future borrowing needs and how future profits and cash flows will be distributed amongst those with an interest in the enterprise and how further finance is likely to be raised.

3 Information about *performance* and the variability of performance of an enterprise is required to assess potential change in economic resources and is useful in predicting the capacity of the enterprise to generate cash flow and its efficiency in employing additional resources.

4 Information about *changes in financial position* is useful in order to assess an enterprise's investing, financing and operating activities.

In order to meet this objective financial statements are prepared on the underlying assumptions of an accruals-based accounting system and that the enterprise is a going concern and will continue in operation for the foreseeable future.

1.8.2 Qualitative characteristics

In order that financial statements should be useful to the users, the following qualitative characteristics should be present and the constraints noted.

1.8.2.1 Understandability

Information should be readily understandable by users who have a reasonable knowledge of business and economic activities and accounting, and a willingness to study the information with reasonable diligence.

1.8.2.2 Relevance

Information is relevant where it influences the economic decisions of users by helping them to evaluate past, present or future events or confirming, or correcting, their past evaluation. The relevance of information is affected by its materiality – i.e. whether its omission or misstatement could influence the economic decisions of users. Materiality provides a threshold or cut-off point for the provision of information.

1.8.2.3 Reliability

Reliability is expressed in terms of freedom from error and bias: information represents what it purports to represent. Within this concept of reliability are issues of faithful representation, substance over form, neutrality, prudence and completeness:

- *faithful representation*: a balance sheet and an income statement should represent faithfully the transactions and other events which meet the recognition criteria;
- *substance over form*: information is presented in accordance with the substance and economic reality and not merely the legal form;
- *neutrality*: information has not been selected or presented so as to encourage a predetermined result or outcome;
- *prudence*: there is a degree of caution in the exercise of judgements such that assets or income are not overstated and liabilities or expenses are not understated, but not permitting the deliberate understatement or overstatement of items;

- *completeness*: information must be complete within the bounds of materiality and cost.

1.8.2.4 Comparability

Financial statements of an entity should be capable of being compared through time. Financial statements of different entities should be comparable for the same period. Measurement and display of the financial effect of similar transactions and other events must be carried out in a consistent way throughout an enterprise and over time for that enterprise and in a consistent way for different enterprises.

1.8.2.5 Constraints on relevant and reliable information

The constraints are timeliness, balanced against benefits and costs. There are also constraints in selecting a balance of qualitative characteristics:

- *timeliness*: if there is undue delay in reporting information it may lose its relevance; management need to balance the relative merits of timely reporting and the provision of reliable information;
- *balance between benefit and cost*: in imposing accounting standards on preparers, accounting standard-setting organizations should apply the constraint that benefits derived from information should exceed the costs of providing it;
- *balance between qualitative characteristics*: there may be constraints in the balance between relevance and reliability – those seeking reliability may ask for more detail than would be considered necessary on grounds of relevance; those emphasizing the relevance of information may have to recognize some sacrifice of reliability.

1.8.3 True and fair view or fair presentation

The IASB framework does not include a discussion of the concept of 'true and fair' but it asserts that the application of the principal qualitative characteristics and of appropriate accounting standards normally results in financial statements that convey what is generally understood as a true and fair view. The framework gives 'presenting fairly' as equivalent wording.

1.8.4 Definition, recognition and measurement

The broad classes of transactions portrayed in financial statements are called elements of financial statements. The elements relating to the measurement of financial position are assets, liabilities, and equity. Those relating to the measurement of performance are income and expenses. For an item to be reported in a balance sheet or income statement it must first of all meet the definition of an element and then satisfy the criteria for recognition. These elements are defined as follows:

- an *asset* is a resource controlled by the enterprise as a result of past events and from which future economic benefits are expected to flow to the enterprise;
- a *liability* is a present obligation of the enterprise arising from past events, the settlement of which is expected to result in an outflow from the enterprise of resources embodying economic benefits;

- *equity* is the residual interest in the assets of the enterprise after deducting all its liabilities;
- *income* is increases in economic benefits during the accounting period in the form of inflows or enhancements of assets or decreases of liabilities that result in increases in equity, other than those relating to contributions from equity participants;
- *expenses* are decreases in economic benefits during the accounting period in the form of outflows or depletions of assets or incurring of liabilities that result in decreases in equity, other than those relating to distributions to equity participants.

An item that meets the definition of an element should be recognized (i.e. incorporated in words and numerical amount in accounting statements) if (and only if):

- it is probable that any future economic benefits associated with the item will flow to or from the enterprise; and
- the item has a cost or value that can be measured with reliability.

Items that meet the definition of an element but fail to meet the criteria for recognition may warrant disclosure in the notes to the financial statements if knowledge of the item is considered to be relevant to the evaluation of the results of the enterprise.

1.8.4.1 Assets

An asset is recognized in the balance sheet when it is probable that the future economic benefit will flow to the enterprise and the asset has a cost or value that can be measured reliably. When expenditure has been incurred that meets the definition of an asset but fails the recognition test because it is considered improbable that economic benefit will flow to the enterprise beyond the current accounting period, the transaction should be recognized as an expense in the income statement.

1.8.4.2 Liabilities

A liability is recognized in the balance sheet when it is probable that an outflow of resources embodying economic benefits will result from the settlement of a present obligation and the amount at which the settlement will take place can be measured reliably.

1.8.4.3 Income

Income is recognized in the income statement when an increase in future economic benefits related to an increase in an asset or decrease of a liability has arisen that can be measured reliably.

1.8.4.4 Expenses

Expenses are recognized in income statements when a decrease in future economic benefits relating to a decrease in an asset or an increase of a liability has arisen that can be measured reliably.

1.8.5 Measurement: concepts of capital maintenance

The IASB framework is least specific when discussing the measurement methods that should be used in recognizing the elements of the financial statements. It merely lists the different measurement bases that are currently used, namely Historical cost; Current cost; Realizable value; and Present value. The framework declines to express a preference for any of these bases of measurement.

In the context of making no recommendation on measurement it is perhaps surprising that the framework ventures into capital maintenance. It offers the guidance that the selection of the appropriate concept of capital (i.e. invested money, invested purchasing power or physical output capacity) and hence the concept of capital maintenance by an enterprise should be based on the needs of the users of its financial statements.

The concept of capital maintenance provides the link between the concepts of capital and profit and imposes some limitation on the measurement processes adopted.

The framework points out that selection from the available concepts of capital maintenance and measurement bases provides a wide range of accounting models that can be used in the preparation of financial statements. It is claimed that the framework is applicable to the range of accounting models and that at present there is no intention to prescribe one particular model for general adoption.

1.9 Multinational companies

It has become common for multinational companies to express their accounting results by reference to an internationally accepted approach. This has been perceived as being more acceptable to the investing public and to stock exchange regulators. At present, many companies have two internationally recognized approaches from which to choose – US GAAP and IFRS.

An example of the use of US GAAP as a global standard is seen in Exhibit 1.14 where Matsushita uses domestic GAAP for individual companies in the group but then applies US GAAP for the group accounts.

The use of IFRS by multinational companies depends on the status of IFRS in the home country of the parent company (see Exhibit 1.15).

Research has shown that companies claiming to comply with IASs in 1996 did not necessarily comply in all respects (Street *et al.*, 1999) and this limited compliance continued into 1999 (Cairns, 1999). It is important for the credibility of the IASB that the claim for compliance is not misleading. Even where companies make clear the areas in which they do not comply, it could nevertheless cause confusion in the minds of those using the accounts. It has been suggested that companies referring to the use of IASs in their financial statements should preferably comply with all material aspects of all IASs (Cairns, 1999).

Exhibit 1.14 Use of US GAAP, Matsushita

---

1. Summary of significant accounting policies

(b) Basis of preparation of Consolidated Financial Statements

The Company and its domestic subsidiaries maintain their books of account in conformity with the financial accounting standards of Japan and its foreign subsidiaries in conformity with those of the countries of their domicile.

The consolidated financial statements presented herein have been prepared in a manner and reflect adjustments which are necessary to conform with accounting principles generally accepted in the United States of America.

Source: Matsushita Electric Industrial Co Ltd, annual report (2004), p. 51.

Exhibit 1.15	Variations in status of IFRS

- IFRS used as national standards, with explanatory material added
- IFRS used as national standards, plus national standards developed for topics not covered by IFRS
- IFRS used as national standards, with some cases of modification for local conditions or circumstances
- National accounting standards separately developed but based on and similar to the relevant IFRS; national standards generally provide additional explanatory material only
- National accounting standards separately developed but based on and similar to the relevant IAS in most cases; however, some standards may provide more or less choice than IFRS; no reference is made to IFRS in national standards
- As in previous case except that each standard includes a statement that compares the national standard with the relevant IFRS
- National standards developed separately
- National standards do not exist at the present time
- No national standards; IFRS not formally adopted but usually used

IAS 1, *Presentation of Financial Statements*, requires that:

An entity whose financial statements comply with IFRSs shall make an explicit and unreserved statement of such compliance in the notes. Financial statements shall not be described as complying with IFRSs unless they comply with all the requirements of IFRSs.

An increasing number of companies now present financial statements that conform with IFRS. However, because of the strict wording of IAS 1 (revised), some are silent because they do not comply as completely as the IAS requires. Four approaches may be identified.

1 In some cases, national requirements conform with IFRS. In such instances there may be no practical problem from the point of view of the company but it is important for the user of the financial statements to know that this is the case. An example is shown in South Africa by Barloworld (Exhibit 1.16).

Exhibit 1.16	Statement of accounting policies, Barloworld

Accounting policies and basis of preparation

The financial statements are prepared in accordance with International Financial Reporting Standards (IFRS), previously referred to as International Accounting Standards (IAS) and with South African Statements of Generally Accepted Accounting Practice. They have been prepared on a basis consistent with the prior year.

Source: Barloworld (South Africa), Annual Report (2003), Notes to the Annual Financial Statements, www.barloworld.com

2 In other cases, IFRS are used where national requirements are silent. This gives partial compliance with IFRSs. Exhibit 1.17 (Saipem) provides an instance of using International Accounting Standards where national accounting standards fail to cover a specific area.

Exhibit 1.17 Accounting policies, Saipem

Preparation criteria

The Consolidated Financial Statements at 31st December 2003 were prepared in accordance with the criteria established in paragraph 3 of Law Decree 127 of 9/4/1991 (hereinafter referred to as "Decree"), and comply with the accounting principles set by the "Consigli Nazionali dei Dottori Commercialisti e dei Ragionieri" (Italian Council of Public Accountants) and, where silent, those set by the International Accounting Standards Board (I.A.S.B.). The true and correct presentation of the Consolidated Balance Sheet and Income Statement has not deviated from paragraph 4 of Decree art.29.

Source: Saipem (Italy), Annual Report (2003), p. 91, www.saipem.eni.it

---

3 Some companies present full financial statements in conformity with IFRS as the main financial statements (see Roche, Exhibit 1.18). Others produce the group financial statements in IFRS but retain national accounting rules for the parent company financial statements (see Stora Enso, Exhibit 1.19).

Exhibit 1.18 Accounting policy for consolidated financial statements, Roche

1. Summary of significant accounting policies

Basis of preparation of the consolidated financial statements

The consolidated financial statements of the Roche Group have been prepared in accordance with International Financial Reporting Standards (IFRS), including standards and interpretations issued by the International Accounting Standards Board (IASB). They have been prepared using the historical cost convention except that, as disclosed in the accounting policies below, certain items, including derivatives and available-for-sale investments, are shown at fair value. They were approved for issue by the Board of Directors on 2 February 2004.

Source: Roche (Switzerland), Annual Report (2003), p. 75. www.roche.com

---

Exhibit 1.19 Accounting principles, Stora Enso

Presentation of financial accounts

Stora Enso prepares annual and interim financial accounts conforming to international financial reporting standards (IFRS). These reports are published in Finnish, Swedish, English and German. In addition, Stora Enso makes an annual reconciliation with US GAAP (Form 20-F).

Extract from auditors' report

In our opinion, the consolidated financial statements prepared in accordance with International Financial Reporting Standards (IFRS) give a true and fair view of the consolidated result of operations, as well as of the financial position of the Stora Enso Group. The

Exhibit 1.19 *(Continued)*

consolidated financial statements have been prepared in accordance with prevailing rules and regulations in Finland and can be adopted.

The parent company's financial statements have been prepared in accordance with the Finnish Accounting Act and other rules and regulations governing the preparation of the financial statements. The parent company financial statements give a true and a fair view, as defined in the Accounting Act, of the Company's result of operations and financial position. The parent company's financial statements can be adopted and the members of the Board of Directors and the Chief Executive Officer of the parent company discharged from liability for the period audited by us. The proposal of the Board of Directors regarding the distributable funds is in compliance with the Finnish Companies' Act.

Helsinki, 13 February, 2004.

Source: Extract from Stora Enso (Finland) Financials (2003) p. 5, p. 107. www.storaenso.com

4 Some companies include in the financial report a reconciliation showing the differences between national accounting practices and the requirements of IFRS or US GAAP (there are examples in later chapters). Stora Enso (Finland) (Exhibit 1.20) provides a reconciliation between IFRS and US GAAP.

Finally, an interesting example of meeting a range of user needs is shown by the Russian company Gazprom (Exhibit 1.21) which produces a statutory consolidated financial

Exhibit 1.20 Reconciliation of IFRS and US GAAP results, Stora Enso

Note 28—Summary of differences between International Financial Reporting Standards and Generally Accepted Accounting Principles in the United States
The Group's consolidated financial statements are prepared in accordance with IFRS, which differ in a number of respects from the accounting principles generally accepted in the United States ("U.S. GAAP"). Such differences include methods for measuring and presenting the amounts shown in the consolidated financial statements, as well as additional disclosures required by U.S. GAAP.

Reconciliation of net profit (loss) and shareholders' equity
The following is a summary of the significant adjustments to net profit (loss) and shareholders' equity required when reconciling such amounts recorded in the Group's consolidated financial statements to the corresponding amounts in accordance with U.S. GAAP. The most significant adjustments relate to the accounting for business combinations. As further detailed below, the business combination of STORA and Enso is accounted for as a uniting of interests under IFRS but is accounted for using the purchase method under U.S. GAAP. This difference affects the valuation of a number of financial statement accounts at the date of the combination. For presentation purposes in the reconciliation, which follow, the "Reverse acquisition" item includes solely the impact of valuation differences that arose using the purchase method under U.S. GAAP. The other reconciling items reflect the pre-and post-combination differences between IFRS and U.S. GAAP.

►

Reconciliation of net profit (loss)

	For the year ended December 31,			
	2001	2002	2003	2003
	€	€	€	$
		(in millions)		
Reconciliation of net profit (loss)				
Net profit (loss) in accordance with IFRS (restated)	917.9	(240.7)	137.9	173.7
U.S. GAAP adjustments:				
a) Employee benefit plans (restated)	2.3	(11.0)	(0.8)	(1.0)
b) Reverse acquisition	(53.3)	(204.5)	(59.7)	(75.2)
c) Acquisition of Consolidated Papers Inc.	(14.6)	(153.1)	7.8	9.8
d) Provision for future reforestation costs	1.8	(1.5)	0.8	1.0
e) Derivative financial instruments	19.8	140.2	133.8	168.5
f) Impairment of goodwill	(10.1)	–	(47.1)	(59.3)
g) Impairment of fixed assets	–	71.8	(4.9)	(6.2)
h) Stock based compensation	(9.2)	9.2	(1.2)	(1.5)
i) Synthetic option hedge	24.2	–	–	–
j) Pension surplus refund	11.9	10.9	2.4	3.0
k) Amortization of goodwill	3.2	148.8	116.1	146.3
l) Restructuring costs	–	–	20.7	26.1
m) Biological assets	–	–	(24.1)	(30.4)
n) Share of results in associated companies	–	–	(10.2)	(12.8)
Deferred tax effect of U.S. GAAP adjustments (restated)	(18.5)	(73.6)	(37.1)	(46.7)
Net income (loss) in accordance with U.S. GAAP	875.4	(303.5)	234.4	295.3

Reconciliation of shareholders' equity

	As of December 31,		
	2002	2003	2003
	€	€	$
		(in millions)	
Reconciliation of shareholders' equity			
Shareholders' equity in accordance with IFRS (restated)	8,034.8	7,952.9	10,018.8
U.S. GAAP adjustments:			
a) Employee benefit plans (restated)	(32.4)	(36.3)	(45.7)
b) Reverse acquisition	658.3	598.6	754.1
c) Acquisition of Consolidated Papers Inc.	257.0	195.8	246.6
d) Provision for future reforestation costs	22.7	23.5	29.6
f) Impairment of goodwill	52.8	5.7	7.2
g) Impairment of fixed assets	64.8	49.4	62.2
h) Stock based compensation	–	(1.2)	(1.5)
j) Pension surplus refund	(3.9)	(1.5)	(1.9)
k) Amortization of goodwill	152.0	268.1	337.7
l) Restructuring costs	–	20.7	26.1
m) Biological assets	–	(886.7)	(1,117.0)
n) Share of results in associated companies	–	(54.2)	(68.3)
Deferred tax effect of U.S. GAAP adjustments (restated)	(21.6)	228.7	288.1
Shareholders' equity in accordance with U.S. GAAP	9,184.5	8,363.5	10,536.0

Source: Stora Enso (Finland) Form 20-F (2003), from pages F-67 and F-69. www.storaenso.com

Exhibit 1.21 Income statements and reconciliation statement, Gazprom

OAO GAZPROM
CONSOLIDATED STATEMENT OF INCOME
for the year ended 31 December 2003
(in million Roubles)

Note		For 2003	For 2002
	INCOME FROM AND EXPENSES ON ORDINARY ACTIVITIES		
	Sales of goods, products, works and services (less value added tax,		
4,15	excise tax and other similar mandatory payments)	844,566	613,745
4,16	Cost of goods, products, works and services sold	(503,535)	(381,665)
4,16	Commercial expenses	(503)	(200)
4,16	Management expenses	(51,312)	(43,748)
	Gross profit from sales	**289,216**	**188,132**
	OTHER INCOME AND EXPENSES		
	Interest income	3,787	4,041
	Interest expense	(31,471)	(29,902)
	Income from investments in other companies	1,121	828
17	Other operating income	821,017	655,957
17	Other operating expenses	(841,251)	(674,294)
18	Non-operating income	81,819	66,353
18	Non-operating expenses	(83,655)	(64,136)
	Profit of associates	10,705	5,754
	Extraordinary income	134	194
	Extraordinary expenses	(157)	(230)
	Profit before profit tax	**251,265**	**152,697**
	Deferred tax assets	(988)	15,108
	Deferred tax liabilities	(28,000)	(32,741)
13	Current profit tax	(41,565)	(23,894)
13	Other similar payments	(7,102)	(9,282)
	Net profit of the reporting period before minority interest	**173,610**	**101,888**
	Minority interest	(2,733)	2,077
	Net profit of the reporting period	**170,877**	**103,965**
	FOR REFERENCE		
	Non-temporary tax liabilities	10,375	4,545
21	Basic profit per share (in roubles)	8.34	4.86

A.B. Miller
Chairman of the Management Committee

E.A. Vasilieva
Chief Accountant

▶

OAO GAZPROM
IFRS CONSOLIDATED STATEMENT OF INCOME
for the year ended 31 December 2003
(in millions of Russian Roubles)

Notes		Year ended 31 December	
		2003	2002
5,22	Sales	819,753	644,687
5,23	Operating expenses	(593,415)	(496,713)
5	**Operating profit**	**226,338**	**147,974**
	Exchange gains	55,564	23,553
	Exchange losses	(40,424)	(32,988)
	Interest income	15,295	10,636
16,17	Interest expense	(32,301)	(29,265)
3	Monetary gain	–	31,380
15,24	Gains on and extinguishment of restructured liabilities	4,007	13,908
	Net monetary effects and financing items	2,141	17,224
11	Share of net income of associated undertakings	3,478	4,285
19	Gains (losses) on available-for-sale investments	5,017	(3,729)
	Profit before profit tax and minority interest	**236,974**	**165,754**
18	Current profit tax expense	(42,368)	(54,187)
18	Deferred profit tax expense	(32,449)	(81,945)
18	Profit tax expense	(74,817)	(136,132)
	Profit before minority interest	**162,157**	**29,622**
29	Minority interest	(3,062)	(667)
	Net profit	**159,095**	**28,955**
26	**Basic and diluted earnings per share (in Roubles)**	**8.02**	**1.39**

A.B. Miller
Chairman of the Management Committee
30 June 2004

E.A. Vasilieva
Chief Accountant
30 June 2004

The accompanying notes are an integral part of these financial statements.

►

Exhibit 1.21 *(Continued)*

OAO GAZPROM
NOTES TO THE IFRS CONSOLIDATED FINANCIAL STATEMENTS – 31 DECEMBER 2003
(in millions of Russian Roubles)

25 RECONCILIATION OF RAR PROFIT TO IFRS NET PROFIT

	Year ended 31 December	
	2003	2002
RAR profit per consolidated statutory accounts	170,877	121,598
Effects of IFRS adjustments:		
Deferred tax expense	(4,229)	(82,242)
Transition period current profit tax expense	6,564	(20,203)
Net effect of additional taxes other than on income	(106)	(6,605)
Impairment provisions and other provisions	(14,813)	(6,883)
Monetary gain	–	31,380
Net effect on indexation of revenues and costs	–	18,593
Discount related to restructured tax and other liabilities	–	4,473
Difference in gains on extinguished restructured tax liabilities	(3,066)	(16,259)
Losses on available-for-sale investments	(2,198)	(4,806)
Gain from sale of treasury shares	(4,679)	(1,057)
Net decrease (increase) in depreciation charge	1,287	(3,596)
Derecognition of income related to penalties and interest	(125)	(4,264)
Other	9,583	(1,174)
IFRS net profit	159,095	28,955

Source: Gazprom, Statutory consolidated financial report (2003) p. 3 and IFRS consolidated financial statements (2003) pp. 4 and 31. www.gazprom.ru/eng/

report, based on Russian GAAP, and an IFRS financial report. These give financial statements of quite different appearance and content. A reconciliation statement is provided, linking reported profit in each system. The reconciliation shows that the IFRS reported profit is considerably more prudent than the RAR profit. The main causes are: recording a deferred tax expense, carrying out an impairment test and reporting the effect of restructured liabilities. The restructured liabilities resulted from an amicable agreement with creditors in 2002. For IFRS purposes, in 2002, the present value of the liabilities was calculated as RR 10,373m and compared with the nominal value of RR 13,211m. The resulting decrease was recognized in the consolidated statement of income for 2002 as a gain arising on the extinguishment of a liability. In subsequent years the carrying amount of the liability increases when the present value is recalculated at the discount rate. The increase in the liability is recognized in the IFRS income statement as an interest expense caused by the discount 'unwinding'

From 2005 the consolidated financial statements of some multinationals are bound by the regulations of their home country, particularly those in the European Union (see Chapter 9). In other parts of the world multinational companies will continue to exercise choice in presenting consolidated financial statements. Time will tell whether US GAAP or IFRS becomes the dominant means by which non-US and non-EU multinational companies will choose to achieve the wider international acceptance of their annual reports.

Summary and conclusions

This chapter has shown that the IASB has made significant steps towards global convergence of accounting standards for listed companies. The expertise and accumulated experience of the IASB and its predecessor IASC has increasingly been recognized by other international standard setters. However, there is a question mark remaining over the likelihood of unconditional acceptance by the most significant stock market regulators and national legislators. Complementing the work of the IASB, there are many organizations working towards achievement of harmonization and standardization. Not all seek to be active at a global level, some being satisfied with regional action. Multinational companies have moved towards use of global accounting standards, either IFRS or US GAAP, but some are selective in mixing international and national practices.

Key points from the chapter:

- The arguments in favour of global accounting standards are expressed in terms of benefits for preparers, investors and regulators in terms of transparency, comparability, cost saving and understandability.

- The arguments against global accounting standards are that apparent comparability of rules may hide underlying real differences in the transactions and events that are reported; national control of standard setting is lost; the standards are being used in developing countries without regard for their specific needs; and giving monopoly position to one organization may reduce quality through lack of competition.

- The work of the IASB is complemented by that of other organizations, such as IFAC, harmonizing related aspects such as auditing, corporate governance, education and training, ethics and stock market regulation.

- The IASB has emerged from a process that began with the IASC forming in 1973; there was constant change in the IASC's methods of working as international standards gained greater acceptance.

- IOSCO's acceptance of international accounting standards in 2000 was the key event leading to acceptance of IFRS as being suitable for developed capital markets.

- The decision of the EU to require IFRS for all listed companies from 2005 was a further key event in encouraging the wider acceptance of IFRS.

- It is important to read the 'accounting policies' notes of any multinational company to know what combination of global standards and national standards has been applied by the company.

Questions

The following questions test your understanding of the material contained in the chapter and allow you to relate your understanding to the learning outcomes specified at the start of this chapter. The learning outcomes are repeated here. Each question is cross-referenced to the relevant section of the chapter.

Discuss the arguments for and against global accounting standards

1 Explain the arguments that support the development of global accounting standards (section 1.2.1).

2 Explain the arguments against the development of global accounting standards (section 1.2.2).

3 Discuss the relative merits of harmonization and standardization as ways of achieving global comparability in accounting rules and practice (section 1.2.3).

Describe the main international organizations that are encouraging international cooperation

4 To what extent does the work of other international organizations complement the work of the IASB (section 1.3)?

5 What are the relative benefits and limitations of regional groupings of accountancy bodies, wider international groupings of accountancy bodies, intergovernmental organizations and representative groupings of interests such as securities markets regulators or financial executives (section 1.3)?

Explain the nature and operations of the IASB

6 To what extent do the stated objectives of the IASC Foundation and the IASB provide something more than the work already done by other international organizations having an interest in accounting matters (section 1.4)?

7 Compare the objectives as stated in the 2000 Constitution with those of the 1973 Constitution. What do you learn about the history of the changing nature of the work of the IASC and the intended future direction of the IASB (sections 1.4 and 1.7)?

8 What are the benefits and potential limitations of having a Standards Advisory Council (section 1.4.4)?

9 What are the benefits and potential limitations of having an International Financial Reporting Interpretations Committee (section 1.4.3)?

Understand the challenges facing the IASB in its work

10 What mechanisms exist to ensure the independence of the IASB as a standard-setting body? Is there any potential risk that the financing arrangements for the IASB might jeopardize its independence? What other factors may influence independence (section 1.4.5)?

11 Is the process for issuing a standard sufficient to ensure that all interested parties are consulted? What are the benefits and potential limitations of the process (section 1.5.1)?

12 Is the IASB able to be effective in enforcing its standards? To what extent do established national practices in developed countries inhibit the work of the IASB (section 1.5.2)?

Understand the key stages of historical development of international accounting standards

13 How and why has the nature of the work of the IASC and IASB changed over time (section 1.7)?

14 Was the 1989 Comparability Project a success (section 1.7.3)?

15 What necessitated the implementation of the core standards programme (section 1.7.4)?

16 What is the purpose of the Improvements project (section 1.7.5.2)?

17 Does the IASB meet the needs of developing economies (section 1.7.6)?

Describe the main features of the Framework for the Preparation and Presentation of Financial Statements

18 Why did the IASC decide it was necessary to issue a Framework in 1989 (section 1.8)?

19 What possible explanations are there for the measurement section being the least well developed section of the Framework (section 1.8.5)?

Explain how multinational companies demonstrate their use of global accounting standards

20 What information should readers look for in understanding the use of global accounting standards by multinational companies (section 1.9)?

References and further reading

Ball, R., Robin, A. and Wu, J.S. (2003) 'Incentives versus standards: properties of accounting income in four East Asian countries', *Journal of Accounting and Economics*, 36: 235–270.

Barth, M.E., Clinch, G. and Shibano, T. (1999) 'International accounting harmonization and global equity markets', *Journal of Accounting and Economics*, 26: 201–235.

Cairns, D. (1999) 'Exceptions to the Rule', *Accountancy International*, November, 84–85, reporting on the *Financial Times International Accounting Standards Survey 1999*, by David Cairns.

Cairns, D. (2002) *A Guide to Applying International Accounting Standards*, 3rd edn. London: Butterworths.

Chamisa, E.E. (2000) 'The relevance and observance of the IASC standards in developing countries and the particular case of Zimbabwe', *International Journal of Accounting*, 35(2): 267–286.

Choi, F.D.S. and Bavishi, V.B. (1982) 'Financial Accounting Standards: A multinational synthesis and policy framework', *International Journal of Accounting*, Fall, 159–183.

Evans, T.G. and Taylor, M.E. (1982) 'Bottom line compliance with the IASC: A comparative analysis', *International Journal of Accounting Education and Research*, Fall, 115–128.

Fleming, P.D. (1991) 'The growing importance of International Accounting Standards', *Journal of Accountancy*, September, 100–106.

Gernon, H., Purvis, S.E.C. and Diamond, M.A. (1990) 'An analysis of the implications of the IASC's Comparability Project', School of Accounting, University of Southern California.

Haller, A. (2002) 'Financial accounting developments in the European Union: past events and future prospects', *The European Accounting Review*, 11(1): 153–190.

Hirshleifer, D. and Teoh. S.H. (2003) 'Limited attention, information disclosure, and financial reporting', *Journal of Accounting and Economics*, 36: 337–386.

Hoarau, C. (1995) 'International accounting harmonization: American hegemony or mutual recognition with benchmarks?', *The European Accounting Review*, 4(2): 217–233.

Holthausen, R.W. (2003) 'Testing the relative power of accounting standards versus incentives and other institutional features to influence the outcome of financial reporting in an international setting', *Journal of Accounting and Economics*, 36: 271–283.

Hove, M.R. (1990) 'The Anglo-American influence on International Accounting Standards: The case of the disclosure standards of the IASC', *Research in Third World Accounting*, Vol. 1. London: JAI Press.

IASC (1989) 'Framework for the Preparation and Presentation of Financial Statements', contained in *International Accounting Standards, 1997*. London: International Accounting Standards Committee.

Kirby, A.J. (2001) 'International competitive effects of harmonization', *International Journal of Accounting*, 36(1): 1–32.

Larson, R.K. and Kenny, S.Y. (1995) 'An empirical analysis of international accounting standards, equity markets, and economic growth in developing countries', *Journal of International Financial Management and Accounting*, 6(2): 130–158.

Leuz, C. (2003) 'IAS versus US GAAP: Information asymmetry-based evidence from Germany's new market'. *Journal of Accounting Research*, 41(3): 445–472.

McKinnon, S.M. and Janell, P. (1984) 'The International Accounting Standards Committee: A performance evaluation', *International Journal of Accounting Education and Research*, Spring, 19–34.

McLeay, S., Neal, D. and Tollington, T. (1999) 'International Standardisation and Harmonisation: A new measurement technique', *Journal of International Financial Management and Accounting*, 10(1): 42–70.

Miles, S. and Nobes, C. (1998) 'The use of foreign accounting data in UK financial institutions', *Journal of Business Finance and Accounting*, 25(3) and (4): 309–328.

Most, K.S. (1984) *International Conflict of Accounting Standards, a Research Report*. Vancouver: The Canadian Certified General Accountants' Research Foundation.

Nair, R.D. and Frank, W.G. (1981) 'The harmonization of International Accounting Standards, 1973–1979', *International Journal of Accounting Education and Research*, Fall, 61–77.

Purvis, S.E.C., Gernon, H. and Diamond, M.A. (1991) 'The IASC and its Comparability Project', *Accounting Horizons*, 5(2), 25–44.

Rahman, S.F. (1998) 'International accounting regulation by the United Nations: a power perspective', *Accounting, Auditing and Accountability Journal*, 11(5): 593–623.

Rivera, J.M. (1989) 'The internationalization of accounting standards: Past problems and current prospects', *International Journal of Accounting Education and Research*, 24(4), 320–341.

Roberts, C.B., Salter, S.B. and Kantor, J. (1996) 'The IASC Comparability Project and current financial reporting reality: An empirical study of reporting in Europe', *British Accounting Review*, 28, 1–22.

Salter, S.B., Roberts, C.B. and Kantor, J. (1996) 'The IASC Comparability Project: A cross-national comparison of financial reporting practices and IASC proposed rules', *Journal of International Accounting and Taxation*, 5(1), 89–111.

Street, D.L., Gray, S.J. and Bryant, S.M. (1999) 'Acceptance and observance of International Accounting Standards: An empirical study of companies claiming to comply with IASs', *International Journal of Accounting*, 43(1), 11–48.

Sunder, S. (2002) 'Regulatory competition among accounting standards within and across international boundaries', *Journal of Accounting and Public Policy*, 21(3): 219–234.

Tarca, A. (2004) 'International convergence of accounting practices: Choosing between IAS and US GAAP', *Journal of International Financial Management and Accounting*, 15(1): 60–91.

Tay, J.S.W. and Parker, R.H. (1990) 'Measuring harmonization and standardization', *Abacus*, March, 71–88.

Wallace, R.S.O. (1990) 'Survival strategies of a global organization: The case of the International Accounting Standards Committee', *Accounting Horizons*, 4(2), 1–22.

Weetman, P., Adams, C.A. and Gray, S.J. (1993) 'Issues in International Accounting Harmonisation: The Significance of UK/US Accounting Differences and Implications for the IASC's Comparability Project', *Research Report*, 33. London: Chartered Association of Certified Accountants.

Zeff, S.A. (2002) '"Political" lobbying on proposed standards: a challenge to the IASB', *Accounting Horizons*, 16(1): 43–54.

This chapter also draws on material contained in IASC and IASB publications, particularly:

IASB/IASC Annual Review (various issues)

IASB/IASC Insight (published several times during a year)

IASB/IASC, International Accounting Standards, published annually

various Exposure Drafts and Statements, as indicated in the chapter

the IASB website www.iasb.org

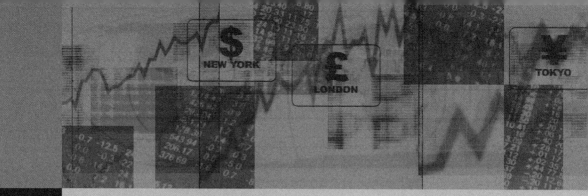

2 International financial reporting standards

Learning outcomes

After reading this chapter you should be able to:

● Explain the key issues and main principles of each international financial reporting standard.

● Understand the aims and achievements of the Comparability Project, the IASC's Core Standards programme and the IASB's Improvements Project in reducing options available under international standards.

● Relate the IFRS to the Framework in categories of assets, liabilities, recognition, measurement, group accounting and special needs of particular user groups.

● Form an opinion on the extent to which a company's stated accounting policies are consistent with IFRS.

2.1 Introduction

The purpose of this chapter is to establish knowledge and understanding of the state of International Financial Reporting Standards (IFRS) at March 2004 which marked the achievement of a 'stable platform' (see section 1.7.5.2). It also explains the process by which successive projects narrowed down the options and removed ambiguities that had existed in earlier versions of standards. For each standard there is an explanation of its development through the Comparability Project of the early 1990s, the Core Standards programme of 1995 to 1999 and the Improvements Project of 2001 to 2004. The chapter will help you to understand the problems of achieving convergence and global acceptance of a single treatment of each accounting issue.

Exhibit 1.10 in Chapter 1 contains a table listing IFRSs in numerical sequence, and then Exhibit 1.11 rearranges them according to the accounting issues they address. This arrangement is used in this chapter.

This chapter summarizes the key issues and main content of each standard. It explains the progression through the Comparability Project of 1989, the Core Standards programme of 1995–99 and the further refinements carried out in the IASB's Improvements Project prior to acceptance of IFRS by those countries which identified 2005 as the target year for implementation.[1]

We explained in Chapter 1 that 'IFRS' is a collective description for the International Financial Reporting Standards issued by the IASB and the International Accounting Standards issued by the predecessor IASC. For clarity in this chapter we use the separate labels 'IFRS' and 'IAS' to reflect the titles of specific standards as at January 2005. It is important to note that, in the language of standard-setting, 'should' is interpreted as 'must', while 'may' is interpreted as 'is permitted'.

2.2 Disclosure and presentation

Disclosure and presentation of information is fundamental to providing the users of financial statements with information which meets their particular needs. IFRS have hitherto taken two routes to disclosure and presentation. One route dealt with general issues and the other with specific aspects. Standards of a general nature covered disclosure of accounting policies, types of information to be presented in financial statements and the presentation of current assets and current liabilities. Standards of a more specific nature focused on the reporting of cash flow; disclosure of fundamental errors; changes in accounting policy; segmental reporting; and the disclosure of related parties and their transactions with the enterprise. The common thread in all these standards is the tension between being open with those who have a legitimate right to information and preserving the commercial confidentiality which gives the enterprise its competitive advantage.

2.2.1 First-time adoption of IFRS (IFRS 1)

IFRS 1 was issued June 2003, effective for the first IFRS financial statements for a period starting on or after 1 January 2004. Earlier application was encouraged.

When an entity applies international standards for the first time it must make an explicit statement of compliance. This must be total compliance; the company may not specify exclusions. It must recognize all assets and liabilities that are required by IFRS and must not recognize assets and liabilities that are not permitted by IFRS. All measurements must follow IFRS. The application must be *retrospective*. That means that in general the company must present the financial statements as if IFRS had always been used by the company. The standard sets out some exemptions from this rule, relating to matters that would be too difficult to reconstruct historically. Comparative figures in the financial statements must comply with IFRS. There must be an explanation of how the transition from previous GAAP to IFRS

---

[1] It is impossible for any text book to be totally up-to-date with the rate at which the international financial reporting standards are developing. You should refer to press releases and summaries on the website of the IASB www.iasb.org and to the analyses and summaries provided by Deloitte Touche Tohmatsu on the website www.iasplus.com.

affected the entity's reported financial position, performance and cash flow. Exhibit 2.1 shows how T-Online reported first-time adoption of IFRS, complying with IFRS 1.

Exhibit 2.1 Presentation of IFRS 1 information, T-Online

Notes to the consolidated financial statements.

Summary of accounting principles.
Commencing with the 2003 financial year, the consolidated financial statements of T-Online International AG, Darmstadt, Germany are prepared in compliance with the International Financial Reporting Standards (IFRS) of the International Accounting Standards Board (IASB), notably IFRS 1 (First Time Adoption of IFRS), the International Accounting Standards (IAS), and the statements of the International Financial Reporting Interpretations Committee (IFRIC).

The criteria for exemption from the obligation to prepare consolidated financial statements in compliance with German accounting rules pursuant to Sec. 292 a of the German Commercial Code (HGB) are met. The consolidated financial statements, in compliance with German Accounting Standard 1 issued by the German Accounting Standards Committee (DRSC), are also consistent with the European Union directive on consolidated accounts (Directive 83/349/EEC). To achieve equivalence with consolidated financial statements prepared in accordance with German commercial law, all material information and notes under German commercial law that extend beyond IASB rules are stated.

From 2003, the consolidated statement of income is classified by the cost of sales format and the consolidated balance sheet is classified by the term of assets and liabilities. The primary basis of segmental reporting in accordance with IAS 14 is geographical. As T-Online's combined business model is based on unified provision of service from access and non-access segments, there is no secondary segmental reporting by product.

Financial Reporting/Auditing
Commencing 2003, under the terms of admission to Frankfurt Stock Exchange's Prime Standard (Exchange Rules, Section 62), the T-Online consolidated financial statements are prepared in accordance with International Financial Reporting Standards (IFRS). T-Online is consequently exempted from preparing financial statements in accordance with the German Commercial Code (HGB).

The consolidated financial statements are made publicly available within 90 days and the quarterly Group reports within 45 days of the reporting date.

Further details on significant accounting regulations are provided in the combined Group Management Report and the notes to the T-Online consolidated financial statements.

Overview
T-Online International AG changed its consolidated accounting method from HGB to IFRS/IAS as of January 1, 2003 and is for the first time presenting its consolidated financial statements for the 2003 financial year in accordance with IFRS. Taking the January 1, 2002 opening balance as our starting point, we thus have IFRS-based asset and earnings figures for 2002 and 2003. We will concentrate in this report on these figures, extended in certain instances to cover a five year period.

▶

Exhibit 2.1 *(Continued)*

[38] Material differences in accounting methods between IFRS/IAS and the German Commercial Code (HGB).

Following first-time adoption of IFRS/IAS in the 2003 financial year, we present a reconciliation of Group net income/loss and Group shareholders' equity from HGB to IFRS for 2002 in the table below.

Millions of €	Group net income/loss 2002	Group shareholders' equity Dec. 31, 2002	Group shareholders' equity Jan. 1, 2002
HGB	**(459.3)**	**5,365.8**	**5,814.0**
Intangible assets	13.2	4.9	(8.3)
Provision for T-Motion	13.9	0.0	0.0
Other provisions	(7.6)	(0.7)	6.9
Revenue deferral	0.5	(0.8)	(1.3)
Deferred taxes	(47.6)	150.6	198.2
Minority interests	(2.8)	(2.1)	(3.7)
IFRS	**(489.7)**	**5,517.7**	**6,005.8**

a) Intangible assets.

In accordance with the principles of IFRS/IAS, the intangible assets acquired from and developed by Deutsche Telekom AG on establishment of the legal predecessor of T-Online International AG (customer base, know-how) are carried at EUR 0.

On meeting the requirements of IAS 38, the development costs of software created by T-Online International AG and T-Online France were–in deviation from the HGB treatment–capitalized and amortized over the software's economic useful life.

b) Provisions.

Some provisions recognized in accordance with HGB are not recognized or are measured differently under IFRS. For example, the pension provisions recognized in the Group financial statements in accordance with HGB and in line with U.S. GAAP (SFAS No. 87) are measured differently in the IFRS/IAS Group financial statements. Provisions for operating expenses are not permissible under IFRS.

c) Deferred taxes.

Differences in income tax effects mostly involve deferred taxes on loss carryforwards, primarily at T-Online International AG. Most importantly, deferred taxes must be capitalized under IFRS/IAS, while recognition of deferred tax assets is optional under Sec. 274 HGB.

Source: T-Online annual report (2003) pages, 16, 70, 98, 121, www.t-online.net

2.2.2 Presentation of financial statements (IAS 1)

IAS 1 was revised in December 2003 to be applied for annual periods beginning on or after 1 January 2005. Earlier application was encouraged.

2.2.2.1 Key issues

The objective of IAS 1 is to ensure comparability of financial statements. This includes both comparability from one period of time to the next for a particular entity and comparability within the same period of time for more than one entity. It prescribes the basis for preparation of general purpose financial statements.

2.2.2.2 Approach in IAS 1

The standard specifies a complete set of financial statements as:

- balance sheet
- income statement
- statement of changes in equity
- cash flow statement
- notes, including a summary of significant accounting policies, significant judgements made by management and the basis of estimates used in the financial statements.

The standard defines 'IFRS' as comprising International Financial Reporting Standards, International Accounting Standards and Interpretations (IFRIC and SIC). It then explains a set of 'Overall Considerations', comprising:

- fair presentation and compliance with IFRSs
- going concern
- accrual basis of accounting
- consistency of presentation
- materiality and aggregation
- offsetting
- comparative information.

The most interesting of these is 'fair presentation'. It is defined in the standard as 'present fairly' without mentioning the phrase 'true and fair' which appeared in the Framework document (para. 46) as an alternative phrase. The change in emphasis could be seen as indirect evidence of a stronger US influence. The US wording is 'fair presentation in accordance with generally accepted accounting principles'. IAS 1 asserts that in virtually all circumstances a fair presentation is achieved by compliance with applicable IFRSs. The words 'true and fair view' may be seen on the one hand as allowing a higher degree of flexibility and judgement but on the other hand as permitting a looser approach to matters of detail. As an apparent compromise, IAS 1 allows that in extremely rare circumstances, where compliance with a standard would be so misleading as to conflict with the objective of fair presentation, a company shall depart from compliance with that requirement.

The 2003 version of IAS 1 prohibits the presentation of items of income and expense as 'extraordinary items'. The Board felt that the nature or function of a transaction or event, rather than its frequency, should determine its presentation within the income statement. Assets and liabilities are classified as current/non-current or else they are presented in order of liquidity.

Illustrative structures of financial statements are appended to IAS 1. The appendix is not part of the proposed standard and is therefore not intended to be mandatory. The use of a suggested format for presentation, even in an appendix, is a new departure for IASs.

The Statement showing changes in equity is a compromise which allows both the US format showing all changes in equity and the UK format showing total recognized gains and losses of the period. The UK approach must be accompanied by a note showing all changes in equity. The US-type format will include as a subtotal the total gains and losses of the period.

2.2.2.3 Reducing the options

The exposure draft E 53, leading to IAS 1 (1997), updated and brought into one document general aspects of disclosure and presentation, taken from earlier versions of IAS 1, IAS 5 (information to be disclosed in financial statements) and IAS 13 (presentation of current assets and current liabilities). IAS 5 and IAS 13 were then withdrawn. E 53 sought to improve comparability and so effectively reduce options in disclosure. However one option remained. IAS 13 had allowed a choice as to whether or not current assets and current liabilities should be presented as separate classifications in the balance sheet. That choice was preserved in E 53 and IAS 1 (1997). It was effectively removed in 2003 by giving precedence to a current/non-current presentation. The alternative is to present assets and liabilities in increasing or decreasing order of liquidity, but this may only be used where it is reliable and more relevant that a current/non-current presentation (e.g. in a financial institution that is lending and borrowing for long-term and short-term periods but does not have a trading cycle of the type found in a manufacturing business).

Comment on E 53 resulted in the inclusion in IAS 1 (1997) of the limited 'fair presentation' override described earlier. It was retained in the 2003 version but with a stronger restriction on the rare circumstances under which it would be necessary.

Prohibiting extraordinary items in IAS 1 (2003) is a further step in reducing the flexibility of accounting under IFRS.

2.2.3 Cash flow statements (IAS 7)

IAS 7 was issued in 1992.

2.2.3.1 Key issues

The purpose of IAS 7 is to provide information which is useful to users of financial statements in making economic decisions. It assumes that economic decisions require an evaluation of the ability of an enterprise to generate cash and cash equivalents and also an assessment of the timing and certainty of the generation of cash. The standard requires an enterprise to present a cash flow statement as an integral part of its financial statements.

2.2.3.2 Approach in IAS 7

Cash flows should be classified according to whether they arise from operating, investing or financing activities.

There are two ways of reporting cash flows from operating activities. The *direct* method requires separate disclosure of each major class of gross cash receipt and gross cash payment. The *indirect* method permits adjustment to the net profit or loss identified in the profit and loss account to eliminate the effects of transactions of a non-cash nature. There is no preference expressed between these alternatives but enterprises are encouraged to report cash flows from operating activities using the direct method.

The total cash flows from operating, investing and financing activities will equal the change in *cash and cash equivalents*, defined as short-term, highly liquid investments (having a maturity of three months or less from the date of acquisition).

The standard also encourages enterprises to disclose, by way of a note to the accounts, additional information that may be relevant to users, including amounts of undrawn borrowing facilities; amounts in each major category of activity relating to joint ventures reported using proportional consolidation; and amounts in each major category of activity for each reported industry and geographical segment.

2.2.3.3 Reducing the options

IAS 7 was fundamentally revised in 1992, superseding a funds flow statement of 1977. The funds flow statement of 1977 dealt with statements of changes in financial position, which concentrated on changes in the funding of the enterprise. IAS 7 concentrates on changes in cash and cash equivalents. In making that change, the IASC was reflecting changing international thinking where it had been recognized that statements covering all changes in financial position were complex and did not help users' understanding so effectively as statements of changes in cash position. The revision allowed choice between the direct and indirect method of preparing the operating cash flow. The indirect method is more commonly used because it is more convenient for companies to prepare this from the existing accounting information. The direct method requires analysis of the cash records.

IAS 7 was acceptable to IOSCO as a core standard.

2.2.4 Accounting policies, Changes in accounting estimates and Errors (IAS 8)

IAS 8 was revised in December 2003 to be applied for annual periods beginning on or after 1 January 2005. Earlier application was encouraged.

2.2.4.1 Key issues

Particular difficulties arise when unusual circumstances cause a change in the outcome of an event already reported. Difficulties for accounting practice are also encountered where a change in one accounting period invalidates comparability with earlier periods. An unusual item arising in one period may cause problems for comparability.

The general proposition underpinning the standard is that all items of income and expense recognized in a period should be included in the determination of the net profit or loss for the period. This proposition is applied in recommending treatment for three difficult areas: the cumulative effect of changes in accounting policy; changes in estimates; and the effect of errors. The common aspect is that all give rise to problems of comparability from one accounting period to the next.

2.2.4.2 Approach in IAS 8

Changes in accounting policy should only be made if required by statute or by accounting standard, or if the change results in more reliable and more relevant information about transactions and events. The required accounting treatment is to adjust the opening balance of retained earnings, or other component of equity, presented as if the new accounting policy had always been applied. Where the change in accounting policy is voluntary, the entity must explain the change, give a reason, and quantify the effect of the change.

Changes in accounting estimates result from the uncertainties of business. Such uncertainties are found in bad debts, warranties, and useful lives of depreciable assets. The effect on profit and loss should be reported in the period of the change, or in that period and future periods if the change takes effect over those periods. The nature and amount of the change should be disclosed.

Errors may arise in measurement, recognition, presentation or disclosure. Material errors that are discovered promptly are corrected before the financial statements are issued. If a material error comes to light after the financial statements are issued, it must be corrected by restating the comparative amounts for the prior period in which the error occurred. If it was even further back in time, the opening balances of the prior period must be adjusted.

2.2.4.3 Reducing the options

IAS 8, issued in 1978 and superseded in 1993, previously covered a larger collection of items in the profit and loss account, particularly extraordinary items, prior period items, fundamental errors and changes in accounting policies. It tried to accommodate those countries that preferred to make adjustments in the current period profit and loss account and those countries that preferred to make adjustments to opening balances of retained profit for the current period. The Comparability Project drew attention to the treatment of adjustments resulting from prior period items. E 32 proposed that the preferred treatment should be an adjustment to opening retained earnings but that an allowed alternative should remain in passing the item through the income statement of the current year. The 1993 version defined 'fundamental errors' and voluntary changes in accounting policies. The benchmark treatment for these was to adjust the opening balance of retained earnings but there was an allowed alternative of reporting the cumulative effect in the current year's profit and loss account. The 2003 revision removes this alternative. It also removes the concept of 'fundamental' errors which was difficult to define. Extraordinary items, formerly dealt with in IAS 8, are now prohibited under IAS 1. The overall result is a considerable tightening of the comparability of profit and loss accounts in representing the results of the period without distortion by the cumulative effects of previous periods.

2.2.5 Discontinued operations (IFRS 5)

IFRS 5 was issued in March 2004 to be applied to periods beginning on or after 1 January 2005. Earlier application was encouraged.

2.2.5.1 Key issues

The full title of IFRS 5 is *Non-current Assets Held for Sale and Discontinued Operations*. Discontinued operations cause the results of a period to be of limited usefulness for forecasting by users of accounts. It would be desirable for companies to give separate disclosure of discontinued operations but this raises questions of what should be disclosed, what should be measured, and what is meant by 'discontinued'.

2.2.5.2 Approach in IFRS 5

The standard deals only with presentation and disclosure. Recognition and measurement principles of other IFRS apply, particularly those on impairments and provisions. A discontinued operation is a component of an entity that has been disposed of or is classified as 'held for sale'. It will represent a separate major line of business or geographical area of operations. It will be part of a single coordinated plan to dispose of a separate major line of business or geographical area of operations, or be a subsidiary acquired exclusively with a view to resale.

There must be separate disclosure in the income statement of revenue, expenses and pre-tax profit of discontinued operations. Net cash flows must also be disclosed separately. This helps those seeking to make forecasts of continuing operations.

2.2.5.3 Reducing the options

IFRS 5 supersedes IAS 35 issued 1998, which in turn superseded part of IAS 8 issued 1992. The revision of IAS 8 in 1992 (see section 2.2.4.3) incorporated a requirement for certain disclosures about discontinuing operations. It resulted in variable practice and did not address the more difficult questions surrounding the recognition and measurement of the gain or loss on discontinuance. One difficult question is to decide on the precise date at which discontinuance should be recognized. A second difficult question is to decide precisely which costs are attributable to the discontinuing operation. The project on Discontinuing Operations was part of the package targeted for completion as a core standard. The title was chosen deliberately to reflect the Board's view that the discontinuance of an operation should be recognized in the financial statements before the process of discontinuing was completed. The Board also agreed, in giving approval for the project, that the operation would be treated as discontinuing once the enterprise was committed to discontinue the operation without any realistic possibilities of withdrawal. A draft Statement of Principles issued in November 1996 added further suggestions relating to disclosure, recognition and measurement. The recognition and measurement aspects were not taken forward in the exposure draft E 58, which preceded IAS 35.

However, IAS 35 was not compatible with the US standard SFAS 144 Accounting for the Impairment or Disposal of Long-Lived Assets (a FASB standard issued in 2001). As part of the project to reduce the differences between IFRS and US GAAP, the IASB moved closer to US GAAP on the subjects of assets held for sale, the timing of the classification of operations as discontinued and the presentation of such operations. The wording changed from 'discontinuing' in IAS 35 to 'discontinued' in IFRS 5. The change in wording reflects the focus on the later stage of the production or service process as recognized in IFRS 5.

2.2.6 Segment reporting (IAS 14)

IAS 14 was revised in 1997.

2.2.6.1 Key issues

Expert users of financial statements will almost always say that the information about segments is by far the most interesting part of the total package. On the other hand, the competitive edge may be lost if business rivals and customers learn too much about the enterprise.

The key issues in segment reporting are concerned with deciding how much detail is desirable and how to define segments so that the information provided is comparable across a range of enterprises and from one period to the next.

2.2.6.2 Approach in IAS 14

IAS 14 applies to enterprises whose securities are publicly traded and other economically significant entities. An enterprise should report financial information by segments – specifically, the different business segments and the different geographical areas in which it operates. *Business segments* are components based on products or services with similar risks and returns. *Geographical segments* are based on a particular economic environment, by location of assets or customers.

IAS 14 requires that an enterprise should look to its internal organizational structure and internal reporting systems for the purpose of identifying those segments. It is likely hat most enterprises will identify their business and geographical segments as the organizational units for which information is reported to the Board of Directors and to the Chief Executive Officer.

Under IAS 14 one basis of segmentation is to be primary and the other secondary. For each primary segment the enterprise must disclose: revenue; operating result; the basis of inter-segment pricing; carrying amount of segment assets and segment liabilities; cost of acquiring property, plant, equipment and intangibles; depreciation; non-cash expenses other than depreciation; and share of profit or loss of equity and joint venture investments. For secondary segments, disclosures are: revenue; assets; and costs of acquiring property.

The sum of the separate segments should equal the aggregate amounts in the financial statements. If that is not the case, a reconciliation statement should be disclosed explaining the difference. Other segmental disclosures are encouraged on a voluntary basis.

2.2.6.3 Reducing the options

IAS 14 was revised in 1997 from a reformatted 1995 version of the previous standard, issued in 1981. Exposure draft E 51, *Reporting Financial Information by Segment*, was issued in June 1996. It reflected many of the reporting requirements of IAS 14 (1981) but added new disclosures and sought to change the way in which segments were identified. It looked to the company's organizational structure and internal reporting system for the purpose of identifying its reportable business and geographical segments. The IASC benefited from the extensive input from financial analysts to this project. The international organizations of analysts had confirmed to the IASC, in various comments prior to the issue of E 51, that segment information was essential to meet the needs of a range of users of financial statements.

The review of IAS 14 was undertaken in parallel with similar reviews of existing requirements in the US and Canada. This was reflected in E 51 by the emphasis on the company's organizational structure and internal reporting system. However, the IASC Board started with the objective of providing insight into how diversity affects the overall risks and returns. This in turn required enterprises to disclose information about segments based on industrial and geographical distinctions. The standard-setters in the US and Canada seek to provide information about business activity. In consequence, they permit an enterprise to disclose segments based on the organizational structure of the enterprise, even where such segments cover a number of different industries or geographical areas.

The IASC Board approved IAS 14 in January 1997 but postponed publication until July 1997 to allow for harmonization efforts by the US and Canadian standard-setters. This resulted in particular in the idea of 'primary' and 'secondary' bases of segmentation. One other tightening of requirements is that the inter-segment transfers must be measured on the basis of the actual transfer pricing practice used in the enterprise (previously a different method could be used for segment disclosure purposes). The accounting policies used for segment reporting must be those of the main financial statements.

2.2.7 Related party disclosures (IAS 24)

IAS 24 was revised in December 2003 to be applied for accounting periods beginning on or after 1 January 2005. Earlier application was encouraged.

2.2.7.1 Key issues

When close relationships exist between one enterprise and another, there may be concerns as to whether the relationship is beneficial or detrimental. Such relationships exist where one party has the ability to control the other party or exercise significant influence over its financial and operating decisions. In the absence of information the user of financial statements cannot make an informed judgement about the relationship or about transactions resulting from the relationship.

The key issues in IAS 24 are the definition of related parties and the specification of what should be disclosed about relationships and the transactions resulting from those relationships.

2.2.7.2 Approach in IAS 24

Parties are considered to be related if one party has the ability to control the other party or exercise significant influence (participation in policy decisions) over the other party in making financial and operating decisions. The detailed definition covers joint control, common control, subsidiaries, associates and joint ventures. 'Significant influence' may be gained by share ownership, statute or agreement. 'Close family members' are defined as family members who may be expected to influence, or be influenced by, an individual in dealings with an entity.

The following relationships are not necessarily related parties:

● companies simply having a director in common;
● providers of finance, trade unions, public utilities, government departments and agencies in their normal dealings with an enterprise;
● business contacts such as a customer, supplier, franchisor, distributor or agent.

Related party relationships where control exists should be disclosed irrespective of whether there have been transactions between the parties. If there have been transactions between related parties, the reporting enterprise should disclose the nature of the related party relationship as well as the type of transaction. Aggregation of similar items can be made unless separate disclosure is necessary for an understanding of the effect on the financial statements.

The standard requires disclosure of the compensation (all employee benefits) of key management personnel, including any director.

2.2.7.3 Reducing the options

The 2003 standard superseded the 1995 reformatting of the standard which was first issued in 1984. IOSCO indicated that IAS 24 was acceptable as a core standard. The 2003 version was strengthened by requiring disclosure of the compensation (employee benefits) of key management personnel and by expanding and clarifying definitions and disclosure requirements of the previous version.

2.2.8 Earnings per share (IAS 33)

IAS 33 was revised in December 2003 to be applied for annual periods beginning on or after 1 January 2005. Earlier application was encouraged.

2.2.8.1 Key issues

The objective of IAS 33 is to set out principles for the disclosure and presentation of earnings per share which will improve performance comparison among different enterprises in the same period and among different accounting periods for the same enterprise. The standard pays particular attention to the number of shares issued, which forms the denominator of the formula for earnings per share.

2.2.8.2 Approach in IAS 33

The standard applies to enterprises whose ordinary shares are publicly traded. The enterprise should disclose basic earnings per share and diluted earnings per share with equal prominence on the face of the income statement. ('Basic earnings per share' indicates the earnings available to existing shareholders, while 'diluted earnings per share' indicates the earnings available if all potential conversions to ordinary shares took place.)

There should be disclosure of the amounts used in calculating the earnings per share. The method of calculation is also prescribed. In particular, a weighted average number of shares in issue should be calculated for use as the denominator. The IASC has worked closely with international organizations of financial analysts on this project.

2.2.8.3 Reducing the options

The 2003 revision superseded the version of 1997 which was the first IAS dealing with earnings per share. Its main achievement was harmonization with the US standard FAS 128, *Earnings per Share* (issued 1997) so far as the denominator (number of shares) is concerned. Initiatives by financial analysts to reach a worldwide consensus on the numerator (definition of earnings) have not yet led to agreement. IAS 33 was part of the agreed work programme of core standards. The 2003 revision gave additional guidance and examples on selected complex matters.

2.2.9 Interim financial reporting (IAS 34)

IAS 34 was issued in 1998.

2.2.9.1 Key issues

National securities regulators have various rules as to which companies should publish interim financial reports and how frequent the interim reporting should be. The key accounting issues are:

- Is the interim financial report intended to help in predicting the current financial year's results, or is it intended to help with projections more generally?
- Where the business activity is spread unevenly over the year, should it be reported as it occurs, or should there be smoothing of revenue and expenses over the year as a whole?

It is for national securities regulators and stock exchanges to decide which companies should be required to publish interim financial reports, and how frequently this should occur.

2.2.9.2 Approach in IAS 34

An interim report should include a condensed balance sheet, condensed income statement, condensed cash flow statement, condensed statement of changes in equity, and selected explanatory notes. Items should be reported in relation to the figures of the period (year-to-date basis) and not in relation to estimated annual data.

The accounting principles must be the same as those used in the company's annual financial statements. The same definitions of assets, liabilities, income and expenses must be used for interim reporting as for annual financial statements. Revenues and costs must be recognized when they occur, and not be anticipated or deferred. The interim tax expenses must be measured using the expected effective annual income tax rate.

The standard applies if an enterprise is required, or elects, to publish an interim report. The standard encourages at least half-yearly reporting for all public companies, within 60 days after the period end.

2.2.9.3 Reducing the options

A Point Outline paper, *Interim Financial Reporting*, issued early in 1996, was the first stage of a major initiative on this subject. The outline paper identified 27 basic issues of this type. The most important issues were to establish comparability with the annual reports and to ensure that the interim statement represents the actual revenues and costs of the period rather than a smoothing of results over the year. The steering committee published a draft Statement of Principles in September 1996, and E 57 followed in August 1997. The standard was issued in February 1998.

2.3 Asset recognition and measurement

Valuation of assets has an impact on reported net income: overstating assets leads to overstating net income. The application of prudence suggests that perceived risk arising from overstatement of assets is greater than perceived risk from understatement of the same magnitude. Standards dealing with asset valuation therefore show a common theme of prudence. Consistency is also an essential feature because users of financial statements need to understand the asset base from which income is generated. Disclosure of the nature of the asset is essential so that users can appreciate the relative risk, subjectivity of valuation and liquidity of the asset. Some or all of these factors are found in each of the IFRSs dealing with assets.

2.3.1 Inventories (IAS 2)

IAS 2 was revised in December 2003 to be applied for accounting periods beginning on or after 1 January 2005. Earlier application was encouraged.

2.3.1.1 Key issues

The valuation of inventories is an important aspect of the determination of profit, or net income, of an enterprise. The standard is based firmly in historical cost accounting. It provides rules for valuation which ensure that profit is not anticipated until it is earned when the inventories are sold. It also ensures that inventories include all the costs of bringing them to their present condition and location.

2.3.1.2 Approach in IAS 2

The standard contains rules for valuation. Key aspects are:

- inventories should be measured at the lower of cost and net realizable value;
- cost should comprise all costs of purchase, cost of conversion and other costs incurred in bringing the inventory to its present location and condition;
- costs include a systematic allocation of fixed and variable production overheads based on the normal capacity of the production facilities; overhead costs are included to the extent that they are incurred in bringing the inventories to their present location and condition;
- in limited circumstances borrowing costs are included in the cost of inventories (*see* IAS 23, section 2.3.4);
- standard cost or the retail method may be used to approximate to cost.

Where specific costs cannot be attributed to identified items of inventory, the standard permits first-in-first-out (FIFO) or weighted average cost formulas.

The standard also contains rules for disclosure.

2.3.1.3 Reducing the options

The 2003 version superseded a 1993 revision of the standard, first issued in 1975. In implementation of the Comparability Project this standard was controversial. E 32 included last-in-first-out (LIFO) as the allowed alternative but the Statement of Intent announced that LIFO and base stock would not be permitted. Subsequent strong opposition from countries using LIFO restored the LIFO approach as the allowed alternative but subject to disclosure of cost using the benchmarked FIFO or weighted average approaches. The standard was acceptable to IOSCO as a core standard. The major change in the 2003 version was removal of LIFO as an allowable measure of inventory cost.

2.3.2 Property, plant and equipment (IAS 16)

IAS 16 was issued in December 2003 to be applied for accounting periods beginning on or after 1 January 2005. Earlier implementation was encouraged.

2.3.2.1 Key issues

The principal issues in accounting for property, plant and equipment are the timing of recognition of the assets, the amount at which they are carried in the balance sheet, and the depreciation to be recorded. The standard also covers disclosure of information.

2.3.2.2 Approach in IAS 16

The standard explains the conditions for recognition of an asset, which follow the general conditions of the IASB Framework. At the point of recognition the asset is measured at cost. Subsequently the entity will choose either the cost model of measurement or the revaluation model. Under the cost model the asset is carried at cost less accumulated depreciation and accumulated impairment losses. Under the revaluation model the asset is carried at fair value less accumulated depreciation and accumulated impairment losses. If revaluation is chosen it must be carried out regularly. If an item of property, plant and equipment is revalued, the entire class to which that asset belongs shall be revalued.

The standard also sets out rules for depreciation, allocating the depreciable amount of an asset on a systematic basis over its useful life.

Extensive disclosure requirements are set out for the primary financial statements and the notes to the accounts.

2.3.2.3 Reducing the options

The 2003 version replaced a 1998 revision of the version issued in 1993, superseding the 1982 version. In the Comparability Project, it was proposed in E 32 that the preferred treatment of gross carrying amount would be historical cost while the allowed alternative would be revaluation, using a prescribed approach. The wording of the 1998 revision of the standard was different, referring to measurement *subsequent* to initial recognition, but the sentiment remained the same in regarding historical cost as the benchmark treatment and revaluation as the allowed alternative.

Depreciation was initially dealt with separately in IAS 4 which was one of the early standards and was very general in nature. It was withdrawn in 1999 because the subject was covered in IAS 16, IAS 22 and IAS 38. The most interesting aspects of depreciation are those relating to property, plant and equipment, now dealt with in IAS 16.

It is stated in IAS 16 that the carrying amount of an item of property, plant or equipment should not exceed its recoverable amount. In order to determine the recoverable amount of an asset it may be necessary to consider the extent of impairment. Impairment became a separate project (see section 2.3.3). IAS 16 was acceptable to IOSCO for the Core Standards programme. The 2003 revision was mainly concerned with providing additional guidance and clarification within the established principles.

2.3.3 Impairment of assets (IAS 36)

IAS 36 was revised in March 2004 to be applied to business combinations with agreement dates on or after 31 March 2004.

2.3.3.1 Key issues

It is an aspect of prudence in accounting that assets should not be overvalued in the balance sheet. There is a risk that this may arise under historical cost accounting. In some cases where fixed assets are depreciated on the basis of historical cost, that depreciation may not take into account a sudden change in circumstances that causes the value of the asset to decrease. Such an unexpected decrease would be an example of impairment of the asset, beyond normal depreciation, which would require recognition in the financial statements. The standard deals with two key questions:

● What are the conditions which show that impairment has occurred?
● What method or methods should be used for measuring the impairment?

2.3.3.2 Approach in IAS 36

An asset is regarded as being impaired if its carrying amount (the net book value in the accounting records) exceeds its recoverable amount. Assets should be reviewed at each balance sheet date for indications of impairment. Where such indications are found, there must be a detailed calculation of recoverable amount, defined as the higher of an asset's fair value (less costs to sell) and its value in use. 'Fair value less costs to sell' is the amount that could be obtained from selling the asset in an arm's length sale, minus the costs of disposal. 'Value in use' is the present value of the future cash flows expected from an asset or a cash-generating unit.

If the carrying amount of an asset or a cash-generating unit exceeds recoverable amount, an impairment loss is recognized. An impairment loss recognized in a prior period should be reversed, and income recognized, if there has been a favourable change in the estimates that were used when the last impairment loss was recognized. The recoverable amount of an intangible asset with an indefinite life must be measured annually, irrespective of whether there is any indication that it may be impaired.

Disclosure of impairment losses during the accounting period should be given for each class of asset. IAS 36 applies to all assets except for inventories, deferred taxes, financial assets, investment property, biological assets, assets arising from construction contracts and employee benefits.

2.3.3.3 Reducing the options

The 2004 version superseded the standard first issued in 1998. Impairment became the subject of a project announced in June 1996. Impairment was already covered in specific standards but had not been coordinated across standards. IAS 36 (1998) followed the exposure draft E 55 in setting general principles to be applied to all assets. The standard was revised in 2004 as part of the IASB's project on business combinations. The effect was to apply a stricter rule to intangible assets with indefinite lives. Some definitions were clarified. The date of implementation was matched to the date of implementing IFRS 3 (see section 2.8.2).

2.3.4 Borrowing costs (IAS 23)

IAS 23 was revised in 1993.

2.3.4.1 Key issues

In most instances, the interest charges on borrowed funds will be reported as an expense of the period in which they arise. There are occasions, however, when companies wish to argue that interest charges are an asset rather than an expense, because they create a benefit for the future. This argument might apply, for example, to interest charged on finance borrowed to pay for a development project.

2.3.4.2 Approach in IAS 23

The standard allows two treatments. One is that borrowing costs should be recognized as an expense in the period in which they are incurred. The alternative treatment is that borrowing costs may be capitalized as part of the cost of an asset where the borrowing costs are directly attributable to the acquisition, construction or production of an asset which necessarily takes a substantial period of time to get ready for its intended use or sale. Reporting the borrowing costs as an asset should cease when substantially all the activities necessary to prepare the asset for its use or sale are complete.

Disclosure is required of the amount of borrowing costs capitalized during the period and the capitalization rate used.

2.3.4.3 Reducing the options

The 1993 revision was based on the first version of the standard, issued in 1984. Prior to the Comparability Project, the standard allowed free choice of capitalizing or not capitalizing borrowing costs incurred on assets being made ready for their intended use. E 32 proposed a preferred treatment and an allowed alternative which were eventually reflected in the revised standard. However, initial reaction to E 32 resulted in a change of thinking by the IASC, indicated in the Statement of Intent, to require capitalization of borrowing costs which met particular criteria. This revised thinking was presented in E 39, which evoked a range of comments. From that point IASC decided to revert, in revising IAS 23, to its proposals as set out in E 32.

IOSCO indicated that IAS 23 was acceptable for the purpose of the Core Standards programme.

2.3.5 Intangible assets (IAS 38)

IAS 38 was revised in March 2004. Early adoption was encouraged.

2.3.5.1 Key issues

An intangible asset is an identifiable non-monetary asset without physical substance. 'Identifiable' means that the asset is separable from the entity or arises from legal rights. The standard sets rules for recognition and measurement.

2.3.5.2 Approach in IAS 38

IAS 38 applies to all intangible assets unless they are within the scope of another standard. An intangible asset shall be recognized if, and only if, it is probable that expected future economic benefits attributable to the asset will flow to the entity; and the cost of the asset can be measured reliably. After initial recognition the entity must make a choice. It can choose either the cost model or the revaluation model. The cost model records the asset at cost less accumulated depreciation and accumulated impairment losses. The revaluation model carries the asset at fair value at the date of revaluation less any subsequent accumulated amortization losses. The frequency of revaluation depends on the volatility of the fair value of the asset.

Some intangible assets may have an indefinite useful life because there is no foreseeable limit to the period over which such assets are expected to generate cash flows. An intangible asset with an indefinite useful life should not be amortized. It should be tested annually for impairment, in accordance with IAS 36.

Internally generated goodwill is not recognized as an asset because it is not 'identifiable' (it is not separable from the entity and does not arise from legal rights). Internally generated intangible assets are classified into a research phase and a development phase. The treatment then follows that set out for research and development expenditure (see section 2.3.6).

2.3.5.3 Reducing the options

IAS 38 was first issued in 1998. The exposure draft E 50 *Intangible Assets*, which preceded IAS 38, had included controversial proposals that all intangible assets should be amortized over a useful life not exceeding 20 years; subsequent measurement should be made, under the allowed alternative treatment, by reference to an active secondary market; and there should be particular restrictions on initial recognition and measurement for intangible assets.

Having considered responses to the exposure draft, the Board announced in July 1996 that it would not impose a 20-year limit on the useful life but that there would be a rebuttable presumption that useful life did not exceed 20 years. Where asset lives were held to exceed 20 years an enterprise would be required to calculate recoverable amount every year in accordance with the Board's proposals on Impairment.

In July 1997 the Board approved a new exposure draft E 60, to include research and development activities. In approving the exposure draft, the Board agreed to require an annual impairment test for internally generated intangible assets that were not yet available for use.

Further changes to E 60 were presented in E 61, prior to issue of IAS 38. IAS 38 (1998) was broadly consistent with E 60 except that the Board withdrew E60's proposal to require an annual impairment test of internally generated intangible assets amortized over more than five years, and withdrew E 60's proposed requirement to disclose the amount of expenditure on certain intangible items recognized as an expense during the period (e.g. software and advertising). For consistency of treating all intangibles, IAS 38 included the definitions and recognition criteria of IAS 9 for research and development.

IAS 38 was revised in 2004 for consistency with IFRS 3 Business Combinations. The main changes are in the definition of an intangible asset, the criteria for initial recognition and the recognition of subsequent expenditure on research and development. The standard allows that an intangible asset might have an indefinite useful life.

2.3.6 Research and development costs (IAS 38)

IAS 38 was revised in March 2004, paragraphs 42–43 and 54–62, superseding IAS 9, issued in 1993, replacing the 1978 version.

2.3.6.1 Key issues

Although research and development is now part of IAS 38, it is dealt with separately here because of its importance. The key issue is whether research and development expenditure should be reported as an expense or as an asset. The standard gives definitions:

- *research* is original and planned investigation undertaken with the prospect of gaining new scientific or technical knowledge and understanding;
- *development* is the application of research findings or other knowledge to a plan or design for the production of new or substantially improved material, devices, products, processes, systems or services prior to the commencement of commercial production or use.

2.3.6.2 Approach in IAS 38

The IAS requires that:

- Expenditure on *research* should be recognized as an *expense* in the period in which it is incurred. No intangible asset should be recognized.
- An intangible asset arising from *development* should be recognized if, and only if, specific conditions can be demonstrated. The conditions, set out in paragraph 57, relate to the reliability of the asset and the expectation of future economic benefits. The amount of development costs recognized as an asset should be amortized and recognized as an expense on a systematic basis so as to reflect the pattern in which the related economic benefits are recognized.
- Financial statements should disclose the amount of research and development costs recognized as an expense in a period. Where the development expenditure is treated as an asset there must be disclosure of the amortization method used and rates used; and a reconciliation of the opening and closing balances of unamortized development costs of the period.

2.3.6.3 Reducing the options

The first standard on this subject was IAS 9, issued in 1978 and revised in 1993. It was withdrawn in 1998 when IAS 38 was issued and included coverage of research and development costs. IAS 9 (1978) permitted development cost to be reported as an asset and amortized, providing that such development cost met specified criteria. There was free choice for companies in this matter. In the Comparability Project, E 32 sought to have the *preferred treatment* as charging all research and development expenditure as an expense of the period, with the *allowed alternative* of recognizing development expenditure as an asset under tightly controlled conditions. The Statement of Intent proposed a harder line, insisting that development cost must be reported as an asset if it met the specified conditions. The revised IAS 9 in 1993 maintained this harder line.

Despite the firmer approach of the revised IAS 9, the standard was included in the list of core standards to be revised by 1998 for the agreement with IOSCO. This reflected concern in some countries that it would be preferable to account for research and development costs as one item, reporting all as an expense of the period. It was agreed in 1997 that the standard on intangible assets should also cover research and development activities for achievement of the Core Standards programme. IAS 38 (1998) did not go so far as to insist on expensing *all* development expenditure but if the development expenditure meets the stated conditions it must be reported as an asset.

2.3.7 Investment property (IAS 40)

IAS 40 was revised in December 2003. Early adoption was encouraged.

2.3.7.1 Key issues

The key issue relates to the measurement of the tangible fixed asset of property, where this is held as an investment for the purpose of earning rental or for an expected increase in value (also called 'capital appreciation'). It is not used in the day-to-day activity of the business. In some countries, including the UK, there is a view that the asset should be valued on a market value basis; in others there is a view that the asset is no different from any other property asset and should be recorded at depreciated cost.

2.3.7.2 Approach in IAS 40

IAS 40 requires enterprises to choose one of two accounting models and to apply the chosen model consistently across all investment properties. The first model is a fair value model and the second is a depreciated historical cost model. Under the fair value model the investment property should be measured at fair value and the changes in fair value should be recognized in the income statement. (That is quite controversial because it puts an unrealized gain in the income statement.) The cost model matches the benchmark treatment of IAS 16 in measuring the asset at depreciated cost, less any accumulated impairment losses. Where the cost model is chosen, the fair value of the investment should be discussed as supplementary information.

A property interest that is held by a lessee under an operating lease may be treated as an investment property provided it meets the definition of an investment property, is accounted for as a finance lease, and uses the fair value of the asset.

2.3.7.3 Reducing the options

IAS 40 was first issued in 2000, replacing part of IAS 25 *Accounting for Investments*. IAS 25 had permitted several different treatments for investment property. IAS 40 narrowed down that choice considerably and also requires more disclosure about investment property. An exposure draft E 64, issued in 1999, proposed that only the fair value model should be allowed. The Board had not previously proposed a fair value model as a sole requirement for any non-financial asset. The comment letters received indicated that there were reservations in some quarters about applying fair value to non-financial assets. By permitting fair value accounting but also leaving a cost model in place, the Board hopes that there will be evolution in the use of the fair value model. The revision in 2004 dealt with an inconsistency between IAS 17 and IAS 40. It was specific to property held by a lessee under an operating lease. The Board discussed the wider issue of removing the choice between fair value and cost models in IAS 40 but concluded that more time was needed for preparers and users to gain experience of using a fair value model.

2.4 Liability recognition and measurement

Reporting of liabilities also has an impact on reported net income: understating liabilities leads to overstating net income. The application of prudence suggests that the risk of understatement of liabilities should be taken very seriously. Standards dealing with liabilities will therefore show a common theme of ensuring that all liabilities are acknowledged as fully as possible. Disclosure of the maturity date of the liability is very important. For longer-term liabilities the user of financial statements will be interested in the commitment of future cash flows to loan interest and capital repayments. There will also be an interest in the gearing (ratio of long-term loans to equity finance).

2.4.1 Events after the balance sheet date (IAS 10)

IAS 10 was revised in December 2003 to be applied for annual periods beginning on or after 1 January 2005. Earlier application was encouraged.

2.4.1.1 Key issues

There are many situations existing at the balance sheet date whose outcome will be determined by future events that may or may not occur. If the likelihood of occurrence is high, the liability will be accrued and reported in the balance sheet. If there is a lesser likelihood of occurrence, the liability may be declared *contingent* and reported in a note to the accounts. Contingent liabilities are treated in IAS 37 (section 2.4.2).

2.4.1.2 Approach in IAS 10

Events that occur after the balance sheet date but before the date on which the financial statements are authorized for issue may indicate a need to make adjustments to assets and liabilities or may require disclosure. The essential test is whether the event provides additional evidence about conditions existing at the balance sheet date or provides information relating to the applicability of the going concern assumption. An example requiring adjustment is the loss on a trade receivable which is confirmed by the bankruptcy of the customer occurring after the balance sheet date.

Dividends of a period that are *proposed or declared* after the balance sheet date but before approval of the financial statements should not be recognized as a liability of the period. Disclosure by way of note is required.

2.4.1.3 Reducing the options

IAS 10 was first issued in 1978, reformatted in 1995 and revised in 1999. The 1978 version of IAS 10 dealt with provisions and contingent liabilities. These were matters of concern to IOSCO for the Core Standards programme and the revision of IAS 10 was seen as essential. This revision was taken to a separate project, resulting in IAS 37 (see section 2.4.2) and leaving IAS 10 covering only events after the balance sheet date. The 2003 revision of IAS 10 strengthened the 1999 version in confirming that proposed dividends should not be recognized as a liability.

2.4.2 Provisions, contingent liabilities and contingent assets (IAS 37)

IAS 37 was issued in 1998.

2.4.2.1 Key issues

The standard prescribes the accounting and disclosure for all provisions, contingent liabilities and contingent assets except for those relating to financial instruments carried at fair value, and some other special applications.

2.4.2.2 Approach in IAS 37

Provisions are defined as liabilities of uncertain timing or amount. A *constructive obligation* arises from actions established by past practice. A *contingent liability* is a possible obligation that arises from past events, in circumstances where the existence of the obligation will be confirmed by future events. A contingent liability also exists where a present obligation exists but there is some uncertainty about its measurement. A *contingent asset* is a possible asset arising from past events whose existence will be confirmed by a future event.

The standard sets conditions for recognition of provisions based on the existence of a present obligation and on the probability of an outflow of resources arising. Contingent liabilities and assets should not be recognized in the financial statements. A provision should be measured as a best estimate of the expenditure required to settle the present obligation at the balance sheet date. Discounted present value should be calculated where the effect of the time value of money is material. The standard contains decision trees and illustrations of how the various items are to be dealt with.

2.4.2.3 Reducing the options

IAS 37 is based on aspects of IAS 10 (1995 revision) which required consideration for the Core Standards programme and it adds some new material. The revision of IAS 10 was an essential element of the Core Standards programme. IOSCO had called for a review of the measurement requirements relating to provisions and contingencies. Guidance was required to define more clearly the nature of contingencies so that the revised standard could provide a basis for distinguishing on-balance-sheet and off-balance-sheet items. There was also a particular concern with the use of provisions in financial statements. A Discussion Paper, produced jointly by a working group of standard-setting bodies in Australia, Canada, the UK, the US and the IASC, served as a basis for developing a revised standard. The project continued as a joint project of the UK Accounting Standards Board

(ASB) and the IASC. E 59, *Provisions, Contingent Liabilities and Contingent Assets*, was issued in August 1997 following from a draft Statement of Principles. The tentative conclusions brought forward in E 59 were that a provision should be recognized when the enterprise had no realistic alternative but to pay out resources. The provision should be measured at the discounted present value of the expected settlement amount. Provision should be made for restructuring when there was a detailed plan and a demonstrable commitment. There should be provision for future losses only in respect of onerous contracts. Eventually the concerns about provisions and contingencies emerged as a separate project leading to IAS 37.

2.4.3 Income taxes (IAS 12)

IAS 12 was revised in 1996.

2.4.3.1 Key issues

Taxes on income are accrued as an expense of the period to which the income and operating expenses relate. To the extent that there are timing differences between an enterprise's accounting income and taxable income (as defined by the relevant tax authorities) the tax effect is included in the tax expense in the income statement and in the deferred tax balance in the balance sheet.

2.4.3.2 Approach in IAS 12

IAS 12 requires that a deferred tax liability should be recognized for all taxable temporary differences (apart from some specified exceptions). A deferred tax asset may be recognized (for the carry-forward of unused tax losses and unused tax credits) to the extent that it is probable that future taxable profit will be available against which the unused tax losses and unused tax credits can be utilized. The term 'temporary differences' is used because it covers temporary timing differences and also some differences between accounting treatment and tax treatment which are not due to timing.

Measurement of current tax liabilities and assets should be at the amount expected to be paid or recovered under law as enacted at the balance sheet date. Measurement of deferred tax liabilities and assets should be at the tax rates which are expected to apply when the liability is settled or the asset is realized.

The standard prohibits discounting of liabilities. It also sets out disclosure requirements for taxes.

2.4.3.3 Reducing the options

IAS 12 was first issued in 1979, reformatted in 1995 and revised in 1996. The 1979 version of IAS 12, *Accounting for Taxes on Income*, permitted either the deferral method or a liability method. IAS 12 (1996) does not permit the deferral method. The revised IAS 12, *Income Taxes*, implements the proposal in exposure draft E 49 (October 1994) that partial application of deferred taxation accounting should not be permitted. In these and other more detailed matters the stricter attitude of the revised IAS 12 contrasts with the permissiveness of the original IAS 12 and the exposure draft E 33.

The approach adopted in the revised IAS 12 has similarities to that used by the FASB in FAS 109, *Accounting for Income Taxes*. The IASC Board consulted major accounting firms and over 100 multinational companies, in arriving at the conclusion that the new approach could be applied internationally.

2.4.4 Leases (IAS 17)

IAS 17 was revised in December 2003 to be applied for annual periods beginning on or after 1 January 2005. Earlier application was encouraged.

2.4.4.1 Key issues

The IASB Framework states that transactions and other events ought to be accounted for and presented in accordance with their substance and financial reality and not merely with their legal form. A finance lease has the effect in substance of a loan-financed purchase, and should therefore be reported as such. The accounting standard covers the lessee and the lessor.

2.4.4.2 Approach in IAS 17

IAS 17 covers aspects of both lessee and lessor accounting. We have included it in the 'liability' section because the main concern has been to record the lessee's liability for a lease. For the lessee the main concern is reporting the full liability of the finance lease, which in turn brings the asset onto the balance sheet. For the lessor the main concerns are reporting revenue from leasing and reporting the value of the lease as an asset.

1 Lessee

The standard requires a finance lease to be reported in the balance sheet as an asset and an obligation. The income statement should report depreciation of the asset and interest on the remaining balance of the liability. The finance lease method must be applied in IAS 40 to investment properties held under operating leases (see section 2.3.7).

An 'operating lease' is any lease other than a finance lease. The full rental payment under the lease should be charged to the income statement over the life of the lease, the allocation being made on a systematic basis that is representative of the time pattern of the user's benefit.

The commitment for minimum lease payments under finance leases and under non-cancellable operating leases with a term of more than one year should be disclosed in summary form, giving the amounts and periods in which the payments will become due.

2 Lessor

The problems lie in reporting income of the period and the nature of the asset. The income of the period should be calculated to achieve a constant rate of return on the lessor's net investment or net cash outstanding over the life of the asset. The asset should be recognized as an account receivable, at an amount equal to the net investment in the lease.

2.4.4.3 Reducing the options

IAS 17 was first issued in 1982 and reformatted in 1995. It was added to the Core Standards programme in June 1996 and revised in 1997. In the Comparability Project, E 32 sought to reduce the flexibility available to lessors in reporting income and also sought to deal with leveraged leases (finance leases structured so as to distribute tax benefits advantageously). The Statement of Intent noted that further work would be required in this area. Consequently IAS 17 was reformatted but without significant change in principles. The options were not reduced as a result of the Comparability Project.

This meant that IAS 17 was among those standards not acceptable to IOSCO as a core standard. IOSCO asked for a review of IAS 17 in three areas considered essential: lessor accounting, leveraged leases and more specific disclosures. Within the work programme an exposure draft was planned to deal with these items in particular, and in the longer term a more fundamental review will be considered. A starting point was a joint Discussion Paper (July 1996) of a working group from the standard-setting bodies of Australia, Canada, New Zealand, the UK and the US, together with the IASC.

Exposure draft E 56 was issued in February 1997, proposing enhanced disclosure by lessees, enhanced disclosure by lessors, and that a lessor should use the net investment method to allocate final income (the net cash investment method would no longer be permitted). The enhanced disclosures were contained in the revised standard issued at the end of 1997. This requires enhanced disclosure by lessees, enhanced disclosure by lessors, and that a lessor should use the net investment method to allocate finance income (the net cash investment method is no longer permitted). The IASC also stated, when it issued the revised standard, that it planned to consider a more fundamental reform of the lease standard once it had finished its Core Standards work programme. This would involve the capitalization of all leases with a term of more than one year. The IASB did not make this fundamental change in the Improvements Project of 2003 because a larger project on leases remained on its agenda. The 2003 revision is consistent with the change to IAS 40 in defining the treatment of investment property held under an operating lease (see section 2.3.7).

2.4.5 Employee benefits (IAS 19)

IAS 19 was amended in 2002.

2.4.5.1 Key issues

In many countries the provision of retirement benefits is a significant element of the remuneration package for an employee. The cost to the employer may fluctuate from one accounting period to the next, depending on the type of plan. Employers also provide other benefits to employees such as paying salaries or wages during periods of absence from work, or bonuses in addition to normal rates of pay. The employer may pay for benefits which continue to be received after the employee has ceased to work for the employer in circumstances other than retirement. The common feature of all these benefits is that the payments made by the employer are not always spread evenly over time. The standard prescribes the amount of the cost that should be recognized and the information to be disclosed in the financial statements of the employing enterprise.

2.4.5.2 Approach in IAS 19

A *defined contribution plan* is a retirement benefit plan under which amounts to be paid as retirement benefits are determined by reference to the earnings of an investment fund which is created from the contributions made. An enterprise's contribution to the fund, in respect of service in a particular period, should be recognized as an expense in that period.

A *defined benefit plan* is an arrangement whereby an enterprise provides benefits for its employees such that the benefits are determined or estimated in advance of retirement from the provisions of a document or from the enterprise's practice. The reported expense in the current period must follow a series of rules which concentrate on the pension obligation as a liability and the assets relating to the plan, measured at fair value.

Extensive disclosures are required.

2.4.5.3 Reducing the options

IAS 19 was issued in 1993 as *Retirement Benefit Costs*. Following exposure draft E 54 (1996) a revised IAS 19, *Employee Benefits*, was issued in 1998 and amended in 2000 and 2002.

The Comparability Project introduced a benchmark and an allowed alternative treatment for a defined benefit plan, in order to limit the free choice existing under the standard as issued in 1993.

Under either approach to a defined benefit plan, the important aspect was the measurement of the expense. Items were reported in the balance sheet in the categories of assets and liabilities. However, these did not necessarily meet the framework document criteria for definition and recognition. The balance sheet entries were a result of the decision about the expense and therefore the standard contradicted the framework to some extent, in allowing the contents of the income statement to determine the nature of an asset or a liability.

Following on from the Comparability Project, it became clear that further work would be required for the Core Standards programme, particularly in considering those balance sheet items resulting from IAS 19 which do not meet the definition of an asset or a liability. There were two particular weaknesses. The nature of retirement benefit arrangements were not consistent in all countries. The standard also provided insufficient guidance on the balance sheet consequences of reporting retirement benefit costs in the income statement. The exposure draft E 54, *Employee Benefits* (1996), proposed a single actuarial method for measuring the expected liability for retirement benefits and also provided accounting procedures for other forms of employee benefits such as paid absences, bonuses and all forms of post-employment benefits. The revised IAS 19 was issued in January 1998. Some amendments of detail were made in 2000 and in 2002.

2.5 Financial instruments: assets and liabilities

The IASB's accounting standards on financial instruments have caused considerable controversy during their development because they have dispensed with traditional approaches to thinking differently about assets and liabilities. An ideal vision of relevance in measurement is that eventually all assets and liabilities should be measured at their fair value at each accounting date, with the changes in fair value recorded as gains or losses of the period. To reach that vision from a starting point of historical cost would take a very long time, particularly where assets and liabilities do not have a readily ascertainable market value. The IASB has started the process of thinking differently about measurement by focusing on the fair value of financial instruments, where there is a market price or there is information that allows a fair value to be estimated. In the course of developing ideas on fair value the IASB and its predecessor IASC found that separating disclosure and presentation from measurement was a practical way of developing the more challenging accounting aspects. Ideally there would be one standard covering disclosure, presentation and measurement.

2.5.1 Financial instruments: disclosure and presentation (IAS 32)

IAS 32 was revised in December 2003 to be applied for annual periods beginning on or after 1 January 2005. Earlier application was permitted.

2.5.1.1 Key issues

International financial markets are changing rapidly, with widespread use of a variety of financial instruments. These could be traditional instruments such as bonds, or they could be derivative instruments such as interest rate swaps. The standard aims to enhance financial statement users' understanding of the significance of on-balance-sheet and off-balance-sheet financial instruments to the financial position, performance and cash flows of an enterprise. The standard deals with presentation and disclosure.

2.5.1.2 Approach in IAS 32

Ideally a standard on this topic should address measurement issues as well as disclosure. It is explained below that the measurement issues are more difficult to resolve. Accordingly, IAS 32 is primarily a disclosure standard but it is coordinated with IAS 39 (see section 2.5.2).

The standard explains in detail matters of classification and presentation. In the balance sheet the reporting enterprise must classify the instrument according to the substance of the contractual arrangement on initial recognition. Where a 'compound' financial instrument contains both a liability and an equity element, the enterprise should classify the component parts separately. The standard gives definitions of financial liability and equity instrument for classification purposes. Interest, dividends, losses and gains relating to a financial instrument must be reported in the income statement. Offsetting a financial asset and a financial liability is permitted only in specific circumstances.

In order to provide an understanding of risk, for each class of financial asset, liability and equity instrument disclosure is required of:

● terms, conditions and accounting policies
● interest rate risk
● credit risk
● fair value
● hedges.

2.5.1.3 Reducing the options

IAS 32 was first issued in 1995. An exposure draft E 48 (January 1994) set out the results of a joint project with the Canadian Institute of Chartered Accountants. Comments from other standard-setting bodies indicated that E 48 was too ambitious and could distance the IASC from those standard-setting bodies which were reluctant to accept some of the proposals.

As a result of these views and of the comments from others on the exposure draft, the IASC decided to separate the disclosure and the measurement aspects into two separate projects. The disclosure aspects resulted in the issue of IAS 32. Recognition and measurement were set to follow as a priority. In March 1997 a Discussion Paper examined major recognition and measurement issues for financial instruments. An exposure draft was expected in October 1997 but somewhat surprisingly a press release from the IASC in September announced that the IASC staff would recommend to the Board that the IASC should adopt the US standards on financial instruments as an interim step, followed by joint work with international standard-setters to agree a harmonized international standard. It was recognized by the IASC staff that it would be impossible to produce an international standard within the timescale for completion of the Core Standards programme. At its meeting in November 1997, the Board decided to develop both a comprehensive standard and an interim standard. The interim standard was issued in 1998 with limited amendments. There were more amendments in 2000, linked to the development of IAS 39. Changes made in 2003 were further technical details.

2.5.2 Financial instruments: recognition and measurement (IAS 39)

IAS 39 was revised in December 2003 to be applied for annual periods beginning on or after 1 January 2005. Earlier application was permitted. An amendment was issued in March 2004. Further modifications were considered by the Board during 2004.[2]

2.5.2.1 Key issues

IAS 39 establishes principles for recognizing and measuring financial assets, financial liabilities and some contracts to buy or sell non-financial items (such as commodities). Presentation is dealt with in IAS 32 (see section 2.5.1). The financial assets and financial liabilities held at the balance sheet date are measured using rules specified in IAS 39. One of these rules is 'fair value'. The fair value is reported in the balance sheet and the change in value is recognized in the profit or loss of the period. This means that IAS 39 may cause significant changes in the appearance and content of the balance sheet and the statement of profit or loss, when compared to traditional historical cost accounting.

In particular IAS 39 sets rules for recognizing and measuring derivatives. Examples seen in annual reports are an interest rate swap, a currency swap, a currency future, a currency forward contract, a commodity future and a commodity forward contract. A derivative is a financial instrument or contract with three characteristics:

1 Its value changes in response to a change in an interest rate, or a commodity price, or a foreign exchange rate, or the price of an equity security (share), or some other underlying variable.
2 It requires no initial investment or involves a relatively small initial investment.
3 It is settled at a future date.

These three characteristics bring risk to the derivative. Investors and others with a stake in companies using such derivatives should know of the risks involved.

2.5.2.2 Approach in IAS 39

Recognition

An entity shall recognize a financial asset or a financial liability on its balance sheet when, and only when, the entity becomes a party to the contractual provisions of the instrument. Tests for recognition and derecognition are explained in terms of risks and rewards of ownership. The initial measurement of a financial asset or financial liability is at fair value.

Four categories of financial instrument are defined in IAS 39:

1 *A financial asset or financial liability at fair value through profit or loss.* This description is applied to a financial asset or liability held for trading.
2 *Held-to-maturity investments.* These are non-derivative financial assets or liabilities that the entity intends to hold to maturity.
3 *Loans and receivables.* These are non-derivative financial assets with fixed payments that are not quoted in an active market.
4 *Available-for-sale financial assets.* These are non-derivative financial assets that are available for sale and not classified under 3, 2, or 1 above.

---

[2] The website www.iasplus.com has a section updating the discussions on IAS 39.

Measurement

Definitions are given for the rules of measurement:

● *Fair value*. This is the amount for which an asset could be exchanged, or a liability set-tled, between knowledgeable, willing parties in an arm's length transaction.
● *Amortized cost*. This is the amount at initial recognition (usually cost) *minus* repayments of principal, *plus or minus* the cumulative amortization caused by allocated interest (the 'effective interest'), *minus* any reduction for impairment or non-collectibility.
● *Effective interest rate*. This is the rate that exactly discounts estimated future cash receipts or payments to the net carrying amount of the financial asset or financial lia-bility. The *effective interest method* then amortizes the asset or liability using the effec-tive interest rate.

Reporting

The rules of measurement and the reporting of the gain or loss depend on the type of financial instrument, as in Exhibit 2.2.

Hedging

A hedging instrument is a designated derivative or a non-derivative financial asset or financial liability whose fair value or cash flows are expected to offset changes in the value of a hedged item. An example of a fair value hedge is holding a financial instru-ment that offsets the risk of a fixed rate loan. An example of a cash flow hedge is the use of a swap to exchange a variable rate interest payment for a fixed rate interest payment. If the hedge arrangements are 'qualifying items' (this means that they meet the very strict tests of 'effectiveness' set by IAS 39) then the gains and losses are 'offset' (matched against each other) and there is no effect on the reported profit or loss of the period. An amendment issued in March 2004 extended the rules on hedging to allow hedging items to be viewed in combination as a 'hedged portfolio'.

The fair value option

IAS 39 (December 2003) allowed companies to designate any financial asset or financial liability as one to be measured at fair value, with changes in fair value reported in profit

Exhibit 2.2 Measurement rules of IAS 39

Type of financial instrument	Measurement	Gain or loss is reported in:
A financial asset or financial liability at fair value through profit or loss	Fair value	Profit or loss
Held-to-maturity investments	Amortized cost using the effective interest method	In profit or loss when the asset or liability is derecognized or impaired
Loans and receivables	Amortized cost using the effective interest method	In profit or loss when the asset or liability is derecognized or impaired
Available-for-sale financial assets	Measurement depends on type	Directly in equity through the statement of changes in equity

or loss. This is described as 'the fair value option'. Some European regulators objected to this option as giving too much freedom to companies to create profits and losses. An exposure draft was issued in April 2004 proposing limits on the types of financial asset and liability to which the option may be applied. In all cases where the option is exercised the fair value must be verifiable.

2.5.2.3 Reducing the options

IAS 39 was first issued in March 1999 and revised in 2000. There was a growing awareness internationally that derivative financial instruments were becoming used more frequently and there was no information in the annual report of the risks carried by companies or the magnitude of the exposure to risk. National standard-setters were starting to deal with the problems of financial instruments. In 1997 the IASC had worked with the Canadian Institute of Chartered Accountants to produce a Discussion Paper on Accounting for Financial Assets and Financial Liabilities. There was some agreement among commentators that fair value was necessary to give consistency and relevance to users but there was unease about reporting unrealized gains in the statement of profit or loss. IAS 39 (1999) was regarded as an interim solution while the IASC continued to work on this problem with the major national standard-setting bodies. Revisions in 2003 provided additional guidance on derecognition, use of fair value, assessment of impairment and some aspects of hedge accounting.

Some commentators were concerned that the rules for identifying hedged items were too strict. These rules did not reflect the idea of having a collection of matched items (called a portfolio hedge or 'macro hedging'). An amendment in March 2004 introduced the idea of a portfolio hedge but the tests of effectiveness remained strictly defined.

Commentators continued to raise objections during 2004, on matters of detail such as the fair value option, to which the IASB responded with an exposure draft in April 2004 (see section 2.5.2.2). The IASB acknowledged further concerns with three detailed exposure drafts in July 2004. Consequently the idea of a 'stable platform' by March 2004 was not achieved in the case of IAS 39. The lack of a stable platform was further complicated in Europe by the reluctance of the European Commission to endorse IAS 39 (see section 9.5.3.1).

2.6 Recognition of economic activity

Recognition is dealt with in the framework document. Recognition becomes particularly significant where an economic activity of the enterprise extends over a period of time: the question arises as to when the economic activity may prudently be reported in the financial statements. Issues of recognition arise for construction contracts, revenue earned, and government grants received ahead of the activity earning those grants.

2.6.1 Construction contracts (IAS 11)

IAS 11 was revised in 1993.

2.6.1.1 Key issues

Construction contracts may extend over more than one accounting period. The standard sets out recognition criteria for the allocation of revenue and costs to more than one period; recognition reflects the percentage of the contract completed in the period.

2.6.1.2 Approach in IAS 11

When the outcome of a construction contract can be estimated reliably, contract revenue and contract costs associated with the construction contact should be recognized as revenue and expenses, respectively, by reference to the stage of completion of the contract activity at the balance sheet date. When it is probable that total contract costs will exceed total contract revenue, the expected loss should be recognized as an expense immediately.

When the outcome of a contract cannot be estimated reliably, revenue should be recognized only to the extent of contract costs incurred that it is probable will be recoverable. Contract costs should be recognized as an expense in the period in which they are incurred.

For all contracts in progress at the balance sheet date, for which costs incurred *plus* recognized profit (*less* recognized losses) exceed progress billings, the net amount should be presented as an asset. Where progress billings exceed costs incurred *plus* recognized profits (*less* recognized losses) the net amount should be presented as a liability.

Disclosures are required to show how these rules have been applied in the period.

2.6.1.3 Reducing the options

IAS 11 was first issued in 1979. Prior to the Comparability Project, IAS 11 allowed free choice in revenue recognition between the percentage of completion method and the completed contract method. Implementation of E 32 in the revised IAS 11 permitted only the percentage of completion method. IAS 11, as revised in 1993, was acceptable to IOSCO as a core standard.

2.6.2 Revenue (IAS 18)

IAS 18 was revised in 1993.

2.6.2.1 Key issues

As a general principle, revenue is recognized when it is probable that future economic benefits will flow to the enterprise and these benefits can be measured reliably. The standard applies this principle to the sale of goods, the rendering of services and the use by others of enterprise assets yielding interest, royalties and dividends.

2.6.2.2 Approach in IAS 18

Revenue should be measured at the fair value of the consideration received or receivable.

Revenue from the *sale of goods* should be recognized when the enterprise has transferred to the buyer the significant risks and rewards of ownership of the goods. The enterprise should not retain a continuing management involvement of the type usually associated with ownership and should not retain effective control over the goods sold.

When the outcome of a transaction involving the *rendering of services* can be estimated reliably, revenue associated with the transaction should be recognized by reference to the stage of completion of the transaction at the balance sheet date. When the outcome of the transaction cannot be estimated reliably, revenue should be recognized only to the extent of the expenses recognized that are recoverable.

Interest should be recognized on a time proportion basis that takes into account the effective yield on the asset. *Royalties* should be recognized on an accrual basis in accordance with the substance of the relevant agreement. *Dividends* should be recognized when the shareholder's right to receive payment is established.

The enterprise should disclose the accounting policies adopted for the recognition of revenue, including the methods adopted to determine the stage of completion of transactions involving the rendering of services and the amount of each significant category of revenue recognized during the period, identifying the amount arising from barter exchange.

2.6.2.3 Reducing the options

IAS 18 was issued in 1982. In the original version of IAS 18 the recognition of revenue on service contracts allowed either the percentage of completion method or the completed contract method. Following the Comparability Project, the revised standard (1993) permitted only the percentage of completion method. The revised standard was acceptable to IOSCO as a core standard.

2.6.3 Accounting for government grants and disclosure of government assistance (IAS 20)

IAS 20 was reformatted in 1995.

2.6.3.1 Key issues

Government grants may be received by the enterprise in advance of the performance of the activity which is financed by the grant. The activity may be the use of a fixed asset purchased with the grant, or the subsidizing of operating costs such as the training of the workforce. Government grants should not be recognized until there is reasonable assurance that:

● the enterprise will comply with the conditions attached to them;
● the grant will be received.

2.6.3.2 Approach in IAS 20

Government grants should be recognized as income over the periods necessary to match them with the related costs which they are intended to compensate, on a systematic basis. They should not be credited directly to shareholders' interest.

A government grant that becomes receivable as compensation for expenses or losses already incurred or for the purpose of giving immediate financial support with no future related costs should be recognized as income of the period in which it becomes receivable.

Government grants relating to assets should be presented in the balance sheet either as deferred income or as a deduction in arriving at the carrying amount of the asset. The standard expresses no preference as to how the grants should be reported in the income statement.

Repayment of a grant relating to income should be first deducted from any deferred credit. The remaining amount of the repayment should be recognized immediately as an expense. Repayment of a grant related to an asset should be recorded by increasing the carrying amount of the asset or reducing the deferred income balance. Any appropriate additional depreciation to date should be recognized immediately as an expense.

Disclosures are also prescribed.

2.6.3.3 Reducing the options

IAS 20 was first issued in 1983. IOSCO accepted IAS 20 as a core standard. However, there were indications that some members of IOSCO would like to propose different treatments for particular types of grants which have come into existence since IAS 20 was issued. At that time it was thought that the IASC would resist any attempt to create exceptions to the general principle of a standard and would expect new types of grant to be reported consistently with the principles stated. This expectation appears to have been confirmed by the lack of any further changes to the standard.

2.6.4 Share-based payment (IFRS 2)

IFRS 2 was issued in February 2004 for annual periods beginning on or after 1 January 2005. Early implementation was encouraged.

2.6.4.1 Key issues

Some entities grant shares or share options to employees or other parties. A share option is the right to buy shares in future at a price fixed today. These shares and share options are part of the remuneration (reward) for directors, senior executives and many other employees. There is no immediate payment of cash, as with wages or salaries. The gain to the employees lies in the future when it is hoped that the share price will rise. The key question is: Should the grant of shares or share options be recognized in profit or loss as a cost to the company?

2.6.4.2 Approach in IFRS 2

IFRS 2 requires an entity to recognize share-based payment transactions in its financial statements. Where an entity makes a share-based payment transaction, it must measure the goods or services received at their fair value. If that fair value can not be measured reliably then the entity must measure value in terms of the equity instruments granted.

For transactions with employees the entity is required to measure the fair value of the equity instruments granted. Estimating the fair value of services received from employees would be very difficult. The fair value is measured at the date when the right is granted.

For other types of transactions the standard assumes, in the first instance, that there will be a reliable fair value for the goods and services provided.

The IFRS sets out various disclosure requirements. These are intended to enable users of financial statements to understand the nature, the value and the effect of share-based payment transactions.

2.6.4.3 Reducing the options

This standard is extremely controversial. The IASB takes the view that having no information means that users of financial statements are at a disadvantage. Those who disagree raise several objections. They say:

- 'The entity is not a party to the transaction. It is the existing shareholders who transfer some of their ownership interest to the employees.'
- 'The employees do not provide services for the option. They have already been paid in cash for their services.'
- 'There is no cost to the entity because there is no sacrifice of cash or other assets.'
- 'Recognizing an expense here is inconsistent with the *Framework* definition of expense.'
- 'Earnings per share is hit twice – once in the income statement and again in the dilution of future earnings per share'.

The IASB rejects all these arguments. The conclusions formed by the IASB are similar to those formed by the FASB in the US, in its standard SFAS 123.

2.7 Measurement of inflation

The Framework document says relatively little about measurement of changing prices. In the separate standards there is a clear preference for historical cost accounting, although some specific alternatives are permitted (e.g. in IAS 16). There were two standards, IAS 15 and IAS 29, dealing particularly with changing prices (inflation). IAS 15 (issued 1981, reformatted 1995) encouraged enterprises to present a supplementary statement reflecting the effects of changing prices. It was withdrawn in December 2003 after consultation. The consultation respondents agreed with the IASB's reasoning that IAS 15 was voluntary and very few companies were using IAS 15. In addition 'the Board does not believe that entities should be required to disclose information that reflects the effects of changing prices in the current economic environment'. This leaves only IAS 29 which insists on the use of the current unit of purchasing power in the primary financial statements where there is a hyperinflationary economy.

Measurement of changing prices was not a significant theme of the agreement with IOSCO on core standards and has taken a relegated position in the IASB's work programme. That ought not to diminish the importance of the issue in economic terms, but does perhaps indicate the dominance of historical cost accounting.

2.7.1 Financial reporting in hyperinflationary economies (IAS 29)

IAS 29 was reformatted in 1995.

2.7.1.1 Key issues

Financial statements of an enterprise that reports in the currency of a hyperinflationary economy should be stated in terms of the measuring unit current at the balance sheet date.

2.7.1.2 Approach in IAS 29

The existence of hyperinflation is indicated by the following characteristics of a country's economic environment:

- the general population prefers to keep its wealth in non-monetary assets or a relatively stable foreign currency;
- amounts of local currency held are immediately invested to maintain purchasing power;
- prices may be quoted in a relatively stable foreign currency;
- sales and purchase on credit take place at a price which compensates for the loss of purchasing power during the period of credit;
- interest rates, wages and prices are linked to a price index;
- the cumulative inflation rate over three years is approaching, or exceeds, 100 per cent.

For accounting records maintained in *historical cost terms*, non-monetary balance sheet items are restated to current monetary units by applying a general price index. Monetary items need no restatement as they are already expressed in monetary units current at the balance sheet date. Each item in the income statement needs to be restated by applying the change in the general price index from the date when that item was initially recorded.

For accounting records maintained in *current cost terms*, most balance sheet items will be expressed in monetary units of currency at the balance sheet date and will not need restating. Cost of sales and depreciation are recorded at current cost of the time they are consumed. Other expenses and all revenues are recorded at monetary amounts of the date they occur. All revenues and expenses must be restated into the measurement unit of the balance sheet date by applying an appropriate general price index.

The gain or loss on the net monetary position should be included in net income and separately disclosed.

2.7.1.3 Reducing the options

IAS 29 was first issued in 1989. It was reformatted in 1995 without any change because it was acceptable to IOSCO as a core standard.

2.8 Group accounting

Many countries which have firm preferences for domestic accounting practices in the financial statements of individual companies turn nevertheless to the IASB for guidance on group accounting. Thus it has been possible to encounter group accounts published under IFRS accounting policies, accompanied by parent company accounts using domestic practices. In some countries there are established domestic standards for group accounting. IFRS deal with many of the problem areas of group accounting, such as foreign exchange rates (IAS 21); the nature of a business combination (IFRS 3); consolidated financial statements and investments in subsidiaries (IAS 27); investments in associates (IAS 28); and interests in joint ventures (IAS 31).

All the standards relating to group accounting were acceptable to IOSCO for the Core Standards programme. Accounting for goodwill, dealt with in IAS 22, was probably the most controversial aspect of acquisition accounting. The IASB identified business combinations as an early target for its Improvements Project.

2.8.1 The effects of changes in foreign exchange rates (IAS 21)

IAS 21 was revised in December 2003 to be applied for annual periods beginning on or after 1 January 2005. Earlier application was encouraged.

2.8.1.1 Key issues

The financial statements of an enterprise may be affected by foreign exchange rates in two ways. The enterprise may undertake transactions in foreign currencies; it may also operate part of its business in a foreign country which has a different currency. The standard sets out procedures for recording transactions undertaken in a foreign currency and translation of financial statements produced in a foreign currency. Each enterprise presents its financial statements in one currency, which is called the 'presentation currency'.

2.8.1.2 Approach in IAS 21

The standard applies two ideas: the '*functional currency*' and the '*presentation currency*'. The functional currency is the currency of the primary economic environment in which the entity operates. An entity does not have a free choice of functional currency; it is determined by the facts of the situation. The presentation currency is the currency in which the financial statements are presented. This can be chosen by the reporting entity.

The standard requires every entity to identify its functional currency and measure its results and financial position in that currency.

A foreign currency transaction may involve buying and selling goods or services priced in another currency. It may involve borrowing or lending where the amounts payable or receivable are denominated in another currency. It may involve buying or selling assets, incurring or settling liabilities, all in a foreign currency. Transactions of this type must be recorded on initial recognition, in the functional currency, by applying the spot rate of exchange at the date of the transaction.

At subsequent balance sheet dates, foreign currency monetary items are translated using the closing rate. Non-monetary items measured in historical cost in a foreign currency are translated using the exchange rate at the date of the transaction. Non-monetary items measured at fair value in a foreign currency are translated using the exchange rates of the date of the valuation.

Exchange differences on the settlement of monetary items or on the translation of monetary items are recognized in the profit or loss of the period in which they arise. When a gain or loss on a non-monetary item is recognized directly in equity, any exchange component is also recognized in equity. When the gain or loss on a non-monetary item is recognized in profit or loss, any exchange component is also recognized in profit or loss.

If the functional currency of an entity is not the presentation currency, then the results and financial position must be translated into the presentation currency. Assets and liabilities are translated at the closing rate at the balance sheet date. Income and expenses are translated at exchange rates at the dates of transactions (average rates for a period are an acceptable compromise). All resulting exchange differences are recognized as a separate component of equity.

If the entity's functional currency is that of a hyperinflationary economy, there are separate rules. The entity must restate its financial statements in accordance with IAS 29 *before* carrying out translation to the presentation currency using the closing rate of exchange for all amounts (assets, liabilities, equity, income, expenses and comparative figures). However, where amounts are translated into the currency of a non-hyperinflationary economy, comparative amounts must be those of the relevant prior year as reported (not adjusted for subsequent changes in the price level or in exchange rates).

On the disposal of a foreign operation, the cumulative amount of the exchange differences deferred in the separate component of equity relating to that foreign operation must be recognized in profit or loss when the gain or loss on disposal is recognized.

The standard prescribed disclosures that help the user of financial statements understand the exchange differences, the functional currency applied and the presentation currency chosen.

2.8.1.3 Reducing the options

IAS 21 was issued in 1983 and revised in 1993. The Comparability Project revised IAS 21 to clarify the required treatment of exchange differences on long-term foreign currency monetary items. It also provided some interim guidance on accounting for hedges, pending the production of an international accounting standard on financial instruments, and it transferred aspects of accounting in hyperinflationary economies to a specific standard on that topic. IAS 21 was acceptable to IOSCO as a core standard. The treatment of hedges was subsequently moved to IAS 39. The revision of IAS 21 in 2003 was part of the IASB's Improvements Project. IAS 21 had given companies freedom to choose one of several functional currencies, which could lead to inappropriate choices. The revised IAS 21 focuses on the underlying economy that determines the pricing of transactions. The revision took the view that an 'integral' foreign subsidiary could not have a functional currency that differed from that of the parent. This eliminated another source of variability in translation of the results of foreign subsidiaries for consolidation with the parent's financial statements. A clearer rule on the treatment of subsidiaries in hyperinflationary economies eliminates the flexibility possible previously.

2.8.2 Business combinations (IFRS 3)

IFRS 3 was issued in March 2004, replacing IAS 22. It applies to accounting for business combinations where the date of the agreement is on or after 31 March 2004.

2.8.2.1 Key issues

Most business combinations involve an acquisition of one enterprise (the acquiree) by another (the acquirer). The result is a combined organization where the location of control is clear, although the separate operations of each enterprise may continue to be identifiable. In relatively rare cases, two enterprises unite their interests in such a way that control continues to be located in the separate entities, but with mutual sharing of risks and benefits. IFRS 3 treats all business combinations as an acquisition. It requires use of the acquisition method. Under this method the acquirer recognizes the acquiree's identifiable assets, liabilities and contingent liabilities at their fair values at the date of acquisition. The acquirer also recognizes goodwill, which is subsequently tested for impairment but is not amortized.

2.8.2.2 Approach in IFRS 3

The standard asserts that in a business combination the result is almost always that one entity, the acquirer, obtains control of one or more other businesses, the acquiree. All business combinations must be accounted for by applying the *acquisition method*.

The acquirer measures the cost of the business combination as the aggregate of the fair values at the date of exchange of the assets given, liabilities taken on and equity instruments issued by the acquirer, in exchange for the acquiree, plus any costs directly attributable to the business combination.

The acquirer recognizes the identifiable assets, liabilities and contingent liabilities of the acquiree at fair value at the date of acquisition.

The acquirer then recognizes goodwill acquired in a business combination as an asset and measures that asset at cost. Cost is calculated as the excess of the cost of the business combination over the net fair value of the identifiable assets, liabilities and contingent liabilities of the acquiree.

After initial recognition the acquirer measures goodwill acquired in a business combination at cost less any accumulated impairment losses.

If the acquirer's interest in the net fair value of the identifiable assets, liabilities and contingent liabilities exceeds the cost of the business combination, the acquirer should reassess the identification and measurement of net fair value. If an excess remains after reassessment, the excess should be recognized immediately in profit or loss. This excess is also known as 'negative goodwill' but the standard does not use the description 'negative goodwill'.

2.8.2.3 Reducing the options

IFRS 3 replaced IAS 22 which was issued in 1983, revised in 1993 and revised again in 1998. This standard has seen many changes, reflecting changing views on accounting for business combinations.

In 1983 there were two approaches to business combinations. One was acquisition accounting and the other was uniting of interests. The Comparability Project tightened up the definition of a uniting of interests in order to reduce the scope for manipulation of reported profits and net assets. In the case of acquisition accounting, the project discontinued the previous practice of permitting goodwill on acquisition to be set against shareholders' interests. Amortization became the required treatment.

The preferred treatment for negative goodwill was proposed as allocation over the relevant assets. The allowed alternative was proposed as recording deferred income to be amortized over a period not normally exceeding five years.

The preferred treatment of minority interests was seen as according more closely with the historical cost basis of accounting. The allowed alternative reflected the opinion of those who regarded the group as a consolidated economic entity.

IOSCO indicated that it would accept IAS 22 as a core standard but nevertheless the IASC decided in 1995 to revise those aspects of IAS 22 dealing with goodwill. The discussion of impairment tests for longer-lived assets and the production of a general standard covering intangible assets both had an impact on the goodwill aspects of IAS 22. In particular, the Board proposed eliminating the allowed alternative for negative goodwill.

In July 1998 the Board reached agreement in principle on IAS 22 (revised) Business Combinations. The revisions were consistent with the proposals in E 61 with regard to the amortization of goodwill, the treatment of negative goodwill and the measurement of the identifiable assets and liabilities of the acquiree at fair value. IAS 22 continued to allow 'pooling of interest' or 'merger accounting' for a merger that was seen as a 'uniting of interests'. This treatment has been eliminated by IFRS 3. IAS 2 also revised the treatment of negative goodwill, presenting it as a negative asset to be released to income according to the circumstances causing the negative goodwill. The treatment of negative goodwill changed again with IFRS 3, to become recognized immediately as a gain.

2.8.3 Consolidated and separate financial statements (IAS 27)

IAS 27 was revised in December 2003 to be applied for annual periods beginning on or after 1 January 2005. Earlier application was encouraged.

2.8.3.1 Key issues

A parent company (i.e. an enterprise that has one or more subsidiary companies that it controls) should normally present consolidated financial statements.

IAS 27 applies the entity concept in regarding all the assets and liabilities of group enterprises as being controlled by the group as an entity. The strength of control requires all the assets and liabilities to be aggregated in the group balance sheet even where the parent company owns less than 100 per cent of the equity of a subsidiary. The minority interest in net assets is presented within the equity section, separately from the parent shareholders' equity.

2.8.3.2 Approach in IAS 27

'Control' in the context of this standard is the power to govern the financial and operating policies of an enterprise so as to obtain benefits from its activities.

A parent need not present consolidated financial statements if, and only if:

- the parent enterprise is itself a wholly-owned subsidiary, or
- the parent is a partially-owned subsidiary of another entity and its other owners do not object; and
- the parent's debt or equity instruments are not traded in a public market; and

- the parent is not filing financial statements with a securities commission for the purpose of issuing financial statements; and
- the ultimate parent or any intermediate parent produces consolidated financial statements for public use that comply with IFRS.

Consolidated financial statements must include all subsidiaries. The only exception is where the subsidiary is acquired with a view to disposal within 12 months and the management is actively seeking a buyer. In preparing consolidated financial statements, intra-group balances and transactions must be eliminated in full. Investments in such excluded subsidiaries should be classified as 'held for trading' and accounted for in accordance with IAS 39. The separate financial statements of the parent and subsidiaries must be prepared as of the same reporting date. Consolidated financial statements must be prepared using uniform accounting policies for like transactions and events in similar circumstances.

When separate financial statements are prepared by the parent company, investments in subsidiaries, jointly controlled entities and associates must be accounted for either at cost or in accordance with IAS 39. The same treatment must be applied for each category of investments.

2.8.3.3 Reducing the options

IAS 27 was issued in 1989 and reformatted in 1995. The first standard on consolidated financial statements was issued in 1976 (IAS 3). This pre-dated the EU Seventh Directive and probably influenced the Directive as well as being available for member states in implementing it. IAS 27, in replacing IAS 3, brought the concept of control into IASs and removed some of the exemptions previously allowed in IAS 3. IAS 27 was acceptable to IOSCO as a core standard. IAS 27 was included in the Improvements Project of IASB. The title was changed to show that its coverage includes subsidiaries, joint ventures, and associates in the separate financial statements of the parent or investor. The revised IAS 27 clarifies the exemption from consolidation, the reporting of minority interests, and the treatment of investments within separate financial statements where these are required by national regulations.

2.8.4 Investments in associates (IAS 28)

IAS 28 was revised in December 2003 to be applied for annual periods beginning on or after 1 January 2005. Earlier application was encouraged.

2.8.4.1 Key issues

Entity *A* may be regarded as an associate of entity *B* where *B* has significant influence and *A* is neither a subsidiary nor an interest in a joint venture. Significant influence is presumed where *B* holds, directly or indirectly, more than 20 per cent of the voting power of *A*. An entity should include in its consolidated financial statements its share of the profits and losses of an associate.

2.8.4.2 Approach in IAS 28

An investment in an associate should be accounted for in consolidated financial statements using the equity method. An exception to this is when the investment is acquired and held exclusively with a view to its disposal within 12 months, in which case it should be classed as 'held for trading and accounted for under IAS 39'. Under the equity method the investment is initially recognized at cost and the carrying amount is increased or decreased to recognize the investor's share of the profit or loss of the investee after the date of acquisition. Associates accounted for using the equity method should be classified as non-current assets and disclosed separately in the balance sheet. The investor's share of the profit or loss of the investee is recognized in the investor's profit or loss. In the investor's separate financial statements the investment in an associate must follow the equity method as described in the standard. Disclosures are prescribed in the standard.

2.8.4.3 Reducing the options

IAS 28 was issued in 1989, reformatted in 1995 and revised in 2000. IAS 28 (1989) replaced the aspects of IAS 3 dealing with associates. It was not revised in the Comparability Project and was acceptable to IOSCO as a core standard. The revisions made in 2000 were for updating and consistency with other standards. IAS 28 was revised in 2003 as part of the Improvements Project, mainly to reduce alternatives in the application of the equity method and in accounting for investments in separate financial statements.

2.8.5 Interests in joint ventures (IAS 31)

IAS 31 was revised in December 2003 to be applied for annual periods beginning on or after 1 January 2005. Earlier application was encouraged.

2.8.5.1 Key issues

The standard identifies three broad types of joint venture structures. Each is characterized by the existence of a contractual arrangement entered into by two or more ventures that establishes joint control (i.e. the agreed sharing of the power to govern the financial and operating policies of an economic activity so as to obtain benefits from it).

An enterprise should include in its consolidated financial statements its proportionate share of assets, liabilities, income and expenses of a jointly controlled entity. The enterprise should also include in its separate financial statements (and hence in the consolidated financial statements) its share of assets and liabilities controlled jointly with other venturers. This requirement for proportional consolidation is in contrast to the normal practice of full consolidation as set out in IAS 27.

2.8.5.2 Approach in IAS 31

Definitions are provided to distinguish various types of joint activity:

- In *jointly controlled operations*, each venturer uses its own assets and incurs its own expenses and liabilities; the joint venture agreement provides a means by which the revenues from the sale of the joint product are shared amongst the venturers.
- For *jointly controlled assets*, there is joint control and ownership of assets constructed or acquired and dedicated for the purpose of the joint venture – each venture takes a share of the output from the assets and each bears an agreed share of the expenses incurred; this does not involve the setting up of a new entity.
- *Jointly controlled entities* involve the creation of a new entity in which each venturer has an interest – this entity owns assets, incurs liabilities and expenses and earns income; each venturer is entitled to a share of the results of the jointly controlled entity, which will maintain its own accounting records and present financial statements.

The accounting treatment of jointly controlled operations and jointly controlled assets is relatively straightforward. For jointly controlled entities there are different approaches available. The venturer may report its interest in a jointly controlled entity using proportionate consolidation. The alternative treatment is that a venturer should report its interest in a jointly controlled entity using the equity method. Although equity accounting is permitted, the standard states that proportionate consolidation better reflects the substance and economic reality of a venturer's interest in a jointly controlled entity.

2.8.5.3 Reducing the options

IAS 31 was issued in 1990, reformatted in 1995 and revised in 2000. IAS 31 did not feature in the Comparability Project of 1989 and was acceptable to IOSCO as a core standard. The revisions made in 2000 related to updating for consistency with other standards. The limited revisions in 2003 were made for consistency with changes to IAS 27 and IAS 28.

2.9 Specialist organizations and industries

The IASB has continued the tradition of the IASC in focusing its attention mainly on general standards rather than industry-specific matters. However, there are some specialist standards, covering retirement benefit plans, banks and similar financial institutions, agriculture and insurance contracts. The agriculture project was initially funded by the World Bank and is important to countries that have an agricultural economy.

2.9.1 Accounting and reporting by retirement benefit plans (IAS 26)

This standard deals with the accounting practices required where a retirement benefit plan exists as a reporting entity separate from the enterprise which employs the persons concerned. There is a separate standard, IAS 19, which sets out the method by which the enterprise accounts for retirement benefit costs in its own financial statements.

2.9.2 Disclosure in the financial statements of banks and similar financial institutions (IAS 30)

The standard recognizes the special needs of banks in reporting matters of solvency, liquidity and relative risk attaching to different types of business. It covers aspects of accounting policies and disclosures which are particularly significant to those who use the financial statements of banks and financial institutions.

2.9.3 Agriculture (IAS 41)

IAS 41 was issued in 2001.

2.9.3.1 Key issues

The key issue is valuing biological assets at fair value rather than historical cost.

The standard sets out the accounting treatment, financial statement presentation, and disclosures related to agricultural activity. It applies to biological assets, agricultural

produce at the point of harvest, and government grants relating to biological assets. It does not apply to products that are the result of processing after harvest. It covers, for example, vines and grapes but not the wine produced. Likewise, it covers dairy cattle and milk but not the cheese manufactured from the milk.

2.9.3.2 Approach in the standard

The standard requires assets to be measured at fair value less estimated point-of-sale costs from initial recognition up to the point of harvest. There is a presumption that fair value can be measured reliably for a biological asset. Where this is not possible, the enterprise should apply cost minus accumulated depreciation and minus any impairment losses.

The change in value of the biological asset must be included in the net profit or loss of the period. This allows the enterprise to report changes in fair value throughout the period up to harvest. An unconditional government grant related to a biological asset must be recognized when it becomes receivable. If the grant is conditional then recognition must wait until the conditions are met.

2.9.4 Insurance contracts (IFRS 4)

The standard specifies the financial reporting for insurance contracts by an insurer as a temporary measure until the Board completes the second phase of its project on insurance contracts. In particular it covers the treatment of insurance liabilities.

Summary and conclusions

This chapter has set out the key issues and approach taken in each of the IFRSs. It has explained how options have been reduced in moving down the route of international harmonization and has indicated the extent to which differences remain. In later chapters, the accounting practices of separate countries will be discussed in the context of adoption and implementation of the IFRSs.

Key points from the chapter:

It is rarely necessary to learn the details of accounting standards because you can usually gain access to a reference manual and check the detail. However, it is useful to know two or three key facts about each standard that will help you think about accounting issues when you read annual reports or compare companies' accounting practices. When you are revising, make a summary of each standard in three sentences, answering the following questions:

● What is the accounting issue addressed in the standard?

● What is the most important requirement of the standard?

● Why might this requirement cause problems for some companies or countries?

If you have this basic set of information clear in your mind, you will then be able to add to it by using reference sources to build more detailed understanding as and when you need it.

Also it is important to update your knowledge. At least once each month check the IASB website, for news of its work programme, and make a note in the margin of the book against any standard that is in the process of being updated, amended or replaced.

Questions

The following questions test your understanding of the material contained in the chapter and allow you to relate your understanding to the learning outcomes specified at the start of this chapter. The learning outcomes are repeated here. Each question is cross-referenced to the relevant section of the chapter.

Explain the key issues and main principles of each international financial reporting standard

1 For each IFRS or IAS, summarize in no more than three sentences the key issues and main principles.

Understand the aims and achievements of the Comparability Project, the IASC's Core Standards programme and the IASB's Improvements Project in reducing options available under international standards

2 To what extent have the Comparability Project, the Core Standards programme and the Improvements Project reduced options in relation to:
   (a) disclosure and presentation?
   (b) asset recognition and measurement?
   (c) liability recognition and measurement?
   (d) financial instruments?
   (e) economic activity?
   (f) group accounting?

3 To what extent is reduction of options necessary or desirable in relation to:
   (a) disclosure and presentation?
   (b) asset recognition and measurement?
   (c) liability recognition and measurement?
   (d) financial instruments?
   (e) economic activity?
   (f) group accounting?

4 Which areas have given the IASC and IASB particular problems in seeking to reduce options in relation to:
   (a) disclosure and presentation?
   (b) asset recognition and measurement?
   (c) liability recognition and measurement?
   (d) financial instruments?
   (e) economic activity?
   (f) group accounting?

5 Which influences appear strongest where there has been resistance to reducing options?

Relate the IFRS to the Framework in categories of assets, liabilities, recognition, measurement, group accounting and special needs of particular user groups

6 Choose one accounting standard in each of the following groups and relate the key issues and content of the standard to relevant aspects of the Framework (as outlined in Chapter 1):
   (a) disclosure and presentation
   (b) asset recognition and measurement
   (c) liability recognition and measurement

(d) financial instruments
(e) economic activity
(f) group accounting

Form an opinion on the extent to which a company's stated accounting policies are consistent with IFRS

7 Obtain the annual report of any listed company and turn to the accounting policies statement. Read the company's statement on compliance with IFRS (if any) and then compare each accounting policy description with the relevant section of this chapter. Assess the company's apparent consistency with IFRS.

The following questions link Chapters 1 and 2

8 To what extent has the 'stable platform' of the IASB's Improvements Project reduced options that remained after completion of the Core Standards programme?

9 To what extent did the Core Standards programme reduce options that were not resolved after the comparability project?

10 Are the circumstances of the Improvements Project sufficiently different from those of the Core Standards programme to allow global acceptance of the IFRS?

11 Why is the position of the US regulators so significant to the global acceptance of IFRS? Which issues attract the particular attention of the US regulators?

12 Which new themes have been added to the IASB's programme since the Core Standards programme was completed? What are the apparent reasons for adding these new themes?

References and further reading

This chapter draws on material contained in IASB publications, particularly:

Annual Review, various issues.

Insight, published several times during a year.

International Financial Reporting Standards, published annually.

Various Exposure Drafts and Statements, as indicated in the chapter.

The IASB website at www.iasb.org

The website of Deloitte Touche Tohmatsu at www.iasplus.com is very useful.

Discussions covering the move towards the IOSCO targets are to be found in:

Cairns, D. (2002) *A Guide to Applying International Accounting Standards*, 3rd edn. London: Butterworths.

3 Confidence and assurance

Learning outcomes

After reading this chapter you should be able to:

- Explain and evaluate the steps taken around the world to improve the credibility of financial reporting.

- Explain and evaluate developments in audit and assurance.

- Explain how the development of corporate governance has affected financial reporting.

- Explain how developments in corporate social responsibility are reflected in financial reporting.

- Explain and evaluate the effectiveness of regulation in ensuring compliance with requirements for financial reporting.

- Explain how research into credibility and assurance is developing.

3.1 Introduction

It has become apparent that developing high-quality international accounting standards is necessary, but not sufficient, to give capital markets sufficient confidence in the reliability of financial reporting. Mechanisms have emerged for encouraging, or enforcing, compliance and for identifying good practice. We explained in section 1.5.2 that the IASB has no powers of enforcement of IFRS. It relies on national governments and regulators to support the adoption of these standards and set a system of penalties on those who fail to comply. This chapter explains how national and international authorities have been working towards supporting high-quality financial reporting. These authorities may be:

- departments of national governments,
- independent bodies supported by governments,
- independent bodies supported by capital market regulators,
- transnational bodies with an interest in the orderly conduct of capital markets,
- transnational bodies with an interest in improving corporate governance,
- transnational bodies with an interest in improving auditing and ethical standards.

The chapter begins with an overview of frameworks proposed for improving the credibility of financial reporting. These frameworks, in seeking to reduce or eliminate the prospect of repeating some of the major crises of recent years, range beyond financial reporting. However, high-quality financial reporting is an essential aspect of the proposals. The chapter describes in more detail the initiatives that have developed in auditing and assurance, corporate governance and corporate social responsibility. It then discusses ways in which these initiatives help those who need to have confidence in corporate financial reports. It concludes with an overview of research directions in this area of study.

3.2 Improving the credibility of financial reporting

Why is it so important to improve the credibility of financial reporting? In the period 1995–2000 the IASC was working on its Core Standards programme, as explained in Chapter 1. During that period the effectiveness of accounting in emerging markets was called into question as a result of the East Asian financial crisis of 1997. The 'financial meltdown', which directly affected Thailand, Malaysia, South Korea, Indonesia, Hong Kong, Singapore and Taiwan,[1] led to questions about the reliability of the financial statements of companies in those countries. The word 'transparency' was linked to calls for internationally recognized standards of accounting and auditing for the private sector. The Chairman of the Securities and Exchange Commission in the US gave a much-publicized speech entitled 'The Numbers Game'. In that speech, where he called for greater transparency and comparability, he said:

> . . . the significance of transparent, timely and reliable financial statements and its importance to investor protection has never been more apparent. The current financial situations in Asia and Russia are stark examples of this new reality. These markets are learning a painful lesson taught many times before: investors panic as a result of unexpected or unquantifiable news.[2]

At that stage the problems of transparency were seen primarily as an issue for emerging markets where the experience and expertise of the long-established markets could be of benefit. It was assumed that supplying international standards for accounting and auditing would bring this expertise to an international stage, to the benefit of all participants. The main focus of the debate was on whether international accounting standards or US accounting standards would give the stronger basis from which to achieve this aim.

It was therefore a much greater shock in November 2001 when a very large US company called Enron announced that it was restating its financial statements for the period from 1997 to 2001 because of 'accounting errors'. As the details of the 'errors' emerged, there was a rapid fall in market confidence and investor trust. By the end of 2001 Enron had filed for bankruptcy.[3] The effects of the collapse of Enron rippled across the world throughout 2002. Questions were asked about the reliability of accounting information, the reliability of audit, the effectiveness of monitoring by major shareholders and the effectiveness of bodies intended to safeguard the rights of employees and investors. In the US there were Congressional enquiries.[4] In July 2002 the US President signed the Sarbanes–Oxley Act which set out a significant expansion of US securities law, regulation of corporate governance, disclosure, reporting and accounting requirements and penalties.[5] The Sarbanes–Oxley Act is very wide-ranging and has an effect on companies and audit firms around the world that have activities in the US (see section 3.2.3).

---

[1] Pilbeam (2001); *Business America* (1998).

[2] Quoted in IASC Insight, October 1998, p. 3. Also available on SEC website at www.sec.gov/news/speech/speecharchive/1998/spch220.txt.

[3] There is a 'links' page on the library section of the Institute of Chartered Accountants in England and Wales that provides a useful guide to Enron sources. The link was archived in May 2004 but may still be effective: www.icaew.co.uk/librarylinks/index.cfm?AUB=TB2I_29490,MNXI_29490.

[4] Congressional Committee (2002).

[5] Hermsen *et al.* (2002).

This section explains how finance ministers and professional accountancy bodies have responded in their respective collective organizations by setting frameworks for action to restore confidence.

3.2.1 The Financial Stability Forum (FSF)[6]

The Financial Stability Forum was established by the finance ministers of the G7 countries in 1999 to identify ways of avoiding or minimizing the effects of crises such as the East Asian financial crisis of 1997/8. The Forum wanted to see strong regulation of capital markets, banking and insurance. It identified 12 'standards' that would be particularly important in achieving this aim.[7] The word 'standard' is used here in a very broad sense of 'regulations or guidelines' that have an international impact. Of these 12 standards, seven relate closely to financial reporting and are listed in Exhibit 3.1. Chapters 1 and 2 have dealt with the first item listed; this chapter explains more on 2, 3, 5 and 7. Items 4 and 6 are specialized for banks and insurance companies.

3.2.2 The International Federation of Accountants (IFAC)[8]

Professional accountancy bodies around the world are members of IFAC. Its secretariat work is funded by membership subscriptions but much of its activity relies on voluntary service from organizations and individuals (see also section 1.3.2). IFAC develops pronouncements on auditing and assurance, ethics, education and public sector accounting.

In October 2002 a Task Force on Rebuilding Public Confidence in Financial Reporting came together at the request of IFAC to consider ways of restoring the credibility of financial reporting and corporate disclosure from an international perspective. The Task Force had to face the loss of credibility caused by high-profile corporate failures, such as Enron, and by the increased frequency of restated financial statements.[9] It also encountered the

---

Exhibit 3.1 Standards relevant to financial reporting, as noted by the Financial Stability Forum

> **1** International Financial Reporting Standards, issued by the IASB
>
> **2** International Standards on Auditing, issued by the IAASB
>
> **3** The OECD Principles of Corporate Governance
>
> **4** The Core Principles for Effective Banking Supervision, issued by the Basel Committee on Banking Supervision
>
> **5** The Objectives and Principles of Securities Regulation, issued by IOSCO
>
> **6** The Insurance Core Principles, issued by the International Association of Insurance Supervisors
>
> **7** Principles on insolvency, being developed by the World Bank

Source: IFAC (2003) extracted from *Rebuilding Public Confidence in Financial Reporting*, Appendix 3

---

[6] IFAC (2003) Appendix 3.

[7] IFAC (2003) Appendix 3.

[8] www.ifac.org.

[9] 'Restatement' means that the company has submitted revised financial statements to the regulator, usually with a lower profit than was first reported.

| Exhibit 3.2 | Task Force on Rebuilding Public Confidence in Financial Reporting |

Recommendations of the Task force:

1 Effective corporate ethics codes, in place and monitored.

2 Effective financial management and controls from corporate management.

3 Reduce incentives to misstate financial information (e.g. pressures to meet analysts' forecasts, or to satisfy management reward schemes).

4 Improved oversight of management, carried out by independent directors.

5 Give attention to the threats to auditor independence.

6 Give greater attention to audit quality control procedures.

7 Codes of conduct for other market participants, such as analysts and credit-rating agencies.

8 Strengthen auditing standards and regulations.

9 Strengthen accounting and reporting practices.

10 Raise the standard of regulation of companies issuing equity in the market.

perception of unfairness where it seemed that business losses had caused hardship for shareholders, employees and those expecting pensions from private pension schemes, while those running companies had made themselves richer despite the losses.[10]

The Task Force made ten recommendations, shown in Exhibit 3.2. The Task Force said that these ten recommendations would need to be taken up at national and international level, to influence legislation and other forms of regulation.

3.2.3 The Sarbanes–Oxley Act 2002

The Sarbanes–Oxley Act was the reaction of US legislators to the crisis of confidence following Enron. It has an international impact because its terms are drawn very widely. It applies to all companies that are registered with the SEC and listed on a US stock exchange and to the auditors of those companies.[11] This section lists the main recommendations of the Act as they affect auditing and the regulation of corporate reporting. An impression of the impact of Sarbanes–Oxley in the US may be gained from the web page devoted to listing the extensive rulemaking and reports that have emerged as a result.[12]

3.2.3.1 Auditing

The Act establishes a Public Company Accounting Oversight Board (PCAOB)[13] as a non-profit corporation subject to administration and oversight by the Securities and Exchange Commission (SEC) of the US. The PCAOB oversees the audits of public companies and related matters. All auditors of public companies must register with the PCAOB. This includes audit firms in other countries where those firms audit parent companies or subsidiaries of companies listed on US stock exchanges. The audit firm must identify public audit clients,

---

[10] IFAC (2003), p. 5.

[11] *Sarbanes–Oxley: A Guide for Europeans*, by Daniel Dooley, www.pwcglobal.com.

[12] *Spotlight on Sarbanes–Oxley Rulemaking and Reports*, www.sec.gov/spotlight/sarbanes–oxley.htm.

[13] www.pcaob.org.

all accountants associated with those clients, list fees earned for audit and non-audit services, explain their audit quality procedures and identify all legal proceedings against the firm in connection with an audit. The PCAOB is required to inspect all professional accountancy firms that audit public companies. All audit committees in companies must consist of independent directors (see section 3.3.3 and section 8.4.3.1). Audit firms are appointed by, and report to the audit committee. The PCAOB is required to adopt standards for auditing, quality control, ethics and independence. It may look to standards established by recognized professional organizations such as the AICPA.[14] The Act restricts consulting work that auditors may undertake for their clients. There is a list of prohibited work. Tax services are not on this list but must be approved by the company's audit committee. The Act requires five-year rotation of the audit partner. An audit firm may not audit a public company whose officers worked for the audit firm within the previous year.[15]

The European Commission objected to the PCAOB's intention to apply its rules to auditors working for any EU company listed on the US Stock exchanges. Registration with the PCAOB would extend to European audit firms engaged by US subsidiaries in Europe if the US subsidiary had turnover that was 20 per cent or more of the group total. The European Commission began discussions with the SEC in August 2003.[16]

3.2.3.2 Executives of a company

The Act requires the company's chief executive officer and chief financial officer to certify the financial statements.[17] This is a serious process involving personal certification of the financial statements (see Exhibit 3.3) with serious penalties if the personal certification is later found to be untrue. The Act prohibits improper influences on auditors and requires executives to forfeit their bonuses and equity gains if financial statements are restated after they have been issued. This condition reflects the growing frequency of such restatement occurring with US companies.

3.2.3.3 Accounting standards and disclosure

The Act requires specific disclosures in financial reports, including information about internal control systems[18] and about off-balance-sheet transactions (which were part of the Enron problem)[19] and it requires the SEC to develop rules on 'proforma' disclosures.[20] This reflects concern over the growing practice of presenting financial statements, as supplementary information, that do not conform to US GAAP. They are used by companies as a preferred form of presentation but users of financial statements have no assurance about the comparability or reliability of such presentations.[21]

The SEC is also required to study the adoption by the US financial reporting system of a 'principles-based accounting system', reporting back within one year of the legislation (see section 8.3.3). This reflects a concern that in Enron the detail of accounting rules

---

[14] www.aicpa.org/index.htm.

[15] *Commission Adopts Rules Strengthening Auditor Independence*, www.sec.gov/news/press/2003–9.htm.

[16] *Accountancy*, August 2003, p. 14.

[17] www.sec.gov/rules/final/33–8124.htm.

[18] *Final Rule: Management's Reports on Internal Control Over Financial Reporting and Certification of Disclosure in Exchange Act Periodic Reports*, www.sec.gov/rules/final/33–8238.htm.

[19] *Final Rule: Disclosure in Management's Discussion and Analysis about Off-Balance Sheet Arrangements and Aggregate Contractual Obligations*, www.sec.gov/rules/final/33–8182.htm.

[20] *Final Rule: Conditions for Use of Non-GAAP Financial Measures*, www.sec.gov/rules/final/33–8176.htm.

[21] *Cautionary Advice Regarding the Use of 'Pro Forma' Financial Information in Earnings Releases*, www.sec.gov/rules/other/33–8039.htm.

Exhibit 3.3 Certification by Chief Executive Officer

CERTIFICATION

I, Carlos M. Gutierrez, certify that:

1. I have reviewed this annual report on Form 10-K of Kellogg Company;

2. Based on my knowledge, this report does not contain any untrue statement of a material fact or omit to state a material fact necessary to make the statements made, in light of the circumstances under which such statements were made, not misleading with respect to the period covered by this report;

3. Based on my knowledge, the financial statements, and other financial information included in this annual report, fairly present in all material respects the financial condition, results of operations and cash flows of the registrant as of, and for, the periods presented in this report;

4. The registrant's other certifying officers and I are responsible for establishing and maintaining disclosure controls and procedures (as defined in Exchange Act Rules 13a-15(a) and 15d-15(e)) for the registrant and have:

a) Designed such disclosure controls and procedures, or caused such disclosure controls and procedures to be designed under our supervision, to ensure that material information relating to the registrant, including its consolidated subsidiaries, is made known to us by others within those entities, particularly during the period in which this report is being prepared;

b) Evaluated the effectiveness of the registrant's disclosure controls and presented in this report our conclusions about the effectiveness of the disclosure controls and procedures, as of the end of the period covered by this report based on such evaluation; and

c) Disclosed in this report any change in the registrant's internal control over financial reporting that occurred during the registrant's most recent fiscal quarter (the registrant's fourth fiscal quarter in the case of an annual report) that has materially affected, or is reasonably likely to materially affect, the registrant's internal control over financial reporting; and

5. The registrant's other certifying officers and I have disclosed, based on our most recent evaluation of internal control over financial reporting, to the registrant's auditors and the audit committee of the registrant's board of directors (or persons performing the equivalent functions):

a) All significant deficiencies and material weaknesses in the design or operation of internal control over financial reporting which could adversely affect the registrant's ability to record, process, summarize and report financial data; and

b) Any fraud, whether or not material, that involves management or other employees who have a significant role in the registrant's internal controls.

/s/ CARLOS M. GUTIERREZ

Carlos M. Gutierrez

Chairman of the Board and Chief Executive Officer of Kellogg Company

Date: March 9, 2004

Source: Kellogg Company, US, annual report on form 10-K for the fiscal year ended 27 December 2003, www.sec.gov

was used to justify inappropriate accounting treatments which would have been less acceptable in a system focusing on the principles of fair presentation.

The Act permits the SEC to recognize standards established by a private-sector standard-setter provided the standard-setter is acceptable to the SEC and 'considers' international convergence in developing standards. FASB meets those conditions. Section 1.5.3 describes the work of the FASB in discussing convergence with the IASB.

3.2.3.4 Protection, penalties and funding

The Act provides legal protection to any employee who assists a federal agency, a member or committee of Congress, or a supervisory employee (this is sometimes described as 'whistleblowing'). This reflects concern that in Enron some employees may have been aware of problems with the company's accounting practices, but were in fear of action against them or loss of employment. It sets criminal penalties for corporate fraud and for shredding documents. This is because documents were allegedly shredded relating to Enron, thus impeding investigation. The cost of this regulatory activity is significant. Some of the costs are carried by registration fees and annual fees paid by accounting firms, while the remaining costs are carried by a fee charged to public companies in proportion to their market capitalization.

3.2.4 The World Bank[22]

The World Bank and the International Monetary Fund (IMF) have together developed a system of benchmarks as an early warning mechanism, based on such international best practices as the World Bank's Principles and Guidelines for Effective Insolvency and Creditor Rights Systems (April 2001).

At the global level, these benchmarks set minimum international standards for transparency, market efficiency, and financial discipline. At the national level, they guide policy reform by identifying economic and financial vulnerability.

Countries are then evaluated against the benchmarks in Reports on the Observance of Standards and Codes (ROSCs).[23] This is a wide-ranging evaluation which includes a Program on Accounting and Auditing.[24] It aims to assess the comparability of national accounting and auditing standards with international accounting and auditing standards and to assist the country in developing and implementing a 'country action plan' for improving the institutional framework that underpins the corporate financial reporting regime in the country. Exhibit 3.4 lists the countries for which ROSC accounting and auditing modules have been published. One of the limitations of the process is that the World Bank only reviews countries that are borrowing money (creditor countries). Donor countries are not scrutinized.

| Exhibit 3.4 | ROSC Accounting and Auditing modules |

Bangladesh	Egypt	Macedonia	Romania
Bulgaria	Jamaica	Mauritius	Slovakia
Colombia	Kenya	Morocco	Sri Lanka
Croatia	Lebanon	Philippines	South Africa
Czech Republic	Lithuania	Poland	Ukraine

Source: www.worldbank.org/ifa/rosc_aa.html at June 2004

---

[22] www.worldbank.org.

[23] www.worldbank.org/ifa/rosc.html.

[24] *Overview of the ROSC Accounting and Auditing Program, January 2004*, www.worldbank.org/ifa/rosc_aa.html.

3.3 Auditing and assurance

Regulation of audit and assurance is a national activity because it relies on national law and enforcement mechanisms. We have shown in section 1.7.5 that the US SEC linked the acceptability of the Core Standards to the rigour of their application. We have also explained in section 3.2 that the East Asian financial crisis and the collapse of Enron in the US both led to questions about the reliability of the assurance process. Assurance comes primarily from independent audit but it comes also from the directors of the company explaining the controls that they have put in place. This section explains international activity to strengthen the quality and reliability of independent audit and also explains how the board of directors gives assurance through an audit committee.

3.3.1 International Auditing and Assurance Standards Board (IAASB)[25]

In 2002 IFAC established the International Auditing and Assurance Standards Board (IAASB). The IAASB is an independent standard-setting body which aims to serve the public interest by setting high-quality auditing standards. It encourages convergence of national and international standards to strengthen public confidence in the global auditing and accounting profession.[26] It was created to accelerate and improve transparency of standard-setting activities in international auditing and assurance.

The IAASB has 18 volunteer members. Most of these are experts from around the world who have significant experience in auditing. There are also 'public members' who may be members of IFAC member bodies but are not engaged in the public practice of auditing. Members were initially appointed by the IFAC Board, with future nominations coming from the Public Interest Oversight Board (see section 3.3.2). Financial support comes from IFAC membership subscriptions and the Forum of Firms. This forum consists of accounting firms who share the aim of promoting high standards of financial reporting and auditing worldwide. A Consultative Advisory Group to the IAASB consists of organizations with an interest in the development of international auditing standards.

3.3.1.1 Widening acceptance of ISAs

In 2002 the IAASB staff began working towards revision of the auditing standards in anticipation that the European Union would adopt International Standards on Auditing (ISAs) for 2005 audits.[27] In its 2003 annual report the IAASB stated that more than 70 countries have indicated that they either have adopted ISAs or noted that there are no significant differences between their national standards and ISAs. ISAs have been translated by member bodies into more than 20 languages, including French, German, Russian and Spanish.

The IAASB Action Plan 2003–04 identified the evidence of growing support for international standards on auditing:

● The European Commission is currently proposing that by 2005 national auditing standards in the European Union (EU) should require auditors of financial statements to comply with ISAs in the performance of their audits. This proposal has been well received by most member states.

---

[25] www.iaasb.org.

[26] *Annual Report, 2003, International Auditing and Assurance Standards Board,* www.iaasb.org.

[27] *IAASB Action Plan 2003–04,* January 2003, www.iaasb.org.

- The International Organization of Securities Commissions (IOSCO) has begun to review ISAs to determine whether they will endorse them for use in international capital markets. The IAASB is working proactively with IOSCO to assist in the review process. IFAC has identified endorsement of ISAs by IOSCO and their adoption by the European Union as major strategic objectives.

- There is an increased support for the development of a worldwide public accounting profession responsive to the demands for a global marketplace and for the convergence of national and international standards, with national bodies continuing to set standards for local regulatory purposes and uniquely local situations.

- There is a rapidly growing demand for audits conducted in accordance with ISAs for cross-border filings and financing activities. Concurrently, a number of national standard-setters in various countries have expressed support for convergence of national and international auditing and assurance standards and have been considering how to achieve convergence of national standards with ISAs, the implications thereof, and the process to be followed to achieve this goal.

- The World Bank and other regional development banks have expressed support for an initiative to establish one set of auditing and assurance standards for both private and public sector entities.

- Launched in 2001, the Forum of Firms (FOF) conducts its business primarily through the Transnational Auditors Committee (TAC). Members of FOF voluntarily agree to meet certain requirements. Commitment to the obligations of membership in the FOF will contribute to raising the standards of the international practice of auditing in the interest of users of the profession's services.

There is no consistent manner in which countries explain how they are harmonizing with ISAs. Exhibit 3.5 gives information on Australia, as an example of a country which is working towards compliance with ISAs but with identified amendments

---

Exhibit 3.5 | Australia

Australian Auditing Standards Board (AuASB) Harmonization Policy

In January 2003, the AuASB issued a release describing their policy on international harmonization. The Australian Accounting Bodies, as members of the International Federation of Accountants (IFAC), are committed to the development of a worldwide accountancy profession with harmonized standards. Consequently, the AuASB endeavours to ensure that Australian auditing and assurance standards cover all matters dealt with in International Standards on Auditing (ISAs). Their objective is that compliance with AUSs should also constitute compliance with ISAs by the beginning of 2005.

In certain circumstances, the Board has had to add extra material by way of footnotes and appendices to respond to local conditions. Occasionally, the Board has to make substantive changes to an ISA to comply with the Australian regulatory environment. Where this happens, the departure from the ISA is highlighted in the text.

The Australian Board issues exposure drafts prepared by the International Auditing and Assurance Standards Board (IAASB) concurrently and makes use of Australian comments in its submission on the exposure draft to the IAASB. In addition the AuASB also provides technical support to Australians who are members of the IAASB.

Source: www.icaa.org.au

Exhibit 3.6	China

In March 2002, the Ministry of Finance adopted four auditing pronouncements formulated by the Chinese Institute of Certified Public Accountants (CICPA). The pronouncements, which took effect from July 1, 2002, and their international counterparts are as follows:

Specific Independent Auditing Standards (SIAS)	Equivalent International Auditing Standard
#26: Attendance of Physical Inventory Counting	#501: Audit Evidence – Additional Considerations for Specific Items
#27: Confirmation	#505: External Confirmation
Independent Auditing Practice Pronouncement (IAPP)	Equivalent International Auditing Standard
#9: Performing Agreed-upon Procedures regarding Financial Information	#920: Engagements to Perform Agreed-upon Procedures regarding Financial Information
#10: Review of Financial Statements	#910: Engagements to Review Financial Statements

All four pronouncements are generally consistent with the principles of the equivalent International Auditing Standards.

Source: IASplus China Newsletter, April 2004.

where these are needed for compliance with national regulation. Exhibit 3.6 gives information on China, where the Ministry of Finance publishes auditing standards using the principles of ISAs. Exhibit 3.7 gives information from Hong Kong on the target of full convergence with ISAs.

3.3.1.2 Obstacles to progress[28]

Progress in harmonizing national auditing standards with ISAs is not as fast as that of harmonizing national accounting standards with IFRS. One reason is that effective regulation of audit requires government backing and for some governments the improvement of financial reporting is not high priority. Effective auditing standards require regulation, an effective auditing profession, a culture of compliance and a sound base of corporate governance. Some governments may not be able to cope with the magnitude of the changes required; others may have vested interests not to make the changes required.

The World Bank in its ROSC process (see section 3.2.4) reviews accounting and auditing standards against IFRS and ISAs as benchmarks. However, while a country is matching its

Exhibit 3.7	Hong Kong

In terms of technical standards, Council issued a mandate three years ago to benchmark Hong Kong's accounting, auditing and ethical standards against international standards. This task will be accomplished by the end of 2004 when Hong Kong standards will be fully converged with international standards.

Source: Extract from members' handbook of the Hong Kong Society of Accountants, www.hksa.org.hk/main.php

---

[28] Street and Needles (2002).

auditing standards to ISAs on paper, this is no guarantee that there is adequate education for professional accountants to know the ISAs or understand how to apply them. The World Bank produces the report but it is for the national government to implement change.

3.3.1.3 Issuing ISAs

IAASB operates 'due process' in developing ISAs. Draft standards and statements are issued as exposure drafts for public review and comment. Comments received are considered prior to finalization of the standard. IAASB meetings are open to the public, with agenda materials being publicly available. The IAASB includes three 'public members' who bring a broader interest to the discussions. All IAASB exposure drafts and standards are available free of charge on the website (see Exhibit 3.8).

ISA 700, *The Auditor's Report on Financial Statements*, requires that the opinion paragraph of the auditor's report should clearly indicate the financial reporting framework used to prepare the financial statements (including identifying the country of origin of the financial reporting framework when the framework used is not International Accounting Standards) and state the auditor's opinion as to whether the financial statements give a true and fair view (or are presented fairly, in all material respects) in accordance with that financial reporting framework and, where appropriate, whether the financial statements comply with statutory requirements.

| Exhibit 3.8 | International Standards on Auditing and other IAASB documents |

AUDITS AND REVIEWS OF HISTORICAL FINANCIAL INFORMATION

100–999 International Standards on Auditing (ISAs)

100–199 INTRODUCTORY MATTERS
120 Framework of International Standards on Auditing

200–299 GENERAL PRINCIPLES AND RESPONSIBILITIES
200 Objective and General Principles Governing an Audit of Financial Statements
210 Terms of Audit Engagements
220 Quality Control for Audit Work
230 Documentation
240 The Auditor's Responsibility to Consider Fraud and Error in an Audit of Financial Statements
250 Consideration of Laws and Regulations in an Audit of Financial Statements
260 Communications of Audit Matters with Those Charged with Governance

300–499 RISK ASSESSMENT AND RESPONSE TO ASSESSED RISKS
300 Planning
310 Knowledge of the Business
315 Understanding the Entity and Its Environment and Assessing the Risks of Material Misstatement
320 Audit Materiality
330 The Auditor's Procedures in Response to Assessed Risks
400 Risk Assessments and Internal Control
401 Auditing in a Computer Information Systems Environment
402 Audit Considerations Relating to Entities Using Service Organizations

Exhibit 3.8   *(Continued)*

500–599 AUDIT EVIDENCE
500 Audit Evidence
500R Audit Evidence
501 Audit Evidence—Additional Considerations for Specific Items
505 External Confirmations
510 Initial Engagements—Opening Balances
520 Analytical Procedures
530 Audit Sampling and Other Selective Testing Procedures
540 Audit of Accounting Estimates
545 Auditing Fair Value Measurements and Disclosures
550 Related Parties
560 Subsequent Events
570 Going Concern
580 Management Representations

600–699 USING WORK OF OTHERS
600 Using the Work of Another Auditor
610 Considering the Work of Internal Auditing
620 Using the Work of an Expert

700–799 AUDIT CONCLUSIONS AND REPORTING
700 The Auditor's Report on Financial Statements
710 Comparatives
720 Other Information in Documents Containing Audited Financial Statements

800–899 SPECIALIZED AREAS
800 The Auditor's Report on Special Purpose Audit

Engagements

1000–1100 International Auditing Practice Statements (IAPSs)

2000–2699 International Standards on Review Engagements (ISREs)

ASSURANCE ENGAGEMENTS OTHER THAN AUDITS OR REVIEWS OF HISTORICAL FINANCIAL INFORMATION

3000–3699 International Standards on Assurance Engagements (ISAEs)

RELATED SERVICES

4000–4699 International Standards on Related Services (ISRSs)

DISCUSSION PAPERS

STUDIES

Source: IAASB website. The full text of all publications, together with additional information on the IAASB, recent developments, and outstanding exposure drafts, are to be found on the IAASB's website at www.iaasb.org

3.3.2 Public Interest Oversight Board (PIOB)

In November 2003 IFAC announced further reforms to increase confidence in the work of IFAC. In particular it set up the mechanism for establishing a Public Interest Oversight Board (PIOB) to oversee the activities of IFAC in setting standards for auditing and ethics. The PIOB takes over the role of nominating members of the IAASB.

3.3.3 Audit committees

Forming an audit committee is part of good corporate governance (see section 3.4). However the presence of an audit committee has not prevented major corporate collapses and questionable conduct by executive directors. Attention has therefore been given in more than one country since 2001 to make audit committees more effective. Exhibit 3.9 summarizes some recent international initiatives on audit committees. Chapters 8, 10 and 11 describe in more details the initiatives in the US, EU and UK to improve the effectiveness of audit committees. In the US there have been several initiatives on audit committees, the most recent coming from Sarbanes–Oxley (see section 8.4.3.1). In the UK the report chaired by Sir Robert Smith set out in detail what is expected of an audit committee (see section 11.6.4).

Exhibit 3.9 **Initiatives on audit committees**

European Union
The High Level Group of Company Law experts (2002) included in their report some recommendations on the nature and role of the audit committee.

US
Sarbanes–Oxley (2002) contained legislation on the role and composition of audit committees.

The New York Stock Exchange (2002) issued new rules on the composition and conduct of audit committees.

Ireland
The Review Group on Auditing made recommendations that were incorporated into the Companies (Audit and Accountancy) (Amendment) Bill 2001.

France
The Bouton Report (2002) 'Promoting better corporate governance in listed companies' set out rules for audit committees.

Canada
There is a mandatory requirement for companies to establish audit committees under the Canada Business Corporations Act.

The Toronto Stock Exchange amended its rules in April 2002 to give guidance on the independence of the external auditor.

Australia
The Corporations Act does not require Australian companies to establish audit committees. However CLERP 9 (2002) recommended mandatory regulation to impose audit committees on the top 500 listed companies, leaving the ASX Corporate Governance Council to develop best practice standards.

Source: Summarized from Appendix III, Smith Report (2003).

3.4 Corporate governance and financial reporting

It appears that equity investors have a keen interest in seeing good quality corporate governance in companies in which they invest. A survey by McKinsey[29] found that investors are willing to pay more for a company that is well-governed. This lowers the cost of capital for the company and so it is in the interests of the company to show good practice in corporate governance.

3.4.1 What is corporate governance?[30]

There is no unique definition of the term 'corporate governance'. Some writers do not attempt to define it. A very simple definition is found in the report of the Cadbury Committee in the UK:

> Corporate governance is the system by which companies are directed and controlled.[31]

For some countries the 'system' may involve laws or regulations imposed by government; for other countries the 'system' may depend largely on private sector market forces in a strong equity market. Corporate governance describes the interaction of shareholders, managers and those who supervise managers in a company, but it also describes the assurance needed to satisfy a wider public interest about the proper conduct of business.

3.4.2 Corporate governance codes

From the late 1990s onwards there has been an explosion of codes of corporate governance. Some are established under the authority of national governments, some are imposed by national securities regulators on listed companies, and many are voluntary codes proposed by institutions or bodies with an interest in improving the way in which companies are managed. In countries where there are competitive capital markets the investment community has shown interest in offering codes of good practice for corporate governance.

Ownership concentration affects the type of corporate governance. Where the ownership of companies is widely spread, there is a wider gap between the shareholders who own the company and the managers who run the company. Some form of supervisory body is required to ensure that the managers act in the interests of the shareholders. In some countries a separate supervisory board oversees the activities of the executive board of directors who carry out the day-to-day management; in other countries there is a single board of directors with a strong representation of independent directors ('non-executives') to balance the activities of the executive directors.

Business practice also affects the approach to corporate governance. One approach to managing a business may involve strong emphasis on co-operative relationships and consensus, with inclusion of employees in the running of the business. A different approach may rely on competition and market forces, with a focus on those who own the business.

The legal system of the country will influence the nature of corporate governance. A country with strong code law will probably have corporate governance regulations based in law. A country with a common law tradition will probably develop corporate

---

[29] *McKinsey Investor Opinion Survey*, June 2000.

[30] *Comparative Study of Corporate Governance Codes Relevant to the European Union and Its Member States.* Section III.A.

[31] Cadbury Report (1992) paragraph 2.5.

governance through private sector self-regulation. (See section 4.4 for further discussion of code law and common law systems.)

3.4.3 What to look for in corporate governance codes

Whatever the form of the regulations for corporate governance, particular features to look for in codes of corporate governance are:

- stakeholder and shareholder interests,
- supervisory and managerial bodies,
- code enforcement and compliance.

This section describes each feature in more detail and then summarises general guidance provided by the OECD. Case studies on specific codes, analysing them in the OECD framework, are provided at the end of this chapter.

3.4.3.1 Stakeholder and shareholder interests

Shareholders are the owners of a company. Good corporate governance will ensure that managers act in the best interests of shareholders (see the research perspectives in section 3.7). It will also require that shareholders take an active interest in how the company is managed. A fair voting system is 'one share, one vote'. Shareholders should then use their votes in general meeting to indicate approval or disapproval of the acts of managers. In practice the voting arrangements, conduct of meetings and activity of shareholders are all very variable between countries and within countries.

The wider stakeholder interest extends to creditors, employees and the public interest in general. Most legislative systems have some protection for creditors but codes of governance may encourage transparency of information for them. In some countries employees have a formal involvement in the management of a company. Accountability to the public interest and the needs of society has become increasingly important.

3.4.3.2 Supervisory and managerial bodies

The first question to ask here is: How do the managers of the company meet to run the business? In some countries the regulation requires a two-tier board structure. There is an executive board of the managers or directors who run the business on a day-to-day basis. There is a supervisory board of experienced business persons who can oversee and guide the executives. This supervisory board may include representatives of employees or lenders as well as shareholders. In other countries the regulation requires a single board structure. In this case the rules of corporate governance usually expect to find a strong representation of independent (non-executive) directors, with wide experience in business, to exercise control over the activities of the executive directors. Corporate governance codes set limits on the number or proportion of each type of director or manager.

The next question to ask is how the roles of the executive and non-executive directors are defined. The non-executives may form the audit committee, and they may set the remuneration of the executive directors. Corporate governance codes define these roles for the non-executive directors and set out the powers they should have to allow them to exercise independence.

The third question is to ask how the directors are accountable for their actions. How do we know that they have carried out the duties expected? Corporate governance codes set out guidance on how frequently, and in how much detail, the directors should report on their activities.

3.4.3.3 Code enforcement and compliance

Codes of governance may rely, partly or totally, on market forces to enforce compliance. Shareholders will vote against the reappointment of directors who do not demonstrate high standards of governance. Other stakeholders may also monitor compliance with codes. There is a growing body of 'watchdog' organizations who monitor, compare and evaluate the corporate governance reports of companies. Evidence of compliance is found in corporate governance reports, usually included in the company's annual report. There may be a requirement for such reports to be audited. However in general the auditor gives an opinon on the process of creating the corporate governance report, not on its content.

3.4.4 Organization for Economic Cooperation and Development (OECD)[32]

In April 2004 the governments of the 30 OECD countries approved a revised version of the OECD's Principles of Corporate Governance. These Principles were first published in 1999. They give a benchmark to the member governments, mainly from developed countries, but are also used by the World Bank in working to improve corporate governance in emerging markets. The Principles emphasize the importance of a regulatory framework in corporate governance that promotes efficient markets, facilitates effective enforcement and defines the responsibilities of the regulatory and enforcement authorities. The Principles cover the following headings:

- Ensuring the basis for an effective corporate governance framework
- The rights of shareholders and key ownership functions
- The equitable treatment of shareholders
- The role of stakeholders in corporate governance
- Disclosure and transparency
- The responsibilities of the board.

These headings are used to analyze specific corporate governance codes in the case studies at the end of this chapter.

3.4.4.1 Ensuring the basis for an effective corporate governance framework

This section of the OECD framework is directed at ensuring an effective regulatory framework. It recommends that the corporate governance framework should promote transparent and efficient markets, be consistent with the rule of law and clearly articulate the divisions of responsibilities among different supervisory, regulatory and enforcement authorities.

3.4.4.2 The rights of shareholders and key ownership functions

This section sets out basic rights for shareholders. These basic rights should allow shareholders to have their ownership registered and to be able to buy and sell shares. The shareholders should be able to obtain relevant and material information about the company on a regular and timely basis. They should be able to participate effectively in the key corporate governance decisions and to vote in general meetings of shareholders. They should be able to use that vote to elect and remove members of the board of directors and to make their views known on the remuneration of directors. Institutional

---

[32] OECD (2004).

investors, who act on a 'good faith' (fiduciary) basis on behalf of their investments, should make clear their attitudes to corporate governance and their voting policies. Shareholders should have the rights to share in the profits of the company. All these rights and obligations may be well-established in developed capital markets, where they are usually contained in company law rather than a voluntary code. Nevertheless they are important points to emphasize in emerging markets.

3.4.4.3 The equitable treatment of shareholders

Equitable treatment means that all shareholders of the same class of shares should be treated equally. All investors should have the same access to information. Minority shareholders should be protected against abusive actions by controlling shareholders. Insider trading should be prohibited. Members of the board of directors should declare their interest in any transaction affecting the company.

3.4.4.4 The role of stakeholders in corporate governance

The corporate governance framework should respect the rights of stakeholders established by law or through mutual agreements. Such stakeholders will include individual employees and their representative bodies. They should be able to communicate their concerns about illegal or unethical practices to the board without risking their rights as employees. Stakeholders will also include creditors. The corporate governance framework should be matched by an efficient insolvency framework and by effective enforcement of the rights of creditors.

3.4.4.5 Disclosure and transparency

This section is particularly relevant to corporate financial reporting and so it describes the OECD recommendations in detail.[33] The corporate governance framework should ensure that timely and accurate disclosure is made on all material matters regarding the company, including the financial situation, performance, ownership and governance of the company. Disclosure should include, but not be limited to, matters relating to:

1 The financial and operating results of the company
2 Company objectives
3 Major share ownership and voting rights
4 Remuneration policy for members of the board and key executives, with information about board members including their qualifications, selection process, other directorships and whether they are regarded as independent directors
5 Related party transactions
6 Foreseeable risk factors
7 Issues regarding employees and other stakeholders
8 Governance structures and policies, particularly the implementation of any code of corporate governance.

From the above list, only item 5, related party transactions, is covered by an IFRS (IAS 24, see section 2.2.7). The remainder of this list indicates the importance of descriptive disclosures that are still largely a matter of national regulation rather than international standards. (See Chapter 15 for further discussion of narrative disclosures.)

The OECD continues by recommending that information should be prepared and disclosed in accordance with high-quality standards of financial and non-financial

---

[33] OECD (2004), section V.

disclosure. An annual audit should be conducted by an independent, competent and qualified auditor, in order to provide an external and objective assurance to the board and shareholders that the financial statements fairly represent the financial position and performance of the company in all material respects. External auditors should be accountable to the shareholders and owe a duty to the company to exercise due professional care in the conduct of the audit. Channels for disseminating information should provide for equal, timely and cost-efficient access to relevant information by users. The corporate governance framework should be complemented by an effective approach that addresses and promotes the provision of analysis or advice by analysts, brokers, rating agencies and others, that is relevant to decisions by investors, free from material conflicts of interest that might compromise the integrity of their analysis or advice.

These recommendations from the OECD are designed to encourage national regulators to incorporate rules for disclosure and transparency in their national frameworks and codes. They also provide a useful starting point for evaluating the extent to which the annual reports of companies appear to be meeting these expectations on disclosure and transparency.

3.4.4.6 The responsibilities of the board

The OECD's final set of recommendations relates to the board of directors. The corporate governance framework should ensure the strategic guidance of the company, the effective monitoring of management by the board, and the board's accountability to the company and the shareholders. In this section the OECD does not specify the details of the structure of the board but it sets out key features of ethical conduct and effective management as follows. Board members should:

- act in the best interests of the company and the shareholders;
- treat all shareholders fairly;
- apply high ethical standards;
- fulfil certain key functions (listed in the report) including ensuring the integrity of the accounting and financial reporting system, including independent audit, and ensuring that appropriate systems of control are in place for risk management, financial and operational control and compliance with law and standards;
- exercise objective independent judgement;
- have access to accurate, relevant and timely information.

3.4.5 National codes of corporate governance

Many countries now have codes of corporate governance. Some are issued by government, others by committees representing key stakeholders having an interest in matters of governance. Exhibit 3.10 lists examples of codes in various countries, showing the name of the body issuing the code. The ECGI website gives a link to each code in English as well as in the national language. The exhibit also gives the website reference for the body issuing the code, where this is available.

3.4.6 Researching international corporate governance

Denis and McConnell (2003) survey research into corporate governance systems around the world. They categorize this research into two 'generations'. The first 'generation' of research investigated corporate governance in US companies and then

Exhibit 3.10 National codes of corporate governance

Australia
Principles of Good Corporate Governance and Best Practice Recommendations
ASX Corporate Governance Council, March 2003
www.asx.com.au/about/l3/AboutCorporateGovernance_AA3.shtm

Brazil
Recomendações sobre Governança Corporativa
Comissão de Valores Mobiliários (CVM) – Securities and Exchange Commission of Brazil
www.cvm.gov.br/

China
Code of Corporate Governance for Listed Companies in China
Issued by: China Securities Regulatory Commission, State Economic and Trade Commission, 7 January 2001
www.csrc.gov.cn/en/homepage/index_en.jsp

France
The Corporate Governance of Listed Corporations: Principles for corporate governance
Based on consolidation of the 1995, 1999 and 2002 AFEP and MEDEF's reports, Association Française des Entreprises Privées (AFEP) and MEDEF (French Business Confederation), October 2003
www.medef.fr/staging/site/page.php

Germany
German Corporate Governance Code
Government Commission, 2003
www.corporate-governance-code.de/index-e.html

Hong Kong
Model Code for Securities Transactions by Directors of Listed Companies: Basic Principles
Hong Kong Stock Exchange Listing Requirements, Appendix 10, June 2001
www.hkex.com.hk/index.htm

Japan
Revised Corporate Governance Principles
Japan Corporate Governance Forum, October 2001
www.jcgf.org/en/index.html

Kenya
Principles for Corporate Governance in Kenya
Private Sector Initiative for Corporate Governance
www.ecgi.org/codes/country_documents/kenya/sample_code.pdf [local website not found]

►

Exhibit 3.10 *(Continued)*

Malaysia
Malaysian Code on Corporate Governance
Securities Commission Malaysia, March 2000
www.sc.com.my/wel.html

The Netherlands
The Dutch corporate governance code
Corporate Governance Committee, December 2003
www.commissiecorporategovernance.nl/

Sweden
The NBK Rules, The Naringslivets Borskommitte
NBK (The Swedish Industry and Commerce Stock Exchange Committee), February 2003
www.stockholmsborsen.se/regulations/index.asp?lank=4&lang=eng
Corporate Governance Policy – guidelines for better control and transparency for owners of companies quoted on the Swedish stockmarket
Sveriges Aktiesparares Riksförbund (The Swedish Shareholders' Association), 26 October 2001
www.aktiespararna.se/

UK
The Combined Code on Corporate Governance
The Financial Reporting Council (FRC), July 2003
www.frc.org.uk/
Audit Committees – Combined Code Guidance (the Smith Report)
A report and proposed guidance by a Financial Reporting Council appointed group chaired by Sir Robert Smith, 2003
www.frc.org.uk/
Review of the role and effectiveness of non-executive director (The Higgs Report),
Department of Trade and Industry, January 2003
www.dti.gov.uk/cld/non_exec_review/

US
Final NYSE Corporate Governance Rules
New York Stock Exchange, November 4, 2003
www.nyse.com
Restoring Trust – The Breeden Report on Corporate Governance for the future of MCI, Inc.
The United States District Court for the Southern District of New York, August 2003
www.nysd.uscourts.gov/

This table contains examples of the codes that exist in a selection of countries. Access to all the codes listed above, and to a more extensive list, is possible through the website of the European Corporate Governance Institute Index of Codes, www.ecgi.org/codes/all_codes.htm
As an additional source of information the home page for the specific codes in this table is shown under each entry. These all have an English language version.

applied the same research methods to study companies in other major world economies, primarily Japan, Germany and the UK. The second 'generation' begins with the work of La Porta *et al.* (1998) in which they present empirical evidence to show that there are significant differences across countries in the degree of investor protection. Countries with low investor protection are generally characterized by a high concentration of equity ownership within firms and a lack of significant public equity markets. La Porta *et al.* (1998) provided valuable data for other researchers by developing objective measures of investor protection across 49 countries. The measures are constructed from variables related to shareholder and creditor rights, and variables related to the rule of law.

3.5 Corporate Social Responsibility

The European Commission has defined Corporate Social Responsibility (CSR) as 'a concept whereby companies integrate social and environmental concerns in their business operations and in their interaction with their stakeholders on a voluntary basis'.[34] This definition was the basis of a Green Paper (a discussion paper) that was intended to launch a debate about the concept of corporate social responsibility and the development of a European framework to promote CSR. It might seem strange to use the word 'voluntary' in the definition and then initiate a debate on a process that is likely to increase compulsion, but the Commission was probably reflecting the momentum already gathering pace from other quarters.

3.5.1 'Triple bottom line' reporting

In its communication on the EU Strategy for Sustainable Development (May 2001) the European Commission invited all publicly-quoted companies with at least 500 staff to publish a 'triple bottom line' in their annual report to shareholders that measures their performance against economic, environmental and social criteria. The three aspects of economic performance, environmental performance and social performance is described as 'the triple bottom line' of CSR reporting. The phrase 'bottom line' is used to link this idea with the traditional financial reporting of earnings for shareholders, often called 'the bottom line' of the statement of profit or loss.

In its communication of July 2002 on CSR,[35] the Commission proposed establishing a Multi-stakeholder Forum on CSR and then inviting the Forum to develop commonly agreed guidelines and criteria for measurement, reporting and assurance.

3.5.2 Sustainability

The idea of 'sustainability' is drawn from the study of ecology, where it represents the degree to which the earth's resources may be exploited without damaging the environment. Sustainable development means planning the long-term use of resources that do not damage the environment. This initial focus on physical resources has been

---

[34] COM (2001) 366.
[35] COM (2002) 347.

extended to thinking about satisfying present needs of society without sacrificing future needs of society. The Global Reporting Initiative (see next section) gives the following explanation:

'Achieving sustainability requires balancing the complex relationships between current economic, environmental and social needs in a manner that does not compromise future needs.'[36]

3.5.3 Global Reporting Initiative (GRI)[37]

The GRI was launched in 1997 as a joint initiative of the US non-governmental organization Coalition for Environmentally Responsible Economies (CERES) and United Nations Environmental Programme with the goal of enhancing the quality, rigour and utility of sustainability reporting. Guidelines were published in 2000 and updated in 2002. In that period GRI developed into a new permanent global institution, creating an accepted disclosure framework for sustainability reporting.

GRI has identified the trends that have caused this rapid movement:

- the search for new forms of global governance;
- reform of corporate governance;
- the global role of emerging economies;
- rising visibility of and expectations for organizations;
- measurement of progress towards sustainable development;
- governments' interest in sustainability reporting;
- financial markets' interest in sustainability reporting;
- emergence of next-generation accounting, such as 'business reporting, 'intangible assets analysis', 'value reporting'.

The GRI report produced by a company will reflect the recommendation of five sections of the Reporting Guidelines:

1 *Vision and strategy*. This section contains a statement of the sustainability vision of the reporting organization and also a statement from the chief executive officer.
2 *Profile*. This covers the profile of the organization, the scope of the report and the profile of the report.
3 *Governance structure and management systems*. This covers details of structure and governance, stakeholder engagement, overarching policies and management systems.
4 *GRI content index*. This is a table identifying the location of each element of the GRI report.
5 *Performance indicators*. These cover economic, environmental and social performance indicators, described in detail in the guidelines. They are intended to reflect the company's particular circumstances and so vary in nature for each organization. Exhibit 3.11 sets out some of the main headings in the GRI Guidelines.

The Guidelines set out Principles for reporting. Transparency and inclusiveness form the starting point. Transparency in reporting is an exercise in accountability, which requires a clear and open explanation of an individual's actions to those who have a right or reason to inquire. Inclusiveness means engaging with stakeholders. These two qualities inform decisions about what information is reported, the quality and reliability of what is reported, and the accessibility of reported information. These in turn lead to qualitative

---

[36] GRI (2002) p. 9.

[37] www.globalreporting.org.

Exhibit 3.11 Headings and examples for CSR performance indicators

Economic performance indicators

Direct impacts

- Monetary flows between the organization and its key stakeholders
- How the organization affects the economic circumstances of those stakeholders

Indirect impacts

- Costs or benefits for a community not fully reflected in the monetary amount of a transaction

Environmental performance indicators

- Materials, e.g. percentage of recycled materials used
- Energy, e.g. energy sources used
- Water, e.g. total water use
- Biodiversity, e.g. activities to protect special habitats
- Emissions, e.g. greenhouse gas emissions

Social performance indicators

- Labour practices and decent work, e.g. labour relations, health and safety
- Human rights, e.g. policies and practices related to international conventions
- Society, e.g. policies to manage impact on community
- Product responsibility, e.g. policies regarding customer health and safety

Source: examples based on Section 5 Performance Indicators, GRI Sustainability Reporting Guidelines (2002)

characteristics of completeness, relevance, sustainability context, accuracy, neutrality, comparability, clarity and timeliness. This list looks very much like the qualitative characteristics of financial reporting set out in the IASB Framework (see Chapter 1). The only unfamiliar phrase is 'sustainability context' which means that the reporting company should seek to place its performance in the larger picture of ecological, social, or other constraints, where this larger picture adds significant meaning to the reported information.

The GRI website lists companies that confirm the use of the GRI Guidelines. Exhibit 3.12 is taken from the annual report of BASF, a German company in the chemicals sector. The Introduction to the annual report explains how sustainability reporting has been combined with other information to give a single corporate report rather than three separate documents. The heading to the GRI Index shows that a further recommendation of the GRI Guidelines has been implemented, with the detail of the index covering more than one page.

3.5.4 The Accountability Rating®[38]

The Accountability Rating® has been developed by AccountAbility and csrnetwork™. AccountAbility is a professional institute whose mission is to promote accountability for sustainable development. It develops innovative and effective accountability tools and

---

[38] www.accountability.org.uk and www.csrnetwork.com.

Exhibit 3.12	Reference in annual report to GRI Guidelines, BASF

About this report

We have further developed BASF's reporting: This Corporate Report combines our sustainability reporting in a single publication. The new report provides information on all three dimensions of sustainable development and thus replaces the three individual reports we have published to date. You can find additional information and data on the Internet. We are orienting our reporting to the recommendations of the Global Reporting Initiative (GRI), and we are actively involved in the discussions to further develop the initiative. Our data and calculations are also based on international standards. In some areas, direct comparison of individual data is made difficult due to portfolio changes, new plant startups and improvements to our data collection method. This is stated in the text where this is the case.

GRI Index

This index shows you where you can find information on the core elements and indicators of the Global Reporting Initiative (GRI) in this report and in our Financial Report (FR). Our online reporting provides additional information on some indicators at www.reports.basf.de. You can find the complete version of the GRI index with all cross-references at www.reports.basf.de/gri-index. Further information on GRI is available at www.globalreporting.org.

Source: BASF Corporate Report (2003) p. 3 Introduction 'About this report'; GRI Index starts p. 69, following 'Glossary'.

standards, called the AA1000 Series. The partner organization, csrnetwork™, is one of the UK's leading corporate social responsibility consultancies. The Accountability Rating® was initially applied to the world's 100 highest-revenue companies. Six areas were scored: strategic intent, governance, performance management, stakeholder engagement, assurance and public disclosure.[39]

3.5.5 Dow Jones sustainability indexes

The Dow Jones sustainability indexes track the performance of market leaders in sustainability. Companies apply to be included in the index and are assessed. The sustainability assessment of each company is based on responses to a questionnaire and the contents of documents provided by the company, including the annual report. Five corporate sustainability principles are applied, covering strategy, innovation, governance, the needs of shareholders and the well-being of employees and other stakeholders.

There is a range of indexes, including

● Dow Jones EURO STOXX^SM Sustainability Index (DJSI EURO STOXX). This consists of the leading 20 per cent of Eurozone companies, evaluated for sustainability, from the Dow Jones STOXX^SM 600 Index.
● Dow Jones STOXX^SM Sustainability Index (DJSI STOXX). This consists of the leading 20 per cent of all companies, evaluated for sustainability, from the Dow Jones STOXX^SM 600 Index,
● Dow Jones Sustainability World Index (DJSI World). This consists of the leading 10 per cent companies, evaluated for sustainability, from the Dow Jones Global Index.

---

[39] The Accountability Rating® 2004. AccountAbility and csrnetwork.

These indexes are defined, and the constituent companies are listed, on the website.[40] These lists give a useful source for planning a research project into companies whose annual report is likely to reflect high standards of sustainability.

3.5.6 FTSE4Good[41]

The FTSE4Good Index Series is designed to create a family of benchmark and tradable indices in response to the growing interest in socially responsible investment around the world. Companies that are included in one of the indices must pass the eligibility criteria detailed in the FTSE4Good Philosophy and Criteria document. There are four benchmark indices:

- FTSE4Good Global Index
- FTSE4Good USA Index
- FTSE4Good Europe Index
- FTSE4Good UK Index.

To be eligible, companies must meet criteria requirements in three areas:[42]

- working towards environmental sustainability;
- developing positive relationships with stakeholders;
- upholding and supporting universal human rights.

3.5.7 Fédération des Experts Comptables Européens (FEE)[43]

In June 2004 FEE called on the Multi-stakeholder Forum to recognize CSR at a level similar to financial reporting. FEE launched an issues paper calling for action. The actions proposed were:

- *Companies* should seek independent assurance on their CSR reports.
- *Companies* and *those providing assurance* should disclose information to stakeholders regarding the independence of those providing assurance.
- *Global Reporting Initiative (GRI)*, as the global standard-setter for sustainability reporting, should ensure that indicators and other disclosures do not preclude assurance. GRI should also encourage disclosures about internal and external assurance.
- *Sustainability indexes*, such as FTSE4Good or the Dow Jones Sustainability Index, when rating a company, should consider whether CSR reports have received assurance.
- *Stakeholder organizations* should increase their members' awareness of the issue of assurance and engage with standard-setters.
- The *European Commission* and national governments should monitor reaction to CSR legislation in France, Denmark and Sweden.
- *IAASB* should develop a specific standard on assurance for sustainability within its assurance framework.

---

[40] www.sustainability-indexes.com.

[41] *Ground Rules for the Management of the FTSE4Good Index Series* (2001), FTSE International Limited. www.ftse.com.

[42] *FTSE4Good Index Series: Inclusion Criteria* (2003). FTSE International Limited.

[43] www.fee.be.

3.5.8 Monitoring for effective reporting

Standard and Poor's[44] is an organization that provides independent financial informa-tion, analytical services and credit ratings to the world's financial markets. It has devel-oped a *Corporate Governance Score* that provides a detailed analysis of a company's corporate governance standards by reference to global practices. In particular it has developed a Transparency and Disclosure Study (for detail see section 15.2.2). The results of surveys published in 2002 and 2003 covered Europe, the US, Asia Pacific and Russian companies.

Laufer (2003) comments on the limitations of retaining a voluntary approach to social accounting. There are those who complain of poor quality and lack of reliability in voluntary reporting; there are others who worry that regulatory intervention would destroy initiative and development. He regrets that the GRI Guidelines do not press for external audit and concludes that decisions to defer third party auditing undermined an appearance of legitimacy. The term 'greenwashing' refers to the idea of using disclosure tactics that appear to meet expectations, because they are supported by reputable bod-ies, but without in reality making any meaningful disclosures.

3.6 Regulating compliance

This section contrasts the direct statutory control imposed by the SEC in the US with the private sector regulation of the UK where there is statutory support for the work of the Financial Reporting Review Panel in taking action on defective accounts and for the work of the Financial Services Authority in maintaining a fair market. The US and the UK present two different approaches to government monitoring of financial reporting by listed companies. The section then explains the initiatives taken by stock market regulators to improve financial reporting across markets. Further details on regulating compliance in separate countries may be found in Chapters 8 to 13.

3.6.1 The US Securities and Exchange Commission (SEC)[45]

The primary mission of the US Securities and Exchange Commission (SEC) is to protect investors and maintain the integrity of the securities markets. It applies a basic principle that all investors, whether large institutions or private individuals, should have access to certain basic facts about an investment prior to buying it. To achieve this, the SEC requires public companies to disclose meaningful financial and other information to the public, which provides a common pool of knowledge for all investors to use to judge for them-selves if a company's securities are a good investment. A steady flow of timely, compre-hensive and accurate information enables people to make sound investment decisions.

The SEC also oversees other key participants in the securities world, including stock exchanges, broker-dealers, investment advisors, mutual funds, and public utility hold-ing companies. Here again, the SEC is concerned primarily with promoting disclosure of important information, enforcing the securities laws, and protecting investors who interact with these various organizations and individuals.

---

[44] www.standardandpoors.com.

[45] www.sec.gov.

3.6.1.1 Enforcement

An important feature of the SEC's effectiveness is its enforcement authority. Each year the SEC brings between 400 and 500 civil enforcement actions against individuals and companies that break the securities laws. Typical infractions include insider trading, accounting fraud, and providing false or misleading information about securities and the companies that issue them.

The Enforcement Division obtains evidence of possible violations of the securities laws from many sources, including its own surveillance activities, other divisions of the SEC, the self-regulatory organizations and other securities industry sources, press reports, and investor complaints.

All SEC investigations are conducted privately. Facts are developed to the fullest extent possible through informal inquiry, interviewing witnesses, examining broker-age records, reviewing trading data, and other methods. Once the Commission issues a formal order of investigation, the Division's staff may compel witnesses by subpoena to testify and produce books, records, and other relevant documents. Following an investigation, SEC staff present their findings to the Commission for its review. The Commission can authorize the staff to file a case in federal court or bring an administrative action. Individuals and companies charged sometimes choose to settle the case, while others contest the charges.

The Chief Accountant is the principal adviser to the Commission on accounting and auditing matters. The Office of the Chief Accountant also works closely with domestic and international private-sector accounting and auditing standards-setting bodies (e.g. the Financial Accounting Standards Board, the International Accounting Standards Board, the American Institute of Certified Public Accountants, and the Public Company Accounting Oversight Board); consults with registrants, auditors, and other Commission staff regarding the application of accounting standards and financial disclosure requirements; and assists in addressing problems that may warrant enforcement actions.

3.6.1.2 Regulation FD[46]

In 2000, the SEC adopted Regulation FD (Fair Disclosure) to address the selective disclosure of information by companies and other issuers. Regulation FD provides that when an issuer discloses material nonpublic information to certain individuals or entities – generally, securities market professionals, such as stock analysts, or holders of the issuer's securities who may well trade on the basis of the information – the issuer must make public disclosure of that information. In this way, the new rule aims to promote the full and fair disclosure.

Whenever an issuer, or any person acting on its behalf, discloses any material non-public information regarding that issuer or its securities to any person in a defined class (such as investors or market participants), the issuer shall make public disclosure of that information:

● simultaneously, in the case of an intentional disclosure; and
● promptly, in the case of a non-intentional disclosure.

---

[46] *Regulation FD – Fair Disclosure*, www.sec.gov/divisions/corpfin/forms/regfd.htm.

3.6.2 UK: FRRP and UKLA

3.6.2.1 The Financial Reporting Review Panel[47]

The Financial Reporting Review Panel (FRRP) is authorized by the Secretary of State to examine departures from the accounting requirements of the Companies Act 1985 and accounting standards. It has the power to appeal to a court of law to require directors to correct and re-issue accounts that do not comply. The FRRP covers the accounts of all public limited companies, whether listed or not, and some large private companies. Its powers are much more limited than those of the SEC but it appears to have influenced financial reporting compliance in the UK.[48]

The Panel considers any matter drawn to its attention from a review of accounts selected by the Panel, or by complainants or press comment. It initially considers whether there is a case to answer. When there is such a case, the Chairman appoints a Group to conduct the enquiry, normally made up of five members including himself and the Deputy Chairman. Other members are chosen from the Panel to provide a balance of experience relevant to the enquiry, excluding any potential conflicts of interest. The Group's discussions with the company are confidential.

The Group puts its concerns to the directors and may discuss them in correspondence and at meetings. The Panel encourages directors to consult with their auditors and to take any other advice they feel they need. The process is informal but is intended to combine efficiency with fairness. As defective accounts could mislead the public, the procedures need to allow for speedy rectification. The Group aims to reach agreement with the directors of the company by persuasion. If the Group is satisfied by the company's explanations, the case is closed and the fact that an enquiry was made remains confidential. Where the directors do agree to take some form of remedial action the Panel issues a Press Notice. The Panel does not comment on or discuss its conclusions.

3.6.2.2 The UK Listing Authority[49]

The Financial Services Authority (FSA) is another private sector body operating under then authority of legislation. When it acts as the competent authority for listing it is referred to as the UK Listing Authority (UKLA), and maintains the Official List. The Financial Services and Markets Act 2000 imposes this requirement on the FSA and gives the necessary powers to the competent authority. By this means the relevant European Community Directives are implemented.

The UKLA has created a set of rules known collectively as the 'Listing Rules'. They reflect requirements that are compulsory under the relevant European Community Directives, and additional requirements of the Financial Services and Markets Act. The UKLA Sourcebook contains the Listing Rules and the UKLA Guidance Manual. The Guidance Manual has been issued to help users understand the application of the Listing Rules. The Combined Code (see section 3.4.5) is a voluntary code that sets out the principles of good governance and a code of practice. It is attached to the Listing Rules for information purposes.

---

[47] www.frc.org.uk/frrp/.

[48] Fearnley *et al.* (2000).

[49] www.fsa.gov.uk/ukla/.

The Sourcebook sets out all the rules for listed companies. Chapter 12[50] contains the rules for Financial Information. The main headings are:

- comparative table and accountants' report (12.1 to 12.20)
- profit forecast and estimate (12.21 to 12.27)
- pro forma financial information (12.28 to 12.36)
- financial information outside comparative table or accountants' report (12.37 to 12.39)
- preliminary statement of annual results and dividends (12.40)
- annual report and accounts (12.41 to 12.43)
- corporate governance and directors' remuneration (12.43A)
- summary financial statements (12.45)
- half-yearly report (12.46)
- change of accounting reference date (12.60).

3.6.3 Associations of stock market regulators

3.6.3.1 International Organization of Securities Commissions (IOSCO)[51]

IOSCO is an international association of securities regulators that was created in 1983. The members of IOSCO are the securities regulators of more than 100 jurisdictions. The SEC in the US is a member of IOSCO. The three core objectives of IOSCO are the protection of investors; ensuring that markets are fair, efficient and transparent; and the reduction of systemic risk. IOSCO sets international standards, called Principles, for securities markets. It claims to be the world's primary forum of international cooperation for securities regulatory agencies. One of the key themes of its technical committee work is 'Disclosure and Accounting', focusing both on multinationals in established markets and on emerging markets.

After the Asian crisis of 1997, IOSCO consolidated its work to that date in a set of Principles of Securities Regulations that were recognized as key standards by the Financial Stability Forum. Following the Enron collapse, three further sets of IOSCO Principles were issued in 2002 to strengthen ongoing disclosure and reporting of material developments by listed companies. Two more were issued in 2003 covering the activities of credit rating agencies and addressing conflict of interest in sell-side analysts.

3.6.3.2 The Committee of European Securities Regulators (CESR)[52]

The Committee of European Securities Regulators (CESR) was established by a European Commission Decision of June 2001. This decision was taken in the light of the recommendation of the Report of the Committee of Wise Men on the Regulation of European Securities Markets (the Lamfalussy Report) as endorsed by the European Council and the European Parliament. CESR is an independent committee bring together senior representatives from national public authorities that act in the field of securities. It adopted the previous work of the Forum of European Securities Commissions (FESCO). CESR reports annually to the European Commission.

The work of CESR is prepared by Expert Groups formed specifically for each project. One of its first actions was to issue, in 2003, a draft recommendation for

---

[50] www.fsa.gov.uk/pubs/ukla/chapt12-3.pdf.

[51] www.iosco.org.

[52] www.europfesco.org.

additional guidance regarding the transition to IFRS in 2005. It was effectively a recommendation from the CESR members to themselves to encourage listed companies to prepare thoroughly for 2005 and communicate the process of preparation. A recommendation was then issued in December 2003.[53] The recommendation covered the information that might be published in the year of transition to IFRS implementation, the accounting framework to be used in interim financial reporting, and achieving comparability in the presentation of comparative figures for previous periods.

3.6.3.3 EU and US cooperation

The CESR and the SEC announced in 2004[54] that they intended to increase cooperation and collaboration so as to identify emerging risks and engage in early discussion of potential regulatory projects. One of their projects for 2004 was to explore an effective infrastructure to support the use of IFRS. The aim was to ensure consistent application, interpretation and enforcement of IFRS, with the objective of avoiding reconciliation from IFRS to national GAAP.

3.7 A research perspective

We have seen from the previous sections that good corporate governance is required to give confidence in financial accounting information, and that reliable disclosure of financial accounting information is an essential aspect of effective corporate governance. This means there are two directions to take in identifying research questions that link corporate governance and financial reporting.

A large body of research starts with an agency theory[55] perspective that the separation of managers from those who own the company can create a potential conflict for the agent (manager). There is a legal duty on the manager, as agent, to serve the needs of the principal (the shareholders) but this legal duty may conflict with self-interested motives where the manager seeks to protect personal remuneration, reputation or job security. The most frequent subject of research concerns the relationship between accounting information and management compensation (remuneration) contracts. That is because a great deal of this kind of research is produced in the US where it is common for managers to receive rewards based on accounting targets and the information is published in the annual report.

Reflecting the two directions identified at the start of this section, there are two different 'schools' of research into governance and financial reporting. One is governance research,[56] which takes the accounting information as given and asks how financial accounting information is used in control mechanisms, mainly management compensation contracts, that promote the efficient governance of companies. The other is contracting research[57] which takes the contract as given and asks how the nature of the contract affects managerial attitudes to accounting information.

Examples of research questions are set out in the next two sections.

---

[53] CESR (2003).

[54] *Accountancy*, July 2004, p. 75, www.sec.gov/news/press/2004-75.htm.

[55] Jensen and Meckling (1976).

[56] Bushman and Smith (2001).

[57] Watts and Zimmerman (1986).

3.7.1 Governance research

This section gives examples of research questions that ask how accounting information is used to control managerial behaviour.

1 How frequently is accounting information used to determine the amount of management compensation in reward schemes? Research shows that accounting numbers have featured strongly in cash-based bonus schemes but in more recent years there has been a rise in reward schemes based on stock price performance (Sloan, 2001: 342).

2 How is accounting information used in the decision to change the chief executive officer? Research finds an inverse relationship between earnings performance and the rate of turnover of chief executives (Conyon and Flourou, 2002).

3 How is accounting information used in debt covenant contracts (Day and Taylor, 1995)? How is accounting information used in other forms of financial contracting, such as using accounting information to restrict a company's ability to pay dividends (Leuz *et al.*, 1998)?

4 How is accounting information used by management to reduce the risk of stockholder litigation caused by accounting disclosure omissions or misstatements? Skinner (1994) suggests that companies will voluntarily disclose bad news rather than cause suspicion in the minds of investors by withholding information.

The academic literature in this area is dominated by papers in the US based on US data. Bushman and Smith (2001), in noting this US dominance, suggest (p. 297) that cross-country analyses are a promising way to assess the effects of financial accounting information on economic performance. One of their reasons is the possibility of observing 'grossly inefficient financial accounting and other regimes' in the sample, which they deem to be unlikely in the US context. That perhaps reflects a pre-Enron perception of US accounting.

3.7.2 Contracting and earnings management

How does the use of accounting information in management compensation contracts affect managerial choices of accounting policies? Watts and Zimmerman (1986: 208) offered the 'bonus plan hypothesis'. This says that, other things being equal, managers of firms with bonus plans are more likely to choose accounting procedures that shift reported earnings from future periods to the current period. One form of this process involves making choices that will not be challenged by the auditors. The accounting policies must conform to acceptable accounting standards and the choice is then exercised within the bounds of the accounting policy. This type of earnings management does not breach accounting standards and so does not attract a qualified audit report. It is not illegal but may be misleading for those who attempt to make forecasts of future accounting figures based on the reported results. It is difficult to research because there is no disclosure. A more extreme form of earnings management involves some form of deception, such as entering dates on sales invoices that are earlier than the date of despatch of goods, in order to increase reported revenue of the period. This type of earnings management leads to headlines in the newspapers when the story emerges. It is difficult to research prior to discovery because it is kept secret. There is therefore a challenge to researchers to find indirect methods of identifying earnings management.

Most of the earnings management literature[58] focuses on identifying whether it exists and if so, what the causes are. The reasons identified are a desire to influence market perceptions, to increase management's compensation, to reduce the likelihood of violating lending agreements (debt covenants) and to avoid regulatory intervention. The literature does not evaluate the extent of earnings management in the population as a whole, and does not identify which accounting standards are most likely to be associated with earnings management.

The models used to test for earnings management are based on the presumption that those who seek to distort reported profits will do so either through working capital adjustments (called 'accruals' in the earnings management literature) or through depreciation adjustments. To overstate profit a company might overstate inventory or receivables, or understate payables. It might also lengthen the life of fixed assets to reduce the depreciation charge. Papers investigating earnings management[59] establish a 'normal' expectation of accruals based on a control group and then compare this outcome with the level of accruals in a set of companies that are believed to be indulging in earnings management.

3.7.3 Other aspects of managerial choice

How do changes in corporate governance regulations affect the voluntary disclosures made by management? In a study of listed firms in Hong Kong, Ho and Wong (2001) found that the existence of an audit committee was significantly and positively associated with greater voluntary disclosure, while the percentage of family members on the board was negatively related to the extent of voluntary disclosure.

3.7.4 Effectiveness of audit committees

A paper by DeZoort *et al.* (2002) provides a useful review of the empirical literature on the effectiveness of audit committees and also gives suggestions for future directions of research. They set out four areas of research investigation:

How does the composition of the audit committee give it adequate independence?

This area of research generally requires the use of survey research methods to discover the independence issues, linked to the information available in the public domain about the composition of the audit committee. It is also possible to observe extreme events such as corporate failure or high levels of earnings management, and attempt to link these to the composition of the audit committee.

How does the audit committee exercise its authority?

This also requires survey research to find out how the audit committees carry out their work. As the corporate governance codes are extended, there may be more information in the public domain describing the work of the audit committee but it is likely that surveys will continue to be important for deeper insight.

---

[58] Healy and Wahlen (1999).
[59] Jones (1991), Dechow *et al.* (1995), Peasnell *et al.* (2000).

Are adequate resources made available to the audit committee?

Resources available include the size of the committee and the support from external and internal auditors. The flow of information to the committee and its access to external advisers are also important resources. Research relates the effectiveness of the audit committee to the resources available to it.

How diligent is the audit committee in its work?

Measuring diligence generally involves measuring the attendance record of committee members. This could be linked to discovery of fraudulent reporting or some other extreme event, but linking to the general efficiency of the company is less easy to quantify.

Summary and conclusions

This chapter has presented a range of the ways in which regulators and voluntary bodies have sought to improve the credibility of corporate reporting through giving more assurance and through encouraging relevant and reliable disclosures. What are the implications of this explosion of assurance and monitoring activity for the person who seeks to analyze the financial statements of companies? The question to ask is: How much assurance is available for this particular set of financial statements? The clues will be found in the annual report and other published documents, or on the company's website. The following list is a suggested system for establishing the assurance underlying an annual report.

● Read the audit report. What are the audit regulations, accounting principles, company law and codes of corporate governance that have been applied?

● Read the report of the directors. What sources of authority do they mention?

● Look for the certification by the directors. What is the wording? Who has signed it personally?

● Read the report of the supervisory board or the independent directors. What level of authority and control have they exercised?

● Read the corporate governance report. Which code has been applied? Is it full or partial application? Is there an audit view on this report?

● Read the corporate social responsibility report. Which guidance has been applied? Is there an audit view on this report?

● Look beyond the annual report to the websites listed in this chapter. Is the company listed as meeting the criteria of any of these evaluations?

Key points from the chapter:

There is a great deal of detail in this chapter and a wide range of bodies either setting regulations or issuing guidance. For revision you will need to bring the detail down to a manageable level. The following list may be helpful in collecting the detail under three themes of auditing, reporting and regulatory control.

Auditing

● International Standards for Auditing are issued by the IAASB.

● Sarbanes–Oxley has set new conditions on the independence and regulation of audit firms that affects audit firms.

- Audit committees show the commitment of independent directors in strengthening the internal controls and the relationship with the external auditor.

Reporting

- Corporate governance initiatives include requirements for companies to report how they are complying with corporate governance codes.
- Corporate social responsibility initiatives require companies to report their policies and practices, with a focus on three themes of economic, environmental and social performance.

Regulatory control

- The Sarbanes–Oxley Act (2002) has set an example that is being imitated in other countries.
- Stock market regulators have taken a strong lead in supporting corporate governance initiatives and supporting global initiatives in accounting and auditing standards.
- Public Company Oversight has become an activity with statutory backing, even in countries that would be regarded as having more of a professional tradition in accounting values.

Case study 3.1　Corporate governance: Germany

The German Corporate Governance Code, revised in 2003, is issued by the Government Commission for the German Corporate Governance Code. It sets statutory regulations for the management and supervision of German listed companies.

Ensuring the basis for an effective corporate governance framework

The code presents statutory regulation. Recommendations are presented using the verb 'shall'. Companies can deviate from recommendations but must disclose this in the annual report. Suggestions are presented using the verbs 'should' or 'can'. Companies can deviate from suggestions without disclosing this. The remaining passages of the Code require compliance under law.

The rights of shareholders and key ownership functions

Shareholders vote at meetings with one vote per share (2.1). The Code sets a procedure for the general meeting (2.2) and the exercise of proxy votes (2.3).

The equitable treatment of shareholders

This is not covered in the Code.

The role of stakeholders in corporate governance

In enterprises having more than 500 employees, the Supervisory Board is one-third employee representatives. Where there are more than 2,000 employees the fraction is one half.

Chapter 3 • Confidence and assurance

Disclosure and transparency

The Management Board and the Supervisory Board shall report each year on the enterprise's corporate governance in the annual report (4.3.5). Transparency is achieved by prompt disclosure of any new facts that could influence the price of the company's securities (6.1) and of specific levels of shareholding (6.2). All information made known to financial analysts shall be disclosed to shareholders without delay (6.4). Information shall be accessible on the company's Internet site and publications shall also be in English (6.8).

The Code asserts (7.1) that shareholders and third parties are mainly informed by the consolidated financial statements, using internationally recognized accounting principles. They shall also be informed by interim reports, also using internationally recognized accounting principles. For corporate law purposes of calculating dividend, for shareholder protection, and for taxation, annual financial statements will be prepared according to the German Commercial Code. The consolidated financial statements shall be prepared by the Management Board and examined by the Supervisory Board, to be publicly accessible within 90 days of the end of the financial year. Interim reports shall be published within 45 days of the end of the reporting period. The consolidated financial statements shall contain information on stock option programmes and on relationships with shareholders as 'related parties'.

The responsibilities of the board

German companies have a dual board system. The Management Board manages the enterprise. The Supervisory Board appoints and advises the members of the Management Board and is involved in decisions of fundamental importance. The Supervisory Board members are elected by shareholders at the annual general meeting. The Management Board and Supervisory Board cooperate closely (3.1 to 3.10). The Management Board has specific tasks and responsibilities (4.1). Its composition, and the remuneration of members, are defined by the Supervisory Board (4.2). There are strict rule applied to the Management Board to prevent conflicts of interest (4.3). The tasks and responsibilities of the Supervisory Board are defined (5.1) as are those of the chairman of the Supervisory Board (5.2). The Supervisory Board shall set up an Audit Committee (5.3.2) and any other committees that increase the efficiency of the Supervisory Board. There are rules for the composition and compensation of the Supervisory Board (5.4) and for the avoidance of conflicts of interest (5.5). It must examine its efficiency on a regular basis (5.6). The Supervisory Board appoints the auditor and determines the audit fee (7.2). It receives the auditor's report and includes the auditor in its discussions on the annual financial statements.

Case study 3.2 Corporate governance: Japan

The Revised Corporate Governance Principles (2001) are set by the Japan Corporate Governance Committee which brings together the interdisciplinary interests of scholars, journalists and economists who wish to reform management.

Ensuring the basis for an effective corporate governance framework

This is a relatively short document setting out principles to be practised by directors, executive managers and shareholders. It does not specify any procedures for enforcement.

The rights of shareholders and key ownership functions

The importance of the general meeting (Principle 13) and good investor relations (Principle 14) are stressed. Executives should be 'enthusiastic' in meeting analysts and others who convey information to investors and shareholders.

The equitable treatment of shareholders

Fairness is to be assured through internal control procedures (Principle 11) and disclosure (Principle 12). There is no guidance on fairness in voting arrangements for shareholders.

The role of stakeholders in corporate governance

The only mention of stakeholders is found in the requirement to make regular disclosures to show shareholders, investors, employees, customers and local communities that the company's business affairs have been efficient and fair (Principle 12).

Disclosure and transparency

The chief executive officer must prepare an annual report on internal audit and control, to be included in the business report and the securities report (Principle 11). The chief executive officer must make prompt disclosure of any information that might affect the stock price, should make regular disclosures of information to stakeholders and should have procedures to announce important information and prevent insider trading (Principle 12).

The responsibilities of the board

Most of the principles are directed towards the board as the body supervising management (Principle 1). There is strong emphasis on the board having oversight over the chief executive officer (Principles 1 and 2). The majority of the board should be 'outside directors' (Principle 3). An 'outside director' is a person who is not an executive or an employee; an 'independent director' is able to make decisions independently of management. An outside director may not be independent of management (e.g. a person who is providing legal services to the company) (Principle 4). A leader of the board of directors is identified as a person separate from the Chief Executive Officer (Principle 5). There should be a nominating committee to appoint directors, a compensation committee to approve the pay of directors and an audit committee. Each committee should consist of three or more directors. The majority of the appointments committee and the compensation committee should be outside directors. The majority of the audit committee should be independent directors (Principle 6). The role of each committee is defined (Principle 7). The role of the chief executive officer is defined (Principle 8) as is the Executive Management Committee working under the CEO (Principle 9). A litigation committee should consider whether to commence litigation against directors or executives when shareholders have made a claim against such persons (Principle 10).

Case study 3.3   Corporate governance: UK

The Combined Code on Corporate Governance was issued by the Financial Reporting Council (FRC) in July 2003. It replaced a previous version issued in 1998 based on the Cadbury[60] and Hampel[61] Reviews of Corporate Governance. The 2003 revision took in the recommendations of the Higgs[62] and Smith[63] reports.

Ensuring the basis for an effective corporate governance framework

The Code is prepared by the Financial Reporting Council which has oversight of the process of setting accounting standards. It is enforced by the requirement of the Financial Services Authority that all listed companies apply the Code as part of the Listing Rules.

The rights of shareholders and key ownership functions

There should be a dialogue with shareholders based on the mutual understanding of objectives (D.1). The board should use the annual general meeting to communicate with investors and encourage their participation (D.2). Proxy votes should be counted and reported. The chairmen of the audit, remuneration and nomination committees should attend the meeting to answer questions.

The equitable treatment of shareholders

In the UK this is an area covered by company law and the takeover code.

The role of stakeholders in corporate governance

Institutional shareholders should enter into a dialogue with companies based on the mutual understanding of objectives (E.1). Institutional shareholders have a responsibility to make considered use of their votes (E.2). The Combined Code does not refer to other stakeholders.

Disclosure and transparency

The Code refers to accountability and audit. The board should present a balanced and understandable assessment of the company's position and prospects (C.1). It should maintain a sound system of internal control to safeguard shareholders' investment and the company's assets (C.2). An audit committee should be established to monitor the integrity of the financial statements and to maintain an appropriate relationship with the company's auditors (C.3).

    The Listing Rules of the Financial Services Authority require companies to include in the annual report a statement on compliance with the Code. Schedule C of the Code sets out detailed guidance on disclosure in this statement. In the first part of the statement the company should explain its governance policies. In the second part it either confirms that it complies with the Code or explains why it does not comply. This is described as a 'comply or explain' approach.

▶

---

[60] Cadbury Report (1992).

[61] Hampel (1998).

[62] Higgs (2003).

[63] Smith (2003).

Case study 3.3 *(Continued)*

The responsibilities of the board

Every company should be headed by an effective board, which is collectively responsible for the success of the company (A.1). The annual report should include a statement of how the board operates, including a high level statement of which types of decisions are to be taken by the board and which are delegated to management (A.1.1). There should be a clear division of responsibilities between the running of the board (the chairman) and the executive responsibility for the running of the company's business (the chief executive). The board should include a balance of executive and non-executive directors so that no individual dominates decisions of the board (A.3). Independence of non-executive directors is defined in the code. Except for smaller companies, at least half the board should be independent non-executive directors. The chairman should be independent at the point of appointment. There should be a transparent procedure for appointing new directors, based on a nominating committee (A.4). The board should receive timely information for its work and should undergo regular training (A.5). It should evaluate its own performance annually (A.6). Regular re-election and refreshing of the board should be planned (A.7).

Case study 3.4 Corporate governance: US

The corporate governance rules of the New York Stock Exchange (NYSE) were approved by the SEC in November 2003. They are codified in Section 303A of the NYSE's Listed Company Manual.

Ensuring the basis for an effective corporate governance framework

Companies listed on the NYSE must comply with these standards of corporate governance. There are penalties for failing to follow a listing standard. The first level of penalty is a public reprimand letter. The ultimate sanction is to suspend trading or delist the company (Rule 13).

The rights of shareholders and key ownership functions

Matters such as voting rights and protection of minority interests are not covered in this guidance.

The equitable treatment of shareholders

These issues are not covered in this guidance.

The role of stakeholders in corporate governance

There is no mention of stakeholders other than shareholders.

Disclosure and transparency

Listed companies must adopt and disclose corporate governance guidelines relating to the responsibilities of directors (Rule 9). The website of each listed company must include its corporate governance guidelines and the charters of its most important committees. The information must be made available in print to any shareholder who requests it. Listed companies must also adopt and disclose a code of business conduct and ethics for directors, officers and employees (Rule 10). Listed foreign private issuers must disclose any significant ways in which their corporate governance practices differ from those followed by domestic companies under NYSE listing standards (Rule 11). This disclosure may be provided on the web site or in the annual report. It must be in English and accessible from the US.

The responsibilities of the board

Listed companies must have a majority of independent directors (Rule 1) who must have no material relationship with the listed company (Rule 2). The non-management directors must meet regularly without the managing directors being present (Rule 3). Some non-management directors may not meet the conditions for being regarded as independent. If so the independent directors should meet separately at least once per year. There must be a nominating committee (Rule 4) and a compensation committee (Rule 5) each consisting entirely of independent directors. There must be an audit committee that meets the standards of the SEC regulations (Rule 6) and this audit committee must have at least three members who must be financially literate and independent (Rule 7). The chief executive officer of each listed company must certify to the NYSE each year that he or she is not aware of any violation by the company of the NYSE corporate governance listing standards (Rule 12).

Case study 3.5   Corporate governance: Kenya

In October 1999, the corporate sector, at a seminar organized by the Private Sector Initiative for Corporate Governance formally adopted a national code of best practice for Corporate Governance to guide corporate governance in Kenya.

Ensuring the basis for an effective corporate governance framework

The code has no statutory power of enforcement. The principles are designed to assist companies formulate their own specific and detailed codes of best practice. The Private Sector Corporate Governance Trust works towards helping corporate organizations develop and improve their corporate governance practices.

The rights of shareholders and key ownership functions

The code describes the duties of shareholders to exercise authority in appointing and overseeing the Board of Directors. Shareholders rights are specified, including the right to obtain relevant information about the company on a timely and regular basis.

The equitable treatment of shareholders

There is specific guidance to the Board of Directors on equitable treatment of shareholders, including minority and foreign shareholders. Members of the Board must disclose material interests in transactions. Self-dealing and insider trading are prohibited.

▶

Case study 3.5 *(Continued)*

The role of stakeholders in corporate governance

The directors are required to recognize the rights of stakeholders as established by law, to develop a code of ethics and monitor the social responsibilities of the company.

Disclosure and transparency

The section of the code on Accounts: Audit and Disclosure reminds directors of their statutory duties, requires an independent audit, and recommends an audit committee be established to review the annual and half-year financial statements before submission to the Board. The audit committee should focus particularly on changes in accounting policy, significant adjustments arising from the audit, and major judgmental areas.

The responsibilities of the board

The code covers the composition of the Board, recommending at least one third non-executives. It recommends a separate chairman and chief executive and also a competent company secretary. Re-election to the Board should take place at least every three years. Service contracts for directors should not exceed three years. There should be an independent remuneration committee. Potential conflicts of interest should be reported to the Board and to the external auditors. Directors should receive formal training. The code also sets out a detailed schedule for board meeting management and procedures.

Case study 3.6   Corporate governance: Poland

The Gdansk Institute for Market Economics issued a Corporate Governance Code in July 2002 It is a self-regulatory process to address loss of confidence faced by the Polish capital market. The Code requires companies to report on compliance or give reasons for non-compliance. There is also a document 'Best Practices in Public Companies in 2002' which describes rules of conduct for all parties involved in the company.

Ensuring the basis for an effective corporate governance framework

The Warsaw Stock Exchange is empowered to make this a formal obligation of listing. The Polish Corporate Governance Forum publishes a corporate governance rating based on the Code.

The rights of shareholders and key ownership functions

The main objective of the company should be to operate in the common interests of all the shareholders, which is to create shareholder value (principle I).

The equitable treatment of shareholders

The shareholders' meeting should be convened and organized so as not to violate the interests and rights of shareholders. The controlling shareholder should not restrict the other shareholders in the effective exercise of their corporate rights (principle IV). The company should not apply anti takeover defences against shareholders' interests. Changes in the company share capital should not violate interests of the existing shareholders (principle V).

The role of stakeholders in corporate governance

The discussion of the shareholders' meeting (expanding on principle IV) criticises instances of manipulative behaviour which has previously deprived minorities of their rights. The Code describes in some detail the standards of good behaviour expected of all shareholders.

Disclosure and transparency

The company should provide effective access to information, which is necessary to evaluate the company's current position, future prospects, as well as the way in which the company operates and applies the corporate governance rules (principle VI). The process for appointing the company's auditor should ensure independence of the auditor's opinion (principle VII).

The responsibilities of the board

The composition of the supervisory board should facilitate objective oversight of the company and reflect the interests of minority shareholders (principle II). The powers of the supervisory board and the company by-laws should ensure an effective supervisory board process and duly secure interests of all the shareholders.

Questions

The following questions test your understanding of the material contained in the chapter and allow you to relate your understanding to the learning outcomes specified at the start of this chapter. The learning outcomes are repeated here. Each question is cross-referenced to the relevant section of the chapter.

Explain and evaluate the steps taken around the world to improve the credibility of financial reporting

1 What were the standards identified by the Financial Stability Forum? (section 3.2.1)

2 What were the recommendations of the IFAC Task Force? (section 3.2.2)

3 What were the main recommendations of Sarbanes–Oxley on auditing and assurance? (section 3.2.3)

4 How does the World Bank contribute to developing accounting practices through ROSCs? (section 3.2.4)

Explain and evaluate developments in audit and assurance

5 What is the role of the IAASB? (section 3.3.1)

6 To what extent are ISAs gaining international acceptance? (section 3.3.1.1)

7 What is the role of the Public Interest Oversight Board of IFAC? (section 3.3.2)

Explain how the development of corporate governance has affected financial reporting

8 What is meant by 'corporate governance'? (section 3.4.1)

9 What is the purpose of corporate governance codes? (section 3.4.2)

10 What are the main features of corporate governance codes? (section 3.4.3)

11 What guidance is provided by the OECD on principles of corporate governance? (section 3.4.4)

12 What is the range of bodies issuing national codes of corporate governance? (section 3.4.5)

Explain how developments in corporate social responsibility are reflected in financial reporting

13 What is meant by 'triple bottom line' reporting? (section 3.5.1)

14 How does the GRI define 'sustainability'? (section 3.5.2)

15 What is the Global Reporting Initiative? (section 3.5.3)

16 What is the Accountability Rating®?(section 3.5.4)

17 How are the Dow Jones sustainability ratings compiled? (section 3.5.5)

18 How is the FTSE4Good Index Series compiled? (section 3.5.6)

19 What are the proposals of FEE in relation to CSR? (section 3.5.7)

20 Does the requirement to report CSR ensure that the reporting is effective? (section 3.5.8)

Explain and evaluate the effectiveness of regulation in ensuring compliance with requirements for financial reporting

21 How does the SEC regulate compliance in financial reporting by US listed companies? (section 3.6.1)

22 How does the UK regulate compliance with accounting standards? (section 3.6.2)

23 How do stock market regulators control standards of reporting by listed companies? (section 3.6.3)

Explain how research into credibility and assurance is developing

24 How does governance research contribute to an understanding of the relationship between accounting information and managerial actions? (section 3.7.1)

25 How does research into contracting and earnings management contribute to an understanding of the relationship between accounting information and managerial actions? (section 3.7.2)

26 How does research evaluate the effectiveness of audit committees? (section 3.7.4)

References and further reading

Bushman, R.M. and Smith, A.J. (2001) 'Financial accounting information and corporate governance', *Journal of Accounting and Economics*, 32: 237–333.

Business America (1998) 'The Asian financial crisis: How did it happen?' July, 119(7): 30–32.

Cadbury Report (1992) Report of the Committee on the Financial Aspects of Corporate Governance (Cadbury Committee), December 1992, available on www.ecgn.org

CESR (2003) European regulation on the application of IFRS in 2005: Recommendation for additional guidance regarding the transition to IFRS. Ref. CESR/03–323e.

COM (2001) 366 *European Commission Green Paper 'Promoting a European Framework for Corporate Social Responsibility'*, www.europa.eu.int/comm/employment_social/soc-dial/csr/csr_index.htm

COM (2002) 347 *Communication from the Commission concerning Corporate Social Responsibility: A business contribution to Sustainable Development*, www.europa.eu.int/comm/employment_social/soc-dial/csr/csr_index.htm

Comparative Study of Corporate Governance Codes Relevant to the European Union and Its Member States. Report by Weil, Gotshal & Manges, LLP in conjunction with EASD (European Association of Securities Dealers) and ECGN (European Corporate Governance Network), January 2002. Published by the European Commission, Internal Market Directorate General, www.europa.eu.int/comm/internal_market/en/company/company/news/corp-gov-codes-rpt_en.htm

Congressional Committee (2002) Committee Report 107–70. *The role of the board of directors in Enron's collapse*. Report prepared by the Permanent Subcommittee on Investigations of the Committee on Governmental Affairs, United States Senate, 107th Congress, 2nd Session, 8 July 2002.

Conyon, M.J. and Flourou, A. (2002) 'Top executive dismissal, ownership and corporate performance', *Accounting and Business Research*, 32(4): 209–244.

Day, J.F.S. and Taylor, P.J. (1995) 'Evidence on the practices of UK bankers in contracting for medium-term debt', *Journal of International Banking Law*, Sept: 394–401.

Dechow, P.M., Sloan, R.G. and Sweeney, A.P. (1995) 'Detecting earnings management', *The Accounting Review*, 70(2): 193–225.

Denis, D.K. and McConnell, J.J. (2003) 'International corporate governance', *Journal of Financial and Quantitative Analysis*, 38(1): 1–45.

DeZoort, F.T., Hermanson, D.R, Archambault, D.S. and Reed, S.A. (2002) 'Audit committee effectiveness: a synthesis of the empirical audit committee literature', *Journal of Accounting Literature*, 21: 38–75.

Fearnley, S., Hines, T., McBride, K. and Brandt, R. (2000) *A peculiarly British institution*. Centre for Business Performance, The Institute of Chartered Accountants in England and Wales.

GRI (2002) *GRI Sustainability Reporting Guidelines*, www.globalreporting.org.

Hampel (1998) *Committee on Corporate Governance: The Final Report*, chaired by Sir Ronald Hampel, London: Gee Publishing.

Healy, P.M. and Wahlen, J.M. (1999) 'A review of the earnings management literature and its implications for standard-setting', *Accounting Horizons*, 13(4): 365–383.

Hermsen, M.L., Niehoff, P.J. and Uhrynuk, M.R. (2002) 'An extraordinary expansion', *Accountancy*, October: 110–112.

Higgs, D. (2003) *Review of the role and effectiveness of non-executive directors*, Department of Trade and Industry, www.dti.gov.uk/cld/non_exec_review.

Ho, S.S.M. and Wong, K.S. (2001) 'A study of the relationship between corporate governance structures and the extent of voluntary disclosure', *Journal of International Accounting, Auditing and Taxation*, 10: 139–156.

IFAC (2003) *Rebuilding Public Confidence in Financial Reporting: An International Perspective*, www.ifac.org

Jensen, M.C. and Meckling, W.H. (1976) 'Theory of the firm: managerial behaviour, agency costs and ownership structure', *Journal of Financial Economics*, 3: 305–360.

Jones, J. (1991) 'Earnings management during import relief investigations', *Journal of Accounting Research*, 29(2): 193–228.

La Porta, R., Lopez-de-Silanes, F. and Shleifer, A. (1998) 'Law and finance', *Journal of Political Economy*, 106(6): 1113–1155.

Laufer, W.S. (2003) 'Social accountability and corporate greenwashing', *Journal of Business Ethics*, 43(3): 253–261.

Leuz, C., Deller, D. and Stabenrath, M. (1998) 'An international comparison of accounting-based payout restrictions in the United States, United Kingdom and Germany', *Accounting and Business Research*, 28(2): 111–129.

137

OECD (2004) *New OECD Principles of Corporate Governance*, Organisation for Economic Cooperation and Development, 22 April 2004, www.oecd.org/daf/corporate/principles

Peasnell, K.V., Pope, P.F. and Young, S. (2000) 'Detecting earnings management using cross-sectional abnormal accruals models', *Accounting and Business Research*, 30(4): 313–326.

Pilbeam, K. (2001) 'The East Asian financial crisis: Getting to the heart of the issues', *Managerial Finance*, 27(1/2): 111–133.

Skinner, D. (1994) 'Why firms voluntarily disclose bad news', *Journal of Accounting Research*, 32: 38–60.

Sloan, R.G. (2001) 'Financial accounting and corporate governance: a discussion', *Journal of Accounting and Economics*, 32: 335–347.

Smith, R. (2003) *Audit Committees: Combined Code Guidance*. A report and proposed guidance by an FRC-appointed group chaired by Sir Robert Smith. Financial Reporting Council, www.frc.org.uk/publications

Street, D.L. and Needles, B.E. (2002) 'An interview with Brian Smith of the International Forum on Accountancy Development (IFAD)', *Journal of International Financial Management and Accounting*, 13(3): 254–273.

Watts, R.L. and Zimmerman, J.L. (1986) 'Compensation plans, debt contracts and accounting procedures', Chapter 9 in *Positive Accounting Theory*. Prentice-Hall International, Inc.

PART 2

Contrasting harmonization and diversity across financial reporting systems

Introduction to Part 2

Given the discussion in Part 1 of the work of the IASB, it would be reasonable for you to ask why, without the IASB, financial reporting would vary from one country to another. After all, accounting presents figures about financial performance and position and these figures might be expected to rise above differences of language (recall, for example, the arguments given in Exhibit 1.1). However, in practice the figures are servants of the influences under which they are created and the process by which they are communicated. Part 2 focuses on the influences on financial reporting rules and practices.

Framework for comparative study

This book uses two frameworks, established in Part 2, to explain why accounting across different countries may show signs of both diversity and harmony. The first framework is that of the institutional and external influences on accounting rules and practice, as explained in Chapter 4. In selecting the basis for a framework, Chapter 4 draws on academic research for justification. The headings used in Chapter 4 are:

- political and economic system
- legal system
- taxation system
- corporate financing system
- accounting profession
- other influences.

Chapter 4 describes general subdivisions within each of these categories and adds some illustrative material. Two case studies at the end of Chapter 4 give added insight relating to countries not covered in subsequent chapters.

The second framework used is that of cultural influences on accounting rules and practice. Chapter 5 leads the reader through general considerations of culture, discusses more specific links between culture and business, and finally addresses specific findings regarding culture and accounting. The chapter draws on the academic literature for its justification but also points to critical evaluation of the extent to which culture influences accounting values and practices.

The accounting values drawn as conclusions for Chapter 5 are:

- professionalism versus statutory control
- uniformity versus flexibility
- conservatism versus optimism
- secrecy versus transparency.

These are applied as a framework of discussion in the country chapters.

Classification of accounting systems

A considerable amount of effort from academics and practitioners has been devoted to classifying accounting systems. In some cases the characteristics of the accounting practices are used as the basis for classification. In other cases the characteristics of the political, economic and legal situations are used for classification. Deductive classification schemes rely strongly on the knowledge or beliefs of the observer who chooses a set of features which vary from one country to the next. Inductive classification systems look to a large body of data, such as that generated by an international survey, and painstakingly generate groups of data which seem to 'belong' together. From the clusters of data which relate closely, the researchers draw conclusions about countries which have accounting similarities and differences.

Chapter 6 describes and explains the research which has created a range of types of classifications of accounting systems.

Measuring the differences and similarities

A full understanding of the existing and potential impact of the IASB requires the measurement of differences and similarities across accounting systems. Differences and similarities can be observed by practical persons but much of the systematic measurement and analysis has been undertaken in the academic sphere. Chapter 7 explains the methods used in academic research to measure international differences. The chapter discusses the importance of observed differences, and explains in simple terms how to measure differences in the figures reported and how to measure differences in the accounting methods used. Academic papers are cited and explained but simple illustrations are also provided so that there is guidance for you if you are considering such analysis in relation to a planned project or dissertation.

Purpose of Part 2

Part 2 is particularly useful as a module on which to base a study of analysis and research methods in comparative financial reporting. It equips students with the analytical framework and research methods that may be used in research projects. It also helps them to understand and evaluate research papers in this field of study.

Learning outcomes

Specific learning outcomes are set out at the start of each chapter but overall, on completion of Part 2, the student should be able to:

- set out a framework of institutional and external influences which could be applied to any country-specific study;
- set out a framework of cultural factors and accounting values to be applied to any country-specific study;
- explain the various approaches to accounting classification;
- carry out a simple measurement of international differences in accounting practices using data provided for the purpose.

4

Institutional and external influences on accounting rules and practices

Learning outcomes

After reading this chapter you should be able to:

- Understand how various aspects of a country's political and economic system have influenced its accounting system.

- Distinguish between common and code law systems and describe how the legal system typically influences the system of accounting regulation.

- Describe the ways in which the tax system can influence accounting rules and practices.

- Identify possible differences in the financing of companies internationally and describe how these differences may help to explain differences in accounting rules and practices.

- Understand how the way in which the accounting profession is organized can influence accounting rules and practices.

- Understand how a country might import or export accounting rules and practices.

4.1 Introduction

This chapter explores some of the reasons why financial accounting rules and practices have differed across countries. Many factors have influenced the development of accounting and there are many reasons why countries have developed different accounting systems.[1] This chapter explores some of the ways in which a society can organize itself and how this has affected the way in which accounting is undertaken. Six different features of a country are explored in this chapter, namely:

- the political and economic system
- the legal system
- the taxation system
- the corporate financing system
- the accounting profession
- religion.

Accounting rules and practices are not only developed inside a country, they may also have been imported into the country. This chapter therefore concludes by looking at the process of importing and exporting accounting rules and practices.

This chapter is primarily concerned with the position before the IASB began to wield a significant influence on practices internationally. It therefore seeks at least partially to answer the question of why moves towards increasing international harmonization have become increasingly important in recent years. It also shows the factors that may continue to influence diversity in areas of accounting and accountability not regulated by the IASB where national influences remain stronger.

The chapter proceeds by introducing a general model that explains the types of factors that influence accounting. It then carries on to look at two of these, namely institutional factors and external factors. Chapter 5 then explores what is meant by 'culture', and looks at how the culture of a country can influence its accounting system.

---

[1] While accounting includes not only financial reporting but also management accounting, auditing and public sector accounting, the term 'accounting system' is used in this book, unless otherwise stated, to mean the financial reporting system. This includes both the rules or regulations and the actual practices of profit-orientated limited liability companies.

4.2 Factors influencing the development of accounting systems

No two countries have identical accounting systems. In a few cases – such as that of the UK and Ireland, or the US and Canada – the differences are relatively few and relatively minor. In other instances, even of geographically proximate countries such as, for example, the UK and France, or the US and Mexico, the differences have been much greater, including some quite fundamental differences. Differences can exist at all levels of the accounting system. For example, if the treatment of assets is considered, a wide range of different rules and practices are found. Countries can adopt different valuation methods, ranging from strict historical cost to full current cost systems or they can adopt quite different definitions of an asset – using either legal ownership- or economic control-based definitions. Differences in the relative importance accorded to different accounting principles – in particular the matching or accruals principle and the prudence or conservatism principle – will also influence the accounting methods used.

Both measurement and disclosure rules vary across countries. Differences in disclosure regulations include differences in the scope of the financial statements (whether only group or group plus individual company accounts), differences in the types of organizations regulated (whether all large organizations or only listed companies), and differences in the amount of information demanded. Many reasons have been given to explain why accounting systems vary so much. Exhibit 4.1 illustrates the range of possible influences.

Exhibit 4.1 The influences on an accounting system

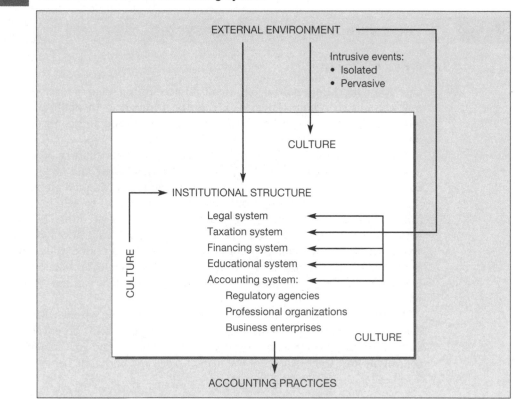

Source: Adapted from Doupnik and Salter (1995).

The accounting system is the outcome of a complex process. It is influenced by and it also influences a number of factors. Governmental or political, economic, legal, tax, educational and financial systems are all important. Factors originating from outside a country can also be important, and its past trading and colonial links and current patterns of foreign investment can influence accounting. The culture of a country is also important. It can perhaps best be seen as a moderating influence that either reinforces or reduces the influence of these other factors. All of the following help to explain the accounting regulations of a country:

- the objectives of accounting regulation, whether the needs of investors, creditors, the government or other users are given precedence;
- the mode of regulation, whether by government, the profession or other group(s); and
- the extent and strictness of regulation.

However, accounting practices are not simply the result of regulations. Voluntary practices are also important. As can be seen in Exhibit 4.1, voluntary practices are also the outcome of a complex process, being influenced by a wide range of factors.

While both internal and external factors are important, in most developed western countries the most important influences on the accounting system have been the institutions of that country – in particular how it organizes its political and economic, legal, financial and professional systems.[2] In contrast, as will be discussed later, factors external to the country have often been as or even more important for many developing countries. It is to the *internal or institutional* factors that we now turn our attention.

4.3 The political and economic system

4.3.1 Types of systems

One of the most important determinants of accounting regulations and practices is the political and economic system of a country. Differences in political systems will be reflected in differences in how the economy is organized and controlled. This will in turn influence the objectives or role of accounting.

What is particularly important to accounting is how a country organizes economic relations. At one extreme, all the processes of production could be jointly owned and controlled by society; prices, outputs, demand and supply would all be determined by centralized plans. Accounting would then serve two roles – to help in centralized planning and to help in controlling the economy. Accounting need then be concerned only with physical units; 'profit' would have no meaning or significance. One example of an accounting system with many of these features was China prior to the economic reforms of the 1980s. The Chinese system is described in Chapter 13, and illustrates an accounting system that was very different from any that exists in western liberal–democratic societies.

At the other extreme would be a capitalist economic system with prices, output, demand and supply all determined in the market place, with no government interference. In practice of course, no country has gone this far, and government regulates and controls at least some aspects of the market place and corporate behaviour.

[2] Puxty *et al.* (1987).

Government control can be manifested in a number of ways. The government may own industrial organizations – in France, Italy and Spain, for example, the state has traditionally owned a range of commercial companies, including large manufacturing enterprises. Alternatively, even if it does not own any businesses, it may play an active role in managing or controlling privately owned businesses. This state control can take several different forms. The government may manage consumer demand with relatively little contact with, or regulation of, business; alternatively, it may manage supply, being actively involved in the regulation and control of businesses.

There are also differences between countries and inside any country over time with respect to the predominant attitude towards business. Business–government relations may be seen both by politicians and the general public mainly in terms of cooperation: business may be seen as generally a 'good thing', operating in the interests of society to generate wealth and employment. Alternatively, business–government relations may be viewed in adversarial terms: large profits will then be seen as the outcome of exploitation of workers, customers or other groups. Government will then regulate more to protect these less powerful groups, whether labour, customers or society in general.

4.3.2 The regulation of accounting

The extent to which the government actively controls the economy, and the means it uses, will influence its willingness to control or regulate accounting, the regulatory structures used and the types of regulation.

If government believes in a 'hands-off' approach with minimal regulation of companies, accounting is also less likely to be heavily regulated by the state. Companies will tend to be left to decide what to report and how to report it. Uniform accounting methods and the reporting of strictly comparable information will be relatively unimportant and accounting regulation will probably be delegated to the profession or other independent bodies.

If, instead, the government believes in a 'hands-on' approach to controlling the economy, it will be much more likely to regulate accounting. Accounting information will now be needed by the government so that it can actively plan and manage corporate behaviour. There is more likely to be a uniform or rigid system of financial reporting imposed upon all companies.

4.3.3 Corporate attitudes towards accounting

The ways in which government–business relations are organized and the government's attitude towards business will affect the attitudes of business managers. If big business is viewed with suspicion, managers are more likely to use financial statements to manage business–society and business–government relationships. Extra disclosures may be seen as a way of demonstrating that the company is acting in socially desirable ways – disclosure may thus be seen as a way of legitimating the actions and activities of business. For example, there has been a significant amount of empirical and theoretical work using legitimacy theory to try to explain social and environmental disclosures by companies.[3] Managers may also be more likely to favour measurement rules and practices that reduce reported earnings.

---

[3] See, for example, the special issue of *Accounting, Accountability and Auditing Journal*, No. 15.3, 2002.

If, on the other hand, business–government relations are generally cooperative and profits are seen as a measure of success, companies will generally be less concerned with trying to justify themselves. There may be less voluntary disclosure of information, especially social information. Companies are also less likely to favour conservative income measurement rules and will instead tend to attempt to maximize rather than minimize their reported earnings (this assumes, of course, that there is no adverse impact on the company's tax bill).

4.3.4 Types of business organization

An important economic feature influencing accounting is the type of business organization that dominates the economy. Two features of business organizations are particularly important in helping to explain accounting rules and practices:

● the complexity of business organizations
● the industrial structure of the country.

4.3.4.1 The complexity of business organizations

The way in which businesses are organized obviously has a major impact on the internal accounting information system and management accounting in general. As a company increases in size and complexity, the need for sophisticated management accounting systems increases – problems of control, performance evaluation and decision making all increase. While less obvious, differences in business complexity also affect the financial accounting system. If companies are generally small or family-owned there is little need for external reporting and there should be relatively few accounting regulations. As companies increase in size, both their impact upon society and their need for external finance, whether by debt or equity, will increase. This means that there is a greater need for external information and the amount of accounting regulation will increase in response. As companies increase in size they are also likely to become more complex. Typically, companies will start to arrange themselves into groups, with subsidiaries, associates and/or joint ventures all becoming more important. Again, accounting regulations will tend to reflect these changes. For example, greater emphasis will be placed upon the regulation of group financial statements and extra disclosure requirements in areas such as segment reporting will be more likely. As size increases, the need for more sophisticated accounting also increases. For example, regulations in the areas of off-balance-sheet finance, hedge accounting, financial instruments and share options should all become increasingly important.

4.3.4.2 The industrial structure of a country

Some accounting issues are industry-specific. Whether or not a country regulates a particular industry-specific issue will obviously depend upon the relative importance of that industry to the economy. For example, if a country is highly dependent upon foreign trade and investment, with many of its companies being multinational, it is more likely to be concerned with the issue of foreign currency transactions and translation and is more likely to issue accounting regulations in this area. Other issues are even more industry-specific. For example, accounting for the oil and gas industry has been an important and contentious issue in the US. Issues of how to account for other extractive industries and agriculture are generally more important in developing countries than in developed countries. Thus, IAS 41 *Agriculture* was a result of pressure from a number of developing countries.

The importance of certain types of industry may also influence wider accounting regulations. For example, the UK standard on research and development was strongly influenced by the potential impact of alternative accounting methods on the behaviour of companies in the aero-engineering and other research and development-dependent industries.[4] Likewise, one of the very few times when the US Congress directly regulated accounting was over the issue of investment tax credits: Congress was concerned that the accounting rules should not adversely affect the investment behaviour of capital-intensive businesses and so impede the economic recovery of the US.[5]

The importance or relevance of other accounting issues depends upon how the economy of a country is structured. For example, accounting for pensions is an important issue in the US, which has a very complex and detailed pension standard. This reflects the particular institutional arrangements of the US, where many companies run employee pension schemes. In other countries, pensions are run entirely by the state or through private arrangements, and accounting for pensions is less important. Likewise, the importance of issues such as leases and financial instruments depends upon the ways in which banks and other financial institutions work and the types of financing they provide.

4.3.5 The importance of inflation

Another important economic influence on accounting is inflation. As inflation rates increase the problems of historical cost accounting also increase. Developed western countries have seldom suffered from high inflation and have tended to view inflation accounting with suspicion, and as a result a system of strict historical accounting is found in much of continental Europe and North America.

Inflation continues to be a serious problem in some countries, though. Mexico, Chile and Brazil, for example, have all had annual inflation rates of over 100 per cent in the past. Obviously, when inflation is running at such levels, the historical cost of an asset soon becomes irrelevant. Thus, various forms of inflation accounting are or have been found in these countries. One interesting example of this is Brazil.[6] A new corporation law was introduced in 1976 which was designed to strengthen the stock market. One of its major concerns was the protection of minority shareholders, so it introduced rules making the payment of dividends obligatory. Therefore, income had to be clearly defined and this was done using a system of monetary corrections: official monthly price indexes were used to update the values of assets, depreciation, cost of sales and owners' equity. These regulations were withdrawn in 1986 as part of a series of anti-inflationary economic measures. Other Central and South American countries have also used various forms of current cost accounting at various times. A description of one such method can be seen in Exhibit 4.2 which reproduces part of the accounting policy statement of the Chilean electricity generation company, Empresa Nacional de Electricidad SA (Endesa Chile).

---

[4] Hope and Gray (1982).

[5] Zeff (1972).

[6] Doupnik (1987).

Exhibit 4.2 Endesa Chile: Price-level statements and accounting policy

Constant currency restatement:
The cumulative inflation rate in Chile as measured by the Chilean Consumer Price Index ("CPI") for the three year period ended December 31, 2002 was approximately 11.2%.

Chilean GAAP requires that the financial statements be restated to reflect the full effect of loss in the purchasing power of the Chilean peso on the financial position and results of operations of reporting entities. The method described below is based on a model that enables calculation of net inflation gains or losses caused by monetary assets and liabilities exposed to changes in the purchasing power of local currency. The model prescribes that the historical cost of all non-monetary accounts be restated for general price-level changes between the date of origin of each item and the year end.

The financial statements of the Company have been price-level restated in order to reflect the effects of the changes in the purchasing power of the Chilean currency during each year. All non-monetary assets and liabilities, all equity accounts and income statement accounts have been restated to reflect the changes in the CPI from the date they were acquired or incurred to year-end.

. . . .

The above-mentioned price-level restatements do not purport to represent appraisal or replacement values and are only intended to restate all non-monetary financial statement components in terms of local currency of a single purchasing power and to include in net income or loss for each year the gain or loss in purchasing power arising from the holding of monetary assets and liabilities exposed to the effects of inflation.

Source: Taken from the financial statements, year ended 31 December 2002, page 98, www.endesa.cl

4.4 The legal system

4.4.1 Types of legal system

Two types of legal systems are found in liberal–democratic countries, namely Romano-Germanic or code law and common law legal systems.

The countries of continental Europe, Latin America and much of Asia have various forms of code law. Laws are generally codified (often using a similar organizational framework to that of the French Napoleonic codes of 1804–11). The philosophy behind the laws in these countries may be described as one where the role of law is to describe and mandate acceptable behaviour. Laws consist of rules and procedures that have to be followed. Typically, commercial codes regulate the behaviour of all commercial organizations, including the regulation of accounting.

The alternative to code law is common law. Here, the philosophy is one where the role of law is to prohibit undesirable behaviour rather than to prescribe or codify desirable behaviour. This system has its origin in England from where it was exported to the US and the Commonwealth, where it takes various forms. In common law countries much of the law is developed by judges or the courts who set case law during the resolution of specific disputes. Statute law does exist, but it tends to be less detailed and more flexible than its equivalent in code law countries.

4.4.2 Accounting and code law legal systems

In code law countries governments have generally regulated accounting as one part of their measures to ensure orderly business conduct. Accounting regulations are one part of a complete system of commercial regulations that apply to all business organizations. Regulations are designed to protect all the parties to any commercial transaction and to ensure orderly business conduct; emphasis is placed upon the protection of outsiders – in particular, creditors. Creditors have been seen as one – and very often the most – important user of financial statements. The tax authorities are often also an important user, and accounting regulations have often been set with their needs in mind. Shareholders have generally not been seen as so important. (This is not surprising when it is realized that most businesses are not listed and do not have many external shareholders.) The financial statements of individual companies have been more highly regulated than are consolidated statements. This is because the tax authorities are interested in the individual company not the group, and most legal contracts with creditors, suppliers or customers also occur at the individual company level.

In most code law countries accounting is regulated primarily through an accounting code which is typically prescriptive, detailed and procedural. Thus, the accounting regulations include not only detailed disclosure rules but also measurement and bookkeeping rules. It is quite common for countries to also have industry-specific regulations or plans.

4.4.3 Accounting and common law legal systems

England is a good example of a common law country. Companies Acts have been concerned mainly with disclosure of information for the protection of the owners of limited liability companies, that is, the shareholders. Not only have companies to follow the specific provisions of the Companies Acts but they also have a general duty to present financial statements that are 'true and fair'. The courts have interpreted this legal requirement to mean that, unless a company can demonstrate otherwise, it must also follow accounting standards as set by the private sector body, the Accounting Standards Board (ASB). The standards set by the ASB are an example of piecemeal regulations – each standard covers one particular issue. They tend to be issued as a reaction to a particular business problem and so are *ad hoc* rather than part of a larger plan. From 2005 the courts will look to the IFRS rather than ASB standards in judging listed companies, but will continue to apply common law principles in forming judgments.

The legislature has an even less important direct role in accounting regulation in some other common law countries. For example, in the US while the legislature in the form of the Congress has ultimate authority for the federal regulation of accounting, it has used this in very few cases. Instead, it has delegated authority to the Securities and Exchange Commission (SEC) which in turn has delegated authority for accounting standard-setting to an independent body, the Financial Accounting Standards Board (FASB) (see Chapter 8).

In contrast to code law countries, the main reason for accounting regulation in common law countries, whether by the state directly or via delegated powers to other bodies, has been the need to protect the owners of companies. Thus, accounting regulations have tended to grow in a piecemeal fashion alongside the growth of limited liability companies and the separation of owners and managers, with an emphasis on accounting and reporting at the group level. Accounting has often been regulated because the free market system has been seen to break down and has not provided sufficient information of an adequate quality. Finally, because the emphasis is on equity providers rather than creditors or taxation authorities, the measurement rules tend to be less conservative than those of code law countries.

4.5 The taxation system

4.5.1 The relationship between tax rules and financial reporting rules

In some countries, the taxation system is an important influence on accounting. In others it has little or no influence on reporting rules and practices. Code law countries tend to have common tax and financial reporting regulations, while common law countries tend instead to keep the tax and financial reporting regulations separate from each other. However, the precise relationship between the two varies across countries and there are always exceptions to these generalizations. (For example, The Netherlands is an important exception to this rule, as discussed in Chapter 10.)

Three types of tax systems can be identified. These are systems where:

● the tax rules and the financial reporting rules are kept entirely, or very largely, independent of each other;
● there is a common system, with many of the financial reporting rules also being used by the tax authorities;
● there is a common system, with many of the tax rules also being used for financial reporting purposes.

4.5.2 Independent tax and financial reporting regulations

One of the best examples of this type of system is the UK. Here, the tax and financial reporting rules are kept separate with the two being set by different bodies. For example, depreciation in the financial statements is based upon a Financial Reporting Standard (FRS), here FRS 15, which requires that the depreciation method used 'should reflect as fairly as possible the pattern in which the asset's economic benefits are consumed by the entity' (paragraph 77). In contrast, the tax charge is based upon a system of predetermined tax-depreciation allowances. Not only is tax depreciation uniform, but the rates often serve economic policy objectives providing investment incentives. For example, the first year capital allowance on fixed assets for small and medium sized enterprises (SMEs) was increased from 40 per cent to 50 per cent for tax year 2004/05. (This is despite a 2001 discussion paper issued by the Inland Revenue suggesting that small companies' taxation should be based upon reported profits.[7])

While many other countries also have largely independent tax and reporting rules, there are often some issues where the tax and accounting rules are not independent of each other. For example, in the US the tax rules do not affect the financial reporting rules or practices with the one exception of stock or inventory valuation. Thus, the 'last-in-first-out' (LIFO) system can be used for tax purposes only if it is also used for financial reporting.

---

[7] Inland Revenue Technical note 12 March 2001.

4.5.3 The use of financial reporting rules by the tax authorities

Many of the countries of the Commonwealth follow the example of the UK with the financial reporting rules being set without direct control or influence of the taxation authorities. (Not only did the UK often export the English common law legal system, it also exported its taxation system.) However, the tax system in many developing Commonwealth countries is not as sophisticated and the rules are not as well developed as they are in the UK. This has meant that the tax authorities have not set detailed and all-embracing rules for the calculation of taxable income. Instead, they have tended to rely wholly or largely upon reported earnings as the basis for calculating tax liabilities. The accounting regulations are therefore by default also the tax regulations.

This has important implications for accounting practice. It means that where there are no accounting regulations, or where the regulations permit some choice, there will be a very much stronger incentive for managers to choose methods that minimize their tax liability. They will prefer not to choose the method that is most informative or the method that best reflects the 'true and fair' position of the company if it leads to a higher tax bill. It also means that companies will be more resistant to new accounting regulations that increase their tax liability, thus making it more difficult to introduce such regulations and, if they are introduced, increasing the problems of non-compliance.

4.5.4 The use of tax rules for financial reporting

The third alternative is where the tax authorities set detailed rules for the calculation of taxable earnings and these rules have to be followed not only in the tax returns but also in the external financial statements. There are variations in exactly how the system works, but this approach can be found in most of the countries of Western Europe. The systems in place in France and Germany will be discussed in Chapter 10. Another example is that of Austria.[8] Commercial law regulates financial reporting. Here, there are several tax allowances that can be claimed only if they are also disclosed in the financial reports; this applies even if the resultant values would not otherwise be allowed by the commercial law. For these items, the tax rules take precedence. Most companies attempt to provide information of most use to external report readers. They therefore show the tax allowances as a separate item in untaxed reserves in the balance sheet rather than treat them as changes in the value of the relevant assets.

For example, Telekom Austria discloses in its Balance Sheet two types of untaxed reserves.[9] One of these is 'Reserves from special depreciation' which contains two items: 'Continuation of special depreciation as per section 8 and 122 of the Austrian Income Tax Act 1972' and 'Transfer of hidden reserves as per Section 12 of the Austrian Income Tax Act'. The second type of untaxed reserve is simply investment allowances as per section 10 of the Austrian Income Tax Act. The consistency between tax and accounting rules is further seen in the income tax notes which states that 'no deferred taxes were recorded in 2003'.

Commercial law may also allow companies to choose between alternative accounting treatments when the tax authorities do not prescribe a particular treatment (e.g. LIFO or FIFO for inventory). In these cases, whichever method is used for financial reporting purposes will also be used by the tax authorities.

---

[8] Wagenhofer (2001).

[9] Telekom Austria, 2003 annual report, available at http://telekom.at.

Tax is calculated at the individual-company rather than at the group level. This is one reason why accounting for the individual company has traditionally been considered more important than group accounting in much of Western Europe. It also means that companies are often far more restricted in their choice of methods of accounting at the individual-company level than at the group level. Thus, the tax rules have been largely responsible for a two-tier system of regulation and reporting in many EU countries, with accounting at the group level converging much more towards an international norm.

4.6 The corporate financing system

Companies can be financed in a variety of ways. Both debt and equity can take many different forms and can be provided by many different types of individuals and institutions. The way in which a company is financed affects accounting in a number of ways. For example, if equity finance is relatively more important than debt finance, accounting regulations are more likely to be designed to provide forward-looking information useful for investment decision-making purposes. If debt financing is relatively more important, accounting measurement rules should be relatively more conservative, being designed to protect creditors. The sophistication of finance providers and the extent to which they have to rely upon financial statements will also impact significantly upon accounting disclosures – both mandatory and voluntary.

4.6.1 Corporate financing patterns

Average debt–equity ratios provide an indication of differences in financing across countries.[10] One study of the relationship between culture and financing patterns in 22 countries[11] found some significant differences in debt–equity ratios even after controlling for differences in performance, legal system, GDP and financial institutions. The highest corporate debt ratios were found in Germany (71 per cent), Italy (65 per cent), The Netherlands (63 per cent), France (62 per cent) and Japan (61 per cent). In contrast, the lowest ratios were found in the US (47 per cent), Australia (45 per cent), Greece (44 per cent), and Taiwan and China (both 42 per cent). Differences in corporate financing patterns will also be reflected in differences in stock market activity. Exhibit 4.3 provides some information on the major stock markets.[12]

Looking first at the number of companies listed, the five largest markets are, perhaps surprisingly, Mumbai followed by the Canadian exchange (TSX), the Spanish exchange, NASDAQ[13] and then London. However, as a measure of the size of the market, the number of companies listed is less important than the number of companies that are actively traded. For Mumbai the value of share trading (turnover) was relatively low, indicating the presence of many inactive stocks. Reflecting the long history of foreign trading and financing in the UK, the London Stock Exchange (LSE) had until very recently, more

---

[10] Average debt–equity ratios only provide an indication of differences. They will be affected by differences in the samples chosen and by differences in the accounting rules used in different countries.

[11] Chui *et al.* (2002).

[12] World Federation of Exchanges website www.world-exchanges.org. Again, a word of warning is in order. Differences in market structures and differences in the methods of data collection mean that these figures are not strictly comparable, although they do indicate important differences.

[13] NASDAQ or the National Association of Securities Dealers Automated Quotation System is a computerized quotation system which allows potential buyers and sellers of securities traded on the over-the-counter (OTC) market to locate the market makers who will buy and sell OTC securities.

Exhibit 4.3	Major equity markets, 2003

Exchange	Domestic market Value ($bn)	Turnover value ($bn)		No. of companies listed		Domestic market capitalization as % of GDP*
		Domestic	International	Domestic	International	
EU						
Euronext	2,076.4	1,911.2	11.1	1046	346	62.7%
Copenhagen	118.2	62.3	1.5	187	7	40.2%
Germany	1,079.0	1,200.9	98.4	684	182	31.2%
Helsinki	170.3	163.4	2.3	142	3	95.4%
Irish	85.1	43.8	0.3	55	11	44.5%
Italian	614.8	708.2	112.3	271	8	36.4%
London	2,460.0	2,143.3	1,463.0	2,311	381	111.0%
Luxembourg	37.3	0.3	0.01	44	198	105.2%
Spanish	726.2	928.3	4.7	3,191	32	63.6%
Stockholm	293.0	260.3	43.0	266	16	66.7%
Vienna	56.5	10.9	0.3	104	21	14.8%
Warsaw	37.4	9.0	<0.1	202	1	14.3%
OTHER						
Australian	585.4	366.9	5.1	1,405	66	91.7%
Hong Kong	714.6	295.2	0.5	1,027	10	286.7%
NSE India	252.9	202.8	0	911	0	23.5%
Korea	298.3	459.0	0	684	0	43.4%
Mexico	122.5	23.9	1.6	158	79	17.5%
Mumbai	278.7	89.1	0	5,644	0	27.2%
NASDAQ	2,844.2	6,703.3	359.9	2,951	343	19.0%
New York	11,323.0	8,778.3	728.4	1,842	466	86.0%
Osaka	1,951.5	106.6	0	1,140	0	35.7%
Shanghai	360.1	251.6	0	780	0	24.8%
Shenzhan	152.9	136.4	0	505	0	12.7%
Singapore	148.5	91.9 total	N/a	475	76	113.6%
South Africa	168.3	70.7	28.1	390	21	88.0%
Switzerland	727.1	564.3	43.0	289	130	183.1%
Taiwan	379.1	591.2	0.4	669	5	93.3%
Tokyo	2,953.1	2,092.1	0.3	2,174	32	49.5%
TSX, Canada	888.7	471.1	0.4	3,561	38	77.3%

* End of 2002

Source: World Federation of Stock Exchanges 2003, Tables 1.1, 1.3, 1.5 and 4.5, www.world-exchanges.org

foreign listings than any other market. Also popular is the second largest by number of companies, NASDAQ, which tends to attract rather smaller foreign companies or foreign companies requiring less financing than does the New York Stock Exchange (NYSE), and Euronext, which tends to attract mainly companies from nearby European countries. Euronext was established in 2000 from the exchanges of Amsterdam, Paris and Brussels. In 2002 the London futures market and the Portuguese stock markets joined.

However, it is not only the number of companies listed that is important; the size of the companies listed is also relevant. One measure of size is the market value of a company's

| Exhibit 4.4 | Stock market capitalization 1990-2002 (US $bn) |

	1990	1992	1994	1996	1998	2000	2002
Euronext			761.0	1105.7	1903.3	2271.7	1538.7
Germany	355.3	346.9	499.3	664.9	1086.7	1270.2	686.0
London	850.0	928.4	1145.3	1642.6	2372.7	2612.2	1856.2
Nasdaq	310.8	618.8	793.7	1511.8	2243.7	3597.1	1994.5
NYSE	2692.1	3798.2	4147.9	6842.0	10277.9	11534.6	9015.3
Tokyo	2928.5	2318.9	3592.2	3011.2	2439.5	3157.2	2089.3
TSX (Canada)	241.9	241.9	315.1	487.0	543.4	766.2	570.2

Source: World Federation of Stock Markets web pages

shares or its stock market capitalization. If we look at the stock market capitalization of domestic companies only, then a rather different pictures emerges. NYSE is now clearly the most important stock market. Indeed, its domestic capitalization is more than the combined value of the next four exchanges (i.e. Tokyo, NASDAQ, London and Euronext). A further measure of the significance of the equity market is the ratio of domestic market capitalization to gross domestic product (GDP) which relates the size of the equity market to the output of the domestic economy. This ratio is shown in the final column of Exhibit 4.3.

Exhibit 4.4 provides details of the domestic capitalization of seven major equity markets in the period 1990–2002. From this, it can be seen that while the NYSE is now much larger than any other exchange, this is a relatively recent phenomenon. Indeed, it was briefly overtaken by Tokyo in the late 1980s/early 1990s. Exhibit 4.4 also shows some other interesting changes in relative capitalization since 1990. These suggest that Euronext has been a success so far. It is also noticeable that only Tokyo has decreased in size over this period. In contrast, London, the German exchange and Canada (TSX) have each approximately doubled in capitalization over this period.

4.6.2 Market liquidity and financial institutions

There are differences not only in the size of the various stock markets but also in their liquidity or depth. In particular, there are differences in the proportion of listed companies that are actively traded and the relative importance of a few large companies. For example, Exhibit 4.5 shows the capitalization and turnover of the most important Swiss companies. In Exhibit 4.3, we saw that the Swiss exchange had 289 domestic companies listed at the end of 2003. So these two tables taken together imply that a significant number of Swiss companies must be hardly traded at all.

There are a number of reasons why some markets are more liquid than others. Cultural factors may affect individuals' saving habits and attitudes to stock market trading. Historical factors affecting the growth of stock markets and the relationships between banks and industrial companies are obviously also important, as are current institutional arrangements. Particularly important here are the costs and ease of trading, the ways in which pensions are organized and the range of financial intermediaries that exist. For example, pension premiums of current employees may be used to finance existing pension commitments; alternatively, they may be held and invested in the stock market until used to finance the future pensions of current employees. Investment trusts and unit trusts are important in some countries, both being designed to allow individuals to invest cheaply and efficiently in the stock market.

Exhibit 4.5 The ten most important shares on the Swiss exchange in 2003

Security	Percentage of total share turnover	Percentage of SWX all share index capitalization
Novartis AG	16.77	18.69
Nestlé AG	13.53	16.38
UBS AG	12.77	12.38
Credit Suisse Group	9.86	7.08
Roche Holding AG	9.83	12.14
Zurich Financial Services	4.90	3.37
Swiss Reinsurance Co.	4.56	3.53
ABB	2.79	*
Adecco SA	2.27	1.30
Swisscom AG	1.64	1.32
Compagnie Financière Richemont AG	*	2.04
Total percentage accounted for by top 10	79.01	78.23%

* Not in top ten for this category.

Source: www.swx.com/markets/reports/2003

At the risk of too much simplification, two models may be identified. In the 'UK model' there is a long history of an active stock market. A wide range of financial intermediaries exists, with pensions being increasingly financed through insurance companies, and investment and unit trusts being important depositories of personal savings. Complementing this is the role of banks, which have traditionally provided only short-term or medium-term financing to industry. This contrasts sharply with what might be termed the 'German model'. Here, the financial system is dominated by approximately 4,000 banks, although commercial banking is dominated by the 'Big Three' of Deutsche Bank, Dresdner Bank and Commerzbank. The banks tend to be less specialized than in the UK, with no distinction between commercial and investment banks, and they increasingly offer life insurance and pension products. While other types of financial institutions do exist, they are far less important than in the UK. The banks are the repository of most personal savings and have tended to have close relationships with industrial companies. They offer more long-term loans than do UK banks, and they often also hold shares in industrial companies as well as acting as proxy shareholders for their private customers. They are also more likely to have representatives on the boards of companies than do their equivalent in the UK.

4.6.3 Equity ownership patterns

From an accounting perspective, what is important is not only the size of the equity market but also its micro-structure. The amount of active trading that occurs, and the types of traders that exist, affect the level of demand for both financial information in general and for particular types of information. For example, if individual small shareholders are active investors then there will be more demand for financial statements orientated to relatively unsophisticated shareholders. If most shares are owned by a small number of pension funds or investment trusts then more emphasis will probably be placed on investor–corporate relationships. Important concerns may then be the protection of private shareholders and the prevention of insider trading.

Exhibit 4.6 provides some information on the popularity of share ownership in eight countries.

Exhibit 4.6	Percentage of individuals owning shares

	1980s	1990–96	1997	1998	1999	2000	2001	2002
Australia	N/A	N/A	20	32	41	40	N/A	37
Hong Kong	N/A	'94 10	16	N/A	16	21	20	20
Korea	N/A	'95 5	6	7	9	9	8	8
Germany	'88 7	'94 6	6	7	8	10	9	8
Switzerland	N/A	N/A	N/A	N/A	N/A	32	N/A	24
Sweden	N/A	N/A	N/A	N/A	N/A	22	22	21
UK	N/A	N/A	28	24	25	25	24	22
Canada	'86 18	'96 37	N/A	N/A	N/A	49	N/A	46

Note: 'The results are not directly comparable because of different time periods in which the data were collected, different definitions, methodologies, sources, and different sample selections, sizes and treatment.' (page 2)

Source: 'International Share Ownership', Australian Stock Exchange, June 2003, p. 2.

The proportion of the population owning shares has tended to remain remarkably stable in most countries over the last few years, and there remain some significant differences across countries. Private share ownership appears particularly common in North America and Australia. In contrast, only approximately one in five of the population in the UK, Switzerland, Sweden or Hong Kong own shares while the figure is much lower in Germany despite its relatively high standard of living. While this table tells us something about the number of individuals owning shares, a more important determinant of the demand for accounting information is the relative importance of private shareholders and other types of shareholders as providers of finance. That is, not only are the number of shareholders important but also important is the size of their shareholdings. Unfortunately, up-to-date information on this is far more difficult to obtain as it is not routinely collected by stock markets. To give some idea of the differences that can be found across countries Exhibit 4.7 gives some data on three very different countries – Sweden, Japan and Thailand. What is most apparent here is simply the differences across the three countries.

The most important differences lie in the relative importance of individuals, financial institutions and non-financial corporations. Thailand shows what is probably a fairly typical picture for a developing country, with most shares owned by individuals or foreigners, with non-financial enterprises holding a much smaller proportion of the stock

Exhibit 4.7	Share ownership in Sweden, Japan and Thailand (all figures are percentages)

	Sweden (2002)	Japan (2003)	Thailand (2003)
Household	18.3	20.5	32.3
Non-financial enterprises	8.0	21.8	15.0
Financial enterprises	30.6	34.5	7.4
Public sector	8.8	0.2	3.6
Foreigners	33.7	21.8	24.8
Other	–	8.7	7.6
Total	100	100	100

Source: World Federation of Stock Exchanges web pages. www.world-exchanges.org

market and financial institutions being a very minor player. Sweden and Japan are more typical of developed countries although it is noticeable how much more important non-financial enterprises are in Japan than in Sweden. This reflects the fact that Japanese companies will often hold, on a long-term basis, relatively small shareholdings in companies in the same group of companies that they do business with to show their long-term commitment and shared interests in maintaining good relationships.

4.7 The accounting profession

A further important influence on the regulation and practice of accounting may be the accounting profession itself. The size, role, organization and importance of the accounting profession all result from the interplay of the various factors discussed earlier in this chapter. For example, the role of the auditor and the way in which the profession is regulated (whether by government or self-regulation) both depend upon the type of legal system in place. Likewise, the importance of the profession – in terms of who it audits and how many audits are conducted – depends upon the types and numbers of companies that exist.

The profession in turn influences the institutions of a country and its accounting system. The way in which the profession is organized and society's attitude towards accountants and auditors will tend to affect auditors' ability to influence or control the behaviour of companies and their reporting systems. The extent to which auditors are independent and their power relative to the companies which they audit are important here. Whether auditors are seen as being independent, powerful professionals, or instead are seen as being under the control or influence of the companies they audit will affect the perceived value of financial statements, and this will happen even if these perceptions are wrong.

4.7.1 Size of the accounting profession

Some idea of the size of the accounting profession in a range of countries can be seen from the data given in Exhibit 4.8. This illustrates some very large differences. The most extreme difference emerges between the UK and Germany: there are approximately 189,000 financial accountants in the UK and Ireland and only 10,000 in Germany. While this example is commonly discussed, it is somewhat misleading. The UK figures are overstated when compared to most other countries. It is common for people to retain membership of an accounting body even if they have moved into industry or commerce – or, indeed, even retired – and this accounts for at least one-half of the UK and Ireland figures. Movement from accounting into industry or commerce on qualification or relatively soon after gaining full membership of an accounting body is common in the UK. In contrast, the German figure is considerably understated compared to most other countries. There are many more tax experts (*Steuerberater*) than accountants (*Wirtschaftsprüfer*). Also excluded from these figures are a second tier of auditors who can audit only private companies. The typical role of the accountant is also smaller in countries such as Germany than in the UK. Many of the tasks undertaken by professional accountants in the UK are undertaken by engineers, lawyers or other professionals in much of Western Europe with the term 'accountant' being more synonymous with the role of the auditor in the UK. However, while some of the differences in the size of the profession are explicable by methods of definition, large differences still remain. In particular, it remains true that the profession tends to be relatively larger in the Commonwealth and the US than it is in Western Europe or Japan.

Exhibit 4.8	The accountancy profession in selected countries

Country	Professional body	Year start	Size	Population (m)
Australia	Institute of Chartered Accountants of Australia (ICAA)	1885	39,100	19.3
	Australian Society of Certified Public Accountants (ASCPA)	1886	102,000	
China	Chinese Institute of Certified Public Accountants	1988	129,000	1,285
France	Ordre des Experts-Comptables et des Comptables Agrées (OECCA)	1952	16,000	59.5
Germany	Institut der Wirtschaftsprüfer (IdW)	1931	10,000	82.0
India	Institute of Chartered Accountants of India	1949	88,400	1,025.1
Japan	Japanese Institute of Certified Public Accountants (JICPA)	1927	13,200	127.3
Netherlands	Nederlands Instituut van Registeraccountants (NIvRA)	1895	13,000	15.9
UK & Ireland*	Institute of Chartered Accountants in England & Wales (ICAEW)	1880	105,800 121,400	63.3
	Institute of CA of Scotland (ICAS)	1854	12,900 15,000	
	Institute of CA of Ireland (ICAI)	1888	11,200 12,500	
	Association of Chartered Certified Accountants (ACCA)	1891	49,100 86,900	
USA	American Institute of Certified Public Accountants (AICPA)	1927	336,800	285.9

* For UK and Ireland the first figure represents number of members in the UK and Ireland and the second figure is the total number of members.

Not only are there major variations in the size of the profession, but there are also a number of other important differences. There are differences in the degree of the profession's independence – in most of the common law countries the profession has traditionally been largely self-regulating, taking responsibility for the licensing of accountants or auditors, including setting entry requirements, training and examinations. (In recent years this self-regulation has been moderated by the establishment of Oversight Boards having statutory powers, for example the PCAOB in the US, as described in section 3.2.3.1.) In contrast, in the code law countries many of these roles are carried out by the state. Similar differences exist with respect to control of the audit – who determines auditing guidelines or standards, and under what authority auditors act.

4.7.2 Accountants' role in regulation

Accounting regulations may or may not be set by the profession. As discussed above, in code law countries accounting regulations are generally set by the government. However, even here the profession often plays a role. It may act as an adviser to the government, providing input into the regulatory process. It may issue standards or recommendations in areas where there are no legal regulations. It may issue pronouncements that explain or expand government regulations. The French profession in the form of the OEC and the CNCC provides a good example of this approach (as discussed in Chapter 10).

In common law countries, the regulation of accounting tends to be delegated by the government to an independent body. The Financial Accounting Standards Board (FASB) in the US, the Australian Accounting Standards Board (AASB) and the UK Accounting Standards Board (ASB) are examples. However, these distinctions are becoming blurred with the establishment of standard-setting bodies such as the German Accounting Standards Board (see section 10.3.3) and the Accounting Standards Board of Japan (see section 12.3.5).

4.8 Other influences

There are a number of other factors which have affected various accounting rules and practices in one or more countries. Particularly important are:

- religion,
- accidents of history,
- the exporting or imposition of accounting rules or practices by more powerful or sophisticated societies,
- the importing of accounting rules or practices from another country or countries.

4.8.1 Religion

The most obvious example of the influence of religion on accounting is with respect to Islam, and in particular, Islamic banking. There has been a significant increase in Islamic banking since it started in the 1960s in Egypt. Now, even several global western banks such as Deutsche Bank and Citibank offer Islamic banking services to their customers.

The most obvious difference from western or secular banks is that under Islamic law, riba or usury is considered to be wrong. This means that banks cannot charge interest. Instead, they have set up a range of alternatives that are designed to share both risks and returns between the borrower and the lender. Also, in manner similar to western ethical funds, the banks will not invest in organizations that do not follow Quranic injunctions. In this case, they will not invest in or lend to non-Islamic banks and companies involved in alcohol, gambling, or rearing pigs.

This obviously affects accounting as there will be no loans or interest, but instead 'participations' and 'investment accounts'. There is considerable debate about whether or not specific accounting standards are required or whether instead IFRS are sufficient. However, many Islamic financial institutions use the accounting standards issued by the Accounting and Auditing Organization for Islamic Financial Institutions rather than IFRS. This organisation was setup in 1993 in Bahrain and has issued 16 standards to date.[14]

---

[14] Drummond (2001); Karim (2001).

4.8.2 Accidents of history

There are numerous examples of accounting rules or practices originating from shocks to the system or accidents of history. For example, much of the early UK company law legislation, including accounting regulations, was the result of financial crises or collapse of companies. Other more significant examples of major economic shocks include the collapse of the US and German stock markets in the 1920s. Similar events in the two countries resulted in very different institutions and regulations. In the US the collapse of the stock market led to the creation of the SEC and increased accounting regulations to protect and encourage share ownership (see section 8.3.1). In Germany, the collapse of the stock market and the resulting increase in debt financing led to regulations which were focused upon creditor protection. The Asian economic crisis of 1997 was a major shock across several countries (see section 3.2) but the most significant shock of recent years for accounting was the failure of the US company Enron (see section 3.2 and Chapter 8).

4.8.3 The exporting/imposition of accounting

Accounting regulations and practices have always been exported and imported from the earliest days of double-entry bookkeeping. Exporting occurs for a number of reasons.[15] The profession itself has always been one source. For example, Price Waterhouse started in London in 1849, but then opened offices in New York and Chicago before it opened its second UK office in Liverpool in 1904. Several US accounting firms were set up by UK-trained accountants. This movement of accountants led to many early similarities between accounting in the UK and the US. International trade in accountants and accounting firms continues to the present time, with the larger firms being active worldwide. This means that they often export their accounting and auditing standards and these are then used where there are no local regulations.

A second major factor in the export of accounting has been colonialism. The UK and France exported many of their legal and administrative structures and their educational systems to their colonies. Following independence, local factors have become more important and the influence of the former colonial powers has declined.[16] But many institutions have not changed very much. For example, all of the Caribbean Economic Community (CARICOM) members (which are English-speaking, former British colonies), with the one exception of Barbados, have Company Acts based upon various UK Companies Acts ranging from the 1829 Act to the 1948 Act.[17] Similar influences can also be seen in the former French colonies of Africa which use accounting codes based upon the French code.[18]

Depending upon the history of a country, the accounting system may show evidence of many different influences. For example, as will be discussed in Chapter 11, Japanese accounting regulations reflect the exporting of both German and US regulations. One particularly interesting example of a country influenced by a large number of other countries

---

[15] See, for example, Parker (1989).

[16] Cooke and Wallace (1990), China and Poullaos (2002).

[17] Chaderton and Taylor (1993).

[18] United Nations (1991).

is Turkey. (See Case study 4.1 for a description of the various external influences on the Turkish accounting system.) Another example of a group of countries that has been influenced by a variety of more developed systems are the ASEAN countries. (See Case study 4.2 for information on these.)

4.8.4 The importing of accounting

Countries may have sought to retain the exported accounting systems in the face of forces for indigenisation of accounting.[19] Alternatively, they may instead have sought actively to import accounting regulations or practices. This may have been done because developing accounting rules is both expensive and time-consuming. It is much less costly to see what other countries have done and to select those rules that most suit your own needs. Thus countries may import an entire set of rules, or specific rules only. The countries of Eastern Europe are a good example of the importation of accounting. Having overthrown communism they sought links with the EU and faced the task of completely overhauling their accounting systems. Most already had a chart of accounts in place from the previous regime, as a basis for bookkeeping, but their accounting regulations had to be rewritten. They tended to look to the countries of Western Europe and the EU for models of regulation. Consequently they imported aspects of EU accounting as well as IASB accounting.[20] In a similar way, individual companies may also import accounting practices from other countries or from the IASB. Below are some examples of the accounting policies used by some European companies:

Use of IFRS compatible local rules and US rules by German companies: Allianz Group (2003):
In accordance with section 292a of the German Commercial Code (HGB) the consolidated financial statements have been prepared in conformity with International Financial Reporting Standards (IFRS). All standards currently in force for the years under review have been adopted in the presentation of the consolidated financial statements.
. . . IFRS do not provide specific guidance concerning the reporting of insurance transactions in annual financial statements. In such cases as envisioned in the IFRS Framework, the provisions embodied under accounting principles generally accepted in the United States of America (US GAAP) have been applied.

Use of IFRS and local rules by Finnish companies: Nokia (2003)
The consolidated financial statements of Nokia Corporation, a Finnish limited liability company with domicile in Helsinki, are prepared in accordance with International Accounting Standards (IAS). The consolidated financial statements are presented in millions of euro (EURm), except as noted, and are prepared under the historical cost convention except as disclosed in the accounting policies below. The notes to the consolidated financial statements also conform with Finnish Accounting legislation.

Use of US GAAP by Dutch companies: Royal Dutch Petroleum Company (2003)
Previously published Financial Statements were presented based on accounting policies which were in accordance with Netherlands and US in all material respects. With effect from 2003, the financial statements are presented in accordance with US GAAP, with separate financial statements presented under Netherlands GAAP.

---

[19] Annisette (2000).

[20] See, for example, King *et al.* (2001) or Daniel *et al.* (2001).

Summary and conclusions

This chapter has provided an overview of many of the factors that influence accounting. It is always dangerous to generalize too much; there will always be exceptions to any generalizations, and there will always be countries that do not follow the typical pattern. As long as this is recognized, there are enough similarities across countries to make generalizations possible. Therefore, in this chapter we have seen how accounting rules and practices are influenced by a large number of quite different factors. Particularly important are the following:

- the political and economic system,
- the legal system,
- the taxation system,
- the corporate financing system,
- the accounting profession.

Finally, we also saw how a country may import and export accounting rules and practices.

Key points from the chapter:

- There is no simple universal relationship between any particular institution and the accounting system. All the factors identified are important as are their interactions.
- Accounting and accountants are influenced by the institutions of a country and by external influences and they in turn can also influence a country's institutions in many complex and changing ways.
- The political and economic system, the taxation system and the corporate financing system all tend to influence the demand for accounting information and the objectives served by the financial reporting system.
- The most important users of financial statements may be shareholders or they may be creditors or taxation authorities.
- The type of legal system a country has and the strength of the accounting profession tend to influence who regulates accounting, and the rigidity of the regulations.
- The regulatory structures and the users both tend in turn to influence the specific measurement rules adopted and the extent of disclosures made, whether mandatory or voluntary.

Case study 4.1 Accounting in Turkey: external influences

Legal requirements that affected accounting entered Turkish business life for the first time with the adoption of the Commercial Code (Law on Commerce) in 1850, which was a translation of the first and third books of the French Commercial Code. By 1864, translation of the whole of the French Commercial Code had been completed.

From 1850 until about 1925, the impact of French accounting on Turkish accounting practice was significant. This was because most of the instructors or authors on accounting and tax in Turkey had received their accounting education in France. Since Italian accounting principles were largely adopted by the French, the so-called Italian System of Accounting practised in Turkey was first introduced through French publications.

In 1926 a new Commercial Code was introduced based mainly on the Commercial Codes of Italy and Germany. However, sections of the new code were taken from the Commercial Codes of Belgium, France, Austria, Hungary, Chile, Argentina, Spain, Romania, Britain and Japan as well as Italy and Germany. The copying of elements of foreign law led to the Turkish Code being piecemeal, and it was therefore not as effective as planned.

During the period 1926–60, Turkish accounting practice was considerably influenced by German accounting. This influence became more pronounced after several well-known German management and accounting professionals emigrated to Turkey in the early 1930s, fleeing the Nazi regime in Germany. In this period, most of the students going abroad went to Germany for accounting education and many Turkish state economic enterprises employed German consultants for the reorganisation of their accounting systems. Another German influence on the Turkish accounting system was the introduction of income tax based on the 1950 German model.

After the defeat of Germany in the Second World War the USA emerged as the main influence. Of particular importance was the Marshall Plan of economic help which marked the beginning of US business involvement on Turkey. More and more students were sent to the USA for business education and special institutions and programmes were established in Turkey to introduce American management theories and practice. The impact of American accounting practice has been even more pronounced over the last three decades.

Source: Cooke and Curuk (1996), p. 341.
European Accounting Review, Taylor & Francis www.tandf.co.uk/journals

Case study 4.2 Accounting in ASEAN: external influences

The comparative analysis of national corporate and companies law within ASEAN suggests four patterns of development: (1) A British approach (adopted by Brunei, Malaysia and Singapore); (2) A Dutch approach (adopted by Indonesia); (3) A US approach (adopted by the Philippines); and (4) A mixed-country approach (adopted by Thailand). Accordingly, Brunei, Malaysia and Singapore (all former British colonies), have each adopted a Companies Act modelled on the UK Companies Act 1948 and the Australian Uniform Companies Act 1961. However, the Companies Act of Singapore has undergone considerable changes since first enacted in 1967. Indonesian Commercial Code, 1848, was patterned on the early Dutch Commercial Code with some minor amendments. Under this system, law is codified, and company legislation prescribes rules in details for accounting and financial reporting. Unfortunately, many of the amendments that have been made in The Netherlands since 1848 were not incorporated in the commercial code in Indonesia. As a result, Indonesia is operating an out of date commercial code adopted in the nineteenth century that is incomputable with today's commercial environment. . . . It is therefore obvious that company laws in ASEAN have been affected strongly by each country's former colonial links despite the appropriateness of such legislation to its environment. [The] British group (Brunei, Malaysia, Singapore) was mainly influenced by [the] British, and [the] non-British group (mainly the Philippines, Thailand and Indonesia)

▶

Case study 4.2 *(Continued)*

was influenced by [the] US, Japan, The Netherlands and Germany, reflecting its important trading links with these major economic powers during the late 1800s and early 1900s. With this backdrop, it is obvious that accounting practice which is a product of accounting education and training in ASEAN has been structured based on the corporate legal environment created by colonial powers during their administration without due regard to local needs and conditions.

Source: Yapa (2003), p.270 (references excluded from quote).

Questions

The following questions test your understanding of the material contained in the chapter and allow you to relate your understanding to the learning outcomes specified at the start of this chapter. The learning outcomes are repeated here. Each question is cross-referenced to the relevant section of the chapter.

Understand how various aspects of a country's political and economic system have influenced its accounting system

1 What are the main institutional influences on accounting practices in general? (section 4.2)

2 Which of the influences identified above are most important in your country? (section 4.2)

3 Why might the importance of the various influences identified differ across countries and over time? (section 4.2)

4 To what extent has the importance of the influences identified above varied over time in your country? (section 4.2)

5 How does the political and economic system of your country fit into the classifications described? (section 4.3)

6 How might the type of political and economic system of a country influence the accounting regulatory system? (section 4.3)

7 How might the type of political and economic system of a country influence the types of accounting measurement rules adopted? (section 4.3)

8 How might the type of political and economic system of a country influence the type of accounting disclosure rules adopted? (section 4.3)

9 How might the type of political and economic system of a country influence the type of accounting measurement and disclosure practices voluntarily adopted by companies? (section 4.3)

Distinguish between common and code law systems and describe how the legal system typically influences the system of accounting regulation

10 How does the legal system of your country fit into the classifications described? (section 4.4)

11 How might the type of legal system of a country influence the accounting regulatory system? (section 4.4)

12 How might the type of legal system of a country influence the types of accounting measurement rules adopted? (section 4.4)

13 How might the type of legal system of a country influence the type of accounting disclosure rules adopted? (section 4.4)

14 How might the type of legal system of a country influence the type of accounting measurement and disclosure practices voluntarily adopted by companies? (section 4.4)

Describe the ways in which the tax system can influence accounting rules and practices

15 How does the taxation system of your country compare to the descriptions given? (section 4.5)

16 How might the type of taxation system of a country influence the accounting regulatory system? (section 4.5)

17 How might the type of taxation system of a country influence the types of accounting measurement rules adopted? (section 4.5)

18 How might the type of taxation system of a country influence the type of accounting disclosure rules adopted? (section 4.5)

Identify possible differences in the financing of companies internationally and describe how these differences may help to explain differences in accounting rules and practices

19 How does the corporate financing system of your country compare to the descriptions given? (section 4.6)

20 How might the type of corporate financing system of a country influence the accounting regulatory system? (section 4.6)

21 How might the type of corporate financing system of a country influence the types of accounting measurement rules adopted? (section 4.6)

22 How might the type of corporate financing system of a country influence the type of accounting disclosure rules adopted? (section 4.6)

23 How might the type of corporate financing system of a country influence the type of accounting measurement and disclosure practices voluntarily adopted by companies? (section 4.6)

Understand how the way in which the accounting profession is organized can influence accounting rules and practices

24 How does the accounting profession in your country compare to the descriptions given? (section 4.7)

25 How might the type of accounting profession of a country influence the accounting regulatory system? (section 4.7)

26 How might the type of accounting profession of a country influence the types of accounting measurement rules adopted? (section 4.7)

27 How might the type of accounting profession of a country influence the type of accounting disclosure rules adopted? (section 4.7)

Understand how a country might import or export accounting rules and practices

28 How do the external influences on accounting practice in your country compare to those described? (section 4.8)

29 How might external influences on a country influence the accounting regulatory system? (section 4.8)

30 How might external influences on a country influence the types of accounting measurement rules adopted? (section 4.8)

31 How might external influences on a country influence the type of accounting disclosure rules adopted? (section 4.8)

32 How might external influences on a country influence the type of accounting measurement and disclosure practices voluntarily adopted by companies? (section 4.8)

References and further reading

Annisette, M. (2000) 'Imperialism and the professions: The education and certification of Accountants in Trinidad and Tobago', *Accounting, Organizations and Society*, 25: 631–659.

Australian Stock Exchange (June 2003) *International Share Ownership (Comparison of Share Owners)*, ASX.

Chaderton, R. and Taylor, P.J. (1993) 'Accounting systems of the Caribbean: Their evolution and role in economic growth and development', *Research in Third World Accounting*, 2: 45–66.

Chua, W.F. and Poullaos, C. (2002) 'The Empire Strikes Back? An exploration of centre–periphery interaction between the ICAEW and accounting associations in the self-governing colonies of Australia, Canada and South Africa, 1880–1907', *Accounting, Organizations and Society*, 27: 409–445.

Chui, A.C.W., Lloyd, A.E. and Kwok, C.C.Y. (2002) 'The determination of capital structure: Is national culture the missing piece to the puzzle?', *Journal of International Business Studies*, 33.1: 99–127.

Cooke, T.E. and Curuk, T. (1996) 'Accounting in Turkey with reference to the particular problems of lease transactions', *European Accounting Review*, 5(2): 339–359.

Cooke, T.E. and Wallace, R.S.O. (1990) 'Financial disclosure regulation and its environment: A review and further analysis', *Journal of Accounting and Public Policy*, 9: 79–110.

Daniel, P., Suranova, V.Z. and de Beedle, I. (2001) 'The development of accounting in Slovakia', *European Accounting Review*, 10(2): 343–359.

Doupnik, T.S. (1987) 'The Brazilian system of monetary correction', *Advances in International Accounting*, 1: 111–35.

Doupnik, T.S. and Salter, S.B. (1995) 'External environment, culture, and accounting practice: A preliminary test of a general model of international accounting development', *International Journal of Accounting*, 30(4): 189–207.

Drummond, J. (2001) 'A risk-free return? Its forbidden', *Accountancy*, April, 98–99.

Hope, T. and Gray, R. (1982) 'Power and policy making: the development of an R&D standard', *Journal of Business Finance and Accounting*, 9(4): 531–558.

Karim, R.A.A. (2001) 'International accounting harmonization, banking regulations and Islamic banks', *The International Journal of Accounting*, 36: 169–193.

King, N., Beattie, A., Critescu, A-M. and Weetman, P. (2001) 'Developing accounting and audit in a transition economy', *European Accounting Review*, 10(1): 149–171.

Parker, R.H. (1989) 'Importing and exporting accounting: The British experience', in Hopwood, A.G. (ed.), *International Pressures for International Change*. London: Prentice Hall/ICAEW, 7–29.

Puxty, A.G., Willmott, H.C., Cooper, D.J. and Lowe, T. (1987) 'Modes of regulation in advanced capitalism: Locating accountancy in four countries', *Accounting, Organisations and Society*, 12(3), 273–291.

United Nations (1991) *Accountancy Developments in Africa: Challenge of the 1990s*. New York: United Nations CTC.

Wagenhofer, A. (2001) 'Austria – Individual accounts', in Ordelheide, D. and KPMG (ed.), *Transnational Accounting*, 2nd edn. London: Macmillan.

Yapa, P.W.S. (2003) 'Accounting education and training in ASEAN: The Western influence and the experience of Singapore, Malaysia, Indonesia and Brunei Darussalam', *Research in Accounting in Emerging Economies*, 5: 267–292.

Zeff, S.A. (1972) *Forging Accounting Principles in Five Countries*. Champaign, IL: Stipes Publishing.

5 Cultural influences on accounting rules and practices

Learning outcomes

After reading this chapter you should be able to:

- Understand what is meant by the term 'culture', and describe the cultural dimensions identified by a number of different researchers.

- Describe the relationship between culture and organizational structures.

- Describe the accounting values identified by Gray, and explain how they might be related to culture.

● Evaluate research which has used these accounting values and assess their significance for those seeking international harmonization.

5.1 Introduction

In Chapter 4 we looked at a range of institutions that can influence accounting rules and practices, and saw how they help to explain why accounting has differed across countries. However, this is not the whole story. This chapter looks at another influence on accounting, namely culture – both the culture of a country and the culture or subculture of accountants.

The institutions of a country are set up and run by people. Accounting regulations are similarly set up by people and accounting is carried out by people. Different people often think and act in different ways. They have different tastes, different beliefs and different attitudes. However, these are not completely random: people often share many similar tastes, beliefs and attitudes. While we will define 'culture' more fully below, we can think of these common attributes as the 'common culture' of a group. The group which shares such a common culture may be the country or society as a whole, or it may be a smaller group of people such as accountants!

If we return to the influences on an accounting system, a similar model is reproduced in Exhibit 5.1. We can see how accounting may be affected or influenced by societal culture and accounting culture. Differences in the culture of a society are reflected in the ways in which society organizes itself. The factors discussed in the previous chapter, namely the ways in which the economic system is organized, the ways in which companies are set up, controlled and financed, the legal system and the organization of professions are all influenced by the culture of the country. But culture also has a more direct influence on accounting. It influences account preparers, regulators, auditors and users, and so influences the types of rules they set out and the practices they follow.

This chapter goes on to explain more fully what is meant by 'culture'. It then looks at some of the evidence on cultural differences across societies, exploring ways in which culture can affect business – in particular how it affects the ways in which businesses are organized, who makes decisions in organizations and what motivates employees. Finally, the cultural values of accountants are discussed and the possible links between accounting and culture are explored.

5.2 Defining culture

5.2.1 The culture of a country

'Culture' in the sense that it is used here refers to the set of common ideas, beliefs and values that are shared by the members of a group of individuals. There are very many alternative definitions of culture and much work has been done in describing and measuring various aspects of culture. However, in the business and accounting literature, the most important work is undoubtedly that carried out by Hofstede, an organizational psychologist. He defined culture as 'the collective programming of the mind which distinguishes the members of one human group from another'.[1]

This definition highlights three important points about culture.

---

[1] Hofstede (1984).

| Exhibit 5.1 | The influences on an accounting system |

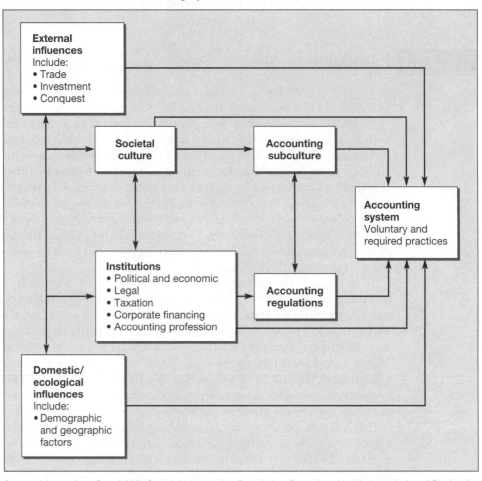

Source: Adapted from Gray (1988). Copyright Accounting Foundation. Reproduced by kind permission of Blackwell Publishers

- Culture is collective, rather than being a characteristic of any one individual.
- It is not directly observable, but it can be inferred from people's behaviour.
- It is of interest only to the extent that it helps to differentiate between groups – due to cultural differences, groups will behave in different and definable ways.

Cultural differences exist at a number of different levels. Hofstede identified four:

1 *Symbols* are the most superficial of the four: they comprise words, gestures, pictures or objects that have particular meanings for a cultural group. An example might be the meaning that different societies tend to attach to Coca-Cola. Coca-Cola can be seen as the most obvious thing to drink on a hot day, or it may be seen as a drink only suitable for the young. It may be seen as being desirable, indicating sophistication and affluence, or it may be seen as an unwelcome example of US international dominance.

2 *Heroes* are individuals (whether real or imaginary) who embody those characteristics that are particularly prized by a society (e.g. Superman in the US, Asterix in France or Tintin in Belgium).

3 At the next level are *rituals* or activities that, of themselves, have little or no extrinsic value but have an essential social or intrinsic value. They range from simple rituals, such as different forms of greeting, through to more complex and formalized rituals such as the Japanese tea ceremony, through to apparently purposive activities such as the ways in which business meetings are conducted. (Indeed, it has been argued[2] that much of accounting is a ritual.)

4 The final core level of culture are *values*. These may be thought of as preferences for particular states of being. Examples include views about what is good or evil, natural or unnatural, desirable or undesirable and honest or dishonest. This does not, of course, mean that everyone acts on these beliefs or that they describe everyone's personal preferences. Instead, they describe general beliefs or social norms.

5.2.2 Subcultures

Culture in terms of shared beliefs and values exists at many levels. There is societal culture or the culture of a country. Inside any country there are a number of distinct, although overlapping, groups with their own cultures (usually referred to as 'subcultures' to distinguish them from the culture of the society as a whole). Different regional areas and ethnic or religious groups may share distinct subcultures. At the level of the company there will also be an organizational or corporate subculture. Indeed, one way that a company can successfully manage uncertainty or instability is by developing a well-defined corporate culture: everyone in the organization should then know and internalize the company's aims, will know what is expected of them and how they should react. This reduces the need for written rules, regulations and procedures and it helps employees to make better decisions in new or unusual circumstances.[3] In addition, each work group and profession, including accountants and the accounting profession, will have its own subculture.

5.2.3 The dimensions of culture

Culture is a complex phenomenon, too complex to be easily described or measured. However, there have been many attempts to unbundle it into a number of underlying dimensions, each of which is less complex. Each dimension covers one aspect of culture which has then been described, measured and quantified. Different cultural or subcultural groups have then been measured on each dimension and compared with each other. There have been a large number of attempts at doing this and while they disagree upon the precise dimensions or factors that are relevant, they all agree that a small number of dimensions or factors are sufficient to compare and describe societies.

The earliest of these attempts was by Kluckholn and Strodtbeck (1961) who used six dimensions developed from asking questions about societies, as shown in Exhibit 5.2. Another anthropologist, Edward Hall, also carried out similar work focusing instead upon only four questions, also shown in Exhibit 5.2.

In what is still the largest cross-country study of employees of any one organization (IBM), Hofstede developed four cultural dimensions, as reproduced in Exhibit 5.3. It is

---

[2] Gambling (1987).

[3] Balaga and Jaeger (1984).

Exhibit 5.2 Possible cultural dimensions

Questions asked by Kluckholn and Strodtbeck:

1 What do members of a society assume about the nature of people? (Good, bad, or some combination?)

2 What do members of a society assume about the relationship between people and the environment? (Live in harmony or subjugate environment?)

3 What do members of a society assume about the relationship between people? (Act as individual, member of group or collective?)

4 What is the primary mode of being? (Accept status quo or not?)

5 What is the conception of space? (Amount of personal space? Public expression of emotions?)

6 What is the dominant temporal orientation? (Past, present or future?)

Dimensions used by Hall:

1 Context: The amount of information that must be explicitly stated if a message or communication is to be successful.

2 Space: Ways of communicating through the specific handling of personal space.

3 Time: Monochronic or sequential handling of tasks versus polychronic or the simultaneous handling of tasks.

4 Information flow: Structure and speed of messages between individuals and organizations.

Source: Taken from: Gannon *et al*. (1994).

Exhibit 5.3 Cultural dimensions identified by Hofstede (1984)

Individualism versus collectivism
Individualism stands for a preference for a loosely knit social framework in society wherein individuals are supposed to take care of themselves and their immediate families only. Its opposite, collectivism, stands for a preference for a tightly knit social framework in which individuals can expect their relatives, clan, or other in-group to look after them in exchange for unquestioning loyalty . . . The fundamental issue addressed by this dimension is the degree of interdependence a society maintains among individuals. It relates to people's self-concept: 'I' or 'we'.

Large versus small power distance
Power distance is the extent to which the members of a society accept that power in institutions is distributed unequally. This affects the behaviour of the less powerful as well as of the more powerful members of society. People in large-power-distance societies accept a hierarchical order in which everybody has a place which needs no further justification. People in small-power-distance societies strive for power equalization and demand justification for power inequalities. The fundamental issue addressed by this dimension is how a society handles inequalities among people when they occur.

Strong versus weak uncertainty avoidance
Uncertainty avoidance is the degree to which the members of a society feel uncomfortable with uncertainty and ambiguity. This feeling leads to beliefs promising certainty and to maintaining institutions protecting conformity. Strong uncertainty-avoidance societies maintain rigid codes of

▶

belief and behaviour and are intolerant towards deviant persons and ideas. Weak uncertainty-avoidance societies maintain a more relaxed atmosphere in which practice counts more than principles and deviance is easily tolerated. The fundamental issue addressed by this dimension is how a society reacts to the fact that time runs only one way and that the future is unknown: whether it tries to control the future or to let it happen.

Masculinity versus femininity (low versus high nurturing)
Masculinity stands for a preference in society for achievement, heroism, assertiveness, and material success. Its opposite, femininity, stands for a preference for relationships, modesty, caring for the weak and the quality of life. The fundamental issue addressed by this dimension is the way in which a society allocates social (as opposed to biological) roles to the sexes.

noteworthy that in this initial work, the four dimensions generated did not, unlike the other two attempts described, include a temporal or time-based dimension.

Hofstede has, rightly, been criticized for his choice of terminology, and in particular the use of the terms 'masculinity versus femininity'. It has been argued by many writers that this terminology reinforces notions of gender differences that may, at best, be considered suspect. Later writers have instead used various terms such as 'human heartedness' or 'nurturing'. Of the alternatives proposed, 'nurturing' best describes the same set of characteristics without ascribing either gender or sex differences to them. We will also use this term instead of masculinity/femininity.

Hofstede measured his four dimensions for each of a range of 50 countries and three geographical groupings of countries.[4] The results obtained by Hofstede for a number of countries discussed in this book are reproduced in Exhibit 5.4. (Note that Hofstede did

| Exhibit 5.4 | Scores and rankings for individual countries from Hofstede's (1984) cultural dimension research |

Country	Individualism versus collectivism		Large power distance versus small power distance		Strong uncertainty avoidance versus weak uncertainty avoidance		Low nurture versus high nurture (masculinity versus femininity in Hofstede)	
	Score	Rank	Score	Rank	Score	Rank	Score	Rank
Australia	90	2	36	41	51	37	61	16
France	71	10/11	68	15/16	86	10/15	43	35/36
Germany	67	15	35	42/44	65	29	66	9/10
Japan	46	22/23	54	33	92	7	95	1
Netherlands	80	4/5	38	40	53	35	14	51
UK	89	3	35	42/44	35	47/48	66	9/10
US	91	1	40	38	46	43	62	15
Arab countries	38	26/27	80	7	68	27	53	23

---
[4] Hofstede (1991).

Exhibit 5.5 Interpretation of Hofstede's scores

Characteristics	Score		Rank	Country
Greatest individualism		91	1	US
Dividing point	50			
Greatest collectivism		6	53	Guatemala
Largest power distance		104	1	Malaysia
Dividing point	44			
Smallest power distance		11	53	Austria
Strongest uncertainty avoidance		112	1	Greece
Dividing point	56			
Weakest uncertainty avoidance		8	53	Singapore
Low nurturing		95	1	Japan
Dividing point	50			
High nurturing		5	53	Sweden

not look at China nor indeed at any of the other then Communist countries, and he looked at only one African country, South Africa, and one Arab country, Iran.)

The interpretation of these scores and rankings is set out in Exhibit 5.5. Hofstede used cluster analysis to identify groupings of countries and from his clusters proposed dividing lines separating one of the pairs of characteristics from the other. Exhibit 5.5 also sets out the dividing points specified by Hofstede. For example, any country scoring more than 50 on the individualism/collectivism dimension could be described as being individualistic. Countries scoring less than 50 would instead be described as being collectivist.

5.2.4 Critique of Hofstede's work

While many researchers in accounting and management have used Hofstede's work, it has not been uncritically received. There has been much debate regarding its usefulness. Some of the criticisms made arise because researchers and writers have used the cultural dimensions or the scores provided by Hofstede in an inappropriate manner, although other criticisms are much more fundamental, calling into question the usefulness of Hofstede's work for understanding culture.

Hofstede (1991) has warned against the inappropriate use of his work. In particular, it must always be remembered that the dimensions are intended to discriminate between national cultures and not between individuals. The 'average' or 'typical' individual does not exist and cultural stereotypes can be more misleading than helpful. Hofstede also argues that the dimensions are not intended to discriminate between sub-cultural groups such as those based upon gender, generation, social class or organization. This might seem to suggest that Hofstede would not support the application of his work to the accounting subgroup as done by Gray. However, this is not what Hofstede is arguing. Gray uses the work to discriminate between accountants or accounting in different countries, a valid comparison, and does not use them to, for example, discriminate between accountants and lawyers in the UK, an invalid use of Hofstede's work.

More fundamental problems with using Hofstede's scores for work seeking to explain accounting differences include the fact that the study took place over the period 1968–72, so it is now more than 30 years old. Over this period, the world has witnessed major changes. In many areas, cultures have moved towards each other, with American cultural values gaining in global importance, while at the same time, other aspects of local or country-specific cultures are gaining more local prominence.[5] In addition, it was administered amongst employees in IBM. IBM was quite a unique company, with very strong corporate culture and therefore it tended to attract certain types of employees.[6] The cultural sub-culture of IBM would have been quite strong, so reducing the size of inter-country differences found in the study. Finally, the study was administered by individuals from a limited range of countries. To quote Hofstede:

> The IBM survey . . . used a questionnaire composed by Western minds. The team that first composed it contained British, Dutch, French, Norwegian, and US members. If the arguments . . . about the cultural relativity of practices and theories are taken seriously, then this restrictive Western input into the research instrument should be a matter of concern. When the surveys were administered, not only Western but also non-Western respondents were confronted with Western questions. They dutifully answered them, but could the results really be supposed to express their values to the full? As a consequence of our own research findings, we [the researchers] have worried about this limitation of our instruments.
>
> (1991, p. 160)

Evidence on this is offered by Michael Bond who developed the Chinese Value Survey (CVS).[7] This was designed to have a Chinese bias, being developed with the help of researchers from Taiwan and Hong Kong and then administered to students in 23 countries worldwide. The CVS again found four significant factors or dimensions – human heartedness, moral discipline, integration and long-term orientation. The first three of these were significantly correlated to three of Hofstede's dimensions, although it is important to realise that they are not direct or one-to-one alternatives or substitutes for Hofstede's dimensions. The most directly comparable was 'human heartedness', significantly related to only one of Hofstede's dimensions – nurturing. 'Moral discipline' and 'integration' were both found to be significantly correlated to the same two of Hofstede's dimensions – power distance and individualism. In contrast, none of the CVS dimensions correlate with uncertainty avoidance which appears not to be universal but instead is unique to western societies. Instead the CVS derived a different dimension – 'Confucian dynamism' or long-term orientation (LTO). This is more similar to the temporal dimension developed by Kluckholn and Strodtbeck. Exhibit 5.6 illustrates the main differences between short- and long-term orientation while Exhibit 5.7 gives the ranks for a number of different countries.

A final criticism of the application of Hofstede's work in empirical studies concerns data availability. While the mean scores for each country are available, it is really necessary to also know the standard deviation or degree of consensus inside each country. If, when comparing two countries, the level of consensus is low inside each country, then culture is unlikely to be a good predictor of differences in accounting systems, even if the mean cultural scores are quite different. In contrast, if the level of consensus is high, culture might be statistically linked to accounting differences even when the mean scores of the two countries are quite similar.

---

[5] See for example Ellwood (2001) or Steger (2003).

[6] Chposky and Leonis (1988); Slater (2002).

[7] Hofstede and Bond (1988).

Exhibit 5.6 Short- versus long-term orientation

Short-term orientation	Long-term orientation
Respect for traditions	Adaptation of traditions to a modern context
Respect for social and status obligations irrespective of cost	Respect for social and status obligations within limits
Social pressure to keep up with others even if this means overspending	Thrift
Small savings, little money to invest	Large savings, funds available for investment
Quick results expected	Perseverance
Concern with 'face'	Willingness to subordinate oneself for a purpose
Concern with possessing the truth	Concern with respecting the demands of virtue

However, even if these practical problems could be solved by, for example, replicating the study now in a different research setting, it would not escape some more fundamental criticisms of the validity of the approach or the conclusions drawn. For example, Baskerville (2003) criticizes the tendency to equate cultural groups with countries as well as arguing that from either an anthropological or sociological perspective, the quantification, measurement and discussion of cultural dimensions is not the best way to think about culture.[8]

Exhibit 5.7 Scores and rankings for individual countries for long-term orientation

	Long-term orientation	
	Score	Rank
Australia	31	15
China	118	1
Germany	31	14
Hong Kong	96	2
Japan	80	4
Netherlands	44	10
Nigeria	16	22
Pakistan	00	23
Philippines	19	21
Taiwan	87	3
United Kingdom	25	18
United States	29	17

Note: Data is available for 23 countries only.

Source: Hofstede (1991), p. 166.

---

[8] See Hofstede (2003) for a reply to Baskerville.

While Hofstede's work has been used by Trompenaars,[9] he argues that there are several problems both with it and the ways in which it is usually interpreted.[10] One danger is that a number of alternative dimensions are ignored. For example, the extent to which emotions are shown is ignored. This is both because of the statistical techniques used and because of the ethnocentric orientation of the work, as illustrated by the genesis of the additional fifth dimension of short/long-term orientation. In addition it uses linear scales which have two ends, both of which preclude the other value construct. In other words, the use of scales sets up a pair of alternates so that the cultural dimensions become thought of as pairs of opposites. In contrast, Trompenaars argues that each end of the dimension is linked to the other and they should be integrated together and thought of in terms of complementarity rather than in terms of opposition.

5.2.5 Hampden-Turner and Trompenaars' dimensions of culture

This type of argument suggests that while it may be valid to use large questionnaires to generate cultural values, it is not valid to then go further and use these constructs to generate linear scales and then map countries on these scales to form the type of two-by-two classifications discussed earlier in this chapter. Indeed, this is the approach taken by Hampden-Turner and Trompenaars (2000) who have sampled some 46,000 managers in 46 countries including a significant number from the ex-communist world and several from Africa and Asia (that is the countries used gave far less of a developed western world bias than does Hofstede's work). Using questions on moral dilemmas and views of how organizations work they generated six dimensions.

These are:

- Universalism (rules, codes, laws and generalizations) and Particularism (exceptions, special circumstances, unique relations);
- Individualism (personal freedom, human rights, competitiveness) and Communitarianism (social responsibility, harmonious relations, cooperation);
- Specificity (atomistic, reductive analytic, objective) and Diffusion (holistic, elaborative synthetic, relational);
- Achieved status (what you've done, your track record) and Ascribed status (who you are, your potential and connections);
- Inner direction (conscience and convictions are located inside) and Outer direction (examples and influences are located outside);
- Sequential time (time is a race along a set course) and Synchronous time (time is a dance of fine coordinations).

5.2.6 Schwartz's dimensions of culture

As argued earlier, one of the, if not the main, reason why the work of Hofstede has been used so much in management and accounting is that he produced quantified measurements of his cultural dimensions which could be used in empirical testing. However, he is not the only one to do this. For example, this type of approach has also been adopted by Schwartz (1994). Using 41 cultural groups he classified national cultures into six types which in turn were summarized into two cultural dimensions.

---

[9] Trompenaars and Hampden-Turner (1997).
[10] Trompenaars (2003).

The value types may be described in the following terms:

Conservatism includes values that are important in close-knit harmonious relationships, in which the interests of the individual are not viewed as distinct from those of the group. These values are primarily concerned with security, conformity, and tradition.

Intellectual and Affective Autonomy are values likely to be important in a society that views the individual as an autonomous entity entitled to pursue his or her own interests. Intellectual autonomy places an emphasis on self-direction and affective autonomy emphasizes stimulation and hedonism.

Hierarchy stresses the legitimacy of hierarchical role and resource allocation.

Mastery accentuates active mastery of the social environment through self-assertion. Such values promote the active efforts of people to change their surroundings and get ahead of others.

Egalitarian Commitment emphasizes the transcendence of selfish interests. The group of values concerns voluntary commitment to help improve the welfare of other people.

Harmony lays emphasis on harmony with nature.

The two cultural dimensions identified can be described as:

Conservatism. This dimension focuses on the extent to which society views the individual as an autonomous entity or as embedded in a social group. Conservatism occurs in societies where values such as harmony and propriety in person-to-group relations are favoured. Values such as moderation, social order, security, tradition, and the reciprocation of favours are seen as crucial in conservative societies. Great importance is placed on the maintenance of the status quo. Also important is the maintenance of harmonious relationships not only within the group, but also within society.

Mastery and Hierarchy. The dimension examines whose interests within society take precedence (ie those of the individual or those of the group). Mastery encompasses values such as being independent, ambitious, successful and choosing one's own goals. Hierarchy reflects wealth, social power, and authority: it is concerned with the use of power to promote individual versus group interests.

(Quoted from Chui *et al.* (2002), pp. 101–103)

While Schwartz's dimensions have been used by Chui *et al.* (2002) to help explain differences in debt–equity ratios, it remains to be seen if this work will be used in the future in the accounting literature.

5.3 Culture and business

5.3.1 Culture and leadership style

Culture affects how a society organizes itself. It will affect businesses and accounting in a variety of ways. If we look first at the relationship between business and culture, Hofstede (1991) suggests that culture influences both the preference for particular leadership styles and organizational structures and the motivation of employers and employees. Hofstede went on to describe how the cultural dimensions he had identified were linked to various organizational characteristics. For example, he argued that leadership styles would be particularly affected by individualism and power distance. If a country is highly individualistic, then leadership styles and structures would tend to be based upon the satisfaction of personal needs. Individual self-interest would feature strongly and personal relationships and loyalties would have relatively little relevance. In collectivist societies leadership would be more of a group phenomenon. Leaders would be successful only if they emphasize the group. Employee welfare would be relatively more important. Culture would also affect the degree of participation – whether extensive and real, consultative, symbolic, or non-existent.

While these differences have little direct impact upon financial accounting, they have obvious implications for management accounting. Leadership style affects who makes what decisions in the company. This affects the accounting information system, which must be designed to ensure that decision-makers receive the relevant information. The performance evaluation system must be designed so that performance measures reflect decision-making authority.

5.3.2 Culture and motivation

Motivation is also affected by culture. Individualism versus collectivism and high versus low nurturing seem to be particularly important. The importance of theories of motivation for financial accounting can be seen, for example, in agency theory. This is one of the most important theories to emerge in accounting in recent years and it has implications for the design of corporate governance systems and the regulation of auditing and financial reporting. The theory seeks to explain the behaviour of corporate managers. Agency theory assumes that managers are motivated by self-interest (high individualism), in particular by their remuneration including perks (low nurturing). Given these assumptions, it follows that managers will maximize their own income even at the expense of the owners of the company. Controls have to be put in place to prevent this happening. These include auditing and financial reporting, both of which monitor the behaviour of managers. However, this monitoring is not sufficient to ensure that managers act in the best interests of owners. Other contracts such as debt covenants are also used to limit managers' freedom of action. Share options and profit-based performance bonuses may, for example, act to bring managers' interests into harmony with those of the external shareholders. Thus, financial reporting and auditing regulations, other contractual arrangements and managers' preferences for particular measurement and reporting practices are all premised upon certain, usually implicit, assumptions about the behaviour of managers.[11]

If the culture of a country is very different from that implicitly assumed by agency theory with, in particular, higher scores on both collectivism and nurturing, agency theory may not provide such a good explanation of managers' behaviour. This means that the optimal amount and type of regulatory structures and rules may also be very different.[12] One example of an obvious and striking cultural difference may be seen in the case of Tanzania. This society is more collectivist than are any of the developed Anglo-American countries, such as the UK, with the extended family being particularly important. Thus, one of the earliest Tanzanian accounting standards (TSSAP 2 issued in 1983) includes extensive disclosure requirements with respect to related parties transactions.[13] What is striking about TSSAP 2 is the relative prominence given to related parties' disclosures and the way in which 'related parties' is defined primarily in personal terms, being mainly seen as family

---

[11] Jensen and Meckling (1976).

[12] Kaplan and Ruland (1991); Ogden (1993).

[13] National Board of Accountants and Auditors (1983).

members. In contrast, in the UK related parties are defined primarily in business terms.[14] While 'members of the close family' fall under the UK definition of related parties, far more emphasis is placed upon business associates and other parties with direct or indirect control or influence (see Case study 5.1 for extracts from the requirements in both countries).

5.3.3 Culture and organizational structures

Finally, culture also affects organizational structures. This has obvious implications for both management and financial accounting. One example is Japanese companies, as will be discussed in more detail in Chapter 11. Japanese corporate groups are often based upon a multitude of relationships such as supplier, customer and debt relationships and common directorships. Rather than there being majority share-ownership by a clearly defined parent company there are often relatively small share cross-holdings throughout the group. This affects the usefulness of group statements which are based upon the assumption that a group is made up of a parent company, subsidiaries and sub-subsidiaries, all organized in a hierarchical structure.

Hofstede argued that the two cultural constructs that most affect how organizations are structured are power distance (which primarily influences superior–subordinate relationships) and uncertainty avoidance (which primarily influences the amount and type of rules in place). Hofstede also identified the types of business organizations which should be most common in particular countries, as illustrated in Exhibit 5.8.[15] (*Note*: This brief and simple description offers only an extremely simplified picture. As with any generalization, many organizations will be structured very differently, and what Hofstede describes may be best thought of as a tendency towards preferring particular styles of organization.)

Exhibit 5.8 shows us that, for example, countries characterized by relatively high power distance and strong uncertainty avoidance should tend to favour organizations run on fully bureaucratic lines. Here, explicit formal rules are more likely to prescribe behaviour. Power and authority tend to depend upon the position held rather than upon personal

---

Exhibit 5.8 Organizational types as identified by Hofstede (1984)

	A	B	C	D
Power distance	Low	High	Low	High
Uncertainty avoidance	Weak	Weak	Strong	Strong
Organization type	Implicitly structured	Personnel bureaucracy	Workflow bureaucracy	Full bureaucracy
Implicit model of the organization	Market	Family	Well oiled machine	Pyramid
Countries	Anglo/US Scandinavian Netherlands	South East Asian	Germany Finland Israel	Latin Med. Islamic Japan

Source: Hofstede (1984) p. 216.

---

[14] Accounting Standards Board (1995).

[15] Hofstede (1984), p. 216.

characteristics. In contrast, in countries such as the UK, the US or Australia, which can be characterized by relatively small power distance and weak uncertainty avoidance, organizations should tend to be at least implicitly modelled upon the market place.

Thus, relatively less emphasis tends to be placed upon formal rules. Personal attributes and performance are both important in determining an individual's power and authority, while performance measures will be based upon the outcomes achieved rather than the actions undertaken.

5.4 Culture and accounting

5.4.1 Accounting subculture

We have seen how societal culture may influence the organizational structures and decision-making processes of companies. These, in turn, will influence the accounting system of the company. But culture also has a more direct impact upon financial accounting. The financial accounting system is set up and run by or for various groups of people, in particular auditors, management accountants or other statement preparers, accounting regulators (who may or may not also be accountants) and statement users.

Each of these groups may be thought of as a distinct group with its own subculture. Some of these groups are not very homogeneous and will not have a well-defined subculture. For example, shareholders range from private individuals to companies holding shares in associates and subsidiaries, to investment trusts and pension schemes. They have little in common beyond perhaps sharing a belief in private ownership of industry, profit maximization by companies and personal wealth maximization. In contrast, accountants are a relatively homogeneous group – they share a common professional education and tend to have common working experiences.

If we return to our model of the influences on accounting rules and practices (Exhibit 5.1) we can see that ecological or environmental and external factors directly influence the institutions and culture of a country. Societal culture also itself influences the institutions of a country, with the two reinforcing each other. When it comes to accounting, the subculture of accountants is influenced by the culture of the wider society while it influences the accounting rules and practices. The system is a dynamic one in the sense that the accounting system provides feedback, influencing society's institutions and culture.

The unique factors influencing accountants will not normally be strong enough to completely override or obliterate society-wide cultural differences. Thus, for example, the culture of the UK is different from the culture of (say) Japan, Germany or Korea and the subculture of UK accountants should therefore also be different from the subculture of accountants from Japan, Germany or Korea. The fact that all these accountants perform similar, although not identical jobs, should not be enough to obliterate all cultural differences between the three groups, although it should reduce them. Given the importance of society wide culture and the influence of this on subcultures, we would expect to find that Hofstede's 'cultural dimensions' are systematically linked to a number of similar 'subcultural dimensions' or 'accounting values'.

5.4.2 Accounting values

If we return to Hofstede's cultural dimensions or values, the two that seem to have the most direct relevance to accounting are 'uncertainty avoidance' and 'individualism'. In a high-uncertainty-avoidance country, institutions will tend to be organized in ways that minimize uncertainty. Rules and regulations will tend to be explicit and prescriptive, they will tend to be detailed, all-embracing and rigid. Low uncertainty avoidance countries will tend to be less concerned with reducing uncertainty, they will tend to have fewer rules, perhaps relying more on general principles, and the rules that exist will be more likely to contain options. Individualism, on the other hand, affects motivation. It should therefore affect preferences for particular earnings measurement rules and disclosure practices. It will also influence the extent to which people are happy to accept rules and controls imposed from above or will be willing to use their personal or professional initiative and be prepared to take risks. This should in turn affects their willingness to accept uniform accounting rules in preference to a more permissive system involving the use of professional discretion.

The work of Hofstede was extended by Gray (1988) who identified four 'accounting values' or 'subcultural dimensions'. '*Professionalism* versus *statutory control*' and '*uniformity* versus *flexibility*' both describe attitudes towards regulation, in particular attitudes towards the type of control system and the level or extent of control that is preferred. '*Conservatism* versus *optimism*' is concerned with attitudes towards measurement. Attitudes towards uncertainty are particularly important here. The final value, '*secrecy* versus *transparency*', is concerned with attitudes towards disclosure. Exhibit 5.9 reproduces Gray's definition of each of these four accounting values.

Gray also argued that Hofstede's societal cultural values will be systematically linked to his accounting values. The hypothesized relationships between the two are illustrated in Exhibit 5.10, which describes which of Hofstede's cultural dimensions are most strongly associated with each of Gray's four accounting values.

The relationships described in Exhibit 5.10 can instead be shown in a diagrammatic way as shown in Exhibit 5.11. This exhibit also shows that Gray hypothesized

---

Exhibit 5.9 Accounting values identified by Gray (1988)

Professionalism versus statutory control
A preference for the exercise of individual professional judgement and the maintenance of professional self-regulation, as opposed to compliance with prescriptive legal requirements and statutory control.

Uniformity versus flexibility
A preference for the enforcement of uniform accounting practices between companies and the consistent use of such practices over time, as opposed to flexibility in accordance with the perceived circumstances of individual companies.

Conservatism versus optimism
A preference for a cautious approach to measurement so as to cope with the uncertainty of future events, as opposed to a more optimistic, *laissez-faire*, risk-taking approach.

Secrecy versus transparency
A preference for confidentiality and the restriction of disclosure of information about the business only to those who are closely involved with its management and financing, as opposed to a more transparent, open and publicly accountable approach.

| Exhibit 5.10 | Association between Hofstede's cultural dimensions and Gray's accounting values |

Gray's accounting values	Cultural dimensions affecting the country's accounting values	
Professionalism *versus* **Statutory control**	Professionalism tends to be associated with: • individualism • weak uncertainty avoidance • small power distance.	Statutory control tends to be associated with: • collectivism • strong uncertainty avoidance • large power distance.
Uniformity *versus* **Flexibility**	Uniformity tends to be associated with: • strong uncertainty avoidance • large power distance • collectivism.	Flexibility tends to be associated with: • weak uncertainty avoidance • small power distance. • individualism.
Conservatism *versus* **Optimism**	Conservatism tends to be associated with: • strong uncertainty avoidance • collectivism • high nurture.	Optimism tends to be associated with: • weak uncertainty avoidance • individualism • low nurture.
Secrecy *versus* **Transparency**	Secrecy tends to be associated with: • strong uncertainty avoidance • large power distance • collectivism • high nurture.	Transparency tends to be associated with: • weak uncertainty avoidance • small power distance • individualism • low nurture.

that the four accounting values influenced different parts of the accounting system. He argued that professionalism and uniformity influenced the regulatory system, in terms of both the institutional arrangements made for regulation and the methods of enforcement used, while conservatism and secrecy instead influenced the practice of accounting in terms of the measurement system adopted and the disclosures made.

| Exhibit 5.11 | The relationship between cultural dimensions and accounting values |

Cultural dimension	Relationship to accounting values			
	Professionalism	Uniformity	Conservatism	Secrecy
Individualism	+	−	−	−
Uncertainty avoidance	−	+	+	+
Power distance	−	+	NR	+
Nurturing	NR	NR	+	+
Accounting practice mainly influenced	Authority	Application	Measurement	Disclosure

Key: + Positive relationship. For example, the *higher* individualism is, the *higher* professionalism will be.
　　− Negative relationship. For example, the *lower* uncertainty avoidance is, the *higher* professionalism will be.
NR No relationship.

5.4.3 Applying cultural analysis to accounting

There have been a large number of attempts to test these hypothesized relationships. However, this is not an easy task. There are problems with using Hofstede's scores, since he based his work on employees of IBM in the period 1968–73, and the scores may not be valid for other groups in the 2000s.[16] For example, he ignored religion which can also affect attitudes towards business and accounting.[17] There are also problems with measuring Gray's accounting values. Auditors or other accountants can be asked their views on various issues, but this is not easy, and when done it tends to be restricted to studies which explore very specific and quite narrow decision-making scenarios.[18] A more common approach is to look instead directly at the accounting system. Thus, for example, rather than looking at attitudes towards conservatism, studies have looked at the importance of conservatism in the measurement rules and practices of countries. They have then tested the hypothesis that, for example, countries that have more uncertainty avoidance and more collectivism will have relatively more conservative measurement rules. This approach implicitly assumes that there is a direct relationship between accounting values and accounting systems. However, as we have seen, accounting systems are influenced by many factors. There may be a relationship between Hofstede's values and accounting systems but the reasons for this may not be correctly specified. Thus, there may be no relationship between Hofstede's dimensions and Gray's accounting values.

5.4.4 An example of a study using accounting values

A number of studies have attempted to measure Gray's accounting values to see whether or not they are linked to Hofstede's cultural values in the ways hypothesized. One of those looking at a large number of countries will be described, that by Salter and Niswander (1995). Gray's accounting values are concerned with values and beliefs of accountants. It is an immense task to measure these directly, especially in the international area. Salter and Niswander instead used indirect measures of accounting values. They assumed that, for example, differences in attitudes towards secrecy or transparency will be reflected in differences in disclosure, while differences in attitudes towards conservatism will be reflected in differences in measurement rules.

The ways in which they measured the four accounting values are described in Exhibit 5.12. This study provides some support for Gray's arguments. As discussed above, Gray argued that the two cultural dimensions most important for accounting are individualism and uncertainty avoidance. Using the scores provided by Hofstede and applying the analysis to 29 countries, Salter and Niswander found that uncertainty avoidance was related to all four of Gray's accounting values. In contrast, individualism helped to explain only one of the four accounting values, namely secrecy: the more individualistic countries tend to disclose the most. There was also little support for the expected relationships between accounting values and either power distance or nurturing.

There have been a number of other studies that have also looked at the relationship between Hofstede's work and accounting. For example, culture has been used to help explain some of the differences in the accounting regulatory systems of the English-speaking countries of the UK, the US, Australia and Canada in comparison to the Asian

---

[16] Trompenaars' work may be more appropriate as it is more up to date and is based on many companies. However, unlike Hofstede, he has not disclosed the full scores of each country.

[17] Hamid *et al.* (1993).

[18] See, for example, Patel *et al.* (2002).

Exhibit 5.12 The measurement of accounting values

Accounting value	Measurement used		
Professionalism	Score for audit perspective + professional structure, where:		
	Audit perspective	1	Conforms with legal requirements
		2	Fairly, consistently present, in conformity with
		3	True and fair, in conformity with
		4	True and fair
	Professional structure	0	Law/legislated
		1	Practitioner body
Uniformity	*De jure*	0	Common law system
		1	Code law system
	De facto		Number of practices with high level of uniformity (less than 25% or greater than 75% compliance rate)
Conservatism	Conservatism 1		Use of various practices that reduce assets or income
	Conservatism 2		Use of various practices that increase assets or income
Secrecy	Disclosure index		Two used, each designed to measure the level of disclosure

Source: Salter and Niswander (1995), p.385. Used with the permission of the *Journal of International Business Studies*.

countries of Singapore, Hong Kong and Taiwan,[19] and New Zealand and India.[20] In each case the two groups of countries are culturally quite dissimilar and the studies were fairly successful in doing this. In contrast, another study, on the contrary, argued that culture fails to explain many of the accounting differences between France and Germany.[21] These two countries are culturally more alike than are the two groups of countries in the former studies. It was also concerned with more detailed features of the accounting systems. Culture has also been used to try to explain levels of disclosure. Again, it appears that culture is helpful in explaining broad patterns or levels of disclosure while there is also some limited evidence that religion as well as Hofstede's cultural dimensions may be a factor affecting disclosure.[22]

5.5 Is culture an important influence on accounting?

There are many supporters of the view that culture has a significant influence on accounting. Indeed, this is fairly incontrovertible: culture, in the sense of how people think and feel and their values, beliefs and attitudes, affects their behaviour. Accounting regulations and practices are an outcome of human behaviour.

---

[19] Kirsch (1994).

[20] Chanchani and Willett (2004).

[21] Fechner and Kilgore (1994).

[22] Zarzeski (1996); Archambault and Archambault (2003).

The models linking accounting and culture suggest that culture acts as an intervening factor. Culture modifies the influence of ecological or environmental and external factors. It also influences the values or subculture of accountants and the institutions of a society. These in turn both influence accounting systems. Given the complexity of these relationships, it would not be too surprising to find that some countries have similar cultures but dissimilar accounting systems, while other countries have similar accounting systems but dissimilar cultures. It is the complex combination or interaction of all these factors that is important.

Even if there is a clear and consistent connection between culture and accounting, researchers may have failed to uncover it. Most studies of accounting rely upon the works of Gray and Hofstede (not least because Hofstede provides quantified measures for a range of countries). Hofstede has reduced a very complex phenomenon down to four dimensions. While these dimensions were statistically significant, they explained just 49 per cent of the differences across the countries in Hofstede's sample. Thus, either there are omitted variables or there is a fairly large amount of unexplainable or random differences across, and presumably also inside, countries. Unfortunately, all we have are the raw or mean scores for each country. We really need more information than this. Anyone using Hofstede's scores really also needs to know how typical or representative the scores are for each cultural dimension. Do most people have very similar beliefs, attitudes and values or not? If the people of a society are culturally very similar, culture is more likely to help to explain their accounting system. If instead a country is culturally heterogeneous with people holding very different views or values, then it is far less likely that a measure of 'average culture' will help to explain the accounting system.

While there are many supporters of Hofstede who argue that his work helps us to understand differences in accounting internationally, there is far from universal support for this. Some of the arguments used by opponents of this approach are summarized by Most (1995), when he argued that:

> he [i.e. Hofstede] used questionnaires to elicit responses designed to identify national groups with attitudes; on the basis of these responses, he found national patterns that led to a classification of organisations and, by inference, of accounting practices.
>
> First, why was this process chosen? The established classification of civilisation allocates each culture to one of these eight classes: Occidental, Muslim, Japanese, Hindu, Confucian, Slavic, African and Latin American. A researcher seeking to identify national patterns of accounting would first attempt to map empirical observations into these classes, investigating any differences that arose. It would be found that modern communications have broken down the strict separations that the categories imply . . . It would doubtless be found that culture is too complex a concept to be analysed using a simple model.
>
> We also find Hofstede's model suspect on other grounds. Power distance and uncertainty avoidance are not unequivocal measures of human characteristics. An individual might accept the uneven distribution of power on the national level but not on the regional, on the regional but not on the tribal, or on the tribal but not within the family. Any society that is based on agriculture, or has a sizeable cultivation sector, must be characterised as one with a low level of 'anxiety . . . in the face of unstructured or ambiguous situations'. Although Hofstede did not make much use of the other 'values', similar criticisms can be levelled at them – individualism versus collectivism has lost much of its significance since his research was done; as for the distinction between masculinity and femininity, the less said, the better. It would appear that the values selected by Hofstede were not found by a process of observation and measurement but simply invented in order to initiate a series of exploratory observations.

The conclusion drawn by Hofstede and his followers, that culture 'dictates' the accounting environment and accounting and auditing judgements, must be rejected as not proven.

Similarly, while there are many who find the work of Gray very helpful in explaining accounting differences, there are problems involved in this work. There are practical problems involved in turning the hypothesis into testable assertions and, even if the theory is correct and there is a significant relationship between societal cultures and accounting systems, it may not be easy to empirically prove such a relationship. Not only are there problems in defining and measuring 'culture', but similar problems exist with respect to the definition and measurement of 'accounting values' and 'accounting systems'.

Culture probably provides a far better explanation of accounting in some countries than it does in others and a far better explanation of some aspects of accounting systems than it does of other aspects.

The previous chapter looked at how accounting has been exported and imported between countries. Even many of the developed countries which have developed systems of regulation and rules over centuries to reflect local needs have imported many of their practices from other countries through a variety of means, as will be discussed later in this book. However, as a generalization it is possible to say that countries such as the UK, Germany or the US have developed their accounting systems over a large number of years as the needs of the country changed. As such, it seems reasonable to hypothesize that there will be a significant relationship between their accounting systems and their country wide culture. Other countries, most particularly many of the developing countries, have imported much or even most of their accounting systems. As such, it might be expected that there is far less relationship, and perhaps even virtually no relationship, between the indigenous culture and the accounting system.

Gray's theory is concerned with the values of accountants. It has two parts to it. First, it hypothesizes that accounting values are linked to societal culture and, secondly, that accountants influence accounting systems. Even if the first of these is correct, the second may not always be correct. The accounting system of a country consists of a number of different parts or subsystems. Authority and enforcement are concerned with the institutions of regulation, while measurement and disclosure are concerned with both the specific rules included in the regulations and the voluntary practices of companies. In some countries, accountants will be important in all three of these. In other countries, accountants may have little or no influence in one, two or even all three of these three subsystems. In these cases, Gray's hypothesis may only hold for parts of, or indeed none of the accounting system.

Summary and conclusions

This chapter has looked at the influence of culture on accounting. We followed Hofstede in defining culture as 'the collective programming of the mind that distinguishes the members of one human group from another'. This was then broken down into the four dimensions of:

- individualism versus collectivism,
- large versus small power distance,
- strong versus weak uncertainty avoidance,
- high versus low nurturing.

The chapter then went on to show how culture can affect business, in particular how it can influence leadership styles, the motivation of employers and employees and organizational structures. Culture can also more directly influence accounting by influencing the subculture of accountants. Four 'accounting values' were described:

- professionalism versus statutory control,
- uniformity versus flexibility,
- conservatism versus optimism,
- secrecy versus transparency.

Finally, the chapter concluded by reviewing a number of empirical studies. From these, and other similar studies, it can be concluded that culture appears to provide a useful first step in understanding or explaining differences between the accounting systems of many countries. This is especially so when we are seeking to explain general patterns across a large number of countries. It may also be helpful in explaining some of the ways in which specific rules or methods are actually applied in different countries. However, as might be expected, it is far less helpful in explaining differences in the accounting systems between relatively similar countries or in explaining differences in specific detailed rules.

Key points from the chapter:

- Culture is defined as the collective programming of the mind which distinguishes the members of one human group from another.
- Culture is collective, not individual. It is not directly observable but can be inferred from people's behaviour.
- Culture in business affects leadership style, motivation and organizational structures.
- Gray (1988) derived four pairs of accounting values from combinations of Hofstede's dimensions of culture.
- Empirical research has found some support for the existence of accounting values as predicted by Gray.
- There are views that support, and views that challenge, the idea that culture is an important influence on accounting.
- There are criticisms of Hofstede's study of cultural dimensions.
- Gray's analysis provides a useful framework for categorizing accounting systems.

Case study 5.1	**Accounting for related parties in the UK and Tanzania**

Tanzania: TSSAP 2

'Related party' transactions

The term 'related party' shall include:

(a) the chief executive of the enterprise, his [*sic*] spouse and children;

(b) every member of the board of directors or their equivalent, however designated, along with each member's spouse and children;

(c) the parents, brothers and sisters of those mentioned in (a) and (b) above, and

(d) any body corporate which has an influence over the composition of the board of directors of the enterprise.

There shall be a full disclosure of loans of every description made during the accounting period or outstanding at any time during the accounting period to or from any person coming within the definition of 'related party' with particulars of:

(a) nature and conditions of such loans;

(b) identity of the party;

(c) maximum amount outstanding at any time during the accounting period;

(d) rate of interest, if any, applicable to the loan;

(e) details of any guarantee or securities available.

There shall be a disclosure of safari [i.e. holiday] and other imprests and all forms of temporary borrowings outstanding on the Balance Sheet date from any person falling within the definition of the 'related party' provided the amount outstanding exceeds five thousand shillings, stating particulars of:

(a) amount outstanding;

(b) purpose of the imprest or other form of temporary accommodation;

(c) how long the amount has been outstanding;

(d) steps taken for the recovery of the amount.

There shall be a disclosure also of the interest of 'related parties' in:

(a) shares and debentures of the enterprise;

(b) contracts in force at any given time during the accounting period or any transaction in which any of the 'related parties' has or had an interest which is of significance to the enterprise.

UK: FRS 8

Guidance on the definition of a related party:

(a) Two or more parties are related parties when at any time during the financial period:

   (i) one party has direct or indirect control of the other party; or

   (ii) the parties are subject to common control from the same source; or

   (iii) one party has influence over the financial and operating policies of the other party to an extent that the other party might be inhibited from pursuing at all times its own separate interests; or

   (iv) the parties, in entering a transaction, are subject to influence from the same source to such an extent that one of the parties to the transaction has subordinated its own separate interests.

(b) For the avoidance of doubt, the following are related parties of the reporting entity:

   (i) its ultimate and intermediate parent undertakings, subsidiary undertakings, and fellow subsidiary undertakings;

   (ii) its associates and joint ventures;

▶

Case study 5.1 *(Continued)*

    (iii) the investor or venturer in respect of which the reporting entity is an associate or a joint venture;

    (iv) directors of the reporting entity and the directors of its ultimate and intermediate parent undertakings; and

    (v) pension funds for the benefits of employees of the reporting entity or of any entity that is a related party of the reporting entity;

(c) and the following are presumed to be related parties of the reporting entity unless it can be demonstrated that neither party has influenced the financial and operating policies of the other in such a way as to inhibit the pursuit of separate interests:

    (i) the key management of the reporting entity and the key management of its parent undertaking or undertakings;

    (ii) a person owning or able to exercise control over 20 per cent or more of the voting rights of the reporting entity, whether directly or through nominees;

    (iii) each person acting in concert in such a way as to be able to exercise control or influence over the reporting entity; and

    (iv) an entity managing or managed by the reporting entity under a management contract.

(d) Additionally, because of their relationship with certain parties that are, or are presumed to be, related parties of the reporting entity, the following are also presumed to be related parties of the reporting entity:

    (i) members of the close family of any individual falling under parties mentioned in (a)–(c) above; and

    (ii) partnerships, companies, trusts or other entities in which any individual or member of the close family of (a)–(c) above has a controlling interest.

Disclosure of transactions and balances

Financial statements should disclose material transactions undertaken . . . with a related party. Disclosure should be made irrespective of whether a price is charged. The disclosure should include:

(a) the names of the transacting related parties;

(b) a description of the relationship between the parties;

(c) a description of the transactions;

(d) the amounts involved;

(e) any other elements of the transactions necessary for an understanding of the financial statements;

(f) the amounts due to or from related parties at the balance sheet date and provisions for doubtful debts due from such parties at that date; and

(g) amounts written off in the period in respect of debts due to or from related parties.

Source: TSSAP 2, *Information Required to be Disclosed in Financial Statements* (National Board of Accountants and Auditors, 1983); FRS 8, *Related Party Disclosures* (ASB, October 1995).

Questions

The following questions test your understanding of the material contained in the chapter and allow you to relate your understanding to the learning outcomes specified at the start of this chapter. The learning outcomes are repeated here. Each question is cross-referenced to the relevant section of the chapter.

Understand what is meant by the term 'culture', and describe the cultural dimensions identified by a number of different researchers

1 What is meant by the terms 'culture' and 'subculture'? Why are the two different? (section 5.2)

2 Why might accountants have a particularly strong subculture? (section 5.2)

3 Describe your country in terms of the cultural dimensions described by Hofstede. (section 5.2)

4 Using the data provided in Exhibits 5.4 and 5.5, describe each of the countries and place them each into relevant groups. (section 5.2)

5 What are the main differences and similarities between the cultural dimensions of Hofstede, Hampden-Turner and Trompenaars, and Schwartz? (section 5.2)

Describe the relationship between culture and organizational structures

6 How might each of Hofstede's cultural dimensions affect corporate leadership styles? (section 5.3.1)

7 How might each of Hofstede's cultural dimensions affect organizational structures? (section 5.3.3)

8 How might each of Hofstede's cultural dimensions affect what factors motivate employees? (section 5.3.2)

Describe the accounting values identified by Gray, and explain how they might be related to culture

9 Describe Gray's four accounting values and describe how they are linked to Hofstede's cultural dimensions. (section 5.4)

10 Describe your country in terms of the four accounting values of Gray. (section 5.4)

11 Does your description of your country's accounting values and cultural dimensions, as defined by Hofstede, support the hypothesized link between the two as described in Exhibit 5.8? (section 5.4)

12 How are Gray's accounting values linked to the system of accounting regulation? (section 5.4.3)

13 How are Gray's accounting values linked to accounting measurement rules and practices? (section 5.4.3)

14 How are Gray's accounting values linked to accounting disclosure rules and practices? (section 5.4.3)

Evaluate research which has used these accounting values and assess their significance for those seeking international harmonization

15 Why does Most criticize Hofstede's work? (section 5.5)

16 Do you agree with these criticisms? Why, or why not? (section 5.5)

17 What are the main practical problems involved in measuring accounting values? (section 5.4.4)

18 Why might Gray's work be more appropriate for developed than developing countries? (section 5.5)

19 Why might Gray's work be more appropriate in explaining general patterns or differences rather than differences in specific measurement and disclosure rules? (section 5.5)

References and further reading

Archambault, J.J. and Archambault, M.E. (2003) 'A multinational test of determinants of corporate disclosure', *International Journal of Accounting*, 38: 173–194.

ASB (1995) *FRS 8, Related Party Transactions*. London: Accounting Standards Board.

Balaga, B.R. and Jaeger, A.M. (1984) 'Multinational corporations: control systems and delegation issues', *Journal of International Business Studies*, Fall, 25–40.

Baskerville, R.F. (2003) 'Hofstede never studied culture', *Accounting, Organizations and Society*, 28: 1–14.

Chanchani, S. and Willett, R. (2004) 'An empirical assessment of Gray's accounting value constructs', *The International Journal of Accounting*, 39: 125–154.

Chposky, J. and Leonis, T. (1988) *Blue Magic: The People, Power and Politics Behind the IBM Personal Computer*, Facts on File Inc.

Chui, A.C.W., Lloyd, A.E. and Kwok, C.C.Y. (2002) 'The determination of capital structure: Is national culture a missing piece of the puzzle?' *Journal of International Business Studies*, 33(1): 99–127.

Ellwood, W. (2001) *The No-Nonsense Guide to Globalization*, Verso.

Fechner, H.H.E. and Kilgore, A. (1994) 'The influence of cultural factors on accounting practice', *International Journal of Accounting*, 29(4): 265–277.

Gambling, T. (1987) 'Accounting for rituals', *Accounting, Organizations and Society*, 12(4): 319–329.

Gannon, M.J. and Associates (1994) *Understanding Global Culture: Metaphorical Journey, through 17 Countries*. London: Sage.

Gray, S.J. (1988) 'Towards a theory of cultural influence on the development of accounting systems internationally', *Abacus*, 24(1): 1–15.

Hamid, S., Craig, R. and Clark, F. (1993) 'Religion: a confounding cultural element in the international harmonisation of accounting?', *Abacus*, 29(2): 131–148.

Hampden-Turner, C.M. and Trompenaars, F. (2000) *Building Cross-Cultural Competence: How to Create Wealth From Conflicting Values*. John Wiley & Sons.

Hofstede, G. (1984) *Culture's Consequences: International Differences in Work-related Values*. Beverly Hills, CA: Sage Publications.

Hofstede, G. (1991) *Cultures and Organisations: Software of the Mind*. London: McGraw-Hill.

Hofstede, G. (2003) 'What is culture? A reply to Baskerville', *Accounting, Organizations and Society*, 28: 811–813.

Hofstede, G. and Bond, M.H. (1988) 'The Confucius connection: From cultural roots to economic growth', *Organizational Dynamics*, 16(1): 5–21.

Jensen, M.C. and Meckling, W.H. (1976) 'Theory of the firm: Managerial behaviour, agency costs and ownership structure', *Journal of Financial Economics*, 3: 305–360.

Kaplan, S.E. and Ruland, R.G. (1991) 'Positive theory, rationality and accounting regulation', *Critical Perspectives on Accounting*, 2: 361–374.

Kirsch, R.J. (1994) 'Towards a global reporting model: Culture and disclosure in selected capital markets', *Research in Accounting Regulation*, 8: 71–110.

Kluckholn, F. and Strodtbeck, F. (1961) *Variations in Value Orientations*. Evanston Row, Paterson.

Most, K. (1995) 'A critique of international accounting theory', *Advances in International Accounting*, 7: 3–11.

National Board of Accountants and Auditors (1983) *Tanzanian Statement of Standard Accounting Practice No.2: Information Required to be Disclosed in Financial Statements*. Dar Es Salaam: NBAA, June.

Ogden, S.G. (1993) 'The limitations of agency theory: The case of accounting-based profit sharing schemes', *Critical Perspectives on Accounting*, 4: 179–206.

Patel, C., Harrison, G.L. and McKinnon, J.L. (2002) 'Cultural influences on judgments of professional accountants in auditor-client conflict resolution', *Journal of International Financial Management and Accounting*, 13(1): 1–31.

Salter, S.B. and Niswander, F. (1995) 'Cultural influence on the development of accounting systems internationally: A test of Gray's [1988] theory', *Journal of International Business Studies*, 26(2): 379–398.

Schwartz, S.H. (1994) 'Beyond individualism/collectivism: New cultural dimensions of values', in Kim, U., Triandis, H.C., Kagitcibasi, C., Choi, S-C. and Yoon, G. (eds), *Individualism and Collectivism: Theory, Method and Applications*, pp. 85–99, Sage Publications.

Slater, R. (2002) *Saving Big Blue: Leadership Lessons and Turnaround Tactics of IBM's Lou Gerstner*. McGraw-Hill.

Steger, M.B. (2003) *Globalization: A Very Short Introduction*. Oxford University Press.

Trompenaars, F. (2003) *Did the Pedestrian Die?* Capstone Publishing.

Trompenaars, F. and Hampden-Turner, C. (1997) *Riding the Waves of Culture: Understanding Cultural Diversity in Business* (2nd edn). London: Nicholas Brealey Publishing.

Zarzeski, M.T. (1996) 'Spontaneous harmonization effects of culture and market forces on accounting disclosure practices', *Accounting Horizons*, 10(1): 18–37.

The classification of accounting systems

Learning outcomes

After reading this chapter you should be able to:

● Explain why it is important to classify accounting systems.

● Distinguish deductive from inductive approaches to classification.

● Distinguish simple from complex classification systems.

● Explain the advantages and limitations of the different types of classification systems.

● Evaluate published research which develops or uses classification systems.

6.1 Introduction

In Chapters 4 and 5 we looked at a range of factors which may influence accounting. This discussion leads to two questions. First, if accounting systems are influenced in systematic ways by environmental factors, then is it possible to find patterns or systematic, explicable differences and commonalities in the accounting systems of different countries? Secondly, which, if any of the many factors discussed in the last two chapters are most important in explaining accounting patterns? This chapter seeks to provide some answers to these questions by classifying or placing accounting systems into groups of similar systems. The chapter will describe the main types of accounting classification systems that exist, and evaluate their usefulness.

We have been asked – why retain this chapter when harmonization with international accounting standards is already widespread and is increasing? Our answer is that accounting systems consist of more than the financial statements and notes that come within the scope of IFRS. Accounting systems provide information beyond the measurement and disclosure rules of accounting standards. The methods of classification described in this chapter can be extended to newly developing aspects of accounting systems and reporting practices.

All systems of classification depend upon being able to differentiate between important and unimportant differences. Only some accounting differences will be important. Others may have a large impact on reported figures, but still not be very important because either the effects on profit or equity is easily seen, or they are transitory differences or they can be changed relatively easily without affecting any other aspects of the accounting system. The use of straight line or accelerated depreciation, for example, may have a large impact on reported profits but the difference is not significant from a theoretical viewpoint. Both are methods of allocating the cost of an asset to the periods that benefit from its use and, as such, are in harmony with each other. Other differences may have relatively little impact upon the reported figures but be important and difficult to standardize. Whether or not a company capitalizes leased assets, for example, may have little effect on its reported profits, but it is very important from a theoretical perspective. The alternative treatments of leased assets reflect very different definitions of an asset. Non-capitalization is based upon a legal definition of assets while capitalization takes an economic perspective instead. These views are not compatible or in harmony with each other.

If we want to gain a complete picture of differences across accounting systems, we must differentiate between significant or fundamental differences and non-significant or non-fundamental differences. Looking only at the impact of differences upon reported figures or only at the number of techniques that are different is not enough.

Classifying accounting systems contributes to this aim. Classifications attempt to place cases (here, the accounting systems of countries) into systematic categories or groups. A good classification system is one where each country's accounting system can be placed in one, and only one, group. The accounting systems of countries in any one group should share the same important or underlying features while also being quite distinct from the accounting systems in the other groups. Differences in unimportant features or transitory differences should not affect the classification system – indeed, the number of differences between countries placed in the same category might be quite large and may even be larger than the number of differences between countries placed in different categories.

6.2 Reasons for classifying accounting systems

There are several reasons for classifying accounting systems. A good classification system should provide a simple way of describing and analysing complex phenomena. In the absence of a classification system, anyone who wants to know about accounting in Italy, for example, must list and describe all the main accounting rules and practices in Italy, such as the methods used to value fixed assets, inventory, intangibles and leases and the rules for consolidation, deferred taxation, foreign currency translation, etc. If the same person then wants to know about accounting in Spain, a similarly long list will be required. A simpler approach would be to turn to classification studies which might show that Italy and Spain are in the same group as France, having government-imposed systems based upon Romanic law with tax rules also influencing the reported figures. While this does not tell us the specific accounting rules of Italy or Spain, we would now have a set of expectations regarding the specific rules and practices of each country. Time and effort can then be concentrated on learning about those rules or practices that are different from what is expected – hopefully a very much smaller list of items.

Classification therefore offers a way to simplify a complex world. Classifications may also help domestic and international standard-setters. At the level of the individual country, standard-setters may be able to look at other countries in the same group for guidance on how they have solved similar problems. This should help them to see which solutions are most likely to be successful, having worked in other countries in the same group, and which will probably be unsuccessful, having failed in other group members. In an international setting, regional or international standard-setters may see which countries should be relatively easy to harmonize (those countries in the same group) and which will probably be the hardest (countries in the most widely separated groups). They can also see which issues should be easy to harmonize (issues that are not fundamental) and which issues will probably be far more difficult (fundamental issues).

6.3 Types of classification schemes

There have been many attempts at classifying accounting systems and many different types of classification schemes have been used. They differ in terms of the type of reasoning used, whether inductive or deductive. They also differ in degree of complexity. Both inductive and deductive classifications vary from the very simple to the complex. The simplest schemes are those which use discrete yes/no or 0/1 categories. More complex schemes may use several different classificatory features or variables, while the most complex involve several layers (or hierarchies).

This chapter will continue by describing the main features of each of these different types of classifications. Once the main types of classification systems have been introduced, some of the more important classification studies will be looked at.

6.3.1 Inductive classifications

Inductive classifications do not rely upon a theory of accounting to develop categories, instead they are data-driven. They start with data in the form of the specific accounting rules or practices of a number of countries. Typically, they use a large number of countries and an even larger number of accounting rules and/or practices. Groups or categories of countries are then generated by a variety of statistical techniques. Some studies have also gone a stage further and tried to explain the resultant categories by reference to the business, economic or cultural features of each country. Typically, data on a range of features such as those discussed in Chapters 4 and 5, that might help explain accounting rules or practices, would also be collected for each country. Various statistical tests would then be run to see which of these features could be used to generate the same country groupings – or, in other words, which features appeared to 'explain' the groups initially found.

6.3.2 Deductive classifications

Deductive classification schemes (sometimes instead called intuitive or *a priori* classifications) decide upon the relevant categories on the basis of the knowledge or beliefs of the classifier. They start with statements such as 'I believe that . . .' or 'I think that the most important features or factors are . . .'. One example of this would be to classify accounting systems on the basis of the valuation system used. For example, all strict historical cost systems would be placed into one category, systems using a modified historical cost system would be placed into a second category, and fully fledged inflation accounting systems would be allocated to the third group. Other examples are that in some accounting systems, the financial statements must comply with all laws; in other systems, information is presented fairly and in conformity with laws and regulations, so that they have to disclose extra information if this is required for 'fair' presentation. A third category is those where the statements must give a true and fair view even if this means that not all rules or regulations are always fully followed.

These are examples of possible classifications that use certain features of the accounting system itself to group countries. However, it is more common to find deductive classifications that instead classify countries on the basis of various of the business or cultural features discussed earlier. Examples include classifications based upon the type of legal system, financial system or cultural values. These classifications are based upon the argument that the accounting system of a country is the outcome of specific business or cultural features. If we choose the correct or relevant features or descriptors, the resulting groups of countries should have accounting rules or practices that are substantially similar inside each group and substantially different across the groups.

Many of the proposed deductive classification schemes have not been tested to check whether or not the accounting systems inside each group are indeed similar to each other while also being dissimilar to those in the other group(s). However, the validity of these classifications can be tested. To do this, countries would be assigned to the hypothesized categories using deductive reasoning. Various statistical tests would then be applied to the accounting rules or practices of the countries in each category to see whether or not the hypothesized or suggested classifications are indeed valid.

6.3.3 Complexity of classification schemes

Within either of the inductive or deductive systems of classification there may be a range of complexity of the classification schemes used. This section describes the increasingly complex approaches that have been taken.

6.3.3.1 Discrete classifications

The simplest inductive and deductive classifications would categorize or place accounting systems into discrete or mutually exclusive groups. For example, some countries use common law while others use code law, so accounting systems could be classified into two systems on the basis of whether the country uses one or other type of legal system. While this is a very simple classification it is intuitively appealing and several deductive classifications have used the legal system as the classification factor, as discussed below. Empirical studies also support the usefulness of this classificatory variable.[1]

The type of legal system is a binary variable – code versus common law – and so it provides a basis for two groups of countries. The advantage of such binary classifications is that they are very simple and easy to use: it is generally clear to which category each accounting system belongs. Other classificatory variables may be used which lead to three or more groups. At least in theory, a classification exercise could result in an infinite number of groups. However, the most useful classifications contain a limited number of groups, since as the classification scheme becomes more complex and the number of groups increases, the problem of deciding which countries fit into which groups also increases.

6.3.3.2 Classifications using continuous variables

An alternative approach to using discrete or categorical variables is to classify countries using continuous classificatory variables. For example, we might use the influence of tax rules as a classificatory variable. Countries could then be placed along a continuum ranging from the complete independence of tax rules and financial reporting rules to complete dependence, where external financial statements are identical to those used for taxation. Even where a continuous grouping or classification factor is used, countries can still be classified into two or more discrete groups. But now a second decision must also be made – namely, where along the continuum do we place the break point(s), or what are the critical value(s) of the grouping variable that differentiates between the groups? If we have chosen a sensible grouping factor, this should be fairly obvious. For example, if countries tend to cluster at the two extremes of 'little or no influence of tax rules' and 'heavy dependence on tax rules', then there are two groups of countries, and it will be fairly obvious which countries fit into which group.

6.3.3.3 Multidimensional mapping

A slightly more complex way of classifying accounting systems is to use 'multi-dimensional mapping'. Rather than classifying on the basis of one grouping factor only, this method groups accounting systems on the basis of a number of factors or features, n, where n can range from 2 to infinity. In effect, an n-dimensional picture or map is produced and countries are located on each dimension depending upon the specific values of each grouping factor. The simplest of these are two-dimensional maps, as illustrated by Exhibit 6.1. Two-dimensional classifications are fairly easy to understand and easy to represent graphically; however, there is no reason why more complex classifications cannot be developed using more dimensions or factors.

The advantage of multidimensional mapping is that it can be used to classify more complex phenomena. For example, a two-dimensional classification might be based upon:

● the independence or interdependence of tax and financial reporting rules, and
● the use of historical or current costs.

While we are using two continuous classification variables we can still place accounting systems into discrete groups. As can be seen in Exhibit 6.1, each accounting system or country is initially placed onto what may be thought of as a map of accounting systems.

---

[1] Salter and Doupnik (1992).

| Exhibit 6.1 | A possible two-dimensional classification |

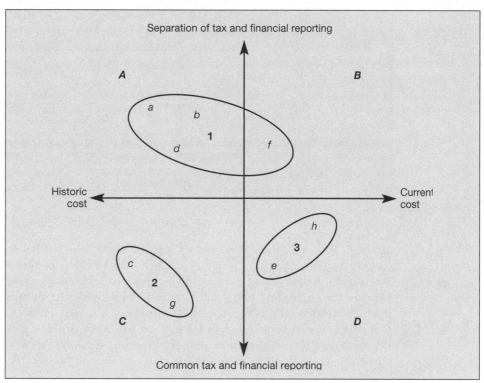

Countries where tax and financial accounting are kept separate, with the latter based upon historical costs, would be placed in sector *A*. Those where tax and financial accounting are kept separate, but the latter uses current costs, would be placed in sector *B*, etc. The exact location of each country in each quadrant would depend upon the strictness of historical cost rules and the extent to which tax rules impact upon financial reporting. Let us assume that the eight countries, *a–h*, have been correctly placed onto the map. As a second stage we can group these countries into discrete categories. From their positions on the map, as shown in Exhibit 6.1 we appear to have three groups or categories. Category or group 1 contains the four countries *a*, *b*, *d* and *f*, group 2 contains the two countries *c* and *g*, while group 3 contains the remaining two countries, *e* and *h*.

6.3.3.4 Hierarchical classifications

All of the possible classification schemes looked at so far place countries' accounting systems into discrete categories or groups. For example, in Exhibit 6.1 we have three groups of countries. Anyone interested in comparing the countries classified might want to know whether an accounting system placed in group 1 was more similar to those in group 2 or those in group 3. They might hypothesize, for example, that groups 2 and 3 are the two groups that are most alike. However, the classification scheme does not tell us this, we have to hypothesize it for ourselves.

Hierarchical classifications attempt to answer this type of question. The use of hierarchical classification systems in accounting was first proposed by Nobes (1984),

| Exhibit 6.2 | A possible hierarchical classification |

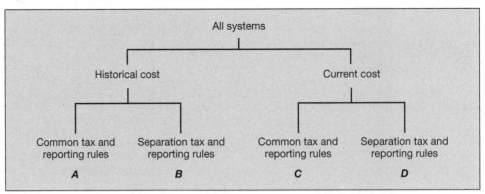

although similar classifications have a long history in the natural sciences. A hierarchical classification using the same two factors as before is presented in Exhibit 6.2. While countries are placed in one of four groups, *A-D*, we can now see the relationship between the groups and understand the linkages between the countries. In particular, this classification tells us that the more important or fundamental classificatory factor is the type of cost system. Countries that are placed in either of groups *A* or *B*, both historical cost, should have more similar accounting systems than would countries that are placed, for example in groups *A* and *C*, both common tax and reporting rules.

6.3.4 Problems of classification in accounting

Despite the large number of attempts at classification in the accounting literature, classification in accounting is contentious. There are obvious technical problems involved in carrying out any classification study. Which is the best statistical method to use? Are the data used of sufficient quantity and quality? But there are also more fundamental problems. In particular, as will be discussed below, while most of the earlier attempts at classification were attempts to classify 'accounting systems', they failed to explain adequately what this means. It could mean a variety of different things – the regulatory system and the rules that apply to all companies, or those that apply to listed companies only or to group accounts only. Alternatively, it could instead encompass the actual practices of companies – either their measurement or disclosure practices, or both. Again, this could be for all companies or just some types of companies. This lack of careful consideration and description of what is meant by an accounting system has been criticized by a number of writers and, in particular, by Roberts (1995).

Roberts argues that if we cannot agree on exactly what an accounting system is, then we have to accept that all we can do is to either classify certain coherent parts of the system, in other words entire subsystems – for example, measurement rules only – or to classify a number of rules or practices which are an incomplete representation of the entire system. In either case, we need to be very clear on why we are classifying and what we are going to do with the classifications. If we are not, then the resultant classifications are likely to be used in inappropriate ways.

6.4 Inductive classifications of accounting systems

Having outlined the main types of classification methods, this section briefly looks at some of the inductive classifications that have been carried out. While there are important differences across these studies, they all follow a similar approach. The primary data source is most often a survey of lots of quite detailed accounting rules or practices, or both. Countries are then allocated to specific groups or categories using various types of statistical analysis.

6.4.1 Use of Price Waterhouse surveys

While now far from recent, most of the inductive classifications have used Price Waterhouse (PW) survey data. PW undertook three surveys in 1973, 1975 and 1979 covering from 38 countries in 1973 to 64 companies in 1979. In each study, PW partners from each country were asked about the use of a variety of accounting practices. The issues covered included both measurement and disclosure issues, varying from a total of 233 items in 1973 to 267 items in 1979.

Two of the studies using the PW data will be briefly described here for illustrative purposes, followed in slightly more detail by a more recent study using an alternative database. The study by Da Costa, Bourgeois and Lawson (1978) is of interest not only because it was the first to use the PW data but, more importantly, because it highlights some of the problems that can occur with this type of classification. Da Costa *et al.* adopted what appears to be a sensible method of classifying accounting systems, but the conclusions reached are very different from what might have been expected. There are several reasons why this study failed to reach what might be termed 'sensible results', and some of these problems were overcome in a later study by Nair and Frank (1980). Despite the fact that this study uses data that are now more than 20 years old, it remains an important inductive classification that now provides interesting perspectives on the historical development of accounting.

6.4.2 Da Costa *et al.*'s study

Da Costa *et al.* (1978) used the subset of the 1973 PW data (100 questions in all). They input these data into a factor analysis computer program. (Factor analysis is a statistical method that summarizes large data sets; it reduces and replaces the underlying data with a much smaller set of factors all of which are linear combinations of original data.) The Da Costa *et al.* study reduced 100 of the PW questions to seven factors. These factors were then each labelled or described as follows:

- **Factor 1**: A measure of financial disclosure
- **Factor 2**: The influence of company law on accounting practice
- **Factor 3**: The importance of income measurement
- **Factor 4**: Conservatism as a guideline policy
- **Factor 5**: The influence of tax law on accounting practice
- **Factor 6**: The importance of inflation
- **Factor 7**: The orientation of information to capital market users.

Many of these factors (and especially factors 2, 4, 6 and 7) are very similar to those identified in various deductive studies. For example, factor 2 (influence of company law) is similar to the code/common law classification, while as we saw earlier, factor 4 (conservatism) was used by Gray (1988). The values for each of these seven factors were then used as inputs into a cluster analysis. (There are many different ways of doing a cluster analysis, but they typically start by placing all the countries into single country groups or clusters. The two groups or countries that are most similar to each other are then moved into a new cluster. The process then continues until a stable position of the minimum number of clusters is reached.) However, the results of this particular analysis were different from what might have been expected. Two groups or clusters emerged – a Commonwealth group and a non-Commonwealth group. The Commonwealth group makes intuitive sense. The problem lies with the second group, which consisted of the USA as well as much of South America and Europe. This group therefore classified countries such as Switzerland and Brazil (both code-based but one strict historical costs and the other an inflation adjusted system) with the USA (a common law system).

There are several possible reasons for these odd results. First, there are problems with the method of data analysis used.[2] Second, there are problems with the data. A limited set of PW data was used. Only 100 of the 233 practices contained in the PW survey were included and different classifications might have been generated if a different subset of questions had been considered.

6.4.3 Some problems of using survey data

There are several problems with the PW or indeed any other data set. The questions asked related to several different types of accounting issues. Exhibit 6.3 lists a few of the questions contained in the 1979 survey.[3]

Exhibit 6.3 Some questions asked in the Price Waterhouse (1979) survey

Question 2
Financial statements are drawn up on the premise that the business will continue in operation indefinitely.

Question 10
Departures from the going concern concept are disclosed.

Question 29
Fixed assets are stated at cost of acquisition or construction, *less* accumulated depreciation.

Question 47
In historical cost statements, revaluation reserves that arise when fixed assets are stated at an amount in excess of cost are available for charges arising on subsequent downward revaluation of fixed assets.

Question 27
The basis on which fixed assets are stated is disclosed.

Question 185
The amount written-off deferred development costs is disclosed.

---

[2] Cluster analysis is a better method to use with the original data. If factor analysis is used, then the factor scores are better used as inputs into a discriminant analysis. (A discriminant analysis is similar to a regression analysis but the independent variable is not continuous but is a 0/1 variable of membership/non-membership of the category.)

[3] Fitzgerald *et al.* (1979).

From this, it can be seen that the PW surveys included questions on broad concepts and underlying principles as well as questions on specific issues inside each of the financial statements – both measurement and disclosure issues. The questions inputed into the statistical analysis are then accorded equal importance. However, some of the questions asked are very important, others are trivial while others cover issues that are of importance to only a few companies. If the survey includes all of these types of questions the statistical analysis cannot differentiate between important and unimportant ones and will treat all questions in the same way. Therefore, unimportant issues may swamp important issues so that the resultant classifications may either be very unstable or incorrect.

If we were to design a database of accounting issues to be used as the basis for developing an inductive classification scheme we would have to decide which issues are important and which are unimportant. To do this, we would have to decide whether to include both regulations and practices or whether instead to limit the database to just regulations or just practices. A classification based upon regulations or *de jure* issues might be quite different from one that was based upon practices or *de facto* issues. As we have seen earlier, in some countries the accounting regulations are set with the needs of the tax authorities or creditors in mind. Discretionary accounting practices and disclosures may instead be designed to meet the needs of stock market participants.

We would also have to consider the question of which types of organization should be covered by our database. In the UK, this is not really a problem. All but the very smallest UK limited liability companies have to follow the same Companies Acts and accounting standards while the stock market requires very few additional disclosures. In other countries, such as the US, there are very different requirements for listed companies (regulated by the Securities and Exchange Commission or SEC) and non-listed companies (regulated at the state rather than the federal or country-wide level). In much of Europe the important distinction is instead between the individual company and the group. In France, for example, group financial statements have been heavily regulated by the stock market. The regulations are mainly aimed at providing information useful for investors and the rules often contain a wide range of choices. In contrast, the financial statements of individual companies have been mainly regulated by the government. The rules are mainly designed to meet the needs of the government, the tax authorities and creditors. They tend not only to result in relatively conservative profit measures but they are also highly uniform, giving companies little discretion or choice in what methods to use. Therefore, if our database of accounting issues was restricted to issues that applied to group financial statements we might find that France, the UK and the US were all placed in the same group. If instead our database was limited to issues applying to individual company financial statements we would probably find that the UK and France were placed into different groups. (The US might even be totally excluded from our database as listed companies have to report only group financial statements.)

6.4.4 Nair and Frank's study

Nair and Frank (1980) argued in a similar way that we should not use all accounting issues to categorize countries. In particular they argued that a classification based upon disclosure issues might be quite different from a classification based upon measurement issues.

They therefore split the 1973 and 1975 PW data into measurement issues and disclosure issues and developed two classifications – one based upon measurement issues and the other based upon disclosure issues. The data were fed into a factor analysis program and groups were formed by allocating countries to categories based upon their highest factor loadings.

To see how this is done, assume that we are classifying three countries 1–3 and, having used factor analysis, we find that the underlying data can be described by three factors, *A–C*. The factor weightings for the countries are as follows:

Factor	*A*	*B*	*C*
1	0.9	0.05	0.05
2	0.4	0.3	0.3
3	0.3	0.4	0.3

If we classify on the basis of the highest factor weightings, as done by Nair and Frank, we would allocate countries 1 and 2 to one group as they each have the highest weighting on factor *A*, and country 3 to the other group. However, if we instead use a rather more sophisticated method, namely discriminant analysis, we would allocate on the basis of their factor loadings on all three factors. Now, country 1 would be allocated to one group and countries 2 and 3 would be allocated to the other group – a result that is more appropriate.

Looking first at Nair and Frank's results for measurement issues, the groups generated from 1973 data are reported in Exhibit 6.4.

Five factors were extracted from the 1973 measurement data. No country had their highest loading on the fifth factor, so four groups were formed. These groups generally appear to make sense. They may be thought of as being:

Group 1: Commonwealth group
Group 2: Latin American group
Group 3: Continental European group
Group 4: United States-led group.

Exhibit 6.4 Nair and Frank's groups based upon measurement issues (1973 data)

1	2	3	4
Australia	Argentina	Belgium	Canada
Bahamas	Bolivia	France	Japan
Fiji	Brazil	Germany	Mexico
Ireland	Chile	Italy	Panama
Jamaica	Colombia	Spain	Philippines
Kenya	Ethiopia	Sweden	USA
Netherlands	India	Switzerland	
New Zealand	Paraguay	Venezuela	
Pakistan	Peru		
Singapore	Uruguay		
South Africa			
Trinidad and Tobago			
UK			
Zimbabwe			

Source: Nair and Frank (1980). Reproduced with kind permission of the American Accounting Association

Exhibit 6.5 Nair and Frank's groups based upon disclosure issues (1973 data)

1	2	3	4	5	6	7
Australia	Bolivia	Belgium	Canada	Argentina	Sweden	Switzerland
Bahamas	Germany	Brazil	Mexico	Chile		
Fiji	India	Colombia	Netherlands	Ethiopia		
Ireland	Japan	France	Panama	Uruguay		
Jamaica	Pakistan	Italy	Philippines			
Kenya	Peru	Paraguay	USA			
New Zealand		Spain				
Singapore		Venezuela				
South Africa						
Trinidad and						
Tobago						
UK						
Zimbabwe						

Source: Nair and Frank (1980). Reproduced with kind permission of the American Accounting Association

The analysis was just as successful when the 1975 data were used, although now six factors were extracted. Five groups were formed, four being quite similar to those found using the 1973 data plus group 5, which contained only one country, Chile. The disclosure-based groups are generally less easy to characterize (although from a purely statistical point of view the classifications are just as successful). As shown in Exhibit 6.5 seven groups were derived from the 1973 disclosure data.

Group 1 is again a Commonwealth group which, with the exception of the omission of The Netherlands, is identical to the 1973 measurement group. Group 4, the US-led group, is again very similar to that found using 1973 measurement data, with the only differences being the addition of The Netherlands and the omission of Japan, which is instead placed in group 2. The other four groups are difficult to explain; in particular there is no clear rationale or explanation for group 2 which contains Japan, two Commonwealth Asian countries (Pakistan and India), two South American countries (Bolivia and Peru) and Germany, a result that has no intuitive appeal. The disclosure groups are generally not very stable, with many countries changing groups between 1973 and 1975, suggesting that the classification is not too successful.

Nair and Frank also attempted to seek explanations for the groups obtained by using 14 cultural and economic variables to discriminate among the 1975 groups of countries. The variables chosen included language variables, which they argued acted as proxies for cultural and historical links, various GNP-based variables reflecting the stage of economic development and a series of trading bloc variables. The analysis met with some success with two trading bloc variables, the use of French and *per capita* income being important in explaining the measurement groups, and the use of German and English, the importance of the agricultural sector and three trading bloc variables helping to explain the disclosure results. However, these explanations of group membership are far from conclusive. Indeed, they had little success when using these variables to predict rather than to explain group membership.

There are several ways in which we can assess the success of these inductive classifications. Statistical analysis is obviously important, and this suggests that Nair and Frank have been at least moderately successful. But more important, we need to ask ourselves: 'Do the groups appear to make sense?' Again, it would appear that the classifications are reasonably successful, but not a total success. Some of the groups found by Nair and Frank make intuitive sense, but others do not. Likewise, some of the groups are fairly stable, but others are not.

There are a number of possible explanations for why the analysis was not more successful. The analysis was based upon the PW data which has been strongly criticized, especially by Nobes (1982). He highlights four problems with these surveys. That they contain a number of mistakes; other answers, while correct, give a misleading picture; the questions chosen tend to exaggerate UK/US differences; and, most importantly, the data were not developed for this purpose. As Nobes (1982, p. 63) argues:

> When classifying plants or animals, biologists largely ignore the most obvious characteristics. That is, they do not carry out factor analysis on animals by weight, colour, number of legs, nature of body covering, length of life, etc. This would merely lead to a classification of that data. It would group man with ostriches, dolphins with sharks, bats with owls, and so on.

A number of later studies have instead used other data sources, including specially developed surveys of accountants[4] and surveys of actual financial statements.[5]

6.4.5 D'Arcy's study

One particularly interesting recent study is by d'Arcy (2001). This study is unusual in that it concentrates solely upon accounting rules for listed companies rather than practices. The data used applies to 14 countries plus the IASC and is based upon the information contained in Ordelheide and KPMG (1995). It therefore has a clear focus – *de jure* harmonization – so meeting many of the concerns of Roberts (1995) regarding the applicability of the databases used and the purpose of the classification.

One problem of course concerns the choice of variables. In this case, that was dictated primarily by data availability. Only those items that could be analyzed into required/forbidden/permitted were included, resulting in 129 variables or 88 topics.[6] This of course raises again the issue of whether or not these are the 'correct' items to be used. Indeed, Nobes (2004) argues that this study also swamped important questions with trivial questions. He gives the examples of six questions on negative goodwill but only two on positive goodwill, or five questions on hyperinflation and none on leasing. While it is undoubtedly true that the database, like any, is not as exhaustive as it might be, d'Arcy (2004) counters that the rules used are important, so that it is not trivia swamping important items, but rather that not all important items are included.

The statistical methods used were a marked improvement upon the prior studies discussed above. Two methods were used, simple matching similarity coefficients, or SM, and cluster analysis. SM counts the number of items for which a pair of countries have the same rules. Not surprisingly, the SM was highest for Austria and Germany (91.5 per cent). The lowest was France and the US (29 per cent), while most pairs ranged between 50 per cent and 70 per cent agreement. Australia was unusual in that all pairs except that with the IASC were less than 60 per cent, so prompting d'Arcy to describe it as having an 'outsider position'.

---

[4] See, for example, Doupnik and Salter (1993).

[5] See, for example, Choi and Bavishi (1980).

[6] These answers were converted into dichotomous or binary data, with 1/0 being required yes and forbidden no, 0/1 being required no and forbidden yes, and 0/0 required no and forbidden no, i.e. the item is permitted.

The cluster analysis was carried out using a variety of different methods and some different non-equal weighting schemes. While there were some differences in terms of exactly when a particular country joined a cluster, each method resulted in the same four quite distinct clusters. Thus, the first pair of countries to 'join' a cluster were Germany and Austria followed by France and Belgium who then joined the other two to form a four country European grouping. This group was later joined by Switzerland, Denmark, Netherlands and the UK to form the cluster one, a European cluster. This was later joined by a rather more heterogeneous group, or cluster two, of Sweden, Spain and Japan. The third cluster, also more heterogeneous than the European group or cluster one, was the three country group of the US, Canada and the IASC. Australia remained a separate one country cluster for the longest time, finally joining the USA group only under a final two cluster solution. This can be seen in Exhibit 6.6 which reproduces the cluster result graphically.

While the methodology applied is clearly a significant improvement upon earlier studies, some results might be thought of as unexpected. First, there is no UK–US group. However, there has been considerable debate recently upon whether or not such a group exists[7] and it can easily be argued that actually this is not a surprising result. Much more surprising is Australia which appears to be quite different from any other country.

Nobes (2004) gives a detailed critique of the work in which he criticized the database used for a number of reasons. In particular that it contains a number of misunderstanding and mistakes. He analyses in detail the mistakes he thinks were made with respect to Australia, the US and the UK and then compares these countries to Germany. Now, instead of finding that of these four countries, the UK and Germany are the most similar, Australia and the UK, Australia and the US, and the UK and the US, are all more similar than

Exhibit 6.6 **Clusters found by d'Arcy (2001)**

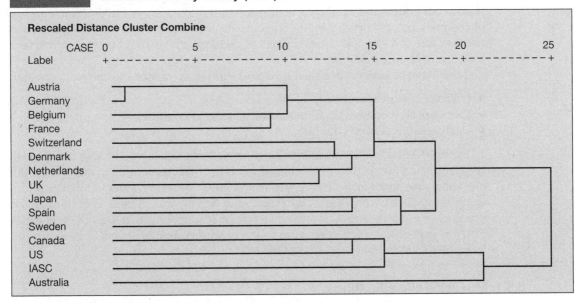

Source: d'Arcy (2001). Fig 1. Dendogram average linkage between groups

---

[7] Alexander and Archer (2000); Nobes (2003).

Germany and the UK. Some of these differences undoubtedly are caused by mistakes, as detailed by Nobes, but some of them also appear to be due to differences in interpretation. D'Arcy (2004) details several of the areas where the differences appear due to interpretation rather than downright mistakes as well as arguing that indeed Australia has had several rules that are quite distinct from those found elsewhere.

6.5 Deductive classifications of accounting systems

Having looked at some of the inductive classification schemes that exist, this section discusses some of the more important deductive classifications that have been proposed in the past.

As discussed in section three, deductive classifications are usually indirect classifications. They use as classificatory factor(s) those characteristics that influence or help explain the accounting systems of countries. Many of the more important influences on accounting were discussed in Chapters 4 and 5. We saw that there were very many influences on accounting and many factors that helped to explain regulations or practices. We therefore need to select the most important factors. Fortunately, this is not quite as difficult as it might at first seem.

Many of the factors that influence accounting are closely related to each other. For example, the legal and tax systems tend to be highly related. Code law countries tend to have far less of a separation between tax and accounting regulations than do common law countries. The same countries will tend to be classified in the same ways whichever of these two factors is used. Therefore, when classifying countries we could choose to use either the legal system or the tax system as a basis for classification, but we would not need to use both. We can also make our task easier by ignoring some countries. Obviously, we would like a classification system that correctly groups all countries and if we cannot correctly classify all countries we should try to refine and improve our analysis. But at this stage in our understanding of comparative accounting systems, we can omit some groups of countries and still develop useful classification schemes. Most of the classifications in the literature, for example, have ignored or excluded the ex-communist countries and most less developed countries.

Three types of factors have been used as classificatory variables in the past, namely:

- the objectives of accounting,
- the political, economic or cultural environments of countries,
- external influences on countries.

Examples of classifications using each of these types of factors will now be explored. However, before doing this, a word of caution is in order. Accounting in many countries has undergone some major changes in recent years. Increasing internationalization of companies and the work of the IASB have led to some major changes in both rules and practices of many countries. It must therefore be remembered that each of these classifications may only apply to one point in time and their results or conclusions may not be equally valid or indeed at all valid now.

6.5.1 Mueller's classifications

Accounting classifications can be traced back to the early work of Hatfield (1966), first published in 1911, who noted similarities between the US and the UK and between France and Germany. The modern work really began with Mueller (1967) who, using casual observation, divided accounting systems into four types – largely, but not exclusively, based upon the objectives of accounting:

1 **Macroeconomic systems**, such as Sweden at that time, where the most important function of accounting was to provide data to facilitate governmental direction of the economy. (*Note*: Since this work was done, the Swedish accounting system has undergone some major changes. Following Sweden's entry into the EU, the accounting system is now less influenced by macroeconomic considerations.)

2 **Microeconomic systems**, such as The Netherlands, where accounting is seen as a branch of business economics, and is aimed primarily at aiding the objectives of the individual business.

3 **Independent discipline systems**, such as the US and the UK, where accounting is seen as a service function derived from business practices and is characterized by the use of professional judgement.

4 **Uniform systems**, such as France or Germany, where accounting is seen as a means of government administration and control.

The grouping variable is fairly complex, involving as it does the ways in which accounting has developed and the ways in which it is viewed in a country. Although Mueller offered typical examples of countries in each category it was often not clear where other countries fit – or, indeed, if they fit at all – into any of the four groups.

While Mueller treated the four groups as distinct categories, placing each country into only one of the four groups, later writers have used his ideas but modified the analysis. Rather than using these concepts to classify countries into four separate groups, they have been used to develop a 2 × 2 classification which combines the characteristics into pairs. One axis is then the micro/macro orientation of the accounting system – whether the primary objective of accounting statements is seen as the provision of information useful for the economy as a whole or information useful to the individual company or corporate stakeholder. The other axis measures the way in which regulations are set – whether a uniform system or a system of independent and flexible rules. For example, Oldham (1987) proposed such a classification, as illustrated in Exhibit 6.7. Illustrating some of the changes occurring in accounting, Oldham produced two different classifications, the one reproduced in Exhibit 6.7, which illustrates the position in the mid-1980s and a second classification, reproduced in Exhibit 6.8, which refers to the position a decade earlier, in the mid-1970s.

6.5.2 Spheres of influence

Mueller's classification was based upon features of the domestic institutional or cultural environment of countries. However, as discussed earlier, the accounting rules and practices of countries are typically influenced also by external factors. In some countries most of the rules and practices have been imported from elsewhere, with little or no local adaptation. Therefore they bear little or no relation to specific features of that country, such as the stage of business development or business complexity. Such a mismatch between the internal business or cultural environment and accounting is likely to be particularly common in developing countries. Cooke and Wallace (1990), for example, provide evidence suggesting that developed and developing countries should be categorized separately. They looked at the financial disclosure regulations of a number of countries and tried to match these with a variety of economic and cultural features. They found that the relationship between disclosure regulations and features

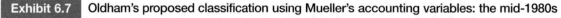

| Exhibit 6.7 | Oldham's proposed classification using Mueller's accounting variables: the mid-1980s |

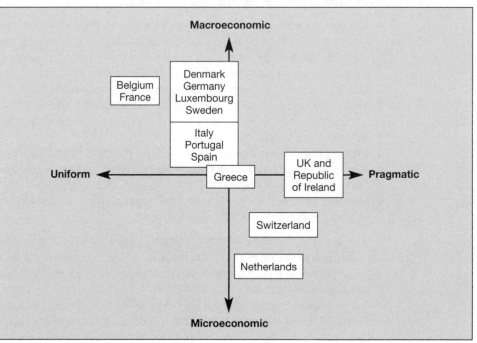

Source: Oldham (1987).

| Exhibit 6.8 | Oldham's proposed classification using Mueller's accounting variables: the mid-1970s |

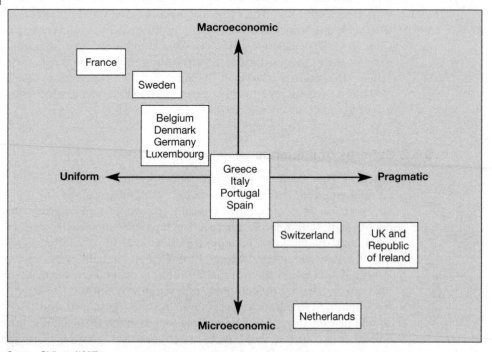

Source: Oldham (1987).

internal to the country was stronger for developed countries than it was for developing countries. Interestingly, and somewhat surprisingly, they also found that the stage of economic development does not help to explain the extent of regulation. This provides clear evidence that, at least for developing countries, we cannot successfully classify if we use only factors that are internal to the country. As discussed in Chapter 4, the accounting regulation of developing countries will often be highly influenced by trade partners or past colonial or other links to particular developed countries.

This idea of exporting or importing accounting rules and practices leads to an alternative type of classification system, which is best illustrated by the work of Seidler (1967). He discussed what he termed 'spheres of influence' and identified three systems:

- **British**: The UK and countries influenced by the UK, including the Commonwealth.
- **American**: The US and areas influenced by the US, such as Israel, Mexico and parts of South America.
- **Continental**: Led by France, and including those parts of southern Europe and South America which base their legal system on the Code Napoléon.

This is a very simple classification system that, in terms of how it is derived, is almost the complete opposite of Mueller's classification schemes in that it ignores all internal factors. Instead, it looks only at external influences and identifies three countries that Seidler argues have had the greatest success in exporting their accounting systems.

While it might appear to be relatively easy to group countries on the basis of external influences, even here a more complex classification is required. Seidler's three categories are clearly not exhaustive and so the proposed classification does not meet one of the requirements of a good classification system. For example, it excludes Scandinavia; also excluded are parts of Africa, which includes former Portuguese colonies which appear to have a quite distinct accounting system following their former colonial ruler.[8] However, more important than these omissions is the fact that the end-product of this type of classification, in terms of the groups developed, will be different depending upon the initial starting point. If we look at what happened in the period from the Second World War until the mid-1960s, when Seidler developed his classification, then it is probably correct to classify US and UK spheres of influence as separate groups. However, if we go back further into history, it can be argued that the UK and US systems are not distinct. The US was originally very influenced by the UK, with many of the leaders of the US profession in its early days being UK-trained.

If we look at what happened to accounting in the 1970s and 1980s, then a far more complex classification scheme would have to be developed. Now EU Directives and European countries would be shown as influencing the UK, while the UK has in turn influenced the EU. Therefore the UK has also influenced accounting in other European countries. A classification developed in the 1990s and 2000s would have to show the increasing international influence of US accounting, both through direct pressures or influences and through its indirect influence via the IASC/IASB and international stock markets. Although these moves towards increasing regional and international harmonization are far from complete, an up-to-date version of the spheres of influence model would have to be far more complex than the model suggested by Seidler. Indeed, it is not at all clear that Seidler's classification helps at all to explain *current* changes in accounting systems.

---

[8] United Nations (1991).

6.5.3 Gray's classification

Slightly more complex than any of the categorial classifications looked at so far are classifications using multidimensional mapping. As discussed earlier, any number of dimensions is possible although the simplest forms are those that use only two dimensions or classificatory factors. One example of a two-dimensional classification was developed by Gray (1988). As discussed in Chapter 5, Gray described four accounting values which he hypothesized were linked to the culture of the country. Using these four accounting values, he went on to suggest two two-dimensional maps of accounting systems. One of the most interesting and important things about this work is how Gray defined two types of 'accounting system'. First, he classified countries on the basis of their system of regulation. Two dimensions were considered – who regulates accounting (statutory control versus the profession) and how flexible are the rules that they set (uniform versus flexible). He also produced a second classification based upon the measurement and disclosure rules themselves. The two dimensions used here were the importance of conservatism or prudence and the openness or transparency of the disclosure rules. Countries were then placed on the maps on the basis of judgment, as shown in Exhibit 6.9.

Gray did not use the maps to develop discrete categories or a classification of countries, being content to place countries into the relevant quadrants. However, the work could be extended fairly easily and countries could be classified or placed into discrete groups on the basis of their location on the maps. If we look at the map of measurement and disclosure systems, for example, we could argue that there are two groups of countries. Those countries placed in the quadrant of relatively high secrecy and conservatism fall into one group, while those countries placed in the quadrant of relatively high optimism and transparency form a second.

6.5.4 AAA's morphology of accounting systems

This idea of multidimensional mapping was also used by the American Accounting Association (AAA) to produce what they called a morphology of accounting systems.[9] This morphology is a systematic attempt to list and describe all of the most important features that influence accounting systems. The AAA's proposed morphology is illustrated in Exhibit 6.10. As can be seen, the AAA identified eight influences on accounting systems, or what it termed 'parameters'. Each of these parameters was then described in terms of a limited number of 'states of nature'. For example, the AAA argued that a country's economic system had an important influence on the accounting system. In addition, the economic system of a country could take one of four possible forms or states of nature: it could be a traditional economy, a market economy, a planned market economy or a planned economy.

Again, this is an indirect way of describing accounting systems in that the parameters identified are not aspects of the accounting system itself. Instead, they are features of the business and economic environment of countries. The main advantage of this approach is that it is a way of describing a very complex construct – the accounting system – in a very much simpler way. Instead of having to describe an almost infinite number of accounting rules and practices we can instead describe a small number of parameters. Accounting systems with the same values for each parameter would

---

[9] American Accounting Association (1977).

Exhibit 6.9 Two-dimensional classifications proposed by Gray

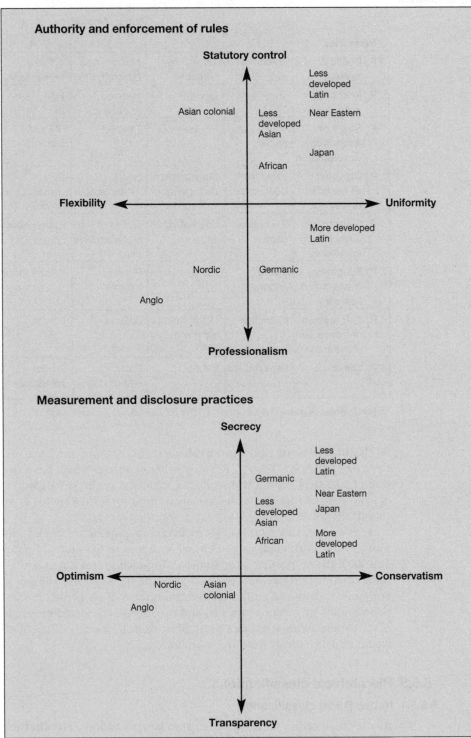

Exhibit 6.10 AAA's proposed morphology of accounting systems

Parameter	States of nature				
	1	2	3	4	5
P_1 Political system	Traditional oligarchy	Totalitarian oligarchy	Modernizing oligarchy	Tutelary democracy	Political democracy
P_2 Economic system	Traditional	Market	Planned market	Plan	–
P_3 Stage of economic development	Traditional society	Pre take-off	Take-off	Drive to maturity	Mass consumption
P_4 Objectives of financial reporting	Investment decisions	Management performance	Social measurement	Sector planning and control	National policy objectives
P_5 Sources of/ authority for standards	Executive decree	Legislative action	Government administrative unit	Public–private consortium	Private
P_6 Education, training and licensing	Public informal	Public formal	Private informal	Private formal	–
P_7 Enforcement of ethics and standards	Executive	Government administrative unit	Judicial	Private	–
P_8 Client	Government	Public	Public enterprises	Private enterprises	–

Source: American Accounting Association (1977), p. 99. Reproduced with permission.

be classified as being in the same category. For example, the UK could be described as P_1^5, P_2^2, P_3^5, P_4^1, P_5^4, P_6^4, P_7^4, P_8^4. Any other countries which have the same combination of parameter values would also be members of the same group as the UK, and it is hypothesized that they will have an accounting system that is essentially similar to that of the UK.

At first sight, this morphology results in an extremely complex and large classification scheme. With eight parameters all with four or five states of nature there are fully 160,000 different possible combinations. In practice, it is not as bad as this, as many of these combinations are not feasible – for example, a country will not have a traditional economic system and a mass consumption stage of economic development. However, the morphology remains untested and no one has calculated how many combinations of the various states of nature exist in practice, or how many different accounting groups would actually emerge from the morphology.

6.5.5 Hierarchical classifications

6.5.5.1 Nobes (1984) classification

All the classification schemes looked at so far are categorial classifications. They all place countries into discrete, non-overlapping and hopefully exhaustive categories. As such, they assume that all the countries in any one category share similar characteristics while also being significantly different from the countries in the other categories. In practice, of course, it is not as simple as this. Instead, differences between countries are a matter of degree and some countries placed in the same group will be more alike than are other countries in the same group. In addition, countries in different groups will share some common characteristics. We therefore want to know which countries or groups of countries are most similar or dissimilar and how similar or dissimilar they are. Answers to these types of questions can be provided by the most complex deductive classifications, which are hierarchical classifications, as illustrated by the work of Nobes (1984). He proposed a classification that sought to classify the measurement practices of listed companies in developed western countries in 1980 – that is, before corporate practices might have changed due to EU harmonization moves. The proposed hierarchy was used to classify 14 countries, as illustrated in Exhibit 6.11, and data on these countries were also collected to test the proposed classification.

As can be seen, this classification has certain similarities with some of the earlier deductive classifications. At the most fundamental level Nobes again argues for two classes of accounting systems, microeconomic- and macroeconomic-based. In the micro class, accounting is seen as serving the needs of the company itself or its specific stakeholders, while in the macro class the orientation is more towards the needs of society as a whole. Each of these two classes splits into two families, with the resultant four families very largely equating with the four groups proposed by Mueller. Similarly, the two species of UK- and US-influenced countries are similar to two of the groups proposed by Seidler.

Exhibit 6.11	Nobes's proposed hierarchical classification of accounting systems (1984)

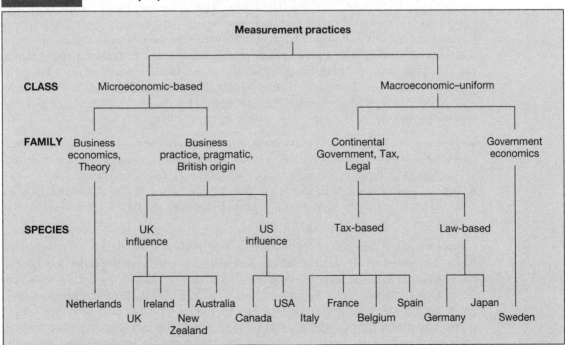

Source: Nobes (1984), p. 94. Reproduced with kind permission of Croom Helm.

This classification was tested by Nobes and the results strongly supported the two classes, although there was relatively little support for the finer categories. The classification was also tested by Doupnik and Salter (1993). They produced an inductive classification applying statistical analysis to data on actual accounting practices. They then assessed whether or not their classification and the categories of countries developed were similar or dissimilar to those suggested by Nobes. While Nobes's original classification scheme was designed to explain measurement practices, Doupnik and Salter tested it using data on both measurement and disclosure practices. In addition, they used data for 1990 rather than 1980 (when the classification was first proposed) and more countries. This is an example of a study that uses cluster analysis as a means of grouping countries.

Despite using very different data from that originally employed by Nobes, Doupnik and Salter's results provide some quite strong support for Nobes's classification. They found two solutions, one with two groups and one with nine groups. At the two-group level, the results clearly support the micro/macro split with the classification being identical to that proposed by Nobes. The nine-group solution also tends to support Nobes's classification.

6.5.5.2 Nobes (1998) study

In a later study, Nobes (1998) sought to instead explain differences in financial reporting practices and to then use this to develop a hypothetical classification of financial reporting systems. He argued that, of the various factors discussed in the first two chapters of this section, the single most important factor in explaining reporting differences is the financing system. Financing systems can vary across countries in terms of two features: the main source of finance, and the relationship between the company and its finance providers. Finance can be mainly in the form of credit (i.e. debt) or in the form of equity (i.e. shares). The providers of both may maintain an arm's length relationship with the company, where they depend upon the financial statements for information and have no means to directly influence the company, or they may be insiders with a privileged or private relationship to the company through, for example, board membership or other long-term close ties. While not inevitable, outsiders tend to be dominant in strong-equity countries and strong-credit countries tend to be countries where insiders are dominant. This results in two types of financial reporting systems:

- **Type A** – strong equity and outsiders dominant: where the financial reporting system is relatively open, being designed to report to those with no access to other information and the rules for reported earnings are relatively non-conservative.
- **Type B** – strong credit and insiders dominant: where the financial reporting system is relatively non-informative and reported earnings are based upon conservative rules.

Nobes argues that other factors are less important, are closely related to the financing system or are not the factors that actually determine the reporting system. For example, while the level of agreement between taxation and reporting rules may differ across countries in a systematic way, it is not the cause of accounting differences. Rather, the need for accounting for other users such as equity providers meant that tax and reporting rules began to diverge, while the lack of competing users of financial reports meant that the two systems could remain in agreement. Similarly, he argues that culture may help to explain the financing system of countries rather than being a direct determinant of the reporting system. However, culture is rather more complex than this, in that two types of countries may be distinguished. In a manner similar to Seidler's spheres of influence, Nobes argues that there are two types of countries, those that are culturally self-sufficient (CSS) and those that are culturally dominated (CD). Culturally dominated countries will have a mismatch between their accounting systems and their financing systems if only one of them has been imported from a culturally self-sufficient country.

These arguments lead to five propositions, three relating to the type of financial reporting system in existence and two being concerned with the process of change in accounting practices:

P1   If a country is culturally self-sufficient with strong equity outsiders dominant then it will have a Type A system.

P2   If a country is culturally self-sufficient with strong credit insiders dominant then it will have a Type B system.

P3   If a country is culturally dominated it will have the accounting system of the dominant country.

P4   As a country develops a strong-equity outsiders market, it will move towards a Type A system.

P5   Strong equity outsiders companies in countries where strong-credit insiders are dominant will move to a Type A system.

Nobes provides a number of examples to support these propositions. It is simplest just to quote him on this:

1 New Zealand is a CD country with wholesale importation of British culture and institutions, including a strong-equity outsider system and Class A accounting. Whether the Class A accounting results from the equity market or from direct cultural pressure is not important to the model, it probably arises from both.

2 China is a country without a strong equity-outsider tradition but which seems to be moving towards such a system. Class A accounting is followed.

3 Malawi is a CD country with very weak equity markets but where the accountancy profession has adopted Class A accounting, consistent with its colonial inheritance from the UK.

4 The Deutsche Bank, Bayer and Nestlé are companies from countries with traditionally weak equity markets. These companies are now interested in world equity-outsider markets, so they are adopting Class A accounting for their group accounts.

(Nobes, 1998, p. 180)

In the light of this analysis, Nobes then went on to update his earlier hypothesized classification, as reproduced in Exhibit 6.12. A number of important changes have been made. In particular, he has responded to a number of the criticisms made by Roberts (1995) and the classification system no longer seeks to classify countries. Instead it classifies the accounts of groups of companies. Therefore, the accounting system is the system of financial reporting rules as they apply to particular groups of companies. For example, one system is US GAAP rather than the US as US GAAP does not apply to companies that are not registered with the SEC. Likewise another group is 'standard French' rather than France, as companies can use IASB rules for group accounts if they wish.

| Exhibit 6.12 | Nobes's proposed hierarchical classification of accounting systems (1998) |

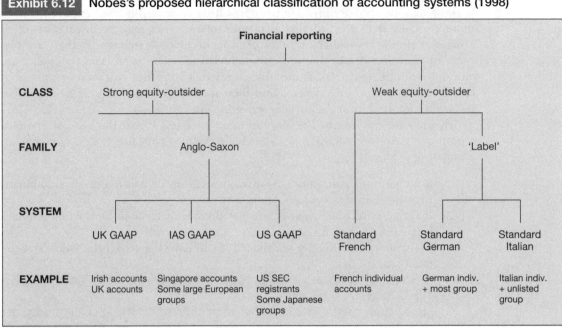

Source: Extract from Nobes (1998), p. 181.

6.6 What conclusions can be drawn?

As we have seen in this chapter, classifications have been developed using a variety of different approaches and there often appears to be little in common between many of the studies. The deductive studies classify on the basis of a wide range of different economic and cultural factors. However, many of these factors are highly correlated so that the resultant groups of countries identified by the various studies are often very similar. These studies suggest, in particular, that there are leading countries in each group. Other countries, often less developed and with historical political and economic links to the leading countries, are influenced by and follow them. When it comes to explaining these groups, the most obvious result is that there are at least two types of accounting systems: a law-based, standardized, macro-based system and a more pragmatic, professionally orientated, micro-based system.

Perhaps the main contribution of the deductive studies is not so much to offer classifications of particular countries, but rather to offer descriptions of the key features of national accounting systems and to suggest which factors are influential in their development.

The inductive studies offer a quite different way of developing a classification. Rather than relying upon deductive or *a priori* arguments they use statistical tests to analyse a large amount of detailed information on accounting rules and/or practices. These studies have a number of weaknesses, particularly the misuse of statistical tests and unthinking use of large data sets. They have also used different types of data and included different countries and different time periods. It is not too surprising, therefore, that the results of the many different classification studies are not always consistent. What is perhaps more surprising is the extent of agreement that there is across the various studies.

Some groups and subgroups clearly emerge from many of the classification studies. In particular, there appear to be:

1 a large Commonwealth group, which may be split into two subgroups of:
   (a) developed Commonwealth, and
   (b) developing Commonwealth;
2 a US-influenced group;
3 a South American group;
4 a European group, which may be split into two subgroups of:
   (a) Central and North Europe, and
   (b) South Europe.

There is also evidence to support the view that no single classification can successfully include all accounting systems, especially when an 'accounting system' is defined to include all aspects of accounting. Disclosure and measurement systems are often sufficiently different to mean that countries need to be classified on the basis of either their disclosure system or their measurement system. While more work needs to be done in this area, different groups will probably also emerge if we consider the practices of different types of companies. For example, countries might be classified quite differently if we looked only at the accounting practices of large listed groups rather than, for example, the practices of individual companies or smaller non-listed groups. In particular, the larger and more international a company is, then the more likely it is to follow internationally accepted practices and the fewer differences there should be across companies from different countries.

There are several possible ways forward. We could use increasingly sophisticated statistical methods alongside databases that have been specifically developed for the purpose of classification. This would undoubtedly lead to better classifications as many of the problems of the existing classifications could be avoided. However, the new classifications will probably not be significantly better or very different from those discussed above. Before we can develop new and significantly improved or more useful data sets of accounting rules and practices we need to decide which rules and practices are important and vary in a consistent and predictable manner across countries, and which occur randomly or are temporary or trivial. The most useful way forward is therefore not to carry on replicating past studies using improved data sets or statistical tests, but instead to concentrate upon detailed individual country case studies. Another useful way forward is to look beyond the financial statements to the aspects of financial reporting and disclosure that will continue to be influenced by national institutional and cultural factors, as explained in Chapter 15.

Summary and conclusions

This chapter has looked at attempts to classify the accounting systems of various countries. All of these classifications attempt to place accounting systems into distinct or non-overlapping groups or categories. The accounting systems inside any one group should share similar characteristics while also being different from the systems placed in the other groups.

The chapter provided an overview of the different types of classifications which are all based upon one or other of two types of reasoning. We saw how deductive or *a priori* classifications start with a theory of accounting or accounting differences which is used to develop the categories. Key features of the accounting system or the economic, institutional or cultural environment of countries are identified on the basis of prior knowledge and theoretical arguments and these are used to guide the classification of accounting systems. Inductive classifications, in contrast, start with the accounting rules or practices themselves and use various statistical techniques to uncover the underlying groups.

Having discussed the different ways in which classifications can be developed, the chapter went on to describe examples of each of the main types of classification. Several of the more important and more influential empirical studies were discussed. These empirical studies cover a range of different countries, use data from very different time periods and even define an 'accounting system' in quite different ways. As such, they have also come to some quite different conclusions regarding the resultant groups of countries. However, they do share a number of common results and this chapter finished by drawing out conclusions regarding the different types of accounting systems that appear to exist internationally.

Key points from the chapter:

- Classification helps simplify a complex world and helps organize ideas.
- Classification systems may be inductive or deductive.
- The complexity of classification systems increases across discrete, continuous multidimensional and hierarchical approaches.
- Inductive methods generate classification systems from large data sets.
- Deductive methods generate classifications from first principles and then apply them to data.

Questions

The following questions test your understanding of the material contained in the chapter and allow you to relate your understanding to the learning outcomes specified at the start of this chapter. The learning outcomes are repeated here. Each question is cross-referenced to the relevant section of the chapter.

Explain why it is important to classify accounting systems

1 Why might users of accounts be interested in classifications of accounting systems? (section 6.2)

2 Why might accounting regulators, both nationally and internationally, be interested in classifications of accounting systems? (section 6.2)

Distinguish simple from complex classification systems and deductive from inductive approaches to classification

3 What are the main types of classification schemes that have been used to classify accounting systems? Give an example of each type. (section 6.3)

4 Which do you think are the most useful? Why? (section 6.3)

5 What types of factors have been used as classificatory variables in deductive classifications? Give an example of the use of each type of factor. (section 6.3.1)

Explain the advantages and limitations of the different types of classification systems

6 What are the strengths and weaknesses of the inductive approach to classification? (section 6.3.1)

7 What are the strengths and weaknesses of the deductive approach to classification? (section 6.3.2)

Evaluate published research which develops or uses classification systems

8 Of the inductive classification studies described in this chapter, which do you think is the best? Why? (section 6.4)

9 If you were to develop an inductive classification, how would you go about doing it? What are the main problems that you think you would encounter? (section 6.4)

10 Of the deductive classification studies described in this chapter, which do you think is the best? Why? (section 6.5)

11 If you were to develop a deductive classification, how would you go about doing it? What are the main problems that you think you would encounter? (section 6.5.)

12 The term 'accounting system' can be taken to mean *de jure* or *de facto* measurement or reporting practices of all companies or certain types of companies. To what extent have the classification studies described in this chapter differentiated between different concepts of an accounting system? (sections 6.4 and 6.5)

13 What evidence is there that the results of classifying countries will be different if different concepts of an accounting system are considered? (For example, to what extent might the groups be different if all companies are considered or if only listed group companies are considered?) (sections 6.4 and 6.5)

14 Which concepts or definitions of an accounting system are likely to be the easiest to empirically classify? Why? (section 6.3.7)

15 Which concepts or definitions of an accounting system are likely to be the hardest to empirically classify? Why? (section 6.3.7)

References and further reading

AAA (1977) 'Committee on international accounting operations and education', *Accounting Review*, Supplement, 65–132. New York: American Accounting Association.

Alexander, D. and Archer, S. (2000) 'On the myth of Anglo-Saxon financial accounting', *International Journal of Accounting*, 33(4): 539–557.

Choi, F.D.S. and Bavishi, V.B. (1980) 'International accounting standards: Issues needing attention', *Journal of Accounting*, March: 62–68.

Cooke, T.E. and Wallace, R.S.O. (1990) 'Financial disclosure regulation and its environment: A review and further analysis', *Journal of Accounting and Public Policy*, 9: 79–110.

D'Arcy, A. (2001) 'Accounting classification and the international harmonization debate – an empirical investigation', *Accounting, Organizations and Society*, 26: 327–349.

D'Arcy, A. (2004) 'Accounting classification and the international harmonization debate: a reply to a comment', *Accounting, Organizations and Society*, 29: 201–206.

Da Costa, R.C., Bourgeois, J.C. and Lawson, W.M. (1978) 'A classification of international financial accounting practices', *International Journal of Accounting*, Spring: 73–86.

Doupnik, T.S. and Salter, S.B. (1993) 'An empirical test of a judgmental international classification of financial reporting practices', *Journal of International Business Studies*, 24(1): 41–60.

Fitzgerald, R.D., Stickler, A.D. and Watts, T.R. (1979) *International Survey of Accounting Principles and Reporting Practices*. London: Price Waterhouse International/Butterworths.

Gray, S.J. (1988) 'Towards a theory of cultural influence on the development of accounting systems internationally', *Abacus*, 24(1): 1–15.

Hatfield, H.R. (1966) 'Some variations in practices in England, France, Germany and the US', *Journal of Accounting Research*, Fall: 169–182.

Mueller, G.G. (1967) *International Accounting*. London: Macmillan.

Nair, R.D. and Frank, W.G. (1980) 'The impact of disclosure and measurement practices on international accounting classifications', *Accounting Review*, July: 426–450.

Nobes, C.W. (1982) 'A typology of international accounting principles and policies: A comment', *AUTU Review*, Spring: 62–65.

Nobes, C.W. (1984) *International Classification of Financial Reporting*. London: Croom Helm.

Nobes, C.W. (1998) 'Towards a general model of the reasons for international differences in financial reporting', *Abacus*, September, 34(2): 162–187.

Nobes, C.W. (2003) 'On the myth of "Anglo-Saxon" financial accounting: a comment', *International Journal of Accounting*, 38(1): 95–104.

Nobes, C.W. (2004) 'On accounting classification and the international harmonization debate', *Accounting, Organizations and Society*, 29: 189–200.

Oldham, K.M. (1987) *Accounting Systems and Practice in Europe*, 3rd edn. London: Gower.

Ordelheide, D. and KPMG (eds) (1995) *Transnational Accounting*, London: Macmillan.

Roberts, A. (1995) 'The very idea of classification in international accounting', *Accounting, Organizations and Society*, 20(7/8): 639–664.

Salter, S.B. and Doupnik, T.S. (1992) 'The relationship between legal systems and accounting practices: A classification exercise', *Advances in International Accounting*, 5: 3–22.

Seidler, L.J. (1967) 'International accounting – The ultimate theory course', *Accounting Review*, October: 775–781.

United Nations (1991) *Accounting Developments in Africa: Challenge of the 1990s*. New York: United Nations CTC.

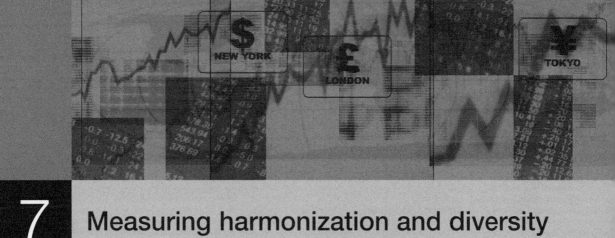

7 Measuring harmonization and diversity

Learning outcomes

After reading this chapter you should be able to:

- Understand how comparability indices are used to measure similarities and differences in reported figures.

- Understand how concentration indices are used to measure similarities and differences in accounting methods.

- Measure the comparability of profits and the level of harmonization, using simple examples.

- Understand the approach taken in market-based research investigating earnings 'conservatism'.

- Evaluate published research which has used these techniques.

7.1   Introduction

Chapters 4 and 5 looked at reasons why countries have adopted different accounting systems and Chapter 6 looked at the ways in which countries can be placed into groups based upon accounting similarities and differences. This chapter looks instead at the ways in which these accounting similarities and differences can be measured. It also looks at some of the empirical studies that have used these techniques and conclusions are drawn regarding both their strengths and weaknesses and the importance of the results achieved.

Differences in the accounting practices of countries are of two types. Similar events can be reported in different ways in different countries. For example, different valuation rules may be used for various assets and liabilities. Second, different events may be reported in different countries (e.g. different off-balance-sheet rules may exclude or include specific transactions). Differences in accounting rules or practices can impose significant direct and indirect costs on providers and users of financial statements. Direct costs include extra preparation or analysis costs, indirect costs arise because different decisions may be taken if different information is available.

This chapter begins by looking at the types of differences that may exist between the accounting systems of countries. It then explores briefly the impact of these differences on the preparers and users of financial accounts. Finally, it looks at the techniques that can be used to quantify or measure the differences and similarities and it explores some of the empirical studies that have tried to do this.

7.2   Sources of differences between accounting systems

The differences between accounting systems fall into three categories:

- differences in the rules of different countries
- differences in the ways in which the rules are interpreted or implemented
- differences in preferred practices (including voluntary disclosure practices).

Each of these types of differences will be briefly explored below.

7.2.1 Differences in accounting rules

The most obvious reason why companies from different countries use different accounting methods or report different information is because the rules or regulations call for different treatments. To illustrate this, some of the differences in rules between IFRS, Dutch national GAAP and US GAAP are shown in Exhibit 7.1.

| Exhibit 7.1 | Some of the differences between accounting regulations of the IASB, The Netherlands and the USA |

	The Netherlands	USA	IASB
Fixed assets (excluding goodwill)	As IASB, cost or revaluation	Must use historical costs	Revaluation permitted
Goodwill amortization	Guidelines as IAS. Civil code options to charge to equity or income	No amortization, instead tested for impairment	Maximum period 20 years
Intangible asset amortization	As IASB	Amortize only if finite life	Amortize over life, presumed not to exceed 20 years
Development costs	As IASB	Deferral as asset not allowed	Should defer if meet specific conditions
Measurement of intangible assets	Cost method required	As The Netherlands	Cost or fair-value revaluation
Joint ventures	Proportionate consolidation or equity method	Equity method only	Proportionate consolidation or equity method

Source: Deloitte & Touche, VNO-NCW (2002), available at www.iasplus.com/dttpubs/iasnlus.pdf

For some of the issues in Exhibit 7.1 the required practices are different under at least two of the three GAAP. For some other issues, there is a greater range of choice under one of the GAAP. For example, The Netherlands and the IASB allow fixed assets to be shown at either historical or current values, while only historical costs are allowed in the US. In this example, a Dutch company could choose to use historical costs, in which case there will be no differences in the accounting methods used by it and by US companies. Alternatively, it could choose to revalue its fixed assets, in which case its statements will not be comparable to those produced by similar US companies.

Alternatively, one country may instead have rules covering some events or transactions that are ignored in the rules of another country. For example, The Netherlands has few rules on financial instruments or pension costs. Again, depending upon the accounting methods actually used by Dutch companies, the statements of companies from the two countries may or may not be comparable.

7.2.2 Differences in the interpretation of accounting rules

Even where the rules of two countries are identical, they may be interpreted or applied in consistently different ways by companies in the two countries. Many areas of accounting entail the use of estimates, forecasts or judgements. For example, to calculate economic depreciation rates you must first decide on the most suitable allocation basis, the useful life of the asset and its residual value. All of these involve the use of estimates, forecasts and judgement. Other accounting rules, by contrast, include ambiguous terms. For example, when deciding whether or not to disclose information on contingencies, a company must decide on exactly what is meant by terms such as 'probable' (does this mean, for example, 95 per cent certain, or is an event with an 85 per cent chance of occurring still probable?) and 'remote' (is this an event with a 10 per cent chance, a 5 per cent chance or only a 2 per cent chance of occurring?)

The use of estimates and the interpretation of ambiguous terminology mean that identical events may be measured and reported in different ways by different companies. Obviously, there may be differences inside a country, but the differences will often be much greater in an international setting. For example, Davidson and Chrisman (1993) looked at the first 24 IASs published in both English and French in Canada. They found that the translations of ambiguous terms such as 'likely', 'normally', 'usually' or 'remote' were not always consistent and that, in almost half of the cases looked at, English- and French-speaking students interpreted the terms in significantly different ways. Similar differences also exist when applying local standards in different countries. For example, Schultz and Lopez (2001) found evidence that auditors from France, Germany and the US interpreted similar domestic rules in different ways. In this case, when asked to decide upon the amount to estimate for warranty costs, the French accountants were the most conservative in their estimates as well as the ones most affected by the way in which the actual question was framed, whether in optimistic or pessimistic terms (similar to the alternatives of describing a glass as being half full or half empty).

Doupnik and Richter (2003) looked both at translations, as Davidson and Chrisman did, and untranslated rules, as did Schulz and Lopez, and supported both sets of conclusions. Using US and German auditors and IAS uncertainty expressions, they found that there was a translation effect in that Germans working in English tended to use less of the continuum of certainty/uncertainty (they were asked to put quantitative measures from 0 to 100 per cent against uncertainty terms) than did German speakers working in German.[1] This was not simply a country effect, in that there were no differences between Swiss, Austrian and German auditors. There was also a culture effect in that native German-speaking accountants working in English and US accountants working in English often attributed significantly different point estimates to the same term.

These findings are probably to be expected. While accounting is often described as a science, implying extremely high levels of objectivity, we saw earlier how accounting rules and practices were influenced by a wide variety of factors. We saw, for example, how the link between taxation and financial reporting and the creditor versus shareholder orientation of the financial statements might affect attitudes towards income measurement. Similarly, it seems reasonable to argue that culture may affect how someone interprets particular rules. For example, a person coming from a society that is relatively unhappy with uncertainty may interpret 'probable' in a more restrictive way than will someone coming from a society that is more comfortable with uncertainty.

---

[1] For more on translation effects see, for example, Evans (2004).

7.2.3 Differences in preferred accounting practices

A distinction must be made between accounting regulations, or *de jure* issues, and actual practices, or *de facto* issues. Accounting regulations often contain a number of options. There may also be a large number of issues which are not covered by accounting regulations at all, giving companies even more choice.

While it is relatively straightforward (although not necessarily easy) to compare the accounting regulations of two countries, this may tell us relatively little about how similar the accounting practices of companies actually are in areas where discretion exists. *De facto* practices may differ considerably across countries, even if there are few *de jure* differences. Alternatively, if all companies, irrespective of country of domicile, choose wherever possible to use similar methods, *de facto* differences may be less than the *de jure* differences.

7.3 The importance of increasing harmonization in accounting systems

7.3.1 Companies as preparers and users of financial statements

Many companies are affected by international accounting differences. A company that engages in any form of international trade may have to use foreign financial statements or prepare financial statements using the rules of other countries. A company that exports or imports goods may want to assess the creditworthiness of its trading partners. A company that wants to borrow money from foreign bankers or other lenders may have to produce financial data using the rules that these potential lenders are familiar with. However, it is multinational companies that will be most affected by international accounting differences.

Local accounting rules will usually have to be used in the financial statements of foreign subsidiaries. These statements may be required by local tax authorities, shareholders or debt providers. However, most countries require companies to produce group accounts using consistent accounting methods across all subsidiaries. This may mean that the company has to produce two sets of financial statements for some of its subsidiaries – one using local GAAP for local reporting purposes and one using parent company GAAP for consolidation. If the rules applicable to external financial statements are different from the rules used by tax authorities, the company may have to produce even more different financial statements for the same subsidiary.

These multiple reporting requirements may involve substantial extra direct costs – there may be additional data collection, collation and auditing costs. There may also be extra indirect costs due to differences in reporting requirements. The existence of different accounting systems may result in the same event being reported in two, or more, very different ways. This may create confusion and dysfunctional behaviour inside the company. If there are two sets of figures each apparently measuring the same events, which is 'correct'? Which one should local management seek to maximize? What should they do if the two accounting systems conflict, so that actions that increase reported earnings under one system reduce earnings reported under the alternative set of rules?

Rather than having different measurement rules, a country may have extra or different disclosure rules. However, companies may be unwilling to provide this extra information. Extra disclosure requirements may involve considerable extra collection, collation, auditing and dissemination costs. Companies may also fear the consequences of disclosing extra information that could be of use to their competitors (usually called 'competitive disadvantage'). Alternatively, the extra information may affect the views or decisions taken by other users, such as governments, trade unions or employees, customers and suppliers.

If the additional costs are substantial they may affect the decisions taken by a company. Without uniform rules companies may invest more in those countries with the least onerous requirements or they may choose where to list their stock based upon differences in local disclosure requirements. Indeed, as discussed in Part 1, this is a major reason for the introduction of more uniform IFRS.

7.3.2 Investors

Shareholders are increasingly investing in foreign companies. Just as in a domestic setting investors can reduce their risk by investing in a diversified portfolio of companies, they can further reduce their risks by investing in companies from many different countries. However, if companies from different countries produce figures using different methods or provide different information, then their statements will not be comparable with each other. Normally, not enough information is given to allow the user to convert the reported figures to those that would have been produced under a different set of accounting rules. The reader of foreign financial statements may thus have great difficulty in understanding what the figures mean.

For example, if a German investor is interested in a UK company, she may compare its financial statements with a similar German company and find that the UK company appears to be more profitable. This may be because the German company really is less efficient than the British one. Alternatively, the German company may be more efficient than the British company, but it uses accounting methods that reduce its reported earnings in comparison to its UK competitor. If the German investor knows that German accounting rules are different, but she cannot measure the impact of these differences, she may decide not to invest in the UK at all or she may decide to invest in British companies only if they appear to be very much more profitable than their German alternatives. Whatever investment decision she finally makes, she will probably have made a different decision from that which she would have made had the German and UK companies used the same accounting methods.

7.3.3 Other groups affected by international differences

If companies or shareholders make different decisions because of international differences in accounting, other groups will also be affected. If differences in disclosure rules affect a company's foreign location decision, then local communities, actual and potential employees and governments will be affected. Similarly, stock market listing decisions affect the stock market(s) themselves, other stock market participants and the balance of payments of countries. Shareholders' investment decisions have secondary impacts or implications for other companies that are not invested in, and for the economy as a whole.

It is not only companies and shareholders that use financial statements. Employees of foreign-owned subsidiaries and their trade union representatives may use financial statements in negotiations on pay or conditions. Host governments may use financial statements to help them in economic planning. Customers, suppliers and lenders may want to gauge the creditworthiness or future prospects of foreign-owned companies. They may not have the power to demand information produced under local rules and they will have to rely upon financial statements produced under unfamiliar foreign rules. This may mean that they have to spend extra resources in learning about the accounting differences and in calculating their impact on the reported figures. Alternatively, they may be unable or unwilling to do this. In this case they are likely to be misled by the financial statements and they may make wrong decisions because of this.

Finally, accountants have to audit the statements of multinational groups, including foreign subsidiaries. The problems and additional expenses involved in having to understand and audit figures produced under multiple accounting jurisdictions may be considerable.

7.3.4 A model of harmonization

There are many pressures on companies to increase the level of harmonization as reflected in the increasing number of companies adopting international accounting standards either as the main set of accounts or as supplementary accounts. The reasons for this are two fold. First, as discussed in Part 1, more and more countries are beginning to use IFRS. For example the EU approved in July 2002 the *Application of International Accounting Standards*, which states that, for each financial year starting on or after 1 January 2005, EU companies must prepare their consolidated financial statements in conformity with IFRSs if they wish to have their securities trading on any EU stock exchange. Also, as discussed previously, many stock exchanges (with the notable exception of those in the US) have permitted the use of either international standards or other non-domestic GAAP. Companies listing in more than one stock market therefore have the obvious financial incentive to use whichever GAAP is accepted in all or as many as possible of the stock markets they list in. Secondly, even without these regulatory pressures, other pressures exist on companies. If companies trade internationally and if they have investors or other users of their accounts domiciled in more than one country, then reporting in unfamiliar GAAP will mean they incur extra direct or indirect costs. If they can use GAAP that is understandable to more than one set of users then they are obviously likely to reduce such costs.

These pressures towards increased harmonization have been shown graphically by Rahman *et al.* (2002) in Exhibit 7.2.

7.4 Similarities and differences in reported figures

One way of comparing financial statements is to measure the extent of the similarities or differences between them. If we can measure and quantify the extent of these, we can see which statements are most alike and which are most different. We can measure changes over time to see if moves towards harmonization are working and we can assess whether or not the differences result in significantly different reported figures.

There are a number of ways to measure the extent of differences or the extent of similarities across financial statements. One approach is to measure the difference in reported earnings and shareholders' funds that are caused by differences in the accounting methods used. Here, we would produce one set of financial statements under local rules and another set for the same company using a different set of rules. An alternative approach is to look instead at the methods or rules used by two companies. Here we would count the number of rules that are the same and the number that are different. Each of these two alternatives will give us some idea of how similar or dissimilar the financial statements are. However, they can often give very different results.

Exhibit 7.2   A model of the pressures towards increased harmonization

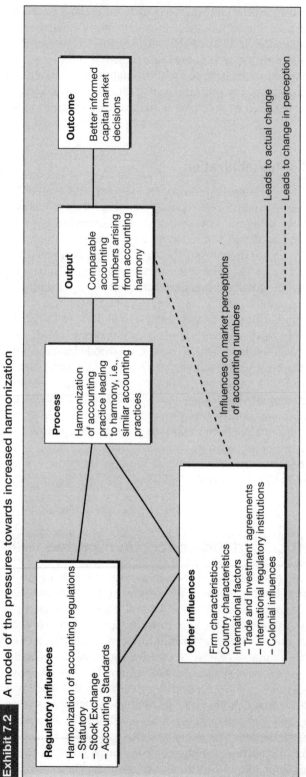

Source: Rahman *et al.* (2002).

There may be a lot of accounting rules that are different between two companies or two countries, but the overall impact of these differences on reported profits and shareholders' funds may be very small. Some of the accounting differences may result in higher profits or shareholders' funds in one country while other differences result in lower figures. The effects may thus cancel each other out. Alternatively, none of the differences in methods or rules may be very important, in that none cause material differences in the figures reported. In other cases there may be very few rules that are different, but each of these different rules may have a significant and consistent impact on profits and shareholders' funds.

When looking at ways of measuring differences in accounting systems we must therefore look at both the differences in the figures reported and the differences in the methods used. The rest of section 7.4 looks at how to measure the extent of similarity or difference in reported figures, while section 7.5 looks at how to measure similarities or differences in the accounting methods used.

7.4.1 Foreign GAAP financial statements

To measure the impact on reported figures of accounting differences you need two sets of figures – one set produced using domestic GAAP and the other set reporting the same events but using an alternative set of principles based upon the GAAP of a second country or the IASB.

A number of companies have done this in the past, and reported two sets of figures, one using domestic GAAP and a second set using the GAAP of a foreign country. As explored further in Part 5 of this book, the main reason for providing foreign GAAP statements is the existence of foreign shareholders and foreign stock market listings. For example, the London stock exchange requires companies to produce annual accounts of an 'international quality'. If a company wishes to list on the London Stock Exchange and its domestic GAAP statements do not meet these quality criteria, the company may be required to produce a second set of financial statements. Statements following UK or US GAAP, IASB standards or EU Directives would all be acceptable. However, this practice is obviously now decreasing in importance as more and or countries introduce rules for consolidated accounts or groups that are consistent with IFRS.

More common than two complete sets of financial statements under different GAAP is a complete set of financial statements under domestic GAAP and a reconciliation statement using foreign GAAP (for more on this see section 14.5.3). Many foreign companies listing on American stock exchanges have to provide a reconciliation statement in their annual form 20-F, filed with the Securities and Exchange Commission, and it is also often reproduced in their domestic country annual report. The reconciliation statements provided by Imperial Tobacco Group (ITG) are reproduced in Exhibit 7.3. As can be seen, these statements start with domestic GAAP profit or net income and shareholders' equity. They then list the significant differences in accounting rules in the UK and the USA. For each of these issues ITG discloses the size of the adjustment or the difference between the figures that would be reported under domestic and US rules. The statements then end up by disclosing net income or profits and shareholders' equity under US GAAP. ITG also provides a statement describing the main differences between the two GAAP (not reproduced here).

If we look at the reconciliation statement of ITG we can see that, for 2003, earnings based upon UK GAAP were £421m, while using US GAAP they were instead £496m. The largest difference between the two was due to differences in the treatment of the amortization of

| Exhibit 7.3 | Reconciliation statement: Imperial Tobacco Group |

in £million	2003	2002
Profit attributable to shareholders under UK GAAP	421	272
US GAAP adjustments:		
Pensions	2	13
Amortization of goodwill	194	48
Amortization of brands/trade marks/licences	(102)	(38)
Deferred taxation	57	16
Mark to market adjustments due to non-designation of hedge accounting	(82)	(10)
Employee share scheme charge to P&L account	6	(4)
Acquisition inventory step-up	–	(42)
Restructuring costs on acquisition	–	44
Net income under US GAAP	496	299
Equity shareholders' funds under UK GAAP	76	(92)
US GAAP adjustments:		
Pensions	345	335
Goodwill	(1,060)	(1,122)
Brands/trade marks/licences	2,921	2,712
Deferred taxation	(1,008)	(967)
Mark to market adjustments	13	95
Proposed dividend	217	167
ESOT shares	(36)	(19)
Employee share schemes	2	(4)
Shareholders' funds under US GAAP	1,470	1,105

Source: ITG Annual Report and Accounts, 2003, p. 90. www.imperial-tobacco.com

goodwill and other intangibles. In the UK goodwill on acquisitions made after the end of 1997 is capitalized and normally amortized over a maximum of 20 years. Goodwill before this date was usually written off against reserves. In the US all identifiable intangible assets are amortized. In this case, most of the intangible asset were brand rights amortised under US GAAP for periods from 25 to 30 years. This meant that US GAAP-based profits were £92m higher in 2003. Other important differences were the treatment of financial instruments (UK allows hedge accounting if derivatives reduce exposures on anticipated future transactions while in the US, only fair value accounting is allowed) and deferred taxation (deferral rules are stricter in the US).

As regards shareholders' equity, the largest item was brands (making US GAAP-based equity £2,921m larger) and goodwill (making US equity lower by £1,060m in contrast). These two were followed by deferred tax differences and pension accounting (only in the US must a company recognize expenses and liabilities when not paying into an over-funded scheme).

7.4.2 The comparability index

In the ITG example in Exhibit 7.3 we saw that earnings were £75m higher under US GAAP than UK GAAP while reserves were £1,394m higher. However, these figures by themselves tell us relatively little. We need a measure of the differences in the reported figures that takes into account their significance – for a company this size, were these differences significant or not? Also, is it more or less important than differences for other companies or countries? Finally, it would be helpful if our measure of difference yielded figures that made some intuitive sense, so we could understand what the measure meant without having to go back to the original financial statements.

One measure which meets these criteria was suggested by Gray,[2] who developed what he called a **conservatism index**. If we use US GAAP earnings (or shareholders' equity) as a benchmark and look at the impact of moving from US GAAP-based figures to those produced under UK GAAP, the index takes the form:

$$1 - \frac{(\text{Earnings}_{USA} - \text{Earnings}_{UK})}{|\text{Earnings}_{USA}|}$$

We do not want an index that is negative simply because the company is making a loss. Therefore absolute earnings is used as the denominator as it ignores the sign of the earnings figures and treats all items as positive. The index will take the value of 1.0 if the two earnings figures are the same, it will be greater than 1.0 if UK GAAP-based earnings are larger than are US GAAP-based earnings, while an index of less than 1.0 means that UK GAAP-based earnings are smaller than are US GAAP-based earnings.

While this index was originally called the 'conservatism index', this term is misleading as accounting methods that result in a lower earnings figure are not always more conservative. For example, the revaluation of fixed assets is not generally thought of as a conservative valuation rule. However, any revaluation will result in higher depreciation charges, and therefore lower earnings. Many other accounting rules are concerned with the question of when costs or revenues are recognized in the income statement rather than being concerned with the amount recognized. Development costs, for example, can be charged to income in the period incurred or capitalized and charged over a number of future periods. These rules therefore result in differences in the pattern of earnings recognition over time but do not affect the total earnings of the entity over its life. This will result in lower earnings in some period(s) but in other period(s) they will result in higher earnings figures. The index is therefore better thought of as an index of how similar or dissimilar the figures are, or how comparable they are. We will therefore instead refer to this index as the **comparability index**.

Just as, in Exhibit 7.3, the difference between US and UK GAAP-based earnings and equity was broken down into its constituent parts, the comparability index can also be broken down into partial indices, each one measuring the impact of one accounting issue. For example, if we want to calculate the partial index due to differences in deferred tax we would calculate the index as follows:

$$1 - \frac{\text{Difference due to deferred tax}}{|\text{Earnings}_{USA}|}$$

An example of the calculation of the index for earnings and shareholders' equity is given in Exhibit 7.4.

Note that the overall index is equal to the sum of the two partial indices *less* 1.0, or if there were N partial indices, it would be equal to the sum of all N partial indexes *less* $(N - 1)$.

This method has been used in a number of studies that have compared accounting practices across different countries. One of these is Weetman *et al.* (1998) who applied this technique to 25 UK companies who provided reconciliations of reported earnings

---

[2] Gray (1980).

Exhibit 7.4   An illustration of the calculation of comparability indices

	£m
Profit attributable to shareholders – UK GAAP	110
Adjustments due to differences in the treatment of:	
Pension costs	10
Deferred tax	(20)
Net income in accordance with US GAAP	100
Shareholders' equity – UK GAAP	800
Adjustments due to differences in the treatment of:	
Goodwill	300
Deferred tax	(100)
Shareholders' equity in accordance with US GAAP	1,000

Comparability index calculations

Earnings:

Total:
$$1 - (Profit_{USA} - Profit_{UK})/\,|\,Profit_{USA}\,|$$
$$1 - (100 - 110)/100 = 1 - (-0.10) \qquad = 1.10$$

Partial:

Pension costs $1 - (10/100) = 1 - 0.10$ $= 0.90$

Deferred tax $1 - (-20/100) = 1 - (-0.20)$ $= 1.20$

Shareholders' equity:

Total: $1 - (1000 - 800)/1000 = 1 - 0.20$ $= 0.80$

Partial:

Goodwill $1 - (300/1000)$ $= 0.70$

Deferred tax $1 - (-100/1000)$ $= 1.10$

to US GAAP-based earnings in both 1988 and 1994. The distribution of values of the total indices is reproduced in Exhibit 7.5.

The indices show that earnings were, on average, less under US GAAP in both years, and that the average difference had actually increased over the period. Some of these differences are not material but fully 18 of the 25 companies had a difference of more than 10 per cent in 1988 and similar differences were found in 21 of the 25 companies in

Exhibit 7.5   Comparison of UK and US GAAP earnings of UK companies

		Number of companies	
	Index value	1988	1994
UK profit less than 90% of US	<0.90	5	4
UK profit between 90 and 95% of US	0.90–0.95	1	1
UK profit between 95 and 105% of US	0.95–1.05	3	2
UK profit between 105 and 110% of US	1.05–1.10	3	1
UK profit more than 110% of US	>1.10	13	17
Total number of companies		25	25
Mean comparability index		1.17	1.25
Range (excluding 2 outliers): Lowest value		0.65	0.75
Highest value		1.79	2.76

1994. Especially important were the differences in treatment of goodwill, financial instruments and leasing. While this study is now somewhat old, it provides a very good illustration of why the work of the IASB is so important. Continuing differences of this type of magnitude are obviously likely to have a significant impact upon both the users and preparers of any accounts that are used in any international setting.

7.4.3 The use of reconciliation statements

The comparability index has also been used in a number of other studies that have looked at the differences in reported figures under various GAAP.[3] However, the index is not without its problems. If the reported earnings figure is very small, the index will often be extremely large, which may be misleading. (This is because the change in earnings is being compared to a very small denominator – the benchmark GAAP-based earnings.) More important than this, though, are the problems of data availability. Reconciliation statements are produced by relatively few companies. These companies are generally among the largest and most international of companies. They may not be typical or representative of other smaller or less international companies. Where alternative methods can be used, these companies may not make the same choices as are made by other companies. No company will want to produce two sets of accounts with very different earnings or equity figures unless they have to. This is because many users of the accounts know very little about accounting and may view the figures – and therefore also the company – with suspicion if it apparently cannot decide how much money it really made. Companies which have to produce reconciliation statements are therefore likely, where possible, to select accounting methods that are acceptable under both domestic and foreign GAAP, so reducing the number of items that are included in the reconciliation statement and the size of the difference between the two sets of figures.

Even if this is not the case, it is always dangerous to make generalizations based upon a few cases. The first German company to list on the New York Stock Exchange (NYSE) was Daimler–Benz, and this example is often quoted to illustrate how large the differences in earnings can be under different GAAP. On listing for the first time, Daimler–Benz's reported earnings fell from a profit of DM615m under German GAAP to a loss of DM1,839m under US GAAP (giving a comparability index of 2.33). However, to quote only this one year and this company is misleading. As can be seen in Case study 7.1 at the end of this chapter, much of the difference was due to a one-off adjustment. In other years the differences in reported figures under the two GAAP were very much less. In 1995, for example, the difference was only DM5m on a German GAAP-based loss of DM5,734m. (Recognizing the importance of producing financial statements under an internationally understood and acceptable set of GAAP if they are to be readily used by international investors, Daimler–Benz changed its accounting policies in 1996. It then started producing its full consolidated financial statements under US GAAP.)

Finally, nearly all of the reconciliation statements provided reconcile domestic GAAP figures to US GAAP figures. Thus, it might be relatively easy, for example, to compare UK and US practices or German and US practices, but it is much more difficult to compare UK and German practices.

[3] See, for example, Adhikari and Emenyonu (1997); Cañibano and Mora (2000); Emenyonu and Gray (1992); Weetman and Gray (1991).

7.4.4 Simulation studies

Given the problems involved in using reconciliation statements, we need to find an alternative way to measure GAAP differences. One possibility is to use simulations. Real companies can be used, or a company can be created using artificial data. The figures can then be recalculated under a number of different accounting methods. If real companies are used, then the samples used can be large enough to be statistically representative of the entire population of companies. If an artificial company is created, we can use average figures derived from all companies or from particular sectors, so creating a typical or average company. Alternatively, we could create an atypical company that illustrates particularly interesting or problematic issues.

A number of simulation studies have been carried out and one of these will be looked at to get an idea of how they work. Walton[4] compared accounting in the UK and France (more information on this study, including the figures generated can be found in Case study 7.2, at the end of this chapter). Walton created an artificial construction company that, among other things, had some foreign operations, extraordinary items and leased assets. The case was presented to a number of accountants in the two countries, who produced balance sheets and income statements for the foreign subsidiary and the parent company. While there were some very significant differences between the average figures generated by the UK and French respondents, for anyone interested in international harmonization, the most important and interesting result (p. 198) was that:

> Variations in treatment within each jurisdiction are quite clear from the results, and it is by no means obvious that a user would obtain a greater consensus by comparing two reports from the same country with each other than by comparing one report from each country.

7.5 Similarities and differences in the accounting methods used

7.5.1 The H-index

So far we have looked at differences in the reported figures of companies that are caused by using different accounting methods. We could instead ignore the actual figures produced and look at the accounting methods used. We would then look at the number of accounting methods that are the same and the number that are different across companies and use this to calculate a measure of how comparable the financial statements are. This method is usually applied only to *de facto* practices because the accounting rules in most countries contain options. However, it could be adapted to measure *de jure* methods. To measure *de jure* methods, where countries allow different ranges of alternatives, we could calculate two measures. The maximum possible level of comparability can be measured using, wherever possible, those alternatives that are the same in both countries. Likewise, the minimum possible comparability level can be measured using, wherever permitted, different alternatives.

The comparability or similarity in the accounting methods used by a group of companies increases as fewer alternative methods are used or as the methods used become more concentrated around one alternative. We can use this idea of 'concentration' to measure comparability. In economics, an industry is said to be more concentrated if a

---

[4] Walton (1992).

small number of companies account for most of the sales of that industry. That is, most customers purchase from the same suppliers. In the same way, financial statements may be said to be more comparable if a small number of alternative accounting methods is used and most companies use the same alternative. That is, most companies choose the same methods. There are many different ways in which industrial concentration can be measured, but one common method is the Herfindahl or H-index. The H-index can also be used to measure the comparability of accounting methods.

The H-index takes the form:

$$\sum_{i=1}^{n} p_i^2$$

where: p_i is the proportion of companies using accounting method i

n is the maximum number of possible methods that can be used.

Exhibit 7.6, panel A, gives numerical illustrations of how to calculate the H-index. This is a simple example of accounting issues 1–3. For each issue two alternative treatments, A and B, are allowed. Assume for the illustration that issue 1 is inventory valuation where the alternatives are (A) FIFO and (B) LIFO. Issue 2 is depreciation where the alternatives are (A) straight line and (B) reducing balance. Issue 3 is development expenditure where the alternatives are (A) capitalize and (B) report as an expense. For issue 1, half of the companies choose method A and the other half use method B, giving an index of 0.50. In contrast, for issue 2 method A is far more popular, being used by 90 per cent of the companies. There is therefore much more consensus and the H-index increases to 0.82. For issue 3 method B is now the more popular, being used by 90 per cent of the companies, so the H-index is again 0.82.

Panel B of Exhibit 7.6 gives information on accounting issues 1–4. For each of these issues four possible alternatives, A–D, exist, although not all are always used in practice. For example, issue 1 is inventory valuation where the alternatives are (A) FIFO, (B) LIFO, (C) average cost and (D) standard cost. Issue 2 is goodwill where the alternatives are (A) write off to revenue reserves, (B) write off to capital reserves, (C) impairment test and

| Exhibit 7.6 | Calculation of the Herfindahl index |

| Panel A | | | | | |
Proportion of companies using method:	A	B	Calculation	H-index
Accounting issue				
1 Inventory valuation	0.50	0.50	$0.5^2 + 0.5^2$	0.5
2 Depreciation	0.90	0.10	$0.9^2 + 0.1^2$	0.82
3 Development expenditure	0.10	0.90	$0.1^2 + 0.9^2$	0.82

| Panel B | | | | | |
Proportion of companies using method:	A	B	C	D	H-index
Accounting issue					
1 Inventory valuation	0.25	0.25	0.25	0.25	0.25
2 Goodwill	0.05	0.25	0.25	0.45	0.33
3 Valuation of land	0	0.33	0.33	0.33	0.33
4 Deferred taxation	0	0	0	1.00	1.00

(D) amortize over useful life. Issue 3 is valuation of land where the alternatives are (A) value in use, (B) replacement cost, (C) cost adjusted for general prices and (D) historical cost. Issue 4 is deferred taxation on asset revaluation where the alternatives are (A) no recognition until sale, (B) partial recognition of short-term deferrals, (C) deduct from asset value and (D) full provision. Now, the lowest-value H-index is 0.25. This is for issue 1, where there is no consensus regarding the best treatment and all four alternatives are equally popular. The highest H-index is 1.0 for issue 4. Here all the companies use method *D*.

We can see from this that the H-index varies from a low of $1/n$ (where n is the maximum number of treatments permitted, in this case 4), to a high of 1.00, when all companies use the same method.

7.5.2 The C-index

The H-index offers a fairly simple way of measuring comparability. However, it is not a perfect measure. There is no one-to-one relationship between the relative popularity of alternative methods and the resultant values of the H-index so that the index value cannot be interpreted in an unambiguous way. For example, in Exhibit 7.6, Panel B accounting issue 2 gives an index of 0.33. The H-index is also 0.33 for issue 3 although the distribution of companies across the alternatives is very different. In addition, the H-index cannot cope with multiple reporting. As discussed above, companies may provide a reconciliation statement or other information which allows the user to see the effects of more than one accounting method. In these cases the H-index would be based upon the method used in the main financial statements and would ignore the supplementary disclosures. This will have the effect of underestimating the comparability of the financial statements. The existence of such multiple reporting led van der Tas[5] to develop what he calls the compatible or C-index. This is a similar type of index but it can cope with multiple reporting.

Rather than looking at the proportion of companies that use each accounting method, the C-index instead looks at the number of financial statements that are compatible with each other. It measures the number of pairs of statements that either apply the same accounting method or provide enough additional information to allow users to make comparisons themselves (that is, the number of compatible reports). The pairs of compatible reports are then compared to the maximum number of possible pairs of reports.

Using a slightly different version of the C-index, one that is slightly easier to use and (it has been argued) is also a better index when many countries are being considered,[6] as developed by Archer *et al.*,[7] the C-index takes the form:

$$\frac{\sum(n_i \times (n_i - 1))}{(N \times (N - 1))}$$

where: n_i is the number of companies using method i
N is the total number of companies.

[5] van der Tas (1988, 1992).
[6] Morris and Parker (1998).
[7] Archer *et al.* (1995).

Exhibit 7.7	Calculation of the C-index

Number of companies using method:					
	A	B	C	Calculation	C-index
Accounting issue					
1 (e.g. depreciation)	15	1	4	$[(15 \times 14) + (1 \times 0) + (4 \times 3)]/[(20 \times 19)]$	0.584
2 (e.g. stock valuation)	7	5	8	$[(7 \times 6) + (5 \times 4) + (8 \times 7)]/[(20 \times 19)]$	0.311

An example of how to calculate the C-index is given in Exhibit 7.7. The methods *A*, *B*, and *C* could represent, for example straight-line, reducing balance and production unit methods of depreciation, or else FIFO, LIFO and average-cost method of valuing stocks of goods.

In this example there are two accounting issues being considered and there are three alternative ways of accounting for each issue. Data are provided on the practices used by 20 companies. There is more consensus over the acceptable treatment for issue 1, where 15 of the 20 companies used method *A*. For issue 2 no single treatment is particularly popular. The C-index reflects this, being 0.584 for issue 1, but falling to only 0.311 for issue 2. As with the H-index, the C-index will vary from a minimum of 0.0 (where each company uses a different method) to a maximum of 1.0 (where all companies use the same method). The actual values taken by the H- and C-indices will be different (except at these two extremes of 0.0 and 1.0), although they converge towards each other as the number of companies considered increases.

A more detailed explanation and example of the C-index is given in Appendix 7.1 at the end of this chapter.

7.5.3 Measurement of international harmony

The H-index and the C-index both measure harmony or compatibility inside a single country. However, we also need a measure of international harmony. There are several ways to think about international harmony and each can be used to develop a compatibility measure.

One approach is to take the world as a whole and have no concern for national boundaries. This might be the perspective taken by an international investor who wants to choose potential investments from a group of companies across a range of countries. To this investor, the home country of each company may not be particularly important. All she wants is to invest in those companies which will provide the best return, irrespective of their country of domicile. To do this, she wants to know the extent to which the financial statements of the group of companies as a whole are compatible. She asks, 'What is the chance that if I pick two companies at random, their accounting practices will be compatible?'

This approach is effectively saying that measuring international harmonization is the same as measuring harmonization in a single country and that the number of countries included is irrelevant. The total C-index would then be applied.

In a study of two or more countries, the total C-index measures *international* harmony defined as the increase in comparability within an international *pool* of accounts brought about when more companies within the pool adopt the same accounting method for an item (Archer *et al.*, 1995). This definition ignores the country of origin of accounts.

A quite different approach is to take account of national boundaries and to ask: 'What is the state of harmonization in each country?', and 'To what extent are companies compatible from one country to the next?' This might be the perspective of a global standard setter who wants to compare the pattern of practices found in different countries.

The question 'What is the state of harmonization in each country?' relates to what Archer *et al.* (1995) call 'within country' harmonization. The question 'To what extent are companies compatible from one country to the next?' relates to what Archer *et al.* call 'between country' harmonization.

For a complete picture of international harmonization, each perspective is valuable. It is therefore helpful to have separate indices measuring each type of harmonization. Archer *et al.* suggest that the C-index can be broken down into these two harmonization measures. To see how this works suppose the world contains two countries. There are 100 companies in total or 50 from each country. A survey shows that 50 companies use the LIFO method of stock valuation while the remaining 50 companies use the FIFO method.

If we ignore the country of origin, the C-index for the 100 companies is 0.49 calculated as:

$$C = \frac{[(50 \times 49) + (50 \times 49)]}{(100 \times 99)} = 0.49$$

Now we decide to instead take note of the national boundaries and we observe the situation as set out in Scenario 1 where the two accounting methods are spread equally across each country.

Scenario 1

	Method A (LIFO)	Method B (FIFO)	Total
Country 1	25	25	50
Country 2	25	25	50
	50	50	100

$$Total \quad C = \frac{[(50 \times 49) + (50 \times 49)]}{(100 \times 99)} = 0.49$$

The within-country C is calculated by estimating

$$\frac{\text{Number of matching pairs in Country 1} + \text{Number of matching pairs in Country 2}}{\text{Maximum matching pairs in Country 1} + \text{Maximum matching pairs in Country 2}}$$

$$= \{(25 \times 24) + (25 \times 24) + (25 \times 24) + (25 \times 24)\}/\{(50 \times 49) + (50 \times 49)\} = \mathbf{0.49}$$

This result should not surprise us because the pattern of choice within each country is the same as the pattern of choice for the world as a whole.

The between-country C is calculated by matching pairs across each country. That is:

$$\frac{\text{Number of matching pairs using method A} + \text{Number of matching pairs using method B}}{\text{Maximum possible number of matching pairs}}$$

$$= \{(25 \times 25) + (25 \times 25)\}/(50 \times 50) = \mathbf{0.5}$$

This result also should not surprise us because the choices are spread evenly across the two countries.

Thus in Scenario 1 the total C-index of 0.49 indicates the extent of worldwide compatibility of accounting practice, while the within-country and between-country indices show that there is similar compatibility within each country and across the countries. An international standard-setting body would have to focus attention on two factors: understanding the reasons for companies in each country making different choices; and understanding the relative strength of the standard-setting body in each country. Both aspects would need to be understood in order to assess the likelihood of reaching a compromise on achieving one universal choice.

Now consider Scenario 2 where there is total agreement on accounting method in each country but no matching at all across the two countries.

Scenario 2

	Method A (LIFO)	Method B (FIFO)	Total
Country 1	50	0	50
Country 2	0	25	50
	50	50	100

$$\text{Total} \quad C = \frac{[(50 \times 49) + (50 \times 49)]}{(100 \times 99)} = 0.49$$

The within-country index is calculated for each country in turn:

$$\frac{\text{Number of matching pairs in Country 1 + Number of matching pairs in Country 2}}{\text{Maximum matching pairs in Country 1 + Maximum matching pairs in Country 2}}$$

$$= \{(50 \times 49) + (0) + (0) + (50 \times 49)\}/\{(50 \times 49) + (50 \times 49)\} = 1.0$$

This is the answer we would expect as there is perfect harmonization within each country.

The between-country index is calculated by matching pairs across each country:

$$= \{(50 \times 0) + (0 \times 50)\}/(50 \times 50) = 0$$

This is again the answer we would expect as there is no harmonization between the two countries.

Scenario 3 shows a calculation where there are three methods of accounting (such as LIFO, FIFO and average cost methods of stock valuation) to be compared across two countries. The overall index is based on the total number of companies using each method. The within-country index is calculated by reading across the line for each country in turn. The between-country index is calculated by reading down each column of figures.

Scenario 3

Country	Method			Number of companies
	1	2	3	
1	2	5	3	10
2	2	3	10	15
Total	4	8	13	25

	Number of comparable pairs	Total number of possible pairs	Index
Overall Index	$((4 \times 3) + (8 \times 7) + (13 \times 12))$ $= 224$	(25×24) $= 600$	0.373
Within-country Index	$((2 \times 1) + (5 \times 4) + (3 \times 2) +$ $(2 \times 1) + (3 \times 2) + (10 \times 9))$ $= 106$	$((10 \times 9) +$ $(15 \times 14))/ 2$ $= 300$	0.420
Between-country Index	$(2 \times 2) + (5 \times 3) + (3 \times 10)$ $= 49$	(10×15) $= 150$	0.327

7.5.4 Measurement of harmonization

While there have been a number of studies that have measured the compatibility of financial statements they have tended to use different indices, different countries, different accounting issues at different levels of fineness and different types of companies.[8] Even without these problems of lack of comparability, there are also some more general problems involved in the interpretation of the C-index.[9] However, while these problems mean that it is difficult to draw anything but very general conclusions from the studies, it is still worth looking at some of the findings.

7.5.4.1 EU harmonization

On of the earliest of these studies, the study by Archer *et al.* (1995), will be described to both give an idea of how C-indices can be used to measure compatibility and to give some ideas on the state of EU comparability prior to the work of the IASB.

The C-index and its two components were used to measure changes in harmony across Europe between 1986/87 and 1990/91. This is a period during which the EU attempted to increase accounting harmonization. If this was successful, the level of harmony achieved, as measured by the C-indices, should have increased. A sample of 89 internationally traded companies from eight countries was used, and data were collected from annual reports. This has the advantage that it means that actual practices were considered; however, financial statements often do not provide much detailed information on exactly which accounting methods have been used. This means that the only issues that can be studied are those where companies usually disclose their exact accounting methods: many potentially important issues cannot be examined.

---

[8] See, for example, Hellman (1993); Herrman and Thomas (1995); Morris and Parker (1998); Rahman *et al.* (1996); Tay and Parker (1990).

[9] See Aisbett (2001); Krisement (1997).

The two areas chosen by this study were deferred tax and goodwill, and five alternative treatments were identified for each (*see* Exhibit 7.8). The study found that the overall level of compatibility was low especially for deferred taxation, where the C-index was only 0.149 in 1986/87 and 0.216 in 1990/91. However, the between-country compatibility had increased quite substantially over the period, from 0.108 to 0.186. This was mainly due to a number of Swedish companies changing their practices, coupled with increasing disclosures by the German and Swiss samples. Particularly striking differences emerged between the practices of companies from France, The Netherlands and Sweden, which tended to use the full provision method, and companies from the UK and Ireland, which instead used the partial provision method. For goodwill, the level of compatibility was considerably higher, at 0.383 in 1986/87 and 0.403 in 1990/91, although major differences still existed. Within-country compatibility actually decreased over the period while between-country compatibility increased, due mainly to a number of German companies changing their methods. The main reason that between-country compatibility was not higher was that capitalization and amortization was the almost universal treatment in Belgium and France while immediate write-off to reserves was instead more common in The Netherlands and the UK. Little consensus existed within the samples from Germany, Sweden and Switzerland.

Exhibit 7.8 Compatibility of European financial reporting practices

Deferred taxation

Possible treatments
A Nil provision or taxes payable approach
B Full provision
C Partial provision
D Deferred tax recognized, method unspecified or recognized for some companies only
E No recognition and not known if deferred tax applicable or not

C-indices

	1986/87	1990/91
Within-country	0.371	0.379
Between-country	0.108	0.186
Total index	0.149	0.216

Goodwill

Possible treatments
A Written-off against profit and loss in year of acquisition
B Written-off against reserves in year of acquisition
C Shown as asset and not amortized
D Shown as asset and amortized over period exceeding one year
E Other or unspecified treatment

C-indices

	1986/87	1990/91
Within-country	0.583	0.539
Between-country	0.347	0.377
Total index	0.383	0.403

This general move towards increased harmonization in Europe appears to have continued beyond the period examined by Archer *et al*. Again using the C-index, this time on 85 international companies from 13 European countries (EU and non-EU) Cañibano and Mora (2000) instead looked at harmonization between 1991/92 and 1996/97 for the four areas of deferred tax, financial leases, goodwill and foreign currency. They found that in all four areas, harmonization increased. The move was greatest for foreign currency (index moved from 0.34 to 0.53) and the least for goodwill (0.31 to 0.38). One of the two areas covered in Archer *et al*. and in this study was deferred taxation. Similar to Archer *et al*., they found that harmonization increased, again with more Swedish companies changing their practices. These, plus a number of German and Norwegian companies moved from nil provision to full provision. However, the differences between the practices of companies from France, The Netherlands, Sweden and now also Germany, which tended to use the full provision method, and companies from the UK, which instead used the partial provision method, remained. The second area both studies considered was goodwill. Here the level of compatibility was higher than that for deferred tax in 1991/92 (0.30), but lower in 1996/97 (0.38). While overall compatibility only increased moderately, there were a significant number of companies who changed their practices. Again, a number of German companies changed from immediate write-off against reserves to amortization. Charging to income in year of purchase did not occur at all in the later period, while several companies from a number of other countries moved from a variety of methods to amortizing over a period in excess of five years.

These results are interesting in the context of institutional moves towards increased harmonization. They are not due to changes in EU rules or domestic standards. Instead, they provide some support for the importance of voluntary harmonization by companies. Of course, while this suggests that at least some companies are recognizing the benefits of increased harmonization, it does not mean that legislative moves towards increased harmonization are not also required.

7.5.4.2 Australia versus the UK and the US

A second example of a similar type of study, by Parker and Morris (2001), throws some further light on the differences between Australian, US and UK GAAP (as discussed earlier in section 6.4.5). Using 1993 accounts and samples matched by industry and size for 40 companies and 11 practices in each of the UK and Australia they measured harmonization using the between-country C-index.

Overall, there was very little international harmony, but there were some areas of considerable harmony inside each country (7 of 11 issues for the UK and 5 of 11 for Australia). Perhaps of more interest was their belief that they would find that Australia was more like the US then the UK as the US had more influence in Australia than it had in the UK. The results supported this, with Australian GAAP being more like US GAAP than UK GAAP for all issues except the valuation of tangible fixed assets and research and expenditure, where the Australian and US standards were different, and interest on construction of assets and identifiable intangibles where there were no Australian standards. Overall, they concluded that the US appears to be the cause of partial international harmonization or harmonization across a limited number of countries only, but this partial geographic harmonization actually hinders international harmonization by the IASB for all issues where the international standards conflict with US GAAP.

7.5.4.3 The success of the IASB

As might be expected, recent studies which have used these techniques have tended instead to look at the question of the success of the IASB in achieving harmonization. For example Murphy (2000) compared a small sample of Swiss companies that did (16) and did not switch (18) from domestic to international GAAP over the period 1988 to 1995 with US, UK and Japanese companies (20 each) which similarly did not use international standards. Any increase in harmonization within the Swiss IAS companies or any increases in harmonization occurring only between the Swiss companies using international standards and the non-Swiss companies could reasonably be thought of as measures of the success of the IASB Comparability Project. However when considering fours items – depreciation, inventory cost method, financial statement cost basis and consolidation – very little evidence of the success of the comparability project was found. Indeed, only in the case of depreciation was the Swiss IAS companies' increase in harmonization significantly greater than that of the non-IAS Swiss companies, while inventory actually became less harmonized in the Swiss IAS companies. When comparing the Swiss and non-Swiss companies it appears that generally practices were becoming more harmonized over the period, but that this applied to both samples of Swiss companies and did not appear therefore to be due solely to the influence of the IASB.

Two aspects of harmonization were included in the measures used in this study, namely, the methods used and the disclosures made. For example, the increasing harmonization of cost basis was due to more Swiss companies disclosing what they actually did. While disclosure is obviously desirable, and indeed essential, if users are to be able to compare companies in an international setting, increased and therefore more comparable or harmonized disclosure is not the same as more harmonized accounting methods. The IASB will only be successful if it can persuade companies to change their accounting methods as well as improve their disclosures. This suggests that we need to look at both rules and practices. The IASC/IASB rules have been examined[10] over the three periods of high flexibility (1973–88), comparability (1989–95) and agreement (1995 onwards) and, not surprisingly found to have become more harmonized over these periods. More work needs to be done comparing the *de jure* position of different countries over these time periods before we can draw very firm conclusions about the success of the IASB over time.

7.6 Similarities and differences in information disclosure

The comparability index and the H- and C-indices are concerned with differences in the accounting techniques used – or, in other words, differences in the measurement system. To gain a complete picture of an accounting system we must also look at disclosure practices, including voluntary disclosure practices. There have been a great number of studies that have looked at disclosure practices inside particular countries. Many of these have tried to model the voluntary disclosure decision by measuring the association between the amount of voluntary disclosure and various company-specific factors. Countries looked at include Japan,[11] Mexico,[12] New Zealand,[13] Nigeria,[14]

---

[10] Garrido *et al.* (2002).

[11] Cooke (1991).

[12] Chow and Wong-Boren (1987).

[13] Hossain *et al.* (1995).

[14] Wallace (1988).

Sweden,[15] Tanzania,[16] and the UK.[17] There is general support for the proposition that disclosure levels increase as companies get larger. Very often, the listing status of the company and the industry it operates in are also important. Profitability and leverage, in contrast, generally appear not to be important.

Far less interest has been shown in the question of whether or not disclosure practices differ across countries. Given our discussion in Chapters 4 and 5, we would expect this to be the case. Mandatory disclosure requirements should vary across countries, just as do mandatory measurement rules. Voluntary disclosure levels will also tend to vary across countries. Both rules and practices will be affected by cultural values. We saw in Chapter 5 that one of Gray's (1988) four accounting values was secrecy versus transparency. We also saw that this accounting value was related to Hofstede's (1984) four cultural dimensions. Gray hypothesized that high transparency or high disclosure levels should be positively related to weak uncertainty avoidance; small power distance; high individualism; and low nurturing. Disclosure practices will also be influenced by the institutions of a country. Particularly important for voluntary disclosures will be the corporate financing system. It would be expected that the more dependent companies are upon equity rather than debt financing, and the more dispersed is that share ownership, then the more the company is likely to disclose in its annual report to shareholders.

Voluntary disclosure practices may also be a function of the level of mandatory rules. If mandatory disclosure levels are set very high there is obviously less scope for voluntary disclosure. However, if mandatory levels are high because of cultural or institutional factors in a country, companies may be willing, as discussed above, to voluntarily disclose more. Thus it is not really clear if high mandatory disclosure levels imply high or low voluntary disclosure levels. However, it is not only the absolute amount of voluntary disclosures that will tend to vary across countries. There will often also be significant differences in the types of disclosure made.

There are a number of ways of measuring the amount of voluntary disclosure made. One of the simplest approaches is to use a scorecard of likely disclosures. If a company discloses the information then it is scored '1', if it has not disclosed the information, but it could have been provided, it is scored '0', while if the item is not relevant for that company then it is not scored but is ignored. Companies can then be compared on the basis of the proportion or percentage of relevant items they each disclose:

$$\frac{\text{Number of items disclosed}}{\text{Maximum number of items that could have been disclosed}}$$

The scores for each company examined from any one country can then be averaged to obtain the country's disclosure score. One of the biggest problems with this approach is deciding what items to include: items that are voluntary in one country or one time period may be required in another, and thus, the items used in surveys in one country and one time period may not be applicable in another. This is a particular problem for cross-national studies of voluntary disclosures. The items included must be voluntary in all countries; however, if the levels of mandatory disclosure are very different, companies in some countries may be disclosing much information voluntarily. But this would not be picked up by the research instrument if they are mandatory in some of the other countries being examined.

---

[15] Cooke (1989).

[16] Abayo *et al.* (1993).

[17] Firth (1979).

This is less of a problem in some areas than in others. It is not a major problem, for example, when looking at social or environmental disclosures, as most countries have few or even no disclosure requirements in this area.

7.6.1 The measurement of environmental and social disclosure

There have been a number of studies that have looked at the disclosure of social and environmental information across different countries.[18] One of the earliest of these was by Roberts (1991), who looked at the disclosures made by large companies in five European countries (France, Germany, The Netherlands, Sweden and Switzerland). Roberts used a simple checklist of 54 items covering nine areas concerned with either the environment or employee-related matters (see Exhibit 7.9).

More recent studies of environmental disclosures have become much more sophisticated, and have used various forms of content analysis. Content analysis-based disclosure checklists are designed to measure whether or not an item is disclosed and also to record the form that disclosure takes. Part of one such content analysis form used to measure environmental disclosures is reproduced in Exhibit 7.10. As can be seen, this is not simply a yes/no checklist of items that may or may not be disclosed. Instead, for each item that might be disclosed, five questions have to be answered, as explained in Exhibit 7.11.

This type of analysis quantifies the number of disclosures made and the types of disclosures made, but it ignores the size of each disclosure. To gain a complete idea of the extent of disclosure you also need to know what types of information are disclosed and how much information is disclosed. For example, if you want to know how important this type of disclosure is to the company itself, then one useful measure might be the relative importance accorded social information versus the importance accorded to financial information. This can be at least partially achieved if the amount of disclosure is also quantified. This may take the form of the number of sentences or pages, either in absolute terms or as a percentage of the total. The analysis can also be extended to include other sources of information and not just the annual report and accounts.[19]

The use of this type of content analysis checklist form means that different types of disclosures can be examined. For example, researchers might be interested in comparing the level of disclosure of financial and non-financial information. Alternatively, it can be used as the basis of a scoring system which rates or scores the disclosures made on the basis of their extensiveness or the quality of the information provided. Thus a company that discloses only qualitative examples of activities for parts of the company might be scored '1'. A company that discloses information about the same activities but provides quantitative data for all of the company might be scored '3', while financial data covering several years might be scored '5'. Again, the score received by a company would be compared to the maximum possible score it could have got, to produce a measure of the relative level of disclosure.

This type of scoring system is often accused of being too subjective. Certainly, it is not always easy to design a good weighting system and different people may have different views on how items should be weighted. However, the problem of how to measure disclosure quality does not go away if it is ignored, and the decision to score all disclosures equally is a subjective decision, as of course is the decision to use a weighted

---

[18] See, for example, Adams *et al.* (1995); Roberts (1990).

[19] See Unerman (2000) for more on this.

Exhibit 7.9   Environment- and employee-related disclosure checklist used by Roberts (1991)

Environment protection statement		4	Energy sources used – costs
1	Policies	5	Improvements achieved – qualitative statements
2	General descriptive statements	6	Improvements achieved – quantitative statements
3	Types of controls employed	7	Improvements achieved – costs
4	Costs incurred	**Political statements**	
5	Outputs/achievements	1	Views on legislation
Process-related information		2	Views on environmental demands
1	Policies	3	Actions undertaken (lobbying, etc.) – specific examples
2	Description of specific examples	4	Actions undertaken – policies
3	Costs incurred	**Employment information**	
4	Outputs/achievements – qualitative statements	1	Disabled employees – numbers/costs/policies
5	Outputs/achievements – quantitative measures	2	Trainee policies
Product-related information		3	Trainee costs
1	Policies	4	Trainee numbers
2	Description of specific examples	5	Trainee hours
3	Outputs/achievements – qualitative statements	6	Pay awards
4	Outputs/achievements – quantitative measures	7	Maternity/paternity leave
Environment-related investments		8	Share/profit schemes
1	Policies	9	Hours worked
2	Description of specific examples	10	Absenteeism
3	Costs incurred	11	Labour turnover
4	Outputs/achievements – qualitative statements	12	Pensioners – numbers/benefits
5	Outputs/achievements – quantitative measures	**Health and safety**	
Research and development activities		1	Policies
1	Policies	2	Description actions undertaken – qualitative
2	Description of specific examples	3	Description actions undertaken – financial
3	Overview of all environment related activities	4	Training activities – qualitative
4	Costs incurred	5	Training activities – quantitative
Energy usage information		6	Accidents – qualitative information
1	Policies	7	Accidents – quantitative
2	Energy sources used – qualitative statements	8	Illness – time lost
3	Energy sources used – quantitative statements		

Source: Roberts (1991).

disclosures score. A more valid reason not to try to weight items according to their importance is the argument that often the extra sophistication is simply not necessary. If we are looking at a fairly large number of items of information, a company that scores relatively high on an equally weighted scoring system will also usually score relatively high on any other type of weighted scoring system. While these are still issues of debate, what is clear is that the disclosure index must, as with the databases used for classifications

Exhibit 7.10 Extract from a content analysis form used to record environmental disclosures

	Type	Time	Area	Extent	Non-narrative
Description of:					
● emission targets					
● other targets					
● external standards					
● legislation					
Achievements re:					
● emission targets					
● other targets					
● external standards					
● legislation					
Non-compliance with:					
● emission targets					
● other targets					
● external standards					
● legislation					
Impacts re:					
● emission levels					
● waste					
● inputs used					
● energy used					
● recycling					
● noise abatement					

Exhibit 7.11 Explanation of content analysis checklist form

Type	Qualitative
	Quantitative or
	Financial information
Time	Time period covered by disclosures
Area	Information given for:
	All of company
	Specific geographical area(s) or
	Specific line(s) of business only
Extent	Describe all relevant activities of the area or give examples of activities carried out only
Non-narrative	Disclose pictures/diagrams/graphs

discussed in Chapter 6, be designed specifically for the purpose it is being used for. If the index is designed for one purpose, but then used without change in a different environment or for a different purpose, it is unlikely to capture what it seeks.[20]

Various different types of content analysis have been used to measure social and environmental disclosures. These studies have mainly been concerned with disclosures in a single country, whether for example UK,[21] USA,[22] India,[23] Singapore[24] or Australia.[25] Far less common are studies comparing the practices in different countries. However, one international study using this type of research instrument replicated and extended Roberts's work.[26] Using annual reports from four years later (i.e. 1992 or 1993) and looking at the same five countries plus the UK, this study came to a somewhat different conclusion. It looked at environmental, employee and ethical information and measured the amount of space devoted to a number of issues in each of these three areas. It also measured the number of items that were disclosed in total and the number of items that were disclosed in quantified or financial terms.

The results of this study were interesting in that it not only found that the six countries disclosed significantly different amounts of information but that the two countries disclosing the most were, first, Germany and, second, the UK. These two countries are very different. Germany has a long history of worker participation in corporate management, with works councils being common. It also has a very active and vociferous Green Party. The UK, in contrast, has a relatively small Green movement, the Green Party has not been very important in domestic politics and the UK has no history of works councils, while the trade union movement has substantially decreased in power and influence over the last decade or so. The authors of this work thus conclude that what motivates the voluntary disclosure of social and environmental information in the two countries is probably very different. In Germany, information may well be disclosed as a reaction to external pressures. In the UK, it is more probable that it is disclosed pro-actively in an attempt to pre-empt such external pressures – if companies can demonstrate that they are acting in socially acceptable ways then perhaps there will be less demand for more regulations and government control of their activities.

More ideas about the reasons for voluntary social and environmental disclosures are provided by Williams (1999) exploring disclosures in seven countries from the Asia–Pacific region. He argued that two of Hofstede's variables are particularly important. While as we saw in Chapter 6, Gray argued that all four of Hofstede's values were linked to secrecy, specifically that 'the higher a country ranks in terms of uncertainty avoidance and power distance and the lower it ranks in terms of individualism and masculinity then the more likely it is to rank highly in terms of secrecy' (Gray, 1988, p. 11), Williams only included uncertainty avoidance and masculinity or nurturing. From the variables discussed in Chapter 5, he also tested the importance of political system, this time in terms of the level of political and civil repression,[27] legal system, economic development and importance of equity financing. However, of these he found only support for the importance of the cultural variables (both of them) and the political system.

---

[20] Coy and Dixon (2004).

[21] Gray, *et al.* (1995a, 2001); Campbell (2004).

[22] Patten (2002); Esrock and Leichty (1998).

[23] Singh and Ahuja (1983).

[24] Tsang (1998).

[25] Deegan and Gordon (1996).

[26] Adams *et al.* (1998).

[27] See Belkaoui (1985) and Goodrich (1986) for more on this possible relationship.

7.6.2 The measurement of other types of disclosure

There have been a number of studies which have been wider in scope, looking at all or most types of voluntary disclosure. Appendix 7.2 gives examples of studies of voluntary disclosure on developed countries and developing countries. It shows how research papers may be summarized in a literature review to bring out the country studied, the date of the study (rather than the date of publication), the number of companies surveyed and the number of data items in the checklist, the variables found to have a significant association with disclosure, and the theories used to explain the findings.

It is difficult to compare these studies or to describe their findings in general terms. They have looked at different countries, different time periods and different types of companies, and have used different disclosure checklists. This section will therefore not attempt to draw generalizations but will instead look at just two of these studies, Meek *et al.* (1995) and Gray *et al.* (1995b), which had a strong influence on the later papers summarized in Appendix 7.2. These two studies looked at a wide range of information of three types – strategic, non-financial and financial – all items being voluntary in both the UK and the US at that time (see Exhibit 7.12). This breakdown of disclosures into three types was necessary as different factors may influence the voluntary disclosure of the different types of information. For example, the disclosure of financial information is likely to be most influenced by corporate financing needs and forms of financing employed. In contrast, disclosure of non-financial information or employee and social information is most likely to be influenced by political and societal pressures for additional disclosures. Thus, companies in one country may tend to disclose relatively large amounts of financial information while companies from another country may instead disclose relatively large amounts of non-financial information.

Gray *et al.* (1995b) looked at large UK and US multinational companies and compared those that were listed only on their domestic stock exchange with those that were internationally listed (i.e. listed on both the London and New York stock exchanges). They were interested in the questions of whether internationally listed companies disclosed more information and disclosed more harmonized information than did domestically listed companies.

For the US sample, they found that internationally listed companies disclosed significantly more information than did domestically listed companies, including significantly more strategic and non-financial information. (This was true after controlling for the possible effect of sample differences with respect to size and multinationality, as measured by the proportion of foreign sales.) For the UK sample, the results were somewhat different, with internationally listed companies disclosing significantly more financial information. They then compared the UK and US samples. For the domestically listed companies, the UK companies disclosed significantly more non-financial information while the US companies disclosed significantly more financial information. For the international group, significant differences also existed, but there was less of a difference between the two countries. Now, the only significant difference was with respect to non-financial information. These results clearly suggest that international listing does not eliminate all country-specific differences in voluntary disclosures. However, it appears to moderate or reduce national differences by, in particular, reducing the difference between the amount of financial information disclosed.

The second study, by Meek *et al.* (1995), looked at the same companies plus a sample of internationally listed European companies from France, Germany and The Netherlands ('internationally listed European companies' were defined as those that listed on either the London or New York stock exchange). Using the same disclosure checklist they modelled

| Exhibit 7.12 | Voluntary disclosure checklist as used by Meek *et al.* (1995) |

Strategic information

1 General corporate information
1 Brief history of company
2 Organizational structure

2 Corporate strategy
3 Statement of strategy and objectives – general
4 Statement of strategy and objectives – financial
5 Statement of strategy and objectives – marketing
6 Statement of strategy and objectives – social
7 Impact of strategy on current results
8 Impact of strategy on future results

3 Acquisitions and disposals
9 Reasons for the acquisitions
10 Reasons for the disposals

4 Research and development
11 Corporate policy on R&D
12 Location of R&D activities
13 Number employed in R&D

5 Future prospects
14 Qualitative forecast of sales
15 Quantitative forecast of sales
16 Qualitative forecast of profits
17 Quantitative forecast of profits
18 Qualitative forecast of cash flows
19 Quantitative forecast of cash flows
20 Assumptions underlying the forecasts
21 Current period trading results – qualitative
22 Current period trading results – quantitative
23 Order book or back-log information

Non-financial information

6 Information about directors
24 Age of directors
25 Commercial experience of executive directors
26 Other directorships held by executive directors
27 Employee information

7 Educational qualifications
28 Geographical distribution of employees
29 Line-of-business distribution of employees
30 Categories of employees, by gender
31 Identification of senior management and their functions
32 Number of employees for two or more years
33 Reasons for changes in employee numbers or categories
34 Amount spent on training
35 Nature of training
36 Categories of employees trained
37 Number of employees trained
38 Data on accidents
39 Cost of safety measures
40 Redundancy information (general)
41 Equal opportunity policy statement
42 Recruitment problems and related policy

8 Social policy and value added information
43 Safety of products (general)
44 Environmental protection programmes – quantitative
45 Amount of charitable donations
46 Community programmes – general
47 Value added statement
48 Value added data
49 Value added ratios
50 Qualitative value added information

Financial information

9 Segmental information
51 Geographical capital expenditure – quantitative
52 Geographical production – quantitative
53 Line-of-business production – quantitative
54 Competitor analysis – qualitative
55 Competitor analysis – quantitative
56 Market share analysis – qualitative
57 Market share analysis – quantitative

10 Financial review
58 Profitability ratios
59 Cash flow ratios
60 Liquidity ratios
61 Gearing ratios
62 Intangible valuations – except goodwill and brands
63 Dividend pay-out policy
64 Financial summary – for at least six years
65 Restatement of financial information to non-UK/US GAAP
66 Off-balance sheet financing information
67 Advertising information – qualitative
68 Advertising information – quantitative
69 Effects of inflation on future operations – qualitative
70 Effects of inflation on results – qualitative
71 Effects of inflation on results – quantitative
72 Effects of inflation on assets – qualitative
73 Effects of inflation on assets – quantitative
74 Effects of interest rates on results
75 Effects of interest rates on future operations

11 Foreign currency information
76 Effects of foreign currency fluctuations on future operations – qualitative
77 Effects of foreign currency fluctuations on current results – qualitative
78 Major exchange rates used in the accounts
79 Long-term debt, by currency
80 Short-term debt, by currency
81 Description of foreign currency exposure management

12 Share price information
82 Market capitalization at year end
83 Market capitalization trend
84 Size of shareholders
85 Types of shareholders

Source: Meek *et al.* (1995), pp. 569–70. Used with the permission of the *Journal of International Business Studies*.

Exhibit 7.13 The disclosure of voluntary information as found by Meek *et al.* (1995)

Info:	Strategic		Non-financial		Financial		Total	
	Mean %	Std dev.	Mean %	Std dev.	Mean %	Std dev.	Mean %	Std dev.
All cos	21.03	13.8	18.06	11.0	16.62	8.9	18.23	7.5
All USA	17.22	10.5	11.89	7.1	16.54	6.8	15.20	5.4
Int. USA	20.03	11.0	14.50	7.4	17.27	7.1	17.09	5.5
Dom. USA	14.43	9.3	9.27	5.7	15.81	6.5	13.32	4.6
All UK	16.83	8.5	25.70	9.1	14.58	9.3	18.73	6.8
Int. UK	17.41	9.7	25.71	10.3	16.92	10.4	19.87	8.0
Dom. UK	16.24	7.3	25.69	8.0	12.24	7.4	17.60	5.2
All Eur	36.52	16.6	23.01	12.4	19.67	11.8	25.16	8.3
Int. Eur	36.51	17.5	21.87	13.3	23.19	9.3	26.23	8.4
Dom. Eur	36.53	15.1	24.16	11.6	16.15	13.2	20.09	8.3

the voluntary disclosure decision through four regression equations (the four dependent variables being: all disclosures; strategic; non-financial; financial information). Exhibit 7.13 reports their findings regarding the amount of disclosure made by the sample companies.

The regression analysis failed to support the hypothesis that disclosure decisions were a function of either profitability or multinationality. All the other independent variables (size, country, industry, leverage and listing status) were significant in at least one of the four regressions. However, none was significant across all four equations (e.g., size was not a significant explanation of the amount of strategic information disclosed). The listing status was significant in explaining the overall level of disclosure and the amount of strategic and financial information. It was not important in explaining the level of disclosure of non-financial information. This, again, supports the assertion that stock market pressures and financing needs are most likely to influence the decision to disclose financial information and other information about the financial and future prospects of the company. In contrast, stock market and financing needs are far less likely to influence decisions regarding the voluntary disclosure of employee and social information.

7.7 Good news, bad news and earnings 'conservatism'

The term 'conservatism' is well known in accounting. It is most commonly used to describe accounting practices that recognize all losses as soon as they are known, but are more cautious about recognizing all gains as soon as they are known. For example, provisions are made against expected losses on long-contracts, but profit is only partly recognized on completion of each certified stage of the contract. The words 'asymmetry' ('lack of symmetry') and 'asymmetric' ('not symmetric') are used to describe this unmatched pattern of behaviour. One of the well-known problems of conservatism is that it has different effects on the balance sheet and the statement of profit or loss. Conservatism in the balance sheet can cause over-optimism in the profit or loss (e.g. understating the value of a fixed asset leads to a lower depreciation charge and so a higher profit). Some writers have given a different description of conservatism as a preference for always choosing the option that leads to lower reported values for shareholders' equity, but this view has been discouraged by standard-setters.

7.7.1 Basu's model of conservatism

Basu (1997) gave a new interpretation of 'conservatism'. He said it captures the accountant's tendency to require a higher degree of verification for recognizing good news than bad news in financial statements (1997, p. 4). This led Basu to an expectation that earnings reflect bad news more quickly than good news. He gave the example that unrealized losses are recognized earlier than unrealized gains. This asymmetry in recognition leads to systematic differences between good news and bad news periods in the 'timeliness' and 'persistence' of earnings. 'Timeliness' measures how quickly an event is reflected in reported earnings. 'Persistence' measures the period of time for which the event continues to have an effect on reported earnings. He used the example of an asset being depreciated over ten years. It is now in its fourth year of operation. Suppose that the enterprise is given the good news that the asset life is now 13 years and so the asset will earn profit for longer. That good news is not reported directly but it results in a lower depreciation charge and so higher earnings. The higher earnings persist for the remainder of the asset life. Suppose instead that the enterprise is given the bad news that the expected asset life is reduced to seven years. The enterprise will apply an impairment test in year 4, causing a sharp reduction in profits in year 4 followed by an even spread of the new depreciation charge on the residual amount. The bad news has a strong immediate effect but less of a persistent effect into future years.

Basu used negative and positive unexpected annual stock returns to represent bad news and good news. Stock returns are measured by the change in share price over a defined period of time. Unexpected returns are the difference between the actual return and the expected return based on a market portfolio and the risk of the specific share. Stock prices reflect market perceptions of a company's performance. Basu

---

Exhibit 7.14 Basu's model of good news, bad news and earnings

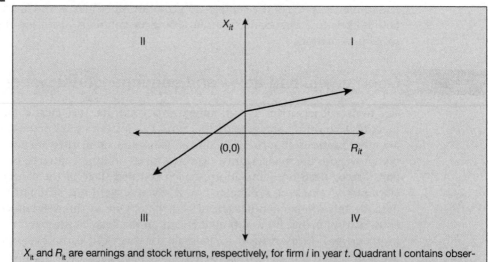

X_{it} and R_{it} are earnings and stock returns, respectively, for firm i in year t. Quadrant I contains observations with positive returns and positive earnings. Quadrant II contains observations with negative returns and positive earnings. Quadrant III contains observations with negative returns and negative earnings. Quadrant IV contains observations with positive returns and negative earnings.

Source: Basu (1997) p. 12.

relied on a body of previous research which indicated that stock prices anticipate accounting earnings by up to four years. This means that stock prices are the 'leading' variable and earnings are the 'lagging' variable. Basu predicted that if a graph is plotted with annual earnings on the vertical axis and unexpected stock returns on the horizontal axis, there will be a correlation between the two but the slope of the graph will be steeper for negative abnormal returns. The 'bad news' on the left-hand side of the graph will cause earnings to fall faster than the 'good news' will cause earnings to rise on the right-hand side. He also predicted that the intercept on the vertical axis (at the point of zero good and bad news) will be positive because even though there is neither good news nor bad news, the persistent effect of any previous good news will remain.

Basu tested his hypothesis using US data from 1963 to 1990. The adjusted R^2 (explanatory power) was higher at 6.6 per cent for negative returns than 2.1 per cent for positive returns, which gave Basu support for his claim that bad news has more impact than good news (although both figures for explanatory power are very low). He also found there were different slopes for the two parts of the graph, as predicted.

Despite the low explanatory power of his results, Basu's paper was significant for comparative research because it led to a series of papers making international comparisons of 'conservatism'.

7.7.2 US/UK comparison

Pope and Walker (1999) applied a similar model in comparing the accounting treatment of extraordinary items in US and UK accounting regimes. Their data covered the period 1976 to 1992 when extraordinary items were a stronger feature in both countries (changes in rules in both countries have subsequently largely eliminated extraordinary items). Their results showed that the degree of 'conservatism' displayed by earnings before extraordinary items under US GAAP was higher than under UK GAAP. However, examination of earnings after extraordinary items showed that the sensitivity of earnings to bad news was higher under UK GAAP than under US GAAP. The explanatory power of their results was 10.5 per cent for earnings after extraordinary items and 13.3 per cent for earnings before extraordinary items. Their results also indicated that an important distinguishing feature of US GAAP conservatism was the relatively slow recognition of good news in earnings.

7.7.3 US, UK, Australia, Canada, France, Germany and Japan

Ball, Kothari and Robin (2000) proposed that earnings would react to good news and bad news at different rates depending on whether the country had a code law or a common law regime. They used the code law/common law distinction as a very crude measure of the extent to which accounting is determined by market supply and demand relative to political forces. Their real interest was in examining how quickly economic income (as indicated by the market's perception of the future prospects of a company) is incorporated into accounting income over time. They analyzed data for companies in Australia, Canada, the US, the UK (as examples of common-law systems) and France, Germany and Japan (as examples of code-law systems) over the period 1985–95. They found that the common-law accounting earnings showed greater timeliness than those of code-law accounting but that this was almost entirely due to greater sensitivity to economic losses (bad news). They linked this to a desire for greater 'transparency' in disclosure and they regard the more timely reporting as 'high-quality' disclosure. The explanatory power was 4.6 per cent for the code-law results and 14.6 per cent for the common-law results. When they split the data into two periods, 1985–90 and 1991–95, they found that all countries except Japan showed increased reaction to bad news and concluded that corporate governance measures around the world were causing pressure for more timely reaction. They seemed somewhat unsure about the explanation for Japan.

Their paper contains a full discussion of the limitations of their analysis (pp. 47–49) and it is important to read this discussion before citing the paper simplistically as a conclusion about code-law and common-law systems. They acknowledge that the most obvious concern is the validity of using stock returns to represent ('proxy' for) economic income. Equating poor public disclosure with uninformed stock prices involves projecting common-law precepts onto code-law institutions. Code-law systems were not designed for public disclosure. Ball *et al.* suggest that this is not a problem as the code law countries will use inside information to inform the market. They assert, without stating the authority (2000, p. 48), that insider-trading laws are fundamentally incompatible with code-law governance. A second concern about their model is that the code-law/common-law categorization is used to represent an economic construct (a variable measure) representing the extent to which accounting is determined by market supply and demand relative to political forces. Their response is that the evidence is consistent with the idea. Another limitation is that their results apply only to listed companies and so are less representative of code-law countries in general, where proportionately more companies are unlisted.

7.7.4 France, Germany and the UK

Giner and Rees (2001) compared France, Germany and the UK, as having two different types of code law and a common-law system, respectively. They studied the period 1990 to 1998. The explanatory power of their results for the 'bad news' sample was 8.5 per cent for Germany, 9.9 per cent for France and 11.4 per cent for the UK. The explanatory powers of the 'good news' sample were 0.6 per cent, 1.7 per cent and 0.9 per cent respectively (2001, p. 1311). They agreed with Ball *et al.* (2000) in concluding that bad news is more rapidly incorporated into earnings than is good news. However Giner and Rees observed higher explanatory power for bad news effects in Germany and France compared to Ball *et al.* They found no significant difference between the three countries, which differs from the main result of Ball *et al.* but is consistent with their findings for the shorter time period of 1991–95. Giner and Rees concluded that the differences were disappearing in more recent years despite the different legal traditions. In further analysis they showed that the results for the German sample also showed characteristics of conservatism in which management always make the choice which leads to lower book value of equity.

7.7.5 Hong Kong, Malaysia, Singapore and Thailand

Ball, Robin and Wu (2003) study the timely recognition of economic losses (measured by negative change in market returns) in Hong Kong, Malaysia, Singapore and Thailand in the period 1984–96 (i.e. before the economic crisis of 1997 in those countries). They make the assumption that these could be described as common law regimes influenced substantially by UK, US and IAS accounting standards and standard-setting institutions. The results are compared with the 'common-law' and 'code-law' findings of Ball *et al.* (2000). Hong Kong shows the highest timeliness and Thailand the lowest. The authors compare this with the more market-oriented reputation of Hong Kong compared to Thailand. All are less timely than the common-law group studied in Ball *et al.* (2000). This is attributed to the incentives facing managers and auditors in companies dominated by family control and personal networking. These companies are characterized by the authors as having strong incentives to hide large profits and large losses by income smoothing. The explanatory power of the results resembles that of Basu (1997) with an R^2 of 4.5 per cent. They conclude that high-quality standards do not guarantee high-quality financial reporting (1997, p. 260) and that the SEC is 'well-advised' (1997, p. 259) in concluding that a condition for acceptance of IAS for financial reporting purposes in the US is that 'the standards must be rigorously interpreted and applied'. This paper lacks the thorough discussion of limitations found in Ball *et al.* (2000) but all those limitations should be considered in evaluating the US-oriented policy conclusions about the quality of financial reporting.

7.7.6 Comment on 'conservatism' research

The limitation of this type of comparative research is that the analysis begins with an unstated presumption that accounting systems that have the characteristics of the US system are a baseline against which to evaluate other accounting systems. It assumes that the stock market is the only consumer of accounting information. It builds on the findings of prior research that accounting earnings lag behind the perceptions of economic earnings that are reflected in market prices. The explanation of accounting earnings reacting to a change in an asset life, which has a direct effect on accounting measures, is generalized by analogy as a reaction to all the information that is contained in the market price of a share. The abnormal returns can be adjusted to allow for other market forces or industry factors that might distort the overall message about the company but it is still possible that the market merely reflects what the company is telling the analysts in briefings that have a horizon of 18 to 24 months into the future. If that is happening then there is perhaps no great surprise that the eventual earnings outcome matches the tentative hints already given to the market. Some of the policy implications drawn in the conclusions sections of these papers are stronger than the underlying evidence supports. The very low explanatory power of the model (up to 10 per cent in most cases) means that 90 per cent of the explanation of earnings has yet to be found.

Summary and conclusions

This chapter has explained the techniques that can be used to measure differences in accounting systems. It has shown how the comparability index can be used to measure the impact of GAAP differences on the reported figures. However, it is not only the difference in reported figures that is important. Standard setters and others interested in international harmonization may also want to measure the degree of difference or similarity in the accounting methods used, as measured by concentration indices. The various ways of measuring voluntary disclosure have been explained and a number of studies reviewed. Finally the chapter has explained comparative studies of 'conservatism' as a link between market returns and the reported earnings of a company.

Key points from the chapter:

- The comparability index can be used to measure differences in both reported earnings and shareholders' equity and it can also be broken down into partial indices used to measure the impact of differences in the treatment of specific issues.
- The H-index and the C-index both measure differences in the accounting methods used by companies.
- The C-index may be broken down into within-country and between-country harmonization.
- The level of voluntary disclosure varies across countries.
- Different considerations appear important in determining the level of disclosure of different types of information, and companies in some countries tend to disclose relatively more financial information while companies in other countries tend instead to disclose relatively high levels of social information, including employee and environmental information.
- Basu's view of conservatism is based on the expectation that company earnings reflect bad news more quickly than good news.
- Research studies show that the rate of reaction of earnings to good news or bad news is different for common law countries compared to code law countries.

Case study 7.1   Daimler–Benz: Reconciliation of earnings from German to US GAAP

Daimler–Benz was the first German company to list on the New York Stock Exchange (NYSE) when it listed in 1993. A number of reasons have been suggested. The company had a mismatch between the importance of its foreign operations and the foreign ownership of its equity. With 40 per cent of its sales coming from outside Germany, only 7.2 per cent of its shares were owned by non-Germans. The company also had a number of significant shareholders, such as Deutsche Bank and the Emirate of Kuwait. If any of these decided to sell a large block of their shares on the German exchanges it could have caused a major fall in the company's share price. Any substantial sale could be better absorbed in the far larger NYSE.

All Figures in DMm	1995	1994	1993	1992	1991	1990
Net income (loss) as reported under						
German GAAP:	(5,734)	895	615	1,451	1,942	1,795
Add changes in appropriated						
retained earnings – provisions,						
reserves and valuation differences	(640)	409	(4,262)	774	64	738
Other adjustments:						
Goodwill and business acquisitions	(2,241)	(350)	(287)	(76)	(270)	(251)
Business dispositions and						
deconsolidations	369	(652)	–	337	(490)	–
Consolidation of non-consolidated						
subsidiaries	–	–	–	–	636	(512)
Pensions and other retirement						
benefits	(219)	(432)	(524)	96	(66)	(153)
Financial instruments	49	633	(225)	(438)	86	35
Securities	238	(388)	–	–	–	–
Deferred taxes	2,621	496	2,627	(646)	(126)	(758)
Other			Various balancing items			
Net income (loss) in accordance						
with US GAAP	(5,729)	1,052	(1,839)	1,350	1,886	884

Source: Daimler–Benz, Form 20-F 1995; Radebaugh et al. (1995).

On listing, the first year's figures based upon US GAAP showed a loss of DM1,839m rather than a profit of DM615m. Much of this change was caused by the write-back of provisions. German law allowed a company to set up provisions to cover the cost of future internal business operations. Under US regulations such provisions are not allowed as there was no external party involved. The massive size of the reconciliation required ensured that Daimler–Benz received a tremendous amount of publicity when it issued these reconciliation statements. The general impression given by this publicity was that German and US accounting regulations were very different, and German requirements were far more conservative. However, many of the differences were one-off adjustments. As can be seen from the figures reproduced in the table, the year of listing, 1993, was something of an atypical year, although the US GAAP-based profits were lower than the German GAAP-based earnings in all years except 1995, when they were virtually identical.

Case study 7.2   A simulation study of UK and French accounting

Walton (1992) explored the impact on the reported figures of differences in the accounting methods used in the UK and France. To do this, he chose a number of accounting issues – some where there are differences in terms of the prescribed rules in the two countries and others where companies have a choice of which methods to use.

The company modelled was a construction company. Specifically, there was a domestic parent company whose premises were compulsorily purchased at a loss and whose new premises were partially financed by a government grant and partially financed by a US-denominated long-term loan. In addition, the parent sold and leased

▶

Case study 7.2 *(Continued)*

back some plant giving the possibility of showing a profit on the disposal. Finally, an overseas subsidiary was set up to carry out a long-term construction contract. Thus, the case included extraordinary items, long-term foreign currency transactions, the capitalisation of interest charges, government grants, leased assets and long-term contracts.

The case study was then presented to a number of auditors and account preparers in both the UK and France. This is not a real company so the results may not apply in practice, but they do provide valuable insights into the types of differences that can exist. The differences in the figures generated by the participants were often very large, especially for the accounts of the subsidiary, as shown in the table. However, the most noticeable, and surprising, conclusion is that for the subsidiary the average responses of the UK participants were more conservative than were the French responses. As shown in the average figures for turnover, profit both before and after interest, net assets and net equity were all less for the UK respondents and often very much less. For example, the average profit before interest calculated by the French sample was 12,793 while for the UK sample it was instead a loss of 12,014.

In contrast, for the parent company, there was little difference in the average figures generated by the UK and French samples – but, this time, the French responses tended to be slightly more conservative and they showed considerably more variability than did the UK responses.

	British sample		French sample		Conservatism
	Mean	Std dev.	Mean	Std dev.	index
Overseas subsidiary					
Turnover	136,644	83,407	185,930	36,432	0.735
Profit before interest	(12,014)	50,759	12,793	23,357	−0.939
Interest	(4,675)	5,619	(4,031)	1,654	0.841
Profit after interest	(16,689)	51,344	8,763	22,812	−1.904
Total net assets	168,711	51,670	208,938	23,091	0.807
Net equity	2,911	51,256	28,763	22,812	0.101
Parent company					
Turnover	1,331,733	44,577	1,345,000	76,572	0.990
Profit before interest	340,340	28,012	352,598	78,076	0.965
Interest	19,478	10,374	33,692	19,950	0.578
Profit after interest	320,862	30,012	318,906	86,169	1.006
Extraordinary items	33,770	24,538	58,182	14,444	0.580
Profit after extraordinary	287,092	19,003	260,724	77,221	1.101
Total net assets	865,802	28,802	860,227	86,214	1.006
Net equity	551,862	18,339	538,895	102,203	1.024

Questions

The following questions test your understanding of the material contained in the chapter and allow you to relate your understanding to the learning outcomes specified at the start of this chapter. The learning outcomes are repeated here. Each question is cross-referenced to the relevant section of the chapter.

Understand how comparability indices are used to measure similarities and differences in reported figures

1 What are comparability and partial comparability indices? (section 7.4.2)

2 How are the comparability and partial comparability indices calculated? (section 7.4.2)

Understand how concentration indices are used to measure similarities and differences in accounting methods

3 What is the H- or Herfindahl index and how is it calculated? (section 7.5.1)

4 What is the C-index and how is it calculated? (section 7.5.2)

5 What is the difference between the H-index and the C-index? Which do you think is more useful? Why? (section 7.5)

6 How can the C-index be disaggregated into two indices it is when used on companies from different countries? (section 7.5.2)

7 Which of the two C-index sub-indices identified above is likely to be of more interest to international investors? Why? (section 7.5.3)

8 Which of the two C-index sub-indices is likely to be of more interest to international standard setters? Why? (section 7.5.3)

Measure the comparability of profits and the level of harmonization, using simple examples

9 If you had to quantify the extent of differences between two countries, how might you go about collecting the required information on each of the three types of differences? (sections 7.4–7.6)

10 What problems might you encounter when collecting this information? (sections 7.4–7.6)

11 If you were asked to measure the comparability of UK and US financial statements using the C-index, how would you set about doing it? What problems do you think that you would encounter? (section 7.5)

12 Use the information provided in the case study on Daimler–Benz and calculate the comparability index and the three most important partial comparability indices for the years 1995, 1993 and 1991. (Case study 7.1)

13 What do your findings tell you about the comparability of German and US GAAP? (Case study 7.1)

14 If you were asked to do a study to measure the comparability of French and US companies, how would you set about doing it? What problems do you think you would encounter? (section 7.4)

Understand the approach taken in market-based research investigating earnings 'conservatism'

15 How does Basu's model of conservatism relate to what is traditionally understood by the word 'conservatism' in accounting? (section 7.7.1)

Evaluate published research which has used these techniques

16 What were the main findings of Weetman *et al.* (1998) when they compared the UK and US GAAP-based earnings of UK companies? (section 7.4.2)

17 Given the discussion in Chapters 4 and 5 on why accounting differs across countries, are the results of Weetman *et al.* what you would have expected, or not? Why? (section 7.4.2)

18 Do you think the results found will apply to most UK and US companies in the mid-2000s? Why, or why not? (section 7.4.2)

19 What were the main findings of Walton when he compared UK and French company earnings? (section 7.4.4)

20 Given the discussion in Chapters 4 and 5 on why accounting differs across countries, are the results of Walton what you would have expected or not? Why? (section 7.4.4)

21 Do you think the results found will apply to most UK and French companies in the mid-2000s? Why, or why not? (section 7.4.4)

22 What were the main findings of Meek, Roberts and Gray when they compared voluntary disclosures of UK and US companies? (section 7.6.2)

23 Given the discussion in Chapters 4 and 5 on why accounting differs across countries, are the results of Meek, Roberts and Gray what you would have expected or not? Why? (section 7.6.2)

24 Do you think the results found will apply to most UK and US companies in the mid-2000s? Why, or why not? (section 7.6.2)

25 How did Ball *et al.* (2000) relate earnings conservatism to code-law and common-law characteristics? (section 7.7.3)

26 How do the findings of Giner and Rees (2001) differ from those of Ball *et al.* (2000)? (section 7.7.4)

27 How do Ball *et al.* (2003) form their conclusions about accounting in Hong Kong, Malaysia, Singapore and Thailand before the Asian economic crisis? (section 7.7.5)

References and further reading

Abayo, A.G., Adams, C.A. and Roberts, C.B. (1993) 'Measuring the quality of corporate disclosure in less developed countries: The case of Tanzania', *Journal of International Accounting Auditing and Taxation*, 2(2): 145–158.

Adams, C.A., Hill, W.Y. and Roberts, C.B. (1995) 'Environmental, employee and ethical reporting in Europe', *Research Report*, 41. London: Chartered Association of Certified Accountants.

Adams, C.A., Hill, W.Y. and Roberts, C.B. (1998) 'Corporate social reporting practices in Western Europe: Legitimating corporate activities?', *British Accounting Review*, 30(1): 1–22.

Adhikari, A. and Emenyonu, E.N. (1997) 'Accounting for business combinations and foreign currency translations: An empirical comparison of listed companies from developed countries', *Advances in International Accounting*, 10: 45–62.

Aisbett, S. (2001) 'Measurment of harmony of financial reporting within and between countries: the case of the Nordic countries', *European Accounting Review*, 10(1): 51–72.

Archer, S., Delvaille, P. and McLeay, S. (1995) 'The measurement of harmonisation and the comparability of financial statement items: Within-country and between-country effects', *Accounting and Business Research*, 25(98): 67–80.

Ball, R., Kothari, S.P. and Robin, A. (2000) 'The effect of international institutional factors on properties of accounting earnings', *Journal of Accounting and Economics*, 29: 1–52.

Ball, R., Robin, A. and Wu, J. (2003) 'Incentives versus standards: properties of accounting income in four east Asian countries', *Journal of Accounting and Economics*, 36: 235–270.

Basu, S. (1997) 'The conservatism principle and the asymmetric timeliness of earnings', *Journal of Accounting and Economics*, 24: 3–37.

Belkaoui, A. (1985) *International Accounting: Issues and Solutions*, Westport, CT: Querum.

Buzby, S.L. (1975) 'Company size, listed vs unlisted stocks, and extent of financial disclosure', *Journal of Accounting Research*, 13(1): 16–37.

Campbell, D. (2004) 'A longitudinal and cross-sectional analysis of environmental disclosure in UK companies – a research note', *British Accounting Review*, 36(1): 107–118.

Cañibano, L. and Mora, A. (2000) 'Evaluating the statistical significance of *de facto* accounting harmonization: A study of European global players', *European Accounting Review*, 9(3): 349–370.

Chow, C.W. and Wong-Boren, A. (1987) 'Voluntary financial disclosure by Mexican corporations', *The Accounting Review*, 62(3): 533–541.

Cooke, T.E. (1989) 'Voluntary corporate disclosure by Swedish companies', *Journal of International Financial Management and Accounting*, 1(2): 1–25.

Cooke, T.E. (1991) 'An assessment of voluntary disclosure in the annual reports of Japanese corporations', *International Journal of Accounting*, 26(3): 174–189.

Coy, D. and Dixon, K. (2004) 'The public accountability index: crafting a parametric disclosure index for annual reports', *British Accounting Review*, 36(1): 79–106.

Davidson, R.A. and Chrisman, H.H. (1993) 'Interlinguistic comparison of international accounting standards: The case of uncertainty expressions', *International Journal of Accountancy*, 28(1): 1–16.

Deegan, C. and Gordon, B. (1996) 'A study of the environmental disclosure practices of Australian companies', *Accounting and Business Research*, 26(3): 187–199.

Deloitte and Touche, VNO-NCW (2002) *Accounting Standards compared: differences between IAS, NL GAAP and US-GAAP.* Deloitte & Touche: available on website www.iasplus.com/dttpubs/iasnlus.pdf

Doupnik, T.S. and Richter, M. (2003) 'Interpretation of uncertainty expressions: a cross-national study', *Accounting, Organizations and Society*, 28: 15–35.

Emenyonu, E.N. and Gray, S.J. (1992) 'EC accounting harmonisation: An empirical study of measurement practices in France, Germany and the UK', *Accounting and Business Research*, Winter: 49–58.

Esrock, S.L. and Leichty, G.B. (1998) 'Social responsibility and corporate web pages: self-presentation or agenda-setting?', *Public Relations Review*, 24(3): 305–319.

Evans, L. (2004) 'Language, translation and the problem of international accounting', *Accounting, Auditing and Accountability Journal*, 17(2): 210–248.

Firth, M.A. (1979) 'The impact of size, stock market listing and auditors on voluntary disclosure in corporate annual reports', *Accounting and Business Research*, 9(36): 272–280.

Garrido, P., Leon, A. and Zorio, A. (2002) 'Measurement of formal harmonization progress: The IASC experience', *International Journal of Accounting*, 37: 1–26.

Giner, B. and Rees, W. (2001) 'On the asymmetric recognition of good and bad news in France, Germany and the United Kingdom', *Journal of Business Finance and Accounting*, 28 (9–10): 1285–1332.

Goodrich, P.S. (1986) 'Cross-national financial accounting linkages: an empirical political analysis', *British Accounting Review*, 18(1): 42–60.

Gray, R., Kouhy, R. and Lavers, S. (1995a) 'Corporate social and environmental reporting: a review of the literature and a longitudinal study of UK disclosure', *Accounting, Auditing and Accountability Journal*, 8(2): 47–77.

Gray, R., Javad, M., Power, D.M. and Sinclair, C.D. (2001) 'Social and environmental disclosures and corporate characteristics: a research note and extension', *Journal of Business Finance and Accounting*, 28(3/4): 327–356.

Gray, S.J. (1980) 'The impact of international accounting differences from a security-analysis perspective: Some European evidence', *Journal of Accounting Research*, 18(1): 64–76.

Gray, S.J. (1988) 'Towards a theory of cultural influence on the development of accounting systems internationally', *Abacus*, 24(1): 1–15.

Gray, S.J., Meek, G.K. and Roberts, C.B. (1995b) 'International capital market pressures and voluntary annual report disclosures by US and UK multinationals', *Journal of International Financial Management and Accounting*, 6(1): 43–68.

Hellman, N. (1993) 'A comparative analysis of the impact of accounting differences on profits and return on equity: Differences between Swedish practice and US GAAP', *European Accounting Review*, 2(3): 495–530.

Herrman, D. and Thomas, W. (1995) 'Harmonisation of accounting measurement practices in the European Community', *Accounting and Business Research*, 25(100): 253–265.

Hofstede, G. (1984) *Culture's Consequences: International Differences in Work-Related Values*. Beverly Hills, CA: Sage Publications.

Hossain, M., Perera, M.H.B. and Rahman, A.R. (1995) 'Voluntary disclosure in the annual reports of New Zealand companies', *Journal of International Financial Management and Accounting*, 6(1): 69–85.

Krisement, V.M. (1997) 'An approach for measuring the degree of comparability of financial accounting information', *European Accounting Review*, 6(3): 465–485.

Meek, G.K., Roberts, C.B. and Gray, S.J. (1995) 'Factors influencing voluntary annual report disclosures by US, UK and continental European multinational corporations', *Journal of International Business Studies*, third quarter: 555–572.

Morris, R.D. and Parker, R.H. (1998) 'International harmony measures of accounting policy: Comparative statistical properties', *Accounting and Business Research*, 29(1): 73–86.

Murphy, A.B. (2000) 'The impact of adopting International Accounting Standards on the harmonization of accounting practices', *International Journal of Accounting*, 35(4): 471–493.

Parker, R.H. and Morris, R.D. (2001) 'The influence of US GAAP on the harmony of accounting measurement policies of large companies in the UK and Australia', *Abacus*, 37(3): 297–328.

Patten, D.M. (2002) 'Media exposure, public policy pressure, and environmental disclosure: an examination of the impact of tri data availability', *Accounting Forum*, 26(2): 152–171.

Pope, P. and Walker, M. (1999) 'International differences in timeliness, conservatism and classification of earnings', *Journal of Accounting Research*, 37(Supplement): 53–87.

Radebaugh, L.H., Gebhardt, G. and Gray, S.J. (1995) 'Foreign stock exchange listings: A case study of Daimler–Benz', *Journal of International Financial Management and Accounting*, 6(2): 158–192.

Rahman, A., Perera, H. and Ganeshanandam, S. (1996) 'Measurement of formal harmonization in accounting: an exploratory study', *Accounting and Business Research*, Autumn.

Rahman, A., Perera, H. and Ganesh, S. (2002) 'Accounting practice harmony, accounting regulation and firm characteristics', *Abacus*, 38(1): 46–77.

Roberts, C.B. (1990) 'International trends in social and employee reporting', *Occasional Research Paper*, 6. London: Chartered Association of Certified Accountants.

Roberts, C.B. (1991) 'Environmental disclosures: A note on reporting practices in mainland Europe', *Accounting, Auditing and Accountability Journal*, 4(3): 62–71.

Schultz, J. and Lopez, T.J. (2001) 'The impact of national influence on accounting estimates: Implications for international accounting standard-setters', *International Journal of Accounting* 36: 271–290.

Singh, D.R. and Ahuja, J.M. (1983) 'Corporate social reporting in India', *International Journal of Accounting*, 18(2): 151–169.

Street, D.L., Nichols, N.B. and Gray, S.J. (2000) 'Assessing the acceptability of International Accounting Standards in the US: An empirical study of the materiality of US GAAP reconciliations by non-US companies complying with IASC standards', *International Journal of Accounting*, 35(1): 27–63.

Tas, L.G. van der (1988) 'Measuring harmonization of financial reporting practices', *Accounting and Business Research*, 18(70): 157–169.

Tas, L.G. van der (1992) 'Evidence of EC financial reporting harmonization: The case of deferred tax', *European Accounting Review*, 1(1): 69–104.

Tay, J.S.W. and Parker, R.H. (1990) 'Measuring harmonization and standardization', *Abacus*, 26(1): 71–88.

Taylor, M.E. and Jones, R.A. (1999) 'The use of International Accounting Standards terminology, a survey of IAS compliance disclosure', *International Journal of Accountancy*, 34(4): 557–570.

Tsang, E.W.K. (1998) 'A longitudinal study of corporate social reporting in Singapore: the case of the banking, food and beverages and hotel industries', *Accounting, Auditing and Accountability Journal*, 11(5): 624–635.

Unerman, J. (2000) 'Methodological issues: reflections on quantification in corporate social reporting content analysis', *Accounting, Auditing and Accountability Journal*, 13(5): 667–680.

Wallace, R.S.O. (1988) 'Corporate financial reporting in Nigeria', *Accounting and Business Research*, 18(72): 352–362.

Walton, P. (1992) 'Harmonization of accounting in France and Britain: Some evidence', *Abacus*, 28(2): 186–199.

Weetman, P., Jones, E.A.E., Adams, C.A. and Gray, S.J. (1998) 'Profit measurement and UK accounting standards: A case of increasing disharmony in relation to US GAAP and IASs', *Accounting and Business Research*, 28(3): 189–203.

Williams, S.M. (1999) 'Voluntary environmental and social accounting disclosure practices in the Asia-Pacific region: an international empirical test of political economy theory', *International Journal of Accounting*, 34(2): 209–238.

Appendix 7.1 **A further explanation of how to calculate the C-index**

The C-index takes the form:

$$\frac{\Sigma(n_i \times (n_i - 1))}{(N \times (N - 1))}$$

where:

n_i is the number of companies using method i

N is the total number of companies.

This formula is based on mathematical combinations.

Take an example of ten companies where six use method 1 (say FIFO stock valuation) and four use method 2 (say LIFO stock valuation).

Company	A	B	C	D	E	F	G	H	J	K
Method	1	1	1	1	1	1	2	2	2	2

The combinations-based approach asks: 'If you picked up two of these company accounts at random, what is the chance they would use the same accounting method?'

The chance is found by dividing the number of matching pairs by the maximum number of pairs that can be formed.

How many companies match on method 1?

AB	AC	AD	AE	AF
	BC	BD	BE	BF
		CD	CE	CF
			DE	DF
				EF

The answer is 15. If you have learned the formulae for combinations you will know that this can be calculated by the formula:

$$\frac{n(n - 1)}{2}$$

where n is the number of companies using the same method (here it is six companies). Calculation:

$$\frac{6 \times 5}{2} = 15$$

How many companies match on method 2?

GH	GJ	GK
	HJ	HK
		JK

The answer is 6. This can also be calculated by the formula:

$$\frac{n(n-1)}{2}$$

Calculation:

$$\frac{4 \times 3}{2}$$
$$= 6$$

The total number of matching pairs is $15 + 6 = 21$.

Now ask the question: What is the maximum number of pairs that could be formed for all companies, disregarding the method used?

									Count
AB	AC	AD	AE	AF	AG	AH	AJ	AK	9
	BC	BD	BE	BF	BG	BH	BJ	BK	8
		CD	CE	CF	CG	CH	CJ	CK	7
			DE	DF	DG	DH	DJ	DK	6
				EF	EG	EH	EJ	EK	5
					FG	FH	FJ	FK	4
						GH	GJ	GK	3
							HJ	HK	2
								JK	1
								Total	45

Calculation:

$$\frac{N(N-1)}{2}$$
$$= \frac{10 \times 9}{2}$$
$$= 45$$

The formula for calculating the C-index is written in full as:

$$\frac{\Sigma(n_i \times (n_i - 1))/2}{(N \times (N - 1))/2}$$

Because both lines have a 'divide by 2' in the formula, this is not shown in the version in section 7.5.2. However, it is important to be consistent. When calculating, either divide by 2 for each line in turn, or calculate both lines of the formula without dividing by 2.

Appendix 7.2 Empirical studies on voluntary disclosure

This appendix compares examples of empirical studies on voluntary disclosure in developed and developing countries. It is extracted from the PhD thesis of Dr Nazli Anum Mohd Ghazali, 'Exploring theoretical explanations of voluntary disclosure by quantitative and qualitative investigation: evidence from Malaysia', University of Strathclyde, 2004. We are grateful to Dr Ghazali for permission to reproduce these tables.

Table 7.1 Examples of empirical studies on total voluntary disclosure in developed countries

	Author	Country	Reporting year	Sample	Disclosure items	Independent variables (statistically significant)	Mheoretical explanation	Non-significant variables
1	Cerf (1961)	US	1956/57	527 companies	31 items (weighted)	*Size (assets) [+]	Information costs, capital need, proprietary costs	
						*Number of shareholders [+]	Political costs, information costs	
						*Profitability (rate of return) [+]	Support continuance and compensation	
						*Listing status [+]	Listing requirements, information costs	
2	Singhvi and Desai (1971)	US	1965/66	55 unlisted and 100 listed companies	34 items (weighted)	*Size (assets) [+]	Information costs, capital need, proprietary costs	
						*Number of shareholders [+]	Political costs, information costs, professional management	
						**Listing status [+]	Listing requirements	
						*Audit firm [+]	Reputation costs	
						*Profitability (rate of return) [+]	Support continuance and compensation	
						*Profitability (earnings margin) [+]	Signalling	
3	Buzby (1975)	US	1970/71	88 companies (44 unlisted OTC, 44 listed NYSE or AMEX)	39 (weighted) [maximum 123.3]	*Size (asset) [+]	Information costs, capital need, proprietary costs, political costs	*Listing status
4	Firth (1979)	UK	1976	40 unlisted and 140 listed companies	48 voluntary items (weighted)	*Listing status [+] *Size (sales) [+]	Capital need Information costs, political costs	*Audit firm
5	McNally et al. (1982)	New Zealand	1979	103 non-financial and non-retail listed companies	54 voluntary	***Size (assets) [+]	Information costs	***Rate of return (net income to total assets), growth, audit firm, industry

►

Table 7.1 (Continued)

	Author	Country	Reporting year	Sample	Disclosure items	Independent variables (statistically significant)	Theoretical explanation	Non-significant variables
6	Cooke (1989)	Sweden	1985	90 non-financial companies (38 unlisted, 33 listed on SSE, 19 multiple listing)	146 voluntary	Listing status [+] Size (assets, number of shareholders, sales) [+] Industry (trading) [−]	Capital need, agency theory Political costs, agency theory 'Bandwagon' effect	Parent company relationship, industry (manufacturing, services, conglomerate)
7	Cooke (1991)	Japan	1988	48 companies (13 unlisted, 25 listed on TSE, 10 multiple listing)	106 voluntary	Size (assets, sales, number of shareholders) [+] Listing status [+] Industry (manufacturing) [+]	Political costs Capital need, agency theory Historical factors, 'bandwagon' effect	Industry (trading, services, conglomerate)
8	Craswell and Taylor (1992)	Australia	1984	86 oil and gas companies	Dichotomous, 1 for disclosers of oil and gas reserves, 0 otherwise	Audit firm [+]	Reputation costs, signalling, agency costs	Leverage, size (assets), cash flow risk, ownership structure (shares held by top 20 shareholders)
9	Malone et al. (1993)	US	1986	125 oil and gas companies (41 listed on NYSE or AMEX; 84 unlisted NASDAQ)	129 (weighted)	Listing status [+] Leverage [+] Number of shareholders [+]	Stock exchange listing requirements Agency theory Agency theory	Size (assets), profitability (rates of return, earnings margin), audit firm, foreign operations, diversification, proportion of outside directors
10	Wallace et al. (1994)	Spain	1991	50 non-financial companies (30 listed and 20 unlisted)	16 mandatory (maximum 146)	Size (assets) [+]	Political costs, information costs	Gearing, earnings return, profit margin, audit firm, industry

#	Study	Country	Year	Sample	Extent	Variables	Theory	Other variables
11	Hossain et al. (1995)	New Zealand	1991	55 listed non-financial companies (40 domestic, 15 domestic + international)	95 voluntary	Size (assets) [+]; Leverage [+]; Listing status (multiple) [+]	Agency theory; Agency theory; Agency theory	Audit firm, assets-in-place
12	Raffournier (1995)	Switzerland	1991	161 listed non-financial companies	30 voluntary	Size (sales) [+]; Internationality (exports/sales) [+]	Proprietary costs, political costs, information costs; Foreign market pressures	Leverage, profitability, ownership structure (shares not held by known shareholders), audit type, percent of fixed assets, industry
13	Inchausti (1997)	Spain	1989–91	49, 47, 42 non-financial listed companies	50 (30 compulsory, 20 voluntary)	Size (assets) [+]	Agency theory, political costs, proprietary costs	Profitability, leverage, industry, dividend payout
14	Adams and Hossain (1998)	New Zealand	1988–93	34 life insurance companies (193 annual reports) [84 mutuals and 109 stocks]	189 voluntary	Organizational form (stock companies) [+]; Size (market value of assets) [+]; Product concentration [–]; Distribution systems (tied agents) [–]; Proportion of non-executive directors [+]; Reinsurance [+]	Agency theory	Assets-in-place, localization of operations
15	Depoers (2000)	France	1995	102 non-financial listed companies	65 voluntary	Size (sales) [+]; Foreign activity [+]; Barriers to entry [+]; Labour pressure [–]	Information costs; Foreign market pressures; Proprietary costs; Political costs	Leverage, ownership structure (proportion of shares held by three largest shareholders), audit firm

▶

Table 7.1 (Continued)

	Author	Country	Reporting year	Sample	Disclosure items	Independent variables (statistically significant)	Theoretical explanation	Non-significant variables
16	Camfferman and Cooke (2002)	UK and The Netherlands	1996	322 companies (161 Dutch and 161 UK)	93 items (specified in the Fourth and Seventh European Union Directives)	Dutch: Size (asset) [+]	Political costs, information costs, capital need	Industry (manufacturing and services), net income margin, ROE, audit firm
						Leverage [+]	Agency theory	
						Current ratio [+]	Signalling	
						Industry (conglomerate +; trading −)	Capital need	
						UK: Industry (manufacturing and conglomerate) [+]	Capital need	Industry (trading and services), leverage, current ratio, ROE
						Size (asset) [+]	Capital need, political costs, information costs	
						Net income margin [−]	Signalling	
						Audit firm [+]	Reputation costs	

Key:
* results obtained using mean scores
** results obtained using both mean scores and multiple regression analysis
*** results obtained using rank order correlations (Spearman's *rho*)
Other results (without asterisks) obtained using multiple regression analysis
OTC – Over the counter
NYSE – New York Stock Exchange
AMEX – American Stock Exchange

Table 7.2 Examples of empirical studies on total voluntary disclosure in developing countries

	Author(s)	Country	Reporting year	Sample	Disclosure items	Independent variables (statistically significant)	Theoretical explanation	Non-significant variables
1	Singhvi (1968)	India	1963 and 1965	45 listed companies	34 (weighted) [maximum 68]	*Size (assets) [+]	Information costs, capital need, proprietary costs	Audit firm, number of shareholders
						*Type of management (foreigner) [+]	(Professional) education	
						*Profitability (rate of return, earnings margin) [+]	Signalling, support continuance	
2	Chow and Wong-Boren (1987)	Mexico	1982	52 manufacturing companies	24 voluntary	Size (MvEq + BvD) [+]	Agency theory	Gearing, assets-in-place
3	Wallace (1988)	Nigeria	1982–86	87 non-financial listed companies	120 mandatory and 65 voluntary	Study examined the extent of disclosure and opinions from six user-groups on different sections of the annual reports and the level of importance of each item of information		
4	Abayo et al. (1993)	Tanzania	1989/90	51 companies	88 mandatory and 44 voluntary	Significant positive relationship was observed between mandatory and voluntary disclosures (those which provided more mandatory disclosure also provided more voluntary information), and between timeliness and audit opinion (companies which received a qualified audit opinion took significantly longer to report than those which received a clean audit report)		
5	Hossain et al. (1994)	Malaysia	1991	67 non-financial listed companies	78 voluntary	Size (market capitalization) [+]	Agency theory	Gearing, assets-in-place, audit firm
						Ownership by top ten shareholders [−]	Agency theory	
						Listing status (multiple) [+]	Capital need, foreign exchange listing requirements	
						Liquidity [−]	Legitimacy (accountability)	
						Listing status (listed) [+]	Stock exchange listing requirements	
6	Ng and Koh (1994)	Singapore	1986	106 listed companies	3 Statement of Recommended Practice	Size [+]	Agency theory, information costs, capital need	Complexity of operation, liquidity
						Profitability [+]	Information costs, political costs	

▶

Table 7.2 (Continued)

Author(s)	Country	Reporting year	Sample	Disclosure items	Independent variables (statistically significant)	Theoretical explanation	Non-significant variables
7 Wallace and Naser (1995)	Hong Kong	1991	80 non-financial listed companies	30 mandatory (maximum 146)	Gearing [+]	Agency theory	Market capitalization, sales, liquidity, earnings return, outside ownership, foreign registered office, gearing
					Auditor type [+]	Reputation	
					Industry (finance, properties, hotels) [−]	Political costs, proprietary costs (secrecy)	
					Size (assets) [+]	Political costs, proprietary costs, information costs	
					Profit margin [−]	Legitimacy (accountability)	
					Scope of business (conglomerate) [+]	Information costs	
8 Ahmed (1996)	Bangladesh	1987/88, 1992/93	59 non-financial listed companies (118 annual reports)	150 (94 statutory, 56 voluntary)	Audit firm [−]	Reputation	Qualification of principal accounting officer, size (sales and assets), total debt
					Audit firm [+]		
					Subsidiaries of MNCs [+]	Political costs, parent company requirements	
					Listing status [+]	Agency theory, capital need	
					Audit firm [+] V: Size [+], audit firm [+]	Signalling	
9 Marston and Robson (1997)	India	1982/83, 1989/90	29 companies (58 annual reports)	17 mandatory and voluntary (maximum 56.5)	Size [+]	Agency theory, political costs	
10 Suwaidan (1997)	Jordan	1992	102 listed companies	75 voluntary	Size (market capital & sales) [+]	Information costs, proprietary costs, political costs, agency theory	Number of shareholders, profitability (ROE & ROA), audit firm (international contact), external financing ratio
					Institutional ownership [+]	Information costs	

#	Author	Country	Year	Sample	Disclosure items	Significant variables	Information costs	Other variables
11	Patton and Zelenka (1997)	Czech Republic	1993	50 joint stock listed companies	66 items (37 narrow, 12 somewhat broader, 17 broader)	Government owner-ship [+]; Industry (insurance) [+]; Audit firm (size) [+]	Proprietary costs, 'follow the leader'; Reputation	Total assets, percentage of intangible assets, leverage, industry
12	Owusu-Ansah (1998)	Zimbabwe	1994	49 listed non-financial companies	214 mandatory	Audit firm [+]; Number of employees [+]; Profitability [+]; Listing status [+]; Size (market capitalisation, assets) [+]	Signalling; Agency theory; Capital need, signalling; Capital need, image; Proprietary costs	Audit firm, industry, liquidity
13	Rahman (1998)	Malaysia	1974, 1984 1994	54 listed companies [162 annual reports]	1974: 97M, 85V; 1984: 141M, 58V; 1994: 149M, 53V	Inside ownership [+]; Company age [+]; Affiliations with MNCs [+]; Profitability [+]; M: size (assets)[+]; V: size (assets) [+]	Learning curve; Political costs; Signalling; Agency theory; Agency theory	Leverage, liquidity, scope of business, audit firm, parent company, type of management, profitability, year-end, outside ownership, image
14	Chen and Jaggi (2000)	Hong Kong	1993 and 1994	87 largest (excluding utilities, finance and non-depository credit institutions) listed companies [174 annual reports]	30 mandatory (weighted) [maximum 142]	Proportion of independent directors on the board [+], stronger for non-family owned companies; Size (assets) [+]; Profitability (ROE) [−]; Conglomerate [−]	Agency theory	Sales, market capitalization, liquidity, gearing, outside ownership, audit firm, year-end

▶

Table 7.2 *(Continued)*

	Authors	Country	Reporting year	Sample	Disclosure items	Independent variables (statistically significant)	Theoretical explanation	Non-significant variables
15	Ho and Wong (2001)	Hong Kong	1997	98 listed companies	20 voluntary	Proportion of family members on the board [−]	Agency theory	Independent directors, dominant personality, leverage, assets-in-place, profitability, industry (conglomerate, banking and finance, others)
						Existence of audit committee [+]	Agency theory	
						Size (assets) [+]	Capital need theory	
						Industry (manufacturing) [+]		
16	Haniffa and Cooke (2002)	Malaysia	1995	138 non-financial listed companies	65 voluntary	Assets-in-place [+]	Agency theory	Proportion of independent directors, role duality, cross director-ships, chair with cross-directorship, Malay FD, Malay Chairperson, Malay MD, qualification of directors, qualification of FD, gearing, complexity of business (number of subsidiaries), institutional investors, industry (trading, plantation and mining), multiple listing, audit firm, listing age, foreign activities
						Ownership by ten largest shareholders [+]		
						Foreign investors [+]	Capital need, agency theory	
						Profitability (ROE) [+]	Signalling theory	
						Industry (consumer and industrial) [−]	Political costs	
						Independent Chair [−]	Agency theory	
						Proportion of family members on the board [−]	Information costs	
						**Proportion of Malay directors on the board [+]	Political costs, legitimacy, Islamic business ethics	
						**Size (assets) [+]		
						**Diversification [+]		
17	Naser et al. (2002)	Jordan	1998/99	84 manufacturing and services listed companies	104 items	Size (market capitalization, sales) [+]	Proprietary costs, capital need	Assets, ROE, number of shareholders, government ownership, individual ownership, foreign ownership, Arab ownership, industry, employees
						Audit firm [+]	Reputation	
						Liquidity [−]	Legitimacy	
						Gearing [+]	Agency	
						Profitability (profit margin) [+]	Signalling	

18	Eng and Mak (2003)	Singapore	1995	158 listed companies	46 voluntary (weighted) [maximum 84]	Managerial ownership [−]	Agency theory	Block ownership, growth, industry, audit firm, analyst following, stock return, profitability (ROE and ROA)
						Government owner-ship [+]	Agency theory	
						Proportion of outside directors [−]	Agency theory	
						Size (sum of market value of ordinary shares, book value of debts and book value of pre-ference shares) [+]		
						Leverage [−]	Agency theory	

Key

* results obtained using mean scores

** statistically significant in the reduced regression model

Other results (without asterisks) obtained using multiple regression analysis

MvEq – market value of equity

BvD – book value of debt

M – mandatory

V – voluntary

Note: Hong Kong and Singapore are generally not regarded as developing countries but are included in this table because they possess many of the corporate characteristics of Asian developing countries such as the dominance of family-owned businesses, owner-managed and government-controlled companies.

References for Tables 7.1 and 7.2

Abayo, A.G., Adams, C.A. and Roberts, C.B. (1993), 'Measuring the Quality of Corporate Disclosure in Less Developed Countries: The Case of Tanzania', *Journal of International Accounting, Auditing and Tax*, 2(2): 145–158.

Adams, M. and Hossain, M. (1998), 'Managerial Discretion and Voluntary Disclosure: Evidence from the New Zealand Life Insurance Industry', *Journal of Accounting and Public Policy*, 17(3): 245–281.

Ahmed, K. (1996), 'Disclosure Policy Choice and Corporate Characteristics: A Study of Bangladesh', *Asia Pacific Journal of Accounting*, 3(1): 183–203.

Buzby, S.L. (1975), 'Company Size, Listed Versus Unlisted Stocks and the Extent of Financial Disclosure', *Journal of Accounting Research*, Spring, 13(1): 16–37.

Camfferman, K. and Cooke, T.E. (2002), 'An Analysis of Disclosure in the Annual Reports of U.K. and Dutch Companies', *Journal of International Accounting Research*, 1: 3–30.

Cerf, A.R. (1961), *Corporate Reporting and Investment Decisions*. University of California, Berkeley, CA.

Chen, C.J.P. and Jaggi, B. (2000), 'Association between Independent Non-Executive Directors, Family Control and Financial Disclosures in Hong Kong', *Journal of Accounting and Public Policy*, 19: 285–310.

Chow, C.W. and Wong-Boren, A. (1987), 'Voluntary Financial Disclosure by Mexican Corporations', *The Accounting Review*, 62(3): 533–541.

Cooke, T.E. (1989), 'Voluntary Disclosure by Swedish companies', *Journal of International Financial Management and Accounting*, 1(2): 171–195.

Cooke, T.E. (1991), 'An Assessment of Voluntary Disclosure in the Annual Reports of Japanese Corporations', *The International Journal of Accounting*, 26: 174–189.

Craswell, A.T. and Taylor, S.L. (1992), 'Discretionary Disclosure of Reserve by Oil and Gas Companies: An Economic Analysis', *Journal of Business Finance and Accounting*, January, 19(2): 295–308.

Depoers, F. (2000), 'A Cost-Benefit Analysis of Voluntary Disclosure: Some Empirical Evidence from French Listed Companies', *The European Accounting Review*, 9(2): 245–263.

Eng, L.L. and Mak, Y.T. (2003), 'Corporate Governance and Voluntary Disclosure', *Journal of Accounting and Public Policy*, 22: 325–345.

Firth, M. (1979), 'The Impact of Size, Stock Market Listing, and Auditors on Voluntary Disclosure in Corporate Annual Reports', *Accounting and Business Research*, Autumn, 9(33): 273–280.

Haniffa, R.M. and Cooke, T.E. (2002), 'Culture, Corporate Governance and Disclosure in Malaysian Corporations', *Abacus*, 38(3): 317–349.

Ho, S.S.M. and Wong, K.S. (2001), 'A Study of Corporate Disclosure Practice and Effectiveness in Hong Kong', *Journal of International Financial Management and Accounting*, 12(1): 75–102.

Hossain, M., Tan, L.M. and Adams, M. (1994), 'Voluntary Disclosure in an Emerging Capital Market: Some Empirical Evidence from Companies Listed on the Kuala Lumpur Stock Exchange', *The International Journal of Accounting*, 29: 334–351.

Hossain, M., Perera, M.H.B. and Rahman, A.R. (1995), 'Voluntary Disclosure in the Annual Reports of New Zealand Companies', *Journal of International Financial Management and Accounting*, 6(1): 69–87.

Inchausti, B.G. (1997), 'The Influence of Company Characteristics and Accounting Regulation on Information Disclosed by Spanish Firms', *The European Accounting Review*, 6(1): 45–68.

McNally, G.M., Eng, L.H. and Hasseldine, C.R. (1982), 'Corporate Financial Reporting in New Zealand: An Analysis of User Preferences, Corporate Characteristics and Disclosure Practices for Discretionary Information, *Accounting and Business Research*, 13(48): 11–20.

Malone, D., Fries, C. and Jones, T. (1993), 'An Empirical Investigation of the Extent of Corporate Financial Disclosure in the Oil and Gas Industry', *Journal of Accounting, Auditing and Finance*, 8(3): 249–273.

Marston, C.L. and Robson, P. (1997), 'Financial Reporting in India: Changes in Disclosure over the Period 1982–1990', *Asia Pacific Journal of Accounting*, 4(1): 109–139.

Naser, K., Al-Khatib, K. and Karbhari, Y. (2002), 'Empirical Evidence on the Depth of Corporate Information Disclosure in Developing Countries: The Case of Jordan', *International Journal of Commerce and Management*, 12(3–4): 122–155.

Ng, E.J. and Koh, H.C. (1994), 'An Agency Theory and Probit Analytic Approach to Corporate Non-Mandatory Disclosure Compliance', *Asia Pacific Journal of Accounting*, 1(1): 29–44.

Owusu-Ansah, S. (1998), 'The Impact of Corporate Attributes on the Extent of Mandatory Disclosure and Reporting by Listed Companies in Zimbabwe', *The International Journal of Accounting*, 33(5): 605–631.

Patton, J. and Zelenka, I. (1997), 'An Empirical Analysis of the Determinants of the Extent of Disclosure in Annual Reports of Joint Stock Companies in the Czech Republic', *The European Accounting Review*, 6(4): 605–626.

Raffournier, B. (1995), 'The Determinants of Voluntary Financial Disclosure by Swiss Listed Companies', *The European Accounting Review*, 4(2): 261–280.

Rahman, A.B.A. (1998), 'Disclosure of Corporate Financial Information in Malaysia', Unpublished PhD Thesis, University of Newcastle.

Singhvi, S.S. (1968), 'Characteristics and Implications of Inadequate Disclosure: A Case Study of India', *International Journal of Accounting Education and Research*, 3(2): 29–43.

Singhvi, S.S. and Desai, H.B. (1971), 'An Empirical Analysis of the Quality of Corporate Financial Disclosure', *The Accounting Review*, 46(1): 129–138.

Suwaidan, M.S. (1997), 'Voluntary Disclosure of Accounting Information: The Case of Jordan, Unpublished PhD Thesis, University of Aberdeen, Aberdeen.

Wallace, R.S.O. (1988), 'Corporate Financial Reporting in Nigeria', *Accounting and Business Research*, 18(72): 352–362.

Wallace, R.S., Naser, K. and Mora, A. (1994), 'The Relationship Between the Comprehensiveness of Corporate Annual Reports and Firm Characteristics in Spain', *Accounting and Business Research*, 25(97): 41–53.

Wallace, R.S.O. and Naser, K. (1995), 'Firm-Specific Determinants of the Comprehensiveness of Mandatory Disclosure in the Corporate Annual Reports of Firms Listed on the Stock Exchange of Hong Kong', *Journal of Accounting and Public Policy*, 14: 311–368.

PART 3

Significant influences on international accounting practices

Introduction to Part 3

In Part 1 you learned about the work of the International Accounting Standards Board and the challenges to listed companies in meeting increased demands for assurance and audit. You saw from Chapter 3 that although there is increasing harmonization in matters of measurement and disclosure in financial statements, there are continuing national differences in the wider sphere of corporate financial reporting. In Part 2 you have studied methods of analysis and research that are used in comparative studies of financial reporting.

Chapters 1 and 2 have explained in detail the most ambitious and far-reaching influence for harmonization, represented by the work of the International Accounting Standards Board. The US system of Generally Accepted Accounting Principles (US GAAP) is a potential rival to the IASB standards as a global accounting system. It has also provided a strong influence on the development of IASB standards. The European Union (EU) represents a group of member states which all have an interest in applying IASB Standards, provided they are able to participate in the process. The EU has a total economy of comparable size to that of the US but has decided to work towards harmonization with IFRS rather than produce 'EU GAAP'. The European Commission also has a history of encouraging harmonization through Directives. Part 3 takes you into a more detailed study of accounting developments in the US and the EU.

Purpose of Part 3

The chapters of Part 3 have two major aims. The first is to explain how the national characteristics of the US and the legal framework of the EU are likely to affect accounting principles and practice. The second is to indicate the extent to which national practice in the US is already close to or in harmony with IASB Standards and to indicate those areas of US national practice that appear to be more resistant to broader desires for harmonization. The chapter on the EU indicates the EU's long-standing experience in harmonization of disclosure through the Fourth and Seventh directives and explains how it has moved towards endorsement of IFRS.

Learning outcomes

Specific learning outcomes are set out at the start of each chapter but overall, on completion of Part 3, the student should be able to:

● describe and evaluate the development of accounting practice in the US;

● discuss the benefits and problems of having US GAAP as a global standard;

● describe and evaluate the development of accounting practice in the EU;

● discuss the benefits and problems of applying IFRS in listed companies of EU member states.

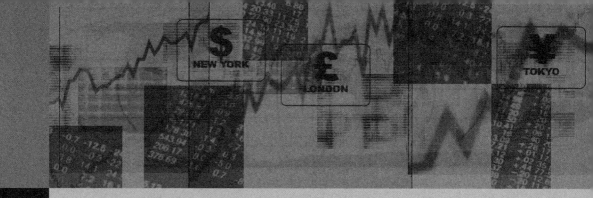

8 The United States of America

Learning outcomes

After reading this chapter you should be able to:

- Explain the development of accounting regulation.
- Understand the impact of the Sarbanes–Oxley Act 2002.
- Explain the key institutional characteristics of the US.
- Make comparisons of US GAAP with IFRS.
- Understand and explain features of the accounting system that illustrate the diversity of US accounting practices.
- Discuss US accounting practices using the analytical framework of Gray's accounting values.

8.1 Introduction

The purpose of this chapter is to explain how the accounting principles and practices of the United States of America (the USA or the US) resemble or differ from the IASB proposals. The US principles and practices are influential beyond the country's national boundary and have, of themselves, provided a means of harmonization for those other countries and business enterprises choosing to follow the US lead. They act also as a block to harmonization where the US regulators will not accept any practices other than those conforming to US standards without a statement of reconciliation of the differences. The source of the widespread influence of US accounting lies in the country's worldwide political and economic dominance and in the importance of its capital market. The market is closely regulated by an agency of the federal government, the Securities and Exchange Commission (SEC). Those companies which seek a listing for their shares must comply with SEC regulations.

Within this framework of close regulation, there is considerable scope for application of professional judgement in accounting matters. Accounting standards are greater in volume and more detailed than those of almost any other country of the world, but they are set by an independent standard-setting body rather than by statute law. The standard-setting body has been well supported financially, and has therefore researched issues to an extent not feasible in other countries.

The combination of US accounting principles and practices is referred to as 'US GAAP', short for 'US generally accepted accounting principles'. The concept of such a set of written principles originates in the US, although the abbreviation is used in reference to other countries also. Accounting disclosure is characterized by transparency and accounting measurement by general conservatism and historical cost. Such conservatism originated in the stock market crash of 1929, modified by business pragmatism and flexibility in response to events of more recent years.

8.2 The country

The US is made up of a land mass stretching from the Atlantic to the Pacific Ocean and includes Alaska and Hawaii as states. There are five major units of physical geography. The coastal plain of the east extends down the entire Atlantic coast. Behind the coastal plain rise the Appalachian mountains in a succession of plateaux and ridges. Moving west, a fertile interior basin is drained by the Mississippi river. Further west again the Rocky Mountains extend from Canada to Colorado and finally the Pacific mountain system contains the Central Valley of California, a rich agricultural area. Mineral resources include iron ore and coal. Agricultural specialization varies according to location and climate. The population is 286 million and has a relatively low growth rate.

The economy showed growth of 3.3 per cent per annum over the period 1991–2000 and general standards of living are high (see Exhibit 8.1).

Gross domestic product (GDP) is created more than three-quarters by services. Manufacturing industry provides approximately one-fifth of GDP. In manufacturing industry, the highest single contribution is provided by machinery and transport but half of manufacturing industry is diversified into a range of activities. Manufacturing is largely concentrated in a belt reaching from New England to the Midwest. This area contains much of the steel industry, the automotive industry, specialized and electrical engineering and the textile and clothing trades.

The main export product is capital goods, excluding vehicles. The main export destination is Canada. Mexico is the most significant trading partner after Canada, with Japan third. The European Union (EU) takes 21 per cent of US exports, spread across all member states, with the UK and Germany being the highest at 5.6 per cent and 4.1 per cent respectively.

The main import product is also capital goods, excluding vehicles. The origins of imports are primarily Canada and Japan. The EU supplies 19 per cent of imports, with Germany being the highest at 5.2 per cent.

Imports exceed exports, giving a negative balance of trade. Inflows of invisibles exceed outflows, reducing the overall negative balance.

From the *Financial Times* annual FT 500 survey there are 227 US companies in the top 500 world companies, measured by market capitalization. The top ten listed US companies are shown in Exhibit 8.2.

Exhibit 8.1	The US: country profile

Population	285.9m
Land mass	9,372,610 km²
GDP per head	US$35,200
GDP per head in purchasing-power-parity	100
Origins of GDP:	%
Agriculture	1.4
Industry	20.3
Services	78.3
	%
Real GDP average annual growth 1991–2000	3.3
Inflation, average annual rate 1996–2002	2.3

Source: *The Economist Pocket World in Figures*, 2004 Edition, Profile Books Ltd.

| Exhibit 8.2 | Top ten listed US companies at March 2004 |

Name	Market cap. $m	Rank in world	Listed UK	Sector
General Electric	299,336.4	1	yes	Electrical Equipment
Microsoft	271,910.9	2	no	Software
Exxon Mobil	263,940.3	3	yes	Oil
Pfizer	261,615.6	4	yes	Pharmaceuticals
Citigroup	259,190.8	5	no	Banks
Wal-Mart Stores	258,887.9	6	no	Discount and Superstores and Warehouses
American International Group	183,696.1	7	yes	Other insurance
Intel	179,996.0	8	no	Semiconductors
Cisco Systems	162,059.7	11	no	Telecommunications Equipment
International Business Machines	157,009.1	14	yes	Software and computer services

Source: 'Survey FT 500', *Financial Times*, 27 May 2004, p. 10.

8.3 Development of accounting regulation[1]

Accounting practices were to some extent imported from the UK by early pioneers establishing business practices in the US.

8.3.1 Early regulation of accounting[2]

The American Association of Public Accountants, formed in 1886, and the Institute of Bookkeepers and Accountants, encouraged a New York State law establishing the profession of Certified Public Accountant in 1896, and similar laws followed in other states. The Association established the *Journal of Accountancy* as a means of professional communication and published a terminology of accounting in 1915. In the early years, maintaining good standards of accountancy practice was very much in the hands of individual practitioners; companies generally did not disclose their accounting practices.

The stock market crash of 1929 caused fundamental changes in many aspects of US business practice. The initial approach was to continue allowing companies relative freedom of choice but to emphasize disclosure. The Securities and Exchange Commission (SEC) was formed by Congress, establishing its rules in 1934 under which it received for filing a copy of the accounts of each listed company. The SEC took a harder line that where listed companies filed accounts which did not have substantial authoritative support, those accounts would not be accepted – effectively, the SEC was deciding on accounting practice.

The American Institute of Accountants (AIA) Committee on Accounting Procedures issued Accounting Research Bulletins (ARBs) between 1939 and 1959. The AIA was renamed as the American Institute of Certified Public Accountants (AICPA) in 1957. Where the SEC

---

[1] Wolk and Tearney (2004), Chapter 3.

[2] Zeff (2003a, 2003b).

felt there was an insufficiently strict approach in the ARBs, it would indicate that filing of accounts might be refused even though the ARBs had been applied. This caused the AICPA to form the Accounting Principles Board (APB) in 1959. However, the ARBs survived in the form of ARB 43, which was a restatement and revision of the first 40 ARBs. Many parts of ARB 43 remain influential on accounting regulations of today.[3]

The APB produced Accounting Research Studies and a series of APB Opinions. These did not dispel the controversies of the earlier periods and there were situations where the SEC indicated dissatisfaction with particular APB Opinions. More generally, it was felt that drafts of APB Opinions were not sufficiently exposed for comment and that resolution of some problems took too long a time. A major enquiry established by the AICPA (called the Wheat Committee) recommended in 1972 the formation of an independent Financial Accounting Standards Board (FASB). In particular, the Wheat Committee noted that the members of the APB were all CPAs, creating a potential conflict of interest; it recommended independence and the broader base of membership seen in the FASB today. A further enquiry, undertaken for the AICPA, by the Trueblood Study Group (AICPA, 1973), identified major objectives of financial statements which were subsequently taken by the FASB as guidance for its approach to standard-setting. The present process is discussed further in section 8.7.1.

The FASB was guided in its work by a series of Statements of Financial Accounting Concepts (SFACs) issued in the late 1970s and early 1980s. These statements emphasize a balance sheet approach of defining and recognizing assets and liabilities. Owners' equity is the residual item in the equation. Changes in assets and liabilities must be reported through the income statement. This tends to lead to fluctuations in reported profit when compared to the alternative approach of matching income and expenses in a way that smooths reported profit from one period to the next.

8.3.2 The Sarbanes–Oxley Act 2002

You have seen in section 3.2.3 how the Sarbanes–Oxley Act of 2002 has changed the procedures for maintaining confidence and assurance in accounting information. These changes have affected all aspects of the US capital market and have affected regulations and practices in many other countries. The Sarbanes–Oxley Act is seen as the most significant piece of securities legislation since the 1930s. This chapter gives more detail of the effect of Sarbanes–Oxley on accounting in the US.

The accounting problems of Enron[4] emerged as headline news towards the end of 2001. In particular there were problems relating to 'special purpose entities' (SPEs). These SPEs are created to carry out a specific purpose or activity, such as a development project. The SPEs may carry tax benefits or attract a lower cost of financing. If the arrangement meets defined conditions, the SPE is 'off-balance-sheet'. That means the investment is recorded at cost and there is no consolidation. At the time of the Enron decline, the conditions for remaining off-balance-sheet were that the assets must be sold to the SPE and that an independent third party which holds a substantive capital investment (at least 3 per cent of the SPE's total capitalization) must control the SPE and carry the risks and rewards of the SPE's assets.

---

[3] Williams, J.R. and Carcello, J.V. (2004) *Miller GAAP Guide 2004*, New York: Aspen, CR.01–02.

[4] Herdman, R., December 2001, Testimony concerning recent events relating to Enron Corporation. Evidence before the Subcommittee on Capital Markets, Insurance and Government Sponsored Enterprises and the Subcommittee on Oversight and Investigation, Committee on Financial Services, US House of Representatives www.sec.gov/news/testimony/1202tsrkh.htm.

In October 2001 Enron announced that shareholders' equity was reduced by $1.2bn because of accounting errors. When one of the SPEs was created, Enron had issued its own shares to the SPE. The intention was that the rising value of the Enron shares would hedge the risk of another investment held by the SPE. In return for the shares issued, Enron received a note (promise) from the SPE. Was this promise an asset for Enron? Initially it was recorded as an asset but in October 2001 Enron and its auditors decided that the item should be deducted from shareholders' equity. This was described at the time as correcting an 'accounting error'.

Enron made a further announcement, in November 2001, that it intended to voluntarily restate its financial statements for 1997 to 2000 and the first two quarters of 2001. The reason was that the company and its auditors had decided that three previously unconsolidated special-purpose entities (SPEs) should have been consolidated under GAAP. Enron concluded that three entities no longer met these conditions and so should be consolidated with the group accounts. Such consolidation makes the extent of borrowings across the group clearer in the group balance sheet but also shows a higher level of gearing. These announcements, and others, caused a loss of market confidence that led rapidly to the company filing for bankruptcy.

The accounting concerns raised by these events caused the Act to require new disclosures in financial reports, relating to off-balance-sheet transactions. Chapter 15 explains in more detail how those disclosures are presented. More generally there were concerns about the emphasis placed on detailed rules. A rules-based approach asks 'how do we stay inside the 3 per cent rule to avoid consolidation?'. A principles-based approach asks 'what gives a fair presentation of the relationship of this special purpose entity to the rest of the group?' The detailed standards and guidance within US GAAP lead down the rules-based approach. Sarbanes–Oxley asked the SEC to study the adoption by the US financial reporting system of a principles-based accounting system.

8.3.3 Rules versus principles[5]

The Sarbanes–Oxley instructions to the SEC on accounting reflected wider concerns of those who asked whether technical compliance with US accounting standards necessarily results in financial reporting that fairly reflects the underlying economic reality of reporting entities.

Three shortcomings of rules-based standards are:

● They contain numerous tests ('bright lines') that may be misused by financial engineers to comply with the letter but not the spirit of standards.
● They contain numerous exceptions ('scope exceptions') to the principles that purport to underlie the standards, resulting in inconsistencies of accounting treatment of transactions and events that have similar economic substance.
● Rules-based standards create a need for detailed implementation guidance, which in turn creates complexity and can even add to uncertainty about the application of the standard.

The SEC reported to the House of Representatives in 2003,[6] as required by Sarbanes–Oxley. The report concluded that neither US GAAP nor international accounting

---

[5] Study pursuant to Section 108(d) of the Sarbanes–Oxley Act of 2002 on the adoption by the United States financial reporting system of a principles-based accounting system. Report prepared by the SEC.
[6] Ibid.

standards, as they existed at that time, were representative of the optimum type of principles-based standard. The SEC had been pointed towards the IFRS as an example of a principles-based system but on close scrutiny they found some IFRS were rules-based standards, while others were principles only and overly general. The SEC defined an optimal standard as making a concise statement of accounting principle where the accounting objective has been specified as an integral part of the standard. There should be few, if any, exceptions or conceptual inconsistencies in the standard. The standard should provide an appropriate amount of implementation guidance. It should also be consistent with a coherent conceptual framework of financial reporting. The SEC called its vision the 'objectives-oriented approach'. It felt that a principles-only approach would provide insufficient guidance to make the standards operational. Increased reliance on the judgements of preparers and auditors could increase the likelihood of disagreements on accounting treatments. This in turn could lead to an increase in litigation.

In the view of the SEC, objectives-oriented standards charge management with the responsibility to capture the economic substance of transactions and events, but defined specifically within the objectives of the standard. The SEC felt that objectives-oriented standards may require less use of judgment than either rules-based or principles-only standards. This would improve consistency and compliance with the intent of the standards.

The SEC explained that an objectives-oriented system would lower the cost to investors and analysts of understanding the standards. They could focus on the objectives of the standard. Quality, consistency and timeliness of financial reporting could be improved. Convergence between US GAAP and international standards would be made easier because standard-setters would agree on a principle more rapidly than they would agree on a highly detailed rule. Finally the SEC demonstrated that the FASB was already beginning the change to objectives-oriented standards.

The FASB responded in July 2004,[7] welcoming the SEC's study and agreeing with the recommendations. The FASB intends to make objectives and principles of standards clearer in writing future standards but also indicated that it intends to continue giving implementation guidance, examples and interpretive guidance. It also acknowledges that the SEC will continue to provide guidance as it deems necessary. The Board felt it would take several years for preparers and auditors to make the behavioural changes necessary to exercise professional judgement rather than request detailed rules. Actions had been taken, in consultation with AICPA and Emerging Issues Task Force (EITF) to make the FASB the only designated standard-setter in the US. This would reduce some of the proliferation of rules that was developing previously. FASB hopes to create a searchable database of authoritative guidance but this would take some years. In the meantime FASB has made its standards accessible by giving free-of-charge access on its website and making existing guidance more accessible. In working with the IASB on coordination projects, the FASB will replace rules-based standards with principles-based standards as they come up within the project.

8.3.4 Consolidated accounting[8]

Consolidated financial statements have been published in the US since the end of the nineteenth century. They are produced so commonly that single-company statements are generally published only by entities having no subsidiaries. There is no law in the US

---

[7] FASB (2004a).

[8] Williams and Carcello (2004), Chapter 4.

that mandates their publication; the requirement to publish has emerged within US GAAP, the most important requirements being ARB 51, dating from 1959, and the more recent SFAS 94. SFAS 94 is close to requiring that all majority-owned subsidiaries be consolidated. Other standards address particular aspects of consolidation and the totality sets the consolidation policy to be followed under US GAAP.

Business combinations are normally accounted for using the purchase (acquisition) method of accounting. On relatively rare occasions, where there is a uniting of interests by exchange of equity shares, the pooling of interests (merger) method has previously been required by APB Opinion 16. Pooling of interests allowed profits to be combined without calculation and amortization of goodwill.

In 1999 the FASB voted to end the pooling of interests method. This reflected the concern of the SEC that pooling of interests had been misused and should not continue. It also voted to reduce the maximum goodwill amortization period from 40 years to 20 years, aligning with the International Accounting Standards. There were objections from industry, led by financial executives through FEI (see section 1.3.5), with appeals to Congress.[9] The chairman of the Senate committee investigating the issue proposed a periodic impairment test as a better solution. Further actions in Senate threatened to delay progress for the FASB. This episode provides an example of the strong political pressure that can be exerted on accounting in the US. The outcome was that in July 2001 the FASB produced SFAS 141, banning pooling of interests in business combinations initiated after that date, and SFAS 142, setting a goodwill impairment test rather than amortization over a specific asset life.[10] SFAS 141 *Business Combinations* supersedes APB Opinion 16. SFAS 142 *Goodwill and other Intangible Assets* supersedes APB Opinion 17.

Also in 1999 the FASB consulted on changing to a consolidation policy focused on the idea of control, which would be a significant change from the traditional approach based on majority ownership. At the end of 1999 FASB reaffirmed a commitment to the idea of control and promised a Statement in due course. However in January 2001 they announced that there was not sufficient support to proceed with a standard.

Joint venture accounting has not been addressed specifically although it is included in the FASB's long-term project on consolidation. The present treatment is that joint ventures are accounted for using equity accounting. Proportionate consolidation is generally not used because the SEC objects; however, the SEC has made an exception for extractive industries such as oil and gas.

8.4 Institutions

8.4.1 Political and economic system

The US is a federal republic of separate states. Each state has its own constitution, but the separate states unite under a federal government operating under a federal constitution. The federal government has the power to impose taxes, the responsibility for national defence and foreign relations, the power to create a national currency and the authority to set countrywide laws regulating commercial and business practice. States also have power to regulate business practice.

The federal constitution divides the federal government into the executive, the legislative and the judicial branches. The President of the US leads the executive

---

[9] Zeff (2002), pp. 51–52.

[10] Williams and Carcello (2004), Chapter 4.

branch, while the legislative branch consists of the Congress, the House of Representatives and the Senate. The judicial branch is led by the Supreme Court and, below it, a system of federal courts. Each of the three branches of the constitution is independent but there are checks and balances. The President has a power of veto over legislation, but the veto may be overcome by a two-thirds majority of both the House of Representatives and the Senate. The judiciary may declare acts of the executive unconstitutional.

The President is elected every four years, and only permitted two terms in total. The members of the House of Representatives and Senate are also elected. One-third of Senate members are elected by rotation every two years; House of Representatives members are elected every two years. Depending on swings in political mood, it is possible for the majority in Senate and the House of Representatives to be of a different political party from the President.

The economic system is that of the open market. Historically, the nature of the economic system has developed and changed as the political climate has changed and as technological change has allowed exploitation of new opportunities. The US has always attracted high wealth in terms of human capital, more than once because persecution elsewhere drove individuals to seek freedom there. Development of the railways opened up the country to industrial production, which has now declined in relation to service industry, though it remains a strong minority element of the economy.

Since the early 1980s the US economy has shown the highest growth rate of gross domestic product (GDP) of the G7 countries; it has been much higher than the OECD average.[11] A technology boom starting around 1997 saw the share prices of 'dot.com' companies soar to unprecedented levels, only to crash in 2000. There was very little growth of GDP in 2001 but after that it started to grow again, driven by household and government spending. The spending was encouraged by low interest rates.[12] US growth has appeared to be faster than that of the Euro area, but if the weaker growth of Germany is taken out of the Euro area analysis, growth in Europe and growth in the US have been similar in recent years.[13]

8.4.2 Legal system

The political doctrine of separation of powers in the federal constitution means that business may be affected by each of the executive, the legislative and the judicial arms. Independent regulatory agencies are also in existence as a fourth arm to the processes of the legal system. However, the chairman and chief accountant of the SEC are appointed by the executive (President). (Regulatory agencies are under the rule of the executive, and so there is not a fourth arm to the constitution; however, the regulatory agencies are approved by Congress.)

Legislation is introduced through committees of each House of Congress. If compromise is required to meet the requirements of each separate House, it will be negotiated in committee before being submitted to the full House of Representatives and Senate. Implementation of the law through the courts begins in federal districts, each having a federal court called a District Court which applies federal law. Appeal from the District

---

[11] OECD (2004).

[12] 'Finance and Economics: off the bottom', *The Economist*, London, 3 July 2004, 372 (8382): 82.

[13] 'Special Report: Mirror, mirror on the wall – Europe v America, America v Europe', *The Economist*, London, 19 June 2004, 371 (8380): 81.

Court is made to the Courts of Appeal, and the Supreme Court reviews decisions of the lower federal courts.

The federal government has general regulatory powers, but much regulation of business enterprises is by state law. One general theme of the federal legislative approach is 'truth in securities', leading to regulation of those who issue shares to the public. Another is free and open competition, leading to what is called 'antitrust legislation'. This makes illegal any restraint of trade created by unfair business combinations, including those established on the basis of what some might regard as mutual trust but others would see as conspiracy.

The legal system of the US is that of the common law family but has developed uniquely American characteristics; it is therefore not surprising to find similarly unique aspects to the development of accounting law in the US.

8.4.2.1 Federal and state law

Federal law deals with matters such as the registration of securities, taxation and antitrust law. Powers not specifically delegated to the US by the constitution are reserved to the states. State laws apply to matters such as enforcement of contract, agency, conveyancing, bills of exchange, and debtor–creditor relationships; they also overlap with federal law on issues such as securities, taxation and antitrust law.

There is some element of competition between federal and state law. This leads also to interesting competition between states in attracting businesses. Many leading companies are registered in Delaware. This is because, in 1913, the state legislature of New Jersey introduced a restrictive approach to corporations. The corporations transferred their registration to Delaware, which had a flexible incorporation law. Delaware has subsequently developed expertise in matters of business law. The restriction in New Jersey was short-lived but the corporations stayed in Delaware.

One important feature of US law is its Freedom of Information Acts, which give access to government papers that might in other countries be locked away. The openness of practices of governmental administration leads to openness in non-governmental organizations (NGOs) also. Information lodged with the government later becomes available as a government paper.

8.4.2.2 Types of business organization

Businesses may operate as sole traders, partnerships or corporations. Corporations are established and governed by the law of the state in which they are incorporated. A foreign company may incorporate in any state, regardless of where the production facilities and management are located. Incorporation is achieved by filing articles of incorporation and bylaws with the relevant state official. State laws will cover matters such as the initial capital required; classes and powers of voting stock; corporate powers; the number of directors and their duties; payment of dividends; requirements for accounting records; and the cessation of the company. A corporation may acquire and hold its own shares.

All corporations have a board of directors elected by the shareholders and responsible to them for the running of the company. Directors and officers have duties of loyalty and care to the corporation. Any shareholder has the right to sue on behalf of the corporation where there has been a perceived breach of duty. The corporation is a taxable entity. The US has many more unlisted than listed companies. The focus of this chapter is on listed companies which are regulated by the SEC. In particular, the SEC prescribes the reporting requirements for published accounting information.

The Chief Executive Officer (CEO) is always a member of the board of the company. The CEO is the focus of attention as the person driving the company; there is relatively little press interest in the directors. Typically a CEO will serve for six to eight years. The directors elect the chairman of the board, although in many cases the CEO is the chairman. Active management is delegated by the directors to paid officials. Directors focus on policy issues.

8.4.2.3 Securities and Exchange Commission (SEC)[14]

The Securities Act 1933 has the intention to create 'truth in securities', aiming to provide information for investors and prohibit misrepresentation. Any company planning to offer its securities for sale must register with the SEC, which imposes regulations based on registration forms requiring extensive disclosure. Domestic US companies must prepare an annual registration form referred to as '10-K'. Foreign companies seeking to offer securities for sale in the US must present an annual registration form called a '20-F' and must restate their financial statements using US GAAP or provide a reconciliation statement. The essential power of the SEC lies in its authority to reject the filing of accounts: without that filing a company cannot continue to have a stock exchange listing. This gives the SEC effective control over accounting practice without being directly a standard-setting body.

The SEC is a federal agency, and has a strong tradition of being activist in its work. There are detailed rules on what information should be provided, where it should be lodged and where it should be sent. The SEC largely controls information issued by companies. It interacts with state law on some matters of specific disclosure but is prevented by the Supreme Court from encroaching too much on state law. The most important disclosure regulations are Regulation S-X, covering financial statements, and Regulation S-K, covering non-financial disclosure about the operations of the business. These are voluminous, and can be found on the SEC's website, www.sec.gov (see also Chapter 15).

The SEC monitors all trading on the stock exchanges. It has an electronic filing system called EDGAR (Electronic Data Gathering Analysis and Retrieval) whereby companies may lodge information electronically. Access to the EDGAR filings is available through the World Wide Web.

The SEC was one of the parties that came under criticism in the many comments on Enron. With its 'activist' reputation, how could the scrutiny by SEC staff have failed to notice that all was not well with the financial statements lodged with them? The Sarbanes–Oxley Act 2002 directed the SEC to take specific actions in relation to its oversight procedures (see section 3.2.3) and in relation to its rules on disclosures (see section 15.3).

The SEC also continues to update its rules on its own initiative. In 2002 it issued a rule requiring all but the smallest domestic listed companies to accelerate filing dates and to require disclosures on website access to reports. From 2002 the filing period for the annual report was reduced progressively, over a period of three years, from 90 days to 60 days. The quarterly report deadline was similarly reduced from 45 days to 35 days. Companies subject to these changes were also required to disclose in their annual reports the company's website address, information on whether the company makes available free of charge, on or through its website, filings such as the 10-K (annual), 10-Q (quarterly) and 8-K (current information) reports.

---

[14] www.sec.gov

One of the problems identified by the SEC in its own internal review is that it had developed a reactive culture that failed to identify danger ahead of time.[15] It was generating one-third of its investigations itself while the remainder were initiated by external sources such as complaints or 'whistleblowers'. The SEC has set a more proactive target of reviewing one-third of reporting companies each year, focusing on the largest. An Office of Risk Assessment has been established to identify and prioritize current risks.

8.4.3 Corporate governance

Corporate governance, as a means of promoting trust, loyalty and commitment among the various parties, has grown in the US over many years but its precise nature has depended on the concerns of the time regarding the behaviour of corporate entities. The most significant *de jure* change to corporate governance regulation in the US is seen in the Sarbanes–Oxley Act of 2002 (see section 3.2.3). Has it had an impact *de facto*? In a survey of 500 companies for the Financial Executives International, second quarter 2004, 49 per cent of respondents said there was no noticeable change; 29 per cent had reduced non-audit business with the audit firm and were using other firms; the quality of internal control had increased significantly in 23 per cent of respondents.

In the 1990s the SEC began to question the way in which some companies appeared to 'manage' their profit figures by techniques such as overstating restructuring charges, using provisions in acquisition accounting to overstate future earnings, recognizing sales before completion or when the customer has the right to reverse the transaction, and deferring expenses as assets (see section 3.2 on 'the numbers game').

8.4.3.1 Audit committees

One result of the SEC's concern about earnings management was the formation of the Blue Ribbon Committee on Improving the Effectiveness of Corporate Audits. The Committee reported in 1999 with recommendations for change which included requiring listed companies to have an audit committee on which at least three directors were independent and financially literate. New rules on audit committees were then produced variously by the SEC, the New York Stock Exchange, the American Stock Exchange, the National Association of Securities Dealers and the FASB. The SEC in particular required a declaration of the independence of the audit committee, the use of an audit committee charter, and the inclusion in the annual proxy statement of report by the audit committee.

However, the presence of audit committees conforming to these rules did not appear to prevent the major corporate collapses of 2001 and 2002, with the result that Sarbanes–Oxley legislated further on the role and composition of audit committees. Key points were:

- The audit committee has responsibility for the appointment, compensation and oversight of any registered public accounting firm employed to perform audit services.
- The audit committee must have a procedure to receive, retain and treat complaints received by the company about accounting, internal controls and auditing.
- The audit committee must have the authority to take independent legal advice or other advice as it deems necessary.
- The company must give appropriate funding to the audit committee.
- The audit committee must approve non-audit services provided by the audit firm.

---

[15] OECD (2004).

- The external auditor must report to the audit committee on all critical accounting policies and practices to be used, all the alternative GAAP discussed with management, and the implications of the choices made.
- Audit committee members must be a member of the board of directors, but otherwise be independent.
- Companies must disclose whether at least one member of the audit committee is a 'financial expert'.

The New York Stock Exchange issued new rules in August 2002. These stated that an audit committee must fulfil a list of functions, as follows:

- Have at least three independent directors, all financially literate and of whom at least one has accounting or financial management expertise.
- Have a formal written charter and code of business conduct, approved by the board of directors.
- Assist the board's oversight of integrity and compliance of the financial statements.
- Hire and fire the external auditors.
- Obtain and review a report by the independent auditors, at least annually, describing the company's internal quality control procedures, any material issues raised about quality control in previous reviews, and all relationships between the independent auditor and the company.
- Discuss the annual financial statements, quarterly financial statements, and management's discussion and analysis (MD&A) disclosures with management and with the independent auditor.
- Discuss earnings press releases and earnings guidance provided to analysts and rating agencies.
- Meet separately, periodically, with management, with internal auditors and with independent auditors.
- Review, with the independent auditor, any audit problems and the response of management.
- Set clear policies for hiring employees or former employees of the independent auditor's firm.
- Report regularly to the board of directors.
- Carry out annual performance evaluation of the work of the board of directors.

This is clearly a demanding list of activities and makes the work of the independent non-executive director more burdensome.

8.4.3.2 Institutional shareholders

The emphasis on 'stakeholders' as a wider constituency encourages corporations to be accountable and report to a wider group. In practice, the market for stocks and shares remains the primary mechanism for corporate governance. In particular, it is noticeable that major institutional shareholders will use their voting power at company meetings to express their views on corporate governance and are aware that they are expected to show an element of social responsibility as well as safeguarding their position as investors.

8.4.3.3 Structure of the board of directors

Members of the board of directors have wide-ranging backgrounds, and the company's operations may be widely dispersed. Directors receive information quite frequently because of the obligation on listed companies to report quarterly to shareholders.

The board of directors meets relatively infrequently, delegating detailed matters to committees of the board. These might cover remuneration packages, finance, public policy, planning, human resources and similar matters. The most important are the audit committee, the compensation committee, the nominating committee and the executive committee.

It is a condition of stock exchange listing that a corporation has an audit committee to review all aspects of external and internal auditing. The audit committee must comprise independent (non-executive) directors. Compensation committees also comprise the independent directors and decide the remuneration packages of senior executives including the CEO. Nominating committees screen policy proposals put forward by the CEO and offer advice on the composition and membership of the board of directors. Executive committees deal with urgent business between meetings of the main board. For corporations progressing at a steady rate, the committee structure is the effective form of governance and the board of directors takes an oversight role, becoming more active in intervention only where a crisis is looming.

8.4.3.4 Remuneration of CEOs

There are often references to the package of remuneration available to the CEO which, in the US, is referred to as 'compensation'. It means the basic salary paid in cash plus all the other benefits received such as membership of a health care scheme; use of a company car; contributions to a retirement benefit package; bonus payments related to corporate performance and profits; and options (rights) to purchase ordinary shares at an agreed price over a stated period of time. The long-term performance-related aspects are a much greater proportion of the total package than in other countries. In 2003 CEO reumneration on average consisted of 18 per cent salary, 19 per cent bonus and 63 per cent long-term incentives.[16] There was a strong correlation between cash payment (salary plus bonus) and company financial performance.

This compensation package has the potential to make the CEO self-seeking where the profits of the company are threatened or the CEO's position in the business is at risk. Restricting the compensation package might reduce the CEO's entrepreneurial spirit, and so the present emphasis in corporate governance is on disclosure to shareholders of the full compensation package and the use of a compensation committee comprising the non-executive members of the board of directors.

8.4.4 Taxation system

The US Congress passes the laws that govern income taxes. The legislation is contained in the Internal Revenue Code and administered by the Internal Revenue Service (IRS). Generally, taxes are imposed on each company separately, but an affiliated group of domestic corporations may file a consolidated return and be taxed as one corporation. It is relatively unusual to find a country allowing tax to be based on the group as a whole.

8.4.4.1 Corporate income tax

Taxable income is determined as the excess of taxable revenue over deductible expenses. The general rule is that all revenue is taxable and expenses are deductible provided they are ordinary and necessary. The resulting taxable profit may differ from the accounting

---

[16] The Wall Street Journal/Mercer Human Resource Consulting 2003 *CEO Compensation Survey and Trends*, May 2004, www.mercerHR.com.

profit because the tax code is intended to generate revenue for the government in a manner consistent with specific social and economic goals, while financial accounting information is intended to be useful to investors and lenders. US corporations are taxable on their worldwide income.

Accrual accounting is used for tax purposes in the US. However, some expenses such as losses on sales of assets (e.g. buildings) must be realized in cash before they are allowed to be deductible. The tax rules also cover revenue recognition, tax rates and tax credits. Some revenue and expenses are not taxable – a fine imposed for an illegal activity, for example, would not be allowable as an expense. Timing differences occur where the expense is recognized differently under tax rules compared with accounting practice, due to accelerated depreciation, delayed revenue recognition and delayed recognition of expenses.

Accelerated depreciation is used for tax purposes but not necessarily for accounting profit. Under the Modified Accelerated Cost Recovery System, assets are placed in one of six groups defining asset life; a depreciation schedule is available for each class. The effect of the acceleration is to write off substantially more than 50 per cent of the cost in the first half of the asset's life: the percentage written off in the early years is greatest for the shortest life group.

An example of delayed revenue is where the business uses the percentage of completion method to report contract profits for accounting purposes but uses the completed contract method for taxation purposes. An example of delayed expenses is a provision for repairs under warranty where the tax rules require the actual repair cost to be incurred.

Companies pay federal taxes and local state taxes, the local taxes being deductible in determining income for federal tax purposes. The federal government may give tax credits, which are direct reductions of the income tax itself, in contrast to tax deductions which reduce the level of taxable income.

8.4.4.2 Tax on distributions

Dividends paid by domestic corporations to US citizens and residents are taxable to such individuals. Dividend income paid to a non-resident alien is generally subject to a withholding tax.

8.4.5 Corporate financing system

8.4.5.1 Equity investors

The US stock exchanges[17] provide an important primary market for raising new capital. They attract listings by foreign registrants which seek to raise capital in the US market. The stock exchanges are also a secondary market for the purchase and sale of shares already in issue. At the end of 2003 there were 2,308 companies having their common stock (ordinary shares) listed on the New York Stock Exchange (NYSE) of which 466 were foreign registrants. On NASDAQ there were 3,294 listed, of which 343 were foreign registrants.[18]

The NYSE share ownership survey[19] showed that households remain a strong influence on the US stock market (see Exhibit 8.3) although the percentage is reducing. (Compare

---

[17] www.nysedata.com/factbook/main.asp.

[18] www.world-exchanges.org/.

[19] *Shareownership 2000*, NYSE, www.nyse.com.

| Exhibit 8.3 | Percentage of corporate stock in the US owned by investor sectors, 1990 and 1998 |

Ownership sector	1990	1998
Direct Household Holdings	51.0%	41.1%
Indirect Household Holdings, through personal trusts and estates, life insurance companies, private pension funds and mutual funds	21.0%	27.5%
Total Household	72.0%	68.3%
Rest of the World	6.9%	7.2%
State and Local Government Retirement Plans	7.6%	11.4%
Defined Benefit Private Pension Plans	8.8%	5.6%
Mutual Funds not owned by Households	1.5%	5.0%
Other Non-Household Investors	3.2%	2.2%

Source: Extracted from Table 16, *Shareownership 2000*, NYSE.

this table with the data for some other countries in Exhibit 4.6.) The survey also shows that there is a relatively low percentage of 'rest of the world' investors. Listed US companies are mainly directing their information at US investors.

Exhibit 4.3 indicates the relative size of the US stock market in relation to those of Europe. New York is now ahead of London in the number of international companies listed. For many years New York had relatively few international listings and this was attributed to the strict reporting requirements in the US, explained later. It might appear that companies are conquering their fears of the US regulatory system. Exhibit 4.4 shows that the US and Japanese markets together dominate world stock markets by size.

The two major national stock exchanges are the New York Stock Exchange (NYSE) and the American Stock Exchange (AMEX), and there are five regional stock exchanges. There is an over-the-counter market (OTC) for unlisted stocks. Dealers in the OTC are regulated by the National Association of Securities Dealers which uses an electronic Automatic Quotation system (NASDAQ). A stock may be listed on an exchange and traded in the OTC market. Trading such stocks in the OTC is called the 'third market'. Transactions may occur directly between buyers and sellers in what is called the 'fourth market'.

The stock exchanges are approved and regulated by the SEC in order to ensure the market's fairness, competitiveness and efficiency. There was concern in the past that investors were not necessarily receiving the best price, and trading rules are now in place to ensure fairness.

8.4.5.2 Bank lending

Commercial banks are prevented from owning controlling blocks of shares in non-banking companies. They may not underwrite issues of shares or link with investment banks which do so. The basis of these restrictions is historical: the banks were blamed significantly for the stock market crash of 1929. Banks do act as trustees, holding shares on behalf of clients, but the banks prefer the clients to exercise their voting rights directly. The main financial link between banks and corporations is therefore that of lender and borrower. However the concept of 'relationship banking', where the bank provides services beyond the loan facility, is relatively unfamiliar; the bank may not always have the closer knowledge of the business which might be found in some continental European companies.

8.4.5.3 Mergers and acquisitions[20]

The ability of corporations to merge is restricted by antitrust legislation which seeks to prevent monopoly positions arising. Where a merger or acquisition is not prevented by antitrust law, the process of acquisition is regulated by state law and federal law. There is no equivalent of the voluntary self-regulation applied by the Takeover Panel in the UK. The SEC requires that acquisitions of 5 per cent or more of voting shares are to be disclosed within ten days; changes of more than 1 per cent thereafter must be notified. Tender offers are regulated by the SEC under the Williams Act 1968. Under a tender offer, the prospective purchaser offers a price for a specified quantity of shares. The company issues the tendered shares at the best price offered.

Contested takeover bids have led to defensive practices which may not be in the best interests of all shareholders – 'Poison pills' allow management, at short notice, to place blocks of shares with friendly persons in order to block a bid; 'Crown jewels' provisions place a desirable asset with a friendly corporation elsewhere; 'Greenmail' means paying a price above the market price for shares held by an investor who is threatening to start a takeover bid; 'Supermajority' means requiring a 75 per cent majority vote to remove directors. All these tactics would be forbidden under the UK Takeover Code. They are contested from time to time under state law, but survive or emerge in a modified form.

8.4.6 The accounting profession

The historical development of the accounting profession has been described in an earlier section. It no longer has a direct role in setting accounting standards, but remains the professional organization to which many of those involved in standard-setting belong. The AICPA retains exclusive authority in the private sector for promulgating auditing rules. The Auditing Standards Board (ASB) of the AICPA issues Statements on Auditing Standards, and members of the AICPA must adhere to all applicable Statements on Auditing Standards in conducting audits. Audit is required by the SEC in the case of listed companies. For other companies, it is voluntary or else carried out at the request of a third party such as a bank lender.

The AICPA has sought to curb what is sometimes called 'opinion shopping', which refers to the practice where listed companies offer the audit to the firm which gives the most sympathetic interpretation of GAAP. As well as strengthening professional standards of conduct, the AICPA has sponsored a major enquiry into the needs of users of financial reporting. The result of this enquiry, referred to as the Jenkins Report, was published in 1994 and is explained in section 8.7.1.6.

On a wider spectrum than the AICPA, specialization has developed in aspects of the accountancy profession. Specialist professional examinations in the US now recognize Certified Public Accountants; Certified Internal Auditors; Certified Management Accountants; and Chartered Financial Analysts. The AICPA itself has membership divisions reflecting various activities, being divided almost equally between public practice (accountancy firms) and industry, as shown in Exhibit 8.4.

---

[20] Sudarsanam (2003).

| Exhibit 8.4 | Membership of the AICPA, 2003 |

Total membership	**335,111**
Public accounting	38.4%
Business and Industry	47.4%
Local, state and federal government	4.1%
Education	2.4%
Retired and Miscellaneous	7.7%

Source: AICPA Annual Report 2002–2003; AICPA website www.aicpa.org

In the 1990s there were six leading accounting firms in the US, often referred to as the 'big 6', which undertook the audits of some 97 per cent of companies listed on the NYSE. These were Andersen Worldwide, Ernst & Young, Deloitte & Touche, KPMG Peat Marwick, Coopers & Lybrand and Price Waterhouse. Merger to form PricewaterhouseCoopers (PwC) led to the 'big 5' and the dissolution of Andersen in the aftermath of Enron reduced this to the 'big 4'. These firms still carry out most of the audits of listed companies, so audit activity has become increasingly concentrated.

8.5 External influences

The US has developed by importing know-how and expertise. That includes accounting, which travelled to the US with early pioneers from the UK. Accounting practice in the US has subsequently been imbued with increasingly national characteristics. (Section 4.8.3 provides more details on this process of import and export of accounting ideas.) In more recent years, the US has exported its brand of accounting to countries under its economic influence, particularly Canada, Central and South America, and countries in South East Asia (see also Case study 4.2). Surveys of the US sphere of influence (Canada, Chile, Mexico compared to UK) are updated regularly.[21]

US influence on Japanese accounting is discussed in Chapter 15. One particularly significant export has been the idea of setting standards through a professional route rather than by government regulation, culminating in an independent standard-setting body.

As a founder member of IASC, the USA has had a significant influence on global accounting practices. Opinions are divided as to whether the US influence has been excessive or not.[22] The transition to the IASB, outlined in Chapter 1, indicates a strong role for continuing US influence.

8.6 Comparison with IFRS

As explained earlier, the regulation of accounting practice lies jointly in the hands of the FASB and the SEC. They have different sets of regulations but the SEC, in accepting filing of financial statements, effectively endorses the authority of the independent FASB. Chapter 1 explains the role of the SEC as a member of the International Organization of Securities Commissions (IOSCO), which has accepted a core set of IASB Standards as common usage

[21] CICA (2002).

[22] Flower (1997); Cairns (1997).

for international companies seeking international listings. However, the SEC has yet to clarify its own position. It has made encouraging sounds in relation to convergence of US GAAP with IFRS but has not indicated a target for acceptance of IFRS in the US.

US interest in international accounting was demonstrated by an act of Congress, signed by the President in October 1996, confirming the importance of IASs in attracting foreign corporations to gain access to listing in the US markets. To that end, Congress urged the SEC to support vigorously the development of high-quality IASs.

The IASB Framework for the Preparation and Presentation of Financial Statements (1989) owes much of its development and direction to the prior work of FASB published earlier in the 1980s as a series of Statements of Financial Accounting Concepts (SFACs). Exhibit 8.5 shows the extent to which US standards are broadly in agreement with IASB Standards, and the key areas of difference.

The IASB and FASB have jointly undertaken a short-term project to eliminate some differences between IFRS and US GAAP. This 'short-term convergence project' was the result of an agreement between the two Boards in September 2002 called the 'Norwalk agreement' (from the place of their meeting). It is essential to refer to a source of information such as the 'iasplus' website[23] for updated briefings on how this project has progressed. Exhibit 8.5 shows the position at March 2004, based on the IASB's 'stable platform' position.

Exhibit 8.5 Comparison of accounting practices in the USA with requirements of IASs: key similarities and differences

Disclosure and presentation		Practice in US
General aspects		
IFRS 1	First-time adoption of IFRS	Not applicable
IAS 1	Presentation of Financial Statements	'Fair presentation' requirement
		Two years' comparative figures required by SEC
		Comprehensive income required by FASB
		Extraordinary items permitted by US
Specific aspects		
IAS 7	Cash Flow Statements	Generally in agreement SFAS 95 Detailed differences on classification of interest received and paid, and overdrafts in cash
IAS 8	Accounting Policies, Changes in Accounting Estimates and Errors	In agreement on restating prior financial statements SFAS 16, APB 20, SFAS 130. Non-mandated changes in accounting policy are not prior year items in US*
IFRS 35	Non-current Assets Held for Sale and Discontinued Operations	Generally in agreement SFAS 144. US less restrictive on definitions of 'discontinued', more disclosures required

▶

---

[23] www.iasplus.com.

Exhibit 8.5 *(Continued)*

Disclosure and presentation		Practice in US
IAS 14	Segment Reporting	Generally in agreement SFAS 131, but limited in secondary disclosure. IASB is taking analysts' advice
IAS 24	Related Party Disclosures	Generally in agreement SFAS 57
IAS 33	Earnings per Share	Generally in agreement SFAS 128. Differences in detail*
IAS 34	Interim Financial Reporting	Differences in approach to measurement APB 28
Asset recognition and measurement		
IAS 2	Inventories	Generally in agreement ARB 43 US does not prohibit costs of idle capacity and spoilage in inventory* US permits LIFO US prohibits reversal of inventory write-downs
IAS 16	Property, Plant and Equipment	Generally in agreement, revaluation not permitted ARB 43, APB 6
IAS 36	Impairment of Assets	Differences in approach SFAS 121
IAS 23	Borrowing Costs	Generally in agreement. SFAS 34 requires capitalization in some circumstances, IAS 23 allows but does not require
IAS 38	Research and Development Costs	Development expenditure may not be capitalized SFAS 2*
IAS 38	Intangible Assets	No amortization, revaluation not permitted, impairment test SFAS 142
IAS 40	Investment Property	Fixed assets must be depreciated ARB 43
Liability recognition and measurement		
IAS 10	Events after the Balance Sheet Date	Discouraged by audit regulations, pro forma revised statement preferred
IAS 37	Provisions, Contingent Liabilities and Contingent Assets	Generally in agreement SFAS 5. US tends towards low end of range of possible amounts
IAS 12	Income Taxes	Generally in agreement SFAS 109 Short-term convergence addressing some details
IAS 17	Leases	Generally in agreement SFAS 13 US gives more detail on lease maturities
IAS 19	Employee Benefits	Generally in agreement SFAS 87, 88, 106 differences in detail
Financial instruments: assets and liabilities		
IAS 32	Financial Instruments: Disclosure and Presentation	Generally in agreement SFAS 133, different treatment of convertible debt instruments

IAS 39	Financial Instruments: Recognition and Measurement	Fair value measurement in primary statements SFAS 133. US does not allow subsequent reversal of an impairment loss
Recognition of economic activity		
IAS 11	Construction Contracts	Generally in agreement ARB 45 Differ on treatment where percentage of completion can not be determined*
IAS 18	Revenue	Generally in agreement SFAC 5 plus specific industry standards. FASB is leading joint project with IASB*
IAS 20	Accounting for Government Grants and Disclosure of Government Assistance	Generally in agreement SFAS 116
IFRS 2	Share-based Payment	SFAS 123 is an agreement on fair value; APB 25 allows intrinsic value*
Measurement of inflation		
IAS 29	Financial Reporting in Hyperinflationary Economies	US would take different approach to subsidiary
Group accounting		
IAS 21	The Effects of Changes in Foreign Exchange Rates	Generally in agreement SFAS 52
IFRS 3	Business Combinations	Generally in agreement on purchase method.Negative goodwill, minority interest, treated differently in US* SFAS 141 bans pooling of interests. SFAS 142 changes amortization of goodwill to impairment test
IAS 27	Consolidated and Separate Financial Statements	ARB 51 Generally in agreement; pooling withdrawn. US focus on majority voting rights.SPEs differently treated. No requirement to conform accounting policies of parent and subsidiary
IAS 28	Investments in Associates	Generally in agreement APB 18. US does not require associate accounting policies to conform to investor
IAS 31	Interests in Joint Ventures	Generally requires equity method* (except for construction and oil and gas industries)

Note: In this exhibit, 'generally in agreement' indicates broad comparability in principle. US accounting standards are very much more detailed in aspects of practical application.

* = the item is under consideration in the joint short-term convergence project with IASB.

Key: ARB, Accounting Research Bulletin
     APB, Accounting Principles Board Opinion
     SFAS, Statement of Financial Accounting Standard

US companies do not specifically acknowledge that their accounting practices are related to the IASB Standards; this may be taken to confirm the relatively low profile of IASB Standards in the scheme of what comprises 'generally accepted accounting principles' (see section 8.7.2.1).

8.7 The accounting system

8.7.1 Current regulations

Since 1973, standards have been set by the FASB. This is an independent, private-sector organization, financed by a spread of contributions from accountancy firms, industry, organizations representing investors and creditors, and other related organizations. The FASB comprises seven members who must maintain total independence of other business activity during their term of office. The seven members of the FASB have diverse business backgrounds, and so could be said to be 'professional' in general terms; they are not all recruited from professional accountancy firms.

There is a substantial secretariat supporting the FASB, and an extensive consultative process, called 'due process', has been put in place. The FASB sponsors systematic and thorough research prior to developing a standard. The principle of openness is an essential element of the work of the FASB, extending to holding public hearings to discuss exposure drafts of standards; their deliberations are open to public attendance.

The 'due process' of consultation on developing standards involves:

- appointing a task force of experts to advise on the project;
- sponsoring research studies and reviewing existing literature on the subject;
- publishing a discussion of issues and potential solutions;
- holding a public hearing;
- issuing an exposure draft for public comment.

The result of the process is a Statement of Financial Accounting Standards (SFAS), and enforcement is effectively through the audit process. Implicitly there is a position of power for the SEC because it may refuse to accept a filing by a corporation where the auditor is not satisfied. The AICPA expects its members to apply FASB pronouncements. The report of the auditors to a public company does not refer directly to SFASs but uses the wording 'fairly present . . . in accordance with generally accepted accounting principles'.

The FASB is complemented by an Emerging Issues Task Force (EITF), which considers new issues requiring rapid guidance. Its views are published and are influential, without carrying the compulsion of an SFAS.

8.7.1.1 Generally accepted accounting principles

A hierarchy of US GAAP is set out in the US Auditing Standard SAS 69 (1992) as follows:

- FASB Statements and Interpretations, APB Opinions and AICPA Accounting Research Bulletins [this is a set of documents for which the IASB equivalent would be IFRS];
- Rules and interpretative releases of the SEC [the UK equivalent would be the FSA Listing Rules];
- FASB Technical Bulletins, AICPA Industry Audit and Accounting Guides and AICPA Statements of Position;

- AICPA AcSEC Practice Bulletins and consensuses of the FASB Emerging Issues Task Force (EITF);
- AICPA accounting interpretations, implementation guides (Qs&As) published by FASB staff and practices that are widely recognized and prevalent either generally or in the industry.

SAS 69 also indicates that other accounting literature may be considered, extending through various professional guidance to textbooks, handbooks and articles. IASs are contained in this miscellaneous grouping.

Acceptance of this list by the FASB was indicated by its inclusion in SFAS 111, 'Rescission of FASB statement no 32 and technical corrections', whereby the wording of SAS 69 was incorporated as a technical correction to APB 20, 'Accounting changes'.

The origins of the phrase 'generally accepted accounting principles' in the US lie in the APB Opinion no. 4 (issued by the AICPA in 1970), which refers to these principles being rooted in 'experience, reason, custom, usage, and . . . practical necessity'. The principles are said there to 'encompass the conventions, rules and procedures necessary to define accepted accounting practice at a particular time'.

The emphasis on GAAP in the USA necessitates having comprehensive and authoritative statements. This in turn has led the FASB to develop a significant volume of Statements of Financial Accounting Standards (SFASs) and an even greater volume of interpretations. The SFASs and the interpretations are quite lengthy in their detail and make a sharp contrast with the IFRS which are primarily statements of broad standards.

8.7.1.2 'Safe harbor' protection for forward-looking statements

The Private Securities Litigation Reform Act of 1995 extends the basic legislation of the Securities Act of 1933 and the Securities Exchange Act of 1934, allowing the SEC to clarify what is called a 'safe harbor' of protection against legal action in respect of forward-looking statements, provided these are made outside the financial statements and notes. To obtain the protection companies must state the factors that could affect the financial performance or cause actual results to differ from any estimates made in forward-looking statements. Companies give the requisite statement in the Form 10-K, with duplication wholly or partly in the published annual report.

8.7.1.3 Frequency of reporting

In addition to the annual report, the SEC requires listed companies to produce quarterly reports. Interim reporting is covered by APB 28. US interim reports usually include both the current interim period and a cumulative year-to-date period, together with comparative figures for the previous year. Each interim period is viewed as an integral part of the annual period. This means that while operating cost and revenues will generally be reported in the interim period to which they relate, discretion exists to allocate other costs across interim periods. When APB 28 was issued there was a dissenting view that it was not sufficiently strict in its guidance on allocation to interim periods. The IASB indicates in IAS 34 a general principle of the 'year-to-date' approach, where the events of the interim period are reported as they occur.

Under APB 28 the cumulative effect of a change in accounting principle is always included in net income of the first interim period of the company's accounting year, regardless of when the accounting change occurred. The IASB indicates in IAS 34 a preference for restatement of the comparative figures for the corresponding previous period so that accounting changes do not appear in any one interim period. The differences between US GAAP and IFRS are not addressed in the short-term convergence project.

8.7.1.4 SEC concerns over flexibility

In 1999 the SEC officials expressed concern over the misuse of accounting policies in order to 'manage' earnings. They indicated that accounting fraud was increasing because of the temptation to sacrifice sound reporting practices in order to meet the expectations of investors. Examples of excessive flexibility were premature recognition of revenue, excessive accruals or manipulation of accruals for loan losses and restructuring charges, improper write-downs of assets that continued to be used in operations, and unreasonable lives for depreciation and amortization. Such matters are not in themselves fraudulent, because the rules allow such flexibility, but if there is an intention to deceive then the acts may become fraudulent. SEC staff reports on investigations are published on the SEC website, www.sec.gov.

8.7.1.5 Tax law and impact on accounting practice

Tax law and accounting law are separate but there may be situations where accountants find it convenient, or even necessary, to use the tax-based approach in the accounting statements. This reduces the flexibility available in principle. An example lies in inventory valuation and the use of LIFO (see section 8.7.3.8).

8.7.1.6 AICPA and FASB projects

The AICPA formed a Special Committee on Financial Reporting in 1991, chaired by E. L. Jenkins, to address two questions:

● What information should companies provide to investors and creditors?
● To what extent should auditors be associated with that information?

The work of the Jenkins Committee was part of the AICPA's broad initiative to improve the value of business information and the confidence of the public in that information. Extensive research was undertaken to ascertain the views of investors and creditors. The Jenkins Committee, reporting in 1994,[24] found that a great deal was right with the present state of business reporting in the US. However, the criticisms offered by users of business reports led to the identification of high-priority areas for improvement. Key recommendations were that, to meet users' changing needs, business reporting must:

● provide more information with a forward-looking perspective, including management's plans, opportunities, risks and measurement uncertainties;
● focus more on the factors that create long-term value, including non-financial measures indicating how key business processes are performing;
● align information reported externally better with the information reported to senior management to manage the business.

The Jenkins Committee designed and illustrated a comprehensive model of business reporting, based on revising the primary financial statements and the MD&A. It was incremental rather than revolutionary, and the report noted that the practical

---

[24] AICPA (1994).

investigation focused on immediate rather than longer-term information needs. That reflected the concern of users with current practice and current problems.

Jenkins noted that the current legal environment in the USA discouraged companies from disclosing forward-looking information and recommended that companies should not expand reporting of forward-looking information until there were more effective deterrents to undesirable legal actions.

The FASB published, in 2001, a research report *Improving Business Reporting: Insights into Enhancing Voluntary Disclosure* to help preparers improve their business reporting by voluntary disclosure.

8.7.1.7 Special industry standards

The FASB sets special industry standards, based on direct action by the FASB rather than the less direct approach of the UK where the ASB franks (approves) the industry's own proposals. FASB industry standards cover the oil and gas industry where there have on occasions been differences of opinion between the FASB and the SEC. The example of SFAS 69, 'Disclosures about oil and gas producing activities', is interesting because it requires disclosure of financially relevant information beyond that conventionally expected in published accounts. In particular, it requires disclosure of proven oil and gas reserve quantities, capitalized costs relating to oil and gas producing activities, costs incurred on oil and gas exploration and development activities, results of production activities, and a discounted cash flow measure of future cash flows expected from proven reserves. The requirement to report proven reserves was given high publicity in 2004 when Royal Dutch/Shell had to revise its estimates downwards four times, causing delay to the annual report for 2003.[25]

Other industries covered by FASB standards include banking and thrift institutions; broadcasters; cable television companies; motion picture films; records and music; franchisors; insurance enterprises; the mortgage banking industry; real estate (property) companies; and regulated industries. These industries may also be subject to other regulatory bodies setting accounting requirements (*see* Exhibit 8.6).

The US approach in developing specific industry standards is quite different from the more general approach of the IASB. The only specialized international standards are IAS 26, 'Accounting and reporting by retirement benefit plans', IAS 30, 'Disclosures in the financial statements of banks and similar financial institutions', IAS 41 'Agriculture' and IFRS 4 'Insurance Contracts'.

8.7.2 Disclosure and presentation

This section explains some of the differences between US GAAP and IFRS or other accounting systems.

8.7.2.1 Fair presentation

The US equivalent of the phrase 'true and fair view' found in European accounting is the somewhat different wording 'fairly presented in conformity with generally accepted accounting principles'. It is different because of the specific emphasis placed on GAAP. The European interpretation of 'true and fair' is not uniform, but the UK view is that 'true and fair' stands above any specific set of rules. Some commentators have drawn the distinction by describing the US approach as highly legalistic when compared with

---

[25] 'Shell accounts get signed off at last', *Financial Times*, 25 May 2004, p. 21.

| Exhibit 8.6 | Southern Co.: summary of significant accounting policies, electricity supply |

Notes to Financial Statements

Note One

Summary of Significant Accounting Policies General

Southern Company is the parent company of five retail operating companies, Southern Power Company (Southern Power), Southern Company Services (SCS), Southern Communications Services (Southern LINC), Southern Company Gas (Southern Company GAS), Southern Company Holdings (Southern Holdings), Southern Nuclear Operating Company (Southern Nuclear), Southern Telecom, and other direct and indirect subsidiaries. The retail operating companies – Alabama Power, Georgia Power, Gulf Power, Mississippi Power, and Savannah Electric – provide electric service in four Southeastern states. Southern Power constructs, owns, and manages Southern Company's competitive generation assets and sells electricity at market-based rates in the wholesale market. Contracts among the retail operating companies and Southern Power – related to jointly owned generating facilities, interconnecting transmission lines, or the exchange of electric power – are regulated by the Federal Energy Regulatory Commission (FERC) and/or the Securities and Exchange Commission (SEC). SCS – the system service company – provides, at cost, specialized services to Southern Company and subsidiary companies. Southern LINC provides digital wireless communications services to the retail operating companies and also markets these services to the public within the Southeast. Southern Telecom provides fiber cable services within the Southeast. Southern Company GAS is a competitive retail natural gas marketer serving customers in Georgia. Southern Holdings is an intermediate holding subsidiary for Southern Company's investments in synthetic fuels and leveraged leases and an energy services business. Southern Nuclear operates and provides services to Southern Company's nuclear power plants.

On April 2, 2001, the spin off of Mirant Corporation (Mirant) was completed. As a result of the spin off, Southern Company's financial statements and related information reflect Mirant as discontinued operations. For additional information regarding Mirant, see Note 3 under "Mirant Related Matters."

The financial statements reflect Southern Company's investments in the subsidiaries on a consolidated basis. The equity method is used for subsidiaries in which the company has significant influence but does not control. All material intercompany items have been eliminated in consolidation. Certain prior years' data presented in the consolidated financial statements have been reclassified to conform with the current year presentation.

Southern Company is registered as a holding company under the Public Utility Holding Company Act of 1935 (PUHCA). Both the company and its subsidiaries are subject to the regulatory provisions of the PUHCA. In addition, the retail operating companies and Southern Power are subject to regulation by the FERC, and the retail operating companies are also subject to regulation by their respective state public service commissions. The companies follow accounting principles generally accepted in the United States and comply with the accounting policies and practices prescribed by their respective commissions. The preparation of financial statements in conformity with accounting principles generally accepted in the United States requires the use of estimates, and the actual results may differ from those estimates.

Also, the Energy Policy Act of 1992 required the establishment of a Uranium Enrichment Decontamination and Decommissioning Fund, which is funded in part by a special assessment on utilities with nuclear plants. This assessment is being paid over a 15-year period, which began in 1993. This fund will be used by the DOE for the decontamination and decommissioning of its nuclear fuel enrichment facilities. The law provides that utilities will recover these payments in the same manner as any other fuel expense. Alabama Power and Georgia Power – based on its ownership interest – estimate their respective remaining liability at December 31, 2003, under this law to be approximately $13 million and $10 million.

Regulatory Assets and Liabilities

The retail operating companies are subject to the provisions of Financial Accounting Standards Board (FASB) Statement No. 71, Accounting for the Effects of Certain Types of Regulation. Regulatory assets represent probable future revenues associated with certain costs that are expected to be recovered from customers through the ratemaking process. Regulatory liabilities represent probable future reductions in revenues associated with amounts that are expected to be credited to customers through the ratemaking process. Regulatory assets and (liabilities) reflected in the Consolidated Balance Sheets at December 31 relate to:

(in millions)	2003	2002	Note
Deferred income tax charges	$ 874	$898	(a)
Loss on reacquired debt	326	313	(b)
DOE assessments	26	33	(c)
Vacation pay	97	98	(d)
Building lease	54	54	(f)
Generating plant outage costs	35	38	(f)
Other assets	75	73	(f)
Asset retirement obligations	(138)	–	(a)
Other cost of removal obligations	(1,269)	(1,944)	(a)
Deferred income tax credits	(409)	(450)	(a)
Accelerated cost recovery	(115)	(229)	(e)
Plant Daniel capacity	(60)	–	(g)
Storm damage reserves	(53)	(38)	(f)
Fuel-hedging liabilities	(13)	(38)	(c)
Environmental remediation reserves	(41)	(42)	(f)
Deferred purchased power	(92)	(63)	(f)
Other liabilities	(13)	(12)	(f)
Total	$(716)	$(1,309)	

Note: The recovery and amortization periods for these regulatory assets and (liabilities) are as follows:

(a) Asset retirement and removal liabilities are recorded, deferred income tax assets are recovered, and deferred tax liabilities are amortized over the related property lives, which may range up to 50 years. Asset retirement and removal liabilities will be settled and trued up following completion of the related activities.

(b) Recovered over either the remaining life of the original issue or, if refinanced, over the life of the new issue, which may range up to 50 years.

(c) Assessments for the decontamination and decommissioning of the DOE's nuclear fuel enrichment facilities are recorded annually from 1993 through 2008. Fuel-hedging assets and liabilities are recorded over the life of the underlying hedged purchase contracts, which generally do not exceed two years. Upon final settlement, actual costs incurred are recovered through the fuel cost recovery clauses.

(d) Recorded as earned by employees and recovered as paid, generally within one year.

(e) Amortized over three-year period ending in 2004.

(f) Recorded and recovered or amortized as approved by the appropriate state public service commissions.

(g) See Note 3 under "Mississippi Power Regulatory Filing."

Source: Southern Co., annual report (2003), pp. 47 and 48

a much more judgemental approach in the UK. This perception is another way of expressing the 'rules versus principles' debate, explained in section 8.3.3.

8.7.2.2 Financial statement formats

In the annual report of US companies there are four primary financial statements:

- balance sheet,
- income statement (statement of earnings, profit and loss account),
- cash flow statement,
- statement of changes in shareholders' equity (stockholders' equity), including comprehensive income.

These four financial statements, augmented by footnotes and supplementary data, are interrelated. Collectively, they are intended to provide relevant, reliable and timely information essential to making investment, credit, and similar decisions, thus meeting the objectives of financial reporting. Companies are required to report comprehensive income under SFAS 130.

Balance sheet

There is no universal form of balance sheet. The objectives are clarity and adequate disclosure of all pertinent and material facts. Some use the account form (a two-sided balance sheet corresponding to debit and credit); others use a report form (where the debit and credit sections of the account form are placed one above the other); and others again use a financial position form which corresponds to the vertical form used in the UK. Within the account form the assets are shown on the left-hand side, starting with cash and proceeding to the least liquid assets. The liabilities are on the right-hand side, starting with current liabilities and proceeding to long-term liabilities and equity. In all cases, there is classification of the main categories of assets and liabilities.

As an example, Sears, Roebuck and Co. uses the report form (Exhibit 8.7), while Altria Inc. uses the account form (Exhibit 8.8).

Income statement

There are essentially two forms of income statement (profit and loss account). One is the multiple-step and the other the single-step approach. Both require columns of comparative figures for two previous years. The multiple-step approach sets out various intermediate balances, including gross profit, as in Altria (Exhibit 8.9). The single-step approach presents one grouping of all revenue items, another grouping of expenses, and a resulting net income figure. Pfizer uses the single-step approach (Exhibit 8.10). Those who favour the single-step approach argue that it is more neutral in its presentation while the multiple-step approach makes assumptions about priority of cost recovery. Combinations of both methods may be used; there is no rigid format or chart of accounts. The title 'statement of income' is most widely used, but not universal. Some use 'statement of earnings' and some use 'operations statement'. Both the single-step and the multi-step income statements have separate sections for discontinued items, extraordinary items and the effect of a change in accounting principle.

Exhibit 8.20 shows the flexibility of income statement presentation. In panel (a) Wachovia segments its net interest income from its fee income on the face of the income statement, which also includes line item details. In panel (b) Colgate-Palmolive presents a highly summarised consolidated statement of income, with supplemental details of line items reported in the notes.

Exhibit 8.7 Sears, Roebuck and Co.: report form of balance sheet

SEARS, ROEBUCK AND CO.
Consolidated Balance Sheets

millions, except per share data	2003	2002
ASSETS		
Current assets		
Cash and cash equivalents	$ 9,057	$ 1,962
Credit card receivables	1,998	32,595
Less allowance for uncollectible accounts	42	1,836
Net credit card receivables	1,956	30,759
Other receivables	733	863
Merchandise inventories	5,335	5,115
Prepaid expenses and deferred charges	407	535
Deferred income taxes	708	749
Total current assets	18,196	39,983
Property and equipment		
Land	392	442
Buildings and improvements	7,151	6,930
Furniture, fixtures and equipment	4,972	5,050
Capitalized leases	609	557
Gross property and equipment	13,124	12,979
Less accumulated depreciation	6,336	6,069
Total property and equipment, net	6,788	6,910
Deferred income taxes	378	734
Goodwill	943	944
Tradenames and other intagible assets	710	704
Other assets	708	1,134
TOTAL ASSETS	$ 27,723	$ 50,409
LIABILITIES		
Current liabilities		
Short-term borrowings	$ 1,033	$ 4,525
Current portion of long-term debt and capitalized lease obligations	2,950	4,808
Accounts payable and other liabilities	7,923	7,485
Unearned revenues	1,244	1,199
Other taxes	609	580
Total current liabilities	13,759	18,597
Long-term debt and capitalized lease obligations	4,218	21,304
Pension and postretirement benefits	1,956	2,491
Minority interest and other liabilities	1,389	1,264
Total Liabilities	21,322	43,656
COMMITMENTS AND CONTINGENT LIABILITIES		
SHAREHOLDERS' EQUITY		
Common shares issued ($.75 par value per share, 1,000 shares authorized, 316.7 and 320.4 shares outstanding respectively)	323	323
Capital in excess of par value	3,519	3,505
Retained earnings	11,636	8,497
Treasury stock – at cost	(7,945)	(4,474)
Deferred ESOP expense	(26)	(42)
Accumulated other comprehensive loss	(1,106)	(1,056)
Total Shareholders' Equity	6,401	6,753
TOTAL LIABILITIES AND SHAREHOLDERS' EQUITY	$ 27,723	$ 50,409

See accompanying notes.

Source: Sears, Roebuck and Co., annual report (2003), p. F-5.

| Exhibit 8.8 | Altria, Inc.: account form of balance sheet |

Consolidated Balance Sheets

(in millions of dollars, except share and per share data)

at December 31,	2003	2002
Assets		
Consumer products		
Cash and cash equivalents	$ 3,777	$ 565
Receivables (less allowances of $135 and $142)	5,256	5,139
Inventories:		
Leaf tobacco	3,591	3,605
other raw materials	2,009	1,935
Finished product	3,940	3,587
	9,540	9,127
Other current assets	2,809	2,610
Total current assets	21,382	17,441
Property, plant and equipment, at cost:		
Land and land improvements	840	710
Buildings and building equipment	6,917	6,219
Machinery and equipment	18,230	16,127
Construction in progress	1,246	1,497
	27,233	24,553
Less accumulated depreciation	11,166	9,707
	16,067	14,846
Goodwill	27,742	26,037
Other intangible assets, net	11,803	11,834
Other assets	10,641	8,151
Total consumer products assets	87,635	78,309
Financial services		
Finance assets, net	8,393	9,075
Other assets	147	156
Total financial services assets	8,540	9,231
Total Assets	**$96,175**	**$87,540**

at December 31,	2003	2002
Liabilities		
Consumer products		
Short-term borrowings	$ 1,715	$ 407
Current portion of long-term debt	1,661	1,558
Accounts payable	3,198	3,088
Accrued liabilities:		
Marketing	2,443	3,192
Taxes, except income taxes	2,325	1,735
Employment costs	1,363	1,099
Settlement charges	3,530	3,027
Other	2,455	2,563
Income taxes	1,316	1,103
Dividends payable	1,387	1,310
Total current liabilities	21,393	19,082
Long-term debt	18,953	19,189
Deferred income taxes	7,295	6,112
Accrued postretirement health care costs	3,216	3,128
Minority interest	4,760	4,366
Other liabilities	7,161	8,004
Total consumer products liabilities	62,778	59,881
Financial services		
Long-term debt	2,210	2,166
Deferred income taxes	5,815	5,521
Other liabilities	295	494
Total financial services liabilities	8,320	8,181
Total liabilities	71,098	68,062
Contingencies (Note 18)		
Stockholders' Equity		
Common stock, par value $0.33\frac{1}{3}$ per share		
(2,805,961,317 shares issued)	935	935
Additional paid-in capital	4,813	4,642
Earnings reinvested in the business	47,008	43,259
Accumulated other comprehensive losses (including		
currency translation of $1,578 and $2,951)	(2,125)	(3,956)
Cost of repurchased stock (768,697,895 and		
766,701,765 shares)	(25,554)	(25,402)
Total stockholders' equity	25,077	19,478
Total Liabilities and Stockholders' Equity	$96,175	$87,540

Source: Altria, Inc., annual report (2003), pp. 42–43. www.altria.com

Exhibit 8.9   Altria, Inc.: multiple-step approach in income statement

Consolidated Statements of Earnings
(in millions of dollars, except per share data)

for the years ended December 31,	2003	2002	2001
Net revenues	$81,832	$80,408	$80,879
Cost of sales	31,870	32,748	33,900
Excise taxes on products	21,128	18,226	17,209
Gross profit	28,834	29,434	29,770
Marketing, administration and research costs	12,602	12,282	12,461
Domestic tobacco legal settlement	202		
Domestic tobacco headquarters relocation charges	69		
Gains on sales of business	(31)	(80)	(8)
Integration costs and a loss on sale of a food factory	(13)	111	82
Asset impairment and exit costs	86	223	19
Provision for airline industry exposure		290	
Litigation related expense			500
Amortization of intangibles	9	7	1,014
Operating income	15,910	16,601	15,702
Gain on Miller Brewing Company transaction		(2,631)	
Interest and other debt expense, net	1,150	1,134	1,418
Earnings before income taxes, minority interest and cumulative effect of accounting change	14,760	18,098	14,284
Provision for income taxes	5,151	6,424	5,407
Earnings before minority interest and cumulative effect of accounting change	9,609	11,674	8,877
Minority interest in earnings and other, net	405	572	311
Earnings before cumulative effect of accounting change	9,204	11,102	8,566
Cumulative effect of accounting change			(6)
Net earnings	$ 9,204	$11,102	$ 8,560
Per share data:			
Basic earnings per share before cumulative effect of accounting change	$ 4.54	$ 5.26	$ 3.93
Cumulative effect of accounting change			(0.01)
Basic earnings per share	$ 4.54	$ 5.26	$ 3.92
Diluted earnings per share before cumulative effect of accounting change	$ 4.52	$ 5.21	$ 3.88
Cumulative effect of accounting change			(0.01)
Diluted earnings per share	$ 4.52	$ 5.21	$ 3.87

Source: Altria, Inc. annual report (2003), p. 44.

Exhibit 8.10   Pfizer: single-step approach in income statement

Consolidated Statement of Income

Pfizer Inc and Subsidiary Companies

(millions, except per common share data)	YEAR ENDED DECEMBER 31		
	2003	2002	2001
Revenues	$45,188	$32,373	$29,024
Costs and expenses:			
Cost of sales	9,832	4,045	3,823
Selling, informational and administrative expenses	15,242	10,846	9,717
Research and development expenses	7,131	5,176	4,776
Merger-related in-process research and development charge	5,052	–	–
Merger-related costs	1,058	630	819
other (income)/deductions – net	3,610	(120)	(95)
Income from continuing operations before provision for taxes on income, minority interests and cumulative effect of change in accounting principles	3,263	11,796	9,984
Provision for taxes on income	1,621	2,609	2,433
Minority interests	3	6	14
Income from continuing operations before cumulative effect of change in accounting principles	1,639	9,181	7,537
Discontinued operations:			
Income from operations of discontinued business and product lines – net of tax	16	278	251
Gains on sales of discontinued business and product lines – net of tax	2,285	77	–
Discontinued operations – net of tax	2,301	355	251
Income before cumulative effect of change in accounting principles	3,940	9,536	7,788
Cumulative effect of change in accounting principles – net of tax	(30)	(410)	–
Net income	$3,910	$9,126	$7,788
Earnings per common share – basic			
Income from continuing operations before cumulative effect of change in accounting principles	$.22	$1.49	$1.21
Discontinued operations:			
Income from operations of discontinued businesses and product lines – net of tax	–	.05	.04
Gains on sales of discontinued businesses and product lines – net of tax	.32	.01	–
Discontinued operations – net of tax	.32	.06	.04
Income before cumulative effect of change in accounting principles	.54	1.55	1.25
Cumulative effect of change in accounting principles – net of tax	–	(.07)	–
Net income	$.54	$1.48	$1.25
Earnings per common share – diluted			
Income from continuing operations before cumulative effect of change in accounting principles	$.22	$1.47	$1.18
Discontinued operations:			
Income from operations of discontinued businesses and product lines – net of tax	–	.05	.04
Gains on sales of discontinued businesses and product lines – net of tax	.32	.01	–
Discontinued operations – net of tax	.32	.06	.04
Income before cumulative effect of change in accounting principles	.54	1.53	1.22
Cumulative effect of change in accounting principles – net of tax	–	(.07)	–
Net income	$.54	$1.46	$1.22
Weighted average shares – basic	7,213	6,156	6,239
Weighted average shares – diluted	7,286	6,241	6,361

Source: Pfizer, annual report (2003), p. 23. www.pfizer.com

Exhibit 8.11 Flexibility in the income statement

(a) WACHOVIA CORPORATION AND SUBSIDIARIES

CONSOLIDATED STATEMENTS OF INCOME

	Years Ended December 31,		
(In millions, except per share data)	2003	2002	2001
INTEREST INCOME			
Interest and fees on loans	$ 9,507	10,296	10,537
Interest and dividends on securities	3,828	3,675	3,534
Trading account interest	724	711	760
Other interest income	1,021	950	1,269
Total interest income	15,080	15,632	16,100
INTEREST EXPENSE			
Interest on deposits	2,360	3,430	4,744
Interest on short-term borrowings	1,219	1,105	1,736
Interest on long-term debt	894	1,142	1,845
Total interest expense	4,473	5,677	8,325
Net interest income	10,607	9,955	7,775
Provision for loan losses	586	1,479	1,947
Net interest income after provision for loan losses	10,021	8,476	5,828
FEE AND OTHER INCOME			
Service charges	1,731	1,698	1,361
Other banking fees	979	945	806
Commissions	2,355	1,783	1,482
Fiduciary and asset management fees	2,258	1,885	1,725
Advisory, underwriting and other investment banking fees	812	681	500
Trading account profits (losses)	85	(109)	345
Principal investing	(139)	(266)	(707)
Securities gains (losses)	45	169	(67)
Other income	1,268	1,087	851
Total fee and other income	9,394	7,873	6,296
NONINTEREST EXPENSE			
Salaries and employee benefits	7,708	6,597	5,810
Occupancy	851	786	730
Equipment	1,021	946	879
Advertising	160	80	66
Communications and supplies	586	545	480
Professional and consulting fees	457	421	359
Goodwill and other intangible amortization	518	628	523
Merger-related and restructuring expenses	443	387	106
Sundry expense	1,448	1,286	877
Total noninterest expense	13,192	11,676	9,830
Minority interest in income of consolidated subsidiaries	143	6	1
Income before income taxes and cumulative effect of a change in accounting principle	6,080	4,667	2,293
Income taxes	1,833	1,088	674
Income before cumulative effect of a change in accounting principle	4,247	3,579	1,619
Cumulative effect of a change in accounting principle, net of income taxes	17	–	–
Net income	4,264	3,579	1,619
Dividends on preferred stock	5	19	6
Net income available to common stockholders	$ 4,259	3,560	1,613

Source: Wachavia Corporation, Annual Report, 2003, p. 79.

(b) COLGATE-PALMOLIVE

For the years ended December 31,	2003	2002	2001
Net sales	$ 9,903.4	$ 9,294.3	$ 9,084.3
Cost of sales	4,456.1	4,224.2	4,234.9
Gross profit	5,447.3	5,070.1	4,849.4
Selling, general and administrative expenses	3,296.3	3,034.0	2,920.1
Other (income) expense, net	(15.0)	23.0	94.5
Operating profit	2,166.0	2,013.1	1,834.8
Interest expense, net	124.1	142.8	166.1
Income before income taxes	2,041.9	1,870.3	1,668.7
Provision for income taxes	620.6	582.0	522.1
Net income	$ 1,421.3	$ 1,288.3	$ 1,146.6
Earnings per common share, basic	$ 2.60	$ 2.33	$ 2.02
Earnings per common share, diluted	$ 2.46	$ 2.19	$ 1.89

15. Supplemental Income Statement Information

Other (Income) Expense, Net	2003	2002	2001
Minority interest	$ 45.2	$ 41.3	$ 40.1
Amortization of intangible assets	12.3	12.5	68.0
Equity losses/(income)	(.3)	.6	(.2)
Gain on sales of non-core product lines, net	(107.2)	–	(10.8)
Restructing activities	59.3	–	–
Other, net	(24.3)	(31.4)	(2.6)
	$ (15.0)	$ 23.0	$ 94.5

Interest Expense, Net	2003	2002	2001
Interest incurred	$ 132.1	$ 158.2	$ 192.4
Interest capitalized	(4.0)	(7.4)	(14.4)
Interest income	(4.0)	(8.0)	(11.9)
	$ 124.1	$ 142.8	$ 166.1
Research and development	$ 204.8	$ 196.6	$ 184.9
Media advertising	$ 514.0	$ 486.6	$ 509.0

Source: Colgate-Palmolive, Annual Report, 2003, pp. 28, 44.

A particular feature of the income statement is the separate disclosure of the results of discontinued operations. IFRS 5 is mostly comparable to SFAS 144 *Accounting for the impairment or disposal of long-lived assets*. The US rules are less restrictive on the definition of a discontinued operation and require information on pre-tax and post-tax income.[26] Historically the the US practice (under APB Opinion No. 30 in 1973) predated the first international standard on the subject in 1992 and probably influenced it, There may be discussion to accompany the financial statement disclosure, as in US Bancorp (see Exhibit 8.12).

| Exhibit 8.12 | Reporting the results of discontinued operations: US Bancorp |

Note 4: Discontinued Operations

On February 19, 2003, the Company announced that its Board of Directors approved a plan to effect a distribution of its capital markets business unit, including the investment banking and brokerage activities primarily conducted by its wholly-owned subsidiary, Piper Jaffray Companies. On December 31, 2003, the Company completed the distribution of all the outstanding shares of common stock of Piper Jaffray Companies to its shareholders. This non-cash distribution was tax-free to the Company, its shareholders and Piper Jaffray Companies. In connection with the December 31, 2003 distribution, the results of Piper Jaffray Companies are reported in the Company's Consolidated Statement of Income separately as discontinued operations.

The following table represents the condensed results of operations for discontinued operations:

Year Ended December 31 (Dollars in Millions)	2003	2002	2001
Revenue	$783.4	$729.0	$800.8
Noninterest expense	716.5	760.3	870.3
Income (loss) from discontinued operations	66.9	(31.3)	(69.5)
Costs of disposal (a)	27.6	–	–
Income taxes (benefit)	16.8	(8.6)	(24.3)
Discontinued operations, net of tax	$ 22.5	$(22.7)	$ (45.2)

(a) The $27.6 million of disposal costs related to discontinued operations primarily represents legal, investment banking and other costs directly related to the distribution.

The distribution was treated as a dividend to shareholders for accounting purposes and, as such, reduced the Company's retained earnings by $685 million. At December 31, 2003, the Consolidated Balance Sheet reflects the non-cash dividend and corresponding reduction in assets and liabilities at that date. In accordance with accounting principles generally accepted in the United States, the Consolidated Balance Sheet for 2002 has not been restated. A summary of the assets and liabilities of the discontinued operations is as follows:

December 31 (Dollars in Millions)	2003	2002
Assets		
Cash and cash equivalents	$ 382	$ 271
Trading securities	656	463
Loans	—	2
Goodwill	306	306
Other assets (a)	1,025	954
Total assets	$2,369	$1,996

---

[26] IAS Plus, *Key Differences Between IFRS and US GAAP*, June 2004.

Liabilities		
Deposits	$ 6	$ 7
Short-term borrowings	905	707
Long-term debt	180	215
Other liabilities (b)	593	458
Total liabilities	$1,684	$1,387

(a) Includes customer margin account receivables, due from brokers/dealers and other assets.
(b) Includes accrued expenses, due to brokers/dealers and other liabilities.

Following the distribution, the Company's wholly-owned subsidiary, USB Holdings, Inc. holds a $180 million subordinated debt facility with Piper Jaffray & Co., a broker-dealer subsidiary of Piper Jaffray Companies. In addition, the Company provides an indemnification in an amount up to $17.5 million with respect to certain specified liabilities primarily resulting from third-party claims relating to research analyst independence and from certain regulatory investigations, as defined in the separation and distribution agreement entered into with Piper Jaffray Companies at the time of the distribution.

Source: US Bancorp annual report (2003), p. 73. www.usbank.com

Cash flow statement

The FASB has prescribed the nature of the cash flow statement in SFAS 95. The reconciliation of operating profit and cash flow from operating activities is generally included as part of the statement rather than as a note. The categories within the cash flow statement and the level of disclosure are very similar to those of IAS 7. IAS 7 is flexible on the classification of interest received and paid, while SFAS 95 requires these items to be classified as an operating activity. IAS 7 allows overdrafts to be included in cash if they form an integral part of cash management. SFAS 95 excludes overdrafts from 'cash'.[27]

Statement of changes in shareholders' equity (stockholders' equity)

This statement is required by SFAS 130 but there is considerable variety of presentation. It may include changes in the following components:

- preferred shares,
- common shares (at par value or at stated value),
- additional paid in capital,
- retained earnings,
- treasury shares (repurchased equity),
- valuation gains and losses unrealized (marketable equity securities),
- cumulative translation gains and losses (foreign operations).

SFAS 130, 'Reporting comprehensive income', was issued in 1997. It requires that comprehensive income items which bypass the income statement should be reported in a financial statement, displayed as prominently as any other financial statement. Such items might include foreign currency translation adjustments and gains or losses on certain securities. There is no format specified for this statement of comprehensive income. A similar idea is already established in the UK with a Statement of total recognized

---

[27] IAS Plus, *Key Differences Between IFRS and US GAAP*, June 2004.

gains and losses. IAS 1 requires a statement of changes in equity but does not specify a presentation of comprehensive income. An example of a statement on comprehensive income is provided by AT&T which emphasizes the changes in shareowners' equity (Exhibit 8.13).

Exhibit 8.13 AT&T Corp.: consolidated statements of changes in shareowners' equity

AT&T CORP. AND SUBSIDIARIES
CONSOLIDATED STATEMENTS OF CHANGES IN SHAREOWNERS' EQUITY

	For the Years Ended December 31,		
	2003	2002	2001
	(Dollars in millions)		
AT&T Common Stock			
Balance at beginning of year	$ 783	$ 708	$ 752
Shares issued (acquired), net:			
Under employee plans	7	6	3
For acquisitions	–	–	9
Settlement of put option	–	–	31
For exchange of AT&T Wireless tracking stock	–	–	(74)
For funding AT&T Canada obligation	–	46	–
Redemption of TCI Pacific preferred stock	–	10	–
Other	2	13	(13)
Balance at end of year	792	783	708
AT&T Wireless Group Common Stock			
Balance at beginning of year	–	–	362
Shares issued:			
Under employee plans	–	–	2
For exchange of AT&T Wireless tracking stock	–	–	438
Conversion of preferred stock	–	–	406
AT&T Wireless Group split-off	–	–	(1,208)
Balance at end of year	–	–	–
Liberty Media Group Class A Common Stock			
Balance at beginning of year	–	–	2,364
Shares issued (acquired), net	–	–	14
Liberty Media Group split-off	–	–	(2,378)
Balance at end of year	–	–	–
Liberty Media Group Class B Common Stock			
Balance at beginning of year	–	–	206
Shares issued (acquired), net	–	–	6
Liberty Media Group split-off	–	–	(212)
Balance at end of year	–	–	–
Additional Paid-In Capital			
Balance at beginning of year	28,163	54,798	93,504
Shares issued (acquired), net:			
Under employee plans	123	328	291
For acquisitions	–	–	862
Settlement of put option	–	–	3,361
For funding AT&T Canada obligation	–	2,485	–

▶

Redemption of TCI Pacific preferred stock	–	2,087	–
Other*	36	31	(1,054)
Gain on issuance of common stock by affiliates	–	–	20
Conversion of preferred stock	–	–	9,631
AT&T Wireless Group split-off	–	–	(20,955)
Liberty Media Group split-off	–	–	(30,768)
AT&T Broadband spin-off	–	(31,032)	–
Exchange of AT&T Wireless tracking stock	–	–	(284)
Beneficial conversion value of preferred stock	–	–	295
Dividends declared – AT&T Common Stock Group	(670)	(569)	(265)
Other	70	35	160
Balance at end of year	27,722	28,163	54,798
(Accumulated Deficit) Retained Earnings			
Balance at beginning of year	(16,566)	(3,484)	7,408
Net income (loss)	1,865	(13,082)	7,715
Dividends declared — AT&T Common Stock Group	–	–	(275)
Dividends accrued — preferred stock	–	–	(652)
Premium on exchange of AT&T Wireless tracking stock	–	–	(80)
Treasury shares issued less than cost	(6)	–	(7)
AT&T Wireless Group split-off	–	–	(17,593)
Balance at end of year	(14,707)	(16,566)	(3,484)
Accumulated Other Comprehensive Income (Loss)			
Balance at beginning of year	(68)	(342)	(1,398)
Other comprehensive income	217	266	1,742
AT&T Wireless Group split-off	–	–	72
Liberty Media Group split-off	–	–	(758)
AT&T Broadband spin-off	–	8	–
Balance at end of year	149	(68)	(342)
Total Shareowners' Equity	$13,956	$12,312	$51,680
Summary of Total Comprehensive Income (Loss):			
Income (loss) before cumulative effect of accounting changes	1,850	(12,226)	6,811
Cumulative effect of accounting changes	15	(856)	904
Net income (loss)	1,865	(13,082)	7,715
Other comprehensive income [net of income taxes of $ (134), $ (169) and $ (1,119)]	217	266	1,742
Total Comprehensive Income (Loss)	$ 2,082	$(12,816)	$ 9,457

AT&T accounts for treasury stock as retired stock. The amounts attributable to treasury stock at December 31, 2003 and 2002, were $(17,026) million and $(17,037) million, respectively.
We have 100 million authorized shares of preferred stock at $1 par value.
*Other activity in 2001 represents AT&T common stock received in exchange for entities owning cable systems.

Source: AT&T Corp., annual report (2003), pp. 36–37. www.att.com

8.7.2.3 Notes to the accounts

There are extensive requirements for notes to the accounts. Cross-referencing from the primary financial statements to the notes is not always clear so that the reader is obliged on occasions to work backwards from the notes rather than forwards from the financial statements. Notes to the accounts may result from FASB standards, SEC regulations, AICPA guidance and other parts of the collection of 'US GAAP'.

Extensive disclosures are required regarding financial instruments and derivative financial instruments, covering many aspects of treasury management within the company. Notes to the accounts give detailed information on the costs of post-retirement benefits, including pensions. Employee stock option plans are described in the notes. Contingent losses and liabilities are reported in the notes where they are reasonably possible. If they are probable, then they must be included in the primary financial statements. SFAS 5 defines 'probable' and 'possible'. Environmental liabilities are to be disclosed, although substantial management judgement is needed in deciding the precise nature of the disclosure. Another important area of disclosure is that of related party transactions where 'related parties' are subject to a wide definition.

8.7.2.4 Earnings per share

The FASB issued SFAS 128, 'Earnings per share' in March 1997. It was the result of an intention to simplify existing standards in the USA and make these compatible with international standards. SFAS 128 requires that entities with simple capital structures present a single figure of 'earnings per common share' on the face of the income statement, whereas those with complex capital structures should present both primary and fully diluted earnings per share.

There had been criticism that the former standard, APB Opinion no. 15, was arbitrary and unnecessarily complex. Although it required companies to report the primary earnings per share and the fully diluted earnings per share, in practice the disclosure note on earnings per share was often of considerable length because the earnings per share figure was reported separately for each class of share and, in each case, before and after discontinued operations. Earnings per share figures were also reported separately for income before extraordinary items, for extraordinary items alone, and for cumulative effects of accounting changes. This variety and detail may have provided an example of professionalism meeting a variety of user needs but in practice it appears to have created potential overload of information. An example of the former complexity of the earnings per share disclosure is provided in the extract from General Motors contrasting the report for 1996 with that of 2003 (see Exhibit 8.14).

There was at one stage a difference of opinion between the FASB and the IASC on the approach to be taken in calculating the fully diluted earnings per share (EPS). The FASB took the view that diluted earnings per share was information on past performance which had predictive value as indirect input to a predictive process. The IASC initially took the view that fully diluted earnings per share provided a forward-looking warning signal. It tried to accommodate both approaches in E 52, but after receiving comment moved towards the US position in issuing IAS 33 in 1997. That in turn allowed the FASB to harmonize by issuing SFAS 128. Differences remain in the US requiring disclosure of more varieties of EPS (considered by IASB in the Improvements Project), in a different calculation of year-to-date diluted EPS (where FASB is considering moving to the IASB approach) and the treatment of contracts that may be settled in ordinary shares or in cash, at the issuer's option (where IASB planned to move to the US approach but then retained its position in the Improvements Project, pending further discussion with FASB.[28]

---

[28] IAS Plus Special Edition, June 2004, p. 12.

Exhibit 8.14   General Motors: earnings per share disclosure

(a) As presented in 1996

Earnings attributable to common stocks (Note 20)	1996	1995	1994
$1-2/3 par value from continuing operations before cumulative effect of accounting changes	$4,589	$5,404	$4,296
Income (loss) from discontinued operations (Note 2)	(5)	105	349
Cumulative effect of accounting changes (Note 1)	–	(52)	(751)
Net earnings attributable to $1-2/3 par value	$4,584	$5,457	$3,894
Income from discontinued operations attributable to Class E (Note 2)	$15	$795	$444
Class H before cumulative effect of accounting change	$283	$265	$249
Cumulative effect of accounting change (Note 1)	–	–	(7)
Net earnings attributable to Class H	$283	$265	$242

Average number of shares of common stocks outstanding (in millions)			
$1-2/3 par value	756	750	741
Class E (Notes 2 and 20)	470	405	260
Class H	98	96	92

Earnings per share attributable to common stocks (Note 20)			
$1-2/3 par value from continuing operations before cumulative effect of accounting changes	$6.07	$7.14	$5.74
Income (loss) from discontinued operations (Note 2)	(0.01)	0.14	0.46
Cumulative effect of accounting changes (Note 1)	–	(0.07)	(1.05)
Net earnings attributable to $1-2/3 par value	$6.06	$7.21	$5.15
Income from discontinued operations attributable to Class E (Note 2)	$0.04	$1.96	$1.71
Class H before cumulative effect of accounting change	$2.88	$2.77	$2.70
Cumulative effect of accounting change (Note 1)	–	–	(0.08)
Net earnings attributable to Class H	$2.88	$2.77	$2.62

Reference should be made to the notes to consolidated financial statements.

Source: General Motors, annual report (1996), p. 59.

(b) As presented in 2003

	2003	2002	2001
Basic earnings (loss) per share attributable to common stocks			
$1-2/3 par value			
Continuing operations	$ 5.10	$ 3.53	$ 2.21
Discontinued operations	$ 2.14	$ (0.16)	$ (0.42)
Earnings per share attributable to $1-2/3 par value	$ 7.24	$ 3.37	$ 1.79
(Losses) per share from discontinued operations attributable to Class H	$ (0.22)	$ (0.21)	$ (0.55)
Earnings (loss) per share attributable to common stocks assuming dilution			
$1-2/3 par value			
Continuing operations	$ 5.03	$ 3.51	$ 2.20
Discontinued operations	$ 2.11	$ (0.16)	$ (0.43)
Earnings per share attributable to $1-2/3 par value	$ 7.14	$ 3.35	$ 1.77
(Losses) per share from discontinued operations attributable to Class H	$ (0.22)	$ (0.21)	$ (0.55)

Source: General Motors annual report (2003), p. 65. www.gm.com

8.7.3 Assets and liabilities

8.7.3.1 Capitalization of borrowing costs

SFAS 34 requires that borrowing costs are normally reported through the income statement. However, in specific circumstances the interest cost may be added to the asset cost (referred to as capitalization of borrowing costs) in order to obtain a measure of acquisition cost that more closely reflects the enterprise's total investment in the asset. Capitalization is also used so as to charge a cost that relates to the acquisition of a resource that will benefit future periods against the revenues of the periods benefited. In the circumstances set out in SFAS 34 the capitalization is mandatory (compulsory). The types of asset to which borrowing costs may be attached are assets under construction or completed investments intended for sale or lease. In contrast, IAS 23 makes capitalization available as a policy choice, without compulsion. This difference is not included in the short-term convergence project.

8.7.3.2 Capitalization of software development costs

SFAS 86 requires that, after technological feasibility has been established, there must be capitalization of all costs incurred for a computer software product that is sold, leased or otherwise marketed. The standard also sets methods for amortization. The Accounting Standards Executive Committee has issued Statement of Position 98-1 *Accounting for the Costs of Computer Software Developed For or Obtained For Internal Use*. The SoP changes previous practice which was to treat such items as an expense of the period. IASB standards do not include this type of industry-specific standard. Exhibit 8.15 (Wal-Mart) shows how the company reported the new accounting policy on the first occasion that it was applied.

8.7.3.3 Depreciation

The definition of depreciation has a long history from ARB 43, emphasizing the allocation of cost. ARB 43 specifically stated that it was a process of allocation, not valuation. For income tax purposes, many companies use accelerated depreciation (as allowed by SFAS 109) but this is used relatively rarely in the published accounts of listed companies. One case, showing use of accelerated depreciation as a means of dealing crudely with the additional cost of asset replacement, is General Motors, giving the explanation set out in Exhibit 8.16.

Exhibit 8.15   Wal-Mart: capitalization of software costs

> **Costs of computer software**
> During fiscal 2000, the Company adopted the Accounting Standards Executive Committee Statement of Position (SOP) 98-1. 'Accounting For the Costs of Computer Software Developed For or Obtained For Internal Use.' This SOP requires the capitalization of certain costs incurred in connection with developing or obtaining software for internal use. Previously, costs related to developing internal-use software were expensed as incurred. Under the new method these costs are capitalized and amortized over a three year life. The impact of the adoption of SOP 98-1 was to capitalize $27 million and $32 million of costs in fiscal 2001 and 2000, respectively, which would have previously been expensed. The impact of the change would not have a material effect on fiscal 1999.

Source: Wal-Mart Stores, Inc., annual report (2000), p. 28. www.wal-mart.com

---

| Exhibit 8.16 | General Motors: accounting policies (extract) |

Depreciation and Amortization

Expenditures for special tools placed in service after January 1, 2002 are amortized using the straight-line method over their estimated useful lives. Expenditures for special tools placed in service prior to January 1, 2002 are amortized over their estimated useful lives, primarily using the units of production method. Replacements of special tools for reasons other than changes in products are charged directly to cost of sales. As of January 1, 2001, the Corporation adopted the straight-line method of depreciation for real estate, plants, and equipment placed in service after that date. Assets placed in service before January 1, 2001 continue generally to be depreciated using accelerated methods. The accelerated methods accumulate depreciation of approximately two thirds of the depreciable cost during the first half of the estimated useful lives of property groups as compared to the straight-line method, which allocates depreciable costs equally over the estimated useful lives of property groups. Management believes the adoption of the straight-line amortization/depreciation method for special tools placed into service after January 1, 2002, and real estate, plants, and equipment placed into service after January 1, 2001, better reflects the consistent use of these assets over their useful lives.

Source: General Motors, annual report (2003), p. 65. www.gm.com

Ford Motor Co. changed its depreciation of property and equipment from accelerated methods to straight line from 1 January 1993. This indicates that comparability cannot be assumed, even within the same industry.

8.7.3.4 Valuation of tangible fixed assets

The prohibition on revaluation of fixed assets dates from ARB 43 and APB 6. It is consistent with the cost model permitted by IAS 16. The prohibition on revaluation extends to investment properties. Some real estate companies (property companies) present historical cost accounts but provide supplementary notes on current value information.

8.7.3.5 Impairment of assets

There is more interest in reduction in the value of fixed assets, referred to as impairment. The current regulation is found in SFAS 144 *Accounting for the impairment or disposal of long-lived assets*. Previous rules in APB 4 and then SFAS 121 were not clear on when and by how much an impairment should be recognized. The test for impairment in SFAS 144 requires that an impairment loss should be recognized if, and only if, the sum of the future *undiscounted* cash flows is less than the carrying amount of the asset. This caused difficulty for the IASC core standards project because the IASC Board believed this test carried too high a risk that the recognition of impairment would be delayed. The Board's rule in IAS 36 is to compare the *discounted* cash flows with the carrying amount, causing earlier recognition.

Where impairment is to be recognized, SFAS 144 states that the recoverable amount is fair value defined as the price for sale or purchase of the asset between willing parties. IAS 36 requires that recoverable amount should be based on the higher of net selling price and value in use. In many cases both approaches will lead to the same answer but IAS 36 may sometimes result in a higher recoverable amount based on value in use.

Finally, SFAS 144 prohibits reversal of an impairment loss where the asset value recovers. IAS 36 specifies circumstances where reversal is required. The differences between SFAS 144 and IAS 36 are not being addressed in the short-term convergence project.[29]

8.7.3.6 Intangible assets

'Intangible assets' are stated at historical cost *less* accumulated amortization. For many years APB 17 prescribed straight-line depreciation over a maximum of 40 years. Even in the case of brand names, where it might be argued that the asset life is longer, the view of the standard was that 40 years was the maximum period. All intangible assets were treated in a similar manner. In 1999 the FASB appeared to be considering reducing the maximum period of amortization from 40 years to 20 years to align with the international standards. Then, in a complete turnaround, FASB took a major change of direction resulting in a new standard SFAS 142 *Goodwill and other intangibles*, issued in 2001, replacing amortization by requiring an annual goodwill impairment test. The change to SFAS 142 received high-profile political attention, as explained in section 8.3.4. It appeared that a more flexible approach to amortization had been offered as a 'sweetener' to the abolition of pooling of interest accounting under SFAS 141.

Intangible assets include marketing costs, which may be treated as an asset where there are demonstrable expectations of future economic benefits. An example is provided by Sears, Roebuck and Co. (Exhibit 8.17). Advertising which does not meet the criteria is reported as an expense of the period.

Exhibit 8.17 Sears, Roebuck and Co.: note on advertising and marketing costs

Advertising

Costs for newspaper, television, radio and other media advertising are expensed the first time the advertising occurs. The total cost of advertising charged to expense was $1.63, $1.67 and $1.59 billion in 1999, 1998 and 1997, respectively.

Direct-Response Marketing

The Company direct markets insurance (credit protection, life and health), clubs and services memberships, merchandise through specialty catalogs, and impulse and continuity merchandise. For insurance and clubs and services, deferred revenue is recorded when the member is billed (upon expiration of any free trial period), and revenue is recognized over the insurance or membership period. For specialty catalog, impulse and continuity merchandise, revenue is recognized when merchandise is shipped.

Membership acquisition and renewal costs, which primarily relate to membership solicitations, are capitalized since such direct-response advertising costs result in future economic benefits. Such costs are amortized over the shorter of the program's life or five years, primarily in proportion to when revenues are recognized. For specialty catalogs, costs are amortized over the life of the catalog, not to exceed one year. The consolidated balance sheets include deferred direct-response advertising costs of $180 and $131 million at January 1, 2000, and January 2, 1999, respectively. The current portion is included in prepaid expenses and deferred charges, the long term portion in other assets.

Source: Sears, Roebuck and Co., annual report (1999), p. 31.

---

[29] IAS Plus, *Key Differences Between IFRS and US GAAP*, June 2004.

Under a separate standard, SFAS 2, research and development (R&D) expenditure is one instance of intangible assets where there is a strong element of conservatism that all expenditure should be reported through the income statement as incurred. It has also been suggested that concern about measurement reliability led in this case to rigid uniformity. This is in contrast to IAS 38, which modifies this approach with a requirement that development costs meeting specific criteria should be capitalized. However, as noted in Chapter 2, there has been continued pressure to base the international practice on expense treatment only.

8.7.3.7 Marketable securities

Marketable securities must be carried in the balance sheet at the lower of cost or market value on a portfolio basis. This is conservative in the overall approach, but less conservative in permitting the loss on one investment to be set against a gain on another. Current and non-current investments must be separated. Reductions in value of the current investment portfolio must be taken through the income statement, but those in relation to non-current investments are taken to a separate component of shareholders' equity. SFAS 133 requires disclosure of the fair value of financial instruments where practicable. SFAS 133 is considerably more detailed and rules-based than IAS 39 but both apply the same principles of fair valuation.

8.7.3.8 Inventory and long-term contracts

Valuation of inventory is covered in ARB 43 (1953), requiring the lower of cost or market value. Cost may be determined using a range of techniques which include FIFO, LIFO and average cost. 'Market value' is defined as current replacement cost subject to an upper limit of net realizable value and a lower limit of net realizable value less a normal profit margin. IAS 2 differs in requiring the lower of cost and net realizable value. In a revision that indicated some independence of the IASB from US influence, IAS 2 (2003) prohibits the use of LIFO. Around two-thirds of US companies use LIFO (see, for example, Eastman Kodak, Exhibit 8.18). A strong factor is that the Internal Revenue Service (IRS) requires that if LIFO is used for tax purposes it must be used for financial reporting purposes.

Accounting for long-term contracts is dealt with in ARB 45 (1955). Both percentage of completion and completed contract methods are permitted, although there is a preference expressed for the former. IAS 11 requires percentage of completion. IAS 2 differs from US GAAP in prohibiting the use of LIFO and in permitting a reversal of inventory write-down. These differences are not considered in the short-term convergence project.

8.7.3.9 Financial instruments

SFAS 133, issued in 1996, specifies disclosure rules for derivative financial instruments and hedging activities. SFAS 137 deferred the date of implementation of SFAS 133 to fiscal years beginning after June 2000, to allow companies time to modify their information systems and to issue SFAS 138, effective with SFAS 133. There are hundreds of pages of guidance on SFAS 133 and its related documents. The fundamental principles are (i) derivative instruments should be reported in financial statements because they meet the definitions of assets and liabilities, (ii) fair value is the only relevant measure, (iii) changes in the fair value of derivative instruments are included in net income, and (iv) special accounting for 'hedged' items should be restricted to qualifying items. Changes in the value of 'fair value' hedges are

| Exhibit 8.18 | LIFO inventory valuation, Eastman Kodak |

NOTE 1: SIGNIFICANT ACCOUNTING POLICIES (extract)

Inventories

Inventories are stated at the lower of cost or market. The cost of most inventories in the U.S. is determined by the "last-in, first-out" (LIFO) method. The cost of all of the Company's remaining inventories in and outside the U.S. is determined by the "first-in, first-out" (FIFO) or average cost method, which approximates current cost. The Company provides inventory reserves for excess, obsolete or slow-moving inventory based on changes in customer demand, technology developments or other economic factors.

NOTE 3: INVENTORIES, NET

(in millions)	2003	2002
At FIFO or average cost		
(approximates current cost)		
Finished goods	$ 818	$ 831
Work in process	302	322
Raw materials	317	301
	1,437	1,454
LIFO reserve	(362)	(392)
Total	$1,075	$1,062

Inventories valued on the LIFO method are approximately 41 per cent and 47 per cent of total inventories in 2003 and 2002, respectively. During 2003 and 2002, inventory usage resulted in liquidations of LIFO inventory quantities. In the aggregate, these inventories were carried at the lower costs prevailing in prior years as compared with the cost of current purchases. The effect of these LIFO liquidations was to reduce cost of goods sold by $53 million and $31 million in 2003 and 2002, respectively.

The Company reduces the carrying value of inventories to a lower of cost or market basis for those items that are potentially excess, obsolete or slow-moving based on management's analysis of inventory levels and future sales forecasts. The Company also reduces the carrying value of inventories whose net book value is in excess of market. Aggregate reductions in the carrying value with respect to inventories that were still on hand at December 31, 2003 and 2002, and that were deemed to be excess, obsolete, slow-moving or that had a carrying value in excess of market, were $75 million and $65 million, respectively.

Source: Eastman Kodak, annual report (2003), pp. 46, 51. www.kodak.com

included in net income. 'Other comprehensive income' is used to report changes in the value of 'cash flow' hedges and foreign currency hedges of net investments in a foreign operation. These rules on reporting hedges are similar to IAS 39 but may cause significant adjustments in reconciliations from GAAP in other countries.

8.7.3.10 Off-balance-sheet transactions

Section 8.3.2 explains the concerns raised about Special Purpose Entities (SPEs) following the collapse of Enron. The SPEs were off-balance-sheet (not consolidated as subsidiaries) because an independent third party (defined as a holding of 3 per cent or more of the equity of the SPE) controlled the entity and carried the risks and rewards. Even before Enron there were warnings that 3 per cent seemed a very low level of outside interest. In 2003 a FASB Intepretation (FIN 46) was introduced to clarify the treatment of 'variable interest entities' (as a new description of SPEs). The variable interest could relate to variability of net income or loss, or to variability of fair values of assets. FIN 46 requires the 'primary beneficiary' of the variable interest to consolidate the results of the variable-interest entity. It also specifies disclosures.

However, the SPE is only one example of off-balance-sheet finance. There is no single standard in the US which deals with off-balance-sheet transactions in general terms. Similarly, the IASB has no specific standard on the subject. Various separate FASB standards address specific issues such as sale and repurchase of products and sale of real estate with conditions attached. Disclosures are required about some long-term obligations which establish commitments to future cash outflows. These and other specific standards restrict the scope for off-balance-sheet transactions in particular situations.

FASB standards continue to take a more flexible approach to consolidation of subsidiary companies which does leave scope for assets and liabilities remaining off-balance-sheet. The usual condition for establishing that control exists is ownership of a majority share-holding. There is no concept of 'dominant interest' or of entities which closely resemble subsidiaries (quasi-subsidiaries), although the FASB has a long-term project in progress. Also, as mentioned earlier, joint ventures are generally reported using equity accounting where the investment appears as a single-line item. Proportional consolidation is rare.

8.7.3.11 Deferred taxation

Consistent with the balance sheet approach of the FASB's conceptual framework, SFAS 109 requires the deferred taxation liability to be accounted for on the basis of the full liability which the enterprise will eventually have to meet. A change in the expected liability will result in an expense in the income statement. The move from the earlier APB 11, based on the matching of income and expenses in any accounting period and having little regard to the resulting balance sheet figure, reflects the FASB's intention to move to a balance sheet approach.

8.7.4 Income statement and economic activity

8.7.4.1 Share-based payments

Share-based payments are described in section 2.6.4. In the US they are called 'stock compensation'. Chapter 2 explains that the accounting treatment of share-based payments in IFRS 2 is controversial. The subject has raised similar controversy in the US. Emerging high-tech companies took advantage of the rapidly rising stock market to pay staff in options rather than expend large amounts of cash. These companies were strongly opposed to reporting an expense that would lower profit, or lead to reported losses and so increase the cost of capital.[30] Under APB 25 the employer can choose to measure the cost as the intrinsic value at the date the option is granted. That is generally zero because the market price is below the amount that the employee must pay to acquire shares under the option agreement. SFAS 123 establishes a method of accounting for stock-based compensation that is based on fair value. Because of the strong opposition SFAS 123 encouraged, but did not require, the use of fair value. SFAS 148 provides transition

---

[30] Wolk and Tearney (2004), p. 395.

alternatives for voluntarily measuring compensation using a fair value method. As part of the convergence process between FASB and IFRS, FASB has indicated that it will move towards the fair value approach only, as in IFRS 2.[31]

8.7.4.2 Extraordinary items

There is a debate in measuring profit about the relative merits of the *all-inclusive concept* and the *current operating performance concept*. The all-inclusive concept takes the view that all items affecting owners' equity, except for dividends and capital transactions, should be included in net income. The current operating performance concept takes the view that net income should report normal, recurring items of profit and loss relating only to the current period. In moving towards comprehensive income the FASB appeared to favour the all-inclusive concept. However it also continues to permit separate disclosure of extraordinary items, which reflects the current operating performance concept. US rules permit the separate reporting of extraordinary items, with strict rules for defining these. Extraordinary items are transactions and other events that are (a) material in nature, (b) unusual in nature, and (c) infrequent in occurrence.[32] Extraordinary items are disclosed separately in the income statement, net of tax. Professional judgment is required to identify extraordinary items. Some areas of GAAP require specific items to be treated as extraordinary. The most common items are expropriations of property, gains or losses due to a major casualty, and losses resulting from prohibition under a new law or regulation.

We explained in section 2.2.2 that IAS 1 prohibits extraordinary items. The reasons given[33] indicate that the IASB prefers the all-inclusive concept of profit.

8.7.5 Group accounting

8.7.5.1 Nature of business combinations[34]

The development of group accounting has been described in section 8.3.4. Differences remain between IFRS and US GAAP, particularly on the definition of a subsidiary and on the treatment of Special Purpose Entities.

Under IAS 27 the basis of consolidation policy is control, looking to governance, risks and benefits. Under US GAAP the focus is on majority voting rights. Companies must also consolidate a 'variable interest equity' where the investor is the primary beneficiary based on assessment of risks and rewards.

For SPEs the IFRS applies the same principles as it does to all other commercial entities in determining whether control exists. In the US consolidation depends on the qualifying criteria. The criteria look to whether the SPE has sufficient equity 'at risk'.

Where reporting dates of parent and subsidiaries differ marginally. IFRS requires adjustment for significant intervening transaction, while US GAAP requires disclosure in notes.

If the parent and subsidiary have different accounting policies, IFRS requires them to conform. In US GAAP there is no requirement to conform policies. In parent-company financial statements IAS 27 prohibits the use of the equity method in accounting for investments in subsidiaries. US GAAP allows the equity method. The minority interest is presented in equity under IFRS but between equity and liabilities in US GAAP.

---

[31] IAS Plus, *Key Differences Between IFRS and US GAAP*, June 2004.
[32] APB 30 paragraph 2.
[33] IAS 1 (2003) paragraphs BC14 to BC18.
[34] Ibid.

The IASB has on its agenda a project on consolidation, including Special Purpose Entities. This project extends into the period beyond the 'stable platform'. The project will include consideration of areas where national practices differ from IFRS.

8.7.5.2 Procedures for acquisition accounting[35]

US GAAP allows only the acquisition method in accounting for a business combination. IFRS 3 also deals the with acquisition method. There are some differences in detail that are being considered by FASB and IASB together. The date on which the consideration is measured may be different. IFRS 3 uses the acquisition date (the date on which control passes) while the US GAAP takes the closing date of the deal, which could be later. The measurement of minority interest is different. IFRS 3 takes the minority's percentage of fair values. US GAAP takes the minority's percentage of the book value (carrying amount) in the accounting records of the acquired company. Negative goodwill is recognized immediately as a gain under IFRS 3. The US procedure allocates the negative goodwill by sharing it across certain non-financial assets acquired. Any excess is recognized as an extraordinary gain.

For entities under common control, US GAAP requires the pooling of interests method to be used. IASB did not reach agreement on this issue by the date of the 'stable platform' in March 2004 and has included it in Phase II of the IASB's business combination project. In the meantime merger accounting continues to be used in such circumstances. The intended convergence with IASB standards took a further step in July 2004 with a FASB publication on 'tentative decisions' as an indication of the direction of FASB thinking.[36] This was not an exposure draft and comments were not invited.

8.7.6 Narrative reporting

8.7.6.1 Basic information package

The requirements of the SEC are considerable, and the most convenient starting point is the basic information package (BIP). The five classes of information in the BIP are:

- market price of, and dividends on, common equity, and related security matters;
- selected financial data;
- management's discussion and analysis (MD&A);
- audited financial statements and supplementary data;
- other information.

The information must be presented in its entirety to the SEC, but there are various ways of achieving this. It may all be included in a form 10-K report, which is then a document of considerable length (as much as 100–200 pages) and generally uninteresting appearance (one type of font and no illustrations or graphics). Alternatively, companies may choose to present some or most of the BIP in the annual report to shareholders, with a much reduced form 10-K in which there is a reference to portions of the annual report and the statement for the annual meeting, which are to be read as part of the 10-K filing. Some information required for the 10-K does not normally appear in the annual report, such as lists of legal proceedings being taken against the company, detailed descriptions of the business and detailed description of land and buildings held by the company.

---

[35] IAS 1 (2003) paragraphs BC 14 to BC 18.
[36] FASB (2004b).

Other information may be included in the proxy statement which accompanies the notice to shareholders convening the annual general meeting. In particular, there is more about directors – their remuneration package ('compensation'); the report of the remuneration committee; information on related-party transactions; and share performance over a period of time. An example is provided by Wal-Mart Stores (Exhibit 8.19).

Exhibit 8.19 Wal-Mart Stores, Inc.: proxy statement (extracts)

SUMMARY COMPENSATION

This table shows the compensation paid during each of the Company's last three fiscal years to Wal-Mart's CEO and the four other most highly compensated executive officers, based on compensation earned during the fiscal year ended January 31, 2004.

Name and position		Annual compensation			Long-term compensation		
	Fiscal year ended Jan. 31,	Salary ($)(1)	Incentive payment ($)(2)	Other annual compensation ($)(3)	Restricted stock awards ($)(4)	Number of Shares underlying options granted (5)	All other compensation ($)(6)
H. Lee Scott, Jr.	2004	1,192,308	4,200,000	82,861	6,700,026	630,413	269,595
President and CEO	2003	1,142,308	3,162,500	85,834	13,134,437	605,327	167,604
	2002	1,123,077	1,784,750	94,682	5,000,000	521,634	133,328
Thomas M. Coughlin	2004	983,894	2,879,565	54,584	2,000,001	279,355	252,082
Vice Chairman of the Board	2003	907,308	2,287,500	40,801	4,211,461	261,832	157,010
	2002	885,769	935,929	45,410	875,000	220,175	152,193
John B. Menzer							
Executive Vice President	2004	816,538	1,856,249	0	1,749,981	225,403	267,013
and President and CEO,	2003	759,231	1,540,000	0	2,605,747	211,865	169,679
International Division	2002	717,308	838,927	0	1,000,000	179,212	72,928
Thomas M. Schoewe	2004	610,384	984,000	0	999,974	119,779	87,324
Executive Vice President	2003	579,615	819,000	0	1,995,190	114,242	55,385
and Chief Financial Officer	2002	561,539	499,730	0	900,000	102,407	45,047
Michael T. Duke							
Executive Vice President and	2004	603,029	852,342	0	999,974	374,050	114,165
President and CEO, Wal-Mart	2003	530,385	749,000	0	1,829,341	110,335	77,085
Stores Division	2002	519,616	458,843	0	750,000	102,407	64,428

(1) This column includes compensation earned during the fiscal year, but some amounts may be deferred. This column also includes compensation for an additional pay period in fiscal year 2002 because fiscal year 2002 had 27 pay periods rather than the normal 26 pay periods.

(2) Incentive payments in this column were made under the MIP in connection with the Company's performance in the January 31, 2002, 2003, and 2004 fiscal years, but were paid during the January 31, 2003, 2004, and 2005 fiscal years, respectively.

(3) The other annual compensation for H. Lee Scott, Jr. includes $82,501 for personal use of a Company aircraft. The other annual compensation for Thomas M. Coughlin includes $49,769 for incentive interest payments on amounts deferred under the ODC Plan. For the other named executive officers, the amounts do not include the value of perquisites and other personal benefits because they do not exceed the lesser of $50,000 or ten percent of any such officer's total annual salary and bonus.

(4) The amounts in this column for fiscal year 2004 include a restricted stock award made on January 5, 2004. While the 2004 restricted stock award occurred during fiscal year 2004, it relates to compensation for the named officers for fiscal year 2005. The amounts in this column for fiscal year 2003 include two restricted stock awards that occurred on March 7, 2002 and January 9, 2003. With respect to the award that occurred on January 9, 2003, the Company awarded restricted stock to the named executive officers in the following amounts: H. Lee Scott, Jr. ($6,500,021), Thomas M. Coughlin ($2,000,010), John B. Menzer ($1,500,021), Thomas M. Schoewe ($1,000,031), and Michael T. Duke ($1,000,031) (the "January Restricted Stock"). While the January Restricted Stock award occurred during fiscal year 2003, it relates to compensation for the named executive officers for fiscal year 2004.

Listed below are the total number of shares of restricted stock owned by each of the following named executives as of January 31, 2004, and the total values thereof based on the market value of the Company's Shares on January 31, 2004: H. Lee Scott, Jr., 674,953 shares of restricted stock ($36,346,219); Thomas M. Coughlin, 292,849 shares of restricted stock ($15,769,919); John B. Menzer, 214,411 shares of restricted stock ($11,546,032); Thomas M. Schoewe 155,726 shares of restricted stock ($8,385,845); and Michael T. Duke 126,049 shares of restricted stock ($6,787,739). Holders of shares of restricted stock receive the same cash dividends as other shareholders owning Shares.

(5) The options shown for 2004 were granted on January 5, 2004.

(6) "All other compensation" for the fiscal year ended January 31, 2004 includes Company contributions to the PS and 401(k) Plan, SERP, above-market interest credited on deferred compensation, and term life insurance premiums paid by Wal-Mart for the benefit of each officer. These amounts are shown in the following table:

Name	PS and 401(k) Plan	SERP contributions	Above-market interest	Life insurance premiums
H. Lee Scott, Jr.	$8,000	$175,062	$ 86,433	$100
Thomas M. Coughlin	$8,000	$129,415	$114,567	$100
John B, Menzer	$8,000	$ 90,869	$168,044	$100
Thomas M. Schoewe	$8,000	$ 51,796	$ 27,428	$100
Michael T. Duke	$8,000	$ 48,549	$ 57,516	$100

RELATED-PARTY TRANSACTIONS

During fiscal year 2004, companies owned by S. Robson Walton, a director, executive officer and beneficial owner of more than five percent of the Shares, John T. Walton, a director and beneficial owner of more than five percent of the Shares, and by Alice L. Walton, Jim C. Walton and Helen R. Walton, each a beneficial owner of more than five percent of the Shares, paid a total of $327,092 to Wal-Mart and its subsidiaries for aviation-related expenses, substantially all of which was for maintenance and fuel at fair market value, as determined by comparable charges to unrelated third parties.

Frank C. Robson, the brother of Helen R. Walton, leased four store locations to Wal-Mart. Wal-Mart paid rent and other expenses of $1,779,049 under the leases for the fiscal year 2004.

During fiscal year 2004, Wal-Mart paid companies owned by John T. Walton, Jim C. Walton, and Helen R. Walton a total of $2,218,393 for commercial products to be sold to the general public by Wal-Mart and its affiliates.

During fiscal year 2004, a banking corporation and its affiliates, collectively owned by Helen R. Walton, S. Robson Walton, John T. Walton, and Jim C. Walton, made payments to Wal-Mart in the amount of $528,294 for banking facility rent and related Automatic Teller Machine surcharges. The banking corporation and its affiliates made additional payments to Wal-Mart pursuant to similar arrangements awarded by Wal-Mart on a competitive-bid basis.

Exhibit 8.19 *(Continued)*

During fiscal year 2004, Springdale Card & Comic Wholesale, which is owned by the son of David D. Glass, a director and executive officer of Wal-Mart, had sales to Mal-Mart in the amount of $2,931,235.

James W. Breyer, a director of Wal-Mart, beneficially owns more than ten percent of the equity of Groove Networks, Inc. During fiscal year 2004, Groove Networks, Inc. provided to Wal-Mart computer software and services in the amount of $1,462,378.

Greg B. Penner, a Senior Vice President of Wal-Mart, is the son-in-law of S. Robson Walton. For fiscal year 2004, Wal-Mart paid Mr. Penner a salary of $268,842 and a bonus of $222,254. Mr. Penner also received a grant of options to purchase 8,732 Shares at an exercise price of $52.40 per Share. In addition, Wal-Mart paid Mr. Penner $246,118 during fiscal year 2004 under an arrangement to repurchase his options of Wal-Mart.com, which Wal-Mart acquired in 2001.

Timothy E. Coughlin, a Regional Loss Prevention Director of Wal-Mart, is the brother of Thomas M. Coughlin, a director and executive officer of Wal-Mart. For fiscal year 2004, Wal-Mart paid Timothy E. Coughlin a salary of $81,139 and a bonus of $19,584. He also received a grant of options to purchase 779 Shares at an exercise price of $52.40 per Share.

Stephen P. Weber, a manager in Wal-Mart's Information System Division, is the son-in-law of Michael T. Duke, an executive officer of Wal-Mart. For fiscal year 2004, Wal-Mart paid Mr. Weber a salary of $67,692 and a bonus of $13,852. Mr. Weber also received a grant of options to purchase 344 Shares and 763 Shares at respective exercise prices of $58.10 and $52.40 per Share.

Christopher J. Williams, a director nominee, is the Chairman of the Board and Chief Executive Officer of The Williams Capital Group, L.P., which company was engaged by Wal-Mart during fiscal year 2004 in customary investment banking services.

Wal-Mart believes that the terms of all of the foregoing transactions are comparable to terms that would have been reached by unrelated parties in arms-length transactions.

STOCK PERFORMANCE CHART

This graph shows Wal-Mart's cumulative total shareholder return during the five fiscal years ended January 31, 2004. The graph also shows the cumulative total returns of the S&P 500 Index and the S&P 500 Retailing Index. The comparison assumes $100 was invested on January 31, 1999 in Shares and in each of the indices shown and assumes that all of the dividends are reinvested.

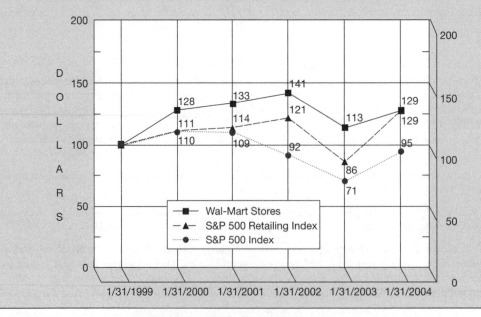

Source: Wal-Mart Stores, Inc., proxy statement (2003), pp. 15, 20–22. www.wal-mart.com

Motorola (2003) illustrates the importance of reading the Form 10-K as well as the annual report The annual report provides only highlights of the financial statements. Full details of financial statements and notes are in the Form 10-K.

It is essential for the interested reader to request the annual report, the 10-K filing and the proxy statement in order to have the benefit of the full BIP intended by the SEC. The main features of each section of the BIP are as follows.

Market price of, and dividends on, common equity, and related security matters

This provides investors with information including the markets in which the stock is traded, the quarterly share price for the past two years, the approximate number of ordinary shareholders, and the frequency and amount of dividends paid over the past two years.

Selected financial data

This is intended to highlight key items including the net sales or operating revenue, income or loss from continuing operations, income (in total and per share) and total assets.

Management's discussion and analysis

The MD&A is explained in more detail in the next section.

Audited financial statements and supplementary data

The company must present income statements and statements of cash flow in respect of the current period and the previous two years. Balance sheets must be presented at the year-end and for the previous year-end. Notes to the accounts are also required.

Other information

This is quite substantial, and covers a brief description of the business; major operating developments such as acquisitions of assets or bankruptcies of parts of the organization; segment information; description of major properties currently owned; description of major active legal proceedings; information about management such as background, remuneration, and major transactions between management and the company; and selected industry-specific disclosures, such as for banking, insurance and other regulated industries.

8.7.6.2 Management discussion and analysis

The management discussion and analysis (MD&A) is a report required by Regulation S-K of the SEC. The full title is the 'Management's discussion and analysis of financial condition and results of operations'. It is one of the most important disclosures made by the company. The full version will in many cases be printed in the annual report. Some companies give an edited summary in the financial report, referring the reader to the 10-K registration for the fuller version.

A flexible format is permitted for the MD&A, but the following five items must be covered:

- specific information about the company's liquidity, capital resources and results of operations;
- the impact of inflation and changing prices on net sales and revenues and on income from continuing operations;

- material changes in line items of the consolidated financial statements compared with the prior-period amount;
- known material events and uncertainties that may make historical financial information not indicative of future operations or future conditions;
- any other information the company believes necessary for an understanding of its financial condition, changes in financial condition, and results of operations.

Although a flexible format is permitted, practice has tended to converge on repetitive and stereotyped paragraphs where the US-resident companies do not always score as highly as foreign registrants seeking to make their mark.[37]

The reference to 'future operations and future conditions' reflects a desire of the SEC to give a forward-looking aspect to the MD&A. The encouragement to give forward-looking information is backed by a 'Safe Harbor' Law which is intended to protect forward-looking statements made in good faith (see section 8.7.1.2).

See also section 15.3.

8.7.6.3 Critical accounting estimates

In a release dated December 2003,[38] the SEC reminded companies of the importance of providing disclosures about critical accounting estimates or assumptions in their MD&A. There had been a previous reminder, in 2001,[39] that under the MD&A requirements at that time companies should address material implications of uncertainties associated with the methods, assumptions and estimates underlying the company's critical accounting measurements. Proposals were made in May 2002 to broaden the rules for such disclosure but these proposals remained under consideration at 2004.

The guidance to companies is that they should consider whether they have made accounting estimates or assumptions which are material in nature and in impact. The additional disclosures should supplement, not duplicate, the description of accounting policies already given in the notes to the financial statements. Exhibit 8.20 shows how American International Group, an insurance company, explains its critical accounting estimates which are in the specific areas of uncertainty relating to insurance risks.

8.7.6.4 Segment reporting

In June 1997 the FASB issued SFAS 131 *Disclosures about segments of an enterprise and related information*. It superseded SFAS 14, which had for some years required segmental disclosure of turnover, profits and assets analysed by industry and geographical segments. SFAS 14, in turn, had been prompted by earlier requirements of the SEC in relation to reports filed on form 10-K. The move to SFAS 131 was prompted by an emerging debate on the definition of segments. The view in the US and Canada has been that the enterprise should be allowed to base segments on the organizational structure of the enterprise, even where such segments cover more than one industry or geographical area. The IASC had, at one stage in its discussion, preferred to concentrate on diversity of industry and geography which requires

---

[37] Collins *et al.* (1993).
[38] SEC (2003).
[39] SEC (2001).

| Exhibit 8.20 | Disclosure of critical accounting estimates, American International Group |

AIG considers its most critical accounting estimates those with respect to reserves for losses and loss expenses, future policy benefits for life and accident and health contracts, deferred policy acquisition costs, and fair value determinations for certain Capital Markets assets and liabilities. These accounting estimates require the use of assumptions about matters, some of which are highly uncertain at the time of estimation. To the extent actual experience differs from the assumptions used, AIG's results for operations would be directly impacted.

Throughout this Management's Discussion and Analysis of Financial Condition and Results of Operations, AIG's critical accounting estimates are discussed in detail. The major categories for which assumptions are developed and used to establish each critical accounting estimate are highlighted below.

Reserves for Losses and Loss Expenses (General Insurance):
- *Loss trend factors:* used to establish expected loss ratios for subsequent accident years based on the projected loss ratio with respect to prior accident years.

- *Expected loss ratios for the latest accident year:* in this case, accident year 2003 for the year end 2003 loss reserve analysis. For low frequency, high severity classes such as Excess Casualty and Directors and Officers' Liability, expected loss ratios generally are utilized for at least the three most recent accident years.

- *Loss development factors:* used to project the reported losses for each accident year to an ultimate amount.

Future Policy Benefits for Life and Accident and Health Contracts (Life Insurance):
- *Interest rates:* which vary by territory, year of issuance and products.

- *Mortality, morbidity and surrender rates*: based upon actual experience by geographical region modified to allow for variation in policy form.

Deferred Policy Acquisition Costs (General Insurance):
- Recoverability based upon the current profitability of the underlying insurance contracts.

Life Insurance and Retirement Services & Asset. Management:
- *Estimated gross profits:* to be realized over the estimated duration of the contracts (non-traditional life). Estimated gross profits include investment income and gains and losses on investments less required interest, actual mortality and other expenses.

Fair Value Determinations of Certain Assets and Liabilities (Financial Services—Capital Markets):
- *Valuation models:* utilizing factors, such as market liquidity and current interest, foreign exchange and volatility rates.

- AIG attempts to secure reliable and independent current market price date, such as published exchange rates from external subscription services such as Bloomberg or Reuters or third party broker quotes for use in this model. When such prices are not available, AIG uses an internal methodology, which includes interpolation or extrapolation from verifiable prices from trades occurring on dates nearest to the dates of the transactions.

Source: American International Group, Form 10-k, pages 19–20.

segmental analysis on this basis. The resulting revision of IAS 14 was a compromise which accommodated the position in SFAS 131, but left some flexibility for other countries which prefer the approach based on geographical and industry-based risk and reward. US GAAP is more flexible than IAS 14 on the accounting basis for reporting. IFRS requires the amounts to be based on IFRS GAAP but US companies base the amounts on whatever basis is used for internal purposes. The reason given by FASB for requiring companies to disclose segment data based on how management makes its decisions was that this was a response to requests from analysts for better information about segments. The IASB will consult financial analysts before reconsidering IAS 14.

8.7.6.5 Voluntary disclosure

The FASB issued a report on voluntary disclosures as a means of improving business reporting.[40] The report was based on an in-depth study of voluntary disclosure by six to eight companies in each of eight industries. It encouraged disclosure of 'critical success factors' and information about unrecognized intangible assets. Voluntary disclosure should disappointments as well as the good news. The metrics used by companies to manage their operations and drive their business strategies were seen as useful voluntary disclosures.

8.8 Gray's accounting values

8.8.1 Professionalism versus statutory control

Gray's (1988) analysis, based on Hofstede's (1984) framework, indicates an expectation of strong professionalism. This means a preference for the exercise of individual professional judgement and professional self-regulation. The practical reality is complex, because the standard-setting process is self-regulatory and makes considerable use of professional expertise. However, standard-setting is subject to indirect statutory control through the SEC which may, if it chooses, exercise a strong influence on particular accounting practices. The accountancy profession is independent and self-regulating so that the institutional arrangements do support the classification of strong professionalism. Professional judgement is exercised in the format of presentation and the use of notes to the accounts; on the other hand, professionalism is limited by industry standards and by some of the factors listed in later sections as indicative of other aspects of Gray's classification.

A litigious society ready to take action against professional accountants and auditors causes them to seek refuge in the protection of statute and regulation. It was hoped that the Private Securities Litigation Reform Act (1995) would put a stop to disgruntled investors bringing frivolous lawsuits against companies and their professional advisers.

8.8.2 Uniformity versus flexibility

Gray's classification, based on Hofstede, indicates high flexibility. By way of contrast it has been suggested[41] that US accounting shows a mixture of both finite uniformity and rigid uniformity. Finite uniformity is seen as the attempt to equate prescribed accounting methods with the relevant circumstances in generally similar situations. The example given is the rule in SFAS 13 on long-term leases where percentages are used to draw the line for capitalization. The percentage is to some extent arbitrary but ensures comparable practice. Another example is the rule on capitalization of borrowing costs in specific circumstances. Rigid uniformity means prescribing one method

---

[40] FASB (2001).

[41] Wolk and Tearney (2004), chapter 9.

for generally similar transactions. An example is SFAS 2, requiring all research and development expenditure to be reported in the income statement as incurred. IAS 38 requires capitalization of development costs that meet specific criteria. This difference may be addressed by FASB in its short-term convergence project.

However, flexibility is evident in matters such as depreciation accounting and inventory valuation and in the separation of tax law from accounting practice.

8.8.3 Conservatism versus optimism

Gray's (1988) classification was one of optimism which is defined in his paper as a *laissez-faire*, risk-taking approach contrasting with conservatism as a cautious approach to measurement. This seems at variance with the US insistence on historical cost accounting and the refusal to allow revaluation. Gray classifies the US as optimistic in relation to countries such as Germany and France. The sources cited date from the 1970s and early 1980s so it may be that his view of relative optimism was based on the absence in the US of the excessive provisions found in some continental European practices prior to the implementation of the Fourth Directive. There is also mention of the practice of secret reserves, existing in continental Europe, not being found in the US or the UK.

The US picture in practice is not totally clear because the caution in banning revaluation, having a long history linked to the 1929 stock market crash, is in contrast to the reluctance to take the harder line on impairment, compared with the preference of the IASB and previously of the IASC. Permitting LIFO stock valuation is probably explained more by the influence of tax law than by the influence of conservatism. Providing in full for deferred taxation could be seen as conservative, but it could also be seen as a professional approach to applying a balance sheet approach consistently. However, the view of a distinguished US academic, commenting on a draft of this section, was 'please do not even try to characterize US accounting as other than conservative. It simply is conservative to the point of being inconsistent in theory.'

Nevertheless, both FASB and the SEC have taken a turn towards fair value since the 1990s. Zeff (1999) traces the progress of both bodies in 'lurching' towards current value accounting based on ideas of 'fair value'.

8.8.4 Secrecy versus transparency

Gray's (1988) classification of US accounting as highly transparent is supported by the extensive disclosure requirements imposed by the SEC, as well as those of the FASB standards. However, it must be remembered that the SEC regulates only listed companies and there are many more unlisted companies in the USA about which much less is known. Research evidence suggests that there is voluntary disclosure by US multinational companies, although less extensive than the voluntary disclosures provided by UK multinational companies.[42] Multinational US companies might reply that they already disclose more under compulsion. Specific elements of secrecy remain in off-balance-sheet transactions which are not regulated by any particular standard. On the other hand, the move towards openness and informativeness is reinforced by the AICPA in the work of the Jenkins Committee.

---

[42] Meek *et al.* (1995).

Summary and conclusions

Using the scores developed by Hofstede (1984), Gray's method of analysis predicts that the accounting system in the US will be characterized by strong professionalism, strong flexibility, strong conservatism and strong transparency. That strong professionalism has been embedded in the historical development of the accountancy profession and the responsibility taken by the profession for setting accounting standards. The FASB continued this professional approach as an independent standard-setter. Statutory control by the SEC was a reserve power, rarely implemented in practice. The collapse of Enron changed the global perception of the professionalism of US accounting and the governance system within which it operated. The Sarbanes–Oxley Act generated an unprecedented amount of new rules and legislation but at the same time questioned the extent to which US accounting had come to rely on detailed rules rather than applying principles to accounting decisions. The FASB survived the investigations and questioning of the system of corporate reporting, but had to promise to reconsider the balance of principles and rules.

'High quality' and 'transparency' are key words used frequently in commentaries and exhortations from the Securities and Exchange Commission. Transparency is seen in the very extensive disclosures required by law and practice, particularly in the basic information package required by the SEC of all listed US companies. Quality is addressed in the SEC's concerns over, and investigations into, earnings management. Flexibility is seen in the lack of prescribed formats of presentation and the separate existence of tax law and accounting law. The traditional insistence on historical cost would place the USA in a highly conservative category, but other aspects of detail in practice, such as capitalization of some expenditure, give glimpses of practices which are not always directed towards conservatism. The developing use of fair values is a further change to the perception of conservatism.

Key points from the chapter:

- The US has given a lead over many years in matters of regulating corporate reporting and setting standards. The Securities and Exchange Commission has been imitated in many countries, the FASB gives a model for an independent standard-setting body, and the Sarbanes–Oxley Act has set new standards for regulation of corporate governance and regulation, notwithstanding the crisis of confidence that made it necessary.

- US GAAP remains as a potential global accounting system to rival IFRS but the FASB and SEC are working with the IASB towards 'converging' the two systems. Section 8.6 shows the main areas of difference that will remain after the short-term convergence projects are completed.

- The 'principles versus rules' debate will continue but it seems unlikely that the US regulators will sacrifice the control they hold through writing detailed rules. These may become 'guidance' or 'interpretations' but there will remain limits on the extent to which professional judgement is exercised.

- When analysing the annual corporate reports of US companies it is essential to cover the full package of annual report, form 10-K and proxy statement.

Questions

The following questions test your understanding of the material contained in the chapter and allow you to relate your understanding to the learning outcomes specified at the start of this chapter. The learning outcomes are repeated here. Each question is cross-referenced to the relevant section of the chapter.

Explain the development of accounting regulation

1 To what extent do early developments in accounting practice indicate the likely directions of professionalism/statutory control, uniformity/flexibility, conservatism/optimism, and secrecy/transparency in current practice? (section 8.3.1)

Understand the impact of the Sarbanes–Oxley Act 2002

2 What were the problems that Sarbanes–Oxley was intended to remedy? (section 8.3.2)

3 How has Sarbanes–Oxley affected corporate governance? (section 8.3.2)

4 What is meant by the 'principles versus rules debate'? (section 8.3.3)

Explain the key institutional characteristics of the US

5 How does the political and economic system of the US fit into the classifications described in Chapter 4? (section 8.4.1)

6 How does the legal system of the US fit into the classifications described in Chapter 4? (section 8.4.2)

7 How does the corporate governance system of the US compare to the descriptions given in Chapter 3? (section 8.4.3)

8 How does the taxation system of the US compare to the descriptions given in Chapter 4? (section 8.4.4)

9 How does the corporate financing system of the US compare to the descriptions given in Chapter 4? (section 8.4.5)

10 How does the accounting profession in the US compare to the descriptions given in Chapter 4? (section 8.4.6)

11 How do the external influences on and by accounting practice in the US compare to those described in Chapter 4? (section 8.5)

12 Which institutional factors are most likely to influence US accounting practice? (section 8.4 generally)

Make comparisons of US GAAP with IFRS

13 In which areas does accounting practice in the US depart from that set out in IASB Standards? (section 8.6)

14 For each of the areas of departure which you have identified, describe the treatment required or applied in the US and identify the likely impact on net income and shareholders' equity of moving from US accounting practice to the relevant IASB Standards. (section 8.6)

15 What explanations may be offered for these departures from IASB Standards, in terms of the institutional factors described in the chapter? (link sections 8.4 and 8.6)

Understand and explain features of the accounting system that illustrate the diversity of US accounting practices

16 What are the most difficult problems facing accounting in the USA in the process of coordinating FASB accounting standards with IFRS? (link sections 8.6 and 8.7)

Discuss US accounting practices using the analytical framework of Gray's accounting values

17 Identify the key features supporting a conclusion that professionalism is a characteristic of US accounting. (link section 8.8.1 to section 8.7)

18 Explain which institutional influences cause professionalism, rather than statutory control, to be a characteristic of US accounting. (link section 8.8.1 to section 8.4)

19 Discuss whether a classification of professionalism is appropriate for present-day accounting practice. (section 8.8.1)

20 Identify the key features supporting a conclusion that flexibility, rather than uniformity, is a dominant characteristic of US accounting. (link section 8.8.2 to section 8.7)

21 Explain which institutional influences cause flexibility, rather than uniformity, to be a dominant characteristic of US accounting. (link section 8.8.2 to section 8.4)

22 Discuss whether a classification of strong flexibility is appropriate for present-day accounting practice. (section 8.8.2)

23 Identify the key features supporting a conclusion that optimism, rather than conservatism, is a dominant characteristic of US accounting. (link section 8.8.3 to section 8.7)

24 Explain which institutional influences cause optimism, rather than conservatism, to be a dominant characteristic of US accounting. (link section 8.8.3 to section 8.4)

25 Discuss whether a classification of optimism is appropriate for present-day accounting practice. (section 8.8.3)

26 Identify the key features supporting a conclusion that transparency, rather than secrecy, is a characteristic of US accounting. (link section 8.8.4 to section 8.7)

27 Explain which institutional influences cause transparency to be a characteristic of US accounting. (link section 8.8.4 to section 8.4)

28 Discuss whether a classification of transparency is appropriate for present-day accounting practice. (section 8.8.4)

References and further reading

Adams, C., Weetman, P., Jones, E.A.E. and Gray, S.J. (1999) 'Reducing the burden of US GAAP reconciliations by foreign companies listed in the United States: the key question of materiality', *The European Accounting Review*, 8(1): 1–22.

AICPA (1973) *Objectives of Financial Statements: Reports of the Study Group on the Objectives of Financial Statements*. American Institute of Certified Public Accountants, New York.

AICPA (1994) *Improving Business Reporting – A Customer Focus: Meeting Information Needs of Investors and Creditors, Comprehensive Report of the Special Committee on Financial Reporting*. New York: American Institute of Certified Public Accountants (The Special Committee was chaired by Edmund L. Jenkins, partner in Arthur Andersen).

Cairns, D. (1997) 'The future shape of harmonisation: A reply', *The European Accounting Review*, 6(2): 305–348.

CICA (2002) *Significant differences in GAAP in Canada, Chile, Mexico, and the United States*, Canadian Institute of Chartered Accountants, regular updating of a Joint study (1995) *Financial Reporting in North America*, undertaken by the Canadian Institute of Chartered Accountants, the Instituto Mexicano de Contadores Públicos, AC, and the Financial Accounting Standards Board of the United States, assisted by KPMG Peat Marwick LLP and published jointly.

Collins, W., Davie, E.S. and Weetman, P. (1993) 'Management discussion and analysis: An evaluation of practice in UK and US companies', *Accounting and Business Research*, 23(90): 123–137.

FASB (2001) *Improving Business Reporting: Insights into Enhancing Voluntary Disclosures*. Business Reporting Research Project, Steering Committee Report. Financial Accounting Standards Board. Available on the FASB website at www.fasb.org.

FASB (2004a) *Response to SEC study on the adoption of a principles-based accounting system*, July 2004. Available on the FASB website at www.fasb.org.

FASB (2004b) *Summary of FASB tentative decisions on business combinations*, July 2004. Available on the FASB website at www.fasb.org.

Flower, J. (1997) 'The future shape of harmonisation: The EU versus the IASC versus the SEC', *The European Accounting Review*, 6(2): 281–303.

Gray, S.J. (1988) 'Towards a theory of cultural influence on the development of accounting systems internationally', *Abacus*, 24(1): 1–15.

Hofstede, G. (1984) *Culture Consequences: International Differences in Work-Related Values*. Beverly Hills, CA: Sage Publications.

Meek, G.K., Roberts, C.B. and Gray, S.J. (1995) 'Factors influencing voluntary annual report disclosures by US, UK and continental European multinational corporations', *Journal of International Business Studies*, Third Quarter: 555–572.

OECD (2004) *Economic Surveys: United States*, May 2004, Vol 2004/7 Organization for Economic Cooperation and Development.

SEC (2001) Cautionary advice regarding disclosures about critical accounting policies, Release no. 33–8040, December 2001.

SEC (2003) Interpretation: Commission guidance regarding management's discussion and analysis of financial condition and results of operations, Release no. 33–8350, December 2003.

Street, D.L., Nichols, N.B. and Gray, S.J. (2000) 'Assessing the acceptability of international accounting standards in the US: An empirical study of the materiality of US GAAP reconciliations by non-US companies complying with IASC standards', *The International Journal of Accounting*, 35(1): 27–63.

Sudarsanam, P.S. (2003) *Creating Value from Mergers and Acquisitions: The Challenges, an Integrated and International Perspective*, FT Prentice Hall.

Weetman, P. and Gray, S.J. (1990) 'International financial analysis and comparative corporate performance: The impact of UK versus US accounting principles on earnings', *Journal of International Financial Management and Accounting*, 2(2/3): 111–129.

Weetman, P. and Gray, S.J. (1991) 'A comparative international analysis of the impact of accounting principles on profits: The US versus the UK, Sweden and The Netherlands', *Accounting and Business Research*, 21(84): 363–379.

Weetman, P., Jones, E.A.E., Adams, C. and Gray, S.J. (1998) 'Profit measurement and UK accounting standards: A case of increasing disharmony in relation to US GAAP and IASs', *Accounting and Business Research*, 28(3): 189–208.

Williams, J.R. and Carcello, J.V. (2004) *Miller GAAP Guide 2004*, New York: Aspen.

Wolk, H.I. and Tearney, M.G. (2004) *Accounting Theory: Conceptual Issues in a Political and Economic Environment*, 6th edn. Ohio: Thomson South-Western.

Zeff, S.A. (1999) 'Sitting on the fence', *Accountancy International*, July: 68–69.

Zeff, S.A. (2002) '"Political" lobbying on proposed standards: a challenge to the IASB', *Accounting Horizons*, 16(1): 43–54.

Zeff, S.A. (2003a) 'How the US accounting profession got where it is today: Part 1', *Accounting Horizons*, 17(3): 189–205.

Zeff, S.A. (2003b) 'How the US accounting profession got where it is today: Part 2', *Accounting Horizons*, 17(4): 267–286.

Journals/professional magazines

Financial Times (UK)

The Journal of Accountancy (US)

OECD, *Economic Surveys*. Paris: Organization for Economic Cooperation and Development.

9 The European Union

Learning outcomes

After reading this chapter you should be able to:

- Explain the origins and nature of the European Union.
- Explain how laws are made in the European Union.
- Explain the effect of the IAS Regulation.
- Understand the main requirements of the EU Fourth and Seventh Directives.
- Explain how the EU is modernizing its approach to accounting legislation and guidance.

9.1 Introduction

The purpose of this chapter is to show an approach to accounting regulation where separate countries surrender some of their power in matters of company law to a supranational body. The reporting practices of member states, and the regulatory framework of financial reporting, have all been influenced by membership of the European Union (EU). Chapter 10 deals with particularly interesting characteristics of a selection of member states. This chapter sets the scene more generally by explaining the origins of the EU, the formation of community law and the common features which bind all member states in matters of accounting.

9.2 Origins and nature of the EU

The present-day EU emerged from the European Communities created in the 1950s by a series of treaties:

- the European Coal and Steel Community (ECSC), 1950 (Treaty of Paris),
- the European Economic Community (EEC), 1957 (Treaty of Rome),
- the European Atomic Energy Community, 1957 (Euratom Treaty).

At that stage the emphasis was on industrial and trading partnerships between member states. The three communities became called collectively the 'European Communities' in 1965. Over the years the emphasis on political linkage, as well as trading cooperation, has become more apparent. The Single European Act of 1986 set the aim of removing all barriers, whether physical, technical or fiscal. The title 'European Union' was adopted in the Treaty on European Union signed at Maastricht in 1991. By the end of 1992, the structure for a Single Market was largely complete.

9.2.1 Purpose of the union[1]

The founders of the European Communities wanted to achieve a closer union among the peoples of Europe. This was stated in terms of achieving freedom of movement of persons, services and capital. The political ambitions varied, with some participants desiring to move eventually to a federation of European states and others more cautiously seeking only commercial benefits. Over the years there have been proposals for European integration and union on an increasingly ambitious scale, within the original aims of freedom of movement of persons, services and capital.

For those concerned with the practice of financial accounting and reporting, the most important of these aims is the freedom of movement of capital. Much of the work of the Council and Commission in the 1970s and 1980s related to bringing company law of member states into closer agreement. In the 1990s, more publicity was given to the harmonization of laws relating to the movement of persons and services, but the work on company law continued to develop. Haller (2002) explains how market forces were driving the harmonization of accounting in advance of the formal decision to require all listed companies to apply IFRS. He discusses the challenges facing the EU regulators in exercising influence on the development of IFRS, the technical challenges facing preparers and users of accounts, and the debate over the best interests of small and medium-sized unlisted companies.

9.2.2 Main institutions[2]

Of the three treaties creating the European Communities, the most significant was the Treaty of Rome which led to the establishment of the European Parliament and the Court of Justice. In 1965 the Merger Treaty established a single Council of Ministers and a single Commission covering all three Communities.

The Council of Ministers is the legislative body, which means that it issues the laws. On receiving a proposal from the Commission (see below), the Council of Ministers will usually consult with the European Parliament before issuing legislation. The Council must act within the scope of the treaties and must base its actions on the proposals of the Commission.

The Commission is the civil service of the EU, and Commissioners have considerable power. The Commission watches over the implementation of the treaties in each member state. It initiates policy and sets in place the procedures to implement policy, it helps Council meetings arrive at an agreed basis for action, and has power to administer some of the rules.

The European Parliament is a body which is consulted on matters for legislation but it does not set legislation. Parliament may question the Commission and may, in theory, dismiss its members. There is also some scope for the exercise of a power of veto, preventing legislation from being issued.

---

[1] Kent (2001), pp. 3–5.

[2] Kent (2001), pp. 15–32.

The Court of Justice is the highest court for matters relating to community law. It examines the legality of Acts of the Council and of the Commission. It can also provide guidance to national courts in the interpretation of community law.

9.2.3 Member countries

The 25 member states of the EU are listed in Exhibit 9.1.

The six countries which signed the Treaty of Rome were Belgium, West Germany, France, Italy, Luxembourg and The Netherlands. In 1972 Denmark, the Republic of Ireland and the United Kingdom joined the European Communities. The 1980s saw a Mediterranean enlargement, bringing into membership Greece (1981), Spain (1986) and Portugal (1986).

Unification of Germany brought the former German Democratic Republic ('East Germany') into membership in 1990. Closer links with countries in the European Free Trade Association (EFTA) brought Sweden, Austria and Finland into membership in 1995. At that point the total membership was 15 countries.

Many East European states signed 'Europe Agreements' following the Copenhagen Summit of 1993. These agreements encouraged a relationship that would lead to convergence and regional cooperation and would eventually provide a route to full membership. It is a condition for new entrants to the EU that they take steps to incorporate the company law directives within their national laws. In March 1998 accession negotiations began with Hungary, Poland, Estonia, the Czech Republic, Slovenia and Cyprus. In October 1999 the Commission recommended member states to open negotiations with Romania, Slovakia, Latvia, Lithuania, Bulgaria and Malta. In May 2004 the Enlargement of the EU admitted ten new member states that had met the conditions for membership. These were the Czech Republic, Cyprus, Estonia, Latvia, Lithuania, Hungary, Malta, Poland, Slovenia and Slovakia. Other countries of Eastern Europe continue to work towards meeting the conditions for membership.

9.2.4 The European Economic Area (EEA)[3]

The Agreement creating the European Economic Area was negotiated between the Community and seven member countries of the European Free Trade Area (EFTA) and signed in May 1992. Subsequently one of these (Switzerland) decided after a referendum

Exhibit 9.1	Member states of the EU from May 2004

The Republic of Austria	The Hellenic Republic (Greece)	The Republic of Poland
The Kingdom of Belgium	The Republic of Hungary	The Portuguese Republic (Portugal)
The Republic of Cyprus	The Republic of Ireland	The Slovak Republic (Slovakia)
The Czech Republic	The Italian Republic	The Republic of Slovenia
The Kingdom of Denmark	The Republic of Latvia	The Kingdom of Spain
The Republic of Estonia	The Republic of Lithuania	The Kingdom of Sweden
The Republic of Finland	The Grand Duchy of Luxembourg	The United Kingdom of Great
The French Republic (France)	The Republic of Malta	Britain and Northern Ireland (UK)
The Federal Republic of Germany	The Kingdom of The Netherlands	

---

[3] http://europa.eu.int/comm/external_relations/eea/.

not to participate, and three others (Austria, Finland and Sweden) joined the Union. The EEA was maintained[4] because of the wish of the three remaining countries – Norway, Iceland and Liechtenstein – to participate in the Single Market, while not assuming the full responsibilities of membership of the EU. The Agreement gives them the right to be consulted by the Commission during the formulation of Community legislation, but not the right to a say in the decision making, which is kept exclusively for member states. All new Community legislation in areas covered by the EEA (which includes the Fourth and Seventh Directives) is integrated into the Agreement through a Joint Committee Decision and subsequently made part of the national legislation of the EEA EFTA States. This means that Norway, Iceland and Liechtenstein are closely related to EU member states in matters of accounting rules.[5]

9.3 How laws are made[6]

There are two aspects to community law. Basic legislation, contained in treaties and protocols, sets out fundamental obligations of member states. When member states agree to accept the basic legislation, they give up some of their sovereign power over national affairs. This basic legislation passes directly into the law of the nation and there is no need for a member state to initiate its own laws. Secondary legislation creates obligations on the governments of member states which citizens of those states may refer to in courts of law. Consequently the member states are expected to incorporate secondary legislation in their national laws.

The levels of legislation encountered in matters of financial reporting are:

1 **Regulation**. A regulation has general application and is directly binding on all member states.
2 **Directive**. A directive explains a set of desirable outcomes, which must be achieved by member states – it indicates to member states a variety of options which they can use to achieve the required outcomes; member states select the option or options which best suit national circumstances.
3 **Decision**. A decision may be issued for a particular purpose such as an antitrust or a competition case – it is binding on the persons to whom it is addressed.
4 **Recommendations and opinions**. Recommendations and opinions are also issued, but do not have binding force.

9.4 Impact of IASB Standards on accounting in the EU

In November 1995, the European Commission announced that it would look to the IASC to carry forward the work of harmonization. This reversed earlier indications by the Commission that it would wish to develop a programme of European standards. The change of approach probably reflected acknowledgement of the continued diversity of measurement practices across EU countries, despite achievements of harmonization in disclosure and presentation. By 1995 it was becoming apparent that only the IASC would be in a position to meet the needs for harmonization within a relatively short timescale.

---

[4] EEA Agreement, updated May 2004, full text on
http://secretariat.efta.int/Web/EuropeanEconomicArea/EEAAgreement/EEAAgreement.

[5] Ibid, Annex XXII.

[6] Kent (2001).

As part of the new accounting strategy adopted by the Commission at the end of 1995, the Contact Committee on the Accounting Directives carried out work to analyze the degree of conformity between rules contained in the IASs and the content of the European Accounting Directives. This was intended to provide information to help each member state decide on whether, and to what extent, national companies could apply the IASs. The major review was carried out in 1995 but was then extended for subsequent issues of IASs. Reports are published on the website of the European Commission.

This strategy was not without its critics in the late 1990s, because the Directives were becoming increasingly out of date. It was suggested that inconsistency with the Directives may not necessarily have reflected badly on an IAS that represented more current thinking on an accounting issue.

The IOSCO endorsement of the IASs in May 2000 and the IASC's agreement on restructuring along lines favoured by the US SEC (see section 1.7.5) were met with newspaper comments suggesting that the regulators would carry on wrangling, and that Brussels had lost its 'voice' in matters of international accounting standards.[7] The first comment reflected a concern that the European Commission would set up committees to carry out a process of reviewing the IASs with a view to taking the 'reconciliation' route as a way of preserving the independence of the Commission in matters of accounting regulation. The second comment led into a suggestion that the future debate on IASs would be one-sided without a strong input from the European Commission.

In June 2000 the Commission published its outline financial reporting strategy to require listed companies to use IASs by 2005. This was part of a wider target to implement the Commission's Financial Services Action Plan by the same date. However, the Commission also indicated that it would apply a two-level endorsement mechanism through political and technical review.[8] One view expressed at the time was that the endorsement mechanism could indicate a desire by the Commission for a Europeanized version of the IASs, which would in turn encourage the US to continue requiring reconciliations to US GAAP. The contrast was made, in comment, between global consensus and regional variation.

The response of the Commission was that endorsement was necessary because it would be unwise to delegate accounting standard-setting unconditionally to a private organization over which the EU had no influence. This response reflected the Commission's continuing concerns about the new IASB, established in 2000, not being representative. The endorsement mechanism was seen as keeping open a dialogue with the IASB. Legislative details published in February 2001 indicated that the Commission would keep a firm control of the political aspects of the process.

For many years the accounting regulation in company law of member states had been affected mainly by two Directives – the Fourth and Seventh Directives. Member states incorporated these two Directives in their national company law. They took options, where available, to reflect national needs. When the EU took the decision to require all listed companies to use international accounting standards in preparing group accounts, the decision was implemented by a Regulation. We explained in section 9.3 that this was more powerful than any Directive and it also took precedence over Directives. So member states were obliged to apply and enforce the Directive as part of their law. The Directives remained effective for companies not

---

[7] Robert Bruce, *The Times*, 25 May 2000; Michael Peel, *Financial Times*, 25 May 2000.

[8] http://europa.eu.int/comm/internal_market/en/company/accounts/news.

required to follow the Regulation. This meant that national company law continued to apply for such companies.

In the following sections we first describe the new Regulation which brings IFRS to European listed companies. We then describe in detail the Fourth and Seventh Directives, which continue to dictate the shape of national legislation for companies not affected by the Regulation.

9.5 The IAS Regulation

In 2002 the European Commission confirmed its target of IAS adoption by 2005. The Regulation (EC) No. 1606/2002 of the European Parliament and the Council (19 July 2002) on the application of international accounting standards is called 'the IAS Regulation'. Its purpose is to harmonize the financial information presented by public listed companies in order to ensure a high degree of transparency and comparability of financial statements. The Regulation is relatively short. For details of its application we have to look to the Comments issued by the Commission in November 2003.[9]

9.5.1 Scope of the Regulation[10]

The Regulation applies to the consolidated financial statements of listed companies[11] for their financial years commencing on or after 1 January 2005. Member states have the option of permitting or requiring the use of IASs for the individual accounts of companies with a listed group and for the accounts of any unlisted groups or individual companies.[12] International accounting standards are defined in the Regulation as IASs, IFRSs, SIC-IFRICs and any other standards issued by the IASB.[13]

As explained earlier, a Regulation is directly applicable in member states. This is different from a Directive, which is an instruction to member states on the content of their national laws. Because the Regulation is directly applicable, member states must ensure that they do not seek to apply to a company any additional elements of national law that are contrary to, or conflict with or restrict a company's compliance with IASs.[14]

9.5.2 Languages

Adopted IFRS and interpretations will be available in all Community languages. They will be published in the *Official Journal* of the EU and will also be available on the website.[15] Some caution will be needed on the part of those using such translations where there is a time lag between the issue of a new IFRS and its adoption by the European Commission. The 'EU endorsed' version of a standard may not necessarily be the most recent update from the IASB.

---

[9] EC (2003b).

[10] EC (2002).

[11] EC (2002) Article 4.

[12] EC (2002) Article 5.

[13] EC (2002) Article 2. Unfortunately the Regulation pre-dates the IASB's decision to use 'IFRS' as the general description – see Chapter 1.

[14] EC (2003b) section 3.1.

[15] http://europa.eu.int/comm/internal_marke/accounting/index_en.htm.

9.5.3 Adopting IFRS in Europe: 'endorsed' IFRS

The Commission decides on the applicability of international accounting standards within the Community.[16] It is assisted by an Accounting Regulatory Committee[17] and is advised by a technical group EFRAG.[18] The tests for adoption[19] are that the standards

- do not contradict specific principles of the Fourth and Seventh Directive,
- are conducive to the European public good, and
- meet the criteria of understandability, relevance, reliability and comparability, required of financial information needed for making economic decisions and assessing the, stewardship of management.

A standard that is adopted is said to be 'endorsed'. If a standard is awaiting endorsement, or is rejected, it may be used as guidance if it is not inconsistent with endorsed standards. If a rejected standard is in conflict with adopted standards, it may not be used. When the European Commission first announced the endorsement process there were fears expressed that this would be used to create 'European IFRS' by selecting some IFRS and rejecting others. The Commission's reply was that the EU cannot give its powers to a body (the IASB) that is not subject to EU jurisdiction, and it is necessary for the EU to endorse standards as part of its duty in setting laws for member states.

9.5.3.1 The Accounting Regulatory Committee

The Accounting Regulatory Committee (ARC) consists of representatives from member states. It is chaired by the Commission. The Committee was set up by the Commission in accordance with the requirements of Article 65 of the IAS Regulation. The ARC has its own procedures, published on the internal market website. Its function is to provide an opinion on Commission proposals to adopt (endorse) an international accounting standard. The IAS Regulation gives a great deal of power to the Commission to control the ARC's agenda because the ARC only gives an opinion, not a decision, and because the ARC has to wait for the Commission to make a proposal. The opinion of ARC may be decided on a majority vote.

The greatest test faced by the ARC in 2004 was the question of endorsing IAS 39. At its meeting in July 2004,[20] the ARC was advised that full endorsement of IAS 39 would be divisive. Some member states supported endorsement, others were opposed. The Commission was exploring an intermediate solution that would endorse IAS 39 with the exception of the fair value option (see section 2.5.2.2) and a limited number of provisions dealing with hedge accounting of core deposits. The chairman of the ARC underlined the exceptional nature of the situation facing the ARC, where he saw the EU having to remedy the inability of the IASB and the European banking industry to come to a mutually satisfactory solution on particular matters of concern to bankers.

---

[16] EC (2002) Article 1.

[17] EC (2002) Article 6.

[18] www.efrag.org/.

[19] Regulation Article 3.2.

[20] Meeting report 9 July 2004, ARC/2004-07-09, website of internal market.

Member states supporting full endorsement asked whether they could adopt it voluntarily, to avoid problems of incomplete application of IFRS.

9.5.3.2 EFRAG

EFRAG is the European Financial Reporting Advisory Group. It is a private institution that was set up in 2001 by organizations active in the area of financial reporting. Its activities are:

- providing proactive advice to the IASB;
- advising the European Commission on the acceptability of IFRS for endorsement in Europe;
- advising the European Commission on any resulting changes to be made to the accounting directives and related topics.

EFRAG differs from ARC. EFRAG is not defined in the IAS Regulation (although there is indirect reference to it), and therefore the European Commission has no obligation to listen to EFRAG. The organizations founding EFRAG believed strongly that it should be recognized by IASB as the body that expresses European positions on matters relating to setting standards. EFRAG itself would like to be acknowledged formally by the Commission as the leading group of technical experts. Within EFRAG there is a Technical Expert Group (TEG) which carries out proactive work and provides endorsement advice via EFRAG. In December 2003 EFRAG issued a consultation document on its role within the endorsement process. EFRAG would like to strengthen and extend its position but that raises issues for the continuing role of national standard-setters.

9.5.4 Formats

The IAS Regulation applies directly to consolidated accounts of listed companies. Member states cannot impose their own formats.[21] The Comment on the IAS Regulation suggests that the application of IAS 1 will lead to balance sheets and profit and loss accounts that follow the same principles as those used in the Directives. The profit and loss account may use disclosure by function or by nature (see Exhibit 9.4 later). The balance sheet will present assets either in order of liquidity or using a current/non-current distinction. The Regulation is less prescriptive than the Directives and so it may be that in future some companies will begin to experiment with new forms of presentation.

9.5.5 Choices for member states

The Comments emphasize the importance of comparability under the IAS Regulation. This will be achieved where member states do not seek additional qualitative or quantitative disclosures. However, additional disclosure may be required by national regulators where such information lies outside the consolidated accounts or falls outside the scope of IASs.[22] Member states must not restrict explicit choices contained in the IASs.[23]

---

[21] EC (2003b) section 4.2.

[22] EC (2003b) section 4.1.

[23] EC (2003b) section 3.1.

9.5.6 Application of national law

Where a company is not subject to the IAS Regulation, it will continue to prepare accounts under national laws that are based on the Fourth and Seventh Directives.[24] A member state might require a particular IAS to be applied by such companies. In such instances the national law would still apply.[25]

9.5.7 Articles of Directives still applying under the IAS Regulation

Some Articles of the Fourth and Seventh Directives deal with publication, audit and other matters that are beyond the scope of International Accounting Standards. These Articles continue to apply, through national law, alongside the IAS Regulation. (There is a detailed list in the Comments document.)

9.6 Company law directives[26]

Company law directives are published under the authority of the Treaty of Rome (Article 54(3)(g)). The Council and the Commission are required to coordinate 'safeguards' to protect the interests of member states and others, in such a way that these safeguards are equivalent across the EU. The safeguards must be consistent with freedom of movement of goods, persons, services and capital. The laws of member states must be brought sufficiently close to allow proper functioning of the common market.

The directives are the practical means of achieving these safeguards. The directives which have been issued in relation to company law are shown in Exhibit 9.2. The date given is that of adoption by the Council of Ministers. Incorporation in national law may take several years from the date of adoption. Where a directive is particularly controversial, such as the Fifth Directive, its adoption may be delayed for a long time. The draft directive on takeovers was first proposed in 1989 but took on greater importance at the 2000 Lisbon European Summit which set a target for implementation of the Financial Services Action Plan.

Information about company law directives, including full texts, is available on the website of the Internal Market Directorate General.[27] In the fields of accounting and statutory audit, the work of the Internal Market Directorate General is directed towards:

● improving the quality, comparability and transparency of the financial information provided by companies, ensuring compatibility between the Accounting Directives and IASB Standards; and
● improving the quality of statutory audit throughout the EU.

It also cooperates closely with international bodies including the International Accounting Standards Board and the International Federation of Accountants.

---

[24] EC (2003b) section 3.4.

[25] Ibid.

[26] Kent (2001).

[27] Website of Internal Market DG in English is at the address:
http://europa.eu.int/comm/internal_market/en/company/company/official/index.htm.

Exhibit 9.2	EU company law directives

Directive	Date of adoption	Main purpose
First	1968	Powers of directors and powers of companies
Second	1976	Requirements for capital when forming a company; maintaining capital; distinction between private and public companies
Third	1978	Reconstructions within public companies
Fourth	1978	Disclosure of financial information and contents of annual accounts of individual companies
Fifth	–	[proposal] Company structure and employee participation
Sixth	1982	Merger and de-merger of public companies
Seventh	1983	Group accounts
Eighth	1984	Qualifications and independence of auditors
Ninth	–	[proposal] Relationships within a group structure
Tenth	–	[proposal] Mergers between plcs
Eleventh	1989	Disclosure in respect of branches of foreign companies located in the member state
Twelfth	1989	Single-member companies – memorandum and articles of association
Thirteenth	2004	Takeover bids

9.6.1 The meaning of equivalence[28]

The purpose of harmonizing company law across member states is to provide equivalent safeguards throughout the EU. The safeguards do not have to be identical. Equivalence allows a variety of options to be inserted in directives. Directives consist of a series of Articles, each containing a separate issue for attention. There are three types of Articles found in directives, namely:

● uniform rules to be implemented identically in all member states;
● minimum rules which may be strengthened by the national government;
● alternative rules giving member states options (choices).

9.6.2 Use of options in national law

Options are negotiated during the drafting of the directives as a result of lobbying or persuasion by the representatives of the various member states in the Council and the Commission. The options reflect areas where it was most difficult to obtain agreement at the negotiation stage.

In some cases the national government decides which options to adopt. As an example of options taken by governments, the Seventh Directive provided various options on the

---

[28] FEE (1993), pp. 15–22.

definition of 'control' for purposes of defining a subsidiary company. The UK government chose one set of options, while the German government chose another. In both cases, companies had to apply the law of their own country.

In other cases the national government preserves the options in its national law and allows the standard-setters or the individual companies to decide which option to apply. It should be noted that the directives provide minimum standards for national law. It is open to national governments to be more exacting in the national legislation. As an example of options within the national law, the Fourth Directive allowed more than one approach to valuation of assets in a balance sheet. The UK government allowed individual companies to choose either historical cost or an alternative valuation method (current cost). The French government did not allow individual companies the choice of departing from historical cost accounting.

9.6.3 The Fourth and Seventh Directives

Accounting rules are contained in the fourth and seventh directives. The Fourth Directive (1978) set the ground rules for the accounts of individual companies, giving standard formats for the balance sheet and profit and loss account.[29] The Seventh Directive (1983) established a common basis of presentation of accounts for groups of companies. Implementation in national law was faster in some countries than in others (Exhibit 9.3) but all member states now have both directives implemented. Member states joining in 2004 were required to incorporate the directives in national law before becoming members. Together the Fourth and Seventh Directives have made a considerable impact on the presentation of companies' financial statements.

Exhibit 9.3 Implementation of Fourth and Seventh Directives in national law

Country	Fourth	Seventh
Denmark	1981	1990
UK	1981	1989
France	1983	1985
Netherlands	1983	1988
Luxembourg	1984	1988
Belgium	1985	1990
Germany	1985	1985
Ireland	1986	1992
Greece	1986	1987
Spain	1989	1989
Portugal	1989	1991
Italy	1991	1991
Sweden	1995	1995
Austria	1995	1995
Finland	1995	1995

---

[29] Watts (1979).

9.6.4 Modernization of company law[30]

In September 2001, the European Commission set up a Group of High Level Company Law Experts to start a discussion on modernization of company law in Europe. The group reported in 2002 on the takeover bids directive and on recommendations for a modern regulatory European company law framework. From their recommendations the Commission produced an Action Plan in May 2003. Its aims were:

- to strengthen shareholders' rights and protection for employees, creditors and the other parties with which companies deal, while adapting company law and corporate governance rules appropriately for different categories of company;
- to foster the efficiency and competitiveness of business, with special attention to some specific cross-border issues.

The Commission did not seek a European Corporate Governance Code but said they would encourage member states towards a common approach on specific aspects such as:

- include a Corporate Governance Statement in the annual report of a company;
- develop legislation to help shareholders to exercise their rights to receive and vote on relevant information;
- promote the role of (independent) non-executive or supervisory directors;
- develop a regulatory regime giving shareholders more transparency and influence over directors' remuneration, which includes receiving detailed disclosure of individual remuneration;
- create a European Corporate Governance Forum.

From comments received in November 2003 the Commission announced its plans for 2004, as:

- a Recommendation aiming at promoting the role of non-executive or supervisory directors (nomination, remuneration and audit committees);
- a Recommendation on directors' remuneration, giving shareholders more information and influence.

Other matters under consideration would follow later.

9.6.5 Other measures

Other community measures which have had an impact on accounting practices include those on:

- admission to listing on a stock exchange;
- mutual recognition of listing particulars (where a company resident in one country is allowed to have its shares listed on the stock exchange of another, without rewriting its financial statements);
- disclosure of major shareholdings;
- insider dealing;
- information contained in a prospectus.

---

[30] http://europa.eu.int/comm/internal_market/en/company/company/modern/index.htm.

9.6.6 Mutual recognition[31]

Stock exchanges each have their own rules to ensure that companies obtaining a listing provide sufficient information to allow a fair market to operate. Prior to 2005 the rules were drawn up in terms of national accounting practices and consequently companies which had a listing on more than one international stock exchange could find themselves preparing more than one set of accounts. To avoid this problem, the stock exchanges in member states agreed that they would recognize accounts prepared under the rules of any other member state. The agreement was 'mutual' because each stock exchange felt it had given something to the financial community by relaxing the rules, and had also gained something from the financial community, by encouraging international listing of shares.

Mutual recognition was based on the reassurance that member states have minimum standards in common because they all apply the Fourth and Seventh Directives. Mutual recognition is less rigorous than the concept of equivalence (explained earlier). Mutual recognition is likely to continue in the areas of financial reporting (such as management discussions) that are not covered by the IAS Regulation.

9.7 The Fourth Directive[32]

Drafting of the Fourth Directive began in 1965[33] when there were only six members of the European Communities but it was completed in 1978 when there were nine members. For Denmark, the UK and Ireland, who all joined the Community in 1978, some relatively late lobbying was required to reflect national concerns. In particular the UK argued forcefully for inclusion of the concept of 'a true and fair view'. The inclusion of the words 'true and fair' caused particular difficulty for translation into the languages of other member states. Not only were the words unfamiliar: the ideas behind the words were unfamiliar in continental Europe, and particular national approaches are dealt with in section 10.7.1. (The influence of German chairmanship in the early stages of drafting the directive is seen in the detailed specification of the format of financial statements; such prescriptive formats were not known in the UK or Ireland prior to the Fourth Directive.)

9.7.1 Objective[34]

The Directive applies to the accounts of an individual company and covers all aspects of the annual accounts. It aims to harmonize accounting principles, presentation, publication and audit by laying down minimum standards to be applied by member states. The intention in preparing the directive was that investors, lenders and suppliers should find it easier to obtain, understand and rely on the accounts of companies in other member states. The Directive was also aimed at promoting fair competition among member state companies: managers of a business anywhere in the EU should be able to find out as much about a competitor company as the competitor can find out about their business. Furthermore, multinational corporations should not base decisions about location on differences in national accounting requirements.

---

[31] FEE (1993), pp. 15–22.

[32] Directive 78/660/EEC of 25 July 1978.

[33] Watts (1979).

[34] Coleman (1984).

9.7.2 'True and fair view'[35]

The Fourth Directive imposes an overriding requirement that the annual accounts (comprising the balance sheet, profit and loss account and notes to the accounts) present a true and fair view. In most cases it would be expected that complying with the requirement of the law would be sufficient. However, it may be necessary for companies to disclose more than the minimum specification in order to present a true and fair view. On relatively rare occasions, companies may have to depart from the requirements of the law in order to give a true and fair view. That is permissible but must be explained in the annual report.

The concept of a 'true and fair view' is essentially Anglo-Saxon in origin[36] and was not readily accommodated within some national practices of continental Europe, particularly where tax legislation had traditionally dominated accounting reporting. The first draft of the directive, issued in 1971, used words such as 'accuracy' and 'principles of regular and proper accounting'. Negotiations following the accession of the UK, the Republic of Ireland and Denmark resulted in the phrase 'true and fair' appearing. The company laws of each member state now include words approximating in translation to 'true and fair view', but the meaning of the words and application of the concept should be considered in the context of juridical tradition and cultural aspects.

It has been suggested that there is a range of positions on the meaning of 'true and fair view'.[37] In the UK and Ireland, it may be used by standard-setters to justify general rules and may be used by companies to justify overriding the specific requirements of law. In Germany, it is clear that the idea of a 'true and fair view' cannot be used to override the requirements of law. Between these two extremes lies a range of interpretations in various member states.

In The Netherlands 'true and fair' may be used by directors and auditors as a basic principle for interpretation of the law and guidelines. It is used in setting guidelines but is not used to override the requirements of the law. In France and Spain 'true and fair' has been used by law makers to allow some move towards substance rather than form. It may be used by companies as a justification for overriding the law, but only very exceptionally. It is used by directors and auditors as a basic principle for interpretation of the law. In Italy 'true and fair' may be used by directors and auditors as a basic principle for interpretation of the law but it is unlikely that it would be used to justify a departure from the law.

9.7.3 Framework of principles

There is no separate European framework of principles. However the Fourth Directive includes Article 31 setting out accounting principles for valuation:

- the company must be presumed to be a going concern unless evidence exists to the contrary;
- methods of valuation must be applied consistently from one period to the next;

---

[35] Parker and Nobes (1994).

[36] Alexander and Archer (2000, 2003), Nobes (2003).

[37] Parker and Nobes (1994), p. 80.

- valuation must be made on a prudent basis and in particular:
  - only profits made may be included in the financial statements;
  - all foreseeable liabilities and potential losses arising in the year should be taken into account, even where they become apparent between the balance sheet date and the date on which it is drawn up;
  - account must be taken of depreciation, irrespective of whether there is a profit or a loss;
- all income and charges must be brought into account (i.e. the accruals concept is applied);
- components of asset and liability items must be valued separately;
- the opening balance sheet of a year must correspond to the closing balance sheet of the previous year.

9.7.4 Disclosure and presentation

The Fourth Directive includes Articles 9, 10 and 23–26, which list items for disclosure in the balance sheet and profit and loss account. The order of presentation may not be varied but there is some latitude allowed, such as the insertion of subtotals. National standard-setting bodies may add further requirements. Companies have the discretion to provide more information than is prescribed by the Directives.

The layout of the annual accounts is prescribed in *formats*. There are descriptions of formats in the Articles of the Fourth Directive setting out the order of line items for one type of balance sheet and two types of profit and loss account, with a choice of horizontal and vertical presentation for both. Examples of some of the prescribed formats are set out in the Appendix to this chapter.

The first example in the Appendix is a full horizontal balance sheet as set out in Article 9. It shows, by using a variety of symbols, information required from all companies, information not required from small companies, and information not required from small companies or in published accounts of medium-sized companies. In that example, each line item carries a label. The major headings are labelled with capital letters A, B, C, and so on. The next level of headings is labelled with roman numerals I, II, III, and so on. The third level of headings is labelled with arabic numerals 1, 2, 3, and so on. Line items labelled with capital letters and roman numerals must appear on the face of the balance sheet. Those labelled with arabic numerals may appear in notes to the accounts. The example in the appendix shows the fullest possible balance sheet where a company places all information on the face of the primary financial statement. Making use of notes to the accounts and the alternative classifications shown for some line items, plus concessions for company size, may reduce the density of information in particular cases.

A full vertical balance sheet is set out in Article 10. The second example in Appendix 9.1 shows the application of Article 10 where a company desires to produce a minimum balance sheet taking advantage of the concessions for small companies and making use of the facility for notes to the accounts.

There are four Articles dealing with formats of the profit and loss account because two quite different approaches are allowed, each in horizontal and vertical form. One approach permits the costs to be analyzed by *type of expenditure* (e.g. purchase of goods, payment of wages and salaries) while the other gives categories based on the *function of the expenditure* (e.g. the function of selling goods is identified as cost of goods sold, while paying wages and salaries is reported as either administrative or distribution functions). This is also called the *operational basis*. These two approaches reflect different national practices in existence when the Directive was written. The resulting differences in presentation occur at the start of each type of profit and loss account, and are set out for comparison in Exhibit 9.4. The *type of expenditure* basis is more detailed on the face of the profit and loss account, but has the disadvantage of not showing the gross profit or loss. Under the *functional basis* more detailed notes to the accounts are required, so the overall provision of information is the same under each.

9.7.5 Recognition and measurement

There are no criteria stated for recognition, but there is the general requirement that profits may only be reported when they are 'made'. The word 'made' is not defined, but has generally been equated with 'realized' (also not defined). The restriction to realization of profit has an inevitable consequence on asset recognition in many instances. The Directive does not define 'made' and hence a great deal of discretion is left to national law and national standard-setters. This area includes potentially controversial issues such as

Exhibit 9.4	Comparison of alternative forms of vertical profit and loss account (based on Articles 23 and 25) (see also Appendix 9.1)

Type of expenditure	Functional basis (Operational basis)
1 Net turnover	1 Net turnover
2 Variations in stocks of finished goods and in progress	
3 Work performed by the undertaking for its own purposes and capitalized	2 Cost of sales (including value adjustments)
4 Other operating income	
5 (a) Raw materials and consumables (b) Other external charges	3 Gross profit or loss

6 Staff costs
    (a) Wages and salaries
    (b) Social security costs, with a separate indication of those relating to pensions
	4 Distribution costs (including value adjustments)

7 (a) Value adjustments in respect of formation expenses and of tangible and intangible fixed assets (b) Value adjustments in respect of current assets, to the extent that they exceed the amount of value which are normal in adjuments undertaking concerned	5 Administrative expenses (including value adjustments)
8 Other operating charges	6 Other operating income
9–21 Same as 7–19 for *functional basis*	7–19 Same as 9–21 for *type of expenditure*

profits on long-term contracts, franchise income, fees received in advance of services rendered, and recognition of income for those who provide finance through leasing arrangements.

The general rule of measurement is that historical cost accounting must be applied, although there is an option in the Fourth Directive (Article 33) by which member states may permit or require companies or any classes of companies to:

- value tangible fixed assets with limited useful economic lives, and stocks, by the replacement value method;
- value by other methods designed to take account of inflation the items shown in the annual accounts, including capital and reserves;
- revalue tangible fixed assets and financial fixed assets.

Where national law provides for use of any these valuation methods, it must define their content and limits and the rules for their application (Article 33).

The Fourth Directive contains specific valuation rules for certain assets:

- fixed assets with a limited useful economic life must be depreciated so as to write off their value systematically over the useful life (Article 35);
- goodwill, research and development costs and formation expenses must in general be written off over five years. In exceptional circumstances, member states may permit a longer period (Article 37.1) (see section 9.8.3 for the treatment of goodwill arising on consolidation);
- current assets must be valued at purchase price or production cost. Value adjustments must be made where the market value is lower than purchase price or production cost (Article 39);
- member states have options on the valuation of stocks of goods. They may permit the purchase price or production cost of stocks of goods of the same category, either on the basis of weighted average prices, or on the basis of first-in-first-out (FIFO) or on the basis of last-in-first-out (LIFO) (Article 40);
- member states have the option to permit use of the equity method of valuing holdings in affiliated companies (the Fourth Directive left open the precise definition of 'affiliated' but the Seventh Directive gave guidance as a holding of 20 per cent or more) (Article 59).

The recognition of liabilities is largely governed by the requirement for prudence, as explained earlier. There are fewer valuation rules than for assets, but particular items are:

- under the heading 'accruals and deferred income', account must be taken of the income and charges of the year, irrespective of the date of receipt or payment (Article 31);
- where the amount repayable under any debt is greater than the amount received (e.g. a discount on issue of a debenture loan) the difference may be shown as an asset and amortized, to be written off no later than the time of repayment of the debt (Article 41);
- deferred taxation liabilities may be recognized, but there is no rule specified for valuation (Article 9/10, Article 43);
- provisions for contingencies and charges must not be in excess of the amount necessary (Article 42).

9.7.6 Measurement approaches

As already explained, the Fourth Directive carries an initial presumption of historical cost accounting. Inflation accounting is considered in the Directive, where member states may permit or require companies or any classes of companies to:

- value tangible fixed assets with limited useful economic lives and stocks by the replacement value method;
- value by other methods designed to take account of inflation the items shown in the annual accounts, including capital and reserves;
- revalue tangible fixed assets and financial fixed assets.

Where national law provides for use of any these valuation methods, it must define their content and limits and the rules for their application (Article 33).

The Fourth and Seventh Directives were written before financial markets developed complex derivative financial instruments. To keep up with such major changes, in May 2001 the Commission published a Directive amending the Fourth and Seventh Directives to align them with IAS 32 and IAS 39. For the first time 'fair value' accounting was permitted under the Directives. It obliged member states to amend national law so as to permit or require companies to adopt fair value accounting methods. It gave member states options to limit the scope of the legislation, such as restricting it to listed companies or to apply it only to consolidated accounts. The use of fair-value accounting does not extend beyond financial instruments on the assets side of the balance sheet, and it does not apply to the 'traditional' types of liability.

9.8 The Seventh Directive[38]

The Fourth Directive deals only with individual companies standing alone. The essential purpose of writing the Seventh Directive was to define a group. This was an extremely controversial matter because of the range of practices in existence across countries and because of the importance of the definition in relation to tax law in some countries.[39] Many of the issues contained in the Fourth Directive, such as presentation, valuation rules and accounting principles, apply equally well to groups of companies. These matters are incorporated in the Seventh Directive by specific reference to the Fourth Directive.

9.8.1 Origins[40]

For some member states, consolidation is a development of recent years. An act of 1965 in Germany required a form of consolidation to be applied by public companies. Listed companies in France were required to apply consolidation from the early 1970s. The Seventh Directive was first published as a draft in 1976 and drew on the long-running experience which could be found in the UK, Ireland and The Netherlands. Consequently the Seventh Directive brought group accounting to some continental European countries which had not previously produced consolidated accounts as a widespread practice.

---

[38] Directive 83/349/EEC of 13 June 1983.

[39] FEE (1993).

[40] Niessen (1993).

The Seventh Directive shows the influence of Anglo-Saxon practice, in contrast to the Fourth Directive which may be seen as having a clear base in continental European law. There are, however, some important indications of continental European influence in the definition of 'control'. Some countries regarded the group as being essentially an economic unit, defined by its economic activity, while others preferred to have strict definitions set out in law, defined by legal contracts. The considerable debate on the content of the Seventh Directive is reflected in the number of options it contains.

9.8.2 Extensive use of options

Options relate to aspects of consolidated accounting which were found to be too controversial to allow any agreement in a Directive. There are more than 50 options which represent political compromises rather than strong points of principle. The extent of the options available to member states means that variety of national practice is wide. The Directive has increased the number of companies that are required to produce consolidated accounts, but has not greatly increased harmonization in the practices of consolidated accounting.

9.8.3 Approach to consolidation

Undertakings are required to draw up consolidated accounts which include subsidiaries irrespective of their location. 'Subsidiaries' are defined in terms of control by voting rights or dominant influence established by contract. Member states have the further option to require consolidation of companies managed on a unified basis and companies over which a dominant influence is exercised in the absence of a specific contract (Articles 1–4). Articles 5–15 begin the process of developing the options which are a particular feature of the Seventh Directive (Exhibit 9.5).

Merger accounting is permitted where any cash payment represents less than 10 per cent of the nominal value of shares issued (Article 20). Minority interests must be shown separately and all income of consolidated companies must be included (Articles 21–23). This means that proportional consolidation of income is not permissible for full subsidiaries.

Exhibit 9.5 Options for consolidation

Member states may exempt financial holding companies that neither manage their subsidiaries nor take part in appointments to the board of directors (Article 5). They may also exempt small and medium-sized groups provided no listed company is involved (Article 6). A company is exempted from the requirement to consolidate its own subsidiaries if it is itself a subsidiary, but member states may insist on consolidation by listed companies, whether or not they are themselves subsidiaries. Other exemptions are available to member states under Articles 7–11. Member states may require horizontal consolidation where companies are managed by the same person (Article 12). Subsidiaries may be excluded from consolidation if they are immaterial, or if there would be disproportionate expense or delay (Articles 13–15).

Various practical rules for consolidation are set out in Articles 24–28. These are very detailed and reflect the lack of widespread experience of the process when the Directive was given approval.

Positive goodwill arising on consolidation must be amortised through the profit and loss account or else written off immediately against reserves. Negative goodwill should be taken to profit only if it is realized or is due to the expectation of future costs or losses (Articles 30, 31).

9.8.4 Similarities to the Fourth Directive

The requirement for a true and fair view is contained in Article 16. Formats of the Fourth Directive are updated and expanded to take account of the additional line items of consolidation (Articles 16 and 17). Goodwill based on fair values should be calculated at the date of first consolidation or at the date of purchase (Article 18).

9.8.5 Valuation rules

The valuation rules of the Fourth Directive must be applied (Article 29). The Article specifies initially that the undertaking which draws up consolidated accounts must apply the same methods of valuation as are used in its individual accounts. However, the Article then provides the option that member states may require or permit the use of other valuation methods in the consolidated accounts, provided such methods are permitted by the Fourth Directive. Most member states give permission for use of other valuation rules, but none requires such an approach. The 'fair value' directive of 2001, explained in section 9.7.6 in relation to the Fourth Directive, applies also to the Seventh Directive.

9.8.6 Associates and joint ventures

Member states may require or permit proportional consolidation for joint ventures (Article 32). Associated companies must be recorded as a single line item, using the equity method of valuation (Article 33). The remainder of the Directive deals extensively with disclosure requirements and transitional provisions.

9.9 Modernization of the Directives

The European Parliament issued a further Directive in June 2003,[41] to set a level playing field between companies in the EU that apply IFRS and those that do not. This Directive stated the desirability of reflecting the IFRS developments in the Fourth and Seventh Directives, particularly in presenting financial statements and applying fair values in accordance with international developments. The Directive set out various instructions and options for member states, requiring them to bring these into force in national legislation by 1 January 2005.

The Directive also introduces a requirement for a 'fair review' in the annual report. This requirement applies to single companies (as an amendment to the Fourth Directive) and to groups (as an amendment to the Seventh Directive). Exhibit 9.6 sets out the requirement in relation to a consolidated annual report.

---

[41] EC (2003a).

| Exhibit 9.6 | Requirement for a fair review in the annual report |

The consolidated annual report shall include at least a fair review of the development and performance of the business and of the position of the undertakings included in the consolidation taken as a whole, together with a description of the principal risks and uncertainties that they face.

The review shall be a balanced and comprehensive analysis of the development and performance of the business and of the position of the undertakings included in the consolidation taken as a whole, consistent with the size and complexity of the business. To the extent necessary for an understanding of such development, performance or position, the analysis shall include both financial and, where appropriate, non-financial key performance indicators relevant to the particular business, including information relating to environmental and employee matters.

In providing its analysis, the consolidated annual report shall, where appropriate, provide references to and additional explanations of amounts reported in the consolidated accounts.

Where a consolidated annual report is required in addition to an annual report, the two reports may be presented as a single report. In preparing such a single report, it may be appropriate to give greater emphasis to those matters which are significant to the undertakings included in the consolidation taken as a whole.

Source: 2003/51/EC Article 2, paragraph 10.

9.10 Recommendation on environmental issues[42]

We explained in section 9.3 the levels of legislation to be encountered in the area of financial reporting. A Recommendation does not have binding force but is an indication of good practice. In May 2001 the Commission issued a Recommendation on the recognition, measurement and disclosure of environmental issues in the annual accounts and annual reports of companies.

The Commission took the view that there was a need to increase and to harmonize the environmental information flowing through corporate annual reports. The Recommendation covers:

- **Recognition of environmental liabilities**. There may be a legal obligation to prevent, reduce or repair environmental damage. There may be a constructive obligation because of past practice or policy of the enterprise. Where reliable estimates of costs can be made, the liability should be recognized. If the costs cannot be estimated reliably, or the obligation has yet to be confirmed, there will be a contingent liability.
- **Recognition of environmental expenditures**. Environmental expenditures should be recognized as an expense of the period in which they are incurred unless they meet the criteria to be recognized as an asset. It may be treated as an asset if it has been incurred to prevent or reduce future damage or conserve resources, and brings future economic benefits.
- **Measurement of environmental liabilities**. The liability is measured as an estimate of the full amount of the liability, based on the expenditure required to settle the present obligation. The estimate should take into account future technical and legal developments, so far as these will probably occur.

---

[42] EC (2001).

- **Disclosures**. There is a detailed list of recommendations on disclosures, covering matters such as policy and programmes for environmental protection, improvements in this area, environmental performance in the business, and descriptions of all environmental liabilities.

Summary and conclusions

This chapter has explained the origins of the EU and the way in which it has expanded and continues to expand as more countries seek membership. It has explained the process by which laws are made, so that the development of national company law may be understood in its impact on national accounting practices. The IAS Regulation imposes IFRS across all EU listed companies from 2005. For entities that do not fall within the IAS Regulation, the most important aspects of EU accounting law are the Fourth and Seventh Directives. The chapter has explained these in some detail so that the practices of individual countries may be understood against this general background. It has also explained how modernization of the Directives is bringing them closer to the IFRS so that eventually it is likely that all companies will apply similar accounting practices, whether listed or not.

Key points from the chapter:

- The IAS Regulation takes precedence over national laws and standards in requiring listed companies in the EU to apply IFRS.
- Member states of the EU have harmonized their national company laws with the Fourth and Seventh Directives. These harmonized national laws continue to apply to companies not covered by the IAS Regulation.
- The EU Commission retains its rights over the process of EU legislation by 'endorsing' IFRS after they are issued by the IASB. The endorsement is carried out by the Commission on the advice of the Accounting Regulatory Committee, which has political representation from all member states. Advice is also taken from technical experts at EFRAG.
- The Fourth and Seventh Directives contain options that give member states flexibility in harmonizing national laws.
- Modernization of the Directives reflects the need to bring them up-to-date on matters such as the use of fair values in reporting financial instruments.
- The Commission is using its influence to encourage harmonization of environmental reporting.

Questions

The following questions test your understanding of the material contained in the chapter and allow you to relate your understanding to the learning outcomes specified at the start of this chapter. The learning outcomes are repeated here. Each question is cross-referenced to the relevant section of the chapter.

Explain the origins and nature of the European Union

1 To what extent is accounting practice in member states likely to be affected by the stated purpose of the EU? (section 9.2)

2 In which ways are each of the main institutions likely to have influence or impact on accounting practice in member states? (section 9.2)

Explain how laws are made in the European Union

3 What are the different levels of legislation that may be applied to accounting? (section 9.3)

Explain the effect of the IAS Regulation

4 Why did the EU abandon the idea of developing 'EU accounting standards'? (section 9.4)

5 What is the status of the IAS Regulation? (sections 9.3 and 9.5)

Understand the main requirements of the EU Fourth and Seventh Directives

6 If a new company law directive were proposed today, what processes would be required? How long might it take for the directive to enter national law of each member state? (section 9.6)

7 Is 'equivalence' the same as 'equality'? (section 9.6)

8 Why is it necessary to have options in directives? What factors might cause options to be allowed in a new directive? (section 9.6)

9 What are the most significant features of the Fourth Directive? (section 9.7)

10 Why may the words 'true and fair' have a different effect in different countries? (section 9.7.2)

11 What are the similarities and differences between the 'type of expenditure' format and the 'functional basis' format of profit and loss account? (section 9.7.5)

12 To what extent do recognition and measurement feature in the Fourth and Seventh Directives? (section 9.7.5)

13 What are the most significant features of the Seventh Directive? (section 9.8)

14 What are the problems in defining a group? (section 9.8.3)

Explain how the EU is modernizing its approach to accounting legislation and guidance

15 Why was there a need to modernize the Fourth and Seventh Directives? (section 9.9)

16 Why did the EU use a Recommendation rather than a Directive to give its views on environmental accounting? (section 9.10)

References and further reading

Alexander, D. and Archer, S. (2000) 'On the myth of "Anglo-Saxon" financial accounting', *The International Journal of Accounting*, 35(4): 539–557.

Alexander, D. and Archer, S. (eds) (2001) *European Accounting Guide*, 4th edn. New York: Aspen Law & Business.

Alexander, D. and Archer, S. (2003) 'On the myth of "Anglo-Saxon" financial accounting: A response to Nobes', *The International Journal of Accounting*, 38(4): 503–504.

Coleman, R. (1984) 'The aims of EEC company law harmonization: Corporate accounting and disclosure issues', in Gray, S.J. and Coenenberg, A.G., *EEC and Accounting Harmonization: Implementation and Impact of the Fourth Directive*. Amsterdam: North-Holland.

FEE (1993) *Seventh Directive Options and their Implementation*. London: Fédération des Experts Comptables Européens/Routledge.

Haller, A. (2002) 'Financial accounting developments in the European Union: past events and future prospects', *The European Accounting Review*, 11(1): 153–190.

Kent, P. (2001) *Law of the European Union*, 3rd edn. London: Longman, Pearson Education.

Niessen, H. (1993) 'The Seventh Directive on consolidated accounts and company law harmonization in the European Community', in Gray, S.J., Coenenberg, A.G. and Gordon, P.D. (eds), *International Group Accounting – Issues in European Harmonization*. London: Routledge.

Nobes, C. (2003) 'On the myth of "Anglo-Saxon" financial accounting: a comment', *The International Journal of Accounting*, 38(1): 95–104.

Ordelheide, D. (ed.) (2001) *Transnational Accounting TRANSACC*, 2nd edn. Basingstoke: Palgrave.

Parker, R.H. and Nobes, C.W. (1994) *An International View of True and Fair Accounting*. London: Routledge.

Watts, T.R. (ed.) (1979) *Handbook on the EEC Fourth Directive: The Impact on Company Accounts in the Nine Member States*. London: The Institute of Chartered Accountants in England and Wales.

Company law and accounting information

Updating news on matters of company law and accounting is available through: http://europa.eu.int/comm/internal_market/accounting/index_en.htm

EC (2001) Commission Recommendation of 30 May 2001 on the recognition, measurement and disclosure of environmental issues in the annual accounts and annual reports of companies. 2001/453/EC.

EC (2002) Regulation (EC) No. 1606/2002 of the European Parliament and of the Council of 19 July 2002 on the application of international accounting standards ('The IAS Regulation').

EC (2003a) Directive 2003/51/EC of the European Parliament and of the Council of 18 June 2003.

EC (2003b) Comments concerning certain Articles of the Regulation (EC) No. 1606/2002 of the European Parliament and of the Council of 19 July 2002 on the application of international accounting standards and the Fourth Council Directive 78/660/EEC of 25 July 1978 and the Seventh Council Directive 83/349/EEC of 13 June 1983 on accounting, Commission of the European Communities, November 2003.

European Union homepage

The starting point for information about the EU is:
http://europa.eu.int/

Appendix 9.1 Formats in the Fourth Directive

Horizontal balance sheet (Article 9)

Assets

A	Subscribed capital unpaid	θ
B	Formation expenses	θ
C	Fixed assets	θ

	I	Intangible assets		⊗
		1 Costs of research and development	φ	
		2 Concessions, patents, licences, trade marks and similar rights and assets	φ	
		3 Goodwill	•	
		4 Payments on account	φ	
	II	Tangible assets		⊗
		1 Land and buildings	•	
		2 Plant and machinery	•	
		3 Other fixtures and fittings, tools and equipment	•	
		4 Payments on account and tangible assets in course of construction	•	
	III	Financial assets		⊗
		1 Shares in affiliated undertakings	•	
		2 Loans to affiliated undertakings	•	
		3 Participating interests	•	
		4 Loans to undertakings with which the company is linked by virtue of participating interests	•	
		5 Investments held as fixed assets	φ	
		6 Other loans	φ	
		7 Own shares	•	

D	Current assets	θ

	I	Stocks		⊗
		1 Raw materials and consumables	φ	
		2 Work in progress	φ	
		3 Finished goods and goods for resale	φ	
		4 Payments on account	φ	
	II	Debtors		⊗

(Amounts becoming due and payable after more than one year
must be shown separately for each item)

1	Trade debtors	φ
2	Amounts owed by affiliated undertakings	•
3	Amounts owed by undertakings with which the company is linked by virtue of participating interests	•
4	Other debtors	φ
5	Subscribed capital called but not paid (unless under A-Assets)	φ
6	Prepayments and accrued income (unless under E-Assets)	•

	III	Investments		⊗
		1 Shares in affiliated undertakings	•	
		2 Own shares	•	
		3 Other investments	φ	
	IV	Cash at bank and in hand		⊗

E	Prepayments and accrued income (unless under D.II.6-Assets)	θ
		θ

Liabilities

A   Capital and reserves   θ

    I   Subscribed capital (unless called-up capital shown under this item)   ⊗
    II   Share premium account   ⊗
    III   Revaluation reserve   ⊗
    IV   Reserves   ⊗

        1   Legal reserve, in so far as required   φ
        2   Reserve for own shares, in so far as required   φ
        3   Reserves provided for by the articles of association   φ
        4   Other reserves   φ

    V   Profit or loss brought forward   ⊗
    VI   Profit or loss for the financial year (unless under F-Assets or E-Liabilities)   ⊗

B   Provisions for liabilities and charges   θ

        1   Provisions for pensions and similar obligations   φ
        2   Provisions for taxation   φ
        3   Other provisions   φ

C   Creditors   θ

(Amounts becoming due and payable within one year and after more than one year must be shown separately for each item and in total)

        1   Debenture loans, showing convertible loans separately   •
        2   Amounts owed to credit institutions   •
        3   Payments received on account of orders in so far as they are
            not shown separately as deductions from stocks   φ
        4   Trade creditors   φ
        5   Bills of exchange payable   φ
        6   Amounts owed to affiliated undertakings   •
        7   Amounts owed to undertakings with which the company
            is linked by virtue of participating interests   •
        8   Other creditors including tax and social security   φ
        9   Accruals and deferred income (unless shown under D-Liabilities)   •

D   Accruals and deferred income (unless shown under
    C.9-Liabilities)   θ
                                                                                                                    θ

Key to symbols
θ   Required from all companies
⊗   Required from all companies
•   Not required for small companies
φ   Not required for small companies or published accounts of medium-sized companies

▶

Minimum vertical balance sheet (Article 10)

C FIXED ASSETS   θ
    I   Intangible assets   ⊗
    II   Tangible assets   ⊗
    III   Financial assets   ⊗

D CURRENT ASSETS   θ
    (showing separately for debtors amounts due in more than one year)

    I   Stocks   ⊗
    II   Debtors   ⊗
    III   Investments   ⊗
    IV   Cash   ⊗

F CREDITORS (due within one year)   (θ)

G NET CURRENT ASSETS   θ

H TOTAL ASSETS LESS CURRENT LIABILITIES   θ

I CREDITORS (due in more than one year)   (θ)

J PROVISIONS FOR LIABILITIES AND CHARGES   (θ)

L CAPITAL AND RESERVES   ⊗

    I   Called-up capital   ⊗
    II   Share premium account   ⊗
    III   Revaluation reserve   ⊗
    IV   Reserves   ⊗
    V   Profit or loss brought forward   ⊗
    VI   Profit or loss for year   ⊗

Notes:
1 Items A, B, E and K are omitted here because national law can permit inclusion within other headings as shown in previous exhibit.
2 For larger companies the above layout assumes that national law requires or allows all items preceded by arabic numerals to be shown in the notes on the accounts.
3 The above layout also shows the form of balance sheet that would be published by small companies if all possible concessions relating to the balance sheet were granted to them (and making assumptions 1 and 2 above).
4 Net current assets will include amounts due from debtors after more than one year.

> *Key to symbols*
> ⊗   Required from all companies
> θ   Required from all companies

Profit and loss account
Type of expenditure basis – vertical (Article 23)

1	Net turnover	φ
2	Variations in stocks of finished goods and work in progress	φ
3	Work performed by the undertaking for its own purposes and capitalized	φ
4	Other operating income	φ
5	(a) Raw materials and consumables	φ
	(b) Other external charges	φ
6	Staff costs	
	(a) Wages and salaries	(•)
	(b) Social security costs, with a separate indication of those relating to pensions	(•)
7	(a) Value adjustments in respect of formation expenses and of tangible and intangible fixed assets	•
	(b) Value adjustments in respect of current assets, to the extent that they exceed the amount of value adjustments which are normal in the undertaking concerned	•
8	Other operating charges	(•)
9	Income from participating interests, with a separate indication of that derived from affiliated undertakings	•
10	Income from other investments and loans forming part of the fixed assets, with a separate indication of that derived from affiliated undertakings	•
11	Other interest receivable and similar income, with a separate indication of that derived from affiliated undertakings	•
12	Value adjustments in respect of financial assets and of investments held as current assets	(•)
13	Interest payable and similar charges, with a separate indication of those concerning affiliated undertakings	(•)
14	Tax on profit on ordinary activities	(•)
15	Profit or loss on ordinary activities after taxation	•
16	Extraordinary income	•
17	Extraordinary charges	(•)
18	Extraordinary profit or loss	•
19	Tax on extraordinary profit or loss	(•)
20	Other taxes not shown under the above items	•
21	Profit or loss for the financial year	•

Key to symbols

φ Small and medium-sized companies may be allowed to combine these items under one item called 'Gross profit or loss'. Small companies may be exempted from publishing, but not from preparing, a profit and loss account.

• Not required for small companies.

Profit and loss account
Functional (operational) basis – vertical (Article 25)

1	Net turnover	φ
2	Cost of sales (including value adjustments)	φ
3	Gross profit or loss	•
4	Distribution costs (including value adjustments)	(•)
5	Administrative expenses (including value adjustments)	(•)
6	Other operating income	•
7	Income from participating interests, with a separate indication of that derived from affiliated undertakings	•
8	Income from other investments and loans forming part of the fixed assets, with a separate indication of that derived from affiliated undertakings	•
9	Other interest receivable and similar income, with a separate indication of that derived from affiliated undertakings	•
10	Value adjustments in respect of financial assets and of investments held as current assets	(•)
11	Interest payable and similar charges, with a separate indication of those concerning affiliated undertakings	(•)
12	Tax on profit or loss on ordinary activities	(•)
13	Profit or loss on ordinary activities after taxation	•
14	Extraordinary income	•
15	Extraordinary charges	(•)
16	Extraordinary profit or loss	•
17	Tax on extraordinary profit or loss	(•)
18	Other taxes not shown under the above items	(•)
19	Profit or loss for the financial year	•

Key to symbols

φ   Small and medium-sized companies may be allowed to combine these items with item 3 under one item called 'Gross profit or loss'. Small companies may be exempted from publishing, but not from preparing, a profit and loss account.

•   Not required for small companies.

PART 4

From national to international standards

Introduction to Part 4

Part 4 brings together the influence of the IASB, the factors causing similarities and differences, and the relative influences of US and EU, to describe the state of financial reporting in a selection of countries. We cover four European countries (France, Germany, The Netherlands and Poland) in a comparative study of the institutional influences and the aspects of accountability which will remain distinctive after harmonization with IFRS in 2005. The UK has a separate chapter in its role as part of what is sometimes called the 'Anglo-American' influence on accounting. Japan was a founder member of the IASC (predecessor of IASB) but has some problems with implementing IFRS because of a perception in Japan that the underlying business structures are so very different from the western corporations for which IFRS appear to have been developed. China is included in our chapter coverage because it is an emerging market, committed to developing its standards under the influence of IFRS, but with many problems of learning how to move from a uniform accounting system to one based on professional judgement.

Purpose of Part 4

The chapters of Part 4 have two major aims. The first is to explain how the national characteristics of a range of countries are likely to affect accounting principles and practice, using a framework derived from the studies explained in Part 2. The second is to indicate the extent to which national practice is already close to or in harmony with IASB Standards (as explained in Part 1) and to indicate those areas of national practice which are particularly influenced by national characteristics, and therefore possibly more resistant to broader desires for harmonization.

Structure of country chapters

Each chapter explains national institutions and characteristics under headings based on Chapter 4:

- the country
- overview of accounting regulations
- institutions, broken down into:

    political and economic system
    legal system
    taxation system
    corporate financing system
    the accounting profession

- external influences.

The influence of institutional factors has been explained in Chapter 4. The effect of cultural influences has been described in Chapter 5. Classifications were summarized in Chapter 6 and measurement of the differences arising from these influences in Chapter 7. Each of the country chapters will refer the reader back to the relevant sections of those chapters. It is important to read those chapters again as each country is studied, so that the reader gains an increased understanding of the relative position of the country and avoids learning about one country in isolation.

The country chapters summarize the overall picture of accounting practice at the present time and then identify key features of interest in national principles and practice. There are discussions of the country's characteristics as represented by Gray's system of classification (described in Chapters 2 and 4) because these forces may cause underlying differences in reality even after adoption of IFRS or US GAAP gives an appearance of harmonization.

Choice of countries

Choosing which countries to include in detail was one of the most difficult aspects of writing this book. The total global diversity of accounting practice creates a classification range which makes international accounting a fascinating subject for study. Describing anything less than the total must necessarily leave the reader with an incomplete picture. However, constraints of time and space necessitate a choice which gives the reader the widest possible taste of the diversity and complexity, leaving an appetite to find out more by using the reference material cited in the chapters.

The choice was influenced by:

- relative size and importance of international capital markets;
- residence of major multinational companies;
- role in the development of International Financial Reporting Standards;
- origins of the accountancy profession;
- distinctive national accounting principles and practice;
- accounting classification systems which indicate an expectation of distinctive characteristics.

The choice of France, Germany, The Netherlands and Poland, within the EU member states, was decided on the basis that their accounting practices have been identified as very different in many comparative studies.

There are emerging markets in the Far East which have derived their accounting practices from very different backgrounds. Japanese accounting practice has established an international reputation based on an international capital market. China is developing internationally orientated accounting practices which will be consistent with its development of international business activity.

Learning outcomes

Specific learning outcomes are set out at the start of each chapter but overall, on completion of Part 3, for each country the student should be able to:

- know, in outline, the key characteristics of each country as summarized in published economic indicators;
- know the origins of accounting regulations and the historical development leading to the present state of practice;

- relate institutional factors for each country to the framework set out in Chapter 1 with particular reference to:
    - the political and economic system,
    - the legal system,
    - the taxation system,
    - the corporate financing system,
    - the accounting profession,
    - external factors;
- relate specific practices to national characteristics and summarize the relative position of the country in the international spectrum of accounting practices.

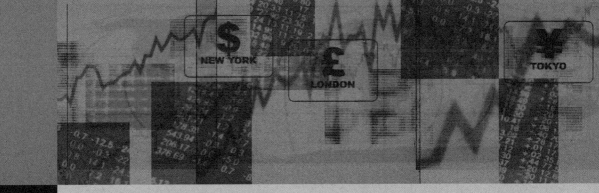

10 Accounting in EU member states

Learning outcomes

After reading this chapter you should be able to:

● Explain how member states of the EU will continue to have a national role, beyond the IAS Regulation, in setting accounting standards.

● Relate the institutional factors and external influences for a selection of member states to the framework set out in Chapter 4.

● Explain and evaluate the state of oversight and assurance in a selection of member states.

● Explain a selection of accounting issues where national differences in accounting are likely to persist.

● Describe how comparative research studies have helped advance understanding of similarities and differences in accounting across Europe.

10.1 Introduction

With the enlargement of the EU to 25 members, and the linking of Norway through the EEA agreement, Switzerland is the only western European country that does not implement the Directives and is not obliged to implement the IAS Regulation. Nevertheless many large Swiss companies apply IFRS by choice. This chapter gives an overview of the national characteristics that have caused accounting diversity in the past and may continue to cause some diversity for listed companies in those areas of financial reporting not subject to the IAS Regulation and those areas not covered by the Directives. As far as possible we draw comparisons across all EU member states; for more detailed discussion we have chosen France, Germany, The Netherlands and Poland. We begin in section 10.2 with economic diversity, since accounting purports to represent the economic substance of transactions and events. In section 10.3 we compare approaches to implementing the IAS Regulation and contrast different approaches to setting national standards. In section 10.4 we expand some of the institutional factors outlined in Chapter 4 by comparing legal systems, the nature of corporate governance, relative strength of equity markets, the nature of professionalism as supported by professional bodies, the influence of taxation, and historical influences. External influences are outlined in section 10.5. Mechanisms of oversight and assurance are discussed in section 10.6.

In section 10.7 we explain and comment on some areas of accounting practice where diversity may persist after 2005. We pay particular attention to Gray's accounting values of transparency or secrecy. Constraints of space make us selective in the issues we consider; our choice reflects matters that show similarities and diversity in annual reports. (For those who wish to know more of the history of accounting development in France, Germany, The Netherlands and Hungary, there are chapter supplements on the website for this text.)

10.2 The countries

Politically all the member states of the EU have systems of government that meet the conditions for acceptance as members, although the precise nature of the democratic process varies. Nobes (1998) suggested that political differences were unlikely to be key explanations of differences in accounting systems across Europe. Economic diversity is greater, especially with the accession of ten new member states in 2004. This leads to the question of whether harmonization of accounting practices creates fictitious comparability because it masks fundamental differences in the underlying economic substance of the business. At present we cannot answer that question from the evidence available but it will undoubtedly provide a subject for future research.

10.2.1 Economic indicators

Exhibit 10.1 shows key economic indicators, separated into the 15 member states prior to 2004 and the ten new members who joined in 2004. The dominant populations are Germany, France, the UK and Spain, with Poland by far the largest of the new members. The gross domestic product (GDP) per head is adjusted to purchasing power parity with the US, applying an adjustment factor to take account of the differences in the price of a standard basket of goods and services. The growth rate of real GDP is shown in the next column, with closer matching among 14 of the 15 older members, but much higher growth in Ireland. The relatively low growth rate in Germany has persisted since unification. Amongst the new members, Poland has the highest growth rate. The Human Development Index (HDI) combines GDP with adult literacy and life expectancy as an index of human development. A score above 80 is considered 'high' in world comparisons but it can be seen in the table that the new member states have relatively lower levels than the pre-2004 members. The final two columns show the export market and the import market having the highest percentage of total exports and imports of the country. The importance of Germany as a trade partner is clear.

10.2.2 Privatization

Political conditions may dictate the extent to which the state takes full or partial ownership in business enterprises. A change in political conditions may lead to privatization where the government of the day seeks to reduce or eliminate state ownership. Governments may start a programme of privatization to reduce public debt or to raise cash for other economic programmes, or they may privatize to move towards a political ideal of free market enterprise. Because the industries under state control are often critical to the economy and security of the country, governments which have privatized enterprises will continue to impose regulations on such enterprises, which may affect their accounting and financial reporting. This section discusses the particular situations of France, as a country with a history of waves of state ownership followed by privatization, and Poland, as a country currently in the transition of privatization of state-owned enterprises.

Some of the largest French companies are partly under state ownership. From 1945 onwards there was a move to reconstruct the economy by creating joint enterprise bodies

Exhibit 10.1 Comparison of economic indicators

	Population	GDP per head $PPP	Annual Growth of GDP 1991–2001	HDI	Largest single export market	Largest single source of imports
Austria	8.1m	26,830	2.2%	92.6	Germany	Germany
Belgium	10.3m	26,150	2.1%	93.9	Germany	Netherlands
Denmark	5.3m	28,490	2.2%	92.6	Germany	Germany
Finland	5.2m	24,030	2.0%	93.0	Germany	Germany
France	59.5m	24,080	1.9%	92.8	Germany	Germany
Germany	82.0m	25,240	1.6%	92.5	France	France
Greece	10.6m	17,520	2.5%	88.5	Germany	Italy
Ireland	3.8m	27,170	7.1%	92.5	UK	UK
Italy	57.5m	24,530	1.6%	91.3	Germany	Germany
Luxembourg	0.4m	48,560	N/a	92.5	N/a	N/a
The Netherlands	15.9m	27,390	2.7%	93.5	Germany	Germany
Portugal	10.0m	17,710	2.7%	88.0	Germany	Germany
Spain	39.9m	20,150	2.7%	91.3	France	France
Sweden	8.8m	23,800	1.7%	94.1	Germany	Germany
UK	59.5m	24,340	2.7%	92.8	US	US
Czech Republic	10.3m	14,320	0.4%	84.9	Germany	Germany
Cyprus	0.8m	21,110	N/a	88.3	N/a	N/a
Estonia	1.4m	9,650	N/a	82.6	N/a	N/a
Latvia	2.4m	7,760	N/a	80.0	N/a	N/a
Lithuania	3.7m	8,350	N/a	80.8	N/a	N/a
Hungary	9.9m	11,990	1.0%	83.5	Germany	Germany
Malta	0.4m	13,140	N/a	87.5	N/a	N/a
Poland	38.6m	9,370	3.4%	83.3	Germany	Germany
Slovenia	2.0m	17,060	2.0%	87.9	Germany	Germany
Slovakia	5.4m	11,780	0.6%	83.5	Germany	Germany

Source: *The Economist Pocket World in Figures*, 2004 Edition, Profile Books Ltd. Figures relate to 2001.

owned by government and private enterprise. That began a tradition of state intervention mixed with private enterprise partnership. France has been subjected to waves of nationalization and privatization of industry, depending on the government in power. A wave of nationalization in the early 1980s was followed by a programme of privatization starting in 1993 but in 1997 a further change of government influenced the process of privatization. Since 1997 the government has raised private-sector capital by selling significant state shareholdings in airline companies, banks, defence, insurance and telecom companies. However, by 2000 the state still owned some 1,500 enterprises, employing over 1 million people. Retaining some major shareholdings in state control was seen as a political compromise of a socialist government facing the pressures of capitalism.[1] By 2003 six companies (Air France, France Télécom, La Poste, EDF/GDF, RATP and SNCF) represented the bulk of the economic weight represented by state-owned firms. Plans to reduce state ownership of these companies further were in place.[2] In particular, the French government announced in September 2004 that it would reduce its holding in France Télécom below

---

[1] *Financial Times* Survey, 'France', 14 June 2000, p. vi.

[2] OECD (2003a), pp. 86–89.

50 per cent, which would allow the company to offer its shares in making future acquisitions, rather than having to offer cash.[3]

In Poland, at the date of accession to membership of the EU, there was a continued State presence in companies being sold as joint-stock companies. An OECD Survey[4] published at that time recommended that the privatization process should be accelerated to reduce public debt, boost productivity and enhance investor confidence. The Survey suggested that where the state has retained an interest, and even a majority holding, in joint-stock companies whose shares are sold on the stock market, this denies the companies the chance of raising equity capital, limits the scope to hire the best staff, and has probably contributed to low offer prices and lack of interest in companies already on sale. Selling off only a minority shareholding in State-controlled enterprises would perpetuate a system of state ownership and politically-appointed managers. The Survey recommended seeking strategic external investors to encourage risk taking and to improve corporate governance.

10.3 International standards; national choices

This section explains how each national regulator intends to implement the IAS Regulation, indicating that there appears to be a continuing role for national standard-setters beyond the consolidated accounts that are covered by the Regulation. We then describe in more detail the national standard-setting systems for France, Germany, The Netherlands and Poland.

10.3.1 Implementing the IAS Regulation

The IAS Regulation (see section 9.5) is compulsory for the consolidated accounts of companies admitted to trading on a regulated market of a member state. However it is not compulsory for the accounts of the individual companies within the group. The Regulation gives member states options to permit or to require individual companies to apply IFRS in their financial statements. Exhibit 10.2 shows the intentions of member states as indicated to the internal markets directorate of the EU at July 2004. Member states appear to have been particularly cautious where the tax system is linked to the accounting system because a change to IFRS could have significant implications for the amount of tax revenue and the distribution of the tax burden. Member states also appear cautious where company law sets rules on distributable profits. The responses of member states on the intended treatment of non-listed groups and individual companies (not shown in the table)[5] are even more cautious.

The spread of answers in Exhibit 10.2 means that national standard-setting bodies will continue to have a role. In some cases that role will cover individual companies within groups; in other cases it will cover consolidated accounts of unlisted companies or individual companies within unlisted groups. In December 2000 the Fédération des Experts Comptables Européens (FEE) published a detailed report in the range of approaches to setting national accounting standards at that time. Exhibit 10.3 summarizes the split between public sector and private sector standard-setting bodies. Sections 10.3.2 to 10.3.5 describe four different types of national standard-setter.

---

[3] *The Financial Times*, 2 September 2004, p. 21.

[4] OECD (2004), p. 18.

[5] http://europa.eu.int/comm/internal_market/en/.

| Exhibit 10.2 | Member states' intentions with regard to individual companies |

Answer	Questions to member state	
	*Will you use the option to **permit** IFRS in the annual accounts for individual listed companies?*	*Will you use the option to **require** IFRS in the annual accounts for individual listed companies?*
Yes	Denmark – yes until 2009 Finland Germany – for information only Ireland – probably Luxembourg (2007 if there is a tax solution) Netherlands UK Iceland Liechtenstein Poland	Denmark – yes after 2009 Italy Portugal Czech Republic Estonia Slovakia Slovenia
No	Austria France, no until tax and legal solution found Greece Hungary Italy Latvia Portugal Spain Sweden Norway Czech Republic Estonia Lithuania Slovakia Slovenia	Austria Finland France, no until tax and legal solution found Germany Greece Ireland Luxembourg Netherlands Spain Sweden UK Norway Iceland Liechtenstein Hungary Latvia Poland
Undecided	Belgium – to consider tax and legal issues Cyprus – no answer Malta – no answer	Belgium – to consider tax and legal issues Cyprus – no answer Malta – no answer

Source: Extract from *Planned Implementation of IAS Regulation*, July 2004, EU internal market website.

10.3.2 France

Under a law passed in 1998, a *Comité de la Réglementation Comptable* (CRC) was set up with 12 members. The CRC is devoted to making mandatory, for all or some enterprises, the accounting standards which are prepared by the Conseil National de la Comptabilité (CNC)[6] or other institutions. For the first time in France, there was a body with the power to impose accounting standards. Previously the CNC had an advisory role under the Ministry of Finance.

---

[6] www.finances.gouv.fr/CNCompta/.

| Exhibit 10.3 | Setting accounting standards in Europe: private or public sector body |

Private sector	Public sector
Austria	Belgium
Denmark	Czech Republic
Germany	Finland
Italy	France
Netherlands	Hungary
Slovenia	Luxembourg
Sweden*	Portugal
Switzerland	Romania
UK and Ireland	Spain
	Sweden*

* Sweden has two standard-setting bodies.

Source: *Accounting standard-setting in Europe*, FEE. December 2000, www.fee.be

The CRC approves all new accounting rules, subject to ratification by the appropriate government ministers. The CRC must act within the framework of the Accounting Law, but is empowered to prepare the necessary rules for applying the law. Prior to 1998, companies could present consolidated accounts according to internationally recognized standards but with considerable flexibility as to what was meant by 'internationally recognized standards'.[7] This resulted in French companies 'shopping around' for the basis of presentation of their group accounts (Ding *et al.*, 2003). The flexibility of French GAAP for consolidated accounts is illustrated in Exhibit 10.4.

The CRC is chaired by the Minister for the Economy, Finance and Industry. Other members are the Minister of Justice, the Secretary of State for the Budget, the presidents

| Exhibit 10.4 | French GAAP in consolidated accounts, Total |

Accounting policies

The Consolidated financial statements of TOTAL and its subsidiaries (together, the Company or Group) have been prepared in accordance with generally accepted accounting principles in France (French "GAAP") and comply with the principles and methodology relative to Consolidated financial statements, Regulation No. 99–02 approved by the decree dated June 22, 1999 of the French Accounting Regulations Committee.

Furthermore, the Company applies the standards issued by the Financial Accounting Standards Board (FASB) which are compatible with the French Regulations and, which contribute, in their current wording, to better reflect the assets and liabilities of the Company and the best comparability with the other oil majors, namely those from North America. The exceptions to the use of FASB standards are presented in the Annual Report as well as in the annual report of the Company under US Generally Accepted Accounting Principles (Form 20-F).

Source: Total annual report (2003), p. 105. www.total.com

---

[7] *FT World Accounting Report*, January 1997, pp. 9–10; May 1997, p. 6.

of the Bourse, the CNC, the CNCC and the OEC, three representatives of enterprise and employer interests and representatives of the civil and criminal courts. During 1999 the CRC adopted a ruling on a new draft of the *Plan Comptable Général* (PCG)[8] and approved a new methodology for consolidated accounts.[9] Ministerial approval remains a final condition for any CRC recommendation. The CNC continues issuing opinions in its advisory role and so it is essential that the CRC and CNC work harmoniously.

10.3.3 Germany

The German Accounting Standards Committee (*Deutsches Rechnungslegungs Standards Committee*, DRSC)[10] was formed in 1998 using the model of the FASB in the US. It takes a legal mandate from the HGB (paragraph 342) and comprises seven independent experts. Its standards are approved by the Ministry of Justice. By mid-2004 the German Accounting Standards Committee had approved 14 accounting standards, as listed in Exhibit 10.5.

Exhibit 10.2 indicates that the Federal Ministry of Justice does not intend to permit or require individual companies to use IFRS in their financial statements for regulatory

Exhibit 10.5 German accounting standards at July 2004

GAS 1	Exempting Consolidated Financial Statements in accordance with § 292a of Commercial Code
GAS 2	Cash Flow Statements
GAS 3	Segment Reporting
GAS 4	Acquisition Accounting in Consolidated Financial Statements
GAS 5	Risk Reporting
GAS 6	Interim Financial Reporting
GAS 7	Group Equity and Total Recognized Results
GAS 8	Accounting for Investments in Associates in Consolidated Financial Statements
GAS 9	Accounting for Investments in Joint Ventures in Consolidated Financial Statements
GAS 10	Deferred Taxes in Consolidated Financial Statements
GAS 11	Related Party Disclosure
GAS 12	Non-current Intangible Assets
GAS 13	Consistency Principle and Correction of Errors
GAS 14	Currency Translation

Source: www.standardsetter.de/drsc/gas.html

---

[8] www.finances.gouv.fr/CNCompta/ Text of PCG in English.

[9] *Accountancy International*, July 1999, p. 57.

[10] www.standardsetter.de (has an option for English language).

purposes, so the DSRC will continue to have a role in developing national standards for individual companies within listed groups and for unlisted companies.

10.3.4 The Netherlands

There are three stages to accounting regulation in The Netherlands. The first is the Civil Code, the second is the Enterprise Chamber (see section 10.6.4) and the third is The Council for Annual Reporting (*Raad voor de Jaarverslaggeving*, or RJ). The RJ is not part of the formal legal system but is an essential element in the implementation of the law. It was established in 1982, replacing an earlier body set up in 1971 at the request of the government, and it operates under the oversight of the Social Economic Council. The RJ acts on behalf of the Foundation for Annual Reporting and comprises representatives of three interest groups – users, preparers and auditors. The users are represented by the two main trade unions and a representative from the Dutch Financial Analysts' Society, the preparers are represented by the principal industrial confederation, and the auditors are represented by their professional body, NIVRA. It is interesting to note the emphasis placed on employees as users.

The Council reviews the accounting principles which are applied in practice and gives its opinion on the acceptability of those principles within the framework of the law. Opinions are published as Guidelines for Annual Reporting. Part of the work of the RJ is to give opinions on IASB Standards.

The composition of the Council for Annual Reporting[11] (RJ) reflects the fundamental legal requirement of financial accounts that the bases underlying the valuation of assets and liabilities and the determination of the financial results comply with standards acceptable in the business environment.

The Council reviews accounting principles used in practice and gives opinions on the acceptability of the principles within the framework of law. It does not in itself have statutory powers or duties and there is no government representative on the Council. The Council's opinions have no statutory backing, although they do provide an important frame of reference for the auditor and for the courts in arriving at views on the application of accounting policies. The Council contains a range of interest groups working together to achieve a consensus. It cannot strictly be proposed as an example of professionalism because the influence of NIVRA is only one of the voices on the Council, but it indicates the potential for interesting social interaction where statutory control is not imposed.

Revaluation to a replacement cost (current cost) basis is allowed as an alternative to historical cost, indicating the flexibility of Dutch accounting *de jure*. However, examples of replacement cost accounting are relatively rare; one case is Heineken (Exhibit 10.6).

10.3.5 Poland[12]

Polish accounting is regulated by the Accounting Act of 1994 with subsequent amendments, particularly those of 2002 and 2004. Together these harmonize with the Fourth and Seventh Directives and bring Polish accounting closer to IFRS. During 2003 the

---

[11] Hoogendoorn (2001), p. 700.
[12] Ernst & Young (2004), p. 27.

Exhibit 10.6   Notes describing replacement cost accounting, Heineken

Tangible fixed assets

Except for land, which is not depreciated, tangible fixed assets are stated at replacement cost less accumulated depreciation. The following average useful lives are used for depreciation purposes:

Buildings	30–40 years
Plant and equipment	10–30 years
Other fixed assets	5–10 years

The replacement cost is based on appraisals by internal and external experts, taking into account technical and economic developments. Other factors taken into account include the experience gained in the construction of breweries throughout the world. Grants received in respect of investments in intangible fixed assets are deducted from the amount of the investment.

Projects under construction are included at cost.

Current assets

Stocks purchased from third parties are stated at replacement cost. based on prices from current purchase contracts and latest prices as at balance sheet date. Finished products and work in progress are stated at manufactured cost based on replacement cost and taking into account the production stage reached.

Stocks of spare parts are depreciated on a straight-line basis taking account of obsolescence. If the recoverable amount or net realizable value of stocks is less than their replacement cost, provisions are formed in respect of the difference. Advance payments on stocks are included at face value.

Receivables are carried at face value less a provision for credit risks and less the amount of deposits on returnable packaging.

Securities are carried at the lower of historical cost and quoted price, or estimated market value in the case of unlisted securities.

Cash is included at face value.

Revaluations

Differences in carrying amounts due to revaluations are credited or debited to group equity, less an amount in respect of deferred tax liabilities where applicable.

Source: Heineken annual report (2003), p. 56. www.heinekeninternational.com

Polish Accounting Committee was established to prepare and issue standards to implement the Act. The first standard was issued by the Committee in September 2003. Polish Accounting Regulations will take into account the specific economic circumstances of Poland as well as the requirements of the EU. In areas unregulated by the Act, reference may be made to IFRS.

From 2005 Polish listed companies follow IFRS completely but as there are relatively few of these the Polish Accounting Regulations remain important for many companies. The reconciliation of Polish accounting standards to IFRS published by Orlen indicates the gap between the two systems (Exhibit 10.7).

Exhibit 10.7 Reconciliation of Polish accounting standards to IFRS, Orlen

34. Transformation for IFRS purposes

The Group companies maintain their accounts in accordance with the accounting principles and practices employed by enterprises in Poland as is required by the Accounting Act and related regulations. The financial statements set out above reflect certain adjustments not reflected in the companies statutory books to present these financial statements in accordance with IFRS effective for 2003, except for non-compliance with IAS 29 and IAS 16 as specified in Note 3.

The adjustments to the consolidated financial statements prepared under Polish Accounting Standards ("PAS") are set out below:

	Net profit for the year ended	
	31.12.2003 in PLN million	31.12.2002 in PLN million
PAS basis consolidated	1,014	479
Distributions from profit for social activity	(4)	–
Borrowing costs capitalisation, less depreciation	(68)	(25)
Amortisation of CPN goodwill	(10)	(11)
IFRS treatment of negative goodwill	17	8
Deferred tax on the above	53	(17)
Other	(15)	(13)
IFRS Consolidated	**987**	**421**

	Net assets 31.12.2003 in PLN million	Net assets 31.12.2002 in PLN million
PAS basis consolidated	9,130	7,927
Distribution from profit for social activity	–	–
Borrowing costs capitalisation less depreciation	458	526
Goodwill on CPN, net	62	72
IFRS treatment of negative goodwill	(54)	(71)
Deferred tax on the above	(87)	(140)
Other	1	15
IFRS Consolidated	**9,510**	**8,329**

a. Distribution from profit for social activity
According to Polish business practice shareholders of the Company have the right to distribute the profit for the employees benefits, i.e. for bonus payment or for the Company's social fund. Such distributions are presented in statutory financial statements, similarly to dividend payments, through the change in capital. In the financial statements prepared in accordance with IFRS such payments are charged to operating costs of the year, that the distribution concerns.

b. Capitalisation of borrowing costs
In accordance with PAS, borrowing costs are written off to the income statement as incurred net of the amount capitalised related to borrowings for specific capital projects. Borrowing costs incurred on general borrowings are always expensed as incurred. Borrowing costs are

Exhibit 10.7 *(Continued)*

> capitalised as a part of the costs of the relevant fixed assets up to the date of commission-
> ing and written off to the income statement over the period in which assets is depreciated.
>
> In these financial statements borrowing costs are subject to capitalisation in accordance with
> allowed alternative treatment of IAS 23 "Borrowing costs" presented in Note 4(i).
>
> *c. Goodwill on shares purchased from former CPN employees*
> The acquisition of CPN's employee shares was recorded for IFRS purposes under the acqui-
> sition method of accounting. As a result the Company recognised goodwill of PLN 107m on
> the acquisition of the 19.43 per cent CPN shares held by the employees.
>
> For PAS, the acquisition of CPN, including the acquisition of the minority shares was pushed
> back to the earliest financial statements presented under pooling of interests' method.
>
> *d. IFRS treatment of negative goodwill*
> According to PAS, before the amended Accounting Act came into force, the Company
> released negative goodwill to income during two to five years period subsequent to acquisi-
> tion. In the IFRS financial statements negative goodwill is recognised in a manner presented
> in Note 4(c).
>
> *e. Deferred tax effects*
> Adjustments related to above mentioned differences between PAS and IFRS are basis for
> deferred tax calculation.
>
> *f. IFRS treatment of revenues*
> In accordance with PAS, the Company and certain of its subsidiaries included excise tax
> charged on the oil product manufactured in their revenues and selling expenses.
>
> For the purpose of these consolidated financial statements prepared under IFRS revenues
> and selling expenses had been presented net of excise tax of PLN 9,309m and PLN 9,426m
> for the years ended 31 December 2003 and 31 December 2002, respectively.

Source: Orlen annual report (2003), pp. 151–153. www.orlen.pl

10.4 Institutional influences

10.4.1 Legal systems

10.4.1.1 Range of legal systems

The characterization of continental European countries as 'code law' systems appears too general when the details are considered. The French legal system is of the Romano-Germanic family but has taken on a European characteristic which is identifiably different from the German legal system. Other countries having a legal system similar to that of France include Belgium, Denmark, Italy, The Netherlands, Portugal and Spain.

The German legal system is of the Romano-Germanic family, with the German approach as a unique branch of the European grouping. Consequently German accounting practice, which is strongly contained in law, might be expected to show unique characteristics.

The Dutch legal system is based on laws, jurisprudence (verdicts), treaties and custom. The laws are passed by Parliament. The courts will recognize international treaties and will use long-established customs as an aid to the interpretation of statutes. The system of law in The Netherlands is within the Romano-Germanic family and of the European tradition, alongside France but distinguished from Germany.

Poland has a code law system. The Polish Commercial Code of 1934 was dormant from 1948 but was gradually reactivated from the 1980s as a market economy began to emerge. It was only in 2000 and 2004 that the Code was modernized in readiness for joining the EU.

10.4.1.2 Types of business organization

Most countries have some form of limited liability company where owners are able to invest in a business and limit their personal loss to the amount of the equity interest in the company. Most countries also distinguish public limited companies from private limited companies (see Exhibit 10.8). As the descriptions suggest, the public limited company has obligations to a wider public as shareholders, lenders, employees, customers, suppliers, and government agencies, while the private limited company has obligations to a narrower range of stakeholders closely connected to the company. Corporate governance obligations, including the requirements of accounting rules, are generally more onerous for public companies.

10.4.2 Corporate governance

The website of the internal market contains a very thorough and detailed comparative study of corporate governance codes across the 15 member states in 2001.[13] This provides an excellent starting point for any comparative study. It can be augmented by reference to the website of the European Corporate Governance Institute (ECGI) where there are links to the codes of separate countries.[14] The rest of

Exhibit 10. 8 Descriptions of public and private limited companies

	Public limited company	Private limited company
France	SA (*Société anonyme*)	SARL (*Société à responsabilité limité*)
Germany	AG (*Aktiengesellschaft*) (joint stock company)	GmbH (*Gesellschaft mit beschränkter Haftung*) (limited liability company)
The Netherlands	NV (*Naamloze vennootschap*) Structure-NV is a larger company having at least 100 employees and a works council	BV (*Besloten vennootschap*) Structure-BV is a larger company having at least 100 employees and a works council
Poland	SA (*spólka akcyjna*) Joint stock company	sp.z.o.o. (*spólka z organiczoną odpowiedzialnością*) Limited liability company

[13] Comparative Study of Corporate Governance Codes Relevant to the European Union and its Member States, on behalf of the European Commission Internal Market Directorate, January 2002.

[14] www.ecgi.org/codes/all_codes.htm.

this section describes some of the key features of corporate governance in France, Germany, The Netherlands and Poland.

10.4.2.1 France

In France, there is a choice of two distinct systems for *Sociétés anonymes*, one having a unitary board and the other a supervisory board. The traditional approach is the unitary board, appointed by the shareholders. A *Président Directeur Générale* (PDG) is the chairman and chief executive. The PDG is elected by the board. As a matter of French law until 2001, the PDG had executive authority and the sole right to represent the company. The *Loi relative aux Nouvelles Régulations Economiques* 2001 (NRE Act) now allows the supervisory and management roles to be separated. The board of directors must decide whether to delegate powers to the president (effectively creating a joint chairman and CEO) or to delegate the powers to a separate manager.[15]

The PDG has traditionally held a strong position of control over the company and the system of corporate governance has been largely dependent on the PDG's personality. Furthermore, the PDG gains support from loyal shareholders and particularly the shareholder representatives who take places on the board of directors. Undertakings not to sell shares may also be given by major shareholders.[16] A typical PDG may be a professional manager who has developed a career with the business, possibly as a founding owner. The PDG may also be a person brought in from outside because of his or her connections, particularly where relations with government are important.

The size of a unitary board varies with company size but at least two-thirds of its members must be non-executive. Traditionally the board did not intervene in the day-to-day running of the business. Its role was to hire and fire the PDG, to authorize the raising of new finance and to authorize mergers or other links; meetings were relatively infrequent. The NRE Act emphasizes the responsibility of the board for supervising the operations of the company.

There is legislation dating from 1966 which allows the alternative of a supervisory board (*conseil de surveillance*) resembling that found in Germany. Management is in the hands of a *Directoire* (two to five members) appointed by the supervisory board to run the company. This alternative system of corporate governance is relatively little used.

Companies over a specified size are required to have a *comité d'entreprise* on which the workforce is represented. This reflects the socialist politics of France in the early 1980s. The committee is not as strongly based as the German works council and the control of the company is very much in the hands of the PDG. One or two members of the *comité d'entreprise* attend meetings of the Board of Directors, but have no voting rights. The board does not deal with day-to-day activities and so it is possible for the PDG to take executive action without extensive consultation with the representatives of the *comité d'entreprise*.

The corporate governance debate in France was encouraged by the publication in 1995 of the report *The Boards of Directors of Public Companies*, from a working group chaired by Marc Viénot. It contained a series of recommendations intended to address the concerns of international investors. In 1999 a review, also chaired by Marc Viénot, made recommendations on the role of chairman and chief executive officer, re-election of directors, executive pay, financial information and audit. It recommended that final consolidated accounts should be available within two months of the period-end and

---

[15] Discussion of individual corporate governance codes relative to the European Union and its member states, p. 64, Annex IV, Weil Gotshal & Manges, 2002.

[16] Charkham (1994), p. 152.

that auditors should advise the board on the choice of accounting framework for the consolidated accounts (IASs or US GAAP where consistent with French GAAP). The recommendations were not mandatory but encouraged voluntary reform and influenced the NRE Act.

Companies in France are allowed by law to distribute voting rights unevenly and may issue new shares during takeover battles without consulting existing shareholders. Such practices are gradually diminishing under pressure from institutional investors. Annual reports contain information on managers' remuneration, including share options.

France has a long history of state involvement in the economy, with waves of nationalization and denationalization. In recent years the state has reduced its holdings in major companies but in some cases the remaining shareholding constrains activity. In the case of France Télécom, legislation has required the state to retain a majority stake. This has inhibited the company in raising equity finance and has led to high borrowing. From a governance perspective there is also a potential question about the capacity of the state to provide effective governance over state-owned enterprises. In moving away from this position, without losing the political principle, a State Ownership Agency was announced (*Agence des participations de l'état*) to watch over state holdings and exercise its rights as a shareholder in state-owned companies.[17]

10.4.2.2 Germany

The German system of corporate governance for companies of a substantial size (all AGs and GmbHs of more than 500 employees) is based on a 'two-tier' principle. This means there are two layers of management control – the shareholders and the employees are stakeholders and share in the appointment of the supervisory board; the supervisory board appoints an executive board. In the case of an AG, this is called a *Vorstand*; in the case of a GmbH, it is called a *Geschäfts-führung*.

There are strict rules on the composition of the supervisory board. For the largest companies, the membership of the supervisory board is split equally between persons appointed by the shareholders and persons appointed by the employees. Where there are fewer than 2,000 employees two-thirds of the members are appointed by the shareholders. The chairman of the board is always drawn from the shareholder representatives, and has the casting vote in a situation of deadlock.

The area of activity of the supervisory board is prescribed by law and covers:

- the company's accounts for a specified period;
- major capital expenditure and strategic acquisitions or closures;
- appointments to the executive board;
- approval of the dividend.

The main function is to ensure the competence of general management, but a second role is the approval of the annual profit and loss account and balance sheet. Both are audited (where the corporation is at least of medium size) and the supervisory board may question the external auditors. The employees' representatives also function effectively because they draw on material provided by the works councils which allows them to play an effective part in the work of the supervisory board.

Banks often take a seat on the supervisory board of a company. They do this as part of the shareholder representation. The banks have traditionally been pre-eminent as suppliers of capital and they also provide a range of other services. There are therefore

---

[17] OECD (2003a), pp. 86–89.

strong personal links with the company beyond the formal links of the supervisory board. The banks themselves have advisory boards of which industrialists are members, and there are therefore some intricately interwoven links between banks and companies. It has been suggested that the combination of direct ownership, deposited share voting rights, length of lending period and breadth of services provides the following benefits:

- deep relationships between companies and banks whereby the bank becomes a counsel and guide to the company on a long-term basis;
- a considerable flow of information into the banks;
- deep knowledge by the banks about sectors of industry which can be used to the advantage of customers;
- development of well-trained staff in the banks;
- banks having the knowledge, motivation and authority to exert influence on company management.[18]

A 1997 law on aspects of corporate governance, the law on Control and Transparency in the Corporate Sector, *Gesetz zur Kontrolle und Transparenz im Unternehmensbereich* (*KonTraG*), aimed to match the corporate governance standards of other countries and was influenced significantly by the report of the Cadbury Committee in the UK.[19] The legislation was a response to problem cases arising in prominent companies in the mid-1990s.

The executive board of directors is a decision-making body which acts collectively and therefore the idea of a powerful chief executive has historically been unusual in Germany. The chair of the board has been held by members of the board in rotation.

Members of the executive board are appointed by the supervisory board, and a two-thirds majority is usually required for this decision. Where such a majority cannot be achieved then a simple majority will suffice, with the chairman having the casting vote. In practice, therefore, shareholders have more potential than employees to influence the composition of the board of directors.

German industrial relations have developed under the principle of co-determination, meaning the right of employees' representatives to participate in decisions that affect them. Central to this is the provision of detailed information, including internal accounting information, at the level of plant, company and group. Co-determination is practised through works councils, which are legally defined trade union bargaining rights and employee board representation. Traditionally, German trade unions have been organized on an industry-by-industry rather than on a craft basis, which tends to encourage industrial harmony. Works councils have existed in Germany since the early 1970s.

In 2001 Professor T. Baums delivered the report of the Baums Commission on corporate governance and the modernization of stock company law. This led to a German code of best practice in 2002, revised 2003 (the Cromme Code, see Case study 3.1). The proposals of the Baums Commission aimed to strengthen accountability and transparency.[20] The 2003 revision of the Cromme Code recommended disclosure of the remuneration of individual directors (as is the practice in the US or UK) but *Company Reporting*[21] found that German companies were resisting this recommendation. These companies disclosed aggregate remuneration of the Board of Management and the

---

[18] Charkham (1994), Chapter 2, p. 43.

[19] *The Corporate Accountant*, April 1997, p. 1.

[20] Available at www.ecgi.org/codes/all_codes.htm.

[21] *Company Reporting*, August 2004, IAS Monitor, pp. 15–18.

Supervisory Board, and the number of directors on each. One company stated that, as the important information had been disclosed, a public discussion of the salaries of individual members would not be expedient. Another said it was contrary to the justified right of privacy of board members.

10.4.2.3 The Netherlands[22]

A Dutch corporation is managed by a *board of management* comprising one or more members. They are all called 'managing directors'. In the UK they would be 'executive directors' and in the US 'executive officers'. These directors are appointed and dismissed by the general meeting. The managing board as a whole is responsible for the proper management of the corporation. For a structure corporation, the supervisory board appoints and dismisses the managing directors.

For structure corporations (large companies) a *supervisory board* is a requirement. Other companies may have a supervisory board if they wish to do so. The functions and responsibilities of the supervisory board are laid down in the Civil Code and include the following powers:

- to appoint and dismiss members of the managing board;
- to determine the financial statements;
- to approve certain decisions of the managing board.

In particular, the supervisory board adopts the annual accounts. It has unrestricted access to the corporate premises and the right to inspect the books and records. Each member of the supervisory board must sign the annual accounts, and members of the supervisory board may be personally liable for the consequences of issuing misleading accounts. Members of the supervisory board of a structure corporation are appointed by co-option (existing members invite new members to join them). The general meeting, the works council and the managing board have the right to recommend for co-option. The general meeting and the works council have the right to object to a recommended co-option.

The *works council* is compulsory for larger companies. Its purpose is to allow the workforce to debate with the executive board twice a year on important issues. The works council must receive the annual accounts and a report on the company's social policy. It must be allowed to give advice when significant plans are being made and it must be consulted on matters regarding conditions of employment.

Audit committees are found in some companies in The Netherlands, as a relatively recent introduction. An important function of the audit committee is to formalize contact between the supervisory board and the internal and external auditors. It appears that the idea originated around 1978 in the supervisory board of Royal Dutch/Shell, drawing on the company's experience in Canada and the US. Its use appears limited to larger listed companies, particularly those in the financial sector. The audit committee will typically comprise a mixture of members of the supervisory board, representatives of the financial management and representatives of the internal audit department. Effectively, the audit committee is a subcommittee of the supervisory board. The audit committee will typically meet prior to the annual audit to discuss the audit plan and shortly after completion of the audit to discuss the results of the audit and the annual financial statements.

---

[22] Hoogendoorn (2001), Klaassen (2001).

Internal audit is a strong aspect of the corporate governance of Dutch companies and the management board places heavy reliance on internal audit. The extension of internal audit work to cover operational control matters and risk assessment indicates the evolution of internal audit towards the status of adviser to senior management on a wide range of aspects of the business.[23]

The *external auditor* is appointed by the general meeting, the supervisory board or the management board (in that order) and may be dismissed by the appointing group or by the general meeting.

In 1997 a committee of the Amsterdam Stock Exchange (the Peters Report) reviewed corporate governance. It made recommendations for companies and their supervisory boards, in a spirit of self-regulation. Many of the recommendations have been adopted voluntarily by listed companies. The Dutch Corporate Governance Code was issued in 2003 by a Corporate Governance Committee (see Exhibit 3.10).

10.4.2.4 Poland

The formal bodies of the joint stock company are the Shareholders' Meeting, the Management Board and the Supervisory Board. The Shareholders' Meeting elects the Supervisory Board, which must have at least three members. The Supervisory Board elects the Management Board. The term of office of members of the Management Board may not exceed five years. Joint stock companies may issue registered shares or bearer shares. Limited liability companies are not required to have an audit or to have a reserve fund. The minimum share capital is lower than that of a joint stock company. The company is run by a Management Board elected by the Shareholders' Meeting.[24] Joint stock companies must have an annual audit and must create a reserve fund for potential losses by transferring 8 per cent of the annual profits until the reserve amounts to one-third of the share capital. There is a minimum level of share capital required.

The Polish Corporate Governance Forum proposed a Corporate Governance Code for Polish listed companies in 2002 (see Case study 3.6). The Best Practices Committee published Best Practices in Public Companies 2002.[25] A survey reported by the Warsaw Stock Exchange at a seminar in 2004 showed that, out of 202 companies listed on the stock exchange, 66 companies declared their observance of every rule of the Best Practices Committee (except Rule 20), 187 were observing at least one rule, 14 observed none and one did not reply.

10.4.3 Equity capital markets

Exhibit 10.9 shows the top 30 European companies, ranked by market capitalization. The columns indicating listing in London and New York show the potential for a strong 'Anglo-Saxon' influence. These largest companies are all in western European countries, apart from Gazprom of Russia which does have a London listing. The largest Polish company, a telecommunications company, was 274th in Europe in 2004. The distribution of the top 500 European companies is shown in Exhibit 10.10. The UK dominates, followed by France and then Germany. Other countries have fewer large listed companies measured on an international scale.

---

[23] Fraser *et al.* (2000).

[24] Ernst & Young (2004), Chapter 3.

[25] Both available in English at www.ecgi.org/codes/all_codes.htm.

Exhibit 10.9	Top 30 European companies, May 2004, with highest Polish company for comparison

Rank in Europe	Name	Country	Market cap. $000m	London listing	NYSE listing	Sector
1	BP	UK	174.6	yes	yes	Oil and gas
2	HSBC	UK	163.6	yes	yes	Banks
3	Vodafone	UK	159.2	yes	yes	Telecoms services
4	Royal Dutch/Shell	NL/UK	158.8	yes	yes	Oil and gas
5	Novartis	Switzerland	115.8	no	yes	Pharmaceuticals and biotechnology
6	GlaxoSmithKline	UK	115.5	yes	yes	Pharmaceuticals and biotechnology
7	Total	France	115.4	yes	yes	Oil and gas
8	Nestlé	Switzerland	101.0	yes	no	Food producer and processor
9	Nokia	Finland	96.4	no	yes	IT hardware
10	Roche	Switzerland	89.6	no	no	Pharmaceuticals and biotechnology
11	Royal Bank of Scotland	UK	88.8	yes	yes	Banks
12	UBS	Switzerland	86.0	no	yes	Banks
13	Deutsche Telekom	Germany	79.8	no	yes	Telecoms services
14	AstraZeneca	UK	76.9	yes	yes	Pharmaceuticals and biotechnology
15	Telefonica	Spain	74.0	yes	yes	Telecoms services
16	ENI	Italy	70.0	no	yes	Oil and gas
17	Unilever NV/plc	NL/UK	65.7	yes	yes	Food producer and processor
18	Siemens	Germany	64.8	yes	yes	Electronic and electrical equipment
19	France Télécom	France	60.5	no	yes	Telecoms services
20	Aventis	France	59.8	no	yes	Pharmaceuticals and biotechnology
21	Barclays	UK	57.0	yes	yes	Banks
22	BNP Paribas	France	54.4	no	no	Banks
23	HBOS	UK	52.3	yes	no	Banks
24	L'Oréal	France	51.1	no	no	Personal care and household products
25	Gazprom	Russia	50.7	yes	no	Oil and gas
26	Santander Central Hispano	Spain	50.6	no	yes	Banks

▶

Exhibit 10. 9 *(Continued)*

Rank in Europe	Name	Country	Market cap. $000m	London listing	NYSE listing	Sector
27	SAP	Germany	48.7	no	yes	Software and computer services
28	Sanofi Synthelabo	France	48.2	no	yes	Pharmaceuticals and Biotechnology
29	Deutsche Bank	Germany	47.4	yes	yes	Banks
30	Telecom Italia	Italy	44.5	no	yes	Telecoms services
274	Telekomunicacja Polska	Poland	5.4	yes	no	Telecoms services

Source: from *Financial Times* FT 500, May 2004.

IOSCO's recommendations to its member bodies in 2000 (see section 1.7.5) encouraged the national stock exchanges of Europe to permit incoming multinational companies to use IAS even before the IAS Regulation came into force in 2005. Haller (2002) summarized the positions reported on the IASB wesbite in 2001 where the stock exchanges of Vienna, Copenhagen, Frankfurt, Milan, Amsterdam, London, Spain, Stockholm, Helsinki and Paris all applied some acceptance of IAS. However the range of permissions was wide: some allowed IAS only for foreign registrants while others allowed IAS also for domestic registrants. Spain and Stockholm required an audited reconciliation of IAS or US GAAP to national GAAP but others did not.

Exhibit 10.10 Europe 500, analyzed by country, May 2004

Country	Number of companies	Market value ($000m)
UK	136	2,067
France	71	1,073
Germany	53	773
Switzerland	30	630
Italy	43	493
The Netherlands	21	397
Spain	31	369
Sweden	24	231
Russia	11	194
Belgium	14	143
Poland	4	17

Source: from *Financial Times* FT 500, May 2004. Other than Poland, countries with fewer than ten companies are excluded.

10.4 3.1 France

Equity investors

Relatively few listed companies in France have widely dispersed shareholdings.[26] Most companies have major shareholders because of a history of flotation as a subsidiary, because of shareholdings by other companies, or because founders have retained their investment. Such shareholdings have in part been designed to discourage takeovers by creation of cross-shareholdings.

Historically, French companies have not generally used the stock market as a source of finance but in more recent years there has been an increase in new equity financing. Use of share options to reward management caused greater interest in the stock market from the 1990s onwards.[27] However, there is a view that shareholders have a conservative view of expectations from dividends. Growth of the company, with corresponding increase in value of the shares, is the preference of many shareholders.[28]

We explain in section 4.6.1 that the French stock exchange is now part of Euronext.[29] Euronext is the world's first cross border exchange business. For regulatory purposes it operates through subsidiaries in the separate countries. Of the 100 companies in the Euronext 100 index, 60 are French and they carry 60 per cent of the weighting of the index.

Almost all shares in quoted companies are held in bearer form. That means the person in possession of the share certificate (the bearer) has ownership. Because this makes share certificates vulnerable to theft and fraud, they are generally held by custodian banks as intermediaries; there is no paper certificate. In 2001 Euroclear[30] took over the national central registry, SICOVAM. Companies do not know who many of their shareholders are, and there is no mailing of information to shareholders, although the annual general meeting is advertised and shareholders have the choice of attending. Dividends are not sent to shareholders. They are paid by Euroclear to intermediaries for onward distribution. Since 1987 there has been a new type of share, the identifiable bearer security (*Titre au porteur identifiable*, TPI). The issuing company may request disclosure of the holder's identity. That request is fulfilled by Euroclear France, which sends it to the account-keeper, which may be the company itself or a financial institution.

There has been some concern that small shareholders may not be paid sufficient attention, and many companies now make efforts to contact their shareholders. Because companies do not know who owns them, communication relies on press announcements and on information given in briefings to analysts meetings, which some companies record for the website.[31]

In France, there is no equivalent to the pension funds of the UK or the US as equity investors. The major insurance companies are significant investors, tending to concentrate their investments, and often having a representative on the company's board of directors.[32]

---

[26] Charkham (1994), pp. 126–127.

[27] Ibid.

[28] Charkham (1994), p. 142.

[29] www.euronext.com.

[30] www.euroclear.com.

[31] www.renault.com/gb/finance/index_finance.htm.

[32] Charkham (1994), p. 147.

There is a tradition of family business in France and some of these family businesses prefer borrowing rather than issuing further shares to raise finance. This, combined with state ownership of some large companies, means that for many years companies preferred to issue bonds to raise new capital, rather than equity.

Regulation of the stock market

The Autorité des marchés financiers (AMF)[33] was established by the Financial Security Act 2003. It is a member of IOSCO, CESR and FSF (see sections 1.3.4 and 3.2.1). It was formed from the merger of the Commission des opérations de bourse (COB), the Conseil des marchés financiers (CMF) and the Conseil de discipline de la gestion financière (CDGF). These bodies were merged to improve the efficiency of France's financial regulatory system and to give it greater visibility. The AMF is an independent public body. Its remit is to safeguard investments in financial instruments and in all other savings and investment vehicles, ensure that investors receive material information, and maintain orderly financial markets. It regulates the activities of Euronext Paris. In particular it monitors companies to ensure that they provide complete, relevant information on a timely basis and in an equitable manner to all market participants (investors, analysts, fund managers, the press, and the general public).

10.4.3.2 Germany[34]

Shares in AG companies have traditionally been in the form of bearer shares, which means that possession is evidence of ownership. Consequently they need to be taken care of, and the usual place for safe custody is a bank. Because they are bearer shares, not carrying the owner's name, it is difficult to gain information on the pattern of share ownership. Towards the end of the 1990s the use of registered shares was becoming increasingly popular, replacing the almost exclusive previous use of bearer shares.

Equity investors

It may be seen from Exhibit 4.3 that the German stock market is third in order of size in the EU, following from London and Euronext. The domestic companies listed have a market capitalization which is a relatively low percentage of GDP, indicating that equity funding is not as significant to the national economy as are the markets in The Netherlands or the UK. From Exhibit 4.6 it is clear that individual investors are not a major factor in the market. The most significant shareholder group is non-financial corporations, a situation where companies hold shares in each other. Such systems of cross-holdings make companies very secure against takeover bids, but also foster secrecy.

Institutional investors are not in general a strong force in the financing and governance of companies. Because shares are in bearer form and held by banks, there is strong power in the hands of the banks when voting at general meetings is required. The banks hold proxy votes authorized by the owners of the shares; banks are obliged to consult the owners of the shares and have dealt with this obligation by asking for a 15-month proxy covering all the shareholdings of the investor. It would not be unusual for the banks collectively to control more than half of the votes cast at an annual general meeting of a major German company. A survey by the Deutsche Bundesbank indicated that 19.4 per cent of shares were held by individuals, 39.3 per cent by miscellaneous companies, 2.7 per cent by insurance companies, 11.4 per cent

---

[33] www.amf-france.org (English language option is available).

[34] Charkham (1994), p. 27; *Accountancy International*, January 2000, p. 67.

by banks, 7.1 per cent by the state and 20 per cent by foreign investors.[35] The introduction of funded pensions is expected to channel savings into equity investments.[36]
Deutsche Post, with Ruhr-Universität Bochum, in 2003 surveyed its 820,000 domestic private investors, holding a total of 10 per cent of the share capital, to find how
they collect information on stocks. They rely mainly on media reports, with the
annual report being relatively low on their list, but 58 per cent read the income
statement.

Regulation of the market

Companies seeking a listing must present a prospectus. Listed companies are also
required to disclose an interim report. The content of this report is regulated by the
Stock Exchange Act (*Börsengesetz*) and the Ordinance regulating Stock Exchange
Listing (*Börsenzulassungsverordnung*).[37] The Deutsche Börse claims to have high transparency in the operation of the market. It has two segments – the General Standard
and the Prime Standard. The General Standard companies must meet the requirements
of German securities laws, such as annual and interim reports and ad-hoc disclosures
in German. The Prime Standard companies must, in addition, give quarterly reports,
use IFRS or US GAAP, publish a financial calendar, hold at least one analyst conference
each year and make ad-hoc disclosures in English as well as in German. Research into
the previous Neuer Market (New Market) showed that companies using IAS or US
GAAP showed 81 per cent average compliance with IAS and 86 per cent average compliance with US GAAP.[38] General concerns about the regulation of the Neuer Market
caused the Deutsche Borse to rearrange its business under the new Prime Standard and
General Standard.

10.4.3.3 The Netherlands

Equity investors

There is an established stock market in Amsterdam and other related markets including the European Options Exchange, the Amsterdam Futures Market, the Rotterdam
Energy Futures Exchange, the over-the-counter (OTC) market and a market for private
arrangements.

The Amsterdam Stock Exchange operates within Euronext and is relatively significant in relation to the GDP of the country. However, its high turnover is mainly attributable to a relatively small number of companies and the Amsterdam exchange is not
a significant source of new capital. The companies listed are relatively large in market
capitalization.

The Amsterdam Stock Exchange allows foreign companies to follow either IASB
Standards or US GAAP without reconciliation to Netherlands GAAP. Prior to 2005,
domestic companies could follow Netherlands GAAP or could apply IASB Standards, US
GAAP, or UK GAAP with a reconciliation to Netherlands GAAP.[39] This indicates the relative flexibility of the stock exchange and perhaps reflects the dominance of a multinational Anglo/Dutch and Belgian/Dutch companies.

---

[35] Rathbone (1997), p. 184.

[36] OECD (2003b), p. 203.

[37] Ballwieser (2001), pp. 1332–1333.

[38] Glaum and Street (2003).

[39] Klaassen (2001), p. 1922.

10.4.3.4 Poland[40]

The Warsaw Stock Exchange is the principal market. In its present form it dates from 1991, with structure and regulation guided by the French system. It is a self-regulatory organization whose rules are approved by the Polish Securities and Exchange Commission.[41] It has three divisions – the main floor, the parallel market and the free floor. The main floor is the primary market, and requires an issuer to publish audited financial statements for the previous three years. The National Depository of Securities registers and keeps in deposit securities introduced to public trading. Any public offering must be approved by the Securities and Exchange Commission.

Poland is a leader in Central Europe in terms of Foreign Direct Investment (FDI). The largest single foreign investor in Poland is France Telecom, followed some way behind by Fiat (Italy, in motor vehicles, insurance and banking), Daewoo (South Korea, in motor vehicles, electrical goods and insurance), HVB (Germany, in banking) and Citigroup (USA, in banking).

10.4.4 Bank lending

10.4.4.1 France

Historically, deposit-taking banks did not participate in the financing of their industrial and commercial customers;[42] merchant banks were the source of lending to business. The two types of banks are, since 1984, similar in status under banking law, all being called *établissements de crédit*. The provision of bank lending is concentrated in a small number of large banks. This factor, in combination with the relative lack of spread of equity shareholding mentioned earlier, means that a few banks are relatively influential in matters of raising corporate finance. Banks also take equity shareholdings in companies. This may be encouraged by the company which sees a source of cheaper capital and a protection against takeover. For the banks, the strategy of increasing their involvement in corporate finance has resulted from comparative evaluation of the systems in Germany and in the UK, with the conclusion favouring the German approach. This gives a long-term orientation to bank financing by loans and by equity investment.[43]

10.4.4.2 Germany

Banks approach lending as a long-term arrangement. This creates what is called 'relationship' banking rather than 'transaction' banking. Bankers have to understand their customers and the industries in which they are located. The major banks have developed a range of services so that a company may receive all types of banking service, including lending, from one source – referred to as *Universalbanken*. Banks take an active part in the corporate governance of companies that they finance. This reduces the information gap between customers and banks and so helps minimize the agency costs of bank lending.

Banks are also shareholders in companies, to a significant extent. This has to some extent happened by accident, because banks will accept equity as repayment of debt when a company falls into difficulties. Because of various regulatory changes in the late

[40] Ernst & Young (2004), pp. 8, 60.

[41] Warsaw Stock Exchange www.wse.com.pl; Polish SEC www.kpwig.gov.pl/index-ang.htm; both with English language versions.

[42] Charkham (1994), pp. 144–145.

[43] Charkham (1994), p. 146.

1990s and capital gains tax changes in 2002 there were expectations that financial institutions would reduce their holdings in non-financial companies but the subdued stock markets discouraged large-scale selling.

Bank financing is relatively more important as a source of finance to the corporate sector than in the US or UK (40 per cent of GDP in Germany in 1999, compared to 12.6 per cent of GDP in the USA).[44] It is commonly asserted in text books that the debt:equity ratios of German companies are higher than those of the USA or the UK but this is not borne out by national income statistics[45] (corporate debt in Germany in 2001 was 7.9 per cent compared to 17.1 per cent in the UK and 19.0 per cent in the US) and is challenged by research (Rajan and Zingales, 1995).

10.4.4.3 The Netherlands

There is an active banking sector. Credit banks grant loans to businesses, and specialist financial institutions offer finance for special purposes such as business start-ups and export finance. Corporate debt was 28.3 per cent of stock market capitalization in 2001.[46] Research into the period 1984–97[47] showed that Dutch companies preferred internal finance over external finance. Among the external finance types they preferred bank loans over shares and preferred shares over bonds.

10.4.4.4 Poland

Traditionally the relationship of Polish banks to companies resembled that of German banks to German companies. However, in recent years banks have become risk averse and have found that they can satisfy their lending plans by lending to the government as a low-risk debtor. So the larger Polish companies have turned to external financing and investment. The very large Polish companies are able to borrow in the US.

10.4.5 Taxation system

A survey of conditions in the early 1990s showed that corporate income tax revenues in most EU countries were low by international standards, as a percentage of GDP. The relatively low yield, and large variations across EU countries with similar statutory tax rates, were attributed to several factors. The differences in accountancy rules were one explanation, but another was extensive political use of tax relief. The tax reliefs substantially reduced the effective tax rates. A Code of Conduct on business taxation was agreed in December 1997 to prevent tax reliefs of one country leading to harmful competition among member states.[48]

The relationship between accounting and taxation systems across Europe was the subject of a special issue of *The European Accounting Review* in 1996 (Vol. 5 supplement). Hoogendoorn (1996) summarized the general relationship between accounting and taxation as shown in Exhibit 10.11.

In the group classed as 'independence' there is a range of relationships between the accounting and taxation systems. Where the tax authorities say that they will accept the profit reported under general commercial accounting principles the preparers of

---

[44] OECD (2003b), p. 201.

[45] OECD (2003b), p. 203.

[46] Ibid.

[47] Haan and Hinloopen (2002).

[48] OECD (2002), pp. 124–125.

| Exhibit 10.11 | The general relationship between accounting and taxation |

Independence	Dependence
Czech Republic	Belgium
Denmark	Finland
Ireland	Germany
Netherlands	Italy
Norway	Sweden
Poland	France
UK	

Source: Hoogendoorn (1996), Table 1, p. 786.

accounts may have taxation consequences in mind when they make their policy selection within general accounting principles. In the group classed as 'dependence' the tax rules may be applied in the commercial accounts and may result in the accounts not conforming to the idea of a 'true and fair view'. Concerns about the relationship between accounting and taxation will continue after 2005 because many countries do not intend to permit or require IFRS for individual companies (see section 10.3.1).

10.4.5.1 France

Companies pay corporation tax based on their accounting profits. The definition of 'profit' for corporate tax purposes is that used for commercial and industrial purposes. Corporate income taxes are paid by individual companies rather than by groups of companies. However, there are some specific rules for groups of companies. For businesses the taxable income is calculated by starting with the accounting profit as determined by the *Plan Comptable Général*. Some further adjustments are made for the purposes of tax law. These adjustments involve the exclusion of expenses which relate to personal items associated with the owner of the business. Gifts to customers, expenses of entertaining and travel, and commissions paid to third parties are examples of transactions which are acceptable. The emphasis is on 'normal business practice', but it is essential that the expense item be included in the financial accounts.

The basis of the depreciation calculation is allocation of cost over the useful life of the asset but accelerated depreciation is allowed for specific assets provided it is used in the financial statements. The civil court (*Conseil d'État*) decided in 1999 that the amortization of goodwill was an allowable deduction when calculating taxable profit, providing the goodwill was a separable asset with a definite end-date to the benefits attached. This clarified previous uncertainty but only where strict conditions are met.[49]

Provisions are widely used in French accounting practice. To be allowable for tax purposes the provision must meet specific criteria which ensure that the provision is probable, that it is specific and that it arises from an event which happened during the year (rather than an event after the balance sheet date).

Capital gains are determined in the same way as for unincorporated businesses, but a company pays a lower long-term rate of capital gains tax if the gain is transferred to special reserves. Short-term investments held by a company are valued at market price at the balance sheet date and a capital gain or loss calculated for tax purposes.

---

[49] *Accountancy International*, January 2000, p. 66.

Dividend distributions are taxed under an imputation system. Where a company makes a distribution of dividend there is an extra payment of 45 per cent of corporate tax but a tax credit of the same amount (*avoir fiscal*) is released for the shareholder. The effective rate of tax on the company increases but the overall tax rate on company and shareholder together is lower than in the absence of distribution.

10.4.5.2 Germany

In Germany, there is a close link between the annual accounts and the tax accounts. The principles of recognition and valuation applied in the commercial accounts must in general be incorporated into the tax balance sheet. On some occasions, tax law requires specific accounting principles which differ from accounting regulations; this is usually to allow a degree of objectivity. The close relationship between accounting and tax principles is referred to as the authoritativeness principle (the *Maßgeblichkeitsprinzip*). (It is also translated in texts as the principle of 'congruency' or 'bindingness'.) The *Maßgeblichkeitsprinzip* states that the generally accepted accounting principles (GoB) form an authoritative basis for tax accounts unless there are other explicit tax rules.[50] Tax accounts are thus derived from commercial accounts. However, the tax legislation is also very detailed in relation to accounting treatment and tax incentives. The availability of tax incentives usually requires the values of tax accounting to be used also in commercial accounting. This has been called 'the reverse authoritativeness principle'. So, in reality, tax practices influence the starting point for preparation of the commercial accounts. In particular there is pressure on German companies to value assets at the lowest amount possible and liabilities at the highest amount possible.[51]

Small businesses in particular prefer to produce one set of accounts which satisfy the tax law as well as the accounting rules. Where the tax burden may be reduced or postponed, businesses will be influenced by that factor in their accounting practice. Tax on companies is levied on each company separately, rather than on a group of companies. Tax reforms agreed by Parliament in July 2000 reduced the corporate tax burden compared to the 1990s and, from 2003, removed capital gains tax on sales of shares by major shareholders, potentially making the capital market more flexible.

10.4.5.3 The Netherlands

In The Netherlands accounting and taxation are formally independent, for both individual accounts and group accounts. Both sets of regulations leave scope for flexibility. Tax law relating to incorporated businesses is contained in the Law on Corporation Tax.

10.4.5.4 Poland

In Poland, taxable income of companies is arrived at by adjusting accounting profits for tax purposes. Tax depreciation rates are prescribed in tax law. There are corporate income tax incentives such as special economic zones. The standard corporate income tax rate was 19 per cent in 2004, which was regarded as a beneficial tax rate.[52] Uncertainty in the tax system has been a significant problem for Polish companies (see Exhibit 10.12).[53] This is because there has been no facility for companies to obtain *ex ante* (in advance) tax

---

[50] Crampton *et al.* (2001).

[51] Ballwieser (2001), pp. 1296–1298.

[52] Ernst & Young (2004), p. 9.

[53] OECD (2004), p. 179.

Exhibit 10.12 Note on uncertainty regarding taxation, Orlen

> **30. Contingent liabilities**
>
> *c. Tax regulations in Poland*
> Poland currently has a number of laws related to excise tax, value-added tax, corporate income tax and payroll (social) taxes. Regulations regarding these taxes are often changed which causes their ambiguity and inconsistency. Implemented regulations are often unclear or inconsistent. Often, differing opinions regarding legal interpretations exist both among and within government ministers and organisations, creating uncertainties and areas of conflict. Tax settlements, together with other legal compliance areas (for example: customs and currency control matters) are subject to review and investigation by a number of authorities, who are enabled by law to impose severe fines, penalties and interest charges. These facts create tax risks in Poland that are substantially higher than those typically found in countries with more developed systems.
>
> There are no formal procedures in Poland to agree the final level of tax charge for a period. Tax settlements may be a subject of review during the subsequent 5 years, from the end of the tax year where tax payments took place. There is a risk that the authorities may have a different opinion from that presented by the entities constituting the Group as to the interpretation of the law which could have significant effect on Group's entities stated tax liabilities.

Source: Orlen S.A. annual report (2003), pp. 144–145. www.orlen.pl

rulings. There has been a lag in time between the passage of a tax law and its enactment, and there have been different interpretations at different local tax offices.

10.4.6 The accounting profession

Baker *et al.* (2001) compared the regulation of the statutory auditor in the UK, France and Germany, and concluded that while there might be a movement towards international harmonization of auditing standards across Europe it is less likely that harmonization of the regulation of statutory auditors will occur. They distinguish significant reliance on recognized professional bodies in the UK from control by quasi-governmental entities in France and Germany. We will see in Chapter 11 that the UK has moved further down the quasi-governmental route since Baker *et al.* carried out their analysis but their observations on the differences in regulation of statutory audit remain instructive. We compare here the nature of the accounting and auditing professions in France, Germany, The Netherlands and Poland.

10.4.6.1 France

The reform of company law in 1967 established the profession of auditor (*Commissaire aux Comptes*). Historically, the profession of auditor had been separate, in the eyes of the law, from that of accountant. However, in practice most auditors also belong to the accountancy profession. A range of professional bodies existed in the latter part of the nineteenth and the early twentieth century. These were rationalized by government action in formation of the *Ordre des experts comptables et des comptables agréés* (OEC) in 1945.[54] This was formed as a two-tier body of the *expert comptable* who was authorized to prepare annual accounts and the *comptable agréé* who operated the bookkeeping system.

---

[54] Scheid and Walton (2001), p. 306.

Ordre des Experts Comptables (OEC)[55]

Only members of the OEC are permitted to call themselves *expert comptable*. They have a monopoly position, protected by law, in the public supply of certain accounting services. Only partners or employees of an accountancy practice may use the title *expert comptable*; those who move to work in industry lose their membership of the professional body. This means there is no professional accountancy body representing accountants working in industry and commerce.

Those seeking membership of the OEC must undergo a period of training and pass professional examinations, including the writing of a dissertation.

In 1996 the OEC published a draft conceptual framework, rejecting the Anglo-Saxon/US/IASC approach of starting with the balance sheet and emphasizing the importance of the profit and loss account as the essential statement of wealth creation.[56]

Compagnie Nationale des Commissaires aux Comptes (CNCC)

The CNCC was formed in 1969 as part of a continuing reform of auditing under government jurisdiction. Although the statutory position of the auditor was established by the law of 1867, there was no professional organization at that time and it was only after a reform of the law in 1935 that the duties of the auditor were extended and professional organizations began to appear.

Formation of the CNCC was related to changes in the law which widened the responsibilities of auditors and fixed their fees in relation to the size of the client. They were required to certify the *regularité* (conforming with legal requirements) and the *sincerité* (application of accepted valuation methods in good faith) of the accounts. Most *commissaires aux comptes* are also *experts comptables*, as members of the OEC.

10.4.6.2 Germany

Audit is required for large corporations and large enterprises. According to the law, only *Wirtschaftsprüfer* and firms of *Wirtschaftsprüfer* may act as auditors. For medium-sized limited liability companies there is a second category, the sworn-in auditors (*vereidigter Buchprüfer*) and their firms. Those seeking to become *Wirtschaftsprüfer* normally require a university degree and to have at least four years of practical auditing experience.[57]

| Exhibit 10.13 | Composition of the German Accountancy profession |

Wirtschaftsprüfer Statutory auditor	9,611
vereidigter Buchprüfer Sworn-in auditors	4,205
Statutory audit firms	1,829
Licensed audit firms	146
Steuerberater Tax accountant	55,000

Source: www.accaglobal.com/members/services/int_mobility/factsheets/germany/composition

[55] Scheid and Walton (2001), p. 306; Standish (2000), Chapter 5.

[56] *FT World Accounting Report*, July 1996, p. 2.

[57] *Wirtschaftsprüferordnung*, section 9, paragraph 1.

There is a demanding final examination. As in most other countries, a high degree of independence is demanded of the *Wirtschaftsprüfer*. Links with the company under audit are forbidden, both for the auditor and for the audit firm. There is a body of tax accountants, the *Steuerberater*, who would like to have the right to audit but their claims are repeatedly rejected by the legislators.

Legislation sets out the legal position of the *Wirtschaftsprüfer* and the sworn-in auditor. The legislation allows the profession to be self-governing. All *Wirtschaftsprüfer* and sworn-in auditors are required to be members of the chamber of *Wirtschaftsprüfer* (*Wirtschaftsprüferkammer*) which is a public law body under the official supervision of the Federal Minister of Economics. With around 10,000 persons entitled to describe themselves as *Wirtschaftsprüfer*, they may be regarded as an elite body. Germany is one of the EU member states (along with Belgium, France and Greece) that restrict membership of the professional associations to those working in public practice. Membership therefore indicates a function rather than an educational background. There is no equivalent professional body for those working in industry or business.

At a conference in 1995 a senior official at the Federal Ministry of Justice invited German accountants to enter detailed discussions about professional standards. The Institute of German Public Accountants and the *Wirtschaftsprüferkammer* entered into detailed negotiations with the ministry. The fruits of the discussions were incorporated in the *KonTraG*.[58] Among other aspects of corporate governance, the law requires German accountants to comment on the company's year-end business report as well as the accounts. They are also required to scrutinize the company's risk management system and mention any risks which might threaten the company as a going concern. This creates a new volume of work and adds new complexity to the statutory audit. Most significant, however, is the change from regarding auditing as an examination of past business alone. The *KonTraG* requires auditors to express a view about ongoing business.

The *Institut Der Wirtschaftsprüfer* (IDW) has for some time issued statements in the form of professional expert opinions. As a result of the *KonTraG*, these are now separated into IDW Auditing Standards (IDWAuS) and IDW Accounting Standards (IDWAcS). Standards are supplemented by non-binding Practice Statements.[59]

As a further result of the *KonTraG*, the Institute of German Auditors (IDW) published new auditing standards in 1999, bringing aspects of the International Auditing Standards into German auditing principles, subject to German law. A structure is recommended for the long form audit report which is required by the HGB. The auditor must evaluate management's assessment of the economic situation and future development of the enterprise.[60]

Some proposals from the Federal Ministry were not incorporated in the new law. A clause requiring rotation of auditors was removed and the Ministry was persuaded against its initial intention of increasing statutory liability. The *KonTraG* stipulates automatic liability of DM2m for statutory audits (previously established at DM500,000 in 1965) and four times that figure for consultancy. In practice lawsuits are rare.

10.4.6.3 The Netherlands[61]

The origins of the accounting profession may be traced to the last decades of the nineteenth century when the role of accountants developed from bookkeeping to auditing

[58] *The Accountant*, May 1997, p. 13.

[59] Crampton *et al.* (2001), p. 15.

[60] *Accountancy International*, November 1998, p. 82; October 1999, pp. 51–52.

[61] Hoogendoorn (2001), Klaassen (2001).

as limited companies grew in importance. The separation of management and ownership of companies created a demand for auditors having independent and professional judgement. Other duties such as internal auditing, governmental auditing and management advisory work also developed.

The Netherlands Institute of Accountants was established in 1895 with the purpose of creating statutory rules for the accounting profession, although the rules did not materialize. No further significant legislative action arose until the Chartered Accountants Act of 1962, which reserved the auditing of financial statements for *registeraccountants (RA)*. The same law created the *Nederlands Instituut van Registeraccountants*, *NIVRA*, as the Dutch institute of chartered accountants. Another body, the *Accountants-Administratieconsulenten (AA)* came into existence in 1974, providing accounting services directed more at SMEs. Implementation of the Eighth Directive in Dutch Law in 1993 gave the right of auditing to both NIVRA and AA, but in practice large companies choose NIVRA members as their auditors.

The education and examination of RAs is considerably more onerous than that required by the Eighth Directive. It lasts from eight to 12 years, embracing undergraduate and postgraduate study as well as professional training.

NIVRA issues auditing guidelines but does not issue accounting standards or guidelines. It does, however, participate in accounting guidelines through membership of the Council for Annual Reporting. However, departures from the Guidelines for Annual Reporting are not referred to in the report of the independent auditor.

10.4.6.4 Poland

The Act on Auditors and their Self-Governing Body (1994) provides a legal framework for the creation, governance and operation of the National Chamber of Statutory Auditors (NCSA). The Ministry of Finance supervises the NCSA.[62] Of about 7,700 NCSA members, some 4,250 are active.[63] NCSA is a member of IFAC, along with the National Board of Chartered Accountants Association in Poland (NBCAAP), created within the Accountants Association of Poland (AAP).[64] AAP is a voluntary organization of accountants, financial specialists, auditors and information technology accounting specialists, existing since 1907. When the Act on Auditors was introduced, the chartered accountant members of AAP were able to register as statutory auditors and NCSA members. The AAP is not a self-regulatory body within the Polish legal framework. There is a code of professional ethics. The NCSA sets auditing standards. If particular issues are not covered by existing standards the NCSA permits the use of International Standards on Auditing. The NCSA is empowered to take disciplinary action for enforcing the code of professional ethics and auditing standards.

10.5 External influences

10.5.1 France

There is a history of independent development of accounting practice in France. Early tendencies towards charts of accounts may be traced to a commission formed in 1918 which included in its remit the idea of standardization. No specific chart appeared in France at

---

[62] Jaruga and Schroeder (2001).

[63] World Bank ROSC report 2002.

[64] www.skwp.org.pl has English language website.

that time but in the 1920s Schmalenbach proposed a model chart of accounts in Germany. The German occupation of France in 1940 brought ideas of German economic organization to industry and administration in France; this drew attention to potential deficiencies in French accounting practice and a code was prepared in 1942 as a detailed manual.

As a founder member of the EU France has influenced the content of the directives affecting company law in the community. It has in turn been influenced by other members joining the EU, particularly the UK request that the Fourth Directive should include the requirement for a 'true and fair view' (see Chapter 11).

Colonization of Africa in the late nineteenth century left a legacy of French accounting tradition in many African countries which are now independent. In particular, that legacy reflects the notion that accounting regulations should apply to all business entities, whether or not incorporated, and that there should be a uniform chart of accounts. It has been suggested that the French approach has made it easier to regulate unincorporated businesses and provide bookkeeping training, provided there is adequate literacy among small traders.[65]

10.5.2 Germany

Historically, accounting practice in Germany has developed independently with distinctive national characteristics.[66] As a founder member of the EU, Germany has had a significant influence on the directives affecting company law. Because of historical political links and continuing commercial links, German accounting has an influence on practices in countries such as Austria and Hungary. During periods of occupation of other countries during wartime, the German influence affected some accounting practices in countries such as France, there is also evidence of a German influence on Japanese accounting. Germany itself was occupied briefly after the Second World War, and there has been a resulting impact on consolidated accounting in some sectors.

As other countries have joined the EU, Germany has found its own approach modified from time to time. This is particularly significant in the case of the 'true and fair view' being imported under UK influence and being seen as an infringement of the tax-driven approach to accounting.

Multinational companies are a vehicle of change in accounting practice. Daimler–Benz, the first German company to obtain a full listing on a US stock exchange (see also Case study 3.1),[67] changed in 1996 to using US GAAP figures both internally and externally as a result of the change of culture caused by taking a full listing.[68] From that time the group accounts have been presented in US GAAP but the parent company accounts have been prepared under the German Commercial Code. Both sets of financial statements are audited by independent auditors.

10.5.3 The Netherlands

The accounting system of The Netherlands is very clearly individualistic and has developed under internal national influences.

As a founder member of the EU, The Netherlands influenced the formation of directives. The Netherlands was also a founder member of the IASC. Former colonies of The

---

[65] Walton, P., 'Special rules for a special case', *Financial Times*, 18 September 1997, p. 11.

[66] Ballwieser (2001), pp. 1224–1227.

[67] *FT World Accounting Report*, June 1997.

[68] *FT World Accounting Report*, June 1997, p. 3.

Netherlands, mainly Indonesia (the former Dutch East Indies), have accounting practices reflecting the Dutch influence. It has been suggested that the Dutch influence made it relatively easy for Indonesia to create national rules closely aligned with IASs.[69]

The large multinational companies which have their base in The Netherlands have created their own mixture of harmonized accounting practices to meet their specific needs and have in some matters influenced domestic practices of competitors.

It has been suggested that a willingness to consider foreign ideas has been a continuing characteristic of Dutch accounting, but uncritical reception has been rare. Until the 1970s unique features of Dutch accounting were a source of pride. Perceptions of the value of harmonization are seen as a feature of more recent years.[70]

10.5.4 Poland[71]

To understand the complexities of accounting developments in Poland it is necessary to understand the history of Poland. It was a significant political and economic entity from the 15th to 17th centuries but was then partitioned progressively in the late 1700s, divided among Russia, Prussia and Austria. The legislation of each of these countries affected the partitioned country. Napoleon Bonaparte created the Grand Duchy of Warsaw in 1807, introducing the Napoleonic Code. His defeat in 1815 left that part of Poland under Russian control. As commercial laws developed, one part of Poland experienced Russian laws while the rest developed under the German Commercial Code. In 1918 at the end of the First World War the Second Republic was created and had to reintegrate the tripartite business and accounting practices. In 1934 the Polish Commercial Code was introduced. From 1939 to 1944 the German system of uniform accounting was imposed in the parts of Poland under German occupation, while Soviet accounting was used in the regions incorporated into the USSR (Russia). The uniform accounting plan adopted in 1946 followed the German model. From the 1950s there was a centrally planned economy under Soviet economic planning. The failure of central planning led to the creation of a social market economy in the 1980s. From the end of the 1980s Poland had the target of EU membership and its accounting laws were changed to reflect the EU directives.

10.6 Oversight and assurance

This section indicates some of the main developments in mechanisms of oversight and assurance in Europe generally and in France, Germany, The Netherlands and Poland in particular. Chapter 3 gives a broader view of processes of oversight and assurance.

10.6.1 EU-wide initiatives

Responsibility for ensuring compliance with accounting standards remains a national responsibility. This section compares the national processes for oversight and assurance and describes some of the developments in the establishment and operation of audit committees.

---

[69] *FT World Accounting Report*, August/September 1996, pp. iii–v.

[70] Klaassen (2001), pp. 1915–1916.

[71] Jaruga and Schroeder (2001), pp. 1596–1599.

10.6.1.1 Public oversight

We have explained in Chapter 3 how the Sarbanes–Oxley Act established a Public Oversight Board in the US. For Europe the question is whether such initiatives should be taken at national level or across the EU. FEE published a discussion paper in 2003 on the European coordination of public oversight. It supported the European Commission's view[72] that the practical implementation of oversight should be at national level.

FEE had previously published an investigation of national oversight systems in 2001. In particular it analyzed the oversight of the consolidated accounts of listed companies where there is a review that extends beyond a formal check of the contents. Exhibit 10.14 shows which body, if any, takes responsibility for overseeing publication of consolidated accounts of listed companies.

The FEE commentary (2003) emphasizes the importance of coordination and recognition of equivalence in quality between the European and US oversight systems. It suggests that this could be achieved through a European Coordination Audit Oversight Board (ECAOB). It would coordinate, rather than duplicate, work at a national level.

10.6.1.2 Audit committees

A comparative study of European corporate governance codes found that by the end of 2001 an audit committee was recommended in, among other countries, Belgium, France, The Netherlands, Spain, Sweden, and the UK.[73] The High Level Group of Company Law Experts[74] presented their final report in November 2002 on a Modern Regulatory framework for company law in Europe. The report provided guidance on the role and composition of audit committees. However it saw corporate governance as a matter for national codes on corporate governance. The report can therefore be seen as a guide against which to evaluate national codes. The report recommends that the

Exhibit 10.14 Mechanisms of institutional oversight for consolidated accounts of listed companies, 2001

Institutional oversight mechanisms				No institutional oversight system
Stock Exchange	Stock Exchange Regulator	Review Panel	Other government	
Sweden Norway Switzerland	Belgium France Italy Portugal Spain	UK (FRRP)	Denmark UK (DTI) Czech Republic	Austria Finland Germany Ireland Luxembourg Netherlands Hungary Slovenia

Source: FEE Survey of Enforcement mechanisms in Europe, 2001, p. 12

---

[72] EC Communication May 2003, *Reinforcing Statutory Audit in the EU.*

[73] Comparative Study (2002) Section V.A.6.

[74] http://europa.eu.int/comm/internal_market/en/company/company/modern/index.htm.

audit committee should comprise non-executive or supervisory directors, the majority of whom should be independent. The responsibilities of the audit committee should be:

- selecting the external auditor for appointment by shareholders;
- setting the terms and conditions for employment of the external auditor;
- monitoring the relationship between the external auditor and the company and its executive management, with particular emphasis on safeguarding auditor independence;
- monitoring the provision of non-audit services, either by prohibiting them or by monitoring them closely;
- meeting the auditors at least once in each quarter, and meeting them annually without the executive directors being present;
- ensuring that the external auditor has all the information required for the audit role;
- receiving the auditors' management letter with comments on the financial statements and considering whether these comments should be disclosed in the financial statements;
- reviewing accounting policies and changes to these;
- monitoring internal audit procedures and the company's risk management system;
- meeting regularly with those who are responsible for the internal audit procedures and risk management systems;
- considering to what extent the findings of the risk management system should be reported in the company's financial statements.

10.6.2 France

The Loi sur la Sécurité Financière (LSF 2003) affects the structure of French accountancy firms, reinforcing the importance of the separation of audit and non-audit activities.[75] It established the Haut Conseil des Commissaires aux Comptes to monitor the audit profession and oversee ethics and independence. It works with the CNCC (see section 10.4.6.1).

The Bouton Report 'Promoting better corporate governance in listed companies' was issued in September 2002. It made recommendations on the constitution and work of audit committees, reflecting the detail of the report of the EU High Level Group of Company Law Experts (see section 10.6.1.2). It required the audit committee to exclude any corporate officer, but only specified that two-thirds of the committee should be independent directors.[76]

The audit report of Pinault-Printemps (Exhibit 10.15) is interesting because of the section 'Justification of our Assessments', required by a change in the law. This section draws attention to particular accounting matters, but without qualifying the audit opinion. This is a variation on the US requirement for directors to draw attention to critical accounting estimates (see Exhibit 15.5).

10.6.3 Germany

The German Corporate Governance Code (2003) is summarized as Case study 3.1. It presents essential statutory regulations for the management and supervision of German listed companies. It is built on the legal requirement in Germany for a dual board system of Management Board and Supervisory Board (section 10.4.2.2) but in the foreword to the Code defends the dual board system as converging with a the type of single board system found in other countries, through the intensive interaction between

---

[75] *International Accounting Bulletin*, Issue 338, 21 November 2003, pp. 1 and 11–14.
[76] Smith (2003), Appendix III.

Exhibit 10.15 Audit report, Pinault Printemps

STATUTORY AUDITORS' REPORT
on the consolidated financial statements
(for the year ended December 31, 2003)

In accordance with our appointment as auditors by your Annual General Meeting, we have audited the consolidated financial statements of Pinault-Printemps-Redoute S.A. for the year ended December 31, 2003.

The consolidated financial statements are the responsibility of the Management Board. Our role is to express an opinion on these financial statements based on our audit.

Opinion on the consolidated financial statements

We conducted our audit in accordance with the professional standards applicable in France. Those standards require that we plan and perform the audit to obtain reasonable assurance that the consolidated financial statements are free of any material misstatement. An audit includes examining, on a test basis, evidence supporting the amounts and disclosures in the financial statements. An audit also includes assessing the accounting principles used and significant estimates made by management. as well as evaluating the overall financial statement presentation. We believe that our audit provides a reasonable basis for our opinion.

In our opinion, the consolidated financial statements give a true and fair view of the financial position and the assets and liabilities of the Group as at December 31, 2003 and the results of its operations for the year then ended in accordance with accounting principles generally accepted in France.

Justification of our assessments

Pursuant to the provisions of Article L.225–235 of the *Code de Commerce* (French Commercial Code) governing the justification of our assessments, which apply for the first time this year, we draw your attention to the following:

● The net book value of goodwill and other intangible assets was subject to review by the Company as described in note 1.8 of the notes to the financial statements. We have verified the validity of the methodology applied, reviewed, where necessary, the documentation drawn up accordingly, and assessed the consistency of the data used, particularly by comparing 2003 forecasts with the corresponding actual figures.

● Your Company presented the commitment to purchase Gucci shares and the related foreign currency risk hedging transactions in notes 25.2 and 23.2 of the notes to the financial statements. As part of our audit of the overall presentation of the financial statements, we reviewed the relevance of the information provided in the notes on these transactions.

These assessments were performed as part of our audit approach for the consolidated financial statements taken as a whole and contributed to the expression of the unqualified opinion in the first part of this report.

Specific procedure

We have also performed certain procedures on the financial information given in the Group's management report, in accordance with professional standards applicable in France. We have no matters to report regarding the fairness of this information or its consistency with the consolidated financial statements.

Paris, March 10, 2004
The Statutory Auditors

KPMG Audit   Deloitte Touche Tohmatsu
Department of KPMG S.A.

Gérard Rivière   Amadou Raimi   Pascale Chastaing-Doblin

This is a free translation into English of the statutory auditors' report issued in the French language and is provided solely for the convenience of English speaking readers. The statutory auditors' report includes for the information of the reader, as required under French law in any auditor's report, whether qualified or not, an explanatory paragraph separate from and presented below the audit opinion discussing the auditors' assessment of certain significant accounting and auditing matters.

These assessments were considered for the purpose of issuing an audit opinion on the financial statements taken as a whole and not to provide separate assurance on individual account caption or on information taken outside of the financial statements. Such report, together with the statutory auditors report addressing financial reporting in management's report on internal control, should be read in conjunction and construed in accordance with French law and French auditing professional standards.

Source: Pinault Printemps annual report (2003) consolidated financial statements, p. 126, www.pprgroup.com

Management and Supervisory Boards. The Code includes requirements for accounting and audit. It is structured as a set of provisions that must be observed under law but also contains Recommendations (using the word 'shall') and Suggestions (using 'should' or 'can'). Companies may deviate from Recommendations but must explain this in the annual report. They may deviate from Suggestions without giving any explanation. The auditor's report on T-Online, a German company, does not refer specifically to the corporate governance code but it does cover the group management report (Exhibit 10.16).

Exhibit 10.16 Audit report, T-Online

Auditor's Report

We have audited the consolidated financial statements of T-Online International AG, Darmstadt, consisting of the balance sheet, the income statement and the statements of changes in equity and cash flows as well as the notes to the financial statements for the business year from January 1 to December 31, 2003. The preparation and the content of the consolidated financial statements according to the International Accounting Standards/International Financial Reporting Standards of the IASB (IAS/IFRS) are the responsibility of the Company's Board of Managing Directors. Our responsibility is to express an opinion, based on our audit, whether the consolidated financial statements are in accordance with IFRS.

We conducted our audit of the consolidated financial statements in accordance with German auditing regulations and generally accepted standards for the audit of financial statements promulgated by the Institut der Wirtschaftsprüfer in Deutschland (IDW). Those standards require that we plan and perform the audit to obtain reasonable assurance about whether the consolidated financial statements are free of material misstatements. Knowledge of the business activities and the economic and legal environment of the Company and evaluations of possible misstatements are taken into account in the determination of audit procedures. The evidence supporting the amounts and disclosures in the consolidated financial statements are examined on a test basis within the framework of the audit. The audit includes assessing the accounting principles used and significant estimates made by the Board of Managing Directors, as well as evaluating the overall presentation of the consolidated financial statements. We believe that our audit provides a reasonable basis for our opinion.

In our opinion, the consolidated financial statements give a true and fair view of the net assets, financial position, results of operations and cash flows of the T-Online Group for the business year in accordance with IFRS.

Our audit, which also extends to the group management report prepared by the Board of Managing Directors for the business year from January 1 to December 31, 2003, has not led to any reservations. In our opinion, on the whole the group management report, together with the other information of the consolidated financial statements, provides a suitable understanding of the Group's position and suitably presents the risks of future development. In addition, we confirm that the consolidated financial statements and the group management report for the business year from January 1 to December 31, 2003 satisfy the conditions required for the Company's exemption from its duty to prepare consolidated financial statements and the group management report in accordance with German accounting law.

Frankfurt am Main, February 13, 2004

PWC Deutsche Revision
Aktiengesellschaft
Wirtschaftsprüfungsgesellschaft

(Laue)
Wirtschaftsprüfer

(ppa. Jerger)
Wirtschaftsprüferin

Source: T-Online, annual report (2003), p. 123. www.t-online.net/ir

10.6.4 The Netherlands

The Enterprise Chamber[77] is a special chamber of the Courts of Justice which gives rulings on allegations of failure to comply with the legal requirements of financial accounting. The verdicts are specific to the cases considered, but may also have a wider influence. The Chamber may state that the financial accounts are incorrect and may give an order to the company containing precise requirements as to the preparation of financial statements, now or in the future. It may also give instructions of a more general nature which may cause a particular accounting policy to become unacceptable. The verdict may include comment on the auditor, which may in turn lead to professional disciplinary action being taken by the professional body. The audit report of a typical Dutch company gives a 'true and fair' opinion but does not refer to the corporate governance code (Exhibit 10.17).

10.6.5 Poland

In 2002 the World Bank produced a Report on the Observance of Standards and Codes (ROSC) with specific coverage of Accounting and Auditing.[78] The conclusions were

---

Exhibit 10.17 Audit report, a typical Dutch company

Independent auditors' report

Introduction
We have audited the financial statements of ABC N.V. for the year 2003. These financial statements are the responsibility of the Company's management. Our responsibility is to express an opinion on these financial statements based on our audit.

Scope
We conducted our audit in accordance with auditing standards generally accepted in The Netherlands. Those standards require that we plan and perform the audit to obtain reasonable assurance about whether the financial statements are free of material misstatement. An audit includes examining, on a test basis, evidence supporting the amounts and disclosures in the financial statements. An audit also includes assessing the accounting principles used and significant estimates made by management, as well as evaluating the overall presentation of the financial statements. We believe that our audit provides a reasonable basis for our opinion.

Opinion
In our opinion, the financial statements give a true and fair view of the financial position of ABC N.V. as at December 28, 2003 and of the result for the year then ended in accordance with accounting principles generally accepted in The Netherlands and comply with the financial reporting requirements included in Part 9 of Book 2 of The Netherlands Civil Code.

XYZ Accountants

Amsterdam, The Netherlands

April, 2004

---

[77] Klaassen (2001) p. 1917

[78] World Bank (2002) www.worldbank.org/ifa/rosc_aa.html.

mainly of the form 'needs to strengthen' which is perhaps not surprising in a system that is developing rapidly to meet international standards. The report is perhaps more interesting in its description of the structures in place with the aim of achieving greater assurance. The Securities and Exchange Commission (SEC) has established a system of monitoring and enforcing disclosure requirements. It reviews financial statements of listed companies and other participants in the securities market, seeks to identify violations of disclosure requirements and imposes penalties. The ROSC report recommended that more reviewers with adequate professional expertise were required to strengthen monitoring activities. The NCSA has power to take disciplinary action to enforce the code of professional ethics and auditing standards. The ROSC report regarded the NCSA as a well-organized professional body but recommended strengthening of practice reviews and more effective training and examination in the application of standards.

An example of an audit report is shown in Exhibit 10.18. The auditors of Orlen include a comment on the treatment of hyperinflation and on the application of IAS 16. They give a 'present fairly' opinion. Corporate governance codes are not mentioned.

Exhibit 10.18 Audit report, Orlen

Independent Auditors' report

To the Supervisory Board of Polski Koncern Naftowy ORLEN SA
We have audited the accompanying consolidated balance sheet of Polski Koncern Naftowy ORLEN SA ("the Company") as of 31 December 2003, and the related consolidated statements of income, cash flows and changes in equity for the year then ended. These consolidated financial statements are the responsibility of the Company's management. Our responsibility is to express an opinion on these financial statements based on our audit.

We conducted our audit in accordance with International Standards on Auditing. Those Standards require that we plan and perform the audit to obtain reasonable assurance about whether the financial statements are free of material misstatement. An audit includes examining, on a test basis, evidence supporting the amounts and disclosures in the financial statements. An audit also includes assessing the accounting principles used and significant estimates made by management, as well as evaluating the overall financial statement presentation. We believe that our audit provides a reasonable basis for our opinion.

International Accounting Standard No. 29 "Financial Reporting in Hyperinflationary Economies" (IAS 29) requires that the carrying amounts of assets and liabilities reported in a period of hyperinflation should be expressed in the measuring unit current at the end of the hyperinflationary period and constitute the basis for the carrying amounts in the subsequent financial statements. The Polish economy was hyperinflationary until the end of 1996 and ceased to be hyperinflationary in 1997. The Company last revalued its fixed assets as of 1 January 1995 to reflect the effects of inflation, in general by applying price indices determined by the Central Statistical Office for individual groups of assets. This revaluation was not performed in accordance with the provisions of IAS 29 since the Company did not use a general price index and did not subsequently revalue its fixed assets as of 31 December 1996. As a result, the cumulative balances of property, plant and equipment as of 31 December 2003, which existed prior to 31 December 1996, have not been expressed in the measuring unit current at the end of 1996. The Company also did not apply International Accounting Standard No 16 "Property, Plant and Equipment" requiring that the revalued amount of fixed assets approximate their fair value as at the date of revaluation.

In our opinion, except for the matter referred to in the paragraph above, the consolidated financial statements present fairly, in all material respects, the consolidated financial position of the Company as of 31 December 2003,

▶

Exhibit 10.18 *(Continued)*

and of the consolidated results of its operations and its cash flows for the year then ended in accordance with International Financial Reporting Standards.

Without further qualifying our opinion, we draw attention to the following:

We also reported separately on the consolidated financial statements of the Company for the year ended 31 December 2003 prepared in accordance with Polish Accounting Standards ("PAS"). The significant differences between PAS and International Financial Reporting Standards as far as they concern the financial statements referred to above are summarized in Note 33 of the accompanying consolidated financial statements.

Warsaw, Poland

19 April 2004

Source: Orlen SA annual report (2003), pp. 94–95. www.orlen.pl

10.7 Accounting issues

The IAS Regulation brought *de jure* harmonization to European listed companies from 2005 but only in those areas where IFRS are applicable. The remainder of the corporate report is open to a mixture of national and international influences. This section considers some of them.

10.7.1 'True and fair view'

The idea of a 'true and fair view' was introduced to the Fourth Directive at a late stage in its development. The translations to the languages of member states reflected different perceptions in each country. Parker and Nobes (1994) explored the meaning of 'true and fair' across a range of European countries. Aisbitt and Nobes (2001) examine the implementation of the true and fair view requirement into the laws of Austria, Finland and Sweden. The translation issue will be no less problematic as IAS 1 is taken into national languages. Evans (2003) examined the nature of the IAS 1 wording on 'present fairly' and discussed the likely interpretation in Germany. This section explains the perceptions of 'true and fair view' in the period immediately prior to adoption of IAS 1 in the EU.

France

The wording used in French legislation is *'une image fidèle'*, translated as 'a faithful picture'. The use of the word 'faithful' had historical precedents and left sufficient ambiguity to satisfy national legislators. Parker and Nobes (1994, p. 80) classify the French approach as allowing the arrival of the true and fair view to permit some change towards substance rather than form. It became available to directors and auditors to be used as a basis for interpretation or for guidance where no rules existed.

Germany

The wording in the law which enacts the fourth directive is *'(unter Beachtung der Grundsätze ordnungsmässiger Buchführung) ein den tatsächlichen Verhältnissen entsprechendes Bild'*. It is translated as '(in compliance with accepted accounting principles) a picture in accordance with the facts'. The German legislators found it difficult to bring the concept of 'true and fair' into German law, and their wording differs from that of the official German-language version of the directive. Parker and Nobes (1994) classify the German approach to 'true and fair' as one which cannot be used to justify a departure from the law.

The Netherlands[79]

The wording of the Dutch law, incorporating the Fourth Directive, uses the phrase *'een getrouw beeld'*, which may be translated as 'a faithful picture'. Nobes's (1984) classification of The Netherlands in respect to 'true and fair view' is that it is used by directors and auditors as the basic principle in interpreting the law and guidelines. The 1970 law had used wording which could be translated as 'presents faithfully, clearly and consistently over time' and also 'presents an insight such that a well-founded opinion can be formed'. Thus in The Netherlands, as in the UK and Ireland, the notion of a true and fair view predated the Fourth Directive.

Poland[80]

We explained earlier that the 1994 Act was revised in 2000, with the majority of revisions only came into force in the financial year beginning 1 January 2002. The true and fair requirement is contained in Article 4(1) of both the old and the revised Act and the Polish words used are unchanged (*rztelnie* and *jasno*). The paragraphs are almost identical, but the revision is substantive and consists of omitting the requirement that accounting principles are applied in a way that is *prawidlowo*, i.e. in accordance with the rules. The explanation of this change lies in a new article 4(2) which was not present in the 1994 Act. It reads:

> *Events, including economic transactions, are included in the books of account and disclosed in the financial statements in accordance with their economic substance.*

Also new from 1 January 2002 is Article 10(3) which reads:

> *In matters not regulated by the provisions of the Act, the entity, when choosing an accounting principle or policy, may use national accounting standards issued by the Accounting Standards Board so authorised by the Act. In the event of the absence of an appropriate national standard, international accounting standards may be used.*

10.7.2 Formats of financial statements

We have explained in section 9.5.4 that it is not entirely clear how formats will develop after 2005. The first evidence may be seen in the 2005 annual reports but it could take longer as companies experiment gradually. Group financial statements are only required to apply IAS 1 which is quite flexible on presentation. Individual companies may continue to be regulated by the Directives.

---

[79] Zeff *et al.* (1999).

[80] We are indebted to Dr Marek Schroeder, University of Birmingham, for the information in this section.

Until the 1990s it was common for groups to include the parent company financial statements in the group annual report published in English. The parent company financial statements followed national practice in presentation and often looked quite different from the group financial statements which took advantage of the flexible approach to consolidated financial statements then existing for companies with foreign listings. Even before 2005 these separate individual financial statements were disappearing from the consolidated annual report. One of the few remaining examples of inclusion of the parent company financial statements is Altcatel (see Exhibit 10.19).

Exhibit 10.19 shows the assets on the left (*actif*) and liabilities and equity on the right (*passif*). Liabilities are categorized by their nature but not by date of maturity. The separation of current and non-current liabilities is given in notes to the accounts. The categories gross cost, accumulated depreciation (or provision for depreciation) and net book value are used for all assets, whether current or fixed. This example shows the potential for different presentations to remain after 2005, because France does not at present intend to require or permit individual companies to apply IFRS rather than national law. It may be that the different presentations will become less apparent to an international readership if the group accounts in English omit the parent company financial statements.

Exhibit 10.19 Balance sheet of parent company, Alcatel

PARENT COMPANY BALANCE SHEETS AT DECEMBER 31, 2003						
ASSETS (in million of euros)	Notes	2003			2002	2001
		Gross value	Amortization and depreciation	Net value	Net value	Net value
Intangible assets		20.3	(16.8)	3.5	4.0	4.6
Land		–	–	–	–	–
Buildings		0.3	(0.3)	–	–	–
Other property, plant and equipment		0.4	(0.3)	0.1	0.1	0.2
Property, plant and equipment		0.7	(0.6)	0.1	0.1	0.2
Investments in subsidiaries and associates	(7)	20,869.2	(11,130.3)	9.738.9	13,659.6	25,735.3
Receivables from subsidiaries and associates	(8)	1.1	(0.6)	0.5	0.5	0.5
Other financial assets	(8)	2,266.0	(236.9)	2,029.1	2,374.8	2,735.6
Investments and other non-current assets		23,136.3	(11,367.8)	11,768.5	16,034.9	28,471.4
TOTAL NON-CURRENT ASSETS		23,157.3	(11,385.2)	11,772.1	16,039.0	28,476.2
Accounts receivable and other current assets	(9)/(16)	10,767.9	–	10,767.9	11,330.8	11,867.5
Marketable securities	(9)	1,330.7	(55.0)	1,275.7	497.4	304.1
Cash	(9)	3,034.7	–	3,034.7	3,584.0	3,439.3
TOTAL CURRENT ASSETS		15,133.3	(55.0)	15,078.3	15,412.2	15,610.9
Prepayments and deferred charges		587.7	–	587.7	257.5	128.8
TOTAL ASSETS	(6)	38,878.3	(11,440.2)	27,438.1	31,708.7	44,215.9

LIABILITIES AND SHAREHOLDERS' EQUITY (in millions of euros)	Notes	2003		2002	2001
		Before appropriation	After appropriation*	After appropriation	After appropriation
Capital stock	(11)	2,568.8	2,568.8	2,529.4	2,481.5
Additional paid-in capital	(12)	21,719.1	7,562.4	21,601.8	21,425.8
Reserves	(12)	2,284.1	2,119.0	2,284.1	2,284.1
Retained earnings		(11,066.4)	–	(11,066.3)	3,555.5
Net income (loss) for the year		(3,255.4)	–	–	–
Statutory provisions		–	–	–	–
SHAREHOLDERS' EQUITY	(12)	12,250.2	12,250.2	15,349.0	29.746.9
OTHER EQUITY	(13)	645.0	645.0	645.0	–
RESERVES FOR LIABILITIES AND CHARGES	(14)	3,485.9	3,485.9	3,467.8	404.5
Bonds convertible into new or existing shares (OCEANE)	(15)/(16)	1,022.4	1,022.4	–	–
Other bonds and notes issued	(15)/(16)	3,782.1	3,782.1	5,324.7	5,968.7
Bank loans and overdrafts	(16)	198.8	198.8	297.4	673.0
Miscellaneous borrowings	(16)	244.7	244.7	190.5	898.4
TOTAL FINANCIAL DEBT		5,248.0	5,248.0	5,812.6	7,540.1
Taxation and social security	(16)	4.8	4.8	3.0	6.0
Other liabilities	(16)	5,794.9	5,794.9	6,431.2	6,472.3
TOTAL LIABILITIES		5,799.7	5,799.7	6,434.2	6,478.3
Currency translation adjustment		9.3	9.3	0.1	46.1
TOTAL		27,438.1	27,438.1	31,708.7	44,215.9

* Proposal.

Source: Alcatel annual report (2003), pp. 84–85. www.alcatel.com

10.7.3 Charts of accounts

10.7.3.1 France[81]

Early attempts had been made at creating a chart of accounts, particularly in 1942 (see also section 8.5). In 1946 the government of France established a commission on accounting standards leading to a code (*Plan Comptable Général*) in 1947 which contained some of the features of the 1942 code. One of the genuinely French features was to have no fixed relationship between management accounts and financial accounts (splitting the chart into two sets of related accounts). The code gradually became standard practice although it was not mandatory under law. It had a strong influence on the training of professional accountants and remained substantially unaltered until the implementation of the Fourth Directive in the 1982 *Plan Comptable Général*.

The national accounting code (*Plan Comptable Général*)[82] is at the heart of financial reporting and accounting. The Code is revised at relatively infrequent intervals, with amendments and additions occurring more frequently. The 1999 PCG was issued by the

---

[81] Griziaux (1999), pp. 1178–1179; Fortin (1991).

[82] Standish (2000); CNC website (2000). www.finances.gouv.fr/CNCompta/

Exhibit 10.20 Main classes of financial accounts

Class 1	Capital accounts
Class 2	Fixed asset accounts
Class 3	Stocks and work in progress accounts
Class 4	Accounts for debts receivable and payable
Class 5	Financial accounts
Class 6	Accounts for charges
Class 7	Income accounts

CRC with approval of the CNC and under ministerial order. There are two central objectives of the *Plan Comptable Général*:

● standardizing the organization of the accounting system of the enterprise;
● standardizing the presentation of financial results and position.

Taken together, these ensure that the accounting records are maintained in a form which permits production of the required form of financial statements.

The *Plan Comptable Général* is very detailed, using a decimal numbering system to specify major headings and greater levels of detail. The highest level of heading is shown in Exhibit 10.20.

The detailed accounts under each heading are also specified using further digits. Two-digit examples are given in Exhibit 10.21. Three-digit and four-digit codes are also used for detailed recording (see Exhibit 10.22). They can be aggregated to the two-digit level in order to present information for financial reporting.

The *Plan Comptable Général* contains the following main sections:

TITLE I	–	OBJECT AND PRINCIPLES OF ACCOUNTING
TITLE II	–	DEFINITION OF ASSETS, LIABILITIES, INCOME AND CHARGES
TITLE III	–	ACCOUNTING RECOGNITION AND VALUATION RULES
TITLE IV	–	KEEPING, STRUCTURE AND FUNCTIONING OF ACCOUNTS (including list of accounts codes)
TITLE V	–	FINANCIAL STATEMENTS (annual account, balance sheet, profit and loss account and notes)

Effectively it is a very detailed manual for the preparation of accounts. It does not have the status of a law, but application of the classification is compulsory. Further-

Exhibit 10.21 Examples of two-digit codes in the *Plan Comptable Général*

21	Tangible fixed assets
40	Suppliers and related accounts
×9	Any two-digit account ending in 9 indicates a provision against an asset

Exhibit 10.22 Examples of three-digit and four-digit codes

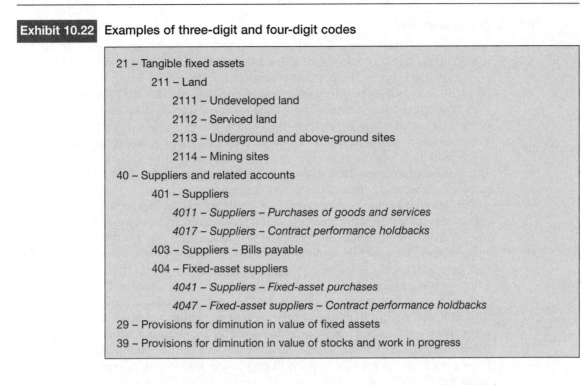

```
21 – Tangible fixed assets
        211 – Land
                2111 – Undeveloped land
                2112 – Serviced land
                2113 – Underground and above-ground sites
                2114 – Mining sites
40 – Suppliers and related accounts
        401 – Suppliers
                4011 – Suppliers – Purchases of goods and services
                4017 – Suppliers – Contract performance holdbacks
        403 – Suppliers – Bills payable
        404 – Fixed-asset suppliers
                4041 – Suppliers – Fixed-asset purchases
                4047 – Fixed-asset suppliers – Contract performance holdbacks
29 – Provisions for diminution in value of fixed assets
39 – Provisions for diminution in value of stocks and work in progress
```

more there are industry-specific versions. The *Plan Comptable Général* requires interpretation of some of the rules and it is not a full source of information on all matters. It does, however, contain extensive guidelines for explanation of the principles.

The general principles of the *Plan Comptable Général* are intended to produce a true and fair view (*image fidèle*) by application of prudence, consistency (*régularité*) and faithful reckoning (*sincérité*). The CNC continues to give advice in the PCG. In April 2000 it issued advice relating to liabilities, covering definitions and valuation.

10.7.3.2 Germany

There are two meanings of the phrase 'chart of accounts' in Germany. One is an accounts framework (*Kontenrahmen*), setting an outline chart for companies in a particular sector. The other is a detailed accounts plan (*Kontenplan*) developed by a business for its own use. Both use a decimal system of classification. Ten classes of accounts, numbered 0–9, are each divided into ten account groups. Each account group has ten account types and each account type has ten sub-accounts; further subdivision is permitted.[83] The numbers so created form the account number.

Charts of accounts have a long history in Germany, first appearing around 1900. A comprehensive system was developed by Schär in 1911, but the leading authority was the work of Schmalenbach published in 1927, called *Kontenrahmen*. Since 1945 it is not mandatory to use a particular *Kontenrahmen* for a sector. Industry frameworks have continued to be issued by the Association of German Industry and have been adapted to take account of the Fourth Directive.

---

[83] www.accaglobal.com/members/services/int_mobility/factsheets/germany/procedures.

10.7.3.3 The Netherlands[84]

The Civil Code deals with financial statements and related matters in Title 9 of Book 2, *Annual Accounts and Directors' Report*. The 15 sections are shown in Exhibit 10.23.

As explained earlier, there are three sources for companies which intend to follow generally acceptable accounting principles in The Netherlands. The word 'acceptable' is used here rather than 'accepted' because there is no specific book of accounting standards such as that found in the US or the UK. The first source is to follow the Civil Code as statute law. The second is to take note of the verdicts of the Enterprise Chamber and the third is to apply the recommendations of the Council for Annual Reporting (RJ). This combination is essential as the key rule for accounting in The Netherlands (comparable to achieving a 'true and fair view' in the UK).

The Enterprise Chamber can only react to complaints – it cannot initiate action. The person making a complaint must prove a direct interest in the financial statements of the company and must state the perceived deficiency. The court hears the complainant, the company's view and the auditor's explanation. Because the Chamber is part of a formal legal process, the number of judgments is relatively small. The formation of the Chamber was seen as being an alternative to creating a supervisory body like the US SEC.

As explained earlier (see section 10.3.4), the recommendations of the Council for Annual Reporting (RJ), published in the form of guidelines, are not a statutory requirement. They are, however, regarded as authoritative pronouncements and an important frame of reference for the auditor in forming an opinion on financial statements. Departures from the guidelines of the RJ are possible and are not referred to in the auditor's report.

Exhibit 10.23	Sections of the Civil Code

1, 2	General provisions
3	Regulations concerning the balance sheet and the notes
4	Regulations concerning the profit and loss account and the notes
5	Special regulations concerning the notes
6	Regulations concerning valuation principles and the principles underlying the determination of financial results
7	Executive directors' report
8	Other data
9	Audit requirements
10	Publication
11	Exemptions based on the size of the company
12	Specific industries
13	Consolidated financial statements
14	Provisions for banks
15	Provisions for insurance companies

---

[84] Klaassen (2001).

10.7.3.4 Poland[85]

Uniform charts of accounts were used from 1940 to 1989. Since then, the Accounting Act requires each entity to prepare its own chart of accounts. Model charts of accounts may be used to unify groups of operations and reduce the work of creating a chart. Model charts may be devised by the SEC for listed companies or by the Ministry of Finance for other companies.

The history of charts of accounts in Poland is described by Jaruga and Szychta (1997), tracing the development and changes from German occupation in the 1940s to the first Polish Uniform Plan of Accounting in 1946–49, a reform in the 1950s to a Soviet plan of accounts and then a return to a more 'continental' approach in the late 1980s. Although the law from 1991 allowed companies to design their own chart, the authors reported a prevailing opinion that a standard chart (such as the Model chart) would facilitate training and application. The counter opinion of the regulatory experts was that greater flexibility would result in a better reflection of economic reality.

10.7.4 Business combinations[86]

A survey by FEE (2002), using a mixture of *de jure* and *de facto* analysis, showed the diversity of national practices across 21 European countries in 1999/2000 in the treatment of business combinations. The survey found that the purchase method was allowed in every country studied while pooling of interest was allowed in most countries but not in Austria, the Czech Republic and Hungary. Of the 96 business combinations examined, 75 used the purchase method and 21 used pooling of interests. Some of the pooling of interest cases were effectively acquisitions but the alternative treatment was allowed under national law.

Most countries required goodwill to be capitalized and amortized. During the period of the survey, nine countries allowed direct write-off against reserves (Austria, the Czech Republic, Denmark, France, Germany, Italy, Luxembourg, The Netherlands and Switzerland). Only one company in the survey used the impairment approach, which had already been established in the US at that time. There was a wide range of amortization periods used by companies, with 20 years being a common period but phrases such as 'up to 20 years' being seen as unhelpful to readers. Some countries presumed a period of five years for amortization in the absence of further information (Belgium, Denmark, Finland, Italy, Poland, Portugal, Sweden).

Some countries allowed IAS or US GAAP for group accounts, giving further flexibility within any country. At the time of the FEE report this flexibility in consolidated accounts applied in Austria, Germany, Finland, the Czech Republic, Denmark, France, Italy and The Netherlands. The application of IFRS to all European listed companies from 2005 was thus a major change in harmonization of group accounting across Europe, in the area of business combinations. Some companies were already applying IFRS, although not always in full.

10.7.5 Secrecy versus transparency

10.7.5.1 France

Gray (1988) classified French accounting as relatively low on the secrecy scale compared with Germany or the less developed Latin countries. This is consistent with the extensive use of notes to the accounts and various types of additional disclosure such as

---

[85] Jaruga and Schroeder (2001), p. 1603.
[86] FEE (2002).

segmental reporting, the management report and the statutory disclosures on corporate social and environmental reporting, sometimes referred to as 'the social balance sheet'.

Notes on the accounts[87]

The balance sheet, profit and loss account and notes to the accounts must be read as a whole. It is specifically stated in the PCG 1999 that the three documents form *un tout*, and it is also stated in the Commercial Code in the phrase *un tout indissociable*.

The notes are regarded as complementing and commenting on the information in the balance sheet and profit and loss account. They may also supply additional information where the rules are not sufficient to give a true and fair view. Their role also covers describing and justifying changes in accounting policies or presentation of information. It is clear from the Commercial Code that the notes should be used to provide the additional information necessary for a true and fair view. Giving additional information in the balance sheet and profit and loss account is not acceptable.

Two sets of notes are required – one for the parent company and one for the group. It should be noted that in English-language versions of group accounts the parent company accounts and notes are often omitted.

Management report

The 1985 Act incorporates the provision of the Seventh Directive for a review of the development of the business and discussion of important post-balance sheet events, likely future developments and research and development. This may be seen as comparable to the Directors' Report in UK companies' annual reports. The stock market regulations require the management report to be published with the half-yearly results as well as with the annual report. Stock market reporting obligations add further recommendations about information such as risk disclosures.[88]

Social and environmental reporting

A law relating to company law reform in non-accounting matters, passed in 1977, required French undertakings having a significant number of employees (more than 300) to present to the staff committee a *bilan social*, or employment report.[89] The *bilan social* is not part of the notes to the accounts but is sometimes published in the annual report. It may be regarded as a type of social balance sheet although it is presented as a narrative report. The information required by the law covered employment, wages and related costs, health and safety conditions, other working conditions, staff training, industrial relations and living conditions where these are the responsibility of the employer.

This long-standing recognition of the importance of social reporting was consolidated in the Law on New Economic Regulations (Nouvelles Régulations Économiques, NRE) passed in 2001 and implemented from 2002. It represented a major update of France's company law framework. All companies listed on the main market must report on a number of social and environmental issues. Information is required about the working conditions of employees, equality policies, health and safety arrangements, community and charity work, use of energy sources, measures to limit the company's impact on the environment, compliance with environmental legislation and reduction of environmental risk.

---

[87] Parker (1996).

[88] Standish (2000), sections 2.1, 2.2.

[89] Parker (1996), p. 335; Scheid and Walton (1992), p. 164.

Public access to information

The Ministry of Justice runs, through the *Tribunaux de Commerce*, the register of commerce. This is where all corporations of any kind must deposit for public access their articles of association. Limited liability corporations must also deposit their annual financial statements.

The *Centrale des Bilans*, run by the Bank of France, receives data voluntarily from 28,000 large companies. The companies receive in return reports about their own relative performance and balance sheets. A further analysis of the company's performance and financial health is available for a fee. The Bank of France also provides information on a company's indebtedness through the *Centrale des risques*. Ratings of companies for use by lenders are derived from the *Centrale des risques* and are available through the *Fichier bancaire des entreprises*.

10.7.5.2 Germany

Gray (1988) classified German accounting as highly secretive by reputation. However, the extent of information provided is quite extensive and the reputation for secrecy may have been created by concentrating on a few items such as hidden reserves. Since 1998 the change in regulation of group accounting and the pressures of competing in international capital markets have resulted in some German companies providing very informative segmental information and detailed management reports. Leuz and Wüstemann (2003) challenge the perception that German accounting is uninformative. They show the importance of private information channels but acknowledge that arm's length or outside investors relying primarily on public disclosures may be less well-informed in the German system than they would be in the Anglo-American economies. They also argue that the voluntary changes to IFRS (prior to 2005) did not fundamentally alter the German accounting system and its reliance on private information channels and insider governance. Accounting standards leave discretion and the exercise of that discretion depends on controlling insiders' incentives. Reform to accounting standards must be accompanied by changes to the institutional framework and strengthening of corporate governance.

Notes on the accounts

Notes on the accounts are a mandatory part of the financial statements. The German view is that the balance sheet, profit and loss account and notes must, taken together, produce a true and fair view. The 'true and fair' test is not applied to each element separately. Particularly important use of notes to the accounts are:

● disclosure of methods of accounting and valuation;
● effects of accounting methods applied solely for tax reasons;
● information on receivables and liabilities;
● information on changes in equity as shown in the statement of appropriation of profit;
● information on employees;
● remuneration and benefits of board members;
● information on shareholdings.

Before 1987, notes had to be prepared and disclosed only by public companies and certain large private companies. The extension of notes to financial statements of all companies is therefore regarded as an important change resulting from the Fourth Directive.

Management report

Companies are required by the law (HGB) to prepare a management report. It must be consistent with the financial statements. Additional requirements may be set by the Deutsche Börse.

10.7.5.3 The Netherlands

Management report[90]

The report by the managing board of directors is prescribed in the Civil Code. The report should contain a general review, information on the dividends and financial results, a balance sheet profile and an indication of prospects. In this way, past, present and future issues are discussed. It reports also on issues of employment and research and development activities. The indication of prospects relates to capital investments, finance, employees' development, circumstances related to net sales development and profitability analysis. The requirement to show a true and fair view applies to this report.

There are therefore similarities with the operating and financial review provided by UK companies, the management report provided by German companies and the management discussion and analysis required in the USA.

Environmental report[91]

The Environmental Management Act (1997) established a requirement for an environmental report to the government. Companies in targeted industries agree ('covenant') with the government to provide an environmental report. It is available to interested parties on demand. The Environmental Reporting Decree (1999) required that certain categories of company (those which have potentially serious effects on the environment) must produce two environmental reports – one for the government and one for the public.

10.8 Comparative research studies

Comparative research studies may focus on similarities and differences in regulation (*de jure* comparisons) or in practice (*de facto* comparisons). Consolidated financial statements of listed companies are the most readily available source of information for *de facto* comparisons. From 2005 onwards the common application of IFRS will change the approach of researchers to *de facto* comparisons. One approach will be to focus on companies that do not apply the IFRS (individual companies within listed groups, or else unlisted groups). This will offer greater challenges in gaining access to the information and to collaboration across researchers with suitable language skills and national knowledge. Another approach will be to use statistical analysis to detect underlying differences among the consolidated accounts of companies that claim to be harmonized with IFRS.

There is a large body of comparative research studies across European countries where the evidence has been taken from information published by companies. Section 10.8.1 explains how harmonization studies have been carried out on the basis of information disclosed by companies.

---

[90] Klaassen (2001), pp. 1999–2000.

[91] Hoffmann (2003).

10.8.1 Harmonization studies

The methods used in harmonization studies are explained in Chapter 7. The technical detail of the results of these studies may no longer reflect accounting practice in the respective countries but the research studies remain useful for two reasons. They show how comparative studies of harmonization may be carried out where accounting practices remain beyond the IFRS harmonization process and they show the extent of diversity that existed prior to the universal application of IFRS in consolidated accounts of listed companies.

In section 7.5.4.1 we discuss in detail the research of Archer *et al.* (1995) based on the C-index and the work of Cañibano and Mora (2000), also based on the C-index. We show in that section how this type of research demonstrated the relative progress of the harmonization process in areas of accounting diversity such deferred taxation, goodwill, finance leases and foreign currency translation.

Hermann and Thomas (1995) used the I- index in their comparative study. They found that, of the countries classed as legalistic (Belgium, France, Germany and Portugal), France had the highest bicountry I index when compared to the fairness-orientated countries (Denmark, Ireland, the UK and The Netherlands). This was explained by Hermann and Thomas as reflecting French use of methods of consolidation influenced by the UK and the US, and the influence of IASs on French group accounting practices. They found that Germany was the only country where all companies sampled used strict historical cost. Depreciation policy in the German sample, based on declining balance in the early years and then straight line in later life, was significantly different from the straight-line approach used by most other companies. This was attributed by Hermann and Thomas to the influence of tax law on accounting practice in Germany. In respect of accounting for goodwill they detected a change in practice in the accounts examined for 1992/93 year ends, with 20 out of 30 companies capitalizing and amortizing goodwill. They found that the bicountry I index was relatively high for pairings within the fairness-orientated grouping (Denmark, Ireland, The Netherlands and The UK).

Emenyonu and Gray (1992) applied harmonization indexes and chi-square tests to 1989 data. They confirmed the flexibility of measurement practices in consolidated accounts of large French companies, compared with those of German and UK companies. The accounting policies examined were inventory valuation, depreciation methods, goodwill, research and development expenditure and foreign currency translation. In bi-country I indices, Germany was second lowest to Portugal in harmonization with other EU countries in this range of accounting matters.

One of the problems faced by Emenyonu and Gray was non-disclosure of information. Some companies fail to explain an accounting policy that has been applied. Pierce and Weetman (2002) demonstrated the adjustments required to the C and H indices to take account of non-disclosure and applied these adjustments in a comparative study of deferred taxation in Ireland and Denmark over the period 1986 to 1993. The apparent increase in harmonization over the period was explained in part by the improvement in disclosure over the period as companies in both countries gave progressively clearer explanations of how they were accounting for deferred taxation.

Comparisons of mid- and eastern European countries tend to be qualitative descriptions and evaluations rather than quantitative studies. There have been more single-country studies than comparative studies but one example of a large-scale comparative study was the special issue of *The European Accounting Review* (1995) Vol. 4(4), covering Eastern Europe.

10.8.2 Statistical analysis

From 2005 consolidated accounts of listed companies in the EU will all apply IFRS. Within some IFRS there will be a range of choices about measurement that will not be disclosed in the annual reports. So statistical analysis of the reported accounting figures will be required to detect any variations in choices. One type of statistical analysis which has been used to make cross-country comparisons follows the 'conservatism' literature (Basu 1997) which applies econometric analysis (see section 7.7).

Giner and Rees (2001) studied companies in France, Germany and the UK over the period 1990 to 1998. They found that in all three countries there was a stronger relationship between bad news and earnings than between good news and earnings.

Lara and Mora (2004) found evidence of balance sheet conservatism and earnings conservatism across eight European countries in the period 1988–2000. They found that code-law-based countries were more balance sheet conservative. They also found that UK companies were more earnings conservative (recognizing bad news fastest compared to good news). While this kind of research still has some technical question marks, especially when it is effectively comparing stock market sentiment more than it is comparing accounting information, it is nevertheless an indication of the way forward in detecting the persistence of national or cultural choices underlying apparent standardization.

Another type of research question that relates accounting to stock market perceptions is to ask: 'What is the value relevance of accounting information constructed under different accounting systems?' Value relevance is measured as the association between stock prices and accounting numbers (measured as earnings and book value of net assets). Share prices reflect, at least in part, the accounting numbers. Arce and Mora (2002) measured value relevance of earnings and book value in eight countries for the period 1990–98. They found that earnings were more value relevant than book value in market-oriented countries, and found the reverse in creditor-oriented countries. They speculated that IFRS could reduce the differences caused by accounting rules, but not those caused by institutional and cultural factors. Repetition of this type of research, once IFRS accounting is established, could give more scope for quantifying institutional and cultural differences across markets.

Summary and conclusions

The EU has made a major contribution to harmonization of accounting disclosure and measurement. The Fourth and Seventh Directives brought significant harmonization of disclosure and have provided a basis for emerging and transition economies to develop their accounting rules in a very short space of time as part of the process of joining the EU. The Directives did not achieve harmonization in measurement. The decision to work towards acceptance of IAS/IFRS rather than develop separate European standards was a major step towards harmonization in measurement as well as in disclosure. The process of endorsement, developing towards 2005, appeared cumbersome and unduly cautious but was justified as protecting regulatory independence of the EU. The disagreements over aspects of IAS 39 were disappointing but overall the movement towards harmonization for listed groups of companies by 2005 was a major achievement for a large and diverse economic grouping that rivals the US in size and potential economic influence.

Key points from the chapter:

● The IAS Regulation takes precedence over national laws and the Fourth and Seventh Directives. It applies to the consolidated financial statements of listed groups.

● National legislation may require or permit other entities to apply the IAS Regulation. In the approach to 2005 there was great caution over such moves because of the potential impact on taxable profits and distributable profits.

● The distinction between common law and code law countries will have less influence on accounting practice that is harmonized under the IAS Regulation but may continue to affect those aspects of corporate reporting and assurance that remain under national direction.

● Corporate governance has developed rapidly in all member states, but it is important for users of financial information to understand the accompanying assurance mechanisms.

● Equity capital markets are taking a role in developing transparency and assurance in financial reporting. Again it is important for users of financial information to understand the processes of specific markets.

● The accounting profession continues to be very different in functions and state of development in different countries. This brings a challenge to the implementation and assurance of harmonized standards.

● There are accounting issues where evidence of diversity will continue, explained by institutional and cultural differences. Examples are the meaning of 'true and fair; the importance of charts of accounts; and the relative transparency of management reports or other narrative disclosures.

Questions

The following questions test your understanding of the material contained in the chapter and allow you to relate your understanding to the learning outcomes specified at the start of this chapter. The learning outcomes are repeated here. Each question is cross-referenced to the relevant section of the chapter.

Explain how member states of the EU will continue to have a national role, beyond the IAS Regulation, in setting accounting standards

1 What is the range of choices made by member states in deciding on whether to require or permit IFRS for individual companies within a listed group? (section 10.3.1)

2 What types of standard-setting body are found in France, Germany, The Netherlands and Poland? (sections 10.3.2 to 10.3.5)

Relate the institutional factors and external influences for a selection of member states to the framework set out in Chapter 4

3 How do the legal systems of France, Germany, The Netherlands and Poland fit into the classifications described in Chapter 4? (section 10.4.1)

4 How do the corporate governance systems of France, Germany, The Netherlands and Poland compare to the descriptions given in Chapter 3? (section 10.4.2).

5 How do the corporate financing systems of France, Germany, The Netherlands and Poland compare to the descriptions given in Chapter 1? (section 10.4.3)

6 How do the taxation systems of France, Germany, The Netherlands and Poland compare to the descriptions given in Chapter 4? (section 10.4.5)

7 How do the accounting professions in France, Germany, The Netherlands and Poland compare to the descriptions given in Chapter 4? (section 10.4.6)

8 How do the external influences on accounting practice in France, Germany, The Netherlands and Poland compare to those described in Chapter 4? (section 10.5)

Explain and evaluate the state of oversight and assurance in a selection of member states

9 What are the enforcement mechanisms used across member states to support the application of IFRS? (section 10.6)

10 How does enforcement differ in France, Germany, The Netherlands and Poland? (sections 10.6.1 to 10.6.4)

Explain a selection of accounting issues where national differences in accounting are likely to persist

11 What are the problems of comparing the meaning of 'a true and fair view' across member states? (section 10.7.1)

12 What are the benefits of the standard formats introduced by the Fourth and Seventh Directives? (section 10.7.2)

13 Why do some countries have charts of accounts but other countries implement accounting standards without such detailed guidance? (section 10.7.3)

14 What are the similarities and differences in narrative reporting in France, Germany, and The Netherlands? (section 10.7.5)

Describe how comparative research studies have helped advance understanding of similarities and differences in accounting across Europe

15 What did research studies find about harmonization in the 1980s and 1990s? (section 10.8.1)

16 What has been discovered in the 'conservatism' studies based on statistical analysis? (section 10.8.2)

References and further reading

Aisbitt, S. and Nobes, C. (2001) 'The true and fair view requirement in recent national implementations', *Accounting and Business Research*, 31(2): 83–90.

Arce, M. and Mora, A. (2002) 'Empirical evidence of the effect of European accounting differences on the stock market valuation of earnings and book value', *The European Accounting Review*, 11(3): 573–599.

Archer, S., Delvaille, P. and McLeay, S. (1995) 'The measurement of harmonization and the comparability of financial statement items: Within-country and between-country effects', *Accounting and Business Research*, 25(98): 67–80.

Baker, C.R., Mikol, A. and Quick, R. (2001) 'Regulation of the statutory auditor in the European Union: a comparative survey of the United Kingdom, France and Germany', *The European Accounting Review*, 10(4): 763–786.

Ballwieser, W. (2001) 'Germany – Individual accounts', in Ordelheide, D. (ed.), *Transnational Accounting TRANSACC*. Basingstoke and New York: Palgrave.

Basu, S. (1997) 'The conservatism principle and the asymmetric timeliness of earnings', *Journal of Accounting and Economics*, 24: 3–37.

Cañibano, L. and Mora, A. (2000) 'Evaluating the statistical significance of *de facto* accounting harmonization: A study of European global players', *European Accounting Review*, 9(3): 349–370.

Charkham, J.P. (1994) *Keeping Good Company: A Study of Corporate Governance in Five Countries*. Oxford: Clarendon Press.

Comparative Study of Corporate Governance Codes Relevant to the European Union and Its Member States. Report by Weil, Gotshal & Manges, LLP in conjunction with EASD (European Association of Securities Dealers) and ECGN (European Corporate Governance Network). January 2002. Published by the European Commission, Internal Market Directorate General. http://europa.eu.int/comm/internal_market/en/company/company/news/corp-gov-codes-rpt_en.htm

Crampton, A., Dorofeyev, S., Kolb, S. and Meyer-Hollatz, W. (2001) *UK: Germany: The main differences between UK and German Accounting Practice*. Deloitte & Touche. www.iasplus.com

Ding, Y., Stolowy, H. and Tenehaus, M. (2003) ' "Shopping around" for accounting practices: the financial statement presentation of French groups', *Abacus*, 39(1): 42–64.

Emenyonu, E.N. and Gray, S.J. (1992) 'EC accounting harmonization: An empirical study of measurement practices in France, Germany and the UK', *Accounting and Business Research*, Winter: 49–58.

Evans, L. (2003) 'The true and fair view and the "fair presentation" override of IAS 1', *Accounting and Business Research*, 33(4): 311–325.

FEE (2002) *FEE Survey on Business Combinations*, March 2002, Fédération des Experts Comptables Européens.

FEE (2003) Discussion paper: *European Enforcement Coordination*.

Fortin, A. (1991) 'The 1947 French accounting plan: Origins and influences on subsequent practice', *Accounting Historians Journal*, 19(2), December: 1–25.

Fraser, I., Henry, W. and Wallage, P. (2000) *The Future of Corporate Governance Insights from The Netherlands*, The Institute of Chartered Accountants of Scotland.

Giner, B. and Rees, W. (2001) 'On the asymmetric recognition of good and bad news in France, Germany and the United Kingdom', *Journal of Business Finance and Accounting*, 28(9–10): 1285–1332.

Glaum, M. and Street, D.L. (2003) 'Compliance with the disclosure requirements of Germany's New Market: IAS versus US GAAP', *Journal of International Financial Management and Accounting*, 14(1): 64–100.

Gray, S.J. (1988) 'Towards a theory of cultural influence on the development of accounting systems internationally', *Abacus*, 24(1): 1–15.

Griziaux, J.-P. (1999) 'France: Individual Accounts' in Ordelheide, D. (ed.) *TRANSACC: Transnational Accounting*. London: Macmillan.

Haan, L. de and Hinloopen, J. (2002) *Ordering the preference hierarchies for internal finance, bank loans, bonds and shares*, Tinbergen Institute Discussion Paper TI 2002–072/2, www.tinbergen.nl

Haller, A. (2002) 'Financial accounting developments in the European Union: past events and future prospects', *The European Accounting Review*, 11(1): 153–190.

Hermann, D. and Thomas, W. (1995) 'Harmonization of accounting measurement practices in the European Community', *Accounting and Business Research*, 25(100), 253–265.

Hoffmann, E. (2003) 'Environmental reporting and sustainability reporting in Europe: an overview of mandatory reporting schemes in The Netherlands and France', Institute for Global Environmental Strategies, www.iges.or.jp/en/be/pdf/report7.pdf

Hoogendoorn, M. (1996) 'Accounting and taxation in Europe – a comparative overview', *The European Accounting Review*, 5 (Supplement): 783–794.

Hoogendoorn, M.N. (2001) 'The Netherlands', in Alexander, D. and Archer, S. (eds), *European Accounting Guide*. 4th edn. New York: Aspen Law and Business.

Jaruga, A. and Schroeder, M. (2001) 'Poland' in Alexander, D. and Archer, S. (eds) *European Accounting Guide*, 4th edn, Aspen Law and Business: 1596–1627.

Jaruga, A. and Szychta, A. (1997) 'The origins and evolution of charts of accounts in Poland', *The European Accounting Review*, 6(3): 509–526.

Klaassen, J. (2001) 'Netherlands – Individual accounts', in Ordelheide, D. (ed.), *Transnational Accounting TRANSACC*. Basingstoke and New York: Palgrave.

Lara, J.M.G and Mora, A. (2004) 'Balance sheet versus earnings conservatism in Europe', *The European Accounting Review*, 13(2): 261–292.

Leuz, C. and Wüstemann, J. (2003) *The Role of Accounting in the German Financial System*, Centre for Financial Studies, Johann Wolfgang Goethe Universität, Frankfurt am Main, No. 2003/16.

Nobes, C.W. (1984) *International Classification of Financial Reporting*. London: Croom Helm.

Nobes, C.W. (1998) 'Towards a general model of the reasons for international differences in financial reporting', *Abacus*, September, 34(2): 162–187.

OECD (2002) *OECD Economic Studies*, Vol. 34, 2002/01, Organisation for Economic Cooperation and Development, Paris.

OECD (2003a) *OECD Economic Surveys: France*, Vol. 2003/11, Organisation for Economic Cooperation and Development, Paris.

OECD (2003b) *OECD Economic Surveys: Germany*, Vol. 2002, Supplement No.4, January 2003, Organisation for Economic Cooperation and Development, Paris.

OECD (2004) *OECD Economic Surveys: Poland*, Vol. 2004/8, June 2004, Organisation for Economic Cooperation and Development, Paris.

Parker, R.H. (1996) 'Harmonising the notes in the UK and France: A case study in *de jure* harmonisation', *European Accounting Review*, 5(2): 317–338.

Parker, R.H. and Nobes, C.W. (1994) *An International View of True and Fair Accounting*. London: Routledge.

Pierce, A. and Weetman, P. (2002) 'Measurement of de facto harmonisation: implications of non-disclosure for research planning and interpretation', *Accounting and Business Research*, 32(4): 259–273.

Rajan, R.G. and Zingales, L. (1995) 'What do we know about capital structure?', *Journal of Finance*, 50(5): 1421–1460.

Rathbone, D. (ed.) (1997) *The LGT Guide to World Equity Markets 1997*. London: Euromoney Publications.

Scheid, J.-C. and Walton, P. (1992) *European Financial Reporting – France*. London: Routledge.

Scheid, J.-C. and Walton, P. (2001) 'France' in Alexander, D. and Archer, S. (eds), *European Accounting Guide*, 4th edn, Aspen Law & Business.

Smith, R. (2003) *Audit Committees: Combined Code Guidance*. A report and proposed guidance by an FRC-appointed group chaired by Sir Robert Smith. Financial Reporting Council www.frc.org.uk/publications. Appendix III surveys other countries.

Standish, P. (2000) *Developments in French Accounting and Auditing 2000*, available at www.experts-comptables.fr/html/countries/gb/index.html

Zeff, S.A., Buijink, W. and Camfferman, K. (1999) '"True and fair" in the Netherlands: *inzicht or getrouw beeld?*', *The European Accounting Review*, 8(3), 523–548.

Newspapers, journals and web-based sources

FT World Accounting Report, published monthly by *Financial Times* Publications.

The Corporate Accountant, Insert in *The Accountant*, UK monthly. London: Lafferty Publications.

Ernst & Young (2004) *Doing Business in Poland*: www.ey.com/global/content.nsf/Poland_E/ Doing_Business_in_Poland_2004

11 The United Kingdom

▶

Learning outcomes

After reading this chapter you should be able to:

- Explain the development of accounting regulation.
- Explain the key institutional characteristics of the UK.
- Discuss the meaning of an 'Anglo-Saxon' system of accounting.
- Explain the structure and processes for oversight and assurance.
- Understand and explain features of the accounting system that illustrate the continuing diversity of UK accounting practices.
- Discuss UK accounting practices using the analytical framework of Gray's accounting values.

11.1 Introduction

Accounting practice in the UK has a strong tradition of professionalism in which statute law and accounting standards set general bounds on requirements but the professional accountant exercises judgement in the application of those requirements. The accounting profession is well established and there is a relatively wide requirement for the audit of company accounts.

Tax law has developed separately from accounting law and there is no requirement that accounting profit must be calculated under fiscal rules to be an acceptable base for taxable profit. Membership of the European Union (EU) from 1972, and the subsequent incorporation of the Fourth and Seventh Directives into company law, brought more specific requirements in the shape of accounting formats not previously known. Group accounting, and in particular consolidated accounting, was well established from 1948 onwards.

Company law concentrates primarily on protection of shareholders and creditors. Other sources of authority indicate a concern with wider stakeholders. From time to time there have been concerns to ensure that the needs of employees are addressed and that the public interest is taken into account. This type of concern depends to some extent on the political views of the government of the day. A major reform of company law, begun in 1998 but taking several years to implement, is bringing narrative reporting under statutory control rather than leaving it to the traditional professional flexibility.

11.2 The country

The UK comprises The United Kingdom of England, Wales, Scotland and Northern Ireland. The Channel Islands and the Isle of Man have their own Treasuries and separate systems of direct taxation. The term 'Great Britain' denotes the main land mass of the

British Isles. Great Britain includes England, Scotland and Wales; it is a geographical description rather than a political unit. The term 'British Isles' is also a geographical description, covering England, Wales, Scotland, all of Ireland and the various islands around the coastline of these countries. Completion of the Channel Tunnel was a significant factor in allowing commercial freight traffic more ready access to continental Europe.

The population is 59.5 million and has a relatively low rate of growth. Population density is greatest in the south-east of England.

The economy has shown growth of 2.7 per cent per annum over the period 1991–2000 (see Exhibit 11.1). Gross domestic product is created 71 per cent by services, 18 per cent by manufacturing industry and 10 per cent by other industry. Agriculture is a relatively small proportion (0.9 per cent) of gross domestic product.

Standards of living are relatively high in terms of life expectancy and a rate of population growth which is lower than the rate of growth of gross domestic product (GDP). The rate of inflation, at 2.4 per cent per annum over the period 1996–2002, reflects a period of activity in the economy where government spending was initially underpinned by the proceeds of privatization.

Visible imports have exceeded exports for several years but in 2001 there remained a small deficit after taking account of the net inflow on invisibles. Exports comprise mainly manufactured and semi-manufactured products. The US remains an important export destination although the EU as a whole takes a larger portion of UK exports. In 2001 the largest single export market in the EU lay in Germany. Imports also came from the EU but a significant amount of trade exists with the US. Trade with Commonwealth countries has fallen significantly since the UK joined the EU.

From the *Financial Times* annual survey, the top 500 world companies at the start of 2004 included 36 UK companies and also three companies registered in both the UK and The Netherlands. The top ten UK listed companies are shown in Exhibit 11.2.

Exhibit 11.1	The UK: country profile

Population	59.5 million
Land mass	242,534 km^2
GDP per head	US$23,920
GDP per head in purchasing power parity	71.0 (USA = 100)
Origins of GDP:	%
Agriculture	0.9
Industry	27.6
Services	71.4
	%
Real GDP average annual growth 1991–2000	2.7
Inflation, average annual rate 1996–2002	2.4

Source: *The Economist Pocket World in Figures*, 2004 Edition, Profile Books Ltd

| Exhibit 11.2 | Top ten UK listed companies |

Name	Market cap. ($000m)	Rank in Europe	Listed US	Sector
BP	174.6	1	yes	Oil
HSBC Holdings	163.6	2	yes	Banks
Vodafone	159.2	3	yes	Wireless Telecommunication
Shell Transport & Trading Company	158.8	4[1]	yes	Oil
GlaxoSmithKline	115.5	6	yes	Pharmaceuticals
Royal Bank of Scotland	88.8	11	yes	Banks
AstraZeneca	76.9	14	yes	Pharmaceuticals
Unilever	65.7	17[1]	yes	Food producer and processor
Barclays	57.0	21	yes	Banks
HBOS	52.3	23	no	Banks

[1] Joint with The Netherlands.

Source: 'Survey FT 500', *Financial Times*, May 2004; www.nyse.com

11.3 Development of accounting regulation

11.3.1 Company law[1]

The first Companies Act was passed in 1844, allowing limited liability companies to form by incorporation as joint stock companies; prior to that time a separate Act of Parliament was required for each company formed. The Companies Act set out basic rules for accounting and auditing, but these were not effective until 1900. The company was seen as a private arrangement involving shareholders and directors, and secrecy in business matters was regarded as a virtue.

From 1907, there was a requirement to produce an audited balance sheet, but no stipulation as to format or content. A major change in public opinion about accounting disclosure resulted from the *Royal Mail Steam Packet* case (1932) (R *v* Lord Kylsant (1932) I KB 442, [1931] 1 All ER Rep 179), where a company produced a false prospectus by drawing on 'secret reserves' to give the appearance of profitability. That change in opinion led to the Companies Act 1948 specifying minimum levels of disclosure in annual accounts; an audited profit and loss account and balance sheet; group accounts; and enhancement of the rights and duties of auditors. The 1948 Act concentrated on disclosure and the protection of shareholders and creditors.

Matters of valuation, formats of financial statements and the method of recording transactions were all left to directors. There persisted a strong philosophy of minimal intervention by government and a defence of the rights of directors and shareholders to take decisions on corporate matters. Some changes extending disclosure were made in 1967, concentrating primarily on the report of the directors and additional notes to the balance sheet, and also including the significant improvement of disclosing turnover (sales). The principles of 1948 remained.

---

[1] Napier (1995); Gordon and Gray (1994), Chapter 2.

The most significant change in approach was taken in 1981 when the Fourth Directive was implemented in UK company law. This brought formats and valuation rules to company law for the first time. Concepts such as prudence, consistency, accruals and going concern were introduced to law, as was the requirement to report only realized profit in the profit and loss account. The 1981 Act was additional to the 1948 and subsequent Acts. All were consolidated in 1985. Implementation of the Seventh Directive was by way of the 1989 Act amending the principal Act of 1985.

The next phase of company law development began in 1998, in the form of an extensive consultation process on Company Law Reform. The Company Law Review Steering Group delivered its Final Report in June 2001.[2] Its aim was to create a modern framework for company law rather than continue to amend a structure created more than 100 years previously. The government issued a White Paper 'Modernising Company Law' containing proposals for company law reform, in July 2002. Subsequently a phased introduction of changes in Company Law began.[3]

11.3.2 Consolidated accounts[4]

Evidence of consolidation by particular companies may be traced to the early years of the twentieth century but it was not until the aftermath of the *Royal Mail Steam Packet* case (1932) that the doubts of accountants were overcome. One aspect of that case had been reporting the results of subsidiaries only on receipt of dividends. Group accounting was made compulsory under the Companies Act 1948, based on definitions of a subsidiary which held until the incorporation of the Seventh Directive in the 1989 Act. The Companies Act 1948 gave no guidance on the method of group accounting; not even consolidation was compulsory. It was left to the professional accountant to determine the method of group accounting, and it would have satisfied the requirements of law to staple together all the accounts of parent and subsidiary. In this context, the influence of leading text book writers was important.

The initial reaction to the Seventh Directive was that UK accounting already satisfied its requirements and the options on definition allowed the approach of the 1948 Act to continue. However, the experiences of the late 1980s, when companies began to avoid consolidation by working round the 1948 definitions, led to adoption of the more widely embracing options in the Seventh Directive which emphasized effective control rather than relying solely on percentage of ownership. The Companies Act 1989 extended the UK definition of a subsidiary and included recommendations on consolidation not previously found in UK law. The problems identified in the US by the aftermath of Enron did not cause the same concerns with the UK regulation of consolidated accounts because the UK already had an accounting standard FRS 5[5] *Reporting the substance of transactions* which required companies to consider the commercial substance of the risks and rewards of investments, rather than focus only on rules based on percentage holdings.

---

[2] DTI (2001).

[3] Department of Trade and Industry website www.dti.gov.uk.

[4] Ma *et al.* (1991).

[5] ASB (1994).

11.3.3 Accounting standards[6]

Prior to 1970 there was no system of written accounting standards in the UK. Professional bodies issued guidance to their members. The Institute of Chartered Accountants in England and Wales (ICAEW) in particular had a detailed Handbook of Recommendations on accounting and auditing matters; these were advisory in nature. Following some well-publicized company failures in the 1960s the major accountancy bodies established the Accounting Standards Committee (ASC), jointly owned by themselves. They each retained the power of veto over any standard and all proposals for new standards had to be approved by the Council of each member body. From 1970 to 1990 Statements of Standard Accounting Practice (SSAPs) were issued by the ASC.

Accounting standards have from time to time tried to meet economic needs of the day. High inflation in the early 1970s stimulated debate and practice in a variety of approaches to the problem. Initial inclinations towards general price levels in current purchasing power accounting then switched to specific price levels in current cost accounting, as advocated by Edwards and Bell (1961).

A major review of the standard-setting process (the Dearing review) recommended that accounting standards should remain, as far as possible, the responsibility of preparers, users and auditors, rather than becoming a matter of regulation by law. An independent standard-setting body was seen to be necessary, with adequate financial support to carry out its work. Dearing also made recommendations about the organization of the standard-setting process.

Most of Dearing's recommendations were adopted in 1990, when the government announced the establishment of the Financial Reporting Council (FRC) to cover, at a high level, a wide range of interests. The chairman is appointed by the Secretary of State for Trade and Industry and the Governor of the Bank of England. The FRC guides the standard-setting body on matters of policy, ensures it is adequately financed, and acts as an influence on good practice. The Accounting Standards Board (ASB) as one arm of the original FRC, is a panel of experts having a full-time chairman and technical director. There are seven other members, all part-time, drawn from the accountancy profession and from business. A two-thirds majority of the Board is required for approval of an accounting standard. A second arm of the original FRC is the Financial Reporting Review Panel (FRRP) which enquires into annual accounts where it appears that the requirements of the Companies Act might have been breached. The ASB is helped by an Urgent Issues Task Force (UITF) in dealing with matters of detail arising out of existing legislation or standards where clarification or a change of practice is required. The ASB adopted all the SSAPs issued by the ASC and remaining in force at 1990. New standards issued for the first time by the ASB are called Financial Reporting Standards (FRSs). Bodies which represent industry sectors may develop Statements of Recommended Practice (SORPs). The ASB does not specifically endorse the SORP, but will give an assurance that the SORP does not appear to conflict with existing standards.

The Company Law Review consultation included consideration of the nature of accounting standard setting in the UK. The outcome was that the government confirmed its satisfaction with the track record of the FRC, extending its responsibilities beyond accounting standards to cover setting and enforcing auditing standards and to oversight of the regulation of the accountancy profession (see section 7.6).

---

[6] Gordon and Gray (1994), Chapter 5; Wilson *et al.* (2001), Chapter 1.

11.4 Institutions

11.4.1 Political and economic system[7]

The UK is a constitutional monarchy, having a parliamentary system of government. There are two Houses of Parliament at Westminster, in London. The House of Commons has over 600 elected members. Called Members of Parliament (MPs), they are elected by the adult population of the UK on a 'first-past-the-post' system. This system of election normally results in one of two political parties taking a clear majority as the basis of government for a term of office lasting up to five years. The House of Lords until 1999 comprised a mixture of hereditary peers of the realm and also life peers appointed in recognition of public service. In 1999 legislation was passed to prevent hereditary peers from sitting or voting and their numbers are in the process of being reduced, leaving an appointed second chamber. There is a continuing debate as to whether the House of Lords should remain an appointed second chamber or should change to elected membership. Legislation originates in the House of Commons and after approval there is passed to the House of Lords. In the House of Lords there may be detailed amendments to the proposed legislation, but only rarely is it defeated completely. The House of Commons has the power to restore legislation opposed by the House of Lords: the House of Lords may consequently modify or delay legislation, but cannot prevent its passage.

The House of Commons is led by the Prime Minister who is usually also the leader of the parliamentary party holding the parliamentary majority. The monarch is head of state, but must act on the advice of the government of the day.

The dominant position of the House of Commons and the lack of conflict between the leader of the government and the majority party in Parliament means that business legislation desired by the government is likely to become law. From 1979 to 1997 the UK had a Conservative government. A marked change of electoral mood led to the election of a Labour government in 1997.

The economic system is generally based on a free market approach. Government regulation is applied to particular aspects of economic activity such as the control of competition, or the prevention of price-fixing arrangements. In 1996 the Bank of England was given independent power to determine interest rates, taking this power from previous control by the government. The purpose of this change was to allow interest rates to move more closely with market forces in the economy.

The period of Conservative government from 1979 saw a policy of privatization of companies which had been in government control, nationalization having dated from the late 1940s. Privatization was seen as a political ideal but also placed large capital funds at the disposal of the government of the day and reduced the borrowing requirements of the public sector. The privatization policy was largely completed before the Labour government came to power, and despite earlier indications that they would reverse this policy, on achieving power the Labour government showed no apparent desire to carry out such reversal. However, regulation of the privatized companies is extensive, particularly for the utilities, covering pricing of products, and provides another means of government control.

Rates of exchange between the pound sterling and other currencies are determined by market forces. The Bank of England has regard to the rate of exchange when setting interest rates. Although the UK is a member of the EU, there has been reluctance to join the European Monetary System (EMS) and take up the Euro as a common currency.

---

[7] Gordon and Gray (1994), Chapter 1.

11.4.2 Legal system[8]

Statute law is established by Parliament and sits alongside common law which has been established by tradition through the courts of law. There is a national system of law for the UK as a whole but there is also a separate legal system in Scotland, derived from the historical position of Scotland as an independent country prior to the Act of Union in 1707. Business law is usually applicable on a UK-wide basis. There are some separate laws established by the UK Parliament to be applied in Northern Ireland and Wales, recognizing their separate historical origins.

In the seventeenth and eighteenth centuries, trading and commercial companies could be formed only by royal charter or by private Act of Parliament. Company law, allowing relatively straightforward incorporation of business companies, came into existence in the middle of the nineteenth century. The law at that stage was not excessively intrusive, taking the view that the regulation of a company was essentially a matter for the shareholders and the directors. A series of business scandals in the early years of the twentieth century led to the view that more intervention was required through business legislation. This led, in the Companies Act 1948, to much more detailed prescription on disclosure of information and general conduct of the business. That legislation survived, with some modification in 1967, until the UK joined the EU and was required to adopt the Fourth and Seventh Directives. Initially, legislation in 1980 and 1981 modified the earlier law but major consolidation of company law resulted in the comprehensive Companies Act 1985. Further legislation in 1989 modified the Companies Act 1985 in respect of the Eighth Directive and made some amendments to the definition of a subsidiary company.

Statute law also covers matters such as insolvency, financial services, and insider trading on the stock market. There is a strong tradition of judge-made law, passed down through decisions in courts of law which are taken as binding precedent for future cases of a similar type.

Although parliamentary process is required for primary legislation, such as the approval of the Companies Act 1985, some amendments to legislation may thereafter be implemented without debate in Parliament. Thus the Companies Act is amended from time to time by Statutory Instrument. This method is used to change disclosure exemption limits, or to delete minor unwanted items of disclosure, or to add new items of detail within an overall existing heading.

The UK legal system may be classified as from the common-law family, and of British type. Within the UK, Scots law is based on Roman law. Laws affecting business are set by the UK Parliament but may have an additional section relating to Scots law.

Unincorporated businesses operate as sole traders or partnerships. Both carry the disadvantage that the owner has unlimited liability for the obligations of the business. The need to grow and seek a larger capital base may eventually force the expanding business to seek incorporation as a limited liability company. There are two types of limited liability company: the public limited company (plc) and the private limited company (Ltd). Exhibit 11.3 sets out the key differences.

11.4.3 Corporate governance[9]

The day-to-day management of companies is in the hands of the Board of Directors. The single-tier board comprises both executive and non-executive directors. It is desirable in

---

[8] Gordon and Gray (1994), Chapter 2.

[9] Charkham (1994), Chapter 6; Davies (1999).

| Exhibit 11.3 | Differences between private and public companies |

Public limited company (plc)	Private company (Ltd)
Minimum two directors	Minimum one director
Minimum share capital £50,000	No minimum share capital
Shares and debentures may be offered to the public by advertisement	Prohibition on offer to the public
Restrictions on making loans to directors	Fewer restrictions on dealing with directors
General prohibition on assisting others to purchase the company's own shares	Giving assistance to purchase own shares is allowed, subject to safeguards for creditors and minority shareholders
Company may purchase its own shares provided fixed capital is not reduced	Own shares may be purchased out of fixed capital

public companies for the chairman and the chief executive to be separate persons. The Board is led by a chairman who is usually a non-executive director. The Board of Directors is expected to act as a single group of persons, all taking collective responsibility for the decisions of the board. In practice, everyday activity is delegated by the board to a senior executive director who leads the other executives in running the company.

Directors are elected, and may be removed, by the shareholders in annual general meetings. Directors are required to act as agents of the shareholders, as a body, and in that context have duties defined by law. The directors must act in good faith in the best interests of the company.

11.4.3.1 Cadbury, Greenbury and Hampel

There have been several reports into corporate governance in the UK. The first, in 1992, known as the 'Cadbury Report',was chaired by Sir Adrian Cadbury.[10] That report set a Code of Best Practice to be followed by company directors. Its recommendations for disclosure of directors' emoluments were taken forward by Sir Richard Greenbury, resulting in the Greenbury Report (1995).[11] The extensive disclosures on directors' remuneration to be found in the annual reports of UK companies reflect the recommendations of Greenbury. The rules for directors' remuneration are now contained in regulation through a statutory instrument.[12] Subsequently, a review chaired by Sir Ronald Hampel (the 'Hampel Report') published a Report in 1998[13] confirming much of the work of Cadbury and Greenbury and setting a Combined Code containing Principles of Good Governance and a Code of Practice. Hampel took the view that entrepreneurship should not be stifled by excessive regulation. Consequently principles are offered rather than detailed rules. The Principles had four sections:

● Guidance for Directors
● Setting and Disclosing Directors' Remuneration
● Relations with Shareholders
● Accountability and Audit.

---

[10] Available at www.ecgi.org/codes/country_pages/codes_uk.htm.
[11] Ibid.
[12] The Directors' Remuneration Report Regulations 2002, www.hmso.gpv.uk/si/si2002/20021986.htm.
[13] Available at www.ecgi.org/codes/country-pages/codes_uk.htm.

Following publication of the Combined Code in 1998, The Institute of Chartered Accountants in England and Wales agreed with the Stock Exchange that it would provide guidance to assist listed companies in implementing the requirements of the Code in relation to internal control. The Internal Control Working Party, chaired by Turnbull, produced a consultation draft in April 1999 and its final report in September 1999.[14] The guidance is now appended to the Combined Code (2003) as *Related Guidance and Good Practice Suggestions*. In particular it explains how the board of directors should make a narrative statement in the annual report explaining how it has applied the Code.

A survey by *Company Reporting* in 2002[15] described the Turnbull recommendations as 'an opportunity lost'. Turnbull encouraged companies to discuss risk management processes and systems of internal control but stopped short of requiring companies to disclose or discuss what the actual results were. In the opinion of the survey, this had led to mundane statements of procedures. It found that only 14 per cent of the companies surveyed had taken the initiative and gone beyond Turnbull to publish substantive risk disclosures.

11.4.3.2 Developments from 2002

The corporate failure of Enron and other companies in the US in early 2002 prompted the UK government to ask: 'Could it happen here?' The answer was, 'Yes it could, although perhaps less likely'.[16] The Chancellor of the Exchequer and the Department of Trade and Industry put in place specific initiatives on accounting and auditing in addition to continuing work on implementing the recommendations of the Company Law Review (2001). These initiatives were:

- the Co-ordinating Group on Audit and Accounting Issues (CGAA), set up February 2002, interim report July 2002, final report January 2003;
- the Higgs investigation of the effectiveness of non-executive directors, set up February 2002, issued consultation paper June 2002, final report January 2003;
- the CGAA, which published an interim report in July 2002, commissioned a separate group, chaired by Sir Robert Smith, to develop Code guidance for audit committees, set up September 2002, final report January 2003;
- Review of the Regulatory Regime of the Accountancy Profession, announced by Secretary of State for Trade and Industry, July 2002, in response to CGAA interim report, consultation document issued October 2002, final report January 2003;
- Government White Paper 'Modernising Company Law' containing proposals for company law reform, issued July 2002.

It seems clear that a great deal of investigation was taking place during 2002, some of it overlapping, with interaction of the various groups involved to allow simultaneous publication of findings in January 2003.

The Combined Code was updated in 2003 when it came under the umbrella of the Financial Reporting Council (FRC).[17] Compliance with the Code is a requirement of the Listing Agreement of the UK Listing Authority.[18] Summaries of the recommendations of Turnbull, Higgs and Smith are appended to the Combined Code as *Related Guidance and Good Practice Suggestions*.

---

[14] Turnbull (1999).

[15] *Company Reporting*, July 2002, pp. 5–8.

[16] Smith (2003), p. 21.

[17] FRC (2003).

[18] Listing Rules, Rule 12.43A, www.fsa.gov.uk/ukla.

As a result of the work of these Corporate Governance initiatives, the annual report of a major UK company will now contain a report from the Remuneration Committee, a statement on Corporate Governance, a statement on internal controls and a statement on the going concern status of the company, as well as a statement of the directors' responsibilities.[19] Exhibit 11.4 shows Kingfisher's corporate governance report.

Exhibit 11.4 **Corporate governance report, Kingfisher**

CORPORATE GOVERNANCE REPORT
For the financial year ended 31 January 2004

Code statement
Kingfisher recognises the importance of, and is committed to, high standards of corporate governance. During the year ended 31 January 2004, it complied with the requirements of the Combined Code as it then applied, including the reduction of the notice period for directors' service contracts to 12 months for all directors from August 2003.

The principles of good governance adopted by Kingfisher have been applied in the following way:

Board of directors
Kingfisher's Board currently comprises the Chairman, the Deputy Chairman, five other independent non-executive directors, the Chief Executive and three other executive directors.

Their biographies and details of Committee memberships, which can be found on pages 2 and 3, illustrate the directors' range of experience, which is intended to ensure an effective Board to lead and control the Group. Non-executive directors are appointed for an initial term of three years. The Company has an identified Senior Independent Director, namely John Nelson, the Deputy Chairman. Each director receives appropriate training.

The Board has adopted a schedule of matters reserved for its decision and is collectively responsible for the strategic direction of the Group. All directors are provided with, and have full and timely access to, information that enables them to make informed decisions on corporate and business issues discussed.

The Board has completed a further independent review of its performance by the Institute of Chartered Secretaries and Administrators. These reviews examine the operation of the Board in practice including its corporate governance and the operation and content of its meetings.

During the year to 31 January 2004, the Board met 11 times to deal with regular business and a further 14 times principally to approve periodic trading statements or in connection with the demerger. The attendance record of individual directors at Board and Committee meetings is detailed below.

| | Board meetings | | Committee meetings | | | Social | |
	Monthly	Ad hoc	Audit	Remuneration	Nomination	responsibility	Finance
Number of meetings in year	11	14	5	10	3	2	24
Francis Mackay	11	10	5	10	3	–	6
Gerry Murphy	11	14	–	–	3	2	21
John Nelson[1]	10	5	2	10	2	–	–
Phil Bentley	11	2	5	–	–	–	–
Ian Cheshire	11	5	–	–	–	1	11
Michael Hepher	11	2	5	9	–	–	–
Hartmut Krämer	11	2	–	–	–	–	–
Jean–Noël Labroue[2]	6	2	–	–	–	1	–
Margaret Salmon	10	2	–	10	2	2	–
Bernard Thiolon[3]	4	1	2	–	–	–	–
Helen Weir[4]	11	13	–	–	–	–	20
Bill Whiting	11	2	–	–	–	2	–

[1] Appointed to Audit Committee November 2003
[2] Resigned 4 July 2003
[3] Resigned 4 June 2003
[4] Resigned 31 January 2004

[19] *Company Reporting*, February 2000, pp. 3–8.

Exhibit 11.4 *(Continued)*

The Board has a schedule of matters reserved for itself, which has been reviewed and updated during the year. In addition the Board has established the following six standing committees with defined terms of reference. The matters reserved and the committees' terms of reference are published on the Company's website at www.kingfisher.com.

- Audit Committee – comprises Phil Bentley (Chairman), plus two other independent non-executive directors and the Chairman of the Board. This Committee provides an independent oversight of the effectiveness of the Group's internal control systems and financial reporting processes. It receives and considers reports from both the internal and external auditors and approves the annual report and financial statements and the half year results announcement. The Committee and the Board reviewed membership against the Combined Code as it will apply for the financial year ending 29 January 2005 (the "new Combined Code") and concluded it was essential for proper control and in the interests of the shareholders for the Chairman (non-executive) of the Board to be a member of the Committee. Each major operating business has its own audit committee, meetings of which are attended by both Kingfisher's Director of Risk and Audit and the external auditors.

- Nomination Committee – comprises Sir Francis Mackay (Chairman), plus two independent non-executive directors and the Chief Executive. The Committee considers and recommends appointments of new directors as and when necessary.

- Remuneration Committee – comprises John Nelson (Chairman) plus two other independent non-executive directors and the Chairman of the Board. The Committee advises the Board on the Company's executive remuneration policy and its costs, and is responsible for its application. The Board and the Committee considered the question of the Company Chairman's membership of the Committee and concluded that it is in the shareholders' best interests and that, as a Non-Executive Chairman and with three independent Non-Executive directors as members, it remained appropriate for him to be a member. The Chairman will not be present when his own remuneration is discussed. Details of the Group's policy and procedures for directors' and certain other senior executives' remuneration can be found in the Remuneration Report.

- Social Responsibility Committee – comprises Margaret Salmon (Chairman) plus the Chief Executive, two other executive directors and representatives of the operating companies. This Committee is responsible for discussing and developing a general policy relating to environmental, community and equal opportunities matters. The Board director with overall responsibility for environmental matters is the Chief Executive.

- The Finance Committee – comprises the Chairman of the Board, the Chief Executive, the Group Finance Director and any one other director. The Committee is responsible for the treasury operations of the Group, the approval and authorisation of financing documents and signature authorities on bank accounts within its terms of reference and the authority limits laid down by the Board. It reviews borrowing arrangements and other financial transactions and makes appropriate recommendations. It also allots new shares in the Company to Group employees following the exercise of share options.

- The Share Option Committee – comprises any two directors or any one director and the Company Secretary. Its role is to consider the Group's share funding policy in respect of share incentive awards and to decide upon the level of contributions to the ESOP and QUEST in respect of the dilution cost when new shares are issued. This Committee also considers the making of loans to the ESOP in respect of grants that are hedged with existing shares. It has no authority in respect of the making of awards which is a matter reserved to the Remuneration Committee.

Company Secretary

All directors have access to, and the services of, the Company Secretary and may take independent professional advice at the Group's expense.

The Company Secretary or the Company Secretary of B&Q plc acts as secretary to all the above Committees.

The Company Secretary is also responsible for facilitating the induction and professional development of Board members as well as ensuring good information flows within the Board, its Committees and between the non-executive directors and senior management.

Directors' remuneration

The Remuneration Committee, on behalf of the Board, aims to ensure that senior executives (including executive directors of the Company) are rewarded for their contribution to the Group and are motivated to enhance returns to shareholders. Full details of individual directors' remuneration are shown on pages 11 to 19.

Relations with shareholders

Kingfisher is committed to an active dialogue with its shareholders through a planned programme of investor relations. This activity is a key component of its corporate communications programme and is headed by the Director of Communications (Ian Harding).

The programme includes formal presentations of full year and interim results, quarterly trading statements on three other occasions during the year and regular meetings between institutional investors and senior management. Shareholders also receive Annual and Interim Reports and, on their dedicated section of the Company website (www.kingfisher.com/shareholders), can access copies of these, all trading updates, press announcements and presentations to shareholders made by the Company.

Following consultation with a number of institutional shareholders the Board believes there are sufficient opportunities for the necessary dialogue between shareholders and the Board. These include regular meetings between investors and management, the availability of all the non-executive directors for meetings if so requested by the shareholders, a standing invitation for the non-executive directors to attend any of the meetings between management and institutional investors and the availability to shareholders of John Nelson, as the Senior Independent Director, if there are concerns that cannot be resolved through normal channels of communication.

Both institutional and private shareholders are welcome at the Annual General Meeting, which will include a short presentation on the business and its latest trading position. The Annual General Meeting also provides an opportunity for shareholders to discuss with executive and non-executive directors any issues they have concerning the Company and its activities.

Auditor independence

Kingfisher has clear rules and authorisation processes for the instruction of the auditors for non-audit work. The overall level in both years was primarily driven by the now completed major restructuring of the Group. In 2003/4 the majority was in relation to the short and long form reports and listing particulars prepared in relation to the demerger of Kesa Electricals. In 2002/3 it was primarily in relation to the rights issue prospectus and offer documentation for Castorama.

Accountability, risk management and internal control

Internal control

The Board considers risk assessment and control to be fundamental to achieving its corporate objectives within an acceptable risk/reward profile. The process for identifying and evaluating the significant risks faced by the Group has been enhanced during the year under review.

The risk assessment process also identifies mitigating actions.

This system of internal control is:
- the Board's overall responsibility;
- regularly and, at least annually, reviewed for its effectiveness by both the Board and the Audit Committee; and
- in compliance with the Turnbull guidance.

However, such a system is designed to manage rather than eliminate the risk of failure to achieve business objectives and can provide only reasonable and not absolute assurance against material misstatement or loss.

The key elements of this process are:

The Board, which:
- has approved a set of policies, procedures and frameworks for effective internal control. These include the provision of quality internal and external reporting and compliance with applicable laws and regulations. They are periodically reviewed and updated;
- regularly updates the Group's strategy and those of its operating companies;
- reviews and assesses the Group's key risks at least annually;

▶

Exhibit 11.4 *(Continued)*

- reviews performance through a comprehensive system of reporting, based on an annual budget with monthly business reviews against actual results, analysis of variances, key performance indicators and regular forecasting;
- has well-defined policies governing appraisal and approval of capital expenditure and treasury operations;
- seeks assurance that effective control is being maintained through regular reports from the Audit Committee and various independent monitoring functions.

The Audit Committee, which:
- oversees the effectiveness of the Group's internal control systems and financial reporting processes;
- supervises the quality, independence and effectiveness of both the internal and external auditors;
- reviews the effectiveness of the Group's risk identification and evaluation procedures and management responses to significant risks;
- reviews the reports made to it by the internal audit committees of each of the operating companies.

The business head of each operating/business area, who:
- maintains systems that continually identify and evaluate significant risks resulting from their strategies and that apply to their areas of the business;
- reviews and monitors the effectiveness of internal control systems through an operating company audit committee and reports from internal and external audit functions;
- has responsibility for their local audit committee;
- self-certifies that internal control processes are in place and that they comply with Group policies. He/she also reports on any control weaknesses or breakdowns that could be material to the Group.

The Internal Audit and Risk Management function, which:
- works with the operating companies to develop, improve and embed risk management tools and processes into their business operations;
- ensures that business risks are identified, managed and regularly reviewed at all levels of the Group and that directors are periodically appraised of the key risks in accordance with the Turnbull guidance;
- provides the Board with independent and objective assurance on the control environment across the Group;
- ensures that the operating companies have appropriate organisation and processes to carry out regular and effective reviews of their internal controls;
- monitors adherence to the Group's key policies and principles;
- provides the Audit Committee with necessary assurances on the control environment.

The directors can, therefore, confirm that they have reviewed the effectiveness of this system of internal control, and that it accords with the guidance of the Turnbull committee on internal control.

By Order of the Board
Helen Jones
Company Secretary
16 March 2004

Source: Kingfisher annual report (2004), pp. 8–10. www.kingfisher.com

11.4.4 Taxation system

Companies pay corporation tax while owners of unincorporated businesses pay income tax. The two types of tax operate under different rules and may have different rates of tax applied. However, for the determination of taxable business profits the rules are similar. The starting point is the reported accounting profit, modified by specific aspects of tax law.

11.4.4.1 Taxable income

A distinction is drawn between income arising from revenue transactions and that arising from capital receipts. Income is subdivided according to its source and different rules are applied to each source. The aggregate amount is subject to corporation tax. For companies the main sources are:

- trading profit
- non-trading income
- chargeable gains.

In March 2004 the Chancellor of the Exchequer confirmed in his Budget[20] that those companies that chose to use IFRS in their individual accounts would be able to use those accounts as the starting point for their tax computations. They would not be required to prepare separate UK GAAP accounts for tax purposes. Under tax law, trading profit is based on reported accounting profit with adjustments specified in tax law. The most significant adjustment is that tax law does not allow accounting depreciation as an expense but substitutes instead a system of capital allowances at prescribed rates. Trading stock may not be valued on a last-in-first-out (LIFO) basis. Profits and losses on the disposal of fixed assets are not included in taxable profits. Provisions are not allowed unless they can be shown to be specific to a defined item of expected loss. Some expenses, such as business entertaining, are not allowed for tax purposes.

Non-trading income includes investment income, rental income, interest and royalties. These are generally taxed on the basis of cash received rather than on an accruals basis.

Chargeable gains are the profits calculated on disposal of fixed assets. Indexation allowances, calculated to eliminate the inflationary element of the gain, were available until 1998.

Accounting profit for tax purposes is reported separately from accounting profit for accounting purposes; separate laws govern each measure of profit.[21]

There is therefore formal independence of the two approaches to measurement of profit, and this permits financial reporting to be flexible without fiscal impact. However, despite formal independence there have developed effective interdependencies, primarily because the judgment of the courts in relation to taxable profit is that it should be based on the profits reported under generally accepted accounting principles. Where flexibility exists under accounting practice, there have therefore been instances of choosing the approach likely to lead to the most favourable taxation outcome, and on occasions this flexibility has been challenged in the courts by the tax authorities. The results of such court decisions have had some influence on subsequent accounting practice in regard to this particular issue.

11.4.4.2 Tax treatment of dividends

Dividends are paid to UK shareholders net of a withholding tax. The individual shareholder may set the amount of the withholding tax against the personal tax bill but large institutional shareholders such as pension funds, which are exempt from tax, may not reclaim the amount withheld. This selective imputation system reflects a change in political power in 1997, ending almost 25 years of a widely applied imputation system. Companies which receive dividend income from other companies may not claim any deduction for the tax withheld and they must pay corporation tax on the dividend income. Relief is available within groups of companies.

---

[20] Budget note REV BN25.

[21] Lamb (1996); McMahon and Weetman (1997).

11.4.5 Corporate financing system[22]

11.4.5.1 Equity investors

A survey of share ownership in the UK (2002) showed that individuals hold only 14 per cent by value of the equity of listed companies (see Exhibit 11.5). More than 60 per cent is held by insurance companies, pension funds and a range of financial institutions including unit trusts. This relative strength of investment by financial institutions is an unusual characteristic by comparison with other countries. Individuals invest indirectly through saving for pensions, taking insurance and buying investment products provided by financial institutions. Institutional investors tend not to become involved in the management of the company, but where strong concerns arise the institutional investors will use their powers in general meeting. They are increasingly expected to be active in their scrutiny of their investments, as part of good corporate governance.

11.4.5.2 London Stock Exchange[23]

The London Stock Exchange dates from the seventeenth century. For a period of time there were regional trading floors but these closed in the mid-1960s and business focused on London. A major change in the nature of trading operations in the 1980s meant that a dealing floor was no longer maintained, and trading now takes place by use of telephones and computer screens. The main market is the London Stock Exchange, on which companies have a full listing. For new, smaller companies there is the Alternative Investment Market (AIM). It is regulated by the London Stock Exchange but has rules which are less onerous. The AIM may provide a step towards full membership.

Movement on share prices is measured by a number of indices, the most frequently mentioned being the FTSE-100 index. This index is operated jointly by the *Financial Times* and the Stock Exchange, based on the 100 largest companies measured by market capitalization.

From May 2000 the UK Listing Authority (UKLA) was transferred from the London Stock Exchange to the Financial Services Authority (FSA).[24] The FSA takes charge of admissions to listing but the Stock Exchange continues to regulate admission to trading. The FSA is a body established under statute law to regulate a wide range of financial services, including the stock market.

The relative importance of the UK stock exchange in Europe can be seen in Exhibit 4.3, although it remains less significant than US and Japanese markets in terms of the market capitalization of listed companies. Exhibit 11.5 shows that individual shareholders are a relatively small group among those investing in equity shares. The 'rest of the world' proportion has doubled over ten years. This is explained in part by international mergers where the new company is listed in the UK. Also, some companies have moved their domicile to the UK. As a technical change to the figures during this period, shareholdings held in UK offshore islands were reclassified as 'rest of the world'. Nevertheless the increase is an indication of the importance of global markets to the major UK companies. Over the same ten-year period the proportion of shares held by pension funds fell from 27.8 per cent to 15.6 per cent, matched by a trend towards investing in bonds.

---

[22] Gordon and Gray (1994), Chapter 3.

[23] London Stock Exchange, *Fact File*, 1997.

[24] www.fsa.gov.uk.

| Exhibit 11.5 | Beneficial ownership of UK shares, 2002 |

Ownership	Percentage of total equity owned
Rest of the world	32.1
Insurance companies	19.9
Pension funds	15.6
Individuals	14.3
Unit trusts	1.6
Investment trusts	1.8
Other financial institutions	10.5
Charities, churches, etc.	1.1
Private non-financial companies	0.8
Public sector	0.1
Banks	2.1
	100.0

Source: *Share Ownership*: *a report on ownership of shares as at 31 December 2002*, Office for National Statistics, www.statistics.gov.uk

11.4.5.3 Bank lending

London is one of the major banking centres of the world. The Bank of England is the central bank, exercising regulatory control over lending by commercial and merchant banks. Commercial banks are reluctant to become involved in ownership of companies and therefore concentrate on very short-term lending to companies. The medium-term and longer-term lending originates with merchant banks or venture capitalists.

Commercial banks also seek to offer services beyond pure lending, particularly for small and medium-sized enterprises (SMEs). They do not play a significant part in corporate governance but may find themselves linked to a customer on a more long-term basis where short-term loans are repeatedly rolled over.

Merchant banks are interested in the larger companies or those medium-sized companies which intend to grow. The merchant banks offer all types of corporate finance services including dealing in foreign exchange markets; swaps; financial futures; forward rate agreements; interest rate and currency options; money market loans and deposits. Strengths of individual banks depend on their chosen specialisms but most will offer advice on takeovers and mergers; corporate reorganization and reconstruction; management buyouts; stock exchange flotations; and bond issues on foreign currency markets.

11.4.5.4 Mergers and acquisitions[25]

Activity in takeovers and mergers varies with economic cycles. Accounting practice distinguishes a true merger from an acquisition, but in practice nearly all business combinations in the UK involve one party acquiring another. Takeover activity is regulated by the Takeover Panel, a self-regulating mechanism which has existed since 1968. It sets a Code of

---

[25] Sudarsanam (2003).

457

practice for takeovers and can impose penalties ranging from a private reprimand to removal of the shares from stock exchange listing. The underlying themes of the Code are openness, timeliness and even-handedness.

Government policy to discourage creation of monopolies is administered by the Competition Commission. The Commission will investigate a proposed acquisition and is required to state whether the proposal is, or is not, against the public interest.

Accounting information often plays an important part in takeovers, especially where these are contested. The Stock Exchange sets out rules for disclosure in circulars issued in connection with a takeover proposal. The Takeover Code dictates who shall receive such information; often companies will voluntarily exceed the minimum requirement and more may be learned about the parties involved than would ordinarily appear in the annual report.

11.4.6 The accounting profession[26]

The UK has a long history of professional accountancy bodies. Over time specialist groupings have emerged. The major professional bodies are:

● The Institute of Chartered Accountants in England and Wales (ICAEW),
● The Institute of Chartered Accountants of Scotland (ICAS),
● The Institute of Chartered Accountants in Ireland (ICAI),
● The Association of Chartered Certified Accountants (ACCA),
● The Chartered Institute of Management Accountants (CIMA),
● The Chartered Institute of Public Finance and Accountancy (CIPFA).

All set examinations as a precondition of membership. Those persons wishing to become company auditors must obtain the status of Registered Auditor which normally means membership of the ICAEW, ICAS, ICAI or ACCA, together with relevant practical experience.

Before 1990 these professional bodies worked together, through the Accounting Standards Committee (ASC), in setting accounting standards. The process was found to be too slow and was accused of being controlled too closely by the profession. In 1990 the ASB was established as an independent authority and the professional bodies lost their power of veto over the issue of a standard. They continue to make representations to the ASB and to contribute indirectly through the work of members.

11.5 External influences

Historically, UK accounting has developed as an approach which has been exported to other parts of the world, particularly the countries which were once colonies but today form part of the Commonwealth.[27] Those countries, on gaining independence, looked to wider global practices and adapted their UK-based accounting systems to include practices found in major trading-partner countries. It has been suggested that accounting in the US is an adaptation, rather than wholesale adoption, of the UK accounting system, carried to that country by pioneering accountants emigrating to the USA.[28]

---

[26] Gordon and Gray (1994), Chapter 5.

[27] Parker (1995).

[28] Parker (1989).

11.5.1 'Anglo-Saxon' influence

The description 'Anglo-Saxon' or 'Anglo-American' is frequently encountered in research studies and professional commentaries. The countries that are linked by this description are primarily the UK, Ireland, the US, Canada, Australia, and New Zealand. Alexander and Archer (2000) suggested, and then challenged, four hypotheses that would support the validity of 'Anglo-Saxon accounting' based on claims for shared characteristics (see Exhibit 11.6). Based on their challenge, they questioned the existence of a single identifiable 'Anglo-Saxon' system.

Exhibit 11.6   Debating the 'Anglo-Saxon' influence

Arguments for and against the existence of an 'Anglo-Saxon' system of accounting

1   True and fair view

For: There is a close relationship between 'true and fair view' (TFV) and 'fair presentation' (FP)

Against: 'True and fair view' in the UK is an overriding requirement. Complying with the law does not guarantee a true and fair view. Professional judgement is needed. Courts of law will regard accounting standards as important evidence of true and fair. However, the views of experts about the opinion of the profession are very important. Professional judgement may choose an answer that does not comply with law or standards.

'Fair presentation' in the US is expressed as 'fair presentation in accordance with US GAAP'. There is a definition of US GAAP based on written standards and guidance (see Chapter 8). So US accounting does not try to go beyond the law and the standards.

2   Conceptual frameworks

For: There is a common practice of developing 'conceptual frameworks' (CF) for financial accounting and reporting.

Against: Alexander and Archer say that conceptual frameworks are created to give an appearance of self-regulation. They have little practical relevance but they create a set of 'beliefs' that make the standard-setters appear independent of the law-makers.

3   Common law system

For: They all share a common law legal system, which distinguishes them from countries having a code law system.

Against: There can be flexibility or rigidity in either kind of legal system. It does not help to define 'Anglo-Saxon' accounting. The US has a very detailed set of financial accounting standards that must be applied, so the legal system is largely irrelevant as a description of accounting practice. The Netherlands is said to have flexible accounting with professional judgement, similar to UK and US accounting, but it has a legal system based on code law. Germany has a code law system but the accounting rules are written with flexibility for interpretation by professional experts.

4   Setting accounting standards

For: Private sector regulation of accounting takes precedence over public sector regulation.

Against: In the US, Congress sets the laws for the SEC. The SEC accepts accounting standards written by FASB. SEC can overrule FASB. Congress can overrule SEC and FASB. So the public sector aspect is very strong.

Source: Based on Alexander and Archer (2000).

Nobes (2003), in support of the idea of an 'Anglo-Saxon' accounting system, suggested a different hypothesis:

> Anglo-Saxon accounting (compared to other forms of accounting) is oriented towards decision-making by investors; it plays down the measurement of taxable income and distributable income; it is less worried about prudence; it is more willing to go beyond legal form.

Alexander and Archer (2003) replied by saying that they felt Nobes underestimated the power and use of the 'true and fair override' and that the 'Rules v principles' debate (see section 8.3.3) was still not resolved.

11.5.2 Influence of EU membership

The most significant inward influence on UK accounting has been membership of the EU.[29] This has required significant changes in company law to adopt the various directives. In particular, the concept of having formats and valuation rules contained in company law was a major change resulting from the Fourth Directive. However, the UK also had an influence on accounting in the EU. At the date of UK membership, the Fourth Directive was still in draft form and did not give any scope for the 'true and fair' approach which was the UK tradition. The 'true and fair' amendment to the Fourth Directive was a very significant concession to UK requests.

Multinational companies are an agent for the import and export of international practices. Where these companies have found themselves producing different sets of financial statements for different jurisdictions, they have tended to choose options which were common to more than one country. Such companies have from time to time referred to their own attempts to find common approaches to specific issues, or frustration at the lack of common approaches.

11.6 Oversight and assurance

11.6.1 Review of the regulatory regime of the accountancy profession[30]

In October 2002 the Secretary of State for Trade and Industry announced a review of the regulatory regime of the accountancy profession, in commenting on the interim report of the Co-ordinating Group on Accounting and Auditing Issues (CGAA)[31] which was set up in response to the corporate failures of WorldCom and Enron in the US. The recommendations of the review, published in 2003, were that:

1 The Financial Reporting Council should take on the functions of the Accountancy Foundation (established in 2000 to oversee the regulation of the profession) to create a unified and authoritative structure with three clear areas of responsibility:

- setting accounting standards;
- enforcement or monitoring of accounting standards;
- oversight of the major professional bodies.

---

[29] Nobes and Parker (1984); Nobes (1993).
[30] Review (2003).
[31] Co-ordinating Group (2003).

2 The independent regulation and review of audit should be strengthened significantly. Responsibility for setting independence standards for auditors and for monitoring the audit of listed companies and other significant entities should be transferred from the accountancy professional bodies to the independent regulator.

The detailed recommendations were that the Financial Reporting Council should have within its 'family' of organizations the two activities it encompassed previously:

- The Accounting Standards Board
- The Financial Reporting Review Panel,

augmented by three new activities (each of which is explained in subsequent sections):

- The Auditing Practices Board
- A Professional Oversight Board
- An Investigation and Discipline Board.

The Secretary of State for Trade and Industry, who has overall responsibility for company law in Great Britain, would delegate specific authority to the FRC and its subsidiaries.

This report spelled the termination of the Accountancy Foundation,[32] which had been established as a result of a previous government initiative begun in 1997 to provide independent and non-statutory oversight of the regulation of the accountancy profession. The report noted concerns about the complexity of the structure of the Accountancy Foundation.

The Companies (Audit, Investigations and Community Enterprise) Act, passed through Parliament in 2004, amended the Companies Acts of 1985 and 1989 as follows:[33]

- Increase the information disclosed by companies about non-audit services received from the external auditor.
- Impose an obligation on employees to disclose information to the auditors and require directors to state that there is no relevant information withheld from the auditors.
- Give new rights to the Financial Reporting Review Panel to monitor accounts or reports required under the Stock Exchange Listing Rules.
- Give the DTI more powers to carry out company investigations.
- Introduce a new kind of company, the 'community interest company' where the profit is used for community benefit and not for private gain. This is intended to offer a vehicle for social enterprise.

11.6.2 The Financial Reporting Council (from 2004)[34]

The Financial Reporting Council is a unified, independent regulator, with three key roles:

- setting accounting and auditing standards;
- pro-actively enforcing and monitoring them;
- overseeing the self-regulatory professional bodies.

The Council itself draws members from across the financial, business and professional communities at the highest levels. Its original remit of setting and enforcing accounting standards has been enlarged so that it takes a more active role in relation to corporate

---

[32] See Review (2003) for detailed description of the Accountancy Foundation.

[33] *Accountancy*, February 2004, p. 114.

[34] www.frc.org.uk/about/.

governance. It seeks a proactive role in relation to compliance with company law and accounting standards and it takes on new responsibilities in relation to audit, auditing standards and the oversight of the self-regulatory professional bodies. Changes in company law give the subsidiary bodies of the FRC new powers to exercise statutory functions in relation to accounting and auditing on behalf of the Secretary of State for Trade and Industry. The FRC has five subsidiary boards, each described in the following sections. The separate boards are independent in exercising their respective functions. A Management Board and a Chief Executive coordinate policy and resource issues. The FRC is funded jointly by the accountancy profession (through the Consultative Committee of Accountancy Bodies), business (through a levy collected by the Financial Services Authority) and the government.

11.6.2.1 The Accounting Standards Board

The Accounting Standards Board was established in 1990 as an independent standard-setting body. There had been criticism of its predecessor, the Accounting Standards Committee (ASC) because of its dominance by professional accountancy bodies and its apparent lack of power to take bold decisions on difficult accounting issues. The ASB spent the first five years of its existence remedying the perceived defects of the UK national standards but from the mid-1990s it engaged increasingly with other national standard setters and the IASC itself, to influence the direction taken by international accounting standards. The ASB has expressed a strong commitment to align UK national standards with IFRS so that eventually all companies will produce financial statements on a similar basis, whether acting under the IAS Regulation or under national standards. The ASB has established experience of developing a separate standard for small companies. This is called the FRSSE (Financial Reporting Standard for Small Enterprises) The advantage for small companies is that if they choose to follow the FRSSE they do not have to be concerned about the detail of the larger body of full standards.

11.6.2.2 The Financial Reporting Review Panel (FRRP)

Accounting standards are defined in the Companies Act 1985 as a result of an amendment introduced in 1989. The Act requires directors of companies, other than small and medium sized enterprises (SMEs), to disclose whether accounts have been prepared in accordance with applicable accounting standards and to explain any departure from those standards. Where the accounts of a company do not comply with the requirements of the Act, the legislation gives power to the Courts to order preparation of a revised set of accounts, at the cost of the directors who approved the defective accounts. The FRRP was established alongside the Accounting Standards Board to exercise this power under the authority of the Secretary of State. This procedure gives statutory support to UK accounting standards, even though the ASB is an independent private body. The FRRP gives relatively few rulings in any one year and the censured companies appear to be average performers suffering temporary performance difficulties, rather than perennial underperformers.[35]

11.6.2.3 The Professional Oversight Board for Accountancy

The Professional Oversight Board for Accountancy contributes to the achievement of the Financial Reporting Council's own fundamental aim of supporting investor,

---

[35] Peasnell *et al.* (2001).

market and public confidence in the financial and governance stewardship of listed and other entities by providing:

- independent oversight of the regulation of the auditing profession by the recognized supervisory and qualifying bodies;
- monitoring of the quality of the auditing function in relation to economically significant entities;
- independent oversight of the regulation of the accountancy profession by the professional accountancy bodies.

11.6.2.4 The Auditing Practices Board

The Auditing Practices Board was established in April 2002, replacing a previous APB that had been in place since 1991. The APB is committed to leading the development of auditing practice in the UK and the Republic of Ireland so as to:

- establish high standards of auditing;
- meet the developing needs of users of financial information;
- ensure public confidence in the auditing process.

The APB issues auditing standards that apply in the UK and Republic of Ireland. It has applied a policy of moving towards the adoption of International Standards on Auditing for accounting periods commencing on or after 15 December 2004. The APB participates in the work of the IAASB (see section 3.3.1) in developing ISAs. During the transition period it has consulted in the UK using the ISA as an exposure draft for comment. When the ISA is issued in the UK it is augmented by reference to specific aspects of UK regulation.

11.6.2.5 The Accountancy Investigation and Discipline Board (AIDB)

The Accountancy Investigation and Discipline Board took over the work of the Joint Disciplinary Scheme operated by ICAEW and ICAS, extending its role to cover the ACCA, CIMA and CIPFA. The ICAI continues to deal separately with Irish accountants to take account of the separate legal and political circumstances. The AIDB focuses on cases of public interest. Other cases continue to be dealt with by the individual accountancy bodies. Accountancy bodies may refer cases to the AIDB but the AIDB may also call in cases that have come to its attention.

11.6.3 Implementing the Modernisation Directive

In March 2004 the Department of Trade and Industry (DTI) issued a Consultation Document[36] on the IAS Regulation and the Modernisation Directive. The main reason for consultation was to allow the DTI to amend the 1985 Companies Act by 1 January 2005. The questions on the IAS Regulation related to the potential for permitting or requiring IFRS beyond the listed groups covered directly by the IAS Regulation. The Government had already announced in July 2003 that publicly traded companies would be permitted to use IAS in their individual accounts and that non-publicly traded companies would be permitted to use IAS in both their individual and consolidated accounts. In relation to the Modernisation Directive the Government intended to take forward its proposals for a statutory Operating and Financial Review (OFR) because these were similar to the analysis of development and performance required by the Directive.

---

[36] DTI (2004) www/dti.gov.uk/consultations.

Changes to the law relating to the OFR, the Directors' report and the ability to use fair values could be made by a 'statutory instrument' which is a useful device for government to use because it does not take up scarce time in Parliamentary debate.

11.6.4 Audit committees

We have explained in section 11.4.3.2 that as part of the process of revising the Code, the Government asked the CGAA to develop guidance on audit committees. A Group was formed under the chairmanship of Sir Robert Smith. The Group reviewed experience in other countries and noted developments in the US, the EU and elsewhere. The Smith report (2003) defined the primary role of audit committees as ensuring the integrity of financial reporting and the audit process by ensuring that the external auditor is independent and objective and does a thorough job, and by fostering a culture and an expectation of effective oversight.[37]

The key functions of audit committees were listed as:

- Monitor the processes which ensure the integrity of the financial statements of the company.
- Review the company's financial control and risk management systems.
- Monitor and review the effectiveness of the company's internal audit function.
- Make recommendations to the board in relation to the appointment of the exterrnal auditor and approve the remuneration and terms of engagement of the external auditor following appointment by the shareholders in general meeting.
- Monitor and review the external auditor's performance, independence and objectivity.
- Develop and implement policy on the engagement of the external auditor to supply non-audit services.

The Smith report recommended that the directors' report in the company's annual report should include a separately identifiable section on the activities of the audit committee. An example of an audit committee's report is given as an appendix to the Smith report, along with specimen terms of reference for the audit committee.

One important aspect of the work of the audit committee is defining the meaning of 'independent' non-executive director. For this, Smith refers to Higgs[38] who states that the director must be independent in character and judgement and there must be no relationships or circumstances that could affect, or appear to affect, the director's judgement. Higgs listed the kinds of relationships that would indicate lack of sufficient independence. The conditions for independence were confirmed in the Combined Code on Corporate Governance (2003).[39]

11.6.5 Non-executive directors

Section 11.4.3.2 explains the establishment of the Higgs review of the role and effectiveness of non-executive directors. The evidence used in the review included the 250 responses received to the consultation paper, survey data on the population of non-executive directors in 2,200 UK listed companies, an opinion poll survey of 605 executive directors, non-executive directors and chairmen of UK listed companies, and in-depth interviews of

---

[37] Smith (2003) paragraph 7.

[38] Higgs (2003) Annex A section A.3.4.

[39] FRC (2003) paragraph A.3.1.

Exhibit 11.7 Topics covered in the Higgs Report on non-executive directors

The board	Tenure and time commitment
The chairman	Remuneration
The non-executive director	Resignation
The senior independent director	Audit and remuneration committees
Independence	Liability of directors
Recruitment and appointment	Relationships with shareholders
Induction and professional development	Smaller listed companies

40 directors of FTSE 350 companies. This evidence was made available on the Review's website. The recommendations of the Higgs Report are now seen in the Combined Code (2003). The areas covered are listed in Exhibit 11.7.

One of the most controversial recommendations of Higgs was that at least half the members of the board, excluding the chairman, should be independent non-executive directors. In the Combined Code this condition is modified for smaller companies to require at least two independent non-executive directors. One of the non-executive directors should be identified as the senior non-executive director. This person should be available to shareholders whose concerns have not been met through the normal channels of chief executive and chairman. The chairman should meet the tests of independence at the time of appointment but it is recognized that the independence diminishes as the chairman becomes more involved in working with the company. There must be separate roles defined by the board for the chairman and for the chief executive.

There were fears that the Higgs Report would deter suitably qualified persons from agreeing to become non-executive directors because of the additional burden and the risk of legal actions against directors of the company. Higgs recommended that companies should be able to provide insurance cover for all directors to cover the costs of defending legal actions. The Tyson report (2003) resulted from a government request for investigation into broadening the base of non-executive directors.[40]

11.7 Accounting issues

11.7.1 True and fair view

There is no definition of the phrase 'a true and fair view' although much has been written about it. The ASB has sought the advice of legal counsel on the matter and that advice is presented as an appendix to the *Foreword to Accounting Standards*. The emphasis is very much on the dynamic nature of the concept. 'What is required to show a true and fair view is subject to continuous rebirth' (Appendix, paragraph 14). The legal opinion is that the courts will hold that compliance with accounting standards is necessary to meet the true and fair requirement. The courts would probably give special weight to the view of the ASB as a standard-setting body.

It thus seems inescapable that accounting standards are a necessary component of a true and fair view, although they may not in themselves be sufficient in all situations. Professional judgement remains an essential additional element. A particular feature of the application of 'true and fair view' is FRS 5 *Reporting the Substance of Transactions*

---

[40] Tyson (2003).

which seeks the commercial substance of transactions and events. In the discussion of the transition to IFRS in 2005, concerns were expressed in the UK that there was no IASB Standard to parallel FRS 5.

The history of accounting practice in the UK is strongly dependent on professional expertise developing practices to satisfy the general requirements of the law. This is consistent with the development of other professions such as law and medicine.

When the law was required to adopt a more prescriptive approach in relation to incorporating the Fourth and Seventh Directives in national law, those drafting the law made extensive use of options in order to preserve the capacity for professional judgement. The preservation of the concept of a 'true and fair view' was a particularly important aspect of the strength of professionalism in the UK, because it allowed continuation of the practice of evolving generally accepted accounting principles.

The Companies Act 1985 used phrases such as 'in accordance with principles generally accepted, at the time when the accounts are prepared' but did not define 'principles generally accepted'. There were strong indications from case law that the Courts of Law would have careful regard to accounting standards set by the ASB. Popularization of the abbreviation 'UK GAAP' may be attributed to the book of that title first published by the accountancy firm of Ernst and Young in the late 1980s and subsequently revised regularly (Davies *et al.*, 1999). The abbreviation may, however, be found earlier than that in the documents lodged with the SEC by companies having a full listing on a major US stock exchange, where the companies were creating terminology which would appear familiar to US readers.

The use of the phrase in the UK must be seen in the context of the statutory requirement for financial statements to present a 'true and fair view' which is widely regarded in UK accounting practice as having a broader range than the US phrase 'fairly present'.

When company law was revised in 1985 the 'true and fair override' was seen as an important principle because there could be occasions when professional judgement would compel the accountant to break compliance with the law in the interests of presenting a true and fair view. A survey by *Company Reporting* in June 2004[41] showed that while one quarter of companies invoked the true and fair override, nine out of ten cases were a consequence of company law not keeping up with accounting standards. This suggests that the UK concern for retaining the 'true and fair override' in IAS 1 (see section 2.2.2) may be overstated since from 2005 the IAS Regulation is the law and so conflict between IFRS and law disappears. An example of the 'true and fair override' in UK accounting standards, prior to the conversion to IFRS, is shown in Exhibit 11.8 where Kingfisher applies the accounting standards SSAP 19 and FRS 10 but in doing so departs from the requirements of the Companies Act. The departure arises because under SSAP 19 investment properties are revalued but not depreciated. FRS 10 allows an impairment test and no amortization. Company law requires depreciation and amortization.

11.7.2 Formats of financial statements

The formats set out in the Fourth Directive were incorporated in the Companies Act 1985 (consolidating earlier legislation). The Act set out two formats of balance sheet and four formats of profit and loss account, thus permitting both vertical and horizontal

---

[41] Company Reporting, June 2004, pp. 3–8.

Exhibit 11.8 True and fair override, Kingfisher

Accounting policies

Accounting conventions

The financial statements of the Company and its subsidiaries are made up to the nearest Saturday to 31 January each year. The financial statements of the Company and its subsidiaries are prepared under the historical cost convention, except for land and buildings that are included in the financial statements at valuation, and are prepared in accordance with applicable accounting standards in the United Kingdom.

However, compliance with SSAP 19 "Accounting for Investment Properties" relating to depreciation on investment properties and FRS 10 "Goodwill and Intangible Assets" relating to the capitalisation and amortisation of goodwill both require a departure from the requirements of the Companies Act 1985 as explained below.

Source: Kingfisher annual report (2004), p. 27. www.kingfisher.com

arrangements. In practice, most companies choose the vertical form of balance sheet, and the vertical form of profit and loss account in the functional version. This allows the matching of cost of goods sold against turnover to report gross profit. A smaller number of companies use the version of the profit and loss account which shows type of expenditure. The IAS Regulation is less prescriptive than the Directives and so it seems likely that UK companies will continue to use their preferred formats for balance sheet and profit and loss account. A cash flow statement was prescribed by FRS 1, first issued in 1991 and amended in 1996 following a review of experience of its use. The revised format contained eight headings, considerably more detailed than IAS 7. From 2005 listed companies revert to the simpler categorization of IAS 7.

In 1993, the ASB proposed the Statement of Total Recognised Gains and Losses (STRGL) as an additional primary financial statement which would report the total of all gains and losses of the reporting entity that are recognized in a period and are attributable to shareholders. The first line of this statement is taken from the profit and loss account which reports the net profit realized for shareholders, but it continues by adding in unrealized items, particularly increases in value of fixed assets and foreign currency translation effects. The information contained in the STRGL could be found in the note of movements on reserves, but these are not easy to find or to understand. The ASB felt that creating a new primary statement, to be presented in close proximity to the profit and loss account, would draw attention to the unrealized gains and losses.

Respondents to the earlier exposure draft had asked that the STRGL should be extended to provide a complete reconciliation of movements in shareholders' funds. The ASB decided the reconciliation would be useful but preferred a separate note which would not divert attention from the components of performance in the STRGL. The appearance of the full page of information is shown for Rentokil Initial plc (Exhibit 11.9).

11.7.3 Measurement of assets

For all limited liability companies the Companies Act 1985 imposed on directors the requirement to present a true and fair view of the financial position and performance of the period. After stipulating that very onerous requirement the legislation left many important decisions to professional judgement.

| Exhibit 11.9 | Statement of total recognised gains and losses and note of historical cost profits and losses, Kingfisher |

CONSOLIDATED STATEMENT OF TOTAL RECOGNISED GAINS AND LOSSES
For the financial year ended 31 January 2004

£ millions	Notes	2004	2003 (restated)
Profit for the financial year		229.6	170.6
Unrealised surplus on revaluation of properties	14	295.7	39.3
Tax on realised revaluation surplus	31	–	(7.4)
Minority interest movement on the issue of shares in Castorama	31	–	(0.9)
Net foreign exchange adjustments offset in reserves	30	(15.1)	(4.1)
Tax effect of exchange adjustments offset in reserves	30	23.4	10.0
Total recognised gains relating to the financial year		533.6	207.5

NOTE OF CONSOLIDATED HISTORICAL COST PROFITS AND LOSSES
For the financial year ended 31 January 2004

£ millions	2004	2003 (restated)
Reported profit on ordinary activities before taxation	426.7	493.4
Prior year property revaluation surplus now realised (see note 30)	20.2	278.6
Difference between historical cost depreciation charge and the actual charge for the year based on the revalued amount	1.4	1.1
Historical cost profit on ordinary activities before tax	448.3	773.1
Historical cost (loss)/ profit for the year retained after taxation, minority interests and dividends	(1,562.8)	198.9

Source: Kingfisher annual report (2004), p. 24. www.kingfisher.com

Unlike some other EU member states, the UK took the maximum flexibility allowed by the Fourth and Seventh Directives on valuation of fixed assets. The Companies Act 1985 permits either historical cost accounting or the use of an alternative basis of valuation. The alternative basis must be current value, as stipulated by the Directives at that time. After many years of debate on the detail of application of alternative valuations within an overall historical cost system, the accounting standard FRS 15 was issued in 1999.[42] Consistent with IAS 16, FRS 15 proposes that where an entity adopts a policy of revaluation, all assets of the same class should be revalued and the revaluations should be kept up to date. Previously companies were not required to revalue regularly and they could choose which assets to revalue. An example of the more regulated nature of valuation may be seen in Kingfisher (Exhibit 11.10) which produces a full fixed assets note.

The ASB's interpretation of 'current value' is generally replacement cost, based on the 'deprival value' ideas from models in accounting theory. The justification for this approach is set out in the Statement of Principles.[43] As IAS 16 allows the use of revaluations, it will be a matter of interest to observe how many UK companies continue to take this option after 2005.

---

[42] ASB (1999a).

[43] ASB (1999b).

Exhibit 11.10 Fixed asset revaluation, Kingfisher

Accounting conventions

The financial statements of the Company and its subsidiaries are made up to the nearest Saturday to 31 January each year. The financial statements of the Company and its subsidiaries are prepared under the historical cost convention, except for land and buildings that are included in the financial statements at valuation, and are prepared in accordance with applicable accounting standards in the United Kingdom.

14 Tangible fixed assets

£ millions	Group Land and buildings	Group Fixtures, fittings and equipment	Group Total	Company Fixtures, fitting and equipment
Cost or valuation				
At 2 February 2003	2,345.3	1,345.8	3,691.1	14.9
Disposal of subsidiary undertakings	(106.9)	(65.4)	(172.3)	–
Transferred with Kesa Electricals on demerger	(344.3)	(304.3)	(648.6)	–
Effect of foreign exchange rate changes	30.3	19.1	49.4	–
Additions	165.4	226.6	392.0	3.7
Disposals	(117.1)	(71.0)	(188.1)	(9.9)
Revaluation surplus	270.1	–	270.1	–
At 31 January 2004	2,242.8	1,150.8	3,393.6	8.7
Depreciation				
At 2 February 2003	58.3	591.9	650.2	10.5
Disposal of subsidiary undertakings	(6.1)	(44.9)	(51.0)	–
Transferred with Kesa Electricals on demerger	(14.8)	(62.3)	(77.1)	–
Effect of foreign exchange rate changes	2.1	11.4	13.5	–
Charge for year	20.1	147.9	168.0	2.0
Disposals	(5.0)	(60.6)	(65.6)	(8.9)
Revaluation surplus	(25.6)	–	(25.6)	–
At 31 January 2004	29.0	583.4	612.4	3.6
Net book amount				
At 31 January 2004	2,213.8	567.4	2,781.2	5.1
At 1 February 2003	2,287.0	753.9	3,040.9	4.4
Assets in the course of construction included above				
At 31 January 2004	208.8	82.6	291.4	–
At 1 February 2003	252.7	62.8	315.5	–

The cost of land and buildings includes £7.3m (2003: £31.1m) in respect of assets held under finance leases. The related accumulated depreciation at the end of the year was £1.9m (2003: £2.4m).

The cost of fixtures, fittings and equipment includes £40.4m (2003: £40.9m) in respect of assets held under finance leases. The related accumulated depreciation at the end of the year was £33.9m (2003: £31.6m).

The amount of interest capitalised in tangible fixed assets during the year was £2.9m (2003: £4.4m). The cumulative total of interest included at the balance sheet date was £15.2m (2003: £19.8m).

Exhibit 11.10 (Continued)

Land and buildings include investment properties as follows:

£ millions	Group
Cost or valuation	
At 2 February 2003	135.9
Additions	0.3
Reclassification to operating properties	(29.0)
Disposals	(99.8)
Revaluation surplus	4.6
At 31 January 2004	12.0

Land and buildings are analysed as follows:

£ millions	Freehold	Long leasehold	Short leasehold	Total 2004	Total 2003
					Group
Land and buildings					
At valuation	1,666.6	15.8	1.3	1,683.7	1,793.4
At cost	350.8	–	208.3	559.1	551.9
	2,017.4	15.8	209.6	2,242.8	2,345.3
Aggregate depreciation	11.2	–	17.8	29.0	58.3
Net book amount					
At 31 January 2004	2,006.2	15.8	191.8	2,213.8	
At 1 February 2003	1,962.6	74.5	249.9		2,287.0

If land and buildings had not been revalued, the cost to the Group would have been:

£ millions	2004	2003
Cost (excluding assets in the course of construction)	1,584.3	1,905.8
Aggregate depreciation	20.6	51.3
Net amount	1,563.7	1,854.5

During each of the last five years a representative sample of at least one-third of the freehold and long leasehold properties owned by B&Q Properties Limited (formerly Chartwell Land plc), the Group's property subsidiary, have been valued by external qualified valuers. CB Richard Ellis (Chartered Surveyors and Valuers) has carried out a valuation of such a representative sample as at 31 December 2003 and, based upon the results of these valuations, there have been internal valuations by qualified valuers employed by the Group of the remainder of B&Q Properties' portfolio.

All properties owned by Castorama France and Brico Dépôt were valued by FPD Savills (Chartered Surveyors and Valuers) and properties of Castorama Poland and Castorama Italy were valued by Cushman & Wakefield Healy Baker (Chartered Surveyors and Valuers) as at 31 December 2003.

Properties with any element of Group occupancy are valued on an existing use value basis, which does not take account of formal lease arrangements with Group companies or the Group's occupation of the premises. Properties without Group occupancy are valued on the basis of open market value. These valuation bases comply with the RICS Appraisal and Valuation Manual.

The directors have resolved to incorporate these valuations in the financial statements and the resulting revaluation adjustments have been taken to the revaluation reserve. The revaluations during the year ended 31 January 2004 resulted in a revaluation surplus of £295.7m (2003: £39.3m).

Source: Kingfisher annual report (2003), p. 28 and note 14, pp. 40–41. www.kingfisher.com

11.7.4 Narrative reporting

11.7.4.1 Notes to the accounts

Notes to the accounts are required by company law and, for listed companies, by stock exchange regulations. Where the primary financial statements fail to show a true and fair view, this cannot be rectified by providing information in the notes to the accounts. The notes provide additional explanation to support what is contained in the financial statements.

There is considerable evidence that leading UK companies make voluntary disclosures well ahead of the minimum requirement of the law. This is particularly so where the companies have multinational activities. The annual reports of such companies are more informative than the basic prescription of law might lead the reader to expect.[44] Such companies are using the annual report to project their image on international stock exchanges.

11.7.4.2 Operating and financial review[45]

The operating and financial review (OFR) has existed since 1993 as a form of disclosure recommended by the ASB in a non-mandatory Statement of best practice. The ASB saw the OFR as a framework for the directors to discuss and analyze the performance of the business and the factors underlying its results and financial position, in order to assist users to assess for themselves the future potential of the business.

There was no standard format for the OFR because directors were encouraged to design the OFR in the manner best suited to the needs of the business and its users. The ASB was keen to avoid the stereotyped image of some of the Management Discussion and Analysis (MD&A) documents issued in the US. Essential features of the OFR were a top-down structure; a balanced and objective account; reference to matters discussed previously which have not turned out as expected; analytical discussion; explanations of ratios calculated; and analysis of trends. In discussing trends it should indicate trends and factors which have affected the results but are not expected to continue in the future, and also known events, trends and uncertainties which were expected to have an impact on the business in the future.

The Final Report of the Company Law Review Steering Group (section 11.3.1) recommended a mandatory OFR. This was taken forward in a draft regulation issued by the government for consultation in May 2004. Section 15.4.6 summarizes the content of the ASB's voluntary OFR and the proposed content of the mandatory OFR. The directors of quoted companies will be required to prepare an OFR. A quoted company is defined as a company whose equity share capital has been included in the 'official list' of the London Stock Exchange, or is officially listed in an EEA State or is admitted to dealing on either the New York Stock Exchange or Nasdaq.[46] This requirement applies whatever the size of the quoted company. Companies trading on the Alternative Investment Market (AIM) will not be covered by this definition and so will not be required to produce an OFR. However they may be large or medium sized companies which need to comply with the requirements of the EU Modernisation Directive.

Company Reporting (2004) surveyed the OFRs of the FTSE 100 companies in their 2003 year-end annual reports.[47] The survey noted the variety of location and content of OFRs

---

[44] Gray and Roberts (1993).

[45] ASB (1993b, 2003).

[46] Section 262, Companies Act 1985.

[47] *Company Reporting*, August 2004, pp. 3–8.

that had emerged under voluntary compliance and questioned the need for the proposed statutory control of the OFR. One strong theme emerging from the financial review sections was the emphasis on risk, with risk disclosures being found in 75 per cent of OFRs. Discussion of critical accounting policies was found in some OFRs but that may reflect the US requirements since the companies given as examples also had a US listing. The survey suggested that the government's draft proposals appeared muddled because they were directed more towards corporate social responsibility issues which companies tend to disclose in CSR reports.

The Financial Times[48] summarized some of the comments on the government's draft proposals. One strongly supportive view was that the OFR will become the spinal column of narrative reporting, with more detailed reports running off it. One broadly supportive commentator nevertheless feared it might be taken over by corporate social responsibility reporting. Another was concerned that a mechanistic approach with boilerplate text would result. Some thought directors would be inhibited in making forward-looking statements because there is no 'safe harbour' provision (see section 8.7.1.2) but the Department of Trade and Industry rejected that idea as unworkable.

11.7.4.3 Interim reporting

Listed companies are required to provide interim reports on a half-yearly basis. Some provide quarterly reports voluntarily. The regulations on disclosure are largely those set by the Stock Exchange, increased at the recommendation of the Cadbury Report. The ASB has issued a non-mandatory Statement of best practice which is consistent with IAS 34.[49] It sets out the recommended timing, contents and measurement basis of interim reports. On timing it encourages publication within 60 days of the interim period-end. The 'discrete' method is recommended, where the interim period is regarded as a distinct accounting period. Seasonal businesses may consequently report markedly different results in each half or quarter of the year.

The regulation of interim reporting is contained in the Listing Rules of the FSA. The UK Accounting Standards Board produced a Statement on Interim Reports in 1997 but it was not mandatory. The Listing Rules require a profit and loss account, balance sheet and cash flow statement. Some details are prescribed but a great deal of choice is left to companies. Implementation of IAS 34 increases the amount of information and the amount of detail compared with the effect of the Listing Rules and the ASB Statement.

A survey[50] of the half-yearly interim reports of 100 UK listed companies in 2002 found that there was a large gap between those companies that provided considerable information in their interim reports and those complying only with the basic requirements. The survey also found that all UK companies would have to make some changes to comply with IAS 34 although this would not be onerous for those already complying with best practice.

11.7.4.4 Corporate social responsibility reporting

The Kingsmill Report into Women's Employment and Pay (2001)[51] contained a range of recommendations for the Government aimed at improving the management of human capital and so tackling the significant earnings gap between men and women in the UK.

---

[48] *Financial Times*, 2 August 2004, Fund Management Weekly Review, p. 3.

[49] ASB (1997).

[50] An Interim Report: Surveying corporate half-yearly reporting (2002), Deloitte & Touche LLP, www.deloitte.co.uk.

[51] www.kingsmillreview.gov.uk/index.cfm.

In relation to corporate reporting she recommended improved reporting of human capital management information by both public and private sector organisations, suggesting the Operating and Financial Review as a possible vehicle for such reporting.

A survey by *Company Reporting* in July 2004[52] found that companies reporting employee information did so in a specific CSR report or in the Directors' Report. Relatively few used the OFR or a separate HCR section. Information in the Directors' Report tended to be the minimum required by legislation. Those following the spirit of the Kingsmill recommendations were largely using a CSR report. The types of information disclosed were: general employee policies, union and labour relations, communication with employees, career development, remuneration, redundancies, and employee satisfaction surveys. Half the companies surveyed addressed health and safety. A few companies produced diversity statistics on gender, ethnicity and disability.

The UK government has established a website as a gateway to Corporate Social Responsibility.[53] It provides links to websites of organizations encouraging 'best practice' in CSR reporting.

11.7.4.5 Preliminary announcements

Under Stock Exchange rules a listed company is required to make an announcement of its results for the year in such a way that the information reaches all stock market participants at the same time. This is done through an organized announcements service; however, the amount of information announced varies from one company to the next. Some give little more than the annual profit and a summary balance sheet; others provide detail almost as great as that of the annual report which follows later. The ASB issued a non-mandatory Statement on preliminary announcements which will improve the timeliness, quality, relevance and consistency of preliminary announcements. The recommendations have similarities to the statement on interim reports.

11.7.4.6 Directors' remuneration[54]

As explained earlier, concerns about corporate governance in the UK led in particular to recommendations of increased disclosure of directors' emoluments and other benefits. The general recommendations of the Cadbury Committee were made specific by the Greenbury Committee and implemented by the Stock Exchange as requirements for listed companies. In 1997, the requirements were extended by Statutory Instrument to all limited companies, although with less demanding rules for unlisted companies. The statutory instrument was subsequently updated as *The Directors' Remuneration Report Regulations 2002*.

11.8 Gray's accounting values

11.8.1 Professionalism versus statutory control

The history of accounting practice in the UK is strongly dependent on professional expertise developing practices to satisfy the general requirements of the law. This is consistent with the development of other professions such as law and medicine.

---

[52] *Company Reporting*, July 2004, pp. 3–8.

[53] csr.gov.uk.

[54] www.hmso.gov.uk/si/si2002/20021986.htm.

When the law was required to adopt a more prescriptive approach in relation to incorporating the Fourth and Seventh Directives in national law, those drafting the law made extensive use of options in order to preserve the capacity for professional judgement. The preservation of the concept of a 'true and fair view' was a particularly important aspect of the strength of professionalism in the UK, because it allowed continuation of the practice of evolving generally accepted accounting principles. The reforms of supervision of the accountancy profession initiated in 2002 have introduced more layers of oversight and accountability but there is still a core expectation of professional values in applying legislation and standards for corporate reporting.

11.8.2 Uniformity versus flexibility

Gray (1988) classified UK accounting as exhibiting strong flexibility. When prescribed formats first appeared, as a result of the influence of the Fourth Directive, there were concerns in the accountancy profession that this would curtail professional freedom. However, the formats allow flexibility and the standard-setting body has taken the presentation of primary financial statements well ahead of the legal minimum prescription (e.g. in devising the STRGL). The formal separation of tax law and accounting law permits flexibility, although in practice it may be constrained by interactions of the two approaches to profit. In relation to defining a group of companies, it was found in the late 1980s that too much flexibility can lead to problems and the definition was tightened. Generally the trends have been away from flexibility in matters reported in financial statements but the surrounding contents of the annual report still leave scope for flexibility of reporting within a framework of accountability.

11.8.3 Conservatism versus optimism

Gray (1988) classified UK accounting practice as demonstrating strong optimism, rather than conservatism. Companies are permitted to revalue upwards from historical cost and at present the rules on matching this with revaluation downwards are under review for tighter procedures. In the 1990s the ASB gradually removed some of the flexibility of accounting treatments and this also reduced the scope for optimism. One example was the case of provisions. These had been given very varied and flexible treatment until FRS 12 tightened up the definitions so that companies could no longer use provisions to smooth out profit trends from one year to the next. Another example was revaluation of fixed assets which had been flexible and tended to be applied only when asset values were rising. The combination of imposing stricter rules for revaluation (FRS 16) and requiring annual impairment tests (FRS 11) reduced the scope for optimism. The mood of the standard setters was to allow optimism only under carefully controlled conditions. The ASB's approach to optimism, as shown in UK standards, had become generally aligned with that of the IFRS before the conversion process of 2005.

11.8.4 Secrecy versus transparency

Gray (1988) classified UK accounting as strongly transparent. Notes to the accounts and additional voluntary disclosures are evidence of such transparency. The operating and financial review, interim reporting, corporate social responsibility reporting and disclosures regarding directors' remuneration are examples of transparency in UK reporting practice. It has been observed for some time now that non-financial disclosures in annual reports of major companies are greater in the UK than in the US or in continental European countries.[55]

Summary and conclusions

In this chapter you have seen how characteristics of accounting principles and practice in the UK are related to the predictions made by Gray and others based upon analysis of accounting values. Gray's (1988) method of analysis may be used to predict that the accounting system in the UK will be characterized by strong professionalism, strong flexibility, strong optimism and strong transparency. The profession has a long history of development in the UK and has traditionally operated in a framework where statutory control is limited to prescribing minimum standards only, leaving the profession to determine best practice. Flexibility has been consistent with this professional approach, uniformity in matters such as presentation of formats being a relatively new feature caused by implementation of directives. Optimism, rather than conservatism, is seen in the use of alternative valuation rules to historical cost accounting. Transparency is seen in the extensive disclosures required of companies by way of notes to the accounts.

UK accounting has developed in its own mould but has also been exported to former UK colonies and trading partners. The UK standard-setting body has been an active participant in the work programme of the IASB.

Key points from the chapter:

- A history of strong professionalism in accounting has been moderated over the years by increasing regulation, initially through standards volunteered by the profession but more recently tending towards direct or indirect statutory control.

- Corporate governance initiatives, comprising Cadbury, Greenbury and Hampel, have provided guidance that has influenced other countries in their corporate governance codes. Higgs and Smith have added to this guidance in the specific areas of non-executive directors and audit committees.

- The Financial Services Authority sets the listing rules for the London Stock Exchange, including disclosure requirements.

- The idea of 'Anglo-Saxon' influence is frequently mentioned in research and professional papers; there are arguments for and against this system existing in reality.

- Oversight mechanisms have been enhanced since 2002 as a result of company law review and the wider role given to the Financial Reporting Council with its new subsidiaries.

- Accounting issues that may continue to show a separate UK characteristic of listed companies include the application of a 'true and fair view', the formats of financial statements, the measurement of tangible fixed assets, and the range of narrative reporting.

- Gray's (1988) method of analysis may be used to predict that the accounting system in the UK will be characterized by strong professionalism, strong flexibility, strong optimism and strong transparency Current practice indicates modified professionalism with less flexibility and less optimism but continued strong transparency.

---

[55] Meek *et al.* (1995).

Questions

The following questions test your understanding of the material contained in the chapter and allow you to relate your understanding to the learning outcomes specified at the start of this chapter. The learning outcomes are repeated here. Each question is cross-referenced to the relevant section of the chapter.

Explain the development of accounting regulation

1 To what extent do early developments in accounting practice indicate the likely directions of professionalism/statutory control; uniformity/flexibility; conservatism/optimism; and secrecy/transparency in current practice? (section 11.3)

Explain the key institutional characteristics of the UK

2 How does the political and economic system of the UK fit into the classifications described in Chapter 4? (section 11.4.1)

3 How does the legal system of the UK fit into the classifications described in Chapter 4? (section 11.4.2)

4 How does the corporate governance system of the UK fit into the classifications described in Chapter 4? (section 11.4.3)

5 How does the taxation system of the UK compare to the descriptions given in Chapter 4? (section 11.4.4)

6 How does the corporate financing system of the UK compare to the descriptions given in Chapter 4? (section 11.4.5)

7 How does the accounting profession in the UK compare to the descriptions given in Chapter 4? (section 11.4.6)

8 How has membership of the EU affected UK accounting? (section 11.5.2)

9 Which institutional factors are most likely to influence UK accounting practice? (sections 11.4 and 11.5)

Discuss the meaning of an 'Anglo-Saxon' system of accounting

10 What are the arguments that support the description 'Anglo-Saxon accounting system'? (section 11.5.1)

11 What are the arguments against the description 'Ango-Saxon accounting system? (section 11.5.1)

Explain the structure and processes for oversight and assurance

12 What was the outcome of the review of the regulatory regime of the accountancy profession in 2002? (section 11.6.1)

13 What is the role of the Financial Reporting Council and its subsidiary boards? (section 11.6.2)

14 How does the role of the Department of Trade and Industry bring statutory control to a professionally-oriented system of accounting? (section 11.6.3)

15 What is the role of an audit committee in giving assurance on corporate reporting? (section 11.6.4)

16 What is the role of non-executive directors in giving assurance on corporate reporting? (section 11.6.5)

Understand and explain features of the accounting system that illustrate the continuing diversity of UK accounting practices

17 Why is there a strong view from the UK that the 'true and fair override' must be preserved in international accounting standards? (section 11.7.1)

18 What is the purpose of a Statement of Total Recognised Gains and Losses? (section 11.7.2)

19 Why is the alternative valuation choice of IAS 16 important for UK companies? (section 11.7.3)

20 What are the aspects of narrative reporting that are characteristic of the UK accounting system? (section 11.7.4)

Discuss UK accounting practices using the analytical framework of Gray's accounting values

21 How are Gray's accounting values demonstrated in UK accounting practices today? (section 11.8)

References and further reading

Alexander, D. and Archer, S. (2000) 'On the myth of "Anglo-Saxon" financial accounting', *The International Journal of Accounting*, 35(4): 539–557.

Alexander, D. and Archer, S. (2003) 'On the myth of "Anglo-Saxon" financial accounting: A response to Nobes', *The International Journal of Accounting*, 38(4): 503–504.

ASB (1994) FRS 5 Reporting the Substance of Transactions, Accounting Standards Board.

ASB (1997) *Interim Reports*, Statement by the Accounting Standards Board.

ASB (1999a) FRS 15 *Tangible Fixed Assets*, Accounting Standards Board, February 1999.

ASB (1999b) *Statement of Principles*, Accounting Standards Board, December 1999.

ASB (2003) *Operating and Financial Review*, Statement issued by the Accounting Standards Board.

ASB (2004) *UK Accounting Standards: A Strategy for Convergence with IFRS*, Accounting Standards Board, March 2004.

Beattie, V. and Pratt, K. (2002) *Voluntary Annual Report Disclosures: What Users Want*, The Institute of Chartered Accountants of Scotland.

Cairns, D. and Nobes, C. (2000) *The Convergence Handbook: A Comparison between International Accounting Standards and UK Financial Reporting Standards*, Institute of Chartered Accountants in England and Wales.

Charkham, J.P. (1994) *Keeping Good Company: A Study of Corporate Governance in Five Countries*. Oxford: Clarendon Press.

Co-ordinating Group on Accounting and Auditing Issues, *Final Report* to the Secretary of State for Trade and Industry and the Chancellor of the Exchequer, January 2003, URN 03/567. www.dti.gov.uk/cld/cgaai-final.pdf

Davies, A. (1999) *A Strategic Approach to Corporate Governance*, Gower: Aldershot.

Davies, M., Paterson, R. and Wilson, A. (1999) *UK GAAP*, 6th edn. London: Macmillan.

DTI (2001) The Company Law Review Steering Group, Final Report, Modern Company Law for a Competitive Economy, Department of Trade and Industry, June 2001. www.dti.gov.uk/cld/review.htm

DTI (2004) Modernisation of Accounting Directives/IAS Infrastructure: A Consultation Document, March 2004. www.dti.gov.uk/cld/current.htm

Edwards, E. and Bell, P. (1961) *The Theory and Measurement of Business Income*, Berkeley, CA: University of California Press.

Emenyonu, E.N. and Gray, S.J. (1992) 'EC accounting harmonisation: An empirical study of measurement practices in France, Germany and the UK', *Accounting and Business Research*, Winter: 49–58.

FRC (2003) The Combined Code on Corporate Governance, Financial Reporting Council, July 2003.

Gordon, P.D. and Gray, S.J. (1994) *European Financial Reporting – United Kingdom*. London: Routledge.

Gray, S.J. (1988) 'Towards a theory of cultural influence on the development of accounting systems internationally', *Abacus*, 24(1): 1–15.

Gray, S. and Roberts, C. (1993) 'Voluntary information disclosure: The attitude of UK multi-nationals', in Gray, S.J., Coenenberg, A.G. and Gordon, P.D. (eds), *International Group Accounting – Issues in European Harmonization*. London: Routledge.

Higgs, D. (2003) *Review of the role and effectiveness of non-executive directors*, Department of Trade and Industry. www.dti.gov.uk/cld/non_exec_review

Hofstede, G. (1984) *Culture's Consequences: International Differences in Work-related Values*. Beverly Hills, CA: Sage.

ICAEW (2003) *Prospective Financial Information: Guidance for UK Directors*. The Institute of Chartered Accountants in England and Wales. www.icaew.co.uk/pfi

Lamb, M. (1996) 'The relationship between accounting and taxation: The United Kingdom', *The European Accounting Review*, 5: Supplement, 933–949.

Ma, R., Parker, R.H. and Whittred, G. (1991) *Consolidation Accounting*. London: Longman Cheshire.

McMahon, F. and Weetman, P. (1997) 'Commercial accounting principles: Questions of fact and questions of tax law', *British Tax Review*, 1: 6–18.

Meek, G.K., Roberts, C.B. and Gray, S.J. (1995) 'Factors influencing voluntary annual report disclosures by US, UK and continental European multinational corporations', *Journal of International Business Studies*, Third Quarter: 555–572.

Napier, C. (1995) 'The history of financial reporting in the United Kingdom', in Walton, P. (ed.), *European Financial Reporting: A History*. New York: Academic Press.

Nobes, C.W. (1984) *International Classification of Financial Reporting*. London: Croom Helm.

Nobes, C. (1993) 'Group accounting in the United Kingdom', in Gray, S.J., Coenenberg, A.G. and Gordon, P.D. (eds), *International Group Accounting – Issues in European Harmonization*. London: Routledge.

Nobes, C. (2003) 'On the myth of "Anglo-Saxon" financial accounting: a comment' *The International Journal of Accounting*, 38(1): 95–104.

Nobes, C.W. and Parker, R.H. (1984) 'The Fourth Directive and the United Kingdom', in Gray, S.J. and Coenenberg, A.G. (eds), *EEC and Accounting Harmonization: Implementation and Impact of the Fourth Directive*. Amsterdam: North-Holland.

Parker, R. (1989) 'Importing and exporting accounting: The British experience', in Hopwood, A.G. (ed.), *International Pressures for Accounting Change*, pp. 7–29. London: Prentice Hall/ICAEW.

Parker, R. (1995) 'Financial reporting in the United Kingdom and Australia', in Nobes, C.W. and Parker, R. (eds), *Comparative International Accounting*, 4th edn. Englewood Cliffs, NJ: Prentice Hall.

Parker, R.H. and Nobes, C.W. (1994) *An International View of True and Fair Accounting*. London: Routledge.

Peasnell, K.V., Pope, P.F. and Young, S. (2001) 'The characteristics of firms subject to adverse rulings by the Financial Reporting Review Panel', *Accounting and Business Research*, 31(4): 291–311.

Review (2003) *Review of the Regulatory Regime of the Accountancy Profession*. Report to the Secretary of State for Trade and Industry, January 2003, URN 03/589, www.dti.gov.uk/cld/accountancy-review.pdf

Smith, R. (2003) *Audit Committees: Combined Code Guidance*. A report and proposed guidance by an FRC-appointed group chaired by Sir Robert Smith. Financial Reporting Council, www.frc.org.uk/publications

Sudarsanam, P.S. (2003) Creating value from mergers and acquisitions: the challenges, an integrated and international perspective, FT Prentice Hall.

Turnbull (1999) Internal Control: Guidance for Directors on the Combined Code, The Institute of Chartered Accountants in England and Wales, www.icaew.co.uk/internalcontrol

Tyson (2003) The Tyson report on the Recruitment and Development of Non-executive Directors. www.london.edu/tysonreport/Tyson_Report_June_2003.pdf

Weetman, P. and Gray, S.J. (1990) 'International financial analysis and comparative corporate performance: The impact of UK versus US accounting principles on earnings', *Journal of International Financial Management and Accounting*, 2(2/3): 111–129.

Weetman, P. and Gray, S.J. (1991) 'A comparative international analysis of the impact of accounting principles on profits: The USA versus the UK, Sweden and The Netherlands', *Accounting and Business Research*, 21(84): 363–379.

Weetman, P., Jones, E.A.E., Adams, C. and Gray, S.J. (1998) 'Profit measurement and UK accounting standards: A case of increasing disharmony in relation to US GAAP and IASs', *Accounting and Business Research*, 28(3): 189–208.

Wilson, A., Davies, M., Curtis, M. and Wilkinson-Riddle, G. (2001) *UK & International GAAP*, 7th edn. Ernst and Young, London: Tolley

Newspapers and professional journals/magazines

FT World Accounting Report, published monthly by *Financial Times Publications*.

The Corporate Accountant, insert in *The Accountant*, UK monthly. London: Lafferty Publications.

The Accountant (UK).

OECD, *Economic Surveys*. Paris: Organization for Economic Cooperation and Development.

Financial Times (UK).

Sources of regularly updated information on accounting standards and related matters

Accounting Standards (annual publication). London: Accountancy Books.

The London Stock Exchange Fact File (annual publication). London: London Stock Exchange.

Financial Reporting: A Survey of UK Reporting Practice. London: Accountancy Books.

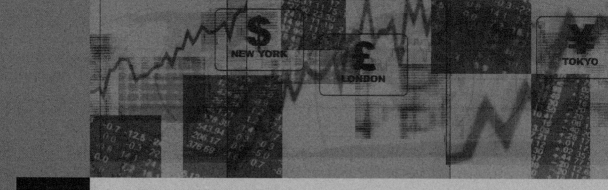

12 Japan

Learning outcomes

After reading this chapter you should be able to:

● Understand the key characteristics of the country as summarized in published economic indicators.

● Explain the origins of accounting regulations and the historical developments leading to the present state of practice.

● Relate institutional factors for the country to the framework set out in Chapter 4.

● Explain the position of national accounting practice in relation to the IFRS described in Chapter 2.

12.1 Introduction

Despite the international pre-eminence of Japanese corporations, it is often quite difficult for a non-Japanese report reader to discover the measurement or disclosure practices of the typical Japanese company. The most obvious reason for this is the problem of language – while most large Japanese companies, including very many not listed on any overseas stock markets, produce English-language annual accounts and reports, these are different from the Japanese language reports. Unlike the statutory Japanese reports, the English language ones are normally glossy documents full of photos and graphics with a PR-style review of activities. More importantly, the financial statements are not the same as those in the Japanese-language statements. They may contain different information, additional notes or even additional statements may be disclosed while other information given in the Japanese accounts is not provided. Japanese financial statements also look somewhat different from UK or US financial statements which can confuse the unsophisticated user. Companies therefore typically recast their financial statements to make the English-language versions look more like a typical set of US financial

| Exhibit 12.1 | Basis of presentation of English-language accounts: Sumitomo Mitsui |

NOTES TO CONSOLIDATED FINANCIAL STATEMENTS

1. Basis of Presentation (extract)

. . . The accompanying consolidated financial statements have been prepared in accordance with the provisions set forth in the Japanese Securities and Exchange Law and its related accounting regulations, and in conformity with accounting principles generally accepted in Japan ("Japanese GAAP"), which are different in certain respects as to application and disclosure requirements of International Financial Reporting Standards.

The accounts of overseas subsidiaries are based on their accounting records maintained in conformity with generally accepted accounting principles prevailing in the respective countries of domicile.

The accompanying consolidated financial statements have been restructured and translated into English (with some expanded descriptions and the inclusion of consolidated statements of stockholders' equity) from the consolidated financial statements of SMFG prepared in accordance with Japanese GAAP.

Some supplementary information included in the statutory Japanese language consolidated financial statements, but not required for fair presentation, is not presented in the accompanying consolidated financial statements.

Amounts less than one million yen have been omitted. As a result, the totals in Japanese yen shown in the financial statements do not necessarily agree with the sum of the individual amounts.

The translation of the Japanese yen amounts into U.S. dollars are included solely for the convenience of readers outside Japan, using the prevailing exchange rate at March 31, 2004, which was ¥105.69 to US$1. The convenience translations should not be construed as representations that the Japanese yen amounts have been, could have been, or could in the future be, converted into US dollars at that rate.

Source: Sumitomo Mitsui Financial Group, annual report, 2004, p. 69. www.smfg.co.jp

statements. This does not affect the reported earnings or equity figures, but many items in the accounts will be re-ordered or re-classified or even produced solely for foreign readers. Exhibit 12.1 provides one example of this. It shows that Sumitomo Mitsui not only re-classifies some of the items but provide a convenience translation and 'some expanded descriptions and the inclusion of consolidated statements of stockholders' equity' in their English language accounts. However the company omits other supplementary information provided in its Japanese language financial statements.

The main problem for the non-Japanese reader will be understanding an unfamiliar set of GAAP, as Japan is not fully compliant with IFRS or US GAAP. A number of companies, especially those listed in the US, therefore adjust the Japanese accounts to reflect US GAAP which is also then used as a basis for the audit of the English-language statements. Many of these companies have been doing this for a large number of years and currently there is no general move towards using IFRS instead of US GAAP. This is a form of restatement and it is not always possible to restate the figures without resorting to various estimates and assumptions. For example Hitachi (2004) state, in its accounting policies, that:

> The consolidated financial statements presented herein have been prepared in a manner and reflect the adjustments which are necessary to conform them with accounting policies generally accepted in the United States of America. Management of the Company has made a number of estimates and assumptions relating to the reporting of assets and liabilities and the disclosure of contingent assets and liabilities to prepare these financial statements. Actual results could differ from those estimates.

Whichever of these two approaches is used, the figures and formats will not be identical to the Japanese-language accounts and, where different accounting rules are used, companies do not generally quantify the impact on reported figures.

12.2 The country

Japan is made up of a number of islands off the coast of China. Much of the land is extremely mountainous and the population resides in the densely populated coastal areas. As can be seen from the figures in Exhibit 12.2, Japan is a highly successful country, with an average *per capita* gross domestic product of over US$32,000 in 2002, the sixth highest of any country.[1] Note however, that Japan has had a very low growth rate over the last ten years, so that it has dropped from third highest per capita gross domestic product in 1998, and, despite negative inflation, it remains a very expensive country so that it is only sixteenth richest in terms of purchasing power, a measure of standard of living.

Japan has achieved remarkable growth since the Second World War. It is a highly industrialized and urbanized country that is dependent for its economic success on large international companies. Much of its success is built on trade, with Japan accounting for 6.3 per cent of the total world exports,[2] with the country being the home of many of the largest companies in the world. For example, the *Financial Times* annual Global 500 survey listed 55 Japanese companies in the top 500 companies in June 2004, measured by market capitalization. (This was second highest after the US with 230 and above the UK with 36.) The top ten of these are shown in Exhibit 12.3.

---

[1] *The Economist* (2004).

[2] *The Economist* (2004). However, trade accounts for only 8.4 per cent of its GDP, one of the lowest figures of any country.

| Exhibit 12.2 | Japan: country profile |

Population	127.3 million
Land mass	377,727 km^2
GDP per head	US$32,520
GDP per head in purchasing power parity	74.5 (USA = 100)
Origins of GDP:	%
Agriculture	1.4
Industry	30.4
Services	68.2
	%
Real GDP average annual growth 1991–2001	1.2
Inflation, average annual rate 1996–2002	−0.1

Source: *The Economist Pocket World in Figures*, 2004 Edition, Profile Books Ltd.

Japan has in the past relied extensively upon exports, resulting in a large balance of payments surplus. Domestic investment has always been high, being approximately 25 per cent of GDP per annum in the early 2000s in comparison to 15–20 per cent in most other developed countries. This has resulted in a low rate of return and calls for a greater amount of inward investment, which has always been exceptionally low (FDI was just 2 per cent of GDP in 2002 compared to 20 per cent in the US and

| Exhibit 12.3 | Top ten Japanese companies June 2004 |

Company	Rank Global 500	Market value $m	Sector	Listed in US	Listed in UK
Toyota Motor	18	128,667	Automobiles and parts	Yes	Yes
NTT DoCoMo	25	102,674	Telecommunications equipment	Yes	Yes
Nippon Telegraph & Telephone	33	89,446	Telecommunications equipment	Yes	Yes
Mitsubishi Tokyo Financial	57	63,299	Banks	Yes	Yes
Nissan Motor	84	48,892	Automobiles and parts	No	No
Mizuho Financial	86	48,589	Banks	No	No
Honda Motor	102	43,366	Automobiles and parts	Yes	Yes
Canon	103	43,116	Electronic and electrical equipment	No	Yes
Sumitomo Mitsui Financial	110	41,371	Banks	No	No
Takedo Chemical Industries	118	39,325	Pharmaceuticals and biotechnology	No	No

Source: www.FT.com, www.NYSE.com, www.Londonstockexchange.com

41 per cent in the UK).[3] However, inward direct investment is still difficult due to legislation such as the mergers and acquisitions rules, corporate and country culture and 'complicated and non-transparent administrative procedures and practices that span several government offices as well as non-transparent administrative guidance and industry practice'.[4]

Despite the limited importation of goods and services, Japan has a long history of importing ideas from other countries. As will be discussed below, this includes accounting principles. Foreign influences can be seen in both the regulatory system and in the rules and practices adopted.

12.3 Development of accounting regulations

12.3.1 Development of the triangular legal system

The Japanese regulatory system is similar to many of the code-based European countries. There are three sources of laws that prescribe financial accounting and reporting. These are: the Ministry of Justice via the Commercial Code, the Ministry of Finance via the Securities and Exchange Law, and the tax authorities which have an important indirect influence, resulting in a system that is often referred to as the 'Triangular Legal System'.[5] While the stock market is important, it does not regulate corporate disclosures itself and the accounting profession has been relatively unimportant except with respect to the auditing rules.

The earliest regulations took the form of Commercial Code regulations administered by the Ministry of Justice. These apply to joint-stock (Kabushiki Kaisha) companies whether publicly listed or not. While there is no code of accounts, the rules are relatively uniform and conservative. The most important objective is to protect creditors. The first Commercial Code of 1899 required all companies to produce five documents:

● an inventory (no longer required),
● a balance sheet,
● an income statement,
● a business report,
● proposals regarding profit distribution and reserve accounts.

These documents had to be audited by a statutory auditor, who does not have to be a CPA. This audit is primarily concerned with ensuring that no fraud has taken place rather than attesting to the 'correctness', 'truthfulness' or 'fairness' of the published accounts. It can be more appropriately thought of as being akin to an internal audit rather than an independent external audit.

The Commercial Code was very largely of Germanic origin, although later amendments have reflected Anglo-American influences. Emphasis was originally placed upon the inventory of assets and liabilities which had to be presented to the annual general meeting. The balance sheet had originally to be created from this inventory, rather than being derived from the original books of account. This reflected the legalistic background of the Commercial Code. The Commercial Code does not include many detailed accounting rules, these instead being prescribed in legal Ordinances which contain detailed rules regarding the form and content of the prescribed statements.

---

[3] OECD (2004); Beattie (2004).

[4] Invest Japan Forum (2002) as reported by Beattie (2004).

[5] www.jicpa.or.jp/n_eng/e-account.html.

Until the latest amendment of the Code, it only applied to single-entity financial statements with companies having to submit an annual report to the AGM containing the balance sheet, income statement, business report, profit appropriation and supporting schedules. For year ends after April 2004, companies will also have to provide designated consolidated statements including the balance sheet and income statement. In addition, the accounting requirements have now been moved from the Code itself to Ministerial regulations, meaning that they no longer need the approval of the Parliament or National Diet, allowing them to be more easily changed.

The Ministry of Finance plays a vital role in regulating listed companies. All listed companies are required, under the SEL, to file audited registration documents and annual and semi-annual accounting reports with both the Stock Exchange and the Ministry of Finance. The registration documents and the annual report contain similar information including a balance sheet, income statement, statement of appropriations and various supporting schedules or notes. These documents are in addition to those required under the Commercial Code. The prescribed form and content are more detailed and the requirements are designed less for creditor protection, instead the needs of shareholders predominate. This means that the SEL accounts include additional disclosures and items may be classified somewhat differently. However, as far as the parent company accounts are concerned, the Commercial Code accounts and the SEL accounts should give the same net income and shareholders' equity figures. These statements have to be audited by a registered independent CPA rather than by the statutory auditors.

Much of the Ministry's work in this regard was passed down to the Business Accounting Deliberation Council, now renamed as the Business Accounting Council (BAC). While this may have appeared to be quite similar to the standard-setting bodies of countries like the UK or US it had certain important differences. In particular it was less independent of the government. Its members were appointed by the Ministry and bureaucrats played an important role in initiating and guiding new rules through the legislative process.

While standards are issued under the SEL regulations, and so have to be complied with by all listed companies, they affect far more companies than the 3,000 or so that fall under the SEL regulations. Their wider significance can be seen in the description of the role played by accounting standards as provided in the foreword to the original 1949 version of 'Financial accounting standards for business enterprises' (reproduced in Exhibit 12.4). This shows that the standards seek to codify GAAP, which the tax law requires all companies to follow, even if they are not regulated by the SEL.

| Exhibit 12.4 | Setting of financial accounting standards for business enterprises |

1 *Financial Accounting Standards for Business Enterprises* is the summary of the accounting conventions which have been generally accepted as fair and proper. It should be followed by all business enterprises, even if it has no statutory binding force.

2 *Financial Accounting Standards for Business Enterprises* is what Certified Public Accountants should follow when they audit financial statements under the Certified Public Accountant Law and the Securities and Exchange Act in Japan.

3 *Financial Accounting Standards for Business Enterprises* should be highly regarded when the law and ordinance affecting business accounting, such as the Commercial Code or the tax law, are enacted, amended, or abolished in the future.

Source: Taken from Hirose (1987), p. 35.

This triangular system is now reduced in importance. The standards-setting process has now moved away from the Ministry of Finance and the BAC to a private sector standard-setting body, the Accounting Standards Board (see section 12.3.5 below).

The history of important accounting and auditing regulations, as seen by the accounting profession is shown in Exhibit 12.5.

12.3.2 Auditing

The regulations governing the scope of auditing are set out in Exhibit 12.6.

Recent changes to the audit rules have brought audit practice significantly into line with International Standards on Auditing. The JICPA have issued a number of implementation guidance notes over the last two years to achieve this, while the CPA law was revised in May 2003 to bring them into line with the US Sarbanes–Oxley Act and to permit the establishment of a CPA and Auditing Oversight Board to enhance auditor oversight.

12.3.3 Early influences on accounting regulations

Before the Meiji era (1868–1912), Japan was a closed country made up of some 2,000 feudal entities with political power shared between the *Shogun* (military leaders) and the *daimyo* (feudal lords). There were no formal courts or written laws, accounting was not regulated and a variety of different types of traditional bookkeeping methods were used. While some of these were extremely sophisticated, they were diary-style single-entry systems. This began to change in the 1860s and 1870s when Japan started to look to the west, to develop international trade and to learn from the experiences of other countries. This included, for example, the introduction of double-entry bookkeeping for the first time in Japan in the Yokosuka Steel Works where it was introduced in collaboration with French naval accountants. Particularly important was the Iwakura Mission in 1871, which included over 1,000 officials who went to Europe and the US to see how businesses were organized and how business–government relationships were structured. Japan also began to import accounting texts from a number of countries and to employ foreign accountants to train local accountants.[6]

The influence of the UK in this period can be seen in the work of Alexander Shand. His system was incorporated into the 1872 National Bank Act which included requirements to prepare annual accounts which had to be examined or audited by government officials. However, continental European influences were more important. The first draft of the Civil Code of 1878 was rejected by Japanese jurists as being too close to the French Code from which it was largely derived. The final 1889 version clearly contained influences from French, German and British law. Similarly, the original draft Commercial Code of 1881 was drafted by a German, and both the final version of the Old Commercial Code of 1890 and its amended version or the New Commercial Code of 1899 retained a strong German flavour. This legal framework remains in place and Japanese accounting in consequence continues to retain certain continental European characteristics.

12.3.4 The development of the accounting profession, BADC and BAC

Significant external influences can also be seen in the regulation of listed companies. Following the defeat of Japan in the Second World War, the allied occupation under the

---

[6] Someya (1989).

Exhibit 12.5 History of the accounting and auditing system

1890	Commercial Code enacted
1948	Securities and Exchange Law enacted Certified Public Accountants Law enacted
1949	Financial Accounting Standards for Business Enterprises issued Japanese Institute of Certified Public Accountants established as a self-disciplinary association
1950	Regulations Concerning the Terminology, Forms & Preparation Methods of Financial Statements issued Auditing Standards & related rules issued
1951	Audit by CPAs required under the Securities and Exchange Law Licensed Tax Accountant Law enacted
1963	Financial Statements of companies with shares traded over-the-counter became subject to audit
1966	JICPA recognized as a special legal body according to amended CPA law requiring all CPAs to be members of JICPA
1967	First audit corporation formed in accordance with amended CPA law
1973	IASC established with JICPA as a founding member
1974	Audit by CPAs required under the Commercial Code
1975	Accounting Standards for Consolidated Financial Statements issued Audit of banks and insurance companies by CPAs required
1977	CPA audit of interim and consolidated financial statements begun IFAC established with JICPA as a founding council member
1979	Accounting standards for foreign currency transactions issued
1981	An IASC board meeting held in Tokyo Scope of audit by CPAs expanded and strengthened in revised Commercial Code Auditing manual issued by JICPA auditing committee
1987	13th World Congress of Accountants held in Tokyo
1988	Disclosure requirements for segments drastically revised Disclosure requirements for related party transactions and market value information for marketable securities amended
1991	Auditing standards and related rules drastically revised
1992	The CPA Law relating to examinations and other issues amended
1993	Commercial Code amended to strengthen shareholders' rights and statutory auditors' authority and to improve procedures for issuing debentures
1995	Accounting Standards for Foreign Currency Transactions amended
1998	Fiftieth anniversary of the CPA Practice in Japan
1999	Accounting standards for Financial Instruments issued Commercial Code amended to set forth new Stock Exchange and Transfer System Accounting Standards for Foreign Currency Transactions revised Accounting Standards for Financial Instruments issued
2001	Accounting Standards Board of Japan (of the Financial Accounting Standards Foundation) established as an accounting standards setter
2002	Business Accounting Council published Opinions concerning Revisions of Auditing Standards, Revisions of Interim Auditing Standards & Accounting Standard for Impairment of Fixed Assets. Commercial Code amended to include Ministerial Decree on Financial Statements of Joint Stock Companies Auditing Standards drastically revised
2003	Certified Public Accountants Law amended

Source: www.jicpa.or.jp (August 2004)

| Exhibit 12.6 | Japanese audit requirements |

Certified public accountants have a commitment to the public to provide and enhance the credibility of financial statements by expressing an audit opinion on such financial statements.

GAAS
The CPA audits have been made in accordance with the Auditing Standards codified by the Business Accounting Council (BAC), and audit practice guidelines issued by the JICPA. The Auditing Standards codified by the BAC together with audit guidelines issued by the JICPA are deemed to be the generally accepted auditing standards (GAAS) in Japan.

In Japan, certified public accountants provide audit services in the following areas:

Statutory Audits
The Commercial Code and Related Laws

- Companies (Kabushiki Kaisha) with outstanding common stock of ¥500 million or more or total liabilities of ¥20,000 million or more
- Mutual insurance companies, credit banks (shinyo kinko), credit cooperatives (shinyo kumiai), and labor banks (rodo kinko) specified by relevant laws

The Securities and Exchange Law

- Companies initially listing and already listed on stock exchanges
- Companies initially registering and already registered with the Japan Securities Dealers Association
- Companies initially offering and have offered to the public securities of at least ¥500 million
- Companies with at least 500 shareholders

Other Statutory Audits

- Private schools receiving subsidy from national or local government
- Labor unions
- Political party's subsidy report prepared in accordance with the Political Party Grant Law.
- Local Governments

Non-Statutory Audits
- Companies in which the Small and Medium Business Investment and Consultation Company has made an investment
- Religious organizations, non-profit organizations, consumers cooperatives, and healthcare organizations
- Audits in connection with mergers, business transfers, and acquisitions
- Other audits not covered above

Cross-Border Audits
- Japanese companies with cross border listings
- Operations in Japan of foreign companies

Source: Japanese Institute of Certified Public accountants web page www.jicpa.or.jp

American General MacArthur set out *inter alia* to reform and restructure Japanese business. An important element of this was the disbanding of the 15 most powerful *zaibatsu* or large financial combines which controlled much of Japanese business and the sale of the shares of the constituent companies to the general public. For this to succeed the stock market, which was not very active, had to be reconstructed to provide external shareholders with sufficient security at an acceptable cost to make share ownership an attractive proposition. The occupation forces naturally turned to the US to provide a model of how to do this and in an albeit modified form, they imported and imposed the relevant US laws. One of the things required was a highly skilled and highly regarded profession of independent auditors to attest the accounts of listed companies.

The CPA law was passed in 1948, leading to the creation of the Japanese Institute of Certified Public Accountants (JICPA). The Securities and Exchange Commission, an independent body designed to oversee the securities market, was also established in the same year. However, this was disbanded in 1953 and its role transferred instead to the Ministry of Finance (MoF). Of long-term importance was the Securities and Exchange Law (SEL) of 1949 which still forms the basis of the regulation of listed companies. Also created was the Investigation Committee on Business Accounting Systems (ICBAS), an independent body charged with developing accounting standards. It began work by issuing, in 1949, two statements: the 'Working Rules for Preparing Financial Statements' and the 'Financial Accounting Standards for Business Enterprises' (also known as the 'Business Accounting Principles'). The latter was very heavily influenced by 'A Statement of Accounting Principles' which had been published by the American AICPA in 1938. In 1952 the ICBAS ceased to be an independent body when it was effectively made a part of the Ministry of Finance. It also changed its name to the Business Accounting Deliberation Council (BADC). While the power to regulate accounting had therefore passed from independent bodies to the government and the bureaucracy, the BADC retained an important role. The profession, in the form of JICPA, was represented on this body, as were academics and representatives from the business community (the *Keidanren*, or the Japanese Federation of Economic Organisations, banks and commercial corporations), the Tokyo Stock Exchange (TSE), the Securities Analysts' Association and various other interested parties. All members were appointed by the Ministry of Finance, which also provided the funding.

The BADC issued a number of standards including:

- 'Financial accounting standards for business enterprises' (first issued in 1949 and amended a number of times since then);
- 'Financial accounting standards on consolidated financial statements' (June 1975 and later amendments, revised June 1997);
- 'Standards for the preparation of interim financial statements';
- 'Accounting standards for foreign currency translation';
- 'Consolidated financial reporting';
- 'Tax effect accounting';
- 'Employee retirement benefits';
- 'Financial instruments'.

It also issued a number of interpretations concerned, *inter alia*, with the problems of reconciling financial accounting standards with Commercial Code and tax law requirements.

In July 2000 there was a further reorganisation with the establishment under the Ministry of Finance of the Financial Services Agency (FSA) with a remit that includes the Securities Exchange law, securities markets trading rules, establishment of business accounting standards, planning and policy on corporate finance and the supervision of CPAs. As part of this, the renamed Business Accounting Council (BAC) was brought under the FSA as an advisory body which 'establishes business accounting standards and audit standards, and at the same time conducts investigations and deliberations concerning the unification of cost accounting and the development and improvement of other aspects of the business accounting system, and reports to the Commissioner of the FSA and others.'[7]

---

[7] www.fsa.go.jp.

12.3.5 The Accounting Standards Board and the Financial Accounting Standards Foundation

Ten private sector organizations including the Keidanren, JICPA and TSE came together in February 2001 to initiate a private sector standard-setting organization. This lead, in July 2001, to the establishment of the Financial Accounting Standards Foundation (FASF) and, underneath this, the Accounting Standard Board of Japan (ASBJ) which then took over from the BAC as the main standard-setting body, while the BAC retained its position as an advisory council to the FSA. The relationship between the FASF and the ASBJ is shown in Exhibit 12.7.

Two main factors led to the creation of this new organization. First, it was recognized that increasing globalization and sophistication of business and financial transactions meant that there was an increased need for new standards and, secondly, it was important to establish a system that could collaborate with and respond quickly and efficiently to the IASB and changes to IFRS. Accordingly, the objective of the FASF is to 'contribute to the sound development of financial practices in Japan and sound capital markets by making recommendations and contributions to the international accounting system by studying, researching, and developing generally accepted accounting standards, and by studying and researching disclosure system and various other practices pertinent to business finance systems'.[8] To do this, the FASF carries out five activities:

- study research and develop generally accepted accounting standards;
- study and research disclosure systems, as well as various other practices pertinent to business finance systems;
- make recommendations based on results of these;
- help develop and improve international accounting standards;
- other business necessary to discharge objectives.

Exhibit 12.7 **Organization of the Financial Accounting Standards Foundation, 2001**

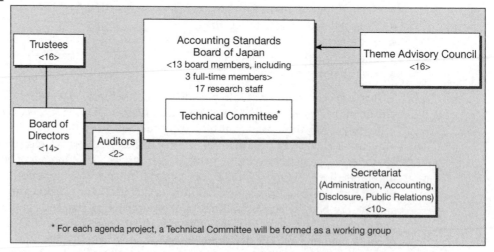

* For each agenda project, a Technical Committee will be formed as a working group

Source: www.asb/or/jp/e_fasf

---

[8] www.asb.or.jp.

Exhibit 12.8 Organization of the ASBJ (2004)

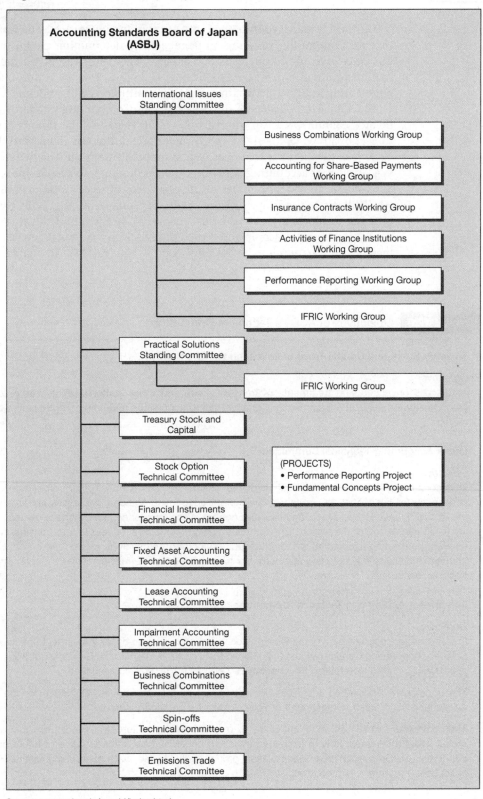

Source: www.asb.or.jp/e_asbj/index.html

The FASF is managed by a Board of Directors and by Trustees. The former are responsible for fund raising, deciding on members and determining the business plan, while the latter give advice on plans and budgets and select the Board members and the Auditors. Currently there are 14 Directors, only one of which is full-time, with the rest representing industry, audit firms, financial institutions and academia.

The ASBJ is responsible for the development of accounting standards via a number of themed committees as shown in Exhibit 12.8. These include various items that are the subject of a BAC Opinion (e.g. Impairment accounting) or changes to the Commercial Code (e.g. Earnings per share), as well as proposals from the Themed Advisory Council (e.g. Fixed asset accounting) and other sources of proposals such as the Koyoto Protocol. Exhibit 12.9 provides examples of the objectives of some of the technical committees which illustrate the sources of the original agenda items. The ASBJ currently has two full-time members plus 11 part-time members. As with the FASF, these include CPAs, academics, business people and representatives from various financial institutions. All members of the founding bodies must comply with the ASBJ standards.

Exhibit 12.9 Objectives of ASBJ's Technical Committees

Treasury Stock and Capital Transactions Technical Committee

Objective
To discuss on accounting treatments of treasury stock and other matters, which was resulted from the amendments on July 2001 Commercial Code restricting acquisition and holding of treasury stock and other matters.

Lease Accounting Technical Committee

Objective
In accordance with the recommendation of the Theme Advisory Council, this committee focuses on the accounting for finance leases. In Japan, the current accounting standard for leases allows alternative treatments that finance leased assets and liabilities can be off-balance-sheet, unless those ownerships are explicitly to be transferred to the lessee. The committee also takes operating leases into consideration and totally reviews the existing accounting standard including whether they shall be recognized on balance sheet. The committee discusses accounting standards for leases based on current practices in Japan and international trends of accounting for leases.

Impairment Accounting Technical Committee

Objective
In response to the publication of the Opinions on Accounting Standards for Impairment of Fixed Assets by the Business Accounting Council (August 9, 2002), ASBJ is going to prepare the Guidance for Impairment of Fixed Assets and decided to establish the Impairment Accounting Technical Committee.

The Impairment Accounting Technical Committee will discuss setting the Guidance for the application of Accounting Standards for Impairment of Fixed Assets for practical issues.

The committee focuses on treatment of detailed issues as illustration of any indication that an asset (asset group) may be impaired, how to estimate net selling prices and basis for estimate of future cash flows, discount rate used in calculating an asset's (asset group's) value in use, ways of grouping assets, treatment for an asset uses in common and goodwill.

Source: www.asb.or.jp

12.3.6 The introduction of consolidated accounting

Many specific accounting rules show the influence of foreign practices. Consolidated accounting provides a particularly good illustration of the conscious importing of a foreign practice.

Until the 1960s, consolidated accounts were not produced. However, the 1960s and 1970s were marked by a number of high-profile bankruptcies which were either caused by or made worse by profit manipulation which remained undetected under single-entity accounting. In addition, the oil crises of the early 1970s led to a number of mergers and takeovers with companies becoming larger and more complex. A number of Japanese companies also had to produce consolidated accounts to achieve a listing on a foreign stock exchange. For example, Sony was the first Japanese company to list on the New York Stock Exchange (NYSE) in 1961, closely followed by Honda, Mitsubishi and Matsushita. The NYSE refused to accept single-entity accounts. Thus, by 1973, more than 60 Japanese companies had had to produce consolidated accounts. Likewise, a number of US companies wanted to list in Japan and they had to gain permission from the Tokyo Stock Exchange to be allowed to list when producing group or consolidated accounts instead of individual company accounts. By the end of 1973 Citicorp, Dow Chemical and First Chicago Corp. had achieved listings on the TSE on this basis.[9]

It has been argued[10] that these factors all meant that the Japanese perceived their accounts to be of a lower quality or status than those of companies from many other countries. It has also been argued that cultural features were particularly important, especially something that has been called the 'shame culture' of Japan.[11] This is a culture where individuals are motivated by the need to avoid the adverse reactions of others: in other words, values are derived from external stimuli. This prompted them to consider the introduction of consolidated accounts. A second cultural feature was also important in helping to explain the process by which consolidated accounts were introduced, namely the wish to avoid conflict, so that harmony and concessional decision making are both important. This meant that non-governmental groups were consulted over the proposed standards, with the BADC playing an important advisory role. Thus, it took fully 12 years and over 60 meetings of the BADC for the MoF to issue Ordinances on consolidated accounts and another five years before they were tightened and increased in scope. The MoF could have unilaterally imposed them as soon as requested by the Diet in 1965, but did not. It is also interesting to note that the *Keidanren* (employers' federation) did not oppose the proposals from any theoretical perspective but instead argued that their implementation would be too difficult.

The 1977 rules were heavily influenced by the rules of other countries, in particular the US, despite controversy over whether or not such rules were appropriate in the Japanese context. (As discussed below, the structure of the typical Japanese group differs quite markedly from the pyramid structure based upon total or majority ownership of subsidiaries and sub-subsidiaries as is typically found in developed western countries.)

Exhibit 12.10 sets out a description of the process that the MoF went through in seeking a consensus over this issue in the period up to the early 1980s.

As consolidation was initially contentious and not supported by the *Keidanren*, the rules when first introduced were something of a compromise and allowed subsidiaries to be

---

[9] McKinnon (1984).

[10] McKinnon (1986).

[11] Cooke (1991).

| Exhibit 12.10 | History of the regulations for consolidated accounts |

1965	Diet requests the Ministry of Finance to improve corporate disclosure under the Securities Exchange Law.
1965	The MoF requests the BADC to prepare an interim report on consolidated financial statements, with the idea of improving corporate disclosure.
1966	The BADC reports to the MoF and the ministry releases an Exposure Draft on Consolidation for public review.
1966	The Keidanren reports that it supports the exposure draft in principle but that it strongly opposes the implementation of consolidation in the near future.
1967	The MoF releases its 'Opinion on Consolidated Statements' which supports the introduction of consolidation.
1971	Diet revises the Securities Exchange Law to require that the financial statement of important subsidiaries be attached to the parent-only statements and calls on the MoF to draft the necessary new provisions and revision clauses for the introduction of consolidation.
1971	The BADC resumes discussion on consolidation.
1975	The BADC releases financial accounting standards for consolidated financial statements.
1976	The MoF issues Ordinances 27 to 30 operational from fiscal periods commencing April 1 1977.
1981	The MoF revises the consolidation Ordinances to make equity accounting mandatory and to tighten the materiality exclusion clause.

Source: McKinnon and Harrison (1985), p. 209.

excluded if they were not material. In this context, 'material' was defined as being less than 10 per cent of both the combined assets and sales of the parent and the consolidated subsidiaries. Earnings were not included in the definition of materiality, as it would have made the requirements too restrictive. However, this exclusion clause was perhaps too successful in reducing the impact of the consolidation requirements. The Ministry of Finance estimated that only 27 per cent of all subsidiaries were actually consolidated in 1979/80, most of the rest being excluded because of liberal interpretations of the materiality exclusion clause. The materiality exclusion clause was tightened in 1981, when a 10 per cent income criterion was also added; this meant that many more subsidiaries had to be consolidated. However, Japanese companies still continued to exclude many subsidiaries from consolidation.

A standard issued in June 1997, effective for fiscal periods starting on or after 1 April 1999, changed this position and brought Japanese practice much more into line with IAS 27. The 1997 standard introduced guideline materiality criteria of between 3 and 5 per cent. Perhaps more importantly it also changed the definition of a subsidiary. Previously, the definition was based exclusively upon ownership. The standard introduced the concept of control into the definition. The standard also had the effect of increasing the amount of information produced in the Japanese-language statements of most companies. It required the consolidated statements, not the parent company statements, to be treated as the more important set of statements and therefore also meant that all companies would produce a consolidated cash flow statement. (Most companies producing English-language statements were already providing a cash flow statement.)

A BAC Statement of Opinion, Accounting for Business Combinations, was issued in 2003 to take effect from 2006. It is described in more detail in section 16.3.4.

12.4 Institutions

12.4.1 Political and economic system

Japan has a liberal-democratic parliamentary system of government and government–business relations may be characterized in terms of cooperation. The government is actively involved in regulating and guiding businesses. A noticeable feature of this system is the bureaucracy, which is far more important and influential than it is in most western democratic societies. Ministerial officials draft legislative bills, brief parliamentary committees and commissions of enquiry and present bills personally to Parliament (the Diet). Particularly important for business is the powerful Ministry of International Trade and Investment (MITI) which, while less influential than many western authors claim, has played a significant role in managing the corporate sector. Also important is the powerful employers' federation, the *Keidanren* which, while not a formal part of the political or government system, plays an important role in influencing government–business relationships and the regulation of business, including the regulation of accounting.

One of the most important features of the economic system that affects accounting is the way in which business is organized. Japanese trade was dominated by powerful trading houses which formed the basis of the *zaibatsu* (large financial combines). These groups were broken up after the Second World War and, in an attempt to stop them re-forming, the 1946 Anti-monopoly Law (modelled on US laws) prohibited holding companies. However, it is not so easy to regulate business behaviour and the *zaibatsu* have been largely replaced by *keiretsu*. Lacking a holding company, the *keiretsu* tend instead to be quite loose networks of related companies which are centred around a bank, trading company (*sogo shosha*) or large manufacturing company. Typically, the size of shareholdings held by the lead company is small, with minority cross-holdings between group members being important. The group is also maintained through interlocking directorships and meetings of key staff. Intergroup sales and purchases are often also important and long credit terms, especially in times of financial difficulty, are not uncommon. The relationships may also be cemented by a number of other activities such as joint research and development projects. In practice, there are four different types of *keiretsu*:[12]

- the six largest corporate groups consisting of three ex-*zaibatso* groups, including Mitsui, Mitsubishi and Sumitomo;
- three bank groups – Fuyo, Sanwa and Daiichi-Kangyo;
- *keiretsu* organized along vertical lines of production (e.g. Toyota); and
- *keiretsu* organized along vertical lines of distribution (e.g. Panasonic).

The example of the cross-holdings of the Mitsubishi Group is shown in Exhibit 12.11. For example, Mitsubishi Corp. holds 1.6 per cent of the Mitsubishi Bank while the latter holds 4.7 per cent of the former.

The impact of the *keiretsu* on accounting has been much debated. It has been argued for example that they have led to lower levels of disclosure to outsiders and lower profits as less efficient management are protected from the rigours of the corporate control market. However, there is also evidence that such insider relationships actually increase the

---

[12] Kumar and Hyodo (2001).

Exhibit 12.11 Mitsubishi Corporation cross-holdings (1994) (all figures are percentages)

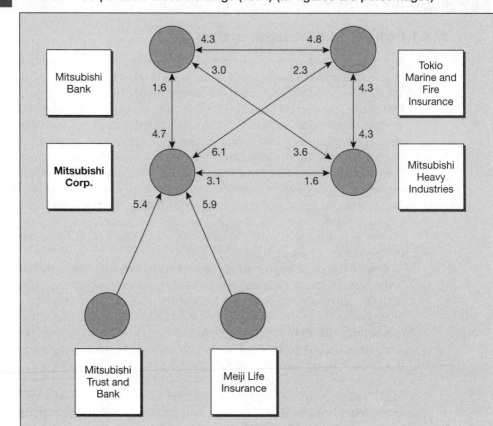

Source: Douthett and Jung (2001), p. 139.

effectiveness of the monitoring of management and decrease the ability of management to manage earnings so increasing the quality and predictability of accounting numbers.[13]

The economic system also impacts upon particular measurement rules. For example, the collapse of Asia–Pacific economies in 1997 had repercussions in Japan which meant that some banks were not able to collect investments in and loans to other countries, while the long period of expansion over a 50-year period saw a pause. This had consequences for accounting and auditing. For example, the poor performance of investments meant that many companies found themselves with large pension-fund obligations which led to a review of the accounting for retirement benefits. This led to the introduction of a new standard which is very similar to IAS 19.

12.4.2 Legal system

The legal system is a code-based legal system. While it has been influenced by other countries, such as France and Germany, it also has some unique features. Like other code law countries, business relationships are regulated by the Commercial Code (CC).

---

[13] See, for example, Cheung *et al.* (1999); Jiang and Kim (2000); Douthett and Jung (2001).

The CC, being set by the Ministry of Justice, is concerned with ensuring that all parties to a contract are protected, especially lenders and other creditors. The emphasis is therefore placed upon single-entity reporting – as it is the legal entity not the group that enters into the legal contracts – and upon prudence or conservatism in reporting performance.

12.4.3 Taxation system

The Japanese corporate tax system has been described as a mixed system. It retains a German influence, seen in the relative importance of the Commercial Code in prescribing methods of tax computation, while it has also been influenced by the US system, seen in its reliance upon GAAP.

The Corporation Income Tax (CT) law does not contain sufficiently detailed rules to enable companies to calculate taxable income. Instead, it relies upon other sources of authority. In particular, it requires companies to use the Commercial Code as the basis for computing much of its taxable income, hence the continental European-style rules that allowances or expenses are permitted for tax purposes only if they are also included in the published accounts. However, the Commercial Code is not exhaustive and does not unambiguously define income. The CT law requires companies to use GAAP if there are no specific regulations and where it does not conflict with the CT law.

There is a clear relationship between reported income and taxable income. If a company changes its methods of calculating reportable income then it will probably also change its taxable income. However, the two income measures are not identical. While the Commercial Code and GAAP form the basis of taxable income, the CT law also prescribes a number of adjustments to reported income, expenses and allowances. There are a number of reasons for this. In particular, CT law is also designed to provide tax incentives to encourage companies to meet the government's economic goals – additional or special depreciation over and above economic or ordinary depreciation, for example, is allowed for under the Special Taxation Measures Law. Special depreciation is recognized as an expense for tax purposes, while under the Commercial Code it is reported as an appropriation of retained earnings. The impact of economic policy considerations can also be seen in a number of other areas of accounting including the further use of reserve accounting. Companies are permitted to set up a number of tax-free reserves. Some of these, such as reserves for bad debts, are permitted under both CT law and the Commercial Code. A considerable number of other tax-free reserves are instead treated as an expense under the Special Taxation Measures Law and so deducted from earnings before taxation, while under Commercial Code they are instead treated as appropriations of retained earnings. While the importance of these measures have declined recently, as Japan has increasingly moved towards an 'equity in taxation' perspective, they still remain important. Just how common these reserves still are is illustrated in Exhibit 12.12, which lists the reserves permitted in the Special Taxation Measurement Law for fiscal year 2003.[14]

The importance of these special tax measures can be seen in the fact that they cost an estimated ¥1,792bn in terms of lost tax revenues in the 2003 fiscal year as shown in Exhibit 12.13.

---

[14] www.mof.go.jp/English/tax/taxes2003e.htm.

| Exhibit 12.12 | Reserves permitted in the Special Taxation Measurement Law |

- Overseas investment loss reserve
- Reserve for prevention of mineral pollution in metal mining
- Reserve for prevention of certain disasters
- Reserve for changing the heat quantity of gas
- Reserve for loss in buying-back computers
- Reserve for preparing for presentations at the Japan International Exhibition
- Used nuclear fuel reprocessing reserve
- Nuclear plant dismantling reserve
- Reserve for extraordinary casualties
- Special reserve for repair ships or furnaces
- Reserve for locating new mineral beds
- Reserve for improvement of urban railway systems
- Reserve for large-scale repair of Shinkansen railways
- Reserve for Kansai or Central Japan International Airport Adjustment
- Reserve for utilisation and accumulation of farmland

Source: Ministry of Finance, www.mof.go.jp/english/tax/taxes2004e.htm

Companies disclose varying amounts of information on taxes, although one particularly interesting example is TDK, which discloses in its March 2004 annual report a reconciliation between the statutory tax rate of 41 per cent and the effective tax rate actually paid of 24 per cent, as illustrated in Exhibit 12.14.

12.4.4 Corporate financing system

The Tokyo Stock Exchange (TSE) is the largest of the Japanese stock markets with 2,174 domestic and 32 foreign companies listed on it at the end of 2003[15] (see Exhibit 4.3).

For a period in the late 1980s the TSE was the largest in the world, as measured by market capitalization. Now, following the recession of the early 1990s and a major fall in share prices,[16] it is the second largest behind the NYSE. However, these figures are slightly misleading. The TSE has a relatively low market turnover with 316,124 million domestic shares and 6,419,000 foreign shares being traded in 2003. This is partly because many shareholdings take the form of cross-holdings and are not actively traded and partly because the personal taxation system encourages long-term shareholdings by taxing dividends at a higher rate than capital gains. Thus, on the basis of market turnover, the TSE is also smaller than NASDAQ and London.

---

[15] Tokyo Stock Exchange annual report (2004).

[16] For example, the NIKKEI share price index fell from an all-time high of 38,916 in December 1990 to a low of 14,390 in August 1992.

Exhibit 12.13	The estimated loss of revenue due to Special Taxation Measures for Corporations, fiscal year 2003

	Billion yen
A. Special depreciation	
1. Special depreciation on specified equipment	
Anti-pollution equipment	6.0
Seacraft etc.	3.0
2. Special depreciation on R&D equipment	79.0
3. Special depreciation on medical equipment etc.	10.0
4. Immediate depreciation on low-value assets	41.0
5. Others	24.0
Sub-total	163.0
B. Reserves	
6. For reprocessing of used nuclear fuels	37.0
7. For removal and disposal of nuclear material used in power generation	14.0
8. Others	25.0
Sub-total	76.0
C. Tax credits and income deduction etc.	
9. Credit for the total amount of research expenses	649.0
10. Tax measures to promote reform of structure of energy supply & demand	25.0
11. Tax measures to improve management fundamentals of SME	10.0
12. Credit for promoting investment by SME	171.0
13. Special depreciation of tax on retained earnings of family corporation	174.0
14. IT investment incentives	517.0
15. Others	7.0
Sub-total	1,553.0
Total revenue loss	1,792.0

Source: Ministry of Finance www.mof.go.jp/english/tax/taxes2004e.htm

The TSE underwent a major structural reform, the so-called 'Japanese Big-Bang', in 1998 to make it more competitive and to make share trading more appealing. This included the introduction of off-exchange trading of listed securities, followed in January 1999 by reductions in the listing requirements for medium-sized companies and, in July 1999, by the introduction of the TDnet (timely disclosure network) which, *inter alia*, means all listed products are traded via a computerized trading system and the information filed with the TSE is also made available on its website. However, while Tokyo is one of the largest and most modern stock exchanges in the world, it differs from most other large stock markets in that international companies are not important. Unlike exchanges such as NYSE, London or Euronext, the number of foreign companies listed has decreased every year since 1998. In 1998 there were 52 listed overseas companies; by the end of 2003 this had fallen to 32, in contrast to the more than 300 in each of Euronext, London, NASDAQ and NYSE (see Exhibit 4.3).

The more important source of finance for most companies has traditionally been bank loans. In the past, these have tended to be short-term loans, although this is changing and the financing patterns of Japanese companies are beginning to resemble more closely those of US or UK companies. Most large companies tend to have close

| Exhibit 12.14 | Income Taxes reconciliation statement of TDK Corporation, 2003 |

Note 7. Income taxes

The Company and its domestic subsidiaries are subject to a national corporate tax of 30 per cent, an inhabitants tax of between 5.2 per cent and 6.2 per cent and a deductible enterprise tax of between 9.6 per cent and 10.1 per cent, which in the aggregate resulted in a statutory rate of approximately 41 per cent in the years ended March 31, 2004, 2003 and 2002.

Amendments to Japanese tax regulations were enacted into law on March 24, 2003. As a result of this amendment, the statutory income tax rate was reduced from approximately 41 per cent to 40 per cent effective from April 1, 2004. Current income taxes were calculated at the rate of 41 per cent, in effect for the years ended March 31, 2004, 2003 and 2002, respectively. Deferred tax assets and liabilities expected to be realized or settled on or after April 1, 2004 have been calculated at the rate of 40 per cent.

The effects of the income tax rate reduction on deferred income tax balances as of March 31, 2003 reduced the net deferred tax asset by approximately ¥1,044 million.

The effective tax rate of the Company for the years ended March 31, 2004, 2003 and 2002, are reconciled with the Japanese statutory tax rate in the following table:

	2004	2003	2002
Japanese statutory tax rate	41.0%	41.0%	41.0%
Expenses not deductible for tax purposes	1.2	0.5	0.2
Non taxable income	(0.0)	(2.4)	(1.0)
Difference in statutory tax rates of foreign subsidiaries	(23.1)	(22.6)	(3.0)
Change in the valuation allowance	6.4	14.8	4.8
Change in enacted tax laws and rates	0.3	5.8	–
Currency translation adjustment	(0.0)	(3.3)	–
Investment tax credit	(1.6)	(4.5)	(1.0)
Other	(0.6)	0.0	2.1
Effective tax rate	23.6%	29.3%	38.9%

Source: TDK annual report (2003), p. 54. www.tdk.co.jp

relationships with a key bank and short-term bank loans are automatically rolled over. (Note that this has the effect of making typical working capital and long-term debt to equity ratios different from what might be expected with UK or US companies.) One of the advantages of being a member of a *keiretsu* is that the central bank is more likely to increase lending in periods of difficulty to prevent a crisis occurring. In many countries, such as the UK, large companies typically have relationships with numerous banks; these may even compete with each other to be the first to call in their loans at the first sign of difficulty.

12.4.5 The accounting profession

The first institute of professional accountants was created in 1927, although the profession in its current form originates in the post-Second World War period as one of the creations of the American occupation forces. The CPA law (1948) required accountants to be suitably trained (in a manner and at a level similar to US accountants). This led to the creation of the Japanese Institute of Certified Public Accountants (JICPA) in 1949, although it was not until 1966 that all CPAs had to be members of the JICPA (see Exhibit 12.5).

All companies regulated by the Securities and Exchange Law, large Commercial Code-regulated companies, financial institutions and various other types of organisations have to be audited by a registered CPA. The profession itself is very small with only 13,226 CPAs plus a further 4,038 junior accountants (having passed stage 2 of the professional exams) and 149 audit corporations at the end of 2000.[17] However, this represents a significant growth over the last two or three decades mirroring the increase in audit requirements. For example, there were 4,162 CPAs and 24 audit corporations in 1970 and 8,799 CPAs and 110 audit corporations in 1990. While this shows a remarkable growth the absolute size of figures is misleading as the tax accountants, who are much larger in number, do much of the work required by the CT Law and they have their own professional body and examinations. A second difference from the UK or US is that far fewer people train as accountants and subsequently leave the profession to join commercial or financial institutions. This difference can largely be ascribed to cultural differences. Japan is famous for lifetime employment, although its importance tends to be overstated in that it applies only to larger companies and to the more skilled workforce. (Even here, people tend to take early retirement and then continue to work after this on a consultancy or short-term contract basis.) However, lifetime employment policies and the philosophy of group membership and loyalty to the company are far stronger in Japan than they are in most other countries – commercial and financial institutions prefer to train their own staff and place far less emphasis upon external training or professional qualifications.

Despite this, the competition to enter the profession has historically been extremely intense and the success rate has correspondingly been low. The examinations are set by the government; the first exam is an entrance exam open to all non-graduates and which tests general literary ability. The second stage allows successful candidates to become junior accountants. The success rate in the second set of examinations has historically been below 10 per cent with only about half of the successful candidates going on to pass the third and final set of examinations in their first sitting at the end of a further minimum of three years of training and practical experience.

The JICPA acts to a large extent as a trade body. The CPA examinations are controlled by the government not the Institute, and the JICPA does not issue accounting standards. Instead, its role is limited to issuing opinions and advice to its members to clarify the legal accounting requirements. It also acts to maintain professional conduct and ethics and sponsors training and professional development of its members and issues auditing guidelines.

12.5 External influences

Section 12.3 above, which described the development of accounting regulation in Japan, is also very largely a history of how Japan has imported help or ideas from overseas. Thus, section 12.3 showed how the early Commercial Codes were heavily influenced by practice in continental Europe while the US played a major role in introducing legislation

---

[17] www.jicpa.or.jp (August 2001).

after the Second World War which created the Securities and Exchange Law, the JICPA and the BADC.

US influence is seen in the English language reports of Japanese companies. When companies were first required to prepare consolidated financial statements in conformity with Japanese GAAP in 1975, some companies were allowed by special regulation to submit US GAAP consolidated financial statements to the Ministry of Finance in place of Japanese GAAP statements. These were companies registered with the US SEC at the time. Over the period of 30 years further companies became registered with the US SEC but they were not named in the special regulation and so had to produce consolidated financial statements under both sets of GAAP. The list was only updated in 2002. The special regulation does not allow IFRS to be substituted for Japanese GAAP.

12.6 Accounting regulations and the IASB

As we saw in section 1.7, Japan was one of the founding members of the IASC in 1973 and JICPA members have a long tradition of involvement in the process of setting international accounting standards. However, active involvement in the work of the IASB does not guarantee compliance with IFRS, and Japan has in the past illustrated this point. The standard-setting process as set up after the Second World War was largely independent of the government. Shortly after this, it was successfully captured by the government and the bureaucracy so that the profession played a relatively minor role in setting standards. Japanese rule setters therefore were not greatly influenced by the work of the IASB. However, this position has changed in the last few years, most obviously with the move to a private sector standard-setting system with the FASF and the ASBJ. Japan was increasingly conscious that its standards were often thought of as being inadequate in comparison to most other major countries. It was also conscious of the importance of the IASB and the need to have a voice in international standard-setting. These two pressures were largely responsible for the establishment of the new system, as described above in section 12.3.5, and the choice of a structure that is similar to other standard setters such as the US and UK as well as the IASB.

Japan has not given a firm or unequivocal commitment to convergence although this does not necessarily mean that it does not intend to converge. Currently, foreign companies listed in Japan can use home or third jurisdiction accounting standards which means that they can use IFRS if they wish. Domestic companies in contrast are not allowed to use IFRS although, as stated by the BAC in June 2004, it is 'open to further consideration to accept IFRS-based consolidated financial statements for Japanese issuers in the future'.[18] Similar support for increasing convergence is seen in a recent statement made by the FSA in its April 2004 pamphlet comparing Japanese GAAP, US GAAP and IFRS (Exhibit 12.15).

The statement by the ASBJ on convergence, reproduced in Exhibit 12.16, explains why Japan has not wholeheartedly endorsed convergence. Indeed, it can be argued that it would be unrealistic given the Japanese culture to expect Japan to fully endorse a system of convergence without firstly knowing exactly what would be involved. As such, it could be argued that this statement is effectively a statement of endorsement.

---

[18] BAC (June 2004).

Exhibit 12.15 FSA statement on convergence, April 2004

Accounting, auditing and disclosure systems in Japan are essentially equivalent to and consistent with internationally recognized systems.

Convergence is an important goal for all market participants to foster confidence and efficiency in global capital markets. In this context, continued efforts towards this goal will be made.

Japanese securities issuers have played an active part in the EU markets. There are approximately 75 Japanese issuers with shares listed and at least 180 issuers with bonds listed within the EU.

Financial statements prepared in accordance with Japanese GAAP and audited in accordance with Japanese GAAS have been widely accepted by investors in the EU markets as well as foreign investors in Japanese markets.

Given these facts, both the EU markets and Japanese securities issuers will benefit from the continued use of financial statements prepared in accordance with Japanese GAAP and audited in accordance with Japanese GAAS.

Source: www.fsa.go.jp/refer/jgaap/e20040419–1/04.pdf

The Japanese accounting and auditing systems have changed quite significantly since 1999. One illustration of this can be seen in the comparison of the 1999 and 2003 accounts of All Nippon Airways Co. Ltd in their English-language annual report. The March 1999 statement, as shown in Exhibit 12.17, lists an large number of differences, covering such important areas such as consolidation deferred taxation, translation, marketable securities and segments. In contrast, the March 2003 accounts, as shown in Exhibit 12.18 describe only two items: leases, and impairment of property and equipment.

Exhibit 12.16 ASBJ Statement on Convergence, April 2003

- International integration of capital markets and that of market systems including accounting standards are two sides of the same coin. Market infrastructures will be fully integrated when domestic capital markets are internationally integrated. We agree with such result as the ultimate goal, and in our view, convergence represents such ultimate and desirable goal. To promote convergence, sufficient discussion and consensus-building among participants in the domestic market are necessary. Therefore, we cannot make commitment that convergence should always come first even for the matters to which we cannot assent on any terms. However, we think it is also true of the countries that announced the intention of convergence, in particular United States and European Countries.

- ASBJ is positively taking part in international discussions and making every effort to improve our own standards, with our mission in our article of organisation, to contribute to development of international accounting standards. ASBJ will continuously make maximum efforts to contribute to convergence of accounting standards and to enhance harmonisation of our own standards with IFRS.

Source: www.asb.or.jp/e_asbj/ifad_report.html

Exhibit 12.17 All Nippon Airways Co. Ltd: consolidated accounts (1999 extract)

The accompanying consolidated financial statements of the Company are principally prepared in conformity with accounting principles and practices generally accepted in Japan, which differ from International Accounting Standards mainly in the following respects:

(a) Consolidation and the equity method of accounting . . .

(b) Tax-effect accounting . . .

(c) Foreign currency translations . . .

(d) Leases . . .

(e) Market value information of marketable securities . . .

(f) Funds in trust . . .

[These are included in current assets and are short-term funds managed by trust banks; they consist mainly of marketable equity securities and interest bearing bonds.]

(g) Employees' retirement benefits . . .

(h) Segment information . . .

(i) Information reflecting changing prices . . .

(j) Related party disclosures . . .

Source: All Nippon Airways, annual report (1999).

Exhibit 12.18 All Nippon Airways Co. Ltd: consolidated accounts (2003 extract)

Accounting principles and practices generally accepted in Japan differ from International Financial Reporting (IFRS) in the following material respects:

(a) Finance leases

IFRS require finance leases to be recognised as assets and liabilities in the balance sheet at an amount equal to the fair value of the leased property at the inception of the lease or, if lower, at the present value of the minimum lease payments.

Accounting principles and practices generally accepted in Japan allow a company either to recognise finance lease as assets and liabilities in the balance sheet as required by IFRS or to account for them as operating leases, unless ownership of the leased property is transferred to the lessee at the end of the lease term. In the latter case, certain information . . . is required to be disclosed.

(b) Impairment of property and equipment

IFRS require a company to carry property and equipment at its cost less any accumulated depreciation, subject to the requirement to write an asset down to its recoverable amount. The carrying amount of property and equipment should be reviewed periodically in order to assess whether the recoverable amount has declined below the carrying amount.

Accounting principles and practices generally accepted in Japan do not require a company to assess the recoverability and recognise impairment of property and equipment, if any.

Source: All Nippon Airways annual report (2003), p. 60. www.ana.co.jp/eng/aboutana/corporate/ir/index_fl.html

Even prior to the establishment of the ASBJ in July 2001, the BADC had issued a number of important statements that essentially harmonized Japanese practice with IASs. These covered, for March 2000 year ends, accounting standards on:

- consolidated financial statements policies and procedures,
- consolidated statements of cash flows,
- interperiod tax allocations,
- research and development costs.

For March 2001 year ends the changes also covered:

- pensions,
- financial instruments,
- interim consolidated financial statements.

At the establishment of the ASBJ, the BAC was tasked with completing those standards it was then considering. Since then, it has issued long awaited standards on the impairment of assets (September 2002) and business combinations (October 2003).

The ASBJ had issued two standards by mid-2004 – Financial Accounting Standard 1 (FAS 1) on Treasury stock and reduction of legal reserves (February 2002) and FAS 2 on Earnings per share (September 2002). It has also issued six implementation guidance statements on the impairment of fixed assets; retirement benefits; treasury stock and legal reserves; distribution of capital surplus; and earnings per share. The technical committees on fixed assets, leases, share options and financial instruments still had not agreed standards by this time.

The FSA issued, in April 2004, a list of the differences that they saw between Japanese GAAP and IFRS. This listed only seven areas: financial instruments; business combinations; impairment of assets; retirement benefits; R&D; consolidated financial statements; and investment properties. While this appears at first sight to be quite an extensive list, many of the items are relatively minor or unimportant for most companies. Only in the case of R&D and goodwill amortization may it be said that the Japanese rules conflict with IFRS, in the other cases it is specific parts of the standards that differ. Exhibit 12.19 lists the differences identified by the FSA.

There are also a number of other inconsistencies between Japanese and IFRS-based statements, because either there are areas where there are no specific Japanese disclosure rules or the two sets of rules are inconsistent. Japan does not have any disclosure requirements for a primary statement of changes in equity although this is normally disclosed in English language reports (see Exhibit 12.1) on the fair value of investment properties or the segment reporting of liabilities. The biggest difference at least for multinational companies is that overseas subsidiaries can apply domestic GAAP if they wish rather than using a consistent set of GAAP throughout the company. Exhibit 12.1 reflects the common practice in this area. There are also a number of other differences, in particular:

- pre-operating costs can be capitalized;
- leases which do not transfer ownership can be treated as operating leases (see Exhibit 12.18);
- inventory can be valued at cost rather than lower of cost or market and can include non-production overheads;
- provisions can be made on the basis of directors' decisions before the obligation arises;

| Exhibit 12.19 | Differences between Japanese GAAP and IFRS, April 2004 |

	Item	Japanese GAAP	IFRS
Financial Instruments	Derecognition of financial asset	Legal isolation required	Legal isolation not required
Business Combinations	Pooling of interest Goodwill	Exceptionally used Strictly amortized with impairment	Prohibited Impairment only
Impairment of Assets	Recognition test	Undiscounted future cash flows	Recoverable amount
	Reversal of impairment loss	Prohibited	Reversed (excl g/w)
Retirement Benefits	Actuarial gain/loss	Strictly amortized, no corridor	Corridor amortization
R&D	Development cost	Expensed when incurred	Capitalized
Consolidated Statements	Presentation of minority interest	Between liability and equity	Equity
Investment property	Measurement	Cost	Fair value or cost

Source: www.iasplus.com/country/japan.html

- extraordinary items are more widely defined;
- segment reporting does not include a primary/secondary basis.

While similar to international audit rules, the audit report is rather different from a UK-style report. The Commercial Code does not contain a complete code of accounts (as, for example, seen in France), and in many areas there are no requirements or, where they exist, they allow companies a wide choice of acceptable methods. However, the accounting system can still best be described as a uniform system of accounting in the sense that the rules have to be applied in the prescribed ways. Thus, the concept of 'true and fair' is not found in Japan. The audit report instead states that the financial statements 'present fairly . . . in conformity with accounting principles generally accepted in Japan'. As we have seen above, these GAAP are codified in many different places – the new ASJ, the Commercial Code, the SEL and the Tax laws. All of these sources of GAAP have to be followed without any possibility of overriding them to produce more useful or relevant information.

The audit report itself tends typically to be very similar to US audit reports with users of Japanese reports having to read them quite carefully to see exactly which GAAP have been used, as illustrated in Exhibit 12.20, the audit report of a typical Japanese listed company.

A second area where laws and practice would be unusual or unfamiliar to a UK reader, or in this case, also a US reader, is with respect to legal reserves. The requirements for legal or statutory reserves is an important aspect of the emphases placed upon creditor protection in the Commercial Code. Companies have to transfer an amount equal

Exhibit 12.20 Audit report, a typical Japanese company

DEF, Auditors

The Board of Directors

PQR, Incorporated

We have audited the accompanying consolidated balance sheets of PQR, Incorporated and consolidated subsidiaries as of March 31, 2004 and 2003, and the related consolidated statements of income, shareholders' equity, and cash flows for the years then ended, all expressed in yen. These financial statements are the responsibility of the Company's management. Our responsibility is to independently express an opinion on these financial statements based on our audits.

We conducted our audits in accordance with auditing standards generally accepted and applied in Japan. Those standards require that we plan and perform the audit to obtain reasonable assurance about whether the financial statements are free of material misstatement. An audit includes examining, on a test basis, evidence supporting the amounts and disclosures in the financial statements. An audit also includes assessing the accounting principles used and significant estimates made by management, as well as evaluating the overall financial statement presentation. We believe that our audits provide a reasonable basis for our opinion.

In our opinion. the financial statements referred to above present fairly. in all material respects. the consolidated financial position of PQR, Incorporated and consolidated subsidiaries at March 31. 2004 and 2003. and the consolidated results of their operations and their cash flows for the years then ended in conformity with accounting principles generally accepted in Japan.

Supplemental Information

As described in Note 3, PQR, Incorporated and its domestic consolidated subsidiaries adopted a new accounting standard for impairment accounting for fixed assets as early adoption of the standard was permitted from the fiscal year ended March 31, 2004.

The U.S. dollar amounts in the accompanying consolidated financial statements with respect to the year ended March 31, 2004 are presented solely for convenience. Our audit also included the translation of yen amounts into U.S. dollar amounts and, in our opinion, such translation has been made on the basis described in Note 2.

June 2004

DEF, Auditors

to at least 10 per cent of cash dividends to a legal reserve each year until that reserve plus, since 2001, any extra paid-in capital amounts to at least 25 per cent of legal capital. This was not distributable. Companies would often also reduce distributable reserves by making relatively large transfers from distributable to appropriated non-distributable reserves. Particularly important are transfers with respect to retirement payments, warranties and repairs. The new rules have somewhat reduced this creditor orientation in that any reserves in excess of the 25 per cent is now distributable.

Also designed to protect creditors are rules with respect to the maximum amounts that can be paid out as interim and final dividends (which are accrued in the balance sheet if declared after year end). Companies will also take full advantage of any tax provisions, as discussed above. An example is shown in TDK (2003) (Exhibit 12.21).

Exhibit 12.21 Legal reserves, TDK

Legal Reserve and Dividends

The Japanese Commercial Code (JCC) had provided that earnings in an amount equal to at least 10 per cent of appropriations of retained earnings to be paid in cash should be appropriated as a legal reserve until such reserve equals 25 per cent of the capital stock by each legal-entity.

Effective October 1, 2001, the JCC was amended to require earnings in an amount to at least 10 per cent of appropriations of retained earnings to be paid in cash should be appropriated as a legal reserve until total additional paid-in capital and legal reserves equals 25 per cent of common stock by each legal-entity. Either additional paid-in capital or legal reserve may be available for dividend by resolution of the shareholders to the extent that the amount of total additional paid-up capital and legal reserve exceeds 25 per cent of common stock of each legal-entity.

Certain foreign subsidiaries are also required to appropriate their earnings to legal reserve, under the laws of the respective countries.

[*The note continues with the amount of the dividend distribution.*]

Source: TDK annual report (2003), p. 61.

12.7 Information disclosure

As we have seen, Japan has imported many of its regulatory structures and accounting rules. However, many features of Japanese society are quite different from those of other countries. Thus, despite a complex system of accounting regulation, there is with some exceptions relatively little emphasis on – or demand for – information disclosure in general purpose annual reports. Debt financing has traditionally been more important than equity financing and the debt providers (the banks) have not required external financial statements as they are able to demand whatever information they require. Other *keiretsu* members likewise have a variety of formal and informal ways of obtaining the information they want. Thus the need for external monitoring via audited annual accounts has been largely replaced by other corporate governance systems. For example, one study of the role of non-executive directors[19] concluded that bankers and other representatives of groups with intercorporate relationships are often appointed in times of financial difficulty and that these board members are important in monitoring and disciplining corporate behaviour. This behaviour is congruent with the culture of the country. Group consciousness and interdependence leads to relatively high levels of mutual trust, so there is less of a perceived need to monitor corporate behaviour externally. For example, in one study it was estimated that, before the new standards of the last few years, Japanese disclosure requirements were only approximately 40 per cent of those in the US.[20]

This lack of disclosure has been compounded by the impacts of patterns of financing, group structures and *keiretsu* membership and cultural values, which all mean that the

---

[19] Kaplan and Minten (1994).
[20] Davis (1989).

Japanese language annual reports, while providing the information required by law, have tended not to go any further by providing extensive amounts of voluntary information. This is less noticeable in many of the English language reports, when companies, and in particular those listed in overseas markets, have tended to disclose rather more information. However, even here, the voluntary disclosure levels tend to be less than those found in the reports of similar US or UK companies, though there is some evidence that the level of voluntary disclosure has been increasing, at least over the three years 1989, 1994 and 1998.[21]

However, one area where Japanese companies provide more information than those from other companies is in the area of forecasts, as required by Japanese law. Such forecasts are generally not produced in the English language reports although one exception to this is the example of Sojitz Group, as shown in Exhibit 12.22. The company issued a forecast in May 2004 at the time of publishing the annual report, but then revised the forecast downwards in September 2004 to reflect an impairment review.

Exhibit 12.22 Forecast information provided by Sojitz Group

Extract from Notice Concerning Revisions to Consolidated and Non-Consolidated Earnings Forecasts for the Fiscal Year Ending March 31, 2005

Following drastic review of its current Business Plan, Sojitz Holdings Corporation (hereinafter referred to as "Sojitz Holdings" or "the Company") has formulated a New Business Plan with the aim of enhancing corporate value by quickly restoring market confidence. Guided by its Business Plan, Sojitz Holdings has decided to write-off an amount totaling approximately ¥400 billion (on a consolidated basis) in an effort to instantaneously restore asset quality. The write-off will cover the loss for the complete withdrawal from low-profit businesses including overseas investments and loans and the disposal of real estate holdings.

As a result of its decision to implement these measures, the Company has revised consolidated and non-consolidated earnings forecasts for the fiscal year ending March 31, 2005 as follows.

Consolidated Earnings Forecasts for the Fiscal Year Ending March 31, 2005

As a result of the Company's decision to write-off the amount as identified in its New Business Plan, mentioned above, Sojitz Holdings has revised its earnings forecasts, which were initially announced on May 13, 2004 together with the Company's fiscal 2003 financial results.

Earnings forecasts for the current fiscal year:

[Consolidated]			Billions of Yen
	Net Sales	Recurring Profit	Net Income (Loss)
Previous Forecast (A)	6,100	85	50
Revised Forecast (B)	5,000	50	−380
Difference (B − A)	−1,100	−35	−430
Difference (%)	−18.0%	−41.2%	−
(Reference) Results of Fiscal 2003	5,861.7	48.5	−33.6

[*The notice continues with information about non-consolidated financial statements.*]

Source: Sojitz Holdings, Notice issued 8 Sept 2004, revised forecast for year ending 31 March 2005, www.Sojitz_holdings.com/eng/

---

[21] Singleton and Globerman (2002).

Summary and conclusions

This chapter has shown that in many respects, Japanese accounting is quite unique. The early continental European (especially German) influences are still important, reflected in the importance of the Commercial Code and its creditor orientation. In contrast, the SEL bears many traces of its roots in the US system of regulation. However, neither German nor US rules or institutions have been adopted wholesale and the imports have been adapted and changed over time to reflect local influences. Overlaid on this is the recent standard-setting system of the Financial Accounting Standards Foundation and the Accounting Standard Board of Japan. This is an independent system with standards set by members of the profession, business and financial institutions, which reflects a deliberate attempt to introduce a standard-setting system that is similar to that of the IASB reflecting the desire of Japan to be involved in and influence the moves towards international convergence. The system thus reflects a mixture of quite disparate influences. Indeed, it is has not really been correct to talk of 'Japanese accounting': instead, there is 'Commercial Code accounting', 'SEL accounting' and 'English-language accounting', although it may be argued that the system is increasingly coalescing into a system that, while not identical to IFRS, is in most respect very similar.

The accounting principles and practices of Japan, at least until the last three or four years when IFRS standards have been an important influence, are related to the predictions made by Gray (1988), based upon analysis of cultural factors. Using the scores developed by Hofstede (1984) which suggested that the most important cultural dimension for accounting was Japan's strong uncertainty avoidance, Gray's work can be used to predict that the Japanese accounting system should exhibit strong statutory control, be uniform rather than flexible, be relatively conservative and be relatively secretive. Many of these predictions have been supported by the analysis of practices in Japan.

Key points from the chapter:

- Japan has a code law legal system and the Commercial Code is used to regulate all businesses.
- The Commercial Code contains a number of rules which apply to all companies, the regulations emphasize creditor protection and require relatively few disclosures.
- Many areas of accounting are not covered by the Commercial Code, many of the more important regulations that affect listed companies being the result of the Securities and Exchange Law (SEL) and, increasingly, accounting standards.
- The taxation system is largely based upon accounting GAAP; however, there are quite a number of areas where the taxation rules have an impact upon accounting and financial reporting practices. In particular, companies typically set up and disclose more special reserves than they would otherwise.
- The accounting profession in Japan is relatively weak in influence.
- Japan has imported many of its institutions from overseas. Many of the early accounting laws were imported from Europe, in particular Germany. Following the

Second World War, new regulations and regulatory structures were introduced based upon the US system, although these have been modified to reflect Japanese influences. The Japanese accounting system has therefore been categorized alongside both the US and Germany.

● While Japan is one of very few countries that has not fully endorsed the IASB convergence project and it has not promised to achieve convergence, Japan is undoubtedly generally in favour of convergence.

● The non-endorsement of convergence is partly a cultural artefact – Japan will not endorse convergence as it is not completely sure of the final output of this process.

Questions

The following questions test your understanding of the material contained in the chapter and allow you to relate your understanding to the learning outcomes specified at the start of this chapter. The learning outcomes are repeated here. Each question is cross-referenced to the relevant section of the chapter.

Understand the key characteristics of the country as summarized in published economic indicators

1 To what extent does the business environment of Japan provide clues as to possible influences on accounting practices? (section 12.2)

Explain the origins of accounting regulations and the historical developments leading to the present state of practice

2 To what extent do early developments in accounting practice indicate the likely current practice? (section 12.3)

Relate institutional factors for the country to the framework set out in Chapter 4

3 How does the political and economic system of Japan fit into the classifications described in Chapter 4? (section 12.4.1)

4 How does the legal system of Japan fit into the classifications described in Chapter 4? (section 12.4.2)

5 How does the taxation system of Japan compare to the descriptions given in Chapter 4? (section 12.4.3)

6 How does the corporate financing system of Japan compare to the descriptions given in Chapter 4? (section 12.4.4)

7 How does the accounting profession in Japan compare to the descriptions given in Chapter 4? (section 12.4.5)

8 Which institutional factors are most likely to influence Japanese accounting practice? (section 12.4)

9 How do the external influences on accounting practice in Japan compare to those described in Chapter 4? (section 12.5)

Explain the position of national accounting practice in relation to the IFRS described in Chapter 2

10 In which areas does accounting practice in Japan depart from that set out in International Financial Reporting Standards? (section 12.6)

11 For each of the issues identified above:

- Describe the treatment prescribed in Japanese GAAP.
- Identify the likely impact on income and shareholders' equity of moving from Japanese GAAP to the relevant IFRS. (section 12.6)

12 What explanations may be offered for these departures from IASs, in terms of the institutional factors described in the chapter? (section 12.4)

13 What are the most difficult problems facing accounting in Japan as it seeks further harmonization with the IASC Core Standards programme? (section 12.6)

References and further reading

Beattie, A. (2004) 'Call for foreigners to help break tradition', *The Financial Times*, 23 March.

Business Accounting Council (2004) *Issues on the International Accounting Standards and Japan's Treatment*, Japan: FSA (24 June).

Cheung, J.K., Kim, J.-B. and Lee, J. (1999) 'The impact of institutional characteristics on return-earnings associations in Japan', *International Journal of Accounting*, 34(4): 571–596.

Cooke, T.E. (1991) 'The evolution of financial reporting in Japan: A shame culture perspective', *Accounting, Business and Financial History*, 1(3): 251–277.

Cooke, T.E. (1993) 'The impact of accounting principles on profits: The USA versus Japan', *Accounting and Business Research*, 23(92): 460–476.

Davis, S.M. (1989) *Shareholder Rights Abroad: A Handbook for the Global Investor*, Washington DC: Investor Responsibility Research Inc.

Douthett, E.B. and Jung, K. (2001) 'Japanese corporate groupings (keiretsu) and the informativeness of earnings', *Journal of International Financial Management and Accounting*, 12(2): 133–159.

The Economist Pocket World in Figures, 2004 Edition. London: Profile Books

Gray, S.J. (1988) 'Towards a theory of cultural influence on the development of accounting systems internationally', *Abacus*, 24(1): 1–15.

Hirose, Y. (1987) 'The promulgation and development of Financial accounting standards in Japan', in Choi, F.D.S and Hiramatsu, K. (eds) *Accounting and Financial Reporting in Japan*, London: Van Rostrand Reinhold.

Hofstede, G. (1984) *Culture's Consequences: International Differences in Work-related Values*. Beverley Hills, CA: Sage Publications.

Jiang, L. and Kim, J.-B. (2000) 'Cross-corporate ownership, information asymmetry and the usefulness of accounting performance measures in Japan', *International Journal of Accounting*, 35(1): 85–98.

Kaplan, S.N. and Minten, B.A. (1994) 'Appointment of outsiders to Japanese boards: Determinants and implications for managers', *Journal of Financial Economics*, 36: 225–258.

Kumar, S. and Hyodo, K. (2001) 'Price–earning ratios in Japan: recent evidence and further results', *Journal of International Financial Management and Accounting*, 12(1): 24–49.

McKinnon, J.L. (1984) 'Application of Anglo-American principles of consolidation to corporate financial disclosure in Japan', *Abacus*, 20(1): 16–33.

McKinnon, J.L. (1986) *The Historical Development and Operational Form of Corporate Reporting Regulations in Japan*. New York: Garland Publishing.

McKinnon, J.L. and Harrison, G.L. (1985) 'Cultural influence on corporate and governmental involvement in accounting policy determination in Japan', *Journal of Accounting and Public Policy*, 4: 201–223.

OECD (2004) *OECD Economic Surveys*: *Japan*, Vol. 2003/18, February 2004, Organization for Economic Cooperation and Development, Paris.

Singleton, W.R. and Globerman, S. (2002) 'The changing nature of financial disclosure in Japan', *International Journal of Accounting*, 37: 95–111.

Someya, K. (1989) 'Accounting "revolutions" in Japan', *The Accounting Historians' Journal*, 16(1): 75–86.

13 China

Learning outcomes

After reading this chapter you should be able to:

● Understand and explain the origins of accounting regulations and the historical development leading to the present state of practice.

● Relate institutional factors for the country to the framework set out in Chapter 4.

● Understand and explain the position of national accounting rules in relation to the IASB standards described in Chapter 2.

● Understand the characteristics of national accounting practice in terms of Gray's accounting values.

● Explain how research papers contribute to understanding accounting practice and accounting values.

We are grateful to Professor Simon Gao, Napier University, and Professor Jason Xiao, Cardiff University, for suggestions and comments on this chapter. Any errors or omissions remain our own.

13.1 Introduction

China has become a major economic force in recent years. With nearly one-quarter of the world's population, China has experienced remarkable growth since it began to liberalize its economy in 1979. Since 1991, annual GDP growth has easily exceeded that of any of the successful but far smaller Asian tiger economies (at an annual real growth rate of 9.8 per cent). This has been accompanied by rapid increases in international trade and inward investment through a variety of vehicles including bonds, equity investment and joint ventures. As we will see in this chapter, this has been accompanied by a massive restructuring of China's economic system including its financial institutions and accounting system. New accounting laws, largely based upon IASB standards, are being introduced and the accounting system is currently undergoing substantial changes.

If you are studying China as an external observer, the current accounting system can be understood only if you first understand the key features of the previous accounting system, which was very different from that of any western capitalist country. This chapter will therefore include an outline of the system of accounting that was in place before the current accounting reforms began. It will then describe the process of continuing development in accounting regulation and practices in China.

13.2 The country

Exhibit 13.1 provides some details about The People's Republic of China (PRC). What is perhaps most striking is the sheer size of the country and its population. This means that it is a country of contrasts – much of the coastal area is highly industrialized and economically successful, with the population having a rapidly rising standard of living. Economic reform began in rural areas with a major government programme to 'Develop the West'. The currency is the renminbi (RMB), also called the yuan.

As can be seen from Exhibit 13.2, China (through Hong Kong) is now home to nine of the FT500 companies.

Recent years have witnessed much debate in the western press about just how successful China has been in restructuring its economy. With such a large country it is difficult to get accurate data and government statistics may be incomplete. From Exhibit 13.1, we can see that *per capita* gross domestic product was only US$900 in 2001, implying that China is still a very poor country. However, this figure is somewhat misleading. With a large rural population (more than 70 per cent of the population live in rural areas) much production is for personal consumption and so is excluded from official statistics. Based upon consumption patterns (e.g. a majority of the urban population have colour TVs and washing machines) and life expectancies, it is estimated that the real GDP is anything up to four times greater than the official statistics, placing China on a par with countries such as Thailand or Turkey. China's largest export market is the US (20 per cent) followed by Hong Kong (18 per cent) and Japan (17 per cent).

The size of the country obviously makes it much more difficult to modernize and reform the economy. Some smaller Asian economies such as Singapore were able to develop rapidly by pursuing a policy of export-led growth. The sheer size of China rules out reliance upon such strategies; instead it must develop mainly through internal growth.

The size of the country also means that it is more difficult to administer and coordinate economic policies. While centralized control of the economy has been of prime importance, in practice the system is often far from uniform. Many of the economic reforms have been applied in a piecemeal fashion. Institutions have been allowed to grow and develop in response to market needs and Government control or regulation has often followed,

Exhibit 13.1   China: country profile

Population	1,285.0 million	
Land mass	9,560,900 km²	
GDP per head	US$900	
GDP per head in purchasing power parity	11.5	(USA = 100)
Origins of GDP:	%	
Agriculture	16.4	
Industry	51.1	
Services	32.5	
	%	
GDP average annual growth 1991–2001	9.8	
Inflation, average annual rate 1996–2002	0.1	

Source: *The Economist Pocket World in Figures*, 2004 Edition, Profile Books Ltd.

Exhibit 13.2 FT500 Chinese companies (including Hong Kong China)

	Name	FT500 rank	Market capitalization US$bn	Listed UK	Listed USA	Sector
1	China Mobile (HK)	65	58,326	No	Yes	Telecommunications services
2	Hutchison Whampoa	165	30,644	No	No	Diversified industrial
3	Hang Seng Bank	203	24,416	No	No	Banks
4	Sun Hung Kai Properties	222	21,957	No	No	Real estate
5	BoC Hong Kong	245	20,152	No	No	Banks
6	Cheung Kong	259	19,472	No	No	Real estate
7	CNOOC	297	17,528	No	Yes	Oil and gas
8	CLP Holdings	403	13,384	No	No	Electricity
9	China Unicom	486	11,366	No	Yes	Telecommunications services

Source: *Financial Times*, FT500 (2004), www.londonstockexchange.com, www.nyse.com

not preceded, market developments. Different parts of the country have been subject to different rules and various government ministries have imposed different sets of rules on the enterprises and institutions under their control. One example of this is Hong Kong. On 1 July 1997, Hong Kong was returned to the control of China. China promised that it would remain as a market-led capitalist system for at least the next 50 years – the 'one country, two systems' policy. That China felt able to do this and that it was prepared to live with such apparently different economic systems co-existing alongside each other is not as remarkable as might at first appear. In an attempt to modernize and increase economic welfare, many of the economic structures of mainland China had already been 'westernized' and China already had experience of running four special economic areas in the coastal region where the economic rules were already far more liberal than those applied elsewhere in the country.

13.3 Development of accounting regulation

13.3.1 Uniform accounting regulation

Prior to reform, the accounting regulations, known as the Uniform Accounting Regulations (UAR), were set either directly by the Department of Administration of Accounting Affairs (a part of the Ministry of Finance) or, in the case of specific industries, by the ministry responsible for that industry and then approved by the Ministry of Finance. The UAR consisted of a system of many uniform plans, each in turn containing detailed rules or regulations covering both costing and financial reporting matters. Accounting was controlled by the Ministry of Finance, because it was seen as only one of the many tools available to ensure the efficient functioning of businesses.

The system was a uniform one, with enterprises having to follow detailed regulations. This may be seen in the treatment of depreciation, for example, with only straight-line depreciation being permitted for most enterprises. Approved useful lives were set by regulation and enterprises were allowed to use different depreciation rates only if they had prior approval. However, while the accounting rules were detailed and rigidly imposed, different systems were developed for enterprises in different sectors or industries.

A major difference from western commercial accounting concerned the use of fund accounting. This is not a type of funds flow statement but rather a way of categorizing accrual based assets and liabilities. The balance sheet categorized both assets and liabilities on the basis of their function. This practice originated because of the need to control the activities of enterprises to ensure that they met the national plan. Three categories were used:

- fixed funds,
- current funds, and
- specific funds.

Fixed funds were similar to fixed assets in that they included the physical assets of the enterprise used by labour to generate output. However, intangible assets were not included and land was also generally excluded. Land is seen as belonging to the people and therefore it cannot be owned by an enterprise although, increasingly, rights to use land were valued and traded. This practice still continues – for example, SVA Electron depreciates land use rights at a rate of 2 per cent per annum on a straight-line basis and has a heading in the fixed assets schedule 'Land use rights and buildings in the PRC'.

Income was calculated in a somewhat different way. Reflecting the state control of the economy, it was calculated after a number of appropriations which would be treated as profit distributions in western companies. Indeed, the current system retains some element of this with transfers from profits to statutory public welfare funds as can be seen in Exhibit 13.3 which explains the movement on reserves and profit distribution policy of SVA Electron. Administration and workshop expenses were also treated as product costs. This was an important difference because many enterprises were producing to centralized plans that could involve stockpiling unsaleable inventory. Including such expenses as product costs meant that they were

---

Exhibit 13.3 **Profit distribution policy statement, SVA Electron Ltd**

Note 26. RESERVES
Movements in reserves are set out in the consolidated statement of changes in equity.

(a) **Pursuant to the relevant PRC regulations and the Articles of Association of the Company, profit after taxation shall be appropriated in the following sequence:**

  (i) Make up accumulated losses;

  (ii) Transfer 10 per cent of which to the statutory surplus reserve. When the balance of the statutory surplus reserve reaches 50 per cent of the paid up share capital, such transfer needs not be made.

  (iii) Transfer 5 per cent to 10 per cent of which to the statutory public welfare fund.

  (iv) Transfer to the discretionary surplus reserve as approved by the shareholders in general meetings.

  (v) Distribute dividends to shareholders.

  The amounts of transfer to the statutory surplus reserve and statutory public welfare fund shall be based on profit after tax in the statutory accounts prepared in accordance with PRC accounting standards.

(b) **Share premium**
  According to the relevant PRC regulations, share premium and surplus reserves can be used to increase share capital.

(c) Statutory surplus reserve and discretionary surplus reserve

According to the relevant PRC regulations, statutory surplus reserve and discretionary surplus reserve can be used to make up losses or to increase share capital. Except for the reduction of losses incurred, other usage should not result in the statutory surplus reserve falling below 25 per cent of the registered capital.

(d) Statutory public welfare fund

According to the relevant PRC regulations, statutory public welfare fund is restricted to capital expenditure for employees' collective welfare facilities. Staff welfare facilities are owned by the Group. The statutory public welfare fund is not normally available for distribution to shareholders except in liquidation.

(e) Profit distribution

Pursuant to the relevant PRC regulations and the Articles of Association of the Company, profit distributable to shareholders shall be the lower of the amount determined in accordance with the PRC accounting standards as stated in the statutory financial statements and that adjusted in accordance with IAS.

In the PRC statutory financial statements as at 31 December 2003, retained profit carried forward amounted to RMB191,374,000 (2002: RMB106,026,000).

Source: SVA Electron annual report (2003), pp. 42–43. www.sva-e.com

not being charged to the income statement but instead appearing as assets in the balance sheet. Not having any overriding principle of conservatism meant that this practice could continue for long periods.

With the economic liberalization of the 1980s which increased enterprises' freedom of action, and with ever more enterprises investing in other enterprises, it became increasingly easy to circumvent the restrictions on the use of the different funds. Also, as enterprises became increasingly free to make their own operating and investment decisions and as private ownership increased in importance, the state had less need to dictate how enterprises should use any particular source of finance. Therefore, the need to use fund accounting decreased greatly, opening the way for the introduction of western accounting principles. At the same time the tradition of uniform accounting rules remained strong.

13.3.2 Stages of financial accounting reforms

The reform of financial accounting can be divided into four phases.[1] The first phase involved regulations for foreign joint ventures. These regulations started in 1979 with the 'Law on Sino-Foreign Joint Ventures'. This was little more than a statement of principles and it was followed by a series of more detailed laws. These included a joint venture income tax law and laws on contracts and foreign exchange. The first accounting-related laws were passed in March 1985, being the 'Accounting Regulations for Sino-Foreign Joint Ventures' and 'Charts of Account and Accounting Statements for Industrial Sino-Foreign Joint Ventures'. Following further changes in the economic system, including the further development of foreign exchange markets, these regulations were replaced, in 1993, by 'Accounting Regulations for Enterprises with Foreign Investments' and 'Charts of Accounts

---

[1] Roberts *et al.* (1995).

and Accounting Statements for Industrial Enterprises with Foreign Investments'. The 1985 regulations were particularly important as they were the first move away from fund accounting towards international practices.

Enterprises started to issue equity shares in 1984. Thus, the second stage of reform involved the introduction of regulations for domestic or Chinese owned public companies. This started in May 1992 when the Ministry of Finance and the National Committee of Economic Structure Reform jointly promulgated 'Accounting Regulations for Share Enterprises'. This was an important development as it was the first set of regulations which adopted international accounting practices for use by purely domestic enterprises.

The third and crucial reform was the 'Accounting System for Business Enterprises (ASBE) (also called the Enterprise Accounting System – EAS) issued in November 1992 and effective from 1 July 1993. The ASBE was a major attempt both to unify the accounting systems used by different industries and to move financial accounting towards international accounting practices.[2]

The fourth stage of reform is still taking place and involves establishing a complete set of accounting standards issued by the Accounting Standards Committee. The ASC was set up in October 1998 by the Ministry of Finance to oversee the development of a complete set of Chinese GAAP. It is a consultative body comprising experts from relevant departments of the Government, local accounting firms and academics. By the completion of this phase all industry-specific regulations will have been phased out and financial reporting should be regulated by a uniform and detailed set of accounting standards.

13.3.3 Accounting regulation from 1992 to 2000

The 1992 Accounting System for Business Enterprises (ASBE) was the first major piece of accounting legislation that applied to all enterprises irrespective of their form of ownership. It was also the first attempt to introduce regulations that applied equally to all industries rather than relying, as in the past, on industry-specific regulations. However, the move from a series of uniform fund-based accounting systems to one western-style system involves major changes for enterprises, and it would have been unrealistic to expect them to be able to change quickly and easily. Thus, there were several transitional arrangements set up, including various voluntary industry-specific accounting systems, each based upon the ASBE but designed to make the move from the respective UAR as simple as possible.

The ASBE involved a change in the function of financial accounting. It has been suggested that prior to the accounting reforms, financial accounting served four objectives:[3]

● to reflect, analyze and assess the implementation of the state plan;
● to reflect the source of funds obtained by enterprises and the ways funds are applied, and to evaluate fund utilization and turnover in operation;
● to ensure legitimacy of the sources of funds and fund application;
● to provide financial and cost information in order to improve operation and management of enterprises for greater economic benefit.

---

[2] Tang *et al.* (1994).
[3] Ibid.

The ASBE introduced the idea of reporting to all external users. Article 11 set out the objectives of accounting information as:

> Accounting information must be designed to meet the requirements of national economic control, the needs of all concerned external users in order to understand an enterprise's financial position and operating results, and the needs of management to strengthen financial practices and administration.
>
> (Tang *et al.* 1994)

It is worth noting that the government was the first-named user group in this objective. It was intended that the ASBE of 1992 would be replaced by a full set of 30 accounting standards within three years. This project was financed by the World Bank with Deloitte Touche Tohmatsu acting as consultants. However, once Deloitte Touche Tohmatsu started work it found that the task was larger than it had originally envisaged and that it would take considerably longer than anticipated to educate many of the State-owned enterprises (SOEs) in the new system and to ensure that they were fully willing and able to introduce new western-style accounting standards. Tang (2000) lists a number of reasons for this. He argues that many accountants did not understand either the theoretical reasoning behind the conceptual frameworks found in a number of other countries or why the old system needed to be changed. In addition, the unique circumstances of China meant that several of the underlying principles found in other countries were inappropriate. The government was identified as an important user; indeed it was thought to be as important as other users. In addition, given a number of past problems caused by false accounting information, it was felt that the concept of reliability was more important than relevance. Thus, there was much more of a need to assess the likely impacts of the proposed standards and to develop professional competence and expertise than was originally realized.

While the ASBE of 1992 introduced western-style financial statements it was not a very detailed set of regulations. They have been considerably strengthened since they were first issued both in terms of rules regarding the operation of the accounting system and in terms of accounting rules themselves. With respect to the former, the Accounting Law was thoroughly revised, effective from July 2000 such that it included:[4]

- an increase in the basic requirements for accounting and bookkeeping, dealing in particular with accounting records kept on computer;
- a clear definition of the responsibilities of the person in charge of a reporting unit;
- a strengthening of the requirements for internal accounting supervision, including the establishment of an effective internal control system by each unit;
- a requirement that accounting personnel must be appropriately qualified;
- increased protection for individuals who report violations of the accounting law; and
- more severe penalties for breaches of the accounting law's requirements.

In the period May 1997 to April 2000, the first ten standards were issued. It was intended that the remaining 20 standards originally envisaged, plus a new batch of a further 17 standards, would be issued by the end of 2005 (although, as explained in section 13.3.4, this intention did not materialize). However, there were also changes in the main accounting laws from 2000, as explained in section 13.3.4.

---

[4] *Accountancy International* (December 1999), p. 52.

13.3.4 The system from 2000

Generally accepted accounting principles in the PRC are set by the Law, the Ministry of Finance and the China Securities Regulatory Commission (CSRC). The Accounting Law of the PRC (revised 1 July 2000) is the highest level of authority. It replaces the previous law of 1992. In 2000 the State Council issued Financial Accounting and Reporting Rules for Enterprises (FARR) which apply to all enterprises except for very small ones that do not raise funds externally.

The Accounting Law gives the Ministry of Finance the power to establish regulations and systems for accounting. In January 2001 the Ministry of Finance adopted an Accounting System for Business Enterprises, described in translation as 'the Accounting System' (see the summary in Appendix 13.1). The Ministry of Finance has also continued to develop accounting standards (see Exhibit 13.4), with the advice of the international accountancy firm, Deloitte Touche Tohmatsu. Although the scope of each PRC standard is different, many of the issues addressed in individual standards are also included in the

Exhibit 13.4 **List of PRC accounting standards issued by the Ministry of Finance**

No.	Subject	Effective date of current version	Applies to
1	Disclosure of related party relationships and transactions	1 January 1997	Listed enterprises
2	Cash flow statements	1 January 2001	All enterprises
3	Events occurring after the balance sheet date	1 January 1998, amendments from July 2003	All who follow ASBE (starting 2003)
4	Debt restructuring	1 January 2001	All enterprises
5	Revenue	1 January 1999	Listed enterprises
6	Investments	1 January 2001	Joint stock limited enterprises (from 2001)
7	Construction contracts	1 January 1999	Listed enterprises
8	Changes in accounting policies and estimates and corrections of accounting errors	1 January 2001	All enterprises from 2001
9	Non-monetary transactions	1 January 2001	All enterprises
10	Contingencies	1 July 2000	All enterprises
11	Intangible assets	1 January 2001	Joint stock limited enterprises
12	Borrowing costs	1 January 2001	All enterprises
13	Leases	1 January 2001	All enterprises
14	Interim financial reporting	1 January 2002	Listed enterprises
15	Inventories	1 January 2002	All who follow ASBE (starting 2003)
16	Fixed assets	1 January 2002	All who follow ASBE (starting 2003)

Source: *IAS Plus Country Updates*, China, July 2004, www.iasplus.com/country/China.htm

Exhibit 13.5	Exposure drafts of accounting standards

> Presentation of financial statements
>
> Earnings per share
>
> Discontinuing operations
>
> Government grants and assistance
>
> Foreign currency translation
>
> Segment reporting

Source: *IAS Plus Country Updates*, China, January 2004, www.iasplus.com/country/China.htm

ASBE, which has wider application. The ASBE is consistent with the standards but there is usually more detail in the individual standards and supporting guidance than there is in the ASBE. The Accounting System for Financial Institutions was adopted in 2002 and an Accounting Guideline for Enterprises Engaging in Publishing Business was issued to take effect from 1 January 2004. These are examples of industry-specific guidance that extend previous experience in China of providing industry guidance.

Exposure drafts under development in 2004 are listed in Exhibit 13.5.

The Ministry of Finance issues authoritative questions and answers on the ASBE. The questions and answers issued in May 2004 covered the following matters:[5]

- share issue costs,
- equity investment difference (goodwill) arising in step acquisitions,
- impairment of equity investments accounted for by the equity method,
- reversal of impairment losses in respect of fixed assets and intangible assets,
- change in the depreciation method for fixed assets,
- derecognition of discounted receivables,
- accounting for the tobacco business tax by tobacco enterprises,
- recognition of provisions and their tax effects,
- accounting by property developers for costs of developing rental property,
- provision for safety costs incurred by coal producing enterprises.

This kind of detailed advice indicates one way in which the application of IFRS in countries might vary in future. Chinese accounting standards are gradually being harmonized with IFRS but there remains a need for more detailed guidance and for industry-specific guidance.

A further source of advice is the Technical Expert Team of the Chinese Institute of CPAs, which issues Guidance Bulletins on detailed matters such as 'accounting for tree planting' and 'classification of rights to collect highway tolls'.[6]

13.4 Institutions

13.4.1 Political and economic system

The Chinese Communist Party dominates the government. The general secretary of the party plays an important leadership role. It was the guidance of Deng Xiaoping that took

---

[5] *IAS Plus Country Updates*, China, July 2004, www.iasplus.com/country/China.htm.
[6] Ibid., January 2004.

China forward into developing a market-based economic system. Jian Zemin followed as leader, continuing the reform policy, and was succeeded in November 2002 by Hu Jintao.

13.4.1.1 Importing a centralized planning system

When the communist party came to power in 1949, the most important task facing it was to achieve rapid socio-economic development without depending in any way on the advanced capitalist nations. The only model then available was the Soviet one, which was imported with almost no major changes. Thus, Soviet-style economic and political institutions were introduced, including centralized planning via a series of five-year plans.

The 1949 revolution resulted in the public ownership of all enterprises. Public ownership existed in two forms: state enterprises and collectives. Collective enterprises were owned by the people who operated them. State enterprises were held by the state and owned ultimately by the entire population. State ownership was considered to be the ideal; collectives were generally converted into state enterprises once they reached a certain size. The government was the main, probably the sole, user of financial statements. The economy was run by means of a compulsory comprehensive economic plan; perceived demand was converted into specific production targets for each enterprise. Capital, labour, equipment and materials were all allocated to enterprises on the basis of production targets. Similarly, prices and customers were strictly controlled via the plan. The only role of accounting was therefore to provide information to the government for planning purposes, for resource allocation decisions and for monitoring of the plan. Each state enterprise can perhaps be best thought of as being equivalent to a cost-centre in a typical western commercial organization. There was no real system of external financial reporting as it is commonly understood. Instead, enterprises had to produce uniform statements describing, among other things, their past production levels and cost data.

The Chinese leadership sought to give the adopted system a Chinese identity. This was seen in the Great Leap Forward of 1958–59 which culminated, most disastrously, in the Cultural Revolution of 1966–76. The Cultural Revolution attempted to ensure that the country retained its socialist nature; in particular, market structures were not to be introduced and no class system was to be allowed to develop. The attempt to prevent a bureaucratic elite developing, by actions such as forcing intellectuals to undertake manual labour and the creation of revolutionary committees of workers to run their factories, resulted in a major collapse of the economy. Following the death of Mao in 1976 the 'Maoist model' was heavily criticized and a new model of socialist development based upon market-orientated principles and institutions began to be created under the leadership of Deng Xiaoping.[7]

Market socialism is a difficult thing to achieve as it involves maintaining the political system and the position of the present political leadership while also undertaking major changes to the economic system. It is difficult to restructure the economy without also calling into doubt the legitimacy and effectiveness of the political system and politicians who ran the previous socialist economic system. This is one of the major reasons why China is adopting a process of piecemeal economic reforms. It also helps to explain why the process is far from smooth and why, at times, political considerations mean that the economic reforms have stalled.

---

[7] White (1993).

13.4.1.2 The start of economic reform

During the initial period of reform the emphasis was mainly on agricultural reform, with dismantling of the commune system. Some reforms were also made in the commodity markets, with state enterprises being allowed to sell some of their output independently and keep some of their income; some goods were removed from price controls and some private businesses were allowed. Some enterprises were also allowed to raise foreign currency loans and to keep a proportion of any foreign currency that they earned.

From the mid-1980s greater emphasis has been placed on state enterprise reforms. This encompasses a large number of different areas. The finance system has been reformed with commercial banks taking over some of the roles of the central bank. Foreign exchange markets have been established, as have stock markets (see below) and even agricultural products and metals futures markets.

13.4.1.3 Membership of the World Trade Organization

The most important event in China's move towards western markets was its admission to membership of the World Trade Organization (WTO) in December 2001. This committed China to unprecedented liberalization of its markets for goods and services. China agreed to overhaul its legal and business systems and to allow more foreign companies and products to enter China's markets.

13.4.2 Legal system

During the period of centralized planning control, the legal system was increasingly seen simply as another tool for the social control of society. Emphasis was placed upon maintaining political control and social order. Other objectives, such as guaranteeing personal liberties or ensuring the smooth functioning of the economy, were given very low priority. Legal reform has also been an important feature of the last two decades. Economic reforms can be successful only if suitable legal controls and protections are developed in parallel with the new market structures. A complete system of contract and commercial law therefore had to be developed almost entirely from the beginning. While there have been a significant number of new codes and statutes introduced, the process is still far from complete.

There are three different levels of legislative power. Accounting has been regulated by institutions at all three levels. Laws are set by the National People's Congress. Below this is the State Council which issues administrative rules and regulations. Finally, national ministries and commissions issue directives and regulations for the particular industries or enterprises under their control. In the past different accounting systems have been employed by different industries and the various ministries have imposed different accounting rules. Recent legal moves have therefore not only involved a move away from the traditional fund based system towards a westernized system, but they have also increasingly dismantled industry specific regulations and moved towards imposing uniform rules on all commercial enterprises, whether foreign owned, joint ventures, equity financed or government owned. However economic reform and government restructuring probably had a stronger influence than legal factors in the abandonment of industry-specific standards in 2000 when the new accounting system was stipulated.

13.4.3 Taxation system

13.4.3.1 Taxation and economic reform

Until the economic reforms began, enterprises were not taxed on their profits or surpluses – all of these were transferred to the state. Starting in 1979, some enterprises were allowed to keep some of their surpluses which, since 1983, have been taxed. Enterprises with foreign investments were treated rather differently. A series of laws were passed starting in 1980, which established the tax structure for these enterprises. Taxable profits were generally the same as reportable profits although there were some differences. Enterprises were given a number of tax incentives while some items were not deductible for tax purposes. Loss carry-forwards were also allowed.

From 1994, the enterprise taxation system has been considerably simplified. State enterprises are now taxed in the same way as other enterprises and the number of different types of taxes substantially reduced. More important for accounting is the fact that there has been a decoupling of tax and accounting. The financial reporting rules may now differ from the rules used to compute taxable earnings. This means that the influence of the tax rules on financial reporting is likely to decrease over time as new financial accounting rules can be introduced without being constrained by their impact upon tax revenues. This period has also witnessed the increasing use of tax incentives to encourage foreign direct investment, especially via the active participation in joint ventures.

13.4.3.2 Business taxes and turnover taxes for foreign investors[8]

Foreign Investment Enterprises based in China are subject to Foreign Enterprise Investment Tax on worldwide income. The national rate is 30 per cent, with an additional local rate of 3 per cent. Foreign Investment Enterprises established in Special Economic Zones pay a lower national rate of 15 per cent. Lower rates also apply to Economic and Technological Development Zones.

VAT applies to sales of goods and services. The rate is generally 17 per cent, with a lower rate of 13 per cent applied to some staple goods such as books and publications. Consumption Tax is an additional turnover tax applied to specific 'luxury goods' such as tobacco, alcohol, jewellery and automobiles.

In all, there are 13 types of Chinese tax applicable to foreign investors. They are Customs Duty, Value Added Tax (VAT), Consumption Tax, Business Tax, Foreign Enterprise Income Tax, Individual Income Tax, Deed Tax, Land Appreciation Tax, Resources Tax, Slaughter Tax, Stamp Duty, Urban Real Estate Tax and Vehicles & Vessels Usage Licence Tax. This variety of taxes, together with the frequent changes of regulation, gives foreign investors the impression that tax is complex. However, the government wishes to encourage foreign investment, so the rules include incentives. These incentives encourage companies to locate in special economic zones, and also encourage export, high-tech and infrastructure projects.

13.4.4 Corporate financing system

13.4.4.1 Listed companies

There are stock markets in the PRC at Shanghai and Shenzhen, and a separate market in Hong Kong.[9] One of the most important differences between the economic reforms of China and those of most of Eastern Europe has been the greater emphasis that China has

---

[8] Grant Thornton Summer 2002 Newsletter, available on www.prctaxman.com.cn.

[9] Hong Kong at www.hkex.com.hk; Shanghai at http://sse.com.cn; and Shenzhen at www.sse.org.cn.

placed upon establishing a suitable financial infrastructure. Thus, rather than starting by privatizing companies and hoping that stock markets and other necessary financial institutions would then develop naturally as they were needed, China instead began much of its economic reforms at the other end, by setting up the required financial institutions. One of the most important of these institutions is a stock market. If companies are no longer to be financed by the government then there needs to be an active and efficient market in which they can raise public debt and equity.

While there was a stock market in China prior to the Communist revolution, it had been closed down in 1949. It was not until the 1980s that moves began to re-establish capital markets. Treasury bonds were first sold to public enterprises in 1981 while, in 1984, state-owned enterprises also started issuing bonds. This was rapidly followed by a number of other developments such as the bond credit rating service of the People's Bank of China, a nation-wide computerized bond trading network (the Securities Trading Automated Quotations System, STAQS) and foreign currency denominated commercial and treasury bonds.

A number of commercial enterprises also started issuing shares in 1984. The Shenzhen stock market opened unofficially on December 1, 1990 and the Shanghai Securities Exchange soon after. The number of companies making equity issues initially increased only slowly. For example by the time Shenzhen stock market officially opened in mid-1991, it had only five listed companies, increasing to 17 by mid-1992. However, the demand for shares was almost limitless. Individuals had to buy application forms before purchasing shares and such was the demand that over one million people gathered in Shenzhen at one point in 1992 to buy these applications forms.

Companies can now list a variety of different types of shares. A-shares are those that are listed and traded in local currency and are available only to Chinese nationals. From December 2002 certain qualified foreign institutional investors (QFII) may purchase A shares on Chinese stock exchanges but they must gain prior approval and must operate within a quota. At December 2003 there were 12 overseas foreign institutions holding QFII licences. In February 2004, China's State Council issued *Guidelines on Promoting Reform, Opening Up and Steady Development of China's Capital Market*. This is part of the programme to build market transparency and increase investor confidence.

B-shares are issued domestically by PRC companies and until 2001 were available only to foreign investors. They are now also available to domestic investors holding foreign currency accounts. In 2003 there were 111 B-share companies but this represented relatively little growth from the 108 listed in 1999. H shares are denominated in Hong Kong dollars and are also available only to foreign investors.

At the end of 2003 there were 1,287 listed companies. Of these, 1,147 issued A shares only, 30 issued A and H shares, 87 issued A and B shares, and 24 issued B shares only. At the same date there were 76 PRC companies listed on the Hong Kong Exchanges and Clearing Limited. Twelve were dually listed in Hong Kong and New York and three were dually listed in Hong Kong and London.[10]

By the end of 1991 the Shanghai Exchange also began to list a number of Chinese companies that traded US dollar-denominated B shares while the Shenzhen Exchange dealt in Hong-Kong dollar-denominated H-shares. Both types of share are designed to attract foreign investors although they cannot gain control of local enterprises and no single investor can acquire more than 5 per cent of an enterprise's share capital without

---

[10] China's Securities and Futures Markets, April 2004, China Securities Regulatory Commission, www.csrc.gov.cn/english/.

central bank permission. While these shares proved to be very popular with non-Chinese investors, a number of other companies instead decided to list on foreign stock markets. The first companies to list on the Hong Kong and New York markets both gained approval for listing in October 1992, less than two years after the first Chinese stock market opened for business.

Increasing numbers of Chinese companies are now listed, not only in Hong Kong, but also in New York and London, as shown in Exhibit 13.6. As discussed later, China has been actively encouraging foreign investment in its own stock markets.

At the end of 2003 the Shanghai Stock Exchange had a total of 780 listed companies offering mainly A shares and a smaller number of B shares. The A shares contributed 98.5 per cent of market capitalization and the B shares contributed 1.5 per cent of

Exhibit 13.6   **Mainland Chinese companies listed in the USA and UK, July 2004**

Company	Industry/Sector	Listed
New York		
Aluminium Corporation of China Limited (*Chalco*)	Aluminium production	December 2001
China Eastern Airlines	Airlines operation	February 1997
China Life Insurance Company	Commercial life insurance	December 2003
China Petroleum and Chemical Corp	Oil refining	October 2000
China Southern Airlines	Commercial airline services	July 1997
China Telecom Corporation Limited	Fixed-line telecommunication	November 2002
China Unicom	Telephone communications	June 2000
CNOOC Limited	Oil and gas	February 2001
Guangshen Railway	Rail transportation	May 1996
Huaneng Power International	Holding co./power plants	October 1994
Jilin Chemical Industrial	Chemical products	May 1995
Petro China	Oil and gas exploration	April 2000
Semiconductor Manufacturing International Corporation	Semiconductor manufacturing	March 2004
Sinopec Beijing Yanhua Petrochemical Company Limited	Petrochemicals production	July 1993
Sinopec Shanghai Petrochemical	Petrochemicals production	July 1993
Yanzhou Coal Mining	Coal mining	March 1998
London		
Beijing Datang Power Generation	Electricity	March 1997
China Petroleum and Chemical Corp	Oil refining	October 2000
Jiangxi Copper Co	Other mineral extraction & mines	June 1997
Zhejiang Expressway Co	Other construction	May 2000
Zhejiang Southeast Electric Power	Electricity	Sept 1997

Source: Based on www.nyse.com (July 2004); www.londonstockexchange.com (July 2004)

capitalization.[11] Share price movements are represented by the SSE 180 index. The Shenzhen Stock Exchange had a total of 507 listed companies. The A shares contributed 95.8 per cent to total market capitalization.[12]

13.4.4.2 Privatization

One factor limiting the expansion of stock market activity is that the state retains substantial shareholdings in companies listed on the stock market. Exhibit 13.7 indicates the presence of the state as controlling shareholder. A report in the *Financial Times* (2003)[13] discusses the lack of genuine investors and low appetite for new stocks. It explains that the government decided to retain a majority share of most listed companies because of the communist party's objections to privatization. As a result, about two-thirds of the shares of Chinese listed companies are non-tradable. Each time the government tries to reduce its holding the market falls rapidly because of investors' fears of a price collapse.

Exhibit 13.7 Statement on use of funds by the controlling shareholder, China Petroleum & Chemical Corporation

---

4 DISCLOSURE OF OTHER SIGNIFICANT EVENTS

(1) Statement in relation to the use of funds by the controlling shareholder and other related parties.

Pursuant to the requirements of the Zheng Jian Fa [2003] No.56 "Notice on listed companies' issues relating to regulating the funding transactions with related parties and the guarantees provided to third parties" issued by the China Securities Regulatory Commission ("CSRC") and the State-owned Assets Supervision and Administration Commission of the State Council, KPMG Huazhen has issued a "Statement in relation to the Use of Funds of China Petroleum & Chemical Corporation by the Controlling Shareholder and other Related Parties for the Year 2003" as shown below:

To the Board of Directors of China Petroleum & Chemical Corporation:

We have accepted the appointment and audited the Company's consolidated balance sheet and balance sheet as at 31 December 2003, and the consolidated income statement and profit appropriation statement, income statement and profit appropriation statement, consolidated cash flow statement and cash flow statement for the year then ended (the "financial statements") in accordance with the China's Independent Auditing Standards of the Certified Public Accountants. We issued an auditors' report with an unqualified audit opinion on these financial statements on 26 March 2004.

Pursuant to the requirements of the "Notice on listed companies' issues relating to regulating the funding transactions with related parties and the guarantees provided to third parties" issued by the China Securities Regulatory Commission and the State-owned Assets Supervision and Administration Commission of the State Council, the Company has prepared the "Summary of the use of funds of China Petroleum & Chemical Corporation by the controlling shareholder and Other Related Parties for the year 2003" (the "Summary"), which is attached in the appendix to this statement.

The Company is responsible for preparing and disclosing the Summary and ensuring its truthfulness, legitimacy and completeness. We are not aware of any inconsistency, in all material respects, when comparing the information contained in the Summary with the financial information verified in the course of our audit and the related contents in the audited financial statements of the Company and its subsidiaries (the "Group") for the Year 2003. Except for the audit procedures performed in the course of our audit of the financial statements for the Year 2003

---

[11] China's Securities and Futures Markets, April 2004, China Securities Regulatory Commission, www.csrc.gov.cn/english/.

[12] Ibid.

[13] Special Report China, *Financial Times*, 16 December 2003.

Exhibit 13.7 *(Continued)*

on the Group's related party transactions, we have not performed any additional audit and other procedures on the information contained in the Summary.

In order to have a better understanding on the use of funds by the Company's controlling shareholder and other related parties for the Year 2003, the Summary should be read together with the audited financial statements.

KPMG Huazhen

Certified Public Accountants Registered in the People's Republic of China, Wu Wei

8/F, Office Tower E2 Oriental Plaza

No.1, East Chang An Ave. Song Chenyang Beijing, The People's Republic of China

Postal Code: 100738

26 March 2004

Source: China Petroleum & Chemical Corporation annual report (2003), Directors' Report, p. 65. www.sinopec.com.cn

13.4.4.3 CSRC regulation of markets

The stock markets are controlled by the Chinese Securities Regulatory Commission (CSRC).[14] This has major powers under a new Securities Law, which became effective in July 1999. Section 3 sets rules for the continuing disclosure of information, stipulating that:

'The documents for the issuing and listing of shares or corporate bonds announced by companies shall be truthful, accurate and complete; they may not contain any falsehoods, misleading statements or major omissions' (Article 59).

Particularly important in this section of the Securities Law are Articles 61 and 62 which regulate the disclosure of information by listed companies. Article 62 requires companies to inform the stock market and the public of any price sensitive or 'major' events. Article 61 requires companies to submit, within four months of the year end, an annual report including:

- a brief account of the company's general situation;
- the company's financial and accounting reports and business situation;
- a brief introduction to the directors, supervisors, managers and senior management and information in their shareholdings;
- details of shares and bonds issued, including names and shareholdings of ten largest shareholders;
- other matters specified by the securities regulatory authority.

The CSRC issues standards that are applicable to all listed companies that specify what these 'other matters' are. At the end of 2003 there were 19 CSRC standards on content and format of information disclosure. The CSRC revised and re-issued *The Standard Form and Content of Information for Disclosure by Companies Making Public Issues No 2: Form and Content of the Annual Report* early in 1999 to increase the amount of disclosure required. A further revision was issued in 2001. It was extended in 2003 to require that managers and financial executives guarantee in writing that the information contained in the financial reports is true and complete. The revised version also standardizes the format of the annual report by including a reporting format in an appendix.[15]

---

[14] Website has pages in English: www.csrc.gov.cn.

[15] *IAS Plus Country Updates*, China, April 2003.

Exhibit 13.8 Corporate governance framework, China Petroleum & Chemical Company

> **Corporate Governance**
>
> The China Petroleum & Chemical Company (Sinopec, the Company) bases its corporate governance on the Code of Corporate Governance for Listed Companies, as issued by the China Securities and Regulatory Commission (CSRC), under the State Economic and Trade Commission; Company Law of the People's Republic of China; Mandatory Provisions for the Articles of Association of Companies to be Listed Overseas; Guidelines for the Articles of Association of Listed Companies; Standards of Corporate Governance of Listed Companies; Sinopec's Articles of Association; and other governing regulations where Sinopec is listed.
>
> This fact sheet is prepared based on our Articles of Association and other documents, and relevant codes, regulations and laws as noted above.
>
> In China, the regulation and enforcement of a company's corporate governance is primarily the responsibility of the Board of Directors and the Supervisory Committee.

Source: Extract from website Corporate Governance Fact Sheet, China Petroleum & Chemical Company, http://english.sinopec.com/en-ir/en-governance/index.shtml, August 2004

The CSRC is particularly concerned to increase the amount of foreign investment in Chinese companies. It has introduced a number of measures to make such investment more attractive. This includes proposals to improve the corporate governance of such companies as well as making information more accessible. For example, its website provided access to English language reports of all companies with listed B shares but this was an exercise for 1998 that has not yet been repeated annually (see www.csrc.gov.cn). It has issued a *Code of Corporate Governance for Listed Companies in China* (issued January 2001)[16] which sets out basic principles for corporate governance, has specified means of investor protection, and has published basic rules of behaviour for directors and senior managers such as *The Guidelines for Introducing Independent Directors to the Board of Directors of Listed Companies* (2001).[17] This emphasis on corporate governance is reflected in company reporting (see Exhibit 13.8).

Under revised CSRC guidelines issued in January 2003, managers and financial executives must guarantee in writing that the reports contain no major errors or misleading information (see Exhibit 13.9). As revised in December 2003 the rules also

Exhibit 13.9 Guarantee by managers and financial executives, SVA Electron

> **Important Note**
>
> The Board of Directors and directors of the company guarantee that the contents of this report contain no false records, misleading statements or major omissions and they will bear individual and joint responsibilities for the truthfulness, accuracy and integrity of the contents. Company board president Mr. Gu Peizhu, general manager Mr. Gu Zhonghui, general accountant Mr. Teng Mingfang and Financial Accounting Dept. manager Mr. Jin Guiyan claim they guarantee the truthfulness and integrity of the financial statements contained in the annual report.

Source: SVA Electron annual report (2003), Important Note and Index, p. 1. www.sva-e.com

---

[16] An English language version is on the CSRC website www.csrc.gov.cn/en/homepage/index_en.jsp.

[17] Ibid.

require additional disclosure in the annual report relating to the use of funds of the listed companies by controlling shareholders and related parties and also provision of financial guarantees to these parties (see Exhibit 13.7 earlier).

The Securities and Futures Ordinance was enacted in 2002 to take effect in 2003, consolidating and modernizing ordinances accumulated over some 30 years.[18]

13.4.5 Accounting profession

As might be expected, one of the problems that China is facing is the extreme shortage of qualified accountants. Until the reforms began all that was required at the enterprise level was people who could follow the prescribed systems and record the required transactions. The only professional accountants were the 10,000 or so who had qualified before the communist revolution.[19]

The Accounting Society of China (ASC) was the first accounting body to be set up after the beginnings of the reforms, in January 1980. The ASC is an academic body which seeks to foster education and research. It was the first body to become involved in standard-setting when, in 1987, it formed a committee to establish a conceptual framework and promote accounting standards. Its work was superseded by Ministry of Finance initiatives when the ministry formed a similar working group. This was the first stage in setting and enforcing authoritative standards.[20]

The main accounting professional body, the Chinese Institute of Certified Public Accountants (CICPA), was set up in 1988. Government influence can be seen most obviously in its membership, with the chair of CICPA being the Ministry of Finance Vice-Minister in charge of accounting affairs. Following merger with the Association of Certified Public Auditors (ACPA) in 1996, the membership rose to approximately 129,000 (1 per 10,000 or so of population in comparison to the UK at 1 per 400) (see Exhibit 4.8).

While the CICPA does not set accounting standards, it has issued a number of important guidelines or codes of conduct on professional ethics, education and training and practice review which all of its members are expected to follow. In 2004 the CICPA established an Auditing Standards Committee, a Discipline Committee, an Appeal Committee and a Rights-protecting Committee. The CICPA drafts 'Independent Auditing Standards' which are issued by the Ministry of Finance.[21] These are generally consistent with IAASB/IFAC standards.

Exhibit 13.10 reproduces the audit report of the China Petroleum & Chemical Corporation. This report, with its reference to 'China's Independent Auditing Standards', and the 'Accounting Standards for Business Enterprises and the Accounting Regulations for Business Enterprises', can be compared with the audit report of CNOOC Ltd as shown in Exhibit 13.11. The report in Exhibit 13.11 is designed for use in the Hong Kong stock exchange and it refers instead to Hong Kong 'Statements of Auditing Standards' and the 'Hong Kong Companies Ordinance'.

The CICPA also assists the Ministry of Finance in organizing the national CPA exams and in approving the registration of CPAs. The 1993 Law of Certified Public Accountants gave the Ministry of Finance power to supervise CPAs, auditing firms and accountancy bodies. It was made responsible for developing the national CPA exams and authorizing the establishment of CPA firms. It has also taken steps to improve professional attitudes.

---

[18] www.hksfc.org.hk/eng (website of the Securities and Futures Commission).

[19] Blake and Gao (1995).

[20] Hao (1999).

[21] Xiao *et al*. (2000).

Exhibit 13.10 Chinese based audit report, China Petroleum & Chemical Corporation

REPORT OF THE PRC AUDITORS

To the Shareholders of China Petroleum & Chemical Corporation:

We have audited the accompanying Company's consolidated balance sheet and balance sheet at 31 December 2003, and the consolidated income statement and profit appropriation statement, income statement and profit appropriation statement, consolidated cash flow statement and cash flow statement for the year then ended. The preparation of these financial statements is the responsibility of the Company's management. Our responsibility is to express an audit opinion on these financial statements based on our audit.

We conducted our audit in accordance with China's Independent Auditing Standards of the Certified Public Accountants. Those standards require that we plan and perform the audit to obtain reasonable assurance as to whether the financial statements are free from material misstatement. An audit includes examination, on a test basis, of evidence supporting the amounts and disclosures in the financial statements, an assessment of the accounting policies used and significant estimates made by the Company's management in the preparation of the financial statements, as well as evaluating the overall financial statements presentation. We believe that our audit provides a reasonable basis for our opinion.

In our opinion, the above-mentioned financial statements comply with the requirements of the Accounting Standards for Business Enterprises and the Accounting Regulations for Business Enterprises issued by the Ministry of Finance of the People's Republic of China and present fairly, in all material respects, the Company's consolidated financial position and financial position at 31 December 2003, and the consolidated results of operations, results of operations, consolidated cash flows and cash flows for the year then ended.

KPMG Huazhen
8/1'; Office Tower E2 Oriental Plaza
No.1, East Chang An Ave.
Beijing, The People's Republic of China
Post Code: 100738

Certified Public Accountants
Registered in the People's Republic of China

Wu Wei
Song Chenyang

26 March 2004

Source: China Petroleum & Chemical Corporation annual report (2003), p. 87.

Exhibit 13.11 Hong Kong based audit report, CNOOC Limited

REPORT OF THE AUDITORS

To the shareholders of
CNOOC Limited
(Incorporated in Hong Kong with limited liability)

We have audited the financial statements of CNOOC Limited (the "Company") and its subsidiaries (the "Group") on pages 53 to 105 which have been prepared in accordance with accounting principles generally accepted in Hong Kong.

Respective responsibilities of directors and auditors

The Companies Ordinance requires the directors to prepare financial statements which give a true and fair view. In preparing financial statements which give a true and fair view it is fundamental that appropriate accounting policies are selected and applied consistently. It is our responsibility to form an independent opinion, based on our audit, on those financial statements and to report our opinion solely to you, as a body, in accordance with Section 141 of the Hong Kong Companies Ordinance, and for no other purpose. We do not assume responsibility towards or accept liability to any other person for the contents of this report.

▶

Exhibit 13.11 *(Continued)*

Basis of opinion

We conducted our audit in accordance with Statements of Auditing Standards issued by the Hong Kong Society of Accountants. An audit includes an examination, on a test basis, of evidence relevant to the amounts and disclosures in the financial statements. It also includes an assessment of the significant estimates and judgements made by the directors in the preparation of the financial statements, and of whether the accounting policies are appropriate to the Company's and the Group's circumstances, consistently applied and adequately disclosed. We planned and performed our audit so as to obtain all the information and explanations which we considered necessary in order to provide us with sufficient evidence to give reasonable assurance as to whether the financial statements are free from material misstatement. In forming our opinion we also evaluated the overall adequacy of the presentation of information in the financial statements. We believe that our audit provides a reasonable basis for our opinion.

Opinion

In our opinion the financial statements give a true and fair view of the state of affairs of the Company and of the Group as at 31 December 2003 and of the profit and cash flows of the Group for the year then ended and have been properly prepared in accordance with the Companies Ordinance.

Ernst & Young
Certified Public Accountants

Hong Kong
15 March 2004

Source: CNOOC Limited annual report (2003), p. 52.

These include reorganizing CPA firms to be independent of Government ownership and to assume legal liability for their work.[22] Under the commitments made for WTO membership, China has allowed CPAs to set up partnerships or independent firms.

13.5 External influences

Accounting in China has a very long history. Both accounting and auditing systems were highly developed, at least as regards the recording of economic and financial transactions, more than 2,000 years ago. Indeed, the emergence of the first form of accounting can be traced back to the Shang Dynasty (1,500 to 1,000 BC). However, accounting failed to develop rapidly after this due at least partially to domestic political upheavals. Thus, until the early part of this century single-entry bookkeeping predominated. Western accounting methods began to be imported into the country in the 1920s although they were still relatively underdeveloped when the People's Republic of China (PRC) was formed in 1949.

With the change to a communist system, China adopted wholesale the Soviet system of accounting. Despite attempts at developing a unique Chinese political and economic system, during the period of both the Great Leap Forward (1958–59) and the Cultural Revolution (1966–76), the accounting system remained largely unchanged until economic liberalization began in the late 1970s.

China is now attempting to find a unique development path combining socialist social structures with capitalist markets. This has involved major changes in the ways in which enterprises are organized with the introduction of profit measures and private ownership.

---

[22] Yunwei and Pacter (2000).

This means that the accounting system has also had to be radically restructured, starting virtually from the beginning. This has encompassed all aspects of accounting, including not only financial accounting and reporting by both domestic enterprises and foreign joint ventures, but also stock market regulations, auditing regulations and accounting education.

As discussed in Chapter 4, it is obviously neither feasible nor sensible to develop a brand new accounting system without reference to the models established elsewhere. This has meant that China has now begun to import western accounting rules as exemplified by, in particular, IFRS. These are being deliberately imported into China by the Chinese authorities rather than being imposed by more powerful players. However the authorities are probably aware of strong encouragement towards IASB standards from joint venture companies, the World Bank, the International Monetary Fund, and foreign accounting firms.[23]

13.6 Accounting regulations and the IASB

CICPA became a member of IFAC and the IASC in May 1997 and China became an observer at IASC Board meetings shortly afterwards. Rather than introducing IASB standards, the intention was to introduce internationally acceptable standards which, while not being identical to IASB standards, would be in harmony with them. The differences between the two can be attributed to the unique circumstances of China (see Exhibit 13.12). A large state-owned enterprise sector and a system of accounting that was very different from western systems, made it impossible to adopt all of the principles endorsed by the IASB. China's socio-economic environment in the 1990s was not appropriate for adoption of IASs on a large scale (Ren and Alexander, 2000). Specifically, it has been found that with Chinese accountants still learning how to work in a market economy and with it sometimes being difficult to translate accounting concepts and terms into Chinese, the new standards are often not only simpler and less sophisticated but also more prescriptive than IASB standards.

Exhibit 13.12 Comparison of accounting practices in China with requirements of IAS/IFRS: key similarities and differences

	Disclosure and presentation	Practice in China
General aspects		
IFRS 1	First-time adoption of IFRS	Not covered
IAS 1	Presentation of Financial Statements	Same set of financial statements, with additional detail (e.g. appropriation of profit to reserves)
Specific aspects		
IAS 7	Cash Flow Statements	PRC standard 2
IAS 8	Accounting Policies, Changes in Accounting Estimates and Errors	PRC standard 8; Ch 10 of Accounting System
IFRS 5	Non-current Assets Held for Sale and Discontinued Operations	Not addressed
IAS 14	Segment Reporting	Business and geographical segments
IAS 24	Related Party Disclosures	PRC standard 1 and Ch 12 of Accounting Systems

---

[23] Xiang (1998); Xiao *et al.* (2000).

Exhibit 13.12 *(Continued)*

IAS 33	Earnings per Share	CSRC gives some guidance on EPS disclosure; differs from IAS
IAS 34	Interim Financial Reporting	PRC standard 14
Asset recognition and measurement		
IAS 2	Inventories	PRC standard 15 and Ch 2 Section 1 of Accounting System
IAS 16	Property, Plant and Equipment	PRC standard 16
IAS 36	Impairment of Assets	Ch 2 Section 5 of Accounting System. No guidance on assets that do not generate cash flows individually
IAS 23	Borrowing costs	PRC standard 12. Must capitalize long-term borrowing costs as part of asset cost
IAS 38	Research and Development costs	Expense all R&D (patent registration and legal costs are capitalized)
IAS 38	Intangible Assets	In non-monetary transaction, measured at carrying amount of asset surrendered
IAS 32, 39	Investments (Financial Instruments)	Short-term investments at lower of cost and market value, using provision for impairment loss; long-term equity investments at cost less impairment
IAS 40	Investment Property	Generally historic cost is required
Liability recognition and measurement		
IAS 10	Events After the Balance Sheet Date	PRC standard 3. Conforms to IAS 10 from July 2003
IAS 37	Provisions, Contingent Liabilities and Contingent Assets	Undiscounted amount of best estimate to settle obligation; provisions arising from restructuring are not addressed
IAS 12	Income Taxes	May use tax payable or tax effect (recognizing deferred tax).
IAS 17	Leases	Measurement rules differ from IAS 17
IAS 19	Employee Benefits	Unfunded liability is not recognized
Financial instruments: Assets and Liabilities		
IAS 32	Financial Instruments: Disclosure and Presentation	Debt/equity classified by legal form
IAS 39	Financial Instruments: Recognition and Measurement	Hedge accounting not addressed
Recognition of economic activity		
IAS 11	Construction Contracts	Borrowing costs never included in cost of construction asset
IAS 18	Revenue	Amount stipulated in contract, rather than fair value
IAS 20	Accounting for Government Grants and Disclosure of Government Assistance	On completion, credit to equity to the extent that grant has been capitalized
IFRS 2	Share-based payments	Not covered

▶

Measurement of inflation		
IAS 29	Financial Reporting in Hyperinflationary Economies	Not covered
Group accounting		
IAS 21	The Effects of Changes in Foreign Exchange Rates	Translation adjustments are deferred in equity
IFRS 3	Business Combinations	No standard, most are acquisitions, some pooling of interest allowed
IAS 27	Consolidated and Separate Financial Statements	Wholly-owned subsidiary must produce own group accounts if it owns other companies. Subsidiaries of dissimilar activities are excluded
IAS 28	Investments in Associates	Goodwill calculated as cost of investment minus share of carrying amounts of net assets acquired
IAS 31	Interests in Joint Ventures	Must use proportionate consolidation

Source: *IAS Plus GAAP differences in your pocket: IAS and GAAP in the PRC*, Deloitte, Touche Tohmatsu (2002); ASBE (2001).

As explained in section 13.3.4, the ASBE (2001) has brought PRC standards closer to IFRS. Exhibit 13.13 shows some of the factors that still cause differences, taking the illustration from SVA Electron. Exhibit 13.14 shows other factors causing differences between PRC accounting and IFRS, as reported by China Petroleum & Chemical Corporation.

Exhibit 13.13 Impact of IAS adjustments, SVA Electron

(II). Impact of IAS adjustments on profit/(loss) after taxation and minority interests and shareholders' equity

The statutory accounts of the Group were prepared in accordance with PRC accounting regulations applicable to joint stock limited companies. These accounting principles differed in certain significant respects from IAS. The effects of these differences on the tax, minority interests for the year ended Dec 31st, 2003 and shareholders' equity at that date were summarized as follows:

	Note	Net profit after tax and minority interest 2003	Shareholders' equity 2003
		RMB (000)	RMB (000)
As determined pursuant to PRC accounting regulations		135,105	2,867,635
Revenue and expense directly recognized as reserve	(a)		
Staff bonus and welfare fund		(10,096)	
Other		1,914	
Intangible asset and its amortization yet to be recognized	(b)	31	(52)

Exhibit 13.13	(Continued)		

Goodwill and its amortization directly recognized as reserve	(c)	2,835	(36,199)
Minority interest	(d)	(2,291)	18,475
As determined pursuant to IAS		127,498	2,849,859

Note:

(a) (1) Staff welfare and benefit fund was appropriated directly from reserve based on the profit after taxation in A Share. The amounts were recognized as expenses in profit and loss account in B Share.

 (2) Account payable repealed by a subsidiary of the Group was credited to capital reserve in A Share and recognized as income in the profit and loss account in B Share.

(b) In A Share, the costs for modification of fixed assets of a subsidiary of the Group were capitalized as long term deferred assets and amortized over 10 years. In accordance with IAS 16, costs without any improvements on the condition of fixed assets were recognized as expenses in the period in which they were incurred.

(c) In accordance with old IAS 22, goodwill arising in prior years on acquisition of subsidiaries was directly dealt with for once.

(d) Adjustment was made because of effects on minority interest due to differences between PRC accounting regulations and IAS

Source: SVA Electron annual report (2003), Section II, pp. 2–3. www.sva-e.com

Exhibit 13.14	PRC accounting rules, China Petroleum & Chemical Corporation

Differences between financial statements prepared under the PRC accounting rules and regulations and IFRS.

Other than the differences in the classifications of certain financial statements captions and the accounting for the items described below, there are no material differences between the Group's financial statements prepared under the PRC Accounting Rules and Regulations and IFRS. The major differences are:

(i) Depreciation of oil and gas properties

Under the PRC Accounting Rules and Regulations, oil and gas properties are depreciated on a straight-line basis. Under IFRS, oil and gas properties are depreciated on the unit of production method.

(ii) Disposal of oil and gas properties

Under the PRC Accounting Rules and Regulations, gains and losses arising from the retirement or disposal of an individual item of oil and gas properties are recognised as income or expense in the income statement and are measured as the difference between the estimated net disposal proceeds and the carrying amount of the asset.

Under IFRS, gains and losses on the retirement or disposal of an individual item of proved oil and gas properties are not recognised unless the retirement or disposal encompasses an entire property. The costs of the asset abandoned or retired are charged to accumulated depreciation with the proceeds received on disposals credited to the carrying amounts of oil and gas properties.

(iii) Capitalisation of general borrowing costs

Under the PRC Accounting Rules and Regulations, only borrowing costs on funds that are specifically borrowed for construction are capitalised as part of the cost of fixed assets. Under IFRS, to the extent that funds are borrowed generally and used for the purpose of obtaining a qualifying asset, the borrowing costs should be capitalised as part of the cost of that asset.

▶

(iv) Acquisition of Sinopec National Star, Sinopec Maoming, Xi'an Petrochemical and Tahe Petrochemical
Under the PRC Accounting Rules and Regulations, the acquisition of Sinopec National Star, Sinopec Maoming, Xi'an Petrochemical and Tahe Petrochemical (the "Acquisitions") are accounted for by the acquisition method. Under the acquisition method, the income of an acquiring enterprise includes the operations of the acquired enterprise subsequent to the acquisition. The difference between the cost of acquiring Sinopec National Star and the fair value of the net assets acquired is capitalised as an exploration and production right, which is amortised over 27 years.

Under IFRS, as the Group, Sinopec National Star, Sinopec Maoming, Xi'an Petrochemical and Tahe Petrochemical are under the common control of Sinopec Group Company, the Acquisitions are considered "combination of entities under common control" which are accounted in a manner similar to a pooling-of-interests ("as-if pooling-of-interests accounting"). Accordingly, the assets and liabilities of Sinopec National Star, Sinopec Maoming, Xi'an Petrochemical and Tahe Petrochemical acquired have been accounted for at historical cost and the financial statements of the Group for periods prior to the Acquisitions have been restated to include the financial statements and results of operations of Sinopec National Star, Sinopec Maoming, Xi'an Petrochemical and Tahe Petrochemical on a combined basis. The considerations paid by the Group are treated as an equity transaction.

(v) Gain from issuance of shares by a subsidiary
Under the PRC Accounting Rules and Regulations, the increase in the Company's share of net assets of a subsidiary after the sale of additional shares by the subsidiary is credited to capital reserve. Under IFRS, such increase is recognised as income.

(vi) Gain from debt restructuring
Under the PRC Accounting Rules and Regulations, gain from debt restructuring resulting from the difference between the carrying amount of liabilities extinguished or assumed by other parties and the amount paid is credited to capital reserve. Under IFRS, the gain resulting from such difference is recognised as income.

(vii) Revaluation of land use rights
Under the PRC Accounting Rules and Regulations, land use rights are carried at revalued amount. Under IFRS, land use rights are carried at historical cost less amortisation. Accordingly, the surplus on the revaluation of land use rights, credited to revaluation reserve, was eliminated.

(viii) Unrecognised losses of subsidiaries
Under the PRC Accounting Rules and Regulations, the results of subsidiaries are included in the Group's consolidated income statement to the extent that the subsidiaries' accumulated losses do not result in their carrying amount being reduced to zero, without the effect of minority interests. Further losses are debited to a separate reserve in the shareholders' funds.

Under IFRS, the results of subsidiaries are included in the Group's consolidated income statement from the date that control effectively commences until the date that control effectively ceases.

(ix) Pre-operating expenditures
Under the PRC Accounting Rules and Regulations, expenditures incurred during the start-up period are aggregated in long-term deferred expenses and charged to the income statement when operations commence. Under IFRS, expenditures on start-up activities are recognised as an expense when they are incurred.

(x) Impairment losses on long-lived assets
Under the PRC Accounting Rules and Regulations and IFRS, impairment charges are recognised when the carrying value of long-lived assets exceeds the higher of their net selling price and the value in use which incorporates discounting the asset's estimated future cash flows. Due to the difference in the depreciation method of oil and gas properties discussed in (i) above, the provision for impairment losses and reversal of impairment loss under the PRC Accounting Rules and Regulations are different from the amounts recorded under IFRS.

Exhibit 13.14 *(Continued)*

(xi) Government grants

Under the PRC Accounting Rules and Regulations, government grants should be credited to capital reserve. Under IFRS, government grants relating to the purchase of equipment used for technology improvements are initially recorded as long term liabilities and are offset against the cost of assets to which the grants related when construction commences. Upon transfer to property, plant and equipment, the grants are recognised as an income over the useful life of the property, plant and equipment by way of reduced depreciation charge.

Effects of major differences between the PRC Accounting Rules and Regulations and IFRS on net profit are analysed as follows:

	Note	2003 RMB millions	2002 RMB millions
Net profit under the PRC Accounting Rules and Regulations		19,011	14,121
Adjustments:			
Depreciation of oil and gas properties	(i)	1,784	2,311
Disposal of oil and gas properties	(ii)	1,260	–
Capitalisation of general borrowing costs	(iii)	389	338
Acquisition of Sinopec Maoming, Xi'an Petrochemical and Tahe Petrochemical	(iv)	326	235
Acquisition of Sinopec National Star	(iv)	117	117
Gain from issuance of shares by a subsidiary	(v)	136	–
Gain from debt restructuring	(vi)	82	–
Revaluation of land use rights	(vii)	18	18
Unrecognized losses of subsidiaries	(viii)	(182)	–
Pre-operating expenditures	(ix)	(169)	–
Effects of the above adjustments on taxation		(1,179)	(825)
Net profit under IFRS*		**21,593**	**16,315**

Analysis of the effects of major differences between the PRC Accounting Rules and Regulations and IFRS on Shareholders' Funds:

	Note	2003 RMB millions	2002 RMB millions
Shareholders' funds under the PRC Accounting Rules and Regulations		162,946	151,717
Adjustments:			
Depreciation of oil and gas properties	(i)	10,885	9,112
Disposal of oil and gas properties	(ii)	1,260	–
Capitalisation of general borrowing costs	(iii)	1,125	736
Acquisition of Sinopec Maoming, Xi'an Petrochemical and Tahe Petrochemical	(iv)	–	9,338
Acquisition of Sinopec National Star	(iv)	(2,812)	(2,929)
Revaluation of land use rights	(vii)	(870)	(822)

▶

Effect of minority interests on unrecognised losses of subsidiaries	(viii)	61	
Pre-operating expenditures	(ix)	(169)	–
Impairment losses on long-lived assets	(x)	(113)	(113)
Government grants	(xi)	(326)	(291)
Effects of the above adjustments on taxation		(4,088)	(2,925)
Shareholders' funds under IFRS*		167,899	163,823

* The above financial information is extracted from the financial statements prepared in accordance with IFRS which have been audited by KPMG.

Source: China Petroleum & Chemical Corporation annual report (2003), pp. 10, 159–160. www.sinopec.com.cn

13.7 The accounting system

This section describes some of the practices where PRC accounting differs from IFRS, or has been different but is now converging. Footnotes give reference to the relevant Articles of the ASBE (2001) which is available in English on the website www.iasplus.com.

13.7.1 Disclosure and presentation

The rules for disclosure and presentation are found mainly in the ASBE (2001).

13.7.1.1 Financial statements

A financial and accounting report of an enterprise comprises the accounting statements, the notes to the accounting statements, and a financial condition explanatory memorandum.[24]

The accounting statements[25] include all the statements normally found in western annual reports, with additional detail as follows:

- a balance sheet,
- an income statement,
- a cash flow statement,
- a statement of provision for impairment of assets,
- a profit appropriation statement,
- a statement of changes in owners' equity,
- a statement of segmental information,
- other relevant supplementary information.

Notes to the accounting statements should at least include details of significant accounting policies and estimates, with an explanation of changes in these; an explanation of any non-compliance with basic accounting principles; details of

---

[24] Article 153.
[25] Article 154.

contingencies and events occurring after the balance sheet date; disclosures of related party relationships and transactions; details of the transfer or disposal of significant assets; details of business combinations and de-mergers; detailed information about significant items in the accounting statements; and other disclosures necessary to enable users to understand and analyze the accounting statements.[26] These requirements do not differ significantly from specific disclosure requirements in relevant IASB standards, although they are generally far less detailed and lack sufficient explanation to be easily and consistently implemented. They reflect a similar Article in previous regulation and illustrate the compromise, and potential confusion, that may arise where IASB standards are introduced by adaptation in parallel to the development of previous legislation.

13.7.1.2 Small-sized enterprises[27]

In April 2004 the MOF issued a new Accounting System for Small Enterprises (ASSE) to take effect from 1 January 2005. Small enterprises are allowed to choose to follow the ASSE or the ASBE. However, if a parent adopts the ASBE then so must the subsidiaries, even if they qualify as small enterprises. The benefit of the ASSE is that it provides simplifications and exemptions compared to ASBE, in areas such as impairment of assets, equity method investments, finance leases, capitalization of borrowing costs, and post-balance-sheet date events. An industrial company is small if it employs less than 300 people, a construction company less than 600 and a retail business less than 100. A small enterprise does not raise funds from the public by issuing shares. This initiative by the MOF recognizes that a lack of specific guidance for small enterprises is one of the problems of IFRS for many developing economies.

13.7.2 Asset recognition and measurement

13.7.2.1 Inventory valuation

This is perhaps the most surprising instance of extreme flexibility. The Accounting System[28] and the new PRC accounting standard both allow the use of first-in-first-out (FIFO), last-in-first-out (LIFO), weighted or moving average, or specific identification methods of valuation. This reflects the flexibility of IAS 2 before it was changed in December 2003 to remove the LIFO option.

Companies should use the lower of cost and net realizable value. Where net realizable value is lower than cost, the difference should be recognized as a provision for decline in value.[29]

13.7.2.2 Depreciation

The Accounting System is similar to IAS 16. It requires depreciation of fixed assets, based on expected useful lives and estimated net residual values that represent the nature and pattern of use of the assets.[30] Fully depreciated assets must not be depreciated further.

---

[26] Article 155.

[27] *IAS Plus Country Update*, China, July 2004.

[28] Article 20(3).

[29] Article 20(5).

[30] Article 36.

An enterprise may choose from different depreciation methods, including straight-line, unit of production, sum-of-years' digits and double declining balance. The flexibility in choice of depreciation method and calculation is new. Previously, enterprises were not free to select either the most appropriate method of depreciation or the economic lives of their assets, and excess depreciation was permitted.

13.7.2.3 Valuation rules – tangible assets

The recording of cost is the same as the IASB preferred treatment, namely cost on acquisition, to include any expenditure necessarily incurred for bringing the fixed asset to working condition ready for use.[31] Interest on borrowings may be capitalized where appropriate. The IASB allowed alternative of revaluation is not mentioned in the PRC regulations or the PRC standard. A fixed asset received as a capital contribution by an investor should be recorded at an amount agreed by all investing parties.[32] Under IAS 16 it would be recorded at fair value. Major overhaul costs may be deferred and amortized under the PRC standard; this would not be allowed under IAS 16. Borrowing costs may be capitalized only on the construction of long-lived fixed assets, not on inventories or service contracts. The latter two are permitted by IAS 23.

13.7.2.4 Investments

The rules for measuring long-term investments in equity securities require equity accounting where the investing enterprise holds 20 per cent or more of the voting shares or has a significant influence.[33] Below that level, the investment is recorded at cost. Long-term debt investments are recorded at cost. Where the recoverable amount of a long-term investment is less than the carrying amount at the end of a period, the difference is recognized as a provision for impairment loss on the long-term investment.[34] Under IAS 39 the long-term investment is equity securities would be measured at fair value, with value changes recognized either in net profit or in equity. Current asset investments should be measured at the lower of cost and market value at the end of a period.[35] If the market value is below cost there should be a provision for decline in current value.[36] Under IAS 39 (see section 2.5.2), investments held for trading and available-for-sale investments are marked to market, while held-to-maturity investments are reduced to estimated recoverable amount either directly or through use of an allowance account.

Previously, the ASBE permitted only the use of historical costs, and did not allow this figure to be written down in recognition of any permanent fall in the value of the investment. Similar rules applied to short-term investments, which also could not be written down below their historical costs. Although the new rules are closer to IFRS, differences remain as illustrated by the wording of the note to the PRC financial statements of China Petroleum & Chemical Corporation (Exhibit 13.15). The different policy does not affect the reconciliation of PRC accounting to IFRS (see Exhibit 13.14 earlier), showing that differences in policy do not necessarily cause a difference in reported financial information. Exhibit 13.15 is also interesting in referring to the 'Questions and Answers' mentioned in section 13.3.4.

---

[31] Article 27.

[32] Article 27(3).

[33] Article 22(2).

[34] Article 24.

[35] Article 16(3).

[36] Articles 16(3) and 52.

Exhibit 13.15	Accounting policy statement for investments, China Petroleum & Chemical Corporation

From Notes to the PRC financial statements

Note (h) Long-term equity investments

The investment income and long-term equity investments related to the Group's investments in the associates and the Company's investments in subsidiaries, associates and jointly controlled entities are accounted for using the equity method. Equity investment difference, which is the difference between the initial investment cost and the Company's share of investors' equity of the investee enterprise, is accounted for as follows:

Any excess of the initial investment cost over the share of shareholders' funds of the investee is amortised on a straight line basis. The amortisation period is determined according to the investment period as stipulated in the relevant agreement, or 10 years if the investment period is not specified in the agreement. The amortisation is recognised as investment loss in the income statement in the relevant period.

Any shortfall of the initial investment cost over the share of shareholders' funds of the investee is recognised in "capital reserve -reserve for equity investment". Such shortfall is amortised on a straight-line basis over 10 years if the investment was acquired before the issuance of Cai Kuai [2003] No.10 "Questions and answers on implementing Accounting Regulations for Business Enterprises and related accounting standards (II)" on 7 April 2003.

An associate is a company in which the Group holds. for long-term purposes, not less than 20 per cent but not more than 50 per cent of Its equity interests and exercises significant Influence in its management. A jointly controlled entity is an entity over which the Group can exercise joint control with other venturers.

Long-term investments in entities in which the Group does not hold more than 20 per cent of their equity interests or those in which the Group holds more than 20 per cent of their equity interests but does not exercise significant influence in their management are stated at cost. Investment income is recognised when an investee enterprise declares a cash dividend or distributes profits.

Disposals or transfers of long-term equity investments are recognised in the income statement based on the difference between the disposal proceeds and the carrying amount of the investments. Long-term equity investments are valued at the lower of the carrying amount and the recoverable amount. A provision for impairment of loss is made when the recoverable amount is lower than the carrying amount.

Source: China Petroleum and Chemical Corporation annual report (2003), Notes on PRC financial statements, pp. 97–98. www.sinopec.com.cn

13.7.2.5 Valuation rules – intangible assets

The Accounting System gives detailed rules on intangible assets and other assets. It prohibits capitalization of internally generated intangibles. Amortization should be spread evenly over the expected useful life or the beneficial period prescribed in the contract, whichever is the shorter. If no period is specified, the amortization period should not exceed ten years.[37] Under IAS 38 the presumption would be a maximum of 20 years.

An example of the prescriptive detail of the Accounting System is seen in land use rights acquired by an enterprise as a transfer from the state. These rights should be accounted for as an intangible asset before construction work commences.[38] The carrying amount then becomes a fixed asset under construction until completion when it is transferred to fixed assets of property, or to the asset of property held for sale. Under IAS 38 the cost of land use rights would be treated as prepaid lease payments under an operating lease.

---

[37] Article 46.

[38] Article 47.

13.7.2.6 Deferred assets

The Accounting System is also optimistic with respect to the recognition and amortization of deferred assets.[39] These are defined as expenses paid by the enterprise, for which the amortization period is more than one year. It includes the cost of overhauling fixed assets. For example, SVA Electron recognizes costs of modification of a fixed asset as a deferred asset in its PRC financial statements, but as an expense in its IAS/IFRS statements, as shown in Exhibit 13.16.

13.7.2.7 Doubtful debts

The Accounting System requires provision for bad debts to be made on accounts receivable at the end of each period.[40] Previously the rules for writing off bad debts tended to be more prescriptive and less prudent than would be found under 'true and fair' accounting.

13.7.2.8 Exchange of assets

In emerging economies it is not unusual for transactions to be settled by an exchange of assets rather than by cash sales and purchases. Where the assets exchanged are not similar there may be no objective measure of the value of each. IAS 16 requires each asset to be measured at fair value unless the exchange transaction lacks commercial substance. If the fair values are different from each other then a gain or loss is recognized. Under the ASBE (2001) if a fixed asset or inventory is obtained by accepting non-cash assets from a debtor to satisfy a debt, then the asset should be recorded at the carrying amount of the debt receivable plus any relevant tax payments and plus or minus any 'boot' paid or received. ('Boot' means that a small amount of cash is paid or received in the transaction.) Using this approach there is no gain or loss recorded on the exchange transaction.

13.7.3 Liability recognition and measurement

Article 66 of the ASBE (2001) carries the definition of a liability which is used in the IASB Framework. The classification into current and long-term liabilities is applied.

Finance leases are recorded on the balance sheet but the fixed asset is recorded at the lower of the carrying amount on the lessor's balance sheet and the present value of the

| Exhibit 13.16 | Treatment of deferred assets, SVA Electron |

The statutory accounts of the Group were prepared in accordance with PRC accounting regulations applicable to joint stock limited companies. These accounting principles differed in certain significant respects from IAS.

....

(b) In A Share, the costs for modification of fixed assets of a subsidiary of the Group were capitalized as long term deferred assets and amortized over 10 years. In accordance with IAS 16, costs without any improvements on the condition of fixed assets were recognized as expenses in the period in which they were incurred.

Source: SVA Electron annual report (2003), Section II, Note 2, p. 3. www.sva-e.com

---

[39] Article 50.

[40] Article 18(5).

minimum lease payments. The undiscounted amount of the minimum lease payment is recorded as long-term accounts payable. The difference between the recorded amount of the asset and the amount of the liability should be recorded as unrecognized finance charges.

Government grants are reported as liabilities when received and transferred to capital reserve on completion of the project (see section 13.7.4.2).

Where a company operates a defined benefit pension plan the unfunded liability is not recognized. The pension expense is recognized when payment is made to retired employees.

13.7.4 Economic activity

13.7.4.1 Revenue recognition

The general principles for revenue recognition (Accounting System, Chapter 5) are similar to those of the IASB in IAS 18 (revised). Previously companies could choose the date of shipping, date of providing a service, date of collecting money, or the date of obtaining the right to collect money.

13.7.4.2 Government grants

When an enterprise receives a grant for a specific project, it should be accounted for as an account payable. On completion of the project the amount should be transferred from account payable to capital reserve. Under IAS 20 the grant would be recognized in income over the project period.

13.7.5 Group accounting

The Accounting System gives relatively little guidance on consolidation. An enterprise should prepare consolidated accounts if:

(a) it holds directly more than 50 per cent of the registered capital of an investee enterprise; or

(b) it holds directly 50 per cent or less of the registered capital of an investee but, in substance, has control over the investee enterprise.

In preparing consolidated accounting statements, an enterprise should comply with the principles and methods relating to compilation of consolidated accounting statements prescribed in the uniform accounting system promulgated by the state. In preparing consolidated accounting statements, an enterprise should consolidate the assets, liabilities, income, expenses, and profits of its joint venture enterprises using the proportionate consolidation method.[41]

Unlike the IASB standards, the Accounting System does not specify the method of accounting that should be used, whether pooling of interests or the purchase method, nor does it give any further guidance on when a subsidiary should be excluded from consolidation. This is an area that will be covered in later standards and, while they will provide more details on how to account for groups, it remains to be seen just how detailed the requirements will be.

---

[41] Article 158.

13.7.6 Narrative disclosures

13.7.6.1 Required disclosures

The financial condition explanatory memorandum could be regarded as similar to the Management Discussion and Analysis required by the SEC in the US. It should at least cover general information about the production and operation of the enterprise; information about the financial performance and profit appropriation; information about financing activities and liquidity; and other events that have a material impact on the financial position, operating results, and cash flows of the enterprise.[42]

13.7.6.2 Voluntary disclosures

As we have seen, the new requirements mark a major change from the old system. In the past enterprises had only to report to the state and they were not expected to produce any more information than that which was required. The Accounting System contains the idea of reporting information useful to all external users. In addition, increasing numbers of enterprises are moving from state ownership and the numbers of listed companies is now increasing quite rapidly. These changes imply that at least some enterprises are likely to begin to disclose extra information voluntarily. However, this is likely to be a slow process and the level of voluntary disclosure by most companies is likely to remain relatively low at least for the next few years. The disclosure standards of the CSRC stipulate detailed requirements which leave little scope for voluntary disclosure.[43]

13.8 Hong Kong China

As discussed above, Hong Kong reverted from British control to Chinese control in July 1997 when it became a Special Administrative Region (SAR) of China. Hong Kong, or as it is now officially termed, Hong Kong China, had been acquired by the British in stages from 1842 and since then it has been economically highly successful, as can be seen from the economic data given in Exhibit 13.17.

13.8.1 Political and economic system

Hong Kong has succeeded not only as a trading nation but also increasingly as an important financial centre. The stock exchange has grown rapidly in recent years (see Exhibit 4.3 for relative size). The economic success of Hong Kong can also be seen in its GDP. With a per capita GDP of over US$23,000, it is the seventeenth richest country in the world, sandwiched between Finland and Germany.

China has promised that Hong Kong will remain as a market-led capitalist system for at least the next 50 years, described as the 'one country, two systems' policy. Given the tiny size of Hong Kong compared to China, the absorption of Hong Kong into China might at first sight to be of little significance to China. However, as we have seen throughout this chapter, China is undergoing a profound process of change. It has introduced many market based laws and regulations and is moving more and more towards

---

[42] Article 156.

[43] Xiao (1999).

Exhibit 13.17 Hong Kong and mainland China: country profile

	China	Hong Kong	
Population	1,285.0 million	7.0 million	
Land mass	9,560,900 km^2	1,075 km^2	
GDP per head	US$900	US$23,260	
GDP per head in purchasing power parity	11.5	74.6	(USA = 100)
Origins of GDP:	%	%	
Agriculture	16.4	0.1	
Industry	51.1	5.5	
Services	32.5	94.4	
	%	%	
GDP average annual growth 1991–2001	9.8	4.0	
Inflation, average annual rate 1996–2002	0.1	–0.7	

Source: *The Economist Pocket World in Figures*, 2004 Edition, Profile Books Ltd.

a market-led capitalist system as exemplified by the economy of Hong Kong. Given the economic success of Hong Kong, it might be expected that Hong Kong will therefore be an important influence upon the rest of China.

13.8.2 Hong Kong Stock Exchange

The securities and futures market in Hong Kong is regulated by the Securities and Futures Commission, which is an independent non-governmental statutory body operating under the authority of the Securities and Futures Ordinance (operational from 2003). It is funded by levies on market transactions and fees charged to the industry.[44] Chinese (PRC) companies which are permitted to issue H shares have their shares traded in Hong Kong. Some PRC companies have a ultimate holding company in the PRC but the listed subsidiary is registered in Hong Kong (see CNOOC, Exhibit 13.18).

There were 1,037 companies quoted on the Hong Kong stock market at the end of 2003, with 80 per cent of the total market value represented by only 51 companies. In the year to September 2002, local investors were the main participants in the Hong Kong stock market, contributing 56 per cent of trading by market value. Overseas investors, all of whom were institutions, contributed 37 per cent. Among overseas investors, UK investors contributed 28 per cent of overseas agency trading, followed by the rest of Europe at 23 per cent and the US at 23 per cent.[45]

13.8.3 Accounting institutions

The institutions of Hong Kong have all been heavily influenced by the British. This includes the legal system and corporate legislation and the accounting profession.

---

[44] See www.hksfc.org.hk (English language option).

[45] *Hong Kong Exchange Fact Book 2002*, www.hkex.com.hk.

Exhibit 13.18 Information on ultimate holding company, CNOOC Limited

> **Corporate Information**
>
> CNOOC Limited (the "Company") was incorporated in the Hong Kong Special Administrative Region ("Hong Kong"), the People's Republic of China (the "PRC") on 20 August 1999 to hold the interests in certain entities thereby creating a group comprising the Company and its subsidiaries. During the year, the Company and its subsidiaries (hereinafter collectively referred to as the "Group") were principally engaged in the exploration, development, production and sale of crude oil, natural gas and other petroleum.
>
> In the opinion of the directors, the ultimate holding company is China National Offshore Oil Corporation ("CNOOC"), a company established in the PRC.

Source: CNOOC Limited annual report (2003), p. 58. www.cnnoltd.com

13.8.3.1 The Hong Kong Society of Accountants (HKSA)

The Hong Kong Society of Accountants (HKSA)[46] has in the past set its examinations in conjunction with the UK based Association of Chartered Certified Accountants (ACCA). The HKSA Qualifying Programme has mutual recognition with the ACCA qualification and with the CPA Australia. Membership of the HKSA is also open, subject to an aptitude test, to accountants that are professionally qualified in the US or a number of British Commonwealth countries including Australia, Canada and South Africa as well as the UK. As in the UK, accounting is mainly regulated via statute or company law and accounting standards. Statute, in the form of the Companies Ordinance 1965, was very largely based upon the UK Companies Act 1948. Thus, it sets out basic requirements to disclose group accounts and directors' reports and details certain disclosures inside both the accounts and the directors' report. As far as accounting is concerned, the Act is very much a disclosure act and it does not include any valuation or measurement rules.

The Professional Accountants (Amendment) Bill was passed in July 2004. It represented a step taken voluntarily by the HKSA to respond to heightened public expectations. It allowed a change of name from HKSA to the Hong Kong Institute of Certified Public Accountants. From the end of 2004, members are designated CPA (Certified Public Accountant).

13.8.3.2 Accounting standards

Accounting standards are set by the Financial Accounting Standards Committee (FASC) of the Hong Kong Society of Accountants (HKSA). The Council of the HKSA requires the FASC to develop accounting standards to achieve convergence with IFRS.[47] However the Council may consider it appropriate to include additional disclosure requirements in a Hong Kong standard, or even deviate from an IFRS. The Urgent Issues and Interpretations Sub-Committee prepares interpretations and guidelines. Accounting standards have tended to fill the gap and cover most measurement issues. Also important are auditing standards; these standards are issued by the Accounting Standards Committee (ASC) and the Auditing Standards Committee (AUSC), both being committees of the HKSA. Standards are thus professionally set; however, the ASC is made up not only of the international auditing firms' employees but also of members from small audit firms, industry and the stock exchange.

---

[46] www.hksa.org.hk.

[47] Preface to Hong Kong Financial Reporting Standards, October 2003.

Exhibit 13.19 Use of Hong Kong GAAP, CNOOC Limited

> **Summary of Significant Accounting Policies**
>
> *Basis of preparation*
> These financial statements have been prepared in accordance with Hong Kong Statements of Standard Accounting Practice, accounting principles generally accepted in Hong Kong ("Hong Kong GAAP") and the requirements of the Hong Kong Companies Ordinance. They have been prepared under the historical cost convention as modified by the revaluation of land and buildings and short term investments.

Source: CNOOC Limited annual report (2003), p. 58. www.cnnoltd.com

These standards have no statutory or legal backing. Instead, the HKSA has made them mandatory on its members. If a company fails to comply with standards, there is no legal sanction that can be taken against the company. However, if the failure to comply is not due to the necessity to report a 'true and fair view' the auditor must qualify the accounts. Failure to issue a qualified report would mean that the auditor can, at least potentially, be held liable to professional misconduct. Exhibit 13.19 gives an example of a PRC-based company, CNOOC, which is registered in Hong Kong (see Exhibit 13.18) and applies Hong Kong GAAP. Exhibit 13.20 sets out the Hong Kong Stock Exchange reporting requirements for PRC companies that use PRC accounting standards.

Exhibit 13.20 Hong Kong Stock Exchange reporting requirements for PRC companies

> **Chapter 4 — Accountants' Reports and Pro Forma Financial Information**
>
> 19A.08 The reporting accountants for a PRC issuer must be qualified and be independent to the same extent as required under rule 4.03 for the reporting accountants of any other issuer.
>
> 19A.09 A report will not normally be regarded as acceptable unless the relevant accounts have been audited to a standard comparable to that required in Hong Kong.
>
> 19A.10 Reports for PRC issuers will normally be required to conform with the requirements as to accounting standards set out in rules 4.11 to 4.13, except that PRC issuers, which adopt IFRS, will not be required to comply with the requirements in (b)(i) and (ii) of rule 4.11.
>
> > *Note: A report for a PRC issuer may, in addition, present in a separate part of the report financial information conforming with applicable PRC accounting rules and regulations provided that the report contains a statement of the financial effect of the material differences (if any) from either of the accounting standards referred to in rule 4.11, as the case may be.*
>
> 19A.11 As indicated in rules 4.14 to 4.16, where the figures in the accountants' report differ from those in the audited annual accounts, a statement of adjustments must be submitted to the Exchange enabling the figures to be reconciled.
>
> Note: Paragraphs 4.11 – 4.13 require companies to provide financial statements in accordance with Hong Kong standards or to disclose and explain departures from such standards. Paragraphs 4.14 to 4.16 require a statement of adjustments made in the accountants' report.

Source: www.hkex.com.hk (August 2004).

13.8.4 Convergence towards IASB standards[48]

Until 1993, the standards issued by the ASC were mainly local adaptations of UK standards. Since then, the standards issued have very largely been local adaptations of IASB standards. Hong Kong has decided not to issue its own standards nor to uncritically accept IASB standards; instead it currently reviews all IASB standards to assess their suitability to the particular circumstances of the country. If they are considered suitable, they are issued as local standards, adapted if necessary to meet any unique local circumstances.

The HKSA has made considerable progress in its target of convergence with IASB standards. This has resulted in the issuance of a large number of revised standards. Exhibit 13.21 indicates that there are relatively few significant differences remaining. Some of these will disappear as the IASB standards themselves are revised in the convergence project. The HKSA now issues exposure drafts contemporaneously with those of the IASB, to keep abreast of developments.

Exhibit 13.21 Comparison of accounting practices in Hong Kong with requirements of IAS/IFRS: key similarities and differences at January 2003

	Disclosure and presentation	Practice in Hong Kong
General aspects		
IFRS 1	First-time adoption of IFRS	Not yet applied
IAS 1	Presentation of Financial Statements	SSAP 1, consistent with some adaptation of detailed disclosures
Specific aspects		
IAS 7	Cash Flow Statements	SSAP 15 consistent
IAS 8	Accounting Policies, Changes in Accounting Estimates and Errors	SSAP 8 consistent
IFRS 5	Non-current Assets Held for Sale and Discontinued Operations	SSAP 33
IAS 14	Segment Reporting	SSAP 26 generally consistent
IAS 24	Related Party Disclosures	SSAP 20 generally consistent
IAS 33	Earnings per Share	SSAP 5 consistent
IAS 34	Interim Financial Reporting	SSAP 25 consistent
Asset recognition and measurement		
IAS 2	Inventories	SSAP 22 allows FIFO/LIFO
IAS 16, IAS 38	Depreciation Accounting	SSAP 17, 29
IAS 16	Property, Plant and Equipment	SSAP 17 generally consistent, with some exemptions in SSAP 17
IAS 36	Impairment of Assets	SSAP 31 consistent
IAS 23	Borrowing costs	SSAP 19 consistent, does not permit full expensing
IAS 38	Research and Development costs	SSAP 29 consistent

▶

---

[48] See *Implementing Hong Kong GAAP: Moving towards IFRS*, Deloitte Touche Tohmatsu, 2003, available on www.iasplus.com

Exhibit 13.21 *(Continued)*

IAS 38	Intangible Assets	SSAP 29 consistent
IAS 32, 39	Investments (Financial Instruments)	Exposure draft issued 2002
IAS 40	Investment Property	SSAP 13 does not permit cost method, movements in value shown in equity
Liability recognition and measurement		
IAS 10	Events After the Balance Sheet Date	SSAP 9 consistent
IAS 37	Provisions, Contingent Liabilities and Contingent Assets	SSAP 28 consistent
IAS 12	Income Taxes	SSAP 12 (revised) generally consistent, includes examples based on Australian standard
IAS 17	Leases	SSAP 14 generally consistent, different treatment of properties held under government leases
IAS 19	Employee Benefits	SSAP 34 consistent
Financial instruments: Assets and Liabilities		
IAS 32	Financial Instruments: Disclosure and Presentation	No equivalent standard, exposure draft issued 2002
IAS 39	Financial Instruments: Recognition and Measurement	SSAP 24, less comprehensive than IAS 39, exposure draft issued 2002
Recognition of economic activity		
IAS 11	Construction Contracts	SSAP 23 consistent
IAS 18	Revenue	SSAP 18 consistent
IAS 20	Accounting for Government Grants and Disclosure of Government Assistance	SSAP 35 consistent
IFRS 2	Share-based payments	Not yet applied
Measurement of inflation		
IAS 29	Financial Reporting in Hyperinflationary Economies	No equivalent standard. Exposure draft issued 2002
Group accounting		
IAS 21	The Effects of Changes in Foreign Exchange Rates	SSAP 11 (revised) generally consistent but less comprehensive
IFRS 3	Business Combinations	SSAP 30 broadly consistent, no pooling of interests, but law allows some exclusions from consolidation
IAS 27	Consolidated and Separate Financial Statements	SSAP 32 broadly consistent, except that Hong Kong law allows some exclusions
IAS 28	Investments in Associates	SSAP 10 broadly similar except some differences in investors' separate accounts
IAS 31	Interests in Joint Ventures	SSAP 21 consistent, permits equity accounting but not proportionate consolidation

Source: Based on *Implementing Hong Kong GAAP: Moving towards IFRS*, Deloitte Touche Tohmatsu, January 2003.

13.9 Gray's accounting values

Chapter 5 explains how Gray (1988) derived accounting values from studies of societal value dimensions by Hofstede (1984). Hofstede (1991) included an additional dimension based on Chinese values relating to a long-term versus a short-term orientation. Gray (1988) concluded that China's accounting development and practice should be in the cluster that supports statutory control, uniform practices, a conservative measurement approach and secrecy in disclosure. Chow *et al.* (1995) analyzed the accounting debate of the 1990s and particularly the adoption of accounting standards from 1993 in moving from a rigid and uniform approach towards a more Anglo-Saxon orientation. They concluded that a continuing mix of uniform system and professional standards would be necessary.

13.9.1 Professionalism versus statutory control

As we have seen, the system of accounting is one which relies exclusively upon statutory control. While accounting standards are issued, they are issued by the Ministry of Finance independently of the profession; the CICPA is limited to setting auditing standards and acting as a trade organization for exams and CPA registration. This position is probably inevitable – the state traditionally closely controlled all enterprises by a system of centralized plans and as one part of this system of control it has imposed a highly regulated set of accounting plans. The state is unlikely to give up this power to a professional body unless there is a very good reason to do so. The profession is also still relatively new, small and powerless and it is currently occupied with the problems involved in meeting the new audit requirements. As such, it is unlikely to be in the position to offer a strong case for why standard setting should be devolved from the state. The interesting question is what might happen in the future. It remains to be seen whether or not, once the profession expands in size and once the full set of basic accounting regulations are in place, the system will rely less exclusively upon statutory control.

13.9.2 Uniformity versus flexibility

While the accounting system lies at an extreme position on the professionalism/statutory control continuum, it is more difficult to place it on the uniformity/flexibility continuum. The UAR was a uniform system giving enterprises no discretion on how to account for particular transactions or events. This philosophy continues into the new regulations although there are a number of areas where enterprises are given almost complete discretion over the methods to use. The result is a dual approach in which China has retained a uniform accounting system in the ASBE while also developing accounting standards based on IFRS. Xiao *et al.* (2004) explain the co-existence of the two approaches to accounting regulation in terms of the special circumstances of a transforming government, strong state-ownership, a weak accounting profession, a weak and imperfect equity market, and the inertial effect of accounting tradition and cultural factors.

13.9.3 Conservatism versus optimism

The concept of conservatism or prudence is a relatively new and controversial concept for most Chinese enterprises. The Accounting System states that an enterprise should comply with the requirements of the prudence concept. An enterprise should not overstate assets or revenue, or understate liabilities or expenses. It should not provide for any hidden reserve.[49] Previously, prudence was in the regulations but was not an overriding concept and was not universally applied. The reasons for this are twofold. First, prudence had always been regarded as a feature of capitalist accounting which could be used by management to manipulate profits and to exploit the workers. As such, criticisms of the concept used to be found in nearly all Chinese accounting text-books until the 1980s. Secondly, prudence tends to result in a reduction in reported surpluses or profits. As these were handed back to the state, the introduction of prudence would have resulted in a fall in state revenues.

When the measurement rules for specific assets are considered it is clear that while the Chinese system has moved towards IASB standards, it is still different from those standards in certain important respects.[50]

13.9.4 Secrecy versus transparency

Chow *et al.* (1995) explain that a society like China with large power distance and strong uncertainty avoidance means that the preference for secrecy is relatively high. On the other hand the collectivist culture requires business enterprises to be accountable to society by way of providing information. The government therefore intervenes to prescribe disclosure requirements. ASBE 2001 has brought greater transparency to PRC accounting.[51] There remains a strong element of secrecy in the limited range of narrative disclosure required and the relatively low level of voluntary disclosure. In business combinations there continue to be exit routes that allow incomplete recognition of assets and liabilities.

13.10 Empirical studies

13.10.1 Classification studies

China has not been included in any of the empirical studies concerned with classifying accounting systems. If it had been included it would have formed an extra or new group. Until the reforms began it would have grouped alongside the USSR and other East European countries. Since the Chinese reforms began, China has moved away from a centralized, socialist and plan based accounting system. Likewise, the countries of East Europe have also been dismantling their accounting systems and replacing them with systems more akin to those in various western countries. If the Chinese accounting reforms described above are compared with those of, for example, Poland, as discussed in Chapter 10, it is clear that the reforms have taken somewhat different directions. We saw in Chapter 10 how Poland has been heavily influenced by the EU and has implemented accounting rules designed to be in harmony with EU rules. China in contrast is attempting to harmonize with the IASB while adapting the standards to meet the continuing unique features of the country. While China has introduced many of the institutions that exist in free markets, state-owned enterprises are still important and the state still maintains its socialist orientation with control

---

[49] Article 11(12).

[50] Pacter (2001).

[51] Ibid.

of the economy and regulation of business being of prime importance. Thus, if China was now to be classified alongside other countries it would probably no longer form a large group with all the countries of Eastern Europe. Instead, it would probably form its own unique group as a country that has a system which shows the influence of international standards while still retaining some characteristics of the pre-reform system.

13.10.2 Comparability measures

We might expect the figures reported by Chinese companies to be quite different from those reported from similar companies from other countries, because of differences in the accounting rules and differences in the environment in which the companies act. As we saw above, the concept of conservatism is a new one in China. While historical costs have been used, assets have not in the past been written down below cost. To the extent that inventories are overvalued and liabilities are not recognized, Chinese profits will be relatively overstated. Similarly, R&D capitalization and the capitalization of self-generated intangibles and pre-operating expenses will also lead to a relative overstatement of earnings. However, there are other accounting methods used in China that will in contrast tend to reduce reported earnings. The use of LIFO, one-off fixed asset revaluations and excess depreciation charges will all reduce reported earnings. Whether the overall effect is one of reducing or increasing earnings in contrast with the equivalent UK or US firm is not obvious.

In the years before the ASBE (2001) there were significant differences between PRC accounting and IAS-based accounting. An idea of the differences between IAS and PRC standards can be gained from the work of Chen *et al.* (1999) who examined the reconciliation statements of between 34 and 50 companies with B shares listed on the Shanghai stock exchange for each of the years 1994–97 (making a total of 165 cases in all). In most cases it was found that IAS based earnings were the more conservative. Thus, in 133 cases PRC-based earnings were the larger and in only 29 cases were they smaller than IAS-based earnings. In no case did restatement to IAS turn a loss into a profit, although in contrast there were 18 cases when the reconciliation turned a profit into a loss. In each year the PRC-reported earnings were, on average significantly larger than the IAS-based earnings. The five items that accounted for the largest differences in the two sets of earnings figures were found to be:

- foreign currency translation,
- bad debts,
- fixed assets valuation, revaluation and depreciation,
- accrued expenses,
- long-term investments.

Although the average differences were large (mean differences varying across the four years from 17.9 per cent to 30.1 per cent) these differences are likely to become less important over time. Five differences are largely eliminated by the ASBE 2001 (inventory valuation, bad debt allowances, long-term investment valuation, deferred tax and use of equity or cost-method). Chen *et al.* (1999) suggest that these five items accounted for approximately 40 per cent of the differences in reported earnings. In addition, the differences in foreign currency treatment were caused by capitalizations created when the monetary reforms were first introduced. These are likely to be fully amortized by now and will no longer affect the earnings figures produced.

13.10.3 Disclosure studies

Ferguson *et al.* (2002) asked: 'What is the level of voluntary disclosure in the annual reports of wholly state-owned PRC enterprises listed on the Hong Kong stock exchange?' This was the first empirical examination of former wholly-owned SOEs (state-owned enterprises) listed internationally. These are the Chinese companies that issue H-shares.

They tested for, and found, greater voluntary disclosure by H-share companies, particularly in financial and strategic disclosures. They suggested several possible reasons:

- Keeping secret might be seen as 'bad news', causing investors to reject the shares ('adverse selection').
- Investors are afraid of things that are kept secret by managers ('information asymmetry').
- The H-share companies do not fear competitors because they have government protection and so do not fear losing cash flows through loss of market share.
- H-share companies want to attract investors.
- H-share companies are not afraid of attracting the attention of regulators ('political costs').
- H-share companies want to raise finance at the lowest cost of capital, so focus on financial and strategic disclosures.

Their second test aimed to show that voluntary disclosure by Red-Chip firms will be lower than that by H-share firms (Red-Chip are the highest rated Hong Kong companies, so called by comparison to 'Blue Chip' which are the highest rated UK companies). Their reasoning was that Red-Chip firms face higher risks from competition (proprietary costs)

The authors suggested that H-share firms may reflect state-initiated disclosure policies rather than management policy. The government of PRC wants to lower the cost of capital in order to raise more capital and expose Chinese companies to investors.

They next compared nine companies issuing H and A shares with 18 companies issuing A shares only, in the consumer electronics industry. Disclosure by the 'H and A' group was significantly higher than that of the 'A alone' group. They concluded that disclosure practices of H-share PRC companies listing in Hong Kong are sensitive to the needs of investors and are not driven by state ownership alone. They also appear to be sensitive to management's assessments of costs and benefits. However there is evidence of state-encouraged disclosure policies. The research is limited by the small size of samples.

Summary and conclusions

This chapter has described a country of contrasts. China has undergone profound changes in recent years. The economic system is still changing and the country is in the midst of introducing many new accounting standards. China has moved from a system of public ownership of all enterprises to a mixed system with increasing private ownership of both small and large companies. Many companies now freely trade their shares on both domestic and overseas stock markets. However, the economic changes are still not completed and many parts of the economy are still owned and controlled by the state.

The communist system led to a uniform accounting system; the recent economic reforms have resulted in the introduction of new accounting laws and regulations, the most recent being the ASBE (2001), plus the first 16 of a set of planned accounting standards. However, the system can still be characterized in terms of low professionalism[52] and high secrecy.[53] It is rather more difficult to characterize the system in terms of conservatism and uniformity. In some areas, the system is still very rigid or uniform. In other areas, the system may be characterized by extreme flexibility. There remains a need for stronger assurance processes, to discourage false accounting or fraudulent reporting. While conservatism or prudence is a new concept, in some areas the system is very conservative, while in other areas it is far from conservative. Finally, there is the fairly large impact of the IASB; while China is not going to introduce IASB standards directly, the new standards are based upon IAS/IFRS. However, it is not intended to issue all the proposed standards before 2005; it remains to be seen how different some of these standards will be from IASB standards – they will tend to be simpler and more prescriptive. How much more simplified and inflexible they will be is currently impossible to tell.

Key points from the chapter:

- The accounting system of China has a strong tradition of a uniform accounting system.
- The uniform accounting system developed under a communist political system to serve the needs of the state and state controlled enterprises.
- Moving to a market-based economy has required major changes in accounting which have developed gradually since the 1980s.
- The Accounting Standard for Business Enterprises (1992) marked a significant stage in the move to a market-based economy.
- China began a process of matching its standards to International Accounting Standards prior to becoming a member of the World Trade Organization.
- The development of PRC standards that are consistent with IFRS continues but China also retains more detailed regulation, particularly the ASBE (2001). This leads to continued differences from IFRS although the gap is considerably narrower from 2001.
- The accounting profession is at a relatively early stage in development and needs the detailed rules of the ASBE as well as the more general standards based on IFRS.
- Hong Kong continues to apply different accounting rules (closer to IFRS) and has its own regulatory system for the stock market. Some PRC companies have their shares traded as 'H' shares on the Hong Kong exchange.

Questions

The following questions test your understanding of the material contained in the chapter and allow you to relate your understanding to the learning outcomes specified at the start of this chapter. The learning outcomes are repeated here. Each question is cross-referenced to the relevant section of the chapter.

Understand and explain the origins of accounting regulations and the historical development leading to the present state of practice

   1 What are the aspects of accounting in China between 1949 and 1980 that may give particular problems in applying western-based international accounting standards? (sections 13.3.1 and 13.3.2)

---

[52] See Xiang (1998).

[53] See Chow *et al.* (1995).

2 Why has accounting in China become of wider interest to western business since the early 1980s? (sections 13.3.2 and 13.3.3)

3 How did accounting in China develop between 1992 and 2000 to meet the requirements for becoming a member of the World Trade Organization? (section 13.3.3)

Relate institutional factors for the country to the framework set out in Chapter 4

4 How does the political and economic system of China fit into the classifications described in Chapter 4? (section 13.4)

5 To what extent does the business environment of China under the communist regime provide clues as to possible influences on accounting practices? (section 13.4)

6 To what extent does the current reform in the business environment of China provide clues as to possible influences on accounting practices? (section 13.4)

7 How does the taxation system of China compare to the descriptions given in Chapter 4? (section 13.4.3)

8 How does the corporate financing system of China compare to the descriptions given in Chapter 1? (section 13.4.4)

9 How does the accounting profession in China compare to the descriptions given in Chapter 4? (section 13.4.5)

10 Which institutional factors are most likely to influence Chinese accounting practice? (section 13.4)

11 How do the external influences on accounting practice in China compare to those described in Chapter 4? (section 13.5)

Understand and explain the position of national accounting rules in relation to the IASB standards described in Chapter 2

12 In which areas does accounting practice in China depart from that set out in International Accounting Standards? (section 13.6)

13 For each of the areas of departure which you have identified, describe the treatment required or applied in China and identify the likely impact on net income and shareholders' equity of moving from Chinese accounting practice to the relevant IASB standard. (section 13.6)

14 What explanations may be offered for these differences from IASB standards, in terms of the institutional factors described in the chapter? (section 13.6)

15 What are the most difficult problems facing accounting in China if it seeks full harmonization with the IASB standards? (sections 13.6 and 13.7)

Understand the characteristics of national accounting practice in terms of Gray's accounting values

16 Identify the key features supporting a conclusion that strong statutory control is a characteristic of Chinese accounting. (section 13.9.1)

17 Identify the key features supporting a conclusion that uniformity, rather than flexibility, is a dominant characteristic of Chinese accounting. (section 13.9.2)

18 Identify the key features supporting a conclusion that conservatism is not a dominant characteristic of Chinese accounting. (section 13.9.3)

19 Identify the key features supporting a conclusion that secrecy is a characteristic of Chinese accounting. (section 13.9.4)

20 Why is the location of Hong Kong China in accounting classification studies likely to remain different from that of mainland China? (sections 13.8 and 13.9)

Explain how research papers contribute to understanding accounting practice and accounting values

21 How might China be located within the classification studies reported in Chapter 4? Why has it not appeared in such classification studies previously? (section 13.10.1)

22 Is it likely that comparability studies may continue to help foreign users to understand accounting information produced by Chinese companies? (section 13.10.2)

23 What may be learned from disclosure studies of Chinese companies reporting in Hong Kong? (section 13.10.3)

References and further reading

Blake, J. and Gao, S. (eds) (1995) *Perspectives on Accounting and Finance in China*. London: Routledge.

Chen, C.J.P., Gul, F.A. and Su, X. (1999) 'A comparison of reported earnings under Chinese GAAP vs IAS: Evidence from the Shanghai Stock Exchange', *Accounting Horizons*, 13(2): 91–111.

Chow, L.M., Chau, G.K. and Gray, S.J. (1995) 'Accounting reforms in China: cultural constraints on implementation and development', *Accounting and Business Research*, 26(1): 29–49.

Ferguson, M.J., Lam, K.C. and Lee, G.M. (2002) 'Voluntary disclosure by state-owned enterprises listed on the stock exchange of Hong Kong', *Journal of International Financial Management and Accounting*, 13(2): 126–152.

Gray, S.J. (1988) 'Towards a theory of cultural influence on the development of accounting systems internationally', *Abacus*, 24(1): 1–15.

Hao, Z.P. (1999) 'Regulation and organisation of accountants in China', *Accounting, Auditing & Accountability Journal*, 12(3): 286–302.

Hofstede, G. (1984) *Culture's Consequences: International Differences in Work-related Values*. Beverly Hills, CA: Sage Publications.

Hofstede, G. (1991) *Cultures and Organisations: Software of the Mind*. London: McGraw-Hill.

Pacter, P. (2001) 'Emerging trends', *Accountancy*, May: 100.

Ren, M. and Alexander, D. (2000) 'Issues in developing accounting standards in China: a contextual perspective', *China Accounting and Finance Review*, 2(3): 108–125.

Roberts, C.B., Adams, C.A., Woo, R.W.K. and Wu, X. (1995) 'Chinese accounting reform: the internationalisation of financial reporting', *Advances in International Accounting*, 8: 201–220.

Tang, Y. (2000) 'Bumpy road leading to internationalisation: A review of accounting development in China', *Accounting Horizons*, 14(1): 93–102.

Tang, Y.W., Chow, L. and.Cooper, B.J. (1994) *Accounting and Finance in China*, 2nd edn. Hong Kong: Longmans.

White, G. (1993) *Riding the Tiger: the Politics of Economic Reform in post-Mao China*. London: Macmillan.

Xiang, B. (1998) 'Institutional factors influencing China's accounting reforms and standards', *Accounting Horizons*, 12(2): 105–119.

Xiao, Z. (1999) 'Corporate disclosures made by Chinese listed companies', *Journal of International Accounting*, 34(3): 349–373.

Xiao, Z., Zhang, Y. and Xie, Z. (2000) 'The making of independent auditing standards in China', *Accounting Horizons*, 14(1): 69–89.

Xiao, Z., Weetman, P. and Sun, M. (2004) 'Political influence and coexistence of a uniform accounting system and accounting standards: Recent developments in China', *Abacus*, 40(2): 193–218.

Yunwei, T. and Pacter, P. (2000) 'Revolution in accounting in China' *Accounting and Business*, January: 18–20.

Appendix 13.1 Accounting System for Business Enterprises

Applicable to Joint Stock Limited Enterprises effective 1 January 2001
Applicable to Foreign Investment Enterprises effective 1 January 2002

The following is a list of the contents of the ASBE and a summary of the general provisions of Chapter 1. The full text in English may be found on the website of Deloitte Touche Tohmatsu at www.iasplus.com/country/china.htm

Chapter 1: General provisions

Article 1. In accordance with 'The Accounting Law of the People's Republic of China', the ASBE (the 'Accounting System') is formulated to prescribe accounting treatments by enterprises and to ensure true and complete accounting information is provided by enterprises.

Article 2. This Accounting System is applicable to all enterprises (including companies) established within the PRC, except for small scale enterprises which do not raise funds externally, and financial and insurance companies.

Article 3. An enterprise should adopt a set of accounting policies and methods suitable for the specific circumstances of the enterprise, in accordance with the requirements of relevant laws and regulations, provided this Accounting System is not violated.

Article 4. An enterprise should prepare accounting vouchers and accounting ledgers, and manage accounting files and records in accordance with the requirements of rules and regulations dealing with these matters.

Article 5. Accounting and financial reports should proceed on the basis that the enterprise is a continuing entity and will remain in operation into the foreseeable future.

Article 6. It should be presumed for accounting purposes that the enterprise is a continuing entity and will remain in normal production and operating activities in the foreseeable future.

Article 7. An enterprise should close the books and prepare financial and accounting reports for separate accounting periods. Accounting periods may be a full year, half-year, a quarter or a month.

Article 8. An enterprise should normally use Renminbi as the recording currency for accounting purposes. A foreign currency can be used if the enterprise's transactions are mainly denominated in foreign currencies, but the foreign currency books must be translated into renminbi for preparing financial and accounting reports.

Article 9. The debit and credit double-entry bookkeeping system should be adopted.

Article 10. Accounting records should be compiled in Chinese. Minority or foreign languages may be used in addition to the Chinese language.

Article 11. An enterprise should comply with the following basic principles for accounting purposes:

1 Accounting information should be based on transactions and events that have actually occurred and should reflect financial position, operating results and cash flows.

2 An enterprise should account for transactions and events according to their economic substance and should not merely refer to their legal form.

3 Accounting information should reflect the financial position, operating results and cash flows of the enterprise in order to meet the needs of users of accounting information.

4 An enterprise should apply accounting treatments consistently throughout different accounting periods. Where changes are necessary, details and reasons should be given, with the amount of the cumulative effect of the change.

5 An enterprise's accounting should comply with prescribed accounting systems. Accounting information should be comparable and be prepared on a consistent basis.

6 Accounting information should be prepared in a timely manner.

7 Accounting information should be prepared in a clear and concise manner, so that it can be readily understood and used.

8 Accounting information should be prepared on an accrual basis.

9 Revenues should be matched against related costs and expenses for accounting purposes.

10 Assets should be recorded at actual costs at the time of acquisition. Provisions for impairment losses, and any other adjustment to carrying amounts of assets, must follow the regulations.

11 Expenditures must be classified as revenue or capital, based on whether the benefits are realized within the accounting period or over several accounting periods.

12 An enterprise should comply with the requirements of the prudence concept for accounting purposes. An enterprise should not overstate assets or revenue, or understate liabilities or expenses. It should not provide for any hidden reserve.

13 An enterprise should comply with the requirements of the materiality concept for accounting purposes . . . [detailed explanations are given]

Chapter 2: Assets

Article 12. An asset is a resource that is (a) owned or controlled by an enterprise as a result of past transactions or events and (b) expected to generate economic benefits to the enterprise.

Article 13. Assets of an enterprise should be classified into current assets, long-term investments, fixed assets, intangible assets and other assets according to their liquidity.

Section 1: Current assets (Articles 14–20)

Section 2: Long-term investments (Articles 21–24)

Section 3: Fixed assets (Articles 25–42)

Section 4: Intangible assets and other assets (Articles 43–65)

Chapter 3: Liabilities

Article 66. A liability is a present obligation arising from past transactions or events; the settlement of such an obligation is expected to result in an outflow from the enterprise of resources embodying economic benefits.

Article 67. A enterprise's liabilities should, according to their liquidity, be classified as current and long-term liabilities.

Section 1: Current liabilities (Articles 68–70)

Section 2: Long-term liabilities (Articles 71–78)

Chapter 4: Owners' equity (Articles 79–83)

Chapter 5: Revenue (Articles 84–98)

Chapter 6: Costs and expenses (Articles 99–105)

Chapter 7: Profit and profit appropriation (Articles 106–112)

Chapter 8: Non-monetary transactions (Articles 113–123)

Chapter 9: Foreign currency transactions (Articles 117–120)

Chapter 10: Accounting adjustments (Articles 121–139)

Chapter 11: Contingencies (Articles 140–146)

Chapter 12: Related party relationships and transactions (Articles 147–150)

Chapter 13: Financial and accounting reports (Articles 151–160)

Appendix 13.2 Differences between Hong Kong GAAP and US GAAP: CNOOC Ltd

Notes to Financial Statements

31 December 2003
(All amounts expressed in Renminbi unless otherwise stated)

39. SIGNIFICANT DIFFERENCES BETWEEN HONG KONG GAAP AND US GAAP

The accounting policies adopted by the Group conform to Hong Kong GAAP, which differ in certain respects from generally accepted accounting principles in the United States of America ("US GAAP").

(a) Net profit and net equity

(i) *Revaluation of land and buildings*

The Group revalued certain land and buildings on 31 August 1999 and 31 December 2000 and the related revaluation surplus was recorded on the respective dates. Under Hong Kong GAAP, revaluation of property, plant and equipment is permitted and depreciation, depletion and amortization are based on the revalued amount. Additional depreciation arising from the revaluation for the year ended 31 December 2003 was approximately RMB9,156,000 (2002: RMB9,156,000). Under US GAAP, property, plant and equipment are required to be stated at cost. Accordingly, no additional depreciation, depletion and amortization from the revaluation is recognized under US GAAP.

(ii) *Short term investments*

According to Hong Kong GAAP, available-for-sale investments in marketable securities are measured at fair value and related unrealized holding gains and losses are included in the current period's earnings. According to US GAAP, such investments are also measured at fair value and classified in accordance with Statement of Financial Accounting Standards ("SFAS") No.115. Under US GAAP, related unrealized gains and losses on available-for-sale securities are excluded from the current period's earnings and included in other comprehensive income.

(iii) *Impairment of long-lived assets*

Under Hong Kong GAAP, impairment charges are recognized when a long-lived asset's carrying amount exceeds the higher of an asset's net selling price and value in use, which incorporates discounting the asset's estimated future cash flows.

Under US GAAP, long-lived assets are assessed for possible impairment in accordance with SFAS No.144, "Accounting for the impairment or disposal of long-lived assets". SFAS No. 144 requires the Group to (a) recognize an impairment loss only if the carrying amount of a long-lived asset is not recoverable from its undiscounted cash flows and (b) measure an impairment loss as the difference between the carrying amount and fair value of the asset. SFAS No. 144 requires that a long-lived asset to be abandoned, exchanged for a similar productive asset, or distributed to owners in a spin-off be considered held and used until it is disposed of.

SFAS No. 144 also requires the Group to assess the need for an impairment of capitalized costs of proved oil and gas properties and the costs of wells and related equipment and facilities on a property-by-property basis. If an impairment is indicated based on undiscounted expected future cash flows, then an impairment is recognized to the extent that net capitalized costs exceed the estimated fair value of the property. Fair value of the property is estimated by the Group using the present value of future cash flows. The impairment was determined based on the difference between the carrying value of the assets and the present value of future cash flows. It is reasonably possible that a change in reserve or price estimates could occur in the near term and adversely impact management's estimate of future cash flows and consequently the carrying value of properties.

In addition, under Hong Kong GAAP, a subsequent increase in the recoverable amount of assets is reversed to the income statement to the extent that an impairment loss on the same asset was previously recognized as an expense when the circumstances and events that led to write-down or write-off cease to exist. The reversal is reduced by the amount that would have been recognized as depreciation had the write-off not occurred. Under US GAAP, an impairment loss establishes a new cost basis for the impaired asset and the new cost basis should not be adjusted subsequently other than for further impairment losses.

For the year ended 31 December 2003, there were no impairment losses recognized under Hong Kong GAAP and US GAAP.

(iv) *Stock compensation schemes*
As at 31 December 2003, the Company has three stock-based employee compensation plans, which are described more fully in Note 31. Prior to 2003, the Company accounted for those plans under the recognition and measurement provisions of APB Opinion No. 25, "Accounting for Stock Issued to Employees", and related interpretations. Since certain of the options granted under those plans had an exercise price below the market value of the underlying common stock on the date of grant, stock-based employee compensation costs of Rmb2,755,000 and Rmb5,632,000 for year ended 31 December 2001 and 2002, respectively, were reflected in previously reported results. During 2003, the Company adopted the fair value recognition provisions of FASB Statement No. 123, "Accounting for Stock-Based Compensation", for stock-based employee compensation. All prior periods presented have been restated to reflect the compensation cost that would have been recognized had the recognition provisions of Statement 123 been applied to all awards granted to employees after 1 January 1995.

Weighted average fair value of the options at the grant dates for awards under the schemes was RMB3.40 per share which was estimated using the Black-Scholes model with the following assumptions: dividend yield of 2.0 per cent, an expected life of five years; expected volatility of 44 per cent; and risk-free interest rates of 5.25 per cent. Weighted average exercise price of the stock options was HK$7.80 per share.

(v) *Provision for dismantlement*
Hong Kong GAAP requires the provision for dismantlement to be recorded for a present obligation whether that obligation is legal or constructive. The associated cost is capitalized and the liability is discounted and accretion expense is recognized using the credit-adjusted risk-free interest rate in effect when the liability is initially recognized.

On 15 August 2001, SFAS No. 143 "Accounting for asset retirement obligation" was released and is effective for the fiscal years beginning after 15 June 2002. SFAS No. 143 requires that the fair value of a liability for an asset retirement obligation be recognized in the period in which it is incurred if a reasonable estimate of fair value can be made. The associated asset retirement costs are capitalized as part of the carrying amount of the long-lived assets. Further, under SFAS No. 143, the liability is discounted and accretion expense is recognized using the credit-adjusted risk-free interest rate in effect when the liability is initially recognized.

The company adopted SFAS No. 143 on 1 January 2003, which resulted in an increase in net property, plant and equipment of RMB863,093,000, an increase in the provision for dismantlement of RMB240,077,000, an increase in retained earnings of RMB436,112,000 and an increase in deferred income tax liabilities of RMB186,904,000 to recognize the cumulative effect of retrospectively applying the new accounting standard.

This adjustment is due to the difference in the method of accruing for dismantlement costs under SFAS No. 143 compared with the method required by SFAS No. 19 "Financial accounting and reporting by oil and gas producing companies", the accounting standard that the Company has been adopted since its establishment. Under SFAS No. 19, the dismantlement costs are accrued on a unit-of-production basis of accounting as the oil and gas is produced. The SFAS No. 19 method matches the accruals with the revenues generated from production and results in most of the costs being accrued early in field life, when production is at the highest level. Because SFAS No. 143 requires accretion of the liability as a result of the passage of time using an interest method of allocation, the majority of the costs will be accrued towards the end of field life, when production is at the lowest level. The cumulative income adjustment described above resulted from reversing the higher liability accumulated under SFAS No. 19 in order to adjust it to the lower present value amount resulting from transition to SFAS No. 143. This amount being reversed in transition, which was previously charged to the income statement under SFAS No. 19, will again be charged to the income statement under SFAS No. 143 in future years. A summary of the changes in the asset retirement obligation during the year is included in the table below:

	2003 RMB'000
Asset retirement obligation upon adoption of SFAS No. 143 on 1 January 2003	2,239,320
Addition of dismantlement cost	314,234
Accretion expenses	93,246
Asset retirement obligation at 31 December 2003	2,646,800

The pro forma effects of the application of SFAS No.143 as if it had been adopted on 1 January 2002 (rather than 1 January 2003) are presented below:

	As reported 31 December 2003 RMB'000	Pro forma 31 December 2002 RMB'000 (Restated)
Net income	11,543,397	9,223,477
Earnings per share		
– Basic	RMB1.41	RMB1.12
– Diluted	RMB1.41	RMB1.12

(vi) *Acquisition of CNOOC Finance*
Under HK GAAP, the Company adopted the purchase method to account for the acquisition of 31.8 per cent equity interest in CNOOC Finance in December 2003. Under the purchase method, the acquired results are included in the consolidated results of operations of the Company from the date of the acquisition.

As the Company and CNOOC Finance are under common control of CNOOC, under US GAAP, the acquisition is considered to be a transfer of businesses under common control and the acquired assets and liabilities are accounted at historical cost in a manner similar to the pooling of interests method. Accordingly, the consolidated financial statements for all periods presented have been retroactively restated as if the current structure and operations had been in existence since inception. The cash consideration paid by the Company is treated as an equity transaction in the year of the acquisition for US GAAP purpose.

CNOOC LIMITED ANNUAL REPORT 2003

Notes to Financial Statements

31 December 2003
(All amounts expressed in Renminbi unless otherwise stated)

39. SIGNIFICANT DIFFERENCES BETWEEN HONG KONG GAAP AND US GAAP (continued)

(a) Net profit and net equity (continued)

The effects on net profit and equity of the above significant differences between Hong Kong GAAP and US GAAP are summarized below:

	Net Profit	
	2003 RMB'000	2002 RMB'000 (Restated)
As reported under Hong Kong GAAP	11,535,490	9,232,827
Impact of US GAAP adjustments:		
– Reversal of additional depreciation, depletion and amortisation charges arising from the revaluation surplus on land and buildings	9,156	9,156
– Equity accounting for the results of CNOOC Finance	30,913	10,663
– Unrealised holding gains from available-for-sale investments in marketable securities	(21,503)	(36,965)
– Realised holding gains from available-for-sale marketable securities	27,088	26,940
– Additional dismantlement based on unit-of-production method	–	(197,079)
– Impact of income tax		59,124
– Recognition of stock compensation cost	(37,747)	(19,144)
Income before cumulative effect of change in accounting policy	11,543,397	9,085,522
Cumulative effect of change in accounting policy for dismantlement liabilities	436,112	–
Net profit under US GAAP	11,979,509	9,085,522
Net profit per share under US GAAP – Basic		
Before cumulative effect of change in accounting policy for dismantlement liabilities	RMB 1.41	RMB 1.11
Cumulative effect of change in accounting policy for dismantlement liabilities	RMB 0.05	–
	RMB 1.46	RMB 1.11

– Diluted
Before cumulative effect of change in
accounting policy for dismantlement liabilities **RMB 1.41** RMB 1.11
Cumulative effect of change in **RMB 0.05** –
accounting policy for dismantlement
liabilities **RMB 1.46** RMB 1.11

	Net Equity	
	2003	2002
	RMB'000	RMB'000
As reported under Hong Kong GAAP	**46,736,532**	40,568,488
Impact of US GAAP adjustments:		
– Reversal of revaluation surplus on land and buildings	**(274,671)**	(274,672)
– Reversal of additional accumulated depreciation, depletion and amortization arising from the revaluation surplus on land and buildings	**35,051**	25,895
– Equity accounting for the results of CNOOC Finance	**41,576**	10,663
– Contribution from CNOOC in respect of CNOOC Finance	**–**	(450,000)
– Dividend distribution made by CNOOC Finance to CNOOC	**(41,576)**	–
– Cumulative adjustment for provision for dismantlement	**–**	(436,112)
Net equity under US GAAP	**46,496,912**	39,444,263

There are no significant GAAP differences that affect classifications within the balance sheet or income statement but do not affect net income or shareholders' equity.

(b) Comprehensive income

According to SFAS No. 130, "Reporting Comprehensive Income", it is required to include a statement of other comprehensive income for revenues and expenses, gains and losses that under US GAAP are included in comprehensive income and excluded from net income.

	2003	2002
	RMB'000	RMB'000
		(Restated)
Net profit under US GAAP	**11,979,509**	9,085,522
Other comprehensive income:		
Foreign currency translation adjustments	**36,243**	(7,948)
Unrealized gains on short-term investments	**21,503**	36,965
Less: Reclassification adjustment for gains included in net income	**(27,088)**	(26,940)
Comprehensive income under US GAAP	**12,010,167**	9,087,599

Roll forward of accumulated other comprehensive income components are as follows:

	Foreign currency translation adjustments RMB'000	Unrealised gains on short term investments RMB'000	Accumulated other comprehensive income RMB'000
Balance at 1 January 2002	(5,648)	43,796	38,148
Current year change	(7,948)	10,025	2,077
Balance at 1 January 2003	(13,596)	53,821	40,225
Reversal of current year realized gains	–	(27,088)	(27,088)
Current year change	36,243	21,503	57,746
Balance at 31 December 2003	22,647	48,236	70,883

(c) Derivative instruments

The Group had a currency swap contract with a financial institution to sell United States dollars in exchange for Japanese Yen in order to hedge certain Japanese Yen denominated loan repayments in the future. The derivative contract was recorded as "Other payable and accrued liabilities" in the consolidated balance sheet at fair value. For the year ended 31 December 2003, the Group recognized related changes in fair value, a gain of RMB10,038,000 (2002: RMB14,485,000), and included the amount in "Exchange (loss)/gain, net" in the consolidated income statement.

During the year, the Group also entered into interest rate swap agreements to partially hedge the fixed-rate debt for interest rate risk exposure management purposes with notional contract amount of US$200 million. The interest rate swap agreements utilized by the Company effectively modifies the Company's exposure to interest risk by converting the Company's fixed-rate debt to a floating rate. These agreements involve the receipt of fixed rate amounts in exchange for floating rate interest payments over the life of the agreement without an exchange of the underlying principal amount. The net gain as of 31 December 2003 related to the ineffective portion of the interest rate swap agreements was approximately Rmb938,000 (2002: nil).

(d) Use of estimates in the preparation of financial statements

The preparation of financial statements in conformity with accounting principles generally accepted in the United States of America requires management to make estimates and assumptions that affect the reported amounts of assets and liabilities and disclosure of contingent assets and liabilities at the date of the financial statements, and the reported amounts of revenues and expenses during the reporting period. The most significant estimates pertain to proved oil and gas reserve volumes and the future development, provision for dismantlement as well as estimates relating to certain oil and gas revenues and expenses. Actual amounts could differ from those estimates and assumptions.

The Group's segment information is based on the segmental operating results regularly reviewed by the Group's chief operating decision maker. The accounting policies used are the same as those used in the preparation of the Group's consolidated Hong Kong GAAP financial statements.

(e) Segment reporting

The group's segment information is based on the segmental operating results regularly received by the Group's chief operating decision maker. The accounting policies used are the same as those used in the preparation of the Group's consolidated Hong Kong GAAP financial statements.

Source: CNOOC Limited annual report (2003), pp. 98–105. www.cnooc.com.cn/enghol

PART 5

Informing international equity markets

Introduction to Part 5

All companies with any international operations, and all users of their financial statements, will be affected by differences in accounting practices internationally – sometimes described as 'accounting diversity'. Accounting diversity can impose extra direct costs on companies. To the extent that companies have to report in multiple jurisdictions, they may have to report under a number of different sets of rules, increasing their accounting and information production costs. If instead, they continue to use domestic rules and follow normal domestic practices, the information reported may be unfamiliar to foreign users, leading to a number of indirect costs to the company. Foreign users will be faced with additional processing costs, as they now have to cope either with unfamiliar types of information or with familiar types of information that are produced in unfamiliar ways. These extra costs of processing information will make foreign users less willing to enter into transactions with the company. This will increase costs to the company – it may have to pay more for capital or offer suppliers and customers better terms. Indeed, at the extreme, if foreign users cannot understand the information provided, they may refuse to enter into any transactions with the company at all.

Chapter 14 focuses first on companies and how international diversity affects a wide range of corporate decisions. It then turns to look at investors and explores two issues – first, how do investors cope with international diversity? and, secondly, how, if at all, do companies change their reporting package when reporting to foreign investors? The chapter also looks at a number of empirical studies that seek to discover how investors in practice choose between companies from different countries.

Chapter 15 turns to transparency, which is a key theme of those seeking high-quality financial reporting, and gives examples of regulation and practice in seeking to improve transparency of financial reporting. It brings out the importance of the narrative sections of corporate reports and the challenges of achieving accountability to stakeholders. It discusses research studies that have explored the nature of disclosure and its relationship to characteristics of reporting entities.

Chapter 16 concludes with a description of accounting practice in three areas where diversity has been greatest under separate national regulation and so IFRS have achieved a great deal in encouraging comparability of regulations and practice. The three areas are business combinations, segmental reporting and foreign currency translation. It is a matter for continuing discussion as to whether this apparent comparability achieved by standardized rules represents comparability of the economic reality underlying the reporting entities.

Purpose of Part 5

Part 5 is a module that permits study of the influence of accounting issue on those participating in capital markets. It encourages consideration of the preparers and users of accounting information and the ways in which they cope with listing and investing outside the national stock exchange. It emphasizes the importance of reading and considering the quality of narrative disclosures within the annual report and it shows how the essential issues of business combinations, segmental reporting and foreign currency translation can be understood sufficiently to allow those using corporate reports to understand the areas of comparability and the questions to be asked about lack of comparability.

Learning outcomes

Specific Learning outcomes are set out at the start of each chapter but overall, on completion of this final part of the book, the student should be able to:

- understand the costs and benefits to companies of listing on foreign stock markets;
- understand the costs and benefits to investors of investing in foreign companies;
- be aware of the investment strategies that investors may adopt to cope with accounting diversity;
- be aware of the reporting strategies that companies may adopt to reduce accounting diversity;
- explain and discuss the developments in corporate reporting that are adding to transparency in disclosure;
- explain and discuss accounting issues facing multinational companies in business combinations, segmental reporting and foreign currency translation.

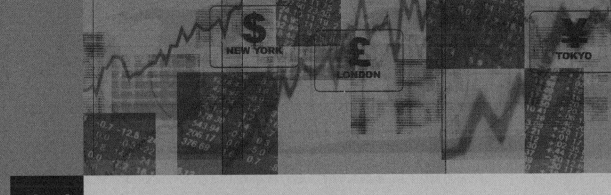

14 Investors and listed companies

Learning outcomes

After reading this chapter you should be able to:

- Understand why investors might want to invest in foreign companies and the approaches they may take.

- Be aware of the reasons why the demand for and supply of foreign equities is likely to continue to increase.

- Understand the reasons why companies might list on foreign stock markets.

- Understand the additional costs of listing on foreign stock markets.

- Evaluate published research seeking to explain the foreign stock market listing choices of companies.

- Understand the different approaches that companies can take when reporting to foreign investors and understand the factors that affect corporate reporting decisions.

14.1 Introduction

As explained in Part 1 of this book, the success of the IASB is due to several factors, but clearly one of the most important has been the growth of international investors coupled with the support of IOSCO for international standards. The growth of international investment by ordinary shareholders and the move towards multiple stock market listings by companies are both likely to increase over the next few years. With the almost universal adoption of IFRS, many of the barriers or additional costs involved in international listing and international equity investing will rapidly fall.

However, this does not mean that all companies will use identical measurement and reporting practices; investors will increasingly be interested in companies with unfamiliar domestic languages and currencies or different views on disclosure.

The chapter begins by looking at investors and explores the reasons why they might want to invest in foreign companies and how they might use (or not use) financial statement information in their investment decision making. It then turns from demand to supply and the decisions of companies to take international listings. The possible reasons for companies to want a foreign listing are explored and some of the additional costs are described. The empirical research on choice of listing location is then reviewed for evidence that the choice of listing location is affected by differences in countries' accounting regulations. While investors are an important user group, others are often also interested in the financial statements of foreign companies. The chapter therefore continues by looking at other users of financial statements, the sorts of decisions they might want to take and their use of financial statement information. Finally, the chapter examines the different approaches that a company can take to reporting to its foreign statement users.

14.2 Approaches to international equity investment

14.2.1 Why shareholders invest internationally

Reading through this book you may gained the impression that prior to the general acceptance of IFRS the sensible investor should not have invested in foreign companies or foreign stock markets, while after the widespread acceptance of IFRS investors can easily invest in companies from any country. Both of these conclusions would be somewhat simplistic. Prior to the introduction of the common platform of standards there were clear economic advantages in investing internationally, which investors understood despite the problems of non-comparable accounting practices. Even after the adoption of IFRS in many countries, some substantive differences in disclosures will persist. In addition, different equity transaction methods, different currencies and different languages all make it more difficult and more expensive to invest in foreign markets.

There are clear benefits to investing in foreign companies and foreign markets. For example, if an investor had invested $1,000 in the US market in 1985 she would have an investment worth $3,818, ten years later. If the investment had been made in the Thai market instead it would have been worth $16,212, or $23,209 in Mexico, $48,023 in the Philippines or $64,707 in Chile.[1] However, this is past history. An investor deciding now to invest in Chile might instead find in ten years' time that this was the worst decision she could have taken. Which stock markets have been particularly good or bad investments in the past is not relevant today. All that is relevant is the fact that stock markets have not all moved together – in any one period, some stock markets will be doing well and others will not be doing so well.

A cautious investor in the domestic stock market would not invest in only one or two companies. No investor can consistently pick winners. To be successful in picking companies, investors must make better or more accurate predictions than do other investors. For example, if you think a company will grow and make lots of profits in the future and if other investors also think the same, they will also buy the shares and the share price will increase now before these profits are made. If in future periods your prediction proves correct and the company is successful the share price will not then increase as this is not new information, but simply something that everyone already expected. It has already been reflected in the share price due to increased demand in earlier periods. You will only benefit if you are better at predicting which companies will perform well in the future than are other investors, in other words if you have special knowledge, insights or skills that others do not have. While you might choose well and make a lot of money, you might equally well choose badly and lose money instead. It is well established that, over time, all the ordinary investor can hope is that they do as well on average as the market does. The semi-strong form of the efficient market hypothesis generally holds in active stock markets of developed countries. Share prices react quickly and correctly to all new information and no investor is able to consistently outguess the market. This means that investors should invest in a well diversified portfolio of shares. This allows them to minimize their risk for any given level of return (or maximize their expected return for any given level of risk). At least in theory investors should diversify across all available shares and invest in the market portfolio. In practice, if they choose different types of companies, a well diversified investment in approximately 40 stocks should be sufficient to gain most of the benefits available from diversification.

Diversification brings benefits because the returns made from different equities are less than perfectly correlated. While some companies might be doing particularly well with rising share prices, other companies will instead be performing less well. Similar considerations apply to international investing. There has been a great deal of interest in the literature in the question of the extent to which different stock markets are cointegrated or the returns from different stock markets are correlated to each other. Studies in the 1970s and 1980s tended to find relatively low levels of correlation. For example, one of

---

[1] Melton (1996), p. 28.

the earliest studies of the benefits of international diversification[2] calculated that this lack of co-integration meant that a well diversified international portfolio would be typically only half as risky as a similar sized portfolio of US shares. However, more and more investors are accessing foreign markets, more companies are listing internationally and many economies are becoming more integrated into the global economy so that the level of cointegration is rising and the benefits from international diversification are falling. For example, Taylor and Tonks (1989) looked at the UK, USA, Japan, The Netherlands and West Germany, from 1973 to 1986, and found that the UK market had become more integrated with the others following the abandonment of exchange controls in the UK in 1989. Similarly, Corhay *et al.* (1993) found that the stock markets of the UK, France, Germany, Italy and The Netherlands had become more integrated during the 1975–1991 period, while Smith (1999), in a study of stock market correlations before and after the 1987 stock market crash, provides evidence that European stock markets became more highly correlated both with each other and with the USA after the 1987 crash.

Exhibit 14.1 reports the correlations between the monthly returns from eight European markets and the US for the 27-year period, January 1974 to January 2001. This shows a picture of very high correlations across all these exchanges. Fraser and Oyefesu (forthcoming) conclude that there is evidence of a common stochastic trend linking all the markets such that, if the period was sufficiently long, there would be perfect correlation across the markets. However, there are significant short-run deviations from this trend, especially with respect to the US and UK markets. This implies that investors can gain from short-term diversification across the markets.

There are a number of reasons why none of the stock markets are perfectly correlated in the short-term. Different economic and political policies, different trade patterns, industrial structures, corporate policies and investor behaviour all mean that companies in different countries will tend, on average, to perform somewhat differently. In any one period companies from one country will tend to perform relatively well, but in other periods, companies from other countries will instead tend to perform better. However, the convergence of stock markets is likely to continue, due at least partially to the increasing use of IFRS which will help reduce market segmentation by reducing barriers to investment caused by different accounting requirements.

| Exhibit 14.1 | Correlation matrix of real stock market returns, 1974–2001 |

	Belgium	Denmark	France	Germany	Italy	US	UK	Spain	Sweden
Belgium	1								
Denmark	0.982	1							
France	0.977	0.982	1						
Germany	0.983	0.989	0.983	1					
Italy	0.945	0.954	0.958	0.954	1				
US	0.877	0.884	0.887	0.881	0.887	1			
UK	0.905	0.917	0.917	0.915	0.918	0.877	1		
Spain	0.942	0.943	0.948	0.944	0.938	0.886	0.907	1	
Sweden	0.940	0.951	0.942	0.946	0.937	0.896	0.910	0.926	1

Source: Fraser and Oyefeso (forthcoming).

---

[2] Solnik (1974).

Exhibit 14.2	Sectoral distribution of the 50 largest companies, selected countries, 2004

	UK	Germany	USA	Japan
Financial sector	11	11	14	10
Mining, oil & gas	6	–	2	–
Computers & IT	–	3	9	7
Telecommunications	3	1	3	3
Utilities	4	3	–	5
Chemicals & pharmaceuticals	3	6	9	2
Auto	–	5	–	7
Industrial	1	12	3	10
Media and Entertainment	5	2	4	1
Food, drink & tobacco	7	1	3	1
Retail	6	1	2	3
Other	4	5	1	1

Source: Derived from FT 500 (May 2004), http://news.ft.com/reports/ft500

Obviously investors cannot invest in all companies in each market. Instead they will chose a smaller number of companies to invest in that approximately replicate international markets. One attraction of investing in a foreign stock market is that the investor can sometimes invest in different types of companies or different industries. For example, a UK investor wanting to invest in an automobile manufacturer could not invest in a UK manufacturer of any significant size but might instead decide to invest in a German or Japanese company. A German or Japanese investor wanting to invest in a large drinks or food manufacturer would have more choice if they look to the UK rather than their own country. Exhibit 14.2 lists the industrial sectors of the 50 largest companies, by market capitalization, from the UK, Germany, the US and Japan. This gives a good idea of differences in the industrial composition of the major companies in these countries.

It is becoming increasingly low cost and a straightforward procedure for investors to invest in foreign stock markets. The simplest way for the ordinary investor to do this is through investing indirectly in foreign markets by buying unit trusts or other similar investments which themselves invest in foreign markets. Exhibit 14.3 lists just some of the types of funds that UK investors can buy, all of which in turn invest in foreign equities and all of which can be bought in pound sterling. This means that individuals or

Exhibit 14.3	Examples of UK funds investing in foreign equities in various countries and groups of countries

Regional funds	World, Europe, North America, Asia Pacific, Far East
Country funds	America, India, Switzerland, Korea, China, Japan
Growth funds	American, Asian, German, Japanese, European growth
Small company funds	American, European, Asian, Global small companies
Tracker	American, Europe, Japan, Pacific
Other	US emerging companies, Far East emerging, Global ethical, European ethical

Source: Based on list of funds in the *Financial Times*, September 2004.

private small investors need not invest directly in the shares of foreign firms. They do not therefore have to bother with the costs and inconvenience of dealing in different currencies or languages. Instead, all they need to do is decide which type of domestic fund they wish to invest in and then choose among the alternative funds. In these cases, the decision is not based upon individual company's financial statement information but is based upon economic data and information about the performance and costs of the competing funds.

However, this does not mean that financial statement information is not used by stock market participants – the investment funds must decide upon suitable companies to invest in. Professional fund managers and analysts will need to compare companies from different countries. The next section therefore looks at the alternative investment strategies that can be adopted by anyone, whether an individual investor or professional fund manager, wishing to invest directly in equities from different countries.

14.2.2 Passive investment strategies

Three different strategies have been identified which investors can use to cope with accounting diversity.[3] At one extreme, investors may decide not to rely upon company specific information at all. Instead, they could adopt a passive or index-based strategy. In the international arena this would involve deciding how much to invest in particular countries on the basis of non-accounting factors. Factors considered might include relative GNP, past and forecast country growth rates and the size of the stock market. The investor would then choose a portfolio of shares from each country that mirrored or represented the country's total stock market. The objective is to match the returns of each stock market invested in, rather than to outperform it. Passive investment strategies are being used increasingly by US and UK institutional investors investing in their domestic stock markets. Such an approach was initially developed as a way of reducing transaction costs as it involves less share trading. Shares are only bought or sold when the portfolio no longer adequately mirrors the market due to changes in the market caused by such factors as new issues, mergers and takeovers. These types of portfolios are often called 'trackers' or 'tracker funds', because they are designed to mirror or track the market.

Because passive investment strategies reduce the need to analyse financial statements, they can also be a useful response to problems of lack of accounting information or lack of understanding of the accounting information provided. They may therefore be particularly useful for investors wishing to diversify into international markets. However, some financial statement information will still be needed when choosing an adequately diversified portfolio and to ensure that it remains well diversified.

14.2.3 Active investment strategies

The opposite approach is to adopt an active investment strategy based, at least partially, on accounting information. Here, investors try to assess whether or not a company will be a good investment. They will use accounting information as well as other information (economic information including forecasts, company information from newspaper reports and stockbroker reports and possibly company visits) to assess the strength and weaknesses

---

[3] Choi and Levich (1997).

of companies and their management and the companies' likely future prospects. Using all of this information they will buy or sell shares whenever they have new information or whenever market conditions change in an attempt to 'beat the market'.

While more and more companies and countries are using IFRS, not all companies are currently doing so. If the statements produced use unfamiliar GAAP and the company itself does not restate these into more familiar GAAP, then the investor can adopt one of two approaches. First, they might restate the figures provided into a more familiar set of accounting principles. This would mean that the figures could then be more easily compared with the figures provided by companies from other countries. This approach is based upon the assumption that stock markets are reasonably well integrated. Companies from different countries can then be compared one with the other: 'Is the company a good investment compared to alternative investments from other countries?' The investors then choose the best companies to invest in irrespective of their home country.

The second approach is to become familiar with various foreign GAAP and then to use a local perspective when analyzing foreign financial statements. This approach is often called a 'multiple principles capability'; it is premised upon the opposite assumption, that markets are not integrated but are segmented. It assumes that companies can be usefully compared only with other companies from the same country and a company's performance should therefore be assessed only in the context of the local market: 'Is the company a good investment inside that market or not?'

14.2.4 Mixed investment strategies

An intermediate investment strategy is also possible which adopts aspects of both a passive and an active approach. This would involve adopting a passive strategy and using an index approach for all of those countries or industries where the investor has insufficient information or where the available information is based upon unfamiliar accounting rules. Where investors are familiar with the information provided and sufficient disclosures are made, they would instead adopt an active investment strategy.

14.2.5 Actual investment strategies

Relatively few studies have looked at how investors actually manage in a world of accounting diversity. Choi and Levich (1996) questioned 400 European institutional investors, 97 of whom replied. Two-thirds of these placed high reliance upon accounting information when selecting foreign equities and only four did not use accounting information at all. Eighty-five percent of the respondents compared investments across countries rather than deciding upon the amount to invest in each country and then selecting from among potential investment targets inside it. When asked about accounting differences, only 23 per cent replied that differences in the quality of financial reporting limited their investments in Europe and 14 per cent cited accounting differences as a reason for limiting investments. (Liquidity, currency and market risks were all mentioned by at least 40 per cent of the sample.) Nearly half (42.3 per cent) of the respondents said that they might increase their investment in Europe if a common set of accounting and reporting concepts were introduced. These respondents were equally divided on whether they would prefer IAS or US GAAP disclosures.

The respondents were also asked about how they dealt with differences in accounting principles and disclosure practices. The findings are reproduced in Exhibit 14.4.

Exhibit 14.4 Dealing with differences in accounting principles and disclosure practices, 1996

	No. of Respondents	Percentage
Differences in accounting principles:		
Place higher weight on other information	64	66.0
Restate foreign accounts	49	50.5
Use information and analysis from investment advisory services	41	42.3
Attach a low weight to accounting information	10	10.3
Differences in disclosure practices:		
Visiting company to collect information	46	47.4
Assigning higher risk rating to company	44	45.4
Attending company road shows	42	43.3
Avoiding investment in companies with less disclosure	34	35.1
Requiring higher expected returns from companies with fewer disclosures	26	26.8
No answer	13	13.4

Source: Choi and Levich (1996), pp. 294–295.

Two different approaches were taken when the accounting principles were different. Respondents either placed more emphasis upon other information, including the services of investment advisors, or attempted to restate the figures using more familiar GAAP. Again when the disclosure practices were different, two approaches were taken. Respondents either sought more information or they changed their investment strategies to cope with the increase in uncertainty. Miles and Nobes (1998) found that fund managers and analysts working in UK financial institutions developed a range of approaches to foreign accounting data and did not all have accounting expertise but used other information to learn about company performance.

14.3 Future demand for and supply of international equity investments

It is argued that the demand for and supply of equity investments will increase in general in the foreseeable future. There are also likely to be some changes in the composition of the demand, with demand for foreign equity investments, in particular, increasing. A number of reasons have been suggested for this.[4]

14.3.1 Pension schemes

Pension schemes are either funded, where pension contributions are invested into a fund that is then used to pay the pension of the contributors at a later date, or unfunded or pay as you go, where current payments are used to pay for current pension commitments and the current contributors to the fund will receive their pensions out of the contributions of future workers. It is estimated that in the EU, 90 per cent of pensions are currently PAYG schemes and only 10 per cent are funded, although the figures vary greatly across the EU with funded schemes being relatively common in the UK and

[4] Price Waterhouse (1997).

The Netherlands. Of the funded schemes that do exist, the proportion of their funds invested in equities also varies greatly from a high of more than 80 per cent in the UK to only 30 per cent in The Netherlands or 10 per cent in Germany.

There is a looming crises in pensions brought about mainly by the growth in the number of old people (e.g. the ratio of workers to pensioners is currently approximately 4:1 in the EU, this is likely to fall to 2.4:1 in the UK and only 1.5:1 in Italy by 2050). If pension schemes remain unchanged then it is estimated that the cost of pensions may rise from 12 per cent to 20 per cent of GNP by 2050. Given this, it is probable that most countries will see at least some moves away from government-based pension schemes and away from unfunded schemes to private sector funded schemes. Similarly, these schemes are likely to invest more of their funds in equities and will become more and more similar to UK-funded schemes with their heavy reliance upon equity investment.[5]

14.3.2 Privatization

The last 20 years or so have been a period of privatization of large companies throughout the world. For example, in 1999, the largest company in most markets except the US was a privatized company. This included both developed countries such as the UK, Japan, Germany and Australia as well as many developing markets (e.g. Mexico, China, Russia, Pakistan, Poland, Korea and Indonesia). Excluding the US, these companies accounted for 21 per cent of non-US total market capitalization at this time.[6]

Large privatization programmes, because of the size and visibility of the companies concerned and their tendency to list on multiple stock markets simultaneously, have tended to attract both more shareholders than other companies and more foreign investors. (For example, international investors bought nearly two-thirds of all privatization issues in 1995.) The number and importance of privatizations must fall over the next few years simply because so many companies have already been privatized. But privatizations will continue, especially in China, East Europe and developing countries as well as part of the EU (see section 10.4.3). This means that the importance of foreign investors is also likely to continue to increase.

14.3.3 Impact of increasing internationalization of equity investment

The changes in the demand for, and supply of, equities discussed above will have different impacts in different countries. To see which countries will be most affected, and how they will be affected, it is necessary to return to the issue of differences in corporate financing systems, as discussed in section 4.6. We saw in Chapter 4 examples of countries with very different corporate financing patterns. While retained earnings is usually the most important source of corporate finance, some countries rely more upon debt and others rely more upon equity finance. This is reflected in differences in the relative size and importance of stock markets. As we also saw in section 4.6, there are also significant differences across countries in terms of the pattern of equity ownership – whether equity is predominantly owned by private shareholders, by financial institutions or by other non-financial corporations.

---

[5] McMorrow and Roeger (2002); Hawksworth *et al.* (2000).

[6] Megginson and Boutchkovo (2000).

Exhibit 14.5	Financial systems and capital structure

	Type of financial system	
	Control-oriented	Arm's length
Share of control-oriented finance	High	Low
Financial markets	Small, less liquid	Large, highly liquid
Share of all firms listed on exchanges	Small	Large
Ownership of debt and equity	Concentrated	Dispersed
Investor orientation	Control-oriented	Portfolio-oriented
Use of mechanisms for separating control and capital base	Frequent	Limited (often by regulation)
Dominant agency conflicts	Controlling v minority shareholders	Shareholder v management
Role of board of directors	Limited	Important
Role of hostile takeovers	Very limited	Potentially important

Source: Berglof (1997)

Based upon these differences, two types of financial systems have been identified. As illustrated in Exhibit 14.5, these may be termed 'control-oriented' and 'arm's length' financial systems.[7]

Other authors have instead discussed similar differences in terms of two different forms of capitalism, namely the 'Anglo-American model' and the 'Rhenish model', otherwise called the Germanic or continental European model.[8]

As with any simple categorization, the divide between the two systems is not always clear-cut. Indeed, the two systems are converging. While UK and US capital markets can be characterized by the relatively greater importance of outside shareholders and by relatively greater interest in short-term financial results, many of the larger companies are actively engaged in promoting and building long-term relationships with their various stakeholders, so reducing the differences between 'outsiders' and 'insiders'. Similarly, many companies in countries such as Germany, France or Japan, all members of the continental European group, are coming to rely more upon outside shareholders for finance and so are becoming more concerned with increasing shareholder value.[9]

While share ownership is increasing in a large number of countries, accounting systems have developed in different ways under different environmental pressures. In particular, as discussed in Chapters 4 and 5, not all countries have developed their accounting system in response to the needs of stock market participants. The possible effects of this on stock market participants has been explored by Ali and Hwang (2000). They explored the value relevance of financial accounting data across 16 countries (i.e. the extent to which accounting earnings and the book value of equity can be

---

[7] Berglof (1997).

[8] Albert, quoted in Price Waterhouse (1997).

[9] Price Waterhouse (1997).

used to explain share returns). They found that the value relevance of accounting information is lower in countries with:

- bank-orientated financial system (i.e. high debt–equity ratios);
- private-sector bodies not involved in the standard-setting process;
- an accounting system belonging to the 'continental' cluster rather than the 'Anglo-American' cluster;
- tax rules that significantly influence financial accounting measurements;
- less spent on external accounting services.

14.4 Benefits of foreign stock market listing

Given the sometimes substantial costs of listing, companies may be reluctant to seek listings in foreign countries. However, as we saw in Chapter 4 (Exhibit 4.3), some stock exchanges have a substantial number of foreign companies listed. Euronext, London, New York and NASDAQ each have over 300 foreign listed companies, while Germany and Luxembourg have nearly 200. Some of these listings are important, with many shares being traded each year, while others are relatively unimportant, with very few shares being traded. Similarly, different companies seek foreign stock market listings for different reasons and companies may list in different countries for different reasons. A number of motives for foreign listing have been suggested.

14.4.1 Public share offerings

Exhibit 14.6 provides some details of the listings of three large European companies. This shows their reliance upon foreign stock exchanges as sources of equity financing. (Note these companies were randomly chosen, they are not unique and many other companies could have been chosen as illustrations.)

The need to raise additional finance is a particular problem for large companies located in countries with relatively small stock markets. The local stock market in many countries is too small and/or too illiquid to absorb very large public share offerings. Thus these companies, if they want to raise equity finance, have to go to foreign stock market(s). However, this option is not always available. Whether or not a foreign company can and will raise money in any particular stock market and whether or not foreign investors can and do enter a stock market depends upon the extent to which stock markets are integrated or segmented.

Stock markets can be completely segmented. Here, foreign investors are unable to invest in the local market and/or foreign companies are unable to list in the local market. This is usually the result of government imposed restrictions. The popularity of measures to restrict entry to domestic stock markets has decreased greatly in recent years and many barriers have been dismantled. However some countries, especially developing ones, still have government imposed restrictions. These can take various forms including foreign currency controls and even the blanket prohibition of foreign ownership of companies.

At the other extreme, stock markets can be completely integrated. Investors from all countries will have equal access to all securities and foreign companies can list freely without incurring more transaction costs than do domestic companies. Foreign and local markets will therefore be equally accessible.

Exhibit 14.6	Selected European companies: listing and ownership patterns

Stock market	Year of entry	Ownership	%
Volvo, Sweden (December 2003)			
Stockholm	1935	Sweden	48.0
London	1972	France	20.3
Hamburg	1974	USA	17.3
USA (NASDAQ)	1985	UK	6.0
		Switzerland	2.2
		Others	6.2
Nestlé, Switzerland (December 2003)			
Swiss		Swiss	42
London		US	22
Paris		UK	10
Frankfurt (until 3/04)		France	8
USA–ADR		Germany	5
		Other	13
Norsk Hydro, Norway (March 2003)			
Oslo			
NYSE		Norway state	44.0
London		Norway private	20.0
Paris		Individuals living in:	
Hamburg		UK	8.3
Stockholm		USA	19.1
(was listed in Switzerland and Amsterdam)		Others	8.5

Source: extracted from annual reports: www.volvo.com, www.Nestle.com, www.hydro.com

Obviously, stock exchanges across different countries are not completely integrated, although there has been significant integration of stock markets with the Paris, Amsterdam, Brussels and Portuguese stock exchanges combining to form Euronext. Most stock markets are partially segmented. Foreign investors and/or companies can trade on foreign markets but they face additional transaction costs or restrictions that are not faced by domestic investors and/or companies. Companies will often find it easier to issue their stock on foreign markets rather than relying upon foreign investors buying their shares on its domestic exchange. In most cases, if a company wants to attract substantial numbers of foreign investors it will have to go to them – the transaction costs faced by the company entering a foreign stock market will be less than the aggregate transaction costs incurred by large numbers of foreign investors all entering the domestic stock exchange.

Exhibit 14.6 provides some anecdotal evidence illustrating the importance of foreign stock markets as a source of finance. For example, 52 per cent of Volvo's and 58 per cent of Nestlé's shares are owned by foreign shareholders, while Norsk Hydro has nearly twice as much of its stock owned by foreign investors as by Norwegian non-state investors.

14.4.2 Other types of share issues

While many companies list on foreign markets to raise finance through a public offering of their shares, there are other reasons why companies might want foreign listing(s).

One of the most publicised foreign listings was Daimler–Benz's listing on the NYSE in 1993 – the first German company to list there. By the time of its merger with Chrysler in 1998 it had still not raised any new finance on the NYSE. Some companies take listings in other countries to support the reputation of their products.

Increasingly, companies issue shares to their employees. Director share options and share-based employee pay schemes are now popular. They are seen as a way of ensuring the long-term loyalty and commitment of the workforce and they may also be tax-efficient. While companies obviously hope that most employees will not sell their shares, they must be given the opportunity to do so. If a company wants to extend these schemes to cover foreign employees they may have to list in the foreign country so that employees have a local market in which they can trade their shares. A company may also wish to issue shares, not for cash, but to finance or partially finance acquisitions. Again, if it wishes to offer shares for foreign takeovers, it may have to provide these potential shareholders with the opportunity to sell their shares in their local stock market(s).

Similarly, a large foreign ownership may help to protect the company from being taken over. Foreign ownership can make takeovers more difficult and more expensive to organize, while shareholders in countries such as Germany, with no history or culture of hostile takeovers, might be less willing to sell their shares to such bidding companies.

14.4.3 Share listing as a signalling device

There are several other potential benefits of a local listing.[10] It may provide the company with extra publicity, which in turn encourages brand recognition and customer loyalty. It may also signal to customers and potential customers the long-term commitment of the company to the country. Again, this may lead to increased sales. Foreign listings may also signal that the company is now a major international player and may therefore increase the company's prestige.

A local listing may also change the perceptions of other groups such as local communities, governments and local authorities and pressure groups. It might help to improve the operating climate facing the company. The political benefits of a local listing may be particularly great in countries that are economically or politically less stable. The company will also want to reduce its risk in these countries, and one way to do this is to ensure that local operations are financed locally. A local listing will mean that the local affiliates can be financed in a more balanced way by local equity as well as local debt. This can be important in reducing the exchange rate or currency risk faced by a company. If all shareholders are situated in the parent's country, the foreign subsidiary's earnings will have to be converted into the parent currency before dividends are paid. Having local shareholders avoids this need to convert currencies, as local earnings can be used to pay local currency dividends.

14.4.4 Additional costs of foreign listings

Selling shares in a foreign country can often be very expensive. There will always be extra direct costs – various registration and listing charges have to be paid and these can be substantial. However, these may be the least of the extra costs incurred. There will often be other costs caused by differences in the regulatory systems:[11]

---

[10] Radebaugh *et al.* (1995).

[11] Hanks (1997).

- different underwriting practices,
- different registration and regulatory requirements,
- different initial and continuing disclosure requirements,
- different control and oversight systems with respect to share dealing practices,
- different clearance and settlement procedures.

This may mean that the company has to plan and organize share issues in different countries in quite distinct ways. Different accounting and reporting systems may also be necessary and extra auditing costs may be incurred.

Once a company has done all this and has managed to issue shares in more than one market, it will be faced with further additional costs if it wants to keep an active presence in the foreign market. If it fails to maintain investor interest there may be substantial share flowback – the shares that were initially issued in the foreign market will be sold back to domestic shareholders. This happened, for example, with some of the UK privatization issues such as British Telecom, with many of the shares that were initially issued in the USA finding their way back to the UK fairly soon after issue.[12] To prevent this happening the company will have to maintain an active investor relations department in the foreign country. This department will be responsible for keeping the press, financial analysts and stockbrokers well informed about the company. Without this activity, there is unlikely to be much press or analyst interest and therefore less interest by ordinary shareholders. Similarly, the interest and loyalty of institutional investors may have to be managed actively. The company will need to organize systematically such measures as company briefings and meetings with financial analysts. This will obviously be far easier and more successful if there is a well organized local investor relations department to manage the relationships.

Different listing and reporting requirements (not only GAAP but also non-financial disclosures and frequency of reporting rules) can result in substantial extra direct and indirect costs. Direct costs are fairly easy to quantify – any extra information production, dissemination and auditing costs. In most cases these will be relatively small, but in those cases where the company's existing information systems have to be redesigned to pick up or process different information there may be very substantial one-off setting up costs. Indirect costs are very much more difficult, if not sometimes impossible, to quantify, and they can be larger than the direct costs.

The provision of any extra information has the potential to induce extra political costs and competitive disadvantage costs. Political costs may arise when the new information causes the perceptions of employees, the general public, pressure groups or the government to change. For example, the company may report higher earnings under foreign GAAP, thus changing perceptions regarding the extent to which the company is exploiting its market position or its labour force. Such changing perceptions may mean that the company is faced with a more difficult operating climate – employees, customers, local communities and the government might become more suspicious and less cooperative. Competitive disadvantage costs arise when a company is made to disclose information that is of value to its competitors. This could happen when a company is forced by foreign reporting requirements to disclose information that is not disclosed by other domestic companies. Examples might include requirements to disclose detailed segment information, research and development and advertising expenditures, or information about environmental contingencies.

---

[12] Tondkar *et al.* (1989).

Political costs will generally be incurred only if foreign GAAP reporting results in larger earnings or the disclosure of particularly sensitive information. In contrast, investor resistance or reluctance to invest can occur whenever the two sets of figures are different. It does not matter if earnings are increased or decreased; all that matters is that they have changed.

14.5 Listing behaviour of companies

14.5.1 General listing patterns

While there is plenty of anecdotal evidence regarding the importance of foreign stock market listings, there has been relatively little work looking at the behaviour of individual companies in any consistent way, and the evidence that does exist is dated. However, it still provides a useful idea of the listing behaviour of companies. One such study[13] looked at the listing of EU companies on all the major European and American exchanges in June 1989: 290 EU companies were quoted on at least one foreign exchange (see Exhibit 14.7). (Some companies are listed on more than one exchange.)

14.5.2 The London Stock Exchange (LSE)

14.5.2.1 LSE listing requirements

The listing requirements of the LSE are influenced by the EU. The EU has issued several Directives on listing which, like the accounting Directives discussed in Chapter 9, have had to be incorporated into the laws of all EU member states.

Several directives are particularly relevant to the harmonization of stock exchanges in the EU.[14] See Exhibit 14.8 for details of these.

Exhibit 14.7 Stock market listing behaviour of EU companies, 1989

Exchange	Country of domicile											Total
	UK	Ger.	Neth.	Belg.	Fr.	Lux.	Ire.	Den.	It.	Gre.	Sp.	
London	–	9	15	–	7	1	–	7	1	–	4	44
Germany	42	–	25	3	20	–	–	2	8	–	12	112
Amsterdam	19	10	–	6	3	4	–	1	3	–	–	46
Brussels	18	8	21	–	11	–	–	–	3	–	–	61
Paris	22	7	4	2	–	–	–	–	1	–	4	40
Luxembourg	7	6	3	8	2	–	–	2	–	–	–	28
Ireland	6	–	–	–	–	–	–	–	–	–	–	6
Scandinavia	1	–	–	–	2	1	–	1	–	–	–	5
Switzerland	19	35	21	6	11	–	1	2	3	2	5	105
Austria	2	17	6	–	–	–	–	–	1	–	–	26
USA	66	1	11	–	3	–	2	1	3	2	7	96
Total number of companies	114	36	44	17	34	5	3	10	8	2	17	290

Note: Totals show number of companies listed on at least one exchange.

Source: Gray *et al.* (1994).

---

[13] Gray *et al.* (1994).

[14] Scott-Quinn (1994).

| Exhibit 14.8 | EU stock exchange directives, 1979–90 |

1979 79/279/EEC	Co-ordinate conditions for admission of securities
1980 80/390/EEC	Co-ordinate information in prospectuses
1982 82/121/EEC	Publication of half-yearly reports
1987 87/345/EEC	Mutual recognition of listing prospectuses
1989 89/298/EEC	Prospectus used for simultaneous public offer all EU states
1990 90/211/EEC	Allow single document for listing and public offers

The first of these Directives, in 1979, established minimum conditions for the admission of securities to a stock market listing. In the following year a second Directive co-ordinated the requirements for the publication of listing particulars. The third, in 1982, set disclosure requirements for interim statements of listed companies. These three Directives had relatively little impact on the London or Paris exchanges. However, they led to significant increases in the disclosure requirements of a number of exchanges including the Amsterdam and the German exchanges.[15] The 1987 Directive was particularly important, as it was the first one to introduce the concept of mutual recognition (see section 9.6.6). It ensured that member states recognized all prospectuses issued by companies listed on any EU member state's exchange as long as the prospectus was approved by the authorities in that country.

Full mutual recognition can be seen clearly in the listing requirements of the LSE. The LSE accepts all documents that have been approved by any competent authority in another EU member state if they are in English or if a certified translation is provided. In addition, its listing requirements are such that it accepts all accounts 'prepared and independently audited in accordance with standards appropriate for companies of international standing and repute'. This would automatically include accounts drawn up under US GAAP or IASs. Other standards are considered on a case-by-case basis.

14.5.2.2 Listing of foreign companies on the LSE

The London Stock Exchange had a position of international prominence by the beginning of the nineteenth century. It helped to finance business in much of the Commonwealth (particularly important was the financing of the South African mining industry) and other parts of the world. For example, up until the mid-1880s much of the US insurance industry, agriculture and railways were financed from London. The importance of the London market can be seen in the example of another US industry, brewing. By 1886 15 American breweries were listed in London[16] (see Exhibit 14.9).

A study by Gray and Roberts (1997) looked at all foreign companies with full listings of equity shares (not debt) on the LSE at the end of 1994. They looked at when the companies were first listed, where they came from and what industries they operated in. The number of companies seeking a new listing increased each year, reaching a peak of new listings per annum in the mid-1980s and declining after that (with 63 of the sample

---

[15] Tondkar *et al.* (1989).

[16] Reckitt (1953).

Exhibit 14.9	American breweries registered on the LSE, 1896

Company	Date of registration
Bartholomay Brewing Co., Rochester NY	April 1889
St Louis Breweries	Dec. 1889
City of Chicago Brewing & Malting Co.	June 1890
San Francisco Breweries	Unknown
City of Baltimore United Breweries	Nov. 1889
Milwaukee & Chicago Breweries	Dec. 1890
United States Brewing Co.	May 1889
New York Breweries	Aug. 1889
New England Breweries	March 1890
Denver Breweries	June 1889
Cincinnati Breweries	Oct. 1889
Springfield Breweries	March 1890
Washington Breweries	April 1888
Indianapolis Breweries	Nov. 1889
Chicago Breweries	April 1888

Source: Reckitt, E. (1953), 'Reminiscences of early days of the accounting profession in Illinois: Illinois Society of Certified Public Accountants' in Zeff, S. A. (ed.) *The US Accounting Profession in the 1890s and Early 1900s* (Garland Publishing), p. 31.

companies having listed during the period 1980–84, 58 in 1985–89 and 34 in 1990–94). The 293 companies identified came from 26 countries. Over one-third (108) came from the US and 63 came from South Africa, while Australia, Bermuda, Canada, Japan and Sweden all had ten or more companies listed on the LSE. The South African companies had generally listed much earlier than had the companies from other countries. This reflects the historical links between the UK and South Africa and the importance of British finance in the development of South African mining. In contrast, the majority of the US companies listed during the 1980s. This was partly due to the break-up of the large telecommunications companies and the creation of a number of smaller companies, known as 'Baby Bells', partly due to the international expansion of US business at this time and probably partly due also to fashion or 'follow-my-leader' behaviour by companies. European companies have a long history of listing in London – Royal Dutch Petroleum and Unilever (The Netherlands) both listed in the 1940s, SKF and Electrolux (Sweden) in the 1950s and Thyssen, Bayer and Hoechst (Germany) in the early 1960s.

The Exchange produces a list of all listed overseas companies and from this it is possible to get an idea of what types of companies are currently listed. Derived from this list, Exhibit 14.10 lists all the countries with more than ten companies listed on either the main market or the newer and smaller Alternative Investment Market (AIM) which was established in 1995 for small and high growth companies.

AIM has been very successful in attracting foreign company listings. For example 20 foreign companies listed in 2002 and were still listed in mid-2004. Of these, 13 were listed on AIM and seven in the main market; for 2003 the figures were eight on the main market and 14 on AIM while for the first half of 2004 there were four on the main market and 20 on AIM. Almost all of these companies come from developed countries – i.e. Europe, North America and Australia or from the off-shore financial centers of Cayman Islands or British Virgin Islands. In contrast, over this period the only companies from other countries were one each from Egypt, South Korea, Chile, Barbados and Poland.

Exhibit 14.10 Number of non-UK corporate issuers on the LSE, July 2004

Country	No. of registrants	Country	No. of registrants
Australia	27	Bermuda	26
Canada	31	Cayman Islands	13
India	17	Ireland	58
Israel	11	Japan	23
The Netherlands	11	South Africa	18
US	60		

Source: Derived from data at www.lse.com, September 2004.

14.5.3 The US

14.5.3.1 American Depository Receipts (ADRs)

Most foreign (non-US) companies trade their shares in the US through American Depository Receipts (ADRs). Rather than offering shares denominated in their own currency they repackage their shares as ADRs. An ADR is a certificate that is evidence of ownership of shares in a company based outside the US. Each certificate is backed by a stated number of shares. The ADRs are popular with US investors because the procedures for sale and purchase are simplified and dividends are paid in US currency. There are various different types of ADRs (see Exhibit 14.11).

ADRs can be sponsored or unsponsored. Sponsored ADRs are administered by one bank only which has been appointed by the issuer. In contrast, unsponsored ADRs allow more than one bank to carry out depository services. Such ADRs usually trade on the over-the-counter (OTC) market and cannot be traded on any stock market.

The easiest and cheapest of these various ADRs are Level One ADRs and Rule 144A offerings. Issuers of Level One ADRs need only file their home country reports with the Securities and Exchange Commission (SEC). However, these ADRs cannot be traded on any US stock market or NASDAQ. Trade can take place only on the electronic bulletin board or the so-called 'pink sheets'. This market tends to be characterised by its expense and trading

Exhibit 14.11 Types of ADR

Level One	Trade over-the-counter (OTC) Not seeking to raise capital, minimal SEC registration, sends SEC the public reporting documents required in its home country
Level Two	Traded on stock exchange or NASDAQ Not seeking to raise capital. Full SEC registration procedures. Reports to SEC on form 20-F
Level Three	Allows issuance of new shares, gives greater visibility in US market Full SEC registration and reporting requirements on form 20-F
Rule 144A	Placed and traded only among Qualified Institutional Buyers SEC registration not required
Global DR	DR structured as combination of Rule 144A private placing and public offering outside USA SEC registration not required

Source: Summarised from *Information on ADRs*, JP Morgan, www.adr.com, September 2004.

margins are typically large. However, it is still an important market. Similarly, Rule 144A offerings cannot be traded on any stock market. Instead, the shares can be offered only as a private placing to a qualified institutional investor. The advantage to the issuing company is again that it avoids the disclosure rules involved in a stock market listing.

A non-US company can go further and issue Level Two or Level Three ADRs on any stock market or on NASDAQ. In these cases, the SEC is very much in favour of a 'level playing field' – in other words, US investors must not be less protected when investing in a foreign company than when investing in a domestic company and US companies must not be disadvantaged in comparison to foreign firms when seeking equity finance. This means that the same measurement and disclosure rules should apply to foreign and domestic companies. However, foreign companies that qualify as foreign issuers[17] (if a majority of shareholders, directors, assets or business is American, the company is treated as a domestic issuer) can opt for Level Two ADRs and take advantage of certain concessions with respect to the information required and the measurement rules used.

If a foreign company wishes to trade shares on the New York Stock Exchange (NYSE), American Stock Exchange (ASE) or Nasdaq, it must also register with the SEC and file its annual report. Since May 2002 this has to be via an electronic submission on EDGAR (see section 8.4.2.3). The annual filing normally meets the requirements of Form 20-F which includes information about the business and financial information as well as other items of information, in particular details of the shares or securities registered (see Exhibit 14.12). This is the equivalent of the Form 10-K lodged by US companies (see section 15.3).

Exhibit 14.12 Information to be included in Form 20-F

PART I

Item 1. Identity of Directors, Senior Management and Advisers

Items 2 & 3 [where 20-F is used for a new offer of shares]. Offer Statistics & Expected Timetable; Key Information

Item 4. Information on the Company
  A. *History and development of the company.*
  B. *Business overview.*
  C. *Organizational structure.*
  D. *Property, plant and equipment.*

Item 5. Operating and Financial Review and Prospects
  A. *Operating results.*
  B. *Liquidity and capital resources.*
  C. *Research and development, patents and licenses, etc.*
  D. *Trend information.*
  E. *Off-balance sheet arrangements.*
  F. *Tabular disclosure of contractual obligations.*
  G. *Safe harbor.*

Item 6. Directors, Senior Management and Employees
  A. *Directors and senior management.*
  B. *Compensation.*

---

[17] Hertz *et al.* (1997).

Exhibit 14.12 *(continued)*

C. *Board practices.*
D. *Employees.*
E. *Share ownership.*

Item 7. Major Shareholders and Related Party Transactions
A. *Major shareholders.*
B. *Related party transactions.*
C. *Interests of experts and counsel.*

Item 8. Financial Information
A. *Consolidated Statements and Other Financial Information.*
B. *Significant Changes.*

Item 9. The Offer and Listing.

Item 10. Additional Information.

Item 11. Quantitative and Qualitative Disclosures About Market Risk.

Item 12. Description of Securities Other than Equity Securities.

PART II

Item 13. Defaults, Dividend Arrearages and Delinquencies.

Item 14. Material Modifications to the Rights of Security Holders and Use of Proceeds.

Item 15. Controls and Procedures.

Item 16A. Audit committee financial expert.

Item 16B. Code of Ethics.

Item 16C. Principal Accountant Fees and Services.

Item 16D. Exemptions from the Listing Standards for Audit Committees.

Item 16E. Purchases of Equity Securities by the Issuer and Affiliated Purchasers.

PART III

Items 17, 18. Financial Statements.

Item 19. Exhibits. [These include the Certification by the officers of the company]

Source: www.sec.gov/about/forms/secforms.htm, Form 20-F.

The rules contain a number of accommodations to the practices of other jurisdictions including:

● interim reporting as per home requirements;
● acceptance of IAS 7 (cash flow accounting), FRS3 (Business combinations) and IAS21 (hyperinflation); and
● acceptance of home country or IAS GAAP plus a reconciliation statement.

The reconciliation statement starts with domestic or IAS earnings and equity and lists all the significant differences between these and US GAAP. Each difference is quantified so that the total difference between the two sets of earnings and equity is explained. Exhibit 7.3 provided an example of the reconciliation statement of a British company, Imperial Tobacco Group. The reconciliation statement must be included in the notes to the accounts, so it is considered by the auditors when they consider their opinion of the financial statements. This means they should declare an exception to the statements if the reconciliation statement does not include all material departures from US GAAP or if the quantification of the effects of the accounting differences are misstated.

Home country GAAP may be used providing they are based on a 'comprehensive body of accounting principles'. While this is not defined, SEC staff have indicated that this is taken to include the principles followed in all OECD member countries.[18]

14.5.3.2 Listing of foreign companies on the NYSE

While relatively few foreign companies have listed in London since 1990, the same cannot be said for New York. New York now has more foreign companies listing on it than does any other stock market, which marks a recent and significant change in listing behaviour.

As at the middle of September 2004, NYSE had 456 foreign companies from 47 countries listing common shares. Exhibit 14.13 provides a list of all countries that are home to at least ten registrants.

It is interesting to see the differences between this list and the pattern of companies listed in London as shown in Exhibit 14.10. As might be expected, far more Central and South American companies are listed on NYSE than on London, as are more companies from Western Europe. In contrast, NYSE has only seven South African companies (of which four listed in 2003 or 2004) and fewer companies from India and Israel than are listed in London.

One significant difference between the two markets lies in the timing of the listings. NYSE has a few companies that have maintained listings from the 1950s or earlier such as Alcan Aluminium and Canadian Pacific from Canada, KLM and Royal Dutch Petroleum from The Netherlands and Shell Transport & Trading from the UK. However, the majority of the listings have occurred since the mid-1980s, although very recent years have seen a fall in the number of foreign registrants. For example, there were 60 new listings of foreign registrants in 2000 followed by 51 in 2001, 33 in 2002, 16 in

Exhibit 14.13 Number of non-US corporate issuers on the NYSE

Country	No. registrants	Country	No. registrants
Argentina	10	Germany	16
Australia	11	Italy	10
Bermuda	22	Japan	19
Brazil	32	Mexico	23
Canada	77	Switzerland	13
Chile	17	The Netherlands	18
China	16	UK	49
France	20		

Source: www.nyse.com, September 2004.

---

[18] Hertz *et al.* (1997).

2003 and eight in the first eight months of 2004. This means that the net increase in the total number of foreign registrants was 40 in 2000, 28 in 2001 and 11 in 2002, followed by a fall of six in 2003 and a fall of 11 in the first eight months of 2004. While most of the new listings in this period came from Europe and Canada, it is noteworthy that several more also came from each of South Africa, China, Brazil, Korea, Taiwan and Puerto Rico.

Only a minority of the foreign companies listed have issued full public offerings on the NYSE. All the Chinese (see Exhibit 14.14) and the majority of companies from South and Central America, India, Hong Kong and from various mainland European countries such as France, Italy and Spain have made public offerings, suggesting that the need for funds was the main reason for seeking a listing. In contrast, relatively few of the companies from Australia, Canada, Japan or the UK have made public offerings, suggesting that the decision to list may not have been driven by a need for new funding. As discussed above, these companies may have sought a listing for a number of other reasons.

It is interesting to look very briefly at the impact of cross listing in the US. The evidence seems to suggest that this is a good thing for the company in that analyst coverage increases as does the accuracy of their forecasts and that is associated with higher valuations.[19] One reason for this may be that such listings seem to encourage firms to adopt a disclosure package more in line with that typically found in the US in that they are also associated with improved disclosures, less aggressive earnings management and the increased willingness to disclose bad as well as good news.[20]

Exhibit 14.14 An example of the information provided by NYSE on its foreign registrants: China

Company	Symbol	Industry	Listing Share	IPO type
CHINA (*16 ADR cos.*)				
Aluminum Corp of China Limited (*Chalco*)	ACH	Aluminum Production	12/11/01	A IPO
China Eastern Airlines Corp Limited	CEA	Airlines Operation	2/4/97	A IPO
China Life Insurance Company (*China Life*)	LFC	Commercial Life Insurance	12/17/03	A IPO
China Petroleum & Chemical Co (*Sinopec*)	SNP	Petroleum & Petrochemical	10/18/00	A IPO
China Southern Airlines Company Limited	ZNH	Commercial Airline Service	7/30/97	A IPO
China Telecom Corporation Limited	CHA	Fixed-Line Telecoms	11/14/02	A IPO
China Unicom	CHU	Telecommunications	6/21/00	A IPO
CNOOC Limited	CEO	Crude Oil & Gas Expl.	2/27/01	A IPO
Guangshen Railway Company Limited	GSH	Rail Transportation	5/13/96	A IPO
Huaneng Power International, Inc.	HNP	Holding Co./ Power Plants	10/6/94	A IPO
Jilin Chemical Industrial Company Limited	JCC	Chemical Products Mfg.	5/22/95	A IPO
PetroChina Company Limited	PTR	Oil and Gas Exploration	4/6/00	A IPO
Semiconductor Manufacturing Internat. Co	SMI	Semiconductor Mfg.	3/17/04	A IPO
Sinopec Beijing Yanhua Petrochemical Co	BYH	Petrochemicals Production	6/24/97	A IPO
Sinopec Shanghai Petrochemical Co	SHI	Petrochemicals Production	7/26/93	A IPO
Yanzhou Coal Mining Company Limited	YZC	Coal Mining	3/31/98	A IPO

Source: www.nyse.com. Data as at 9 September 2004.

---

[19] Lang *et al.* (2003a).

[20] Lang *et al.* (2003b); Khanna *et al.* (2004).

14.5.3.3 NYSE Global Shares

The NYSE has developed Global Shares, which can be traded on either the NYSE or the home-country market without converting the shares traded in one market for shares traded in another. Canadian companies have used this model to trade in the US since 1883. The Global Share enables other non-US companies to also trade on the same terms as North American equities. They are intended to enable virtually seamless cross-border trading, allowing non-US companies to increase liquidity and pricing efficiency in the US market while permitting US investors access to the home-market shares on the same terms as local investors.

An example of the use of Global Shares may be seen in DaimlerChrysler. The merger between Daimler-Benz AG and Chrysler Corporation in November 1998 marked the first time a company outside the US or Canada directly listed the same common shares on both a US exchange and its home stock exchange. The principal features of the DaimlerChrysler share are as follows:

- The DaimlerChrysler (NYSE: DCX) Global Shares trade on the NYSE, the Frankfurt Stock Exchange, and multiple exchanges around the world.
- DaimlerChrysler shares are quoted in US dollars on the NYSE and local currencies on other markets.
- Dividends are payable in euros or US dollars. For American shareholders, a New York transfer agent handles the conversion and payment process.
- Separate transfer agents in the US and Germany clear trades via a computer link between the New York custodian of shares (Depositary Trust Company – DTC) and the Frankfurt custodian (Deutsche Börse Clearing – DBC).

Global Shares provide an alternative to the ADR facility for non-US companies but have the advantage that buyers may make direct purchase of equity in a company, obtaining lower costs than through intermediaries. The shares function in the same way as those of US companies and allow US investors to trade a non-US security outside market hours and receive dividends at the same time as shareholders in the company's home country.

14.6 Empirical research into stock market listing choices

Several studies have looked at the factors that help to explain listing choices or where and why companies list on foreign stock exchanges. One of the first of these studies was by Saudagaran (1988), who tested four hypotheses. These were that the likelihood that a company has a foreign listing is a function of:

- the relative size of the company in its domestic stock market (capitalization or market value of company's equity to total market capitalization);
- importance of foreign sales (foreign sales to total sales);
- importance of foreign investment (investment in foreign countries as a proportion of total investment);
- importance of foreign employees (employees in foreign countries as a proportion of total employees).

Looking at 223 companies with shares listed in at least one of eight foreign countries, the study found support for the importance of the company in its domestic local stock exchange and the importance of foreign sales. It failed to find any support for the other two hypotheses (foreign investment and foreign employees).

Later studies have looked instead at the importance of disclosure levels in different countries. Biddle and Saudagaran (1989), using a similar sample, found support for the hypothesis that companies tend to be indifferent across exchanges with levels of disclosure that are less than domestic disclosure levels. In contrast, they are progressively less likely to list on exchanges in countries with higher disclosure levels. Alternative explanations of listing behaviour were also considered – the importance of industry membership; geographic location (whether located in the same geographic area or not); importance of country of listing as an export market (industry exports to country as proportion of industry exports to all sample countries); and the relative importance of the company to its domestic stock market. Even when all of these alternative explanations were also taken into account, disclosure levels still helped to explain listing choice. These results were confirmed by a later study (Saudagaran and Biddle, 1995), which looked at the listing behaviour of 459 multinational companies from the same eight countries (Canada, France, Germany, Japan, Switzerland, the UK and the US) in 1992.

While these are interesting results, some care should be taken in interpreting them. It should not be assumed that the results will always hold across all countries and all time periods. This type of study suffers from two serious limitations. First, it looks only at the position at one point of time. It tries to explain the decision to list – a decision that may have been taken many years earlier – by looking at contemporary economic, corporate and accounting factors. Secondly, these studies have looked only at certain countries.

One other study (Gray and Roberts, 1997) suggests that the factors determining listing choices may differ across companies from different countries. Gray and Roberts instead tried to explain the number of registrants from each foreign country that were listed on the LSE in 1994. They ran a regression with the dependent variable being number of companies listed from country x and the independent variables being:

- disclosure level (more or less than UK),
- size of economy (GDP),
- economic development of country (*per capita* GDP),
- importance of national stock market (market capitalization to GDP),
- trade with the UK (exports and imports to UK as a proportion of all exports and imports of country),
- level of domestic investment (domestic investment to GDP),
- cultural affinity to the UK (English-speaking, EU member or Commonwealth member).

While the model was relatively successful in explaining the number of foreign registrants (adjusted R^2 of 61 per cent) Gray and Roberts found no evidence to suggest that disclosure levels were significant. Instead, the only factors that helped to explain the number of companies listed were GDP, stock market capitalization and domestic investment rates. More companies were listed from countries that were large, had relatively important stock markets and high needs for capital as measured by domestic investment levels.

A single country study by Yamori and Baba (2001) on the opinions of Japanese managers in 1996 found that the managers believed strongly in the favourable effect of overseas listing in terms of increasing prestige and widening the shareholder base, but regarded disclosure and financial reporting requirements as the main obstacles to overseas listing. They pointed out that the subsequent moves in Japan to align more closely with IFRS, together with the economic impact of the recession that occurred after 1996, would require their conclusions to be tested against the change of circumstances.

14.7 Other users of financial statements

The identity of users of financial statements has been debated for many years. The Trueblood committee of the AICPA in the US (1971) listed 12 objectives of financial accounting, one of which was that financial statements should provide information useful to investors and creditors.[21] While investors are one of the most important groups that a company will want to report to, a wide range of other report users can also be identified. An early and influential report of the UK standard–setting body[22] identified seven user groups (see Exhibit 14.15).

The IASB in its Framework reflects the broad spectrum of users listed in *The Corporate Report*[23] but says that while all the information needs of these users cannot be met by financial statements, there are needs which are common to all users. Providing information that meets the needs of investors will also meet the needs of most other users that the financial statements can satisfy.[24]

While we have concentrated upon foreign equity investors so far in this chapter, many companies also have foreign financial statement users belonging to each of the other groups listed. Many of the motives for raising debt or loans in foreign countries will be the same as the motives for raising foreign equity. Some companies may raise foreign loans, as they see this as a way of reducing the costs of capital. This may be part of an active treasury management policy designed to minimize costs – or, in some cases, even as part of a strategy to actively speculate on foreign currency markets.[25] Other companies will raise foreign debt as a way of reducing risk. As with equity, if debt is raised in the same countries as the money is invested, the company can use local currency earnings to repay the debt. If instead debt is raised in one country and employed in another, the company will have to convert its earnings into a different currency before they can be used to repay the debt, and may therefore be adversely affected by exchange rate changes.

Virtually all large companies have to source some of their supplies from foreign suppliers and similarly sell some of their outputs in foreign markets. Most companies,

Exhibit 14.15 Users of corporate reports, as identified by *The Corporate Report* (1975)

Equity-investor group	Existing and potential shareholders
Loan creditor group	Debentures, loan stock, long- and short-term loan providers
Employee group	Existing, past and potential employees
Analyst–adviser group	Financial analysts, stockbrokers, trade unions, journalists, etc.
Business contact group	Customers, suppliers, competitors
Government	Taxation, supervision commerce and industry, local authorities
Public	Consumers, tax payers, local community, environmental groups, etc.

---

[21] AICPA (1973).

[22] ASSC (1975).

[23] IASB Framework (1989) paragraph 9.

[24] IASB Framework (1989) paragraph 10.

[25] Discussion of this issue is outside the scope of this text, but useful texts in this area include Buckley (2000) and Buckley *et al.* (1998).

whether manufacturing or service sector companies, go further than this and also operate overseas.[26] This means that foreign customers, suppliers, employees, governments, local communities and various special interest and pressure groups are all likely to be interested in the activities of, and performance of, the company.

Some of the groups identified can demand whatever information they want. Governments, stock markets, large loan or debt providers and important customers and suppliers may all be able to demand the information they want. However, providing extra information is not costless and if any of these groups demands a great deal of information they may find that foreign companies are not prepared to trade with them or operate in their countries. In other cases the users cannot or will not impose specific reporting or measurement requirements on foreign companies. Instead, companies are free to decide the extent to which they will meet the specific needs of foreign users. A number of alternative strategies are available to a company, ranging from doing nothing to producing statements that are the same as those generally produced by domestic companies. These different alternatives are all briefly examined below.

14.8 Methods of reporting to foreign users

14.8.1 Foreign language statements

Obviously, companies could just ignore the fact that many users are from other countries and are used to different accounting methods, different types of narrative disclosures, different currencies or different languages. However, there may be substantial indirect or hidden costs in this approach. If potential lenders cannot even understand the language in which the reports are written they are far less likely to buy the shares. Many companies therefore translate their web pages and their annual reports and accounts into foreign language(s). This might be just an abridged report (typically the financial statements, the accounting policies, the Chair's statement and a very brief overview of activities) or a complete word-for-word translation of the entire annual accounts and report. Most large European companies produce complete English-language versions of their annual report including all the narrative disclosures.

The only costs involved are the cost of translation and any additional printing costs, so it tends to be a fairly cheap alternative. It is therefore an acceptable method of reporting to foreign users if:

- the foreign users are relatively unimportant, or
- the accounting and reporting systems of the two countries are very similar to each other.

If there are relatively few foreign users or they are relatively unimportant, it will not be worth spending any more on any of the more expensive alternative ways of reporting to foreign users – the additional costs would outweigh the advantages. Alternatively, the foreign readers may be very knowledgeable about the differences in the accounting systems internationally. As we saw in section 14.2.3 above, some investors are able to adopt a multiple principle capability and are able to cope with differences in accounting methods. Here, there would be no advantages to the company in using other more sophisticated but more expensive reporting methods. Finally, there may be little point

---

[26] Again, the reasons why companies become international are outside the scope of this text, but useful texts in this area include Caves (1996), Dunning (1988) and Pitelis and Sugden (1991).

in doing more if there are few material differences between domestic and foreign GAAP statements. Leventis and Weetman (2004) found that listed companies in Greece reporting in Greek and English produce, on average, a larger amount of voluntary disclosure than those reporting only in Greek. This suggests that the target of producing the English language report may drive the content of the Greek language report.

14.8.2 Convenience translations

Even if a shareholder is presented with a complete set of accounts in their own language, they may still be confused by the use of a different or unfamiliar currency. While this is obviously less likely to be a problem, the use of a different currency can make it more difficult to get an accurate impression of what is going on. Some companies therefore go one stage further and also translate the currency they report in – the 'convenience translation', so called as it is not a complete method of foreign currency translation, such as the closing rate or temporal method. Instead, all the figures, both the current year and past year(s), are translated at one exchange rate.

Convenience translations are relatively rarely found in European reports, but many large Japanese companies provide such statements. Exhibit 12.1 (Sumitomo Mitsui) illustrated the provision of a convenience translation for the latest year for the notes to the accounts. As is common with Japanese companies, this company actually goes slightly further and also reformatted its accounts to present them in a form more familiar to foreign (US) readers. In many cases this is not simply a case of presenting the same information in a slightly different form, but also involves the provision of additional information.

14.8.3 Reconciliation statements

One example of this is the reconciliation statement produced by many companies listed in the US, as described above in section 14.5.3. The benefits of this type of reconciliation statement depend upon several factors. Some companies would argue that there are no benefits. Instead, they would argue that producing two sets of figures will increase uncertainty. However, if the users are relatively sophisticated they should be able to understand why two sets of GAAP may result in different earnings or equity figures and should not be deterred from dealing with the company. Indeed, some users are sufficiently powerful to demand statements drawn-up in familiar GAAP. For example, banks when lending large sums of money will often be able to demand whatever information they require. Similar powers are held by governments and tax authorities.

It appears that the SEC insistence on the preparation of a reconciliation to US GAAP (except by Canadian companies) may partly reflect a concern for insufficiently conservative accounting practices, as well as a desire to see extensive disclosure. In its response to the SEC on the acceptability of IASs, FASB in June 2000 recommended that companies using IASs should provide reconciliations to US GAAP.

There has been a considerable amount of interest in the academic literature on the usefulness of reconciliation statements. There is a high level of agreement that when a company produces two sets of accounts – in particular US GAAP full sets of accounts as well as domestic GAAP accounts, then both sets of accounts contain useful information in the sense that the markets react to both sets of accounts. There is rather less agreement on the usefulness of US GAAP reconciliation statements with much of the evidence suggesting that such statements are not informationally useful.[27] However, others suggest that they are useful, but that the usefulness depends, as might be expected, at least partially upon the time period being considered and upon the country of the disclosing company.[28]

Street *et al.* (2000) used a comparability index (see Chapter 7) to examine the US GAAP reconciliations of 33 companies whose annual reports complied with international accounting standards in 1997. From the three years of data available in the 20-F they found that the overall adjustments were significant only in 1996 with an adjustment of 20 per cent from IAS profit to US GAAP. They concluded that the gap between IAS and US GAAP was narrowing. They also found examples of noncompliance with IAS, some of which were material in relation to the reported earnings. They pointed out that if the SEC were to be persuaded to abandon the requirement for a reconciliation there would need to be greater assurance from the preparers and auditors of accounts.

Studies of the impact of reconciliation statements have generally examined the impact of disclosures upon share returns, although one more recent study has instead explored the issue of the impact of disclosure upon analysts. In that study, Hora *et al.* (2003) tested the effect of foreign GAAP earnings and the 20-F reconciliations on the revision of analysts' forecasts. The data related to the years 1988 to 1995. They found abnormal revisions around the announcement date of earnings prepared under foreign GAAP and around the filing of Form 20-F. They concluded that the foreign earnings and the reconciliations convey information to the analysts. One problem with this research design is that the Form 20-F contains a mass of information alongside the reconciliation statement, so the analysts may have been reacting to some other aspect of the Form 20-F.

These studies are generally taken to mean that US GAAP information is of a better quality than are other GAAP. However, all that can really be concluded is that US GAAP statements and reconciliation statements provide different, new information.

14.8.4 Use of IFRS

Until recently, the IASB listed on its web pages all companies that voluntarily stated their compliance with international standards. This list was then used in a number of studies to examine the questions of how good was the compliance with international standards and who actually complied with the standards voluntarily. From this it is clear that, prior to IFRS1, many companies claimed compliance when this was less than complete. For example, the 2000 survey of 1999 accounts identified 165 companies claiming compliance with international standards, however, only 102 of these were fully compliant with the rest adopting various levels of compliance of 'IAS lite' as shown in Exhibit 14.16.

An earlier survey of 1996 accounts was used to look in detail at 49 companies' accounts.[29] This identified the areas of non-compliance, with the areas of the highest non-compliance shown in Exhibit 14.17.

One obvious question is 'which companies do not comply fully with International Standards?' Street and Bryant (2000) suggest that the level of compliance is associated with a number of factors. In particular, compliance is higher on average amongst companies that are listed in the US or that file in the US than amongst companies that

---

[27] See for example Rees and Elgers (1997); Chan and Seow (1996).

[28] See Fulkerson and Meek (1998) or Rees (1995).

[29] Street *et al.* (1999); see also Taylor and Jones (1999).

Exhibit 14.16 Types of compliance with IASs

		Number of companies
1	Full IAS Compliance	102
2	Full compliance with national standards that comply with IASs	4
3	Full compliance with exceptions specified in the accounting policies	10
4	Full compliance with exceptions specified in the notes, but outside the policies	3
5	Accounting policies comply with IASs or are based on IASs or the principles in IASs	4
6	As 5 but with specified exemptions from full compliance	4
7	IAS used only when there are no equivalent domestic standards	12
8	IAS used only for selected items or when permitted by domestic requirements	13
9	Reconciliations from domestic GAAP to IASs	6
10	Summary IAS financial statements	4
11	Unquantified description of differences from IAS treatments	5
Total		165

Source: *Accountancy*, May 2001, pp. 98–99.

Exhibit 14.17 Level of non-compliance with International Standards

Standard	Area	Number of companies
IAS 2 Inventories	Use of 'lower of cost and market' rather than 'lower of cost and net realizable value'	13 of 47
IAS 8 Net profit/loss	All items of income and expense included in net profit /loss	13 of 49
	Strict definition extraordinary items	10 of 10
IAS 9 R&D	Disclose accounting policy	10 of 43
	Disclose amount charged to expense of period	10 of 43
IAS 16 Property, plant & equipment	Reconcile carrying amount at beginning and end of each period	15 of 49
IAS 18 Revenue	Disclose accounting policy	27 of 49
IAS 19 Retirement plans	Disclose general description of plan	14 of 23
IAS 21 Foreign currency	Disclose amount of exchange difference included in net profit /loss	15 of 48
IAS 22 Business combinations	Disclose cost of acquisition	11 of 31
	If useful life of goodwill exceeds five years, justify period	14 of 38
	Reconcile beginning and end period goodwill	13 of 42
IAS 23 Borrowing costs	Disclose capitalization rate	14 of 14

Source: Derived from Street *et al*. (1999).

are not either listed or filed in the US. Obviously, one reason for this may be the US listing per se, but it may be instead that US listing status is highly correlated with some other variable such as size or country of domicile, which is the real reason for the level of compliance. Further testing using multiple regression found that compliance was positively associated with listing status as well as with the type of audit report compliance statement and the use of international auditing standards. In other words, the main factors were the extent to which the company's auditors, and presumably therefore the company, are serious about the use of international standards. Surprisingly, they did not find that variables such as size, profitability or industry helped explain compliance.

A second important question that could be asked about the impact of international standards is which companies claim to follow international standards (even if this compliance is less than complete)? Again using the IASB list of companies following IASs in 1996, El-Gazzar *et al.* (1999) found that the most important variable appearing to explain whether or not a company complied voluntarily was internationality, as measured by the percentage of foreign sales. Also important were membership of the EU, size, profitability, debt ratio and the number of stock markets listed on. Different stock markets have different listing requirements. In most cases, companies can choose whether to follow local GAAP, international GAAP or some other internationally accepted GAAP such as US GAAP. Which of these three a company will choose depends upon the costs of compliance or non-compliance. Obviously, as a company increases the number of stock markets it lists on the costs of using local GAAP in each market will increase, so that it becomes more and more advantageous to use just one GAAP. However, this need not be IASB GAAP, it could be US GAAP. Ashbaugh (2001) provides evidence to suggest that the decision on whether to use IASB or US GAAP will depend upon the particular circumstances of the company. In most cases, they will prefer whichever of these two alternatives is the easiest or cheapest to do, namely the alternative that requires the least number of accounting changes from their domestic GAAP.

Probably the most important question is simply, is IAS information useful to the market? There is some limited evidence on this. Harris and Muller (1999) looked at the impact of 20-F reconciliation statements that recast information from IAS to US GAAP. They found that the impact on reported figures was generally smaller for their sample than was reported in studies of domestic GAAP to US GAAP reconciliations, implying that US GAAP was more similar to IAS GAAP than it was to GAAP in many other countries. The results on market impact were not unambiguous, differing somewhat depending upon the models used to measure the impact. However, they conclude that there is some evidence that US GAAP reconciliations are useful even from IAS GAAP, in that they were value relevant when using models based upon returns rather than prices per shares. This does of course necessarily imply that US GAAP is somehow 'better' than IAS GAAP, simply that it may provide different information.

One interesting study that throws further light on the question of whether US or IAS GAAP is more informationally efficient was carried out by Leuz (2003) who looked at companies on the German Neuer Markt (new market), a market for smaller high-growth companies. These companies were allowed to use either US or IAS GAAP. Neither of these was used for taxation purposes and the decision on which to use did not affect any other features of the regulatory environment they face. He found no evidence of any significant differences in information asymmetry; in other words there were no significant differences between companies that used US or IAS GAAP in terms of bid-ask spreads, share turnover, analysts forecast dispersion or initial public offering under pricing.

Ashbaugh and Pincus (2001) instead looked at the question of the impact of IAS adoption on analysts forecasts. While this study used voluntary adoptees of IAS during the period 1990–93, a period when IAS standard offered significant choice, they did find that the voluntary adoption of IAS resulted in improved forecasts and that the improvement was greater for those companies with the greatest change in GAAP.

These findings support the conclusions drawn by Barth *et al.* (1999) in a study that uses mathematical proofs to show that international harmonization, of itself, is not necessarily a good thing. Rather it depends upon whether or not greater harmonization results in more or less precise GAAP and increasing or decreasing price informativeness of the resultant information. The empirical studies here show that moving from domestic to IAS GAAP is generally perceived by the market as being desirable. However, stock markets would probably have found the move from a position of international disharmony to the widespread adoption of US GAAP informationally useful as well. The question of whether or not US GAAP or IAS GAAP would have been found most useful in the context of stock market informativeness remains currently unresolved.

Summary and conclusions

This chapter looked at the effects of international diversity in accounting practices. In particular, it sought to provide answers to the questions of how do investors cope with accounting diversity? And how can companies adapt their listing behaviour and their disclosure policies to cope with accounting diversity?

Given the often very different figures that can be produced under different GAAP, it is not immediately obvious why investors would want to cope with the additional problems and uncertainty involved in investing in foreign companies. However, we saw that the benefits can be substantial and, at least for the individual or private investor, it is getting easier and easier to invest in foreign companies indirectly through the ever-increasing number of investment funds that exist. However, this does not remove the problem of how to cope with accounting diversity – the investment trusts still have to decide which companies they should invest in. The chapter therefore looked at the somewhat limited evidence there is regarding how investors cope with accounting diversity. This suggests that foreign investment might well increase as accounting diversity is reduced. We also saw that the demand for international investments are likely to increase and the number of companies seeking foreign listing also looks likely to continue to increase, at least over the next few years.

The chapter then moved on to look at the listing behaviour of companies. Taking as its starting point the evidence presented in Chapter 4 (Exhibit 4.3), showing that many companies list on foreign exchange(s), the chapter looked at the reasons for this phenomenon.

Key points from the chapter:

● Companies may have to list on a larger exchange if they want to raise a large amount of equity capital. This is especially the case for companies from relatively small countries or countries with relatively inactive stock markets.

● Taking a listing can be a problem for any company seeking a great deal of capital – as seen, for example, in a number of privatization issues from many countries including the UK. Companies also list on foreign exchanges for a range of reasons including risk management, issuing shares to employees and for takeovers, and signalling to customers, the general public or governments.

- The US demands the highest level of disclosure from foreign registrant companies – requiring, for example, a reconciliation statement explaining differences from US GAAP.

- The reconciliation affects direct and indirect costs were discussed and the ways in which the US has reduced these costs by allowing a variety of different methods of selling of shares.

- Studies on stock market listing behaviour provide clear evidence that differences in listing requirements have been important; however, this is not the only consideration and given the rapidly increasing importance of the US to foreign companies and the rapidly increasing number of foreign companies raising new equity finance in the US, the extra disclosure costs do not appear to be an insurmountable barrier.

- Increasingly more companies are likely to face the question of how best to report to foreign users. Existing practices range from translation into foreign languages, through translation of the currencies and account formats, to complete statements under foreign GAAP.

Questions

The following questions test your understanding of the material contained in the chapter and allow you to relate your understanding to the learning outcomes specified at the start of this chapter. The learning outcomes are repeated here. Each question is cross-referenced to the relevant section of the chapter.

Understand why investors might want to invest in foreign companies and the approaches they may take

1 Why might investors wish to invest in foreign companies? (section 14.2.1)

2 Describe the composition of the optimal portfolio that an investor can invest in and describe how they might go about investing in a suitable portfolio. (section 14.2)

3 Identify and describe the alternative investment strategies an investor can adopt when deciding which shares to invest in and, in each case, describe the role and use of financial statement information. (section 14.2)

Be aware of the reasons why the demand for and supply of foreign equities is likely to continue to increase

4 Describe the reasons there are for believing that the number of companies listing on foreign stock markets is likely to increase over the next few years. (section 14.3)

5 Describe the reasons there are for believing that the demand for foreign equities will continue to increase over the next few years. (section 14.4)

Understand the reasons why companies might list on foreign stock markets

6 Why do companies list on foreign stock markets? (section 14.4)

7 What actions might a company have to take to ensure that it maintains a large active shareholder base in a foreign country? (section 14.4)

8 Which types of companies are particularly likely to seek a listing on a foreign stock market? (section 14.4)

9 If a company wanted to trade its shares in the US, what alternative methods are available to it? What would you advise it to do? (section 14.5.3)

Understand the additional costs of listing on foreign stock markets

10 What are likely to be the main additional direct costs incurred by a company seeking a listing on a foreign stock market? (section 14.4.4)

11 What are likely to be the main additional indirect costs incurred by a company seeking a listing on a foreign stock market? (section 14.4.4)

Evaluate published research seeking to explain the foreign stock market listing choices of companies

12 What is the empirical evidence of foreign listing behaviour on UK stock markets? (section 14.5.2)

13 What is the empirical evidence of foreign listing behaviour in the US? (section 14.5.3)

14 What does the empirical research tell you about the factors that affect a company's choice of where to list? (section 14.6)

15 If you wanted to test empirically for the factors that affect a company's choice of where to list, how would you go about getting the information you needed? What problems do you think you would encounter? (section 14.6)

Understand the different approaches that companies can take when reporting to foreign investors

16 Describe each of the main methods that a company could adopt when reporting to its foreign users. (section 14.8)

17 Describe the relative advantages and disadvantages of each of the methods identified above. (section 14.8)

References and further reading

ASSC (1975) *The Corporate Report*. London: Accounting Standards Steering Committee.

Albert, M. (1997) *Capitalism against Capitalism*, quoted in Price Waterhouse (1997).

Ali, A. and Hwang, L.-S. (2000) 'Country-specific factors related to financial reporting and the value relevance of accounting data', *Journal of Accounting Research*, Spring; 1–21.

AICPA (1973) *Objectives of Financial Statements*, American Institute of Certified Public Accountants.

Ashbaugh, H. (2001) 'Non-US firms' accounting standard choices', *Journal of Accounting and Public Policy*, 20: 129–153.

Ashbaugh, H. and Pincus, M. (2001) 'Domestic accounting standards, international accounting standards, and the predictability of earnings', *Journal of Accounting Research*, 39(3): 417–434.

Barth, M.E., Clinch, G. and Shibano, T. (1999) 'International accounting harmonization and global equity markets', *Journal of Accounting and Economics*, 26: 201–235.

Berglof, E. (1997) 'Reforming corporate governance: Redirecting the European agenda', *Economic Policy*, April: 91–117.

Biddle, G.C. and Saudagaran, S.M. (1989) 'The effect of financial disclosure levels on firms' choices among alternative foreign stock exchange listings', *Journal of International Financial Management and Accounting*, 1(1): 55–87.

Buckley, A. (2000) *Multinational Finance*, 4th edn. Hemel Hempstead: Prentice Hall.

Buckley, A., Ross, S.A., Westerfield, R.W. and Jaffe, J.F. (1998) *Corporate Finance Europe*. London: McGraw-Hill.

Caves, R.E. (1966) *Multinational Enterprise and Economic Analysis*, 2nd edn. Cambridge: Cambridge University Press.

Chan, K.C. and Seow, G.S. (1996) 'The association between stock returns and foreign GAAP earings versus earnings adjusted to US GAAP', *Journal of Accounting and Economics*, 21: 139–158.

Choi, F.D.S. and Levich, R.M. (1996) 'Accounting diversity', in Steil, B. (ed.) *The European Equity Markets*. London: Royal Institute of International Affairs.

Choi, F.D.S. and Levich, R.M. (1997) 'Accounting diversity and capital market decisions', in Choi, F.D.S. (ed.) *International Accounting and Finance Handbook*, 2nd edn. New York: John Wiley.

Corhay, A., Rad, A.T. and Urbain, J.P. (1993) 'Common stochastic trends in European stock markets', *Economics Letters*, 42: 385–390.

Dunning, J.H. (1988) *Explaining International Production*, London: Unwin Hyman.

El-Gazzar, S.M., Finn, P.M. and Jacob, R. (1999) 'An empirical investigation of multinational firms' compliance with international accounting standards', *International Journal of Accounting*, 34(2): 239–248.

Fraser, P. and Oyefeso, O. (forthcoming) 'US, UK and European stock market integration', *Journal of Business Finance and Accounting*.

Fulkerson, C.L. and Meek, G.K. (1998) 'Analysts' earnings forecasts and the value relevance of 20-F reconciliations from non-US to US GAAP', *Journal of International Financial Management and Accounting*, 9(1): 1–15.

Gray, S.J. and Roberts, C.B. (1997) 'Foreign company listings on the London Stock Exchange: Listing patterns and influential factors', in Cooke, T.E. and Nobes, C.W. (eds), *The Development of Accounting in an International Context*. London: Routledge.

Gray, S.J., Meek, G.K. and Roberts, C.B. (1994) 'Financial deregulation, stock exchange listing choice, and the development of a European capital market', in Zimmerman, V.K. (ed.), *The New Europe: Recent Political and Economic Implications for Accountants and Accounting*. Urbana–Champaign, IL: Center for International Education and Research in Accounting, University of Illinois.

Hanks, S. (1997) 'Globalization of world financial markets: Perspective of the US Securities and Exchange Commission', in Choi, F.D.S. (ed.) *International Accounting and Finance Handbook*, 2nd edn. New York: John Wiley.

Harris, M.S. and Muller, K.A. (1999) 'The market valuations of IAS versus US-GAAP accounting measures using Form 20-F reconciliations', *Journal of Accounting and Economics*, 26: 285–312.

Hawksworth, J., Vause, N., Petitt, D., Lee, J. and Barker, T. (2000) *The European pensions and savings revolution: our vision for the future*, PWC.

Hertz, R.H., Dittmar, N.W., Lis, S.J., Decker, W.E. and Murray, R.J. (1997) *The Coopers and Lybrand SEC Manual*, 7th edn. New York: John Wiley.

Hora, J., Tondkar, R.H. and McEwen, R.A. (2003) 'Effect of foreign GAAP earnings and Form 20-F reconciliations on revisions of analysts' forecasts', *The International Journal of Accounting*, 38: 71–93,

Khanna, T., Palepu, K.G. and Srinivasan, S. (2004) 'Disclosure practices of companies interacting with US markets', *Journal of Accounting Research*, 42(2): 475–525.

Lang, M., Lins, K.V. and Miller, D.P. (2003a) 'ADRs, analysts, and accuracy: does cross listing in the United States improve a firm's information environment and increase market value?' *Journal of Accounting Research*, 41(2): 317–345.

Lang, M., Raedy, J.S. and Yetman, M.H. (2003b) 'How representative are firms that are cross-listed in the United States? An analysis of accounting quality', *Journal of Accounting Research*, 41(2): 363–386.

Leuz, C. (2003) 'IAS versus US GAAP: Information asymmetry-based evidence from the German new market', *Journal of Accounting Research*, 41(3): 445–472.

Leventis, S. and Weetman, P. (2005) 'Impression management: Dual language reporting and voluntary disclosure' (forthcoming), *Accounting Forum*.

McMorrow, K. and Roeger, W. (2002) 'EU pensions reform: an overview of the debate and an empirical assessment of the main policy reform options', *EC Director General for Economic and Financial Affairs*, Economic Papers No. 162: January.

Megginson, W.L. and Boutchkovo, M.K. (2000) 'The impact of privatization on capital market development and individual share ownership', *Working Paper*, FEEM.

Melton, P. (1996) *The Investor's Guide to Going Global with Equities*. London: FT/Pitman Publishing.

Miles, S. and Nobes, C. (1998) 'The use of foreign accounting data in UK financial institutions', *Journal of Business Finance and Accounting*, 25(3–4): 309–328.

Pitelis, C.N. and Sugden, R. (eds) (1991) *The Nature of the Transnational Firm*, London: Routledge.

Price Waterhouse (1997) *Converging Cultures: Trends in European Corporate Governance*. London: Price Waterhouse Europe (April).

Radebaugh, L.H., Gebhart, G. and Gray, S.J. (1995) 'Foreign stock exchange listings: A case study of Daimler–Benz', *Journal of International Financial Management and Accounting*, 6(2): 158–192.

Reckitt, E. (1953) 'Reminiscences of early days of the accounting profession in Illinois: Illinois Society of Certified Public Accountants', reprinted in Zeff, S.A. (ed.) *The US Accounting Profession in the 1890s and Early 1900s*, pp. 165–314. New York: Garland Publishing.

Rees, L. and Elgers, P. (1997) 'The market's valuation of nonreported accounting measures: reconciliations of Non-US and US GAAP', *Journal of Accounting Research*, 35(1): 115–127.

Rees, L. (1995) 'The information contained in reconciliations to earnings based on US accounting principles by non-US companies', *Accounting and Business Research*, 25(100): 301–310.

Saudagaran, S.M. (1988) 'An empirical study of selected factors influencing the decision to list in foreign stock exchanges', *Journal of International Business Studies*, Spring: 101–127.

Saudagaran, S.M. and Biddle, G.C. (1995) 'Foreign listing location: A study of MNCs and stock exchanges in eight countries', *Journal of International Business Studies*, 26(2): 319–342.

Scott-Quinn, B. (1994) 'EC securities markets regulation', in Steil, B. (ed.) *International Financial Market Regulation*, pp. 121–166. Chichester: John Wiley.

Smith, K.L. (1999) 'Major world equity market interdependence a decade after the 1987 crash: Evidence from cross spectral analysis', *Journal of Business Finance and Accounting*, April/May: 365–392.

Solnik, B. (1974) 'Why not diversify internationally?' *Financial Analysts Journal*, July/August: 48–54.

Street, D.L., Gray, S.J. and Bryant, S.M. (1999) 'Acceptance and observance of International Accounting Standards: an empirical study of companies claiming to comply with IASs', *International Journal of Accounting*, 34(1): 11–48.

Street, D.L. and Bryant, S.M. (2000) 'Disclosure levels and compliance with IASs: a comparison of companies with and without US listing and filings', *International Journal of Accounting*, 35(3): 305–329.

Street, D.L., Nichols, N.B. and Gray, S.J. (2000) 'Assessing the acceptability of international accounting standards in the US: An empirical study of the materiality of US GAAP reconciliations by non-US companies complying with IASC standards', *The International Journal of Accounting*, 35(1): 27–63.

Taylor, M.E. and Jones, R.A. (1999) 'The use of International Accounting Standards: A survey of IAS compliance disclosure', *International Journal of Accountancy*, 34(4): 447–570.

Taylor, M.P. and Tonks, I. (1989) 'The internationalization of stock markets and the abolition of UK exchange controls', *The Review of Economics and Statistics*, 71: 332–336.

Tondkar, R.H., Adhikari, A. and Coffman, E.N. (1989) 'The internationalisation of equity markets: Motivations for foreign corporate listing and filing and listing requirements of five major stock markets', *International Journal of Accounting*, Fall: 143–163.

Yamori, N. and Baba, T. (2001) 'Japanese management views on overseas exchange listings: survey results', *Journal of International Financial Management and Accounting*, 12(3): 286–316.

15 Transparency and disclosure

Learning outcomes

After reading this chapter you should be able to:

- Explain the problems of defining 'transparency' in disclosure. ▶

- Explain the requirements of narrative reporting in the US.
- Explain how management reports are produced outside the US.
- Explain and evaluate the initiatives being taken on developing CSR reports.
- Explain the nature and evaluate the usefulness of remuneration reports.
- Explain and contrast methods used to carry out research into disclosure.

15.1 Introduction

The purpose of this chapter is to explain and illustrate the steps that have been taken in many countries to respond to calls for transparency of corporate disclosure. Those calls originated in the US, particularly following the Asian economic crisis of 1997, take on greater significance following the failure of Enron. We have explained in Chapter 3 the range of regulations on governance which affected corporate reporting after Enron and how this rippled around the world from the Sarbanes–Oxley Act. In this chapter we give more detail on the nature of the resulting corporate disclosures and the work done by market participants and by academic researchers in assessing the relative achievement of transparency in disclosure. In particular we give examples of corporate social responsibility reports and we discuss remuneration reports. We finish with a description of the methods being used by academic researchers to investigate disclosure.

15.2 The meaning of 'transparency'

In section 3.2 we explained how 'transparency' came to the fore as a criterion of the SEC in the US, following the Asian financial crisis. It became widely used by policy makers in comments on questionable accounting practices. Being a policy-related issue made it a useful motivation for accounting research. There has been an explosion of documents using the word 'transparency'. Unfortunately it is one of those words that is assumed to have a common basis of understanding, but in fact is used in different ways by different people. Even more unfortunately some omit to explain what they think transparency means.

A policy-oriented definition is provided by the Global Reporting Initiative (GRI):

> It requires that, regardless of the format and content of reports, users are fully informed of the processes, procedures and assumptions embodied in the reported information. For example, a report must include information on the stakeholder engagement processes used in its preparation, data collection methods and related internal auditing and scientific assumptions underlying the presentation of information.
>
> (GRI Sustainability Reporting Guidelines, page 24; see also section 3.5.3 of this book.)

A research-oriented definition is applied by Bushman *et al.* (2004) as '. . . the availability of firm-specific information to those outside publicly traded firms'. They acknowledge 'the multifaceted nature of corporate transparency' and then define two facets for their investigation. They describe 'financial transparency' as the intensity and timeliness of financial disclosures, and their interpretation and dissemination by analysts and the media. They further describe 'governance transparency' as the intensity of governance disclosures used by outside investors to hold officers and directors accountable. Their descriptions are based on data which are available to researchers using large data sets. We describe the method of their research in section 15.7.1.1. At the research conference where the paper was discussed, there were comments on the lack of a theoretical basis to support the view of 'transparency' taken by the paper (Miller, 2004). The authors claimed that they were examining relationships without making predictions based on theory.

IFAC's annual report 2002 is entitled 'Promoting transparency and the public interest'. From page 8 we find that this 'transparency' refers to the openness of the processes used by IFAC in holding public meetings, permitting public access to documents and carrying out due process of consultation. The 2003 annual report of the IAASB is entitled 'transparency, quality and the public interest'. This refers to the transparency of the process for setting international auditing standards.

15.2.1 Standard & Poor's study[1]

Standard & Poor's (S&P), in 2002 and 2003, published the results of studies on relative transparency and disclosure in global markets. This was part of an S&P initiative to introduce new governance information and analytical services. The methodology lists the questions used but does not give a specific definition of 'transparency'. It would appear from the description that greater transparency is associated with covering greater amounts of information from the defined checklist. The S&P study identifies 98 disclosure items classified into three broad categories:

- ownership structure and investor rights;
- financial transparency and information disclosure;
- board and management structure and process.

The study found that companies with a higher disclosure ranking had lower market risk. They also tended to have higher ratios of market value to book value. The conclusion was that companies can lower the cost of equity capital by providing higher transparency and disclosure. One potential limitation of the S&P study is that it focuses mainly on English-language reports and so tends to be biased towards companies that are seeking to appeal to an English-speaking readership. That in turn may encourage companies towards US or UK guidance on disclosure.

Exhibit 15.1 shows the S&P scores for companies across a range of global markets. The S&P analysis brings out the importance of reading all regulatory filings in countries where the annual report gives an incomplete picture. For US companies in particular it is essential to read the annual report, Form 10-K and the proxy statement because the annual report alone gives incomplete disclosure in many cases. S&P also use additional regulatory filings for its evaluation of companies in Japan and France.

15.2.2 The language of account

The language in which accounting information is reported is an issue that is not discussed in papers that originate in the US. However it is an important aspect of transparency for global investment generally. Parker (2001) discusses the problems of choosing a 'language of account' for European companies. The number of official languages of member states is considerably greater than the number of member states themselves. English is the dominant language of account of the early twenty-first century – but whose English should be

---

[1] www.governance.standardandpoors.com Transparency and Disclosure: overview of methodology and study results – United States (October 2002); Transparency and Disclosure Study: Europe (April 2003).

Exhibit 15.1 Distribution of transparency and disclosure rankings based on annual reports and other regulatory filings for global markets

Country/region	Composite	Ownership structure and investor rights	Financial transparency	Board process and structure	No. of companies
France	68	63	73	66	45
Germany	56	44	76	44	32
Italy	55	43	68	50	26
The Netherlands	65	58	69	65	23
Spain	55	44	68	49	17
Sweden	62	53	73	57	18
Switzerland	59	44	74	54	16
UK	71	57	79	73	127
US (annual report only)	42	25	66	31	500
US (combined)	70	52	77	78	50
Japan	61	70	76	37	150
Asia-Pacific	48	41	60	42	99
Latin America	31	28	58	18	89
Emerging Asia	40	39	54	27	253

Source: *Transparency and Disclosure Study*: Europe, April 2003, Table 2, p. 9 of 16.

Exhibit 15.2 Glossary of UK and US accounting terms, BT

Term used in UK annual report	US equivalent or definition
Accounts	Financial statements
Associates	Equity investees
Capital allowances	Tax depreciation
Capital redemption reserve	Other additional capital
Creditors	Accounts payable and accrued liabilities
Creditors: amounts falling due within one year	Current liabilities
Creditors: amounts falling due after more than one year	Long-term liabilities
Debtors: amounts falling due after more than one year	Other non-current assets
Employee share schemes	Employee stock benefit plans
Finance lease	Capital lease
Financial year	Fiscal year
Fixed asset investments	Non-current investments
Freehold	Ownership with absolute rights in perpetuity
Gearing	Leverage
Interests in associates and joint ventures	Securities of equity investees
Investment in own shares	Treasury shares
Loans to associates and joint ventures	Indebtedness of equity investees not current
Net book value	Book value
Operating profit	Net operating income
Other debtors	Other current assets

Own work capitalized	Costs of group's employees engaged in the construction of plant and equipment for internal use
Profit	Income
Profit and loss account (statement)	Income statement
Profit and loss account (under "capital and reserves" in balance sheet)	Retained earnings
Profit for the financial year	Net income
Profit on sale of fixed assets	Gain on disposal of non-current assets
Provision for doubtful debts	Allowance for bad and doubtful accounts receivable
Provisions	Long-term liabilities other than debt and specific accounts payable
Recognized gains and losses (statement)	Comprehensive income
Reserves	Shareholders' equity other than paid-up capital
Share based payment	Stock compensation
Share premium account	Additional paid-in capital or paid-in surplus (not distributable)
Shareholders' funds	Shareholders' equity
Stocks	Inventories
Tangible fixed assets	Property, plant and equipment
Trade debtors	Accounts receivable (net)
Turnover	Revenues

Source: BT annual report and Form 20-F (2004), p. 154.

used? Parker illustrates the European divide between preferences for 'British' English and preference for 'US' English. He also discusses the moves to resist English, and particularly the efforts in past years to find French descriptions that would avoid the 'anglicization' of the national language. Translation of regulations into the language of member states will not be an easy task. The difficulties of translating 'true and fair view' are already well researched but the IFRS have their own language of instruction – 'may' and 'should' as well as many shades of uncertainty phrases. The problems of understanding accounting in UK English and US English are well illustrated in the Glossary provided by BT in its 'US information package' within the annual report and Form 20-F (Exhibit 15.2).

15.3 Narrative reporting in the US

Every US company listed on a national stock exchange must comply with the regulations of the Securities and Exchange Commission (SEC). The SEC requires companies to produce an annual report on Form 10-K. This is a public document and is available free of charge on EDGAR.[2] However if you try to download a Form 10-K from EDGAR you may find it takes up considerable storage space on your computer. The narrative reporting required in Form 10-K is extensive in detail and the Form 10-K report may contain several hundred pages. The requirements for Form 10-K are set out in Regulation S-K.[3]

---

[2] www.sec.gov and select link to EDGAR.

[3] www.sec.gov/divisions/corpfin/forms/regsk.htm.

An extract from the table of contents of Regulation S-K is set out in Exhibit 15.3. One complication of the SEC regulation for Form 10-K is that the requirements may be met by cross-referencing. So you may find that one company produces a Form 10-K containing all this information in full, while another company gives only the headings and then makes a cross-reference to the published annual report or the 'proxy statement' (a document issued to shareholders prior to the annual general meeting).

15.3.1 Management discussion and analysis

You will see from Exhibit 15.3 that a 'Management discussion and analysis' is one of the items of disclosure required by Regulation S-K. This disclosure is frequently abbreviated as 'MD&A'. The requirement for US companies to produce an MD&A has existed since

Exhibit 15.3 Extract from Table of Contents of Regulation S-K

Subpart 229.100 — Business

229.101 (Item 101) Description of Business

229.102 (Item 102) Description of Property

229.103 (Item 103) Legal Proceedings

Subpart 229.200 — Securities of the Registrant

229.201 (Item 201) Market Price of and Dividends on the Registrant's Common Equity and Related Stockholder matters

229.202 (Item 202) Description of Registrant's Securities

Subpart 229.300 — Financial Information

229.301 (Item 301) Selected Financial Data

229:302 (Item 302) Supplementary Financial Information

229.303 (Item 303) Management's Discussion and Analysis of Financial Condition and Results of Operations

229.304 (Item 304) Changes in and Disagreements with Accountants on Accounting and Financial Disclosure

229.305 (Item 305) Quantitative and Qualitative Disclosures About Market Risk

229.306 (Item 306) Audit Committee Report

229.307 (Item 307) Controls and Procedure

229.308 (Item 308) Internal Controls Over Financial Reporting

Subpart 229.400 — Management and Certain Security Holders

229.401 (Item 401) Directors, Executive Officers, Promoters and Control Persons

229.402 (Item 402) Executive Compensation

229.403 (Item 403) Security Ownership of Certain Beneficial Owners and Management

229.404 (Item 404) Certain Relationships and Related Transactions

229.405 (Item 405) Compliance With Section 16(a) of the Exchange Act

229.406 (Item 406) Code of Ethics

Source: Extracted from SEC Regulation S-K at December 2003.

1980 and it has given a basis for development of similar discussions in other countries. The benefit of having a Regulation to define the content of the MD&A is that all companies must comply and all use the same headings, so comparison is relatively straightforward. The limitation is that companies may be tempted to 'boilerplate' which means that over a period of time they develop a standard form of wording that is used regardless of circumstances. The section of Regulation S-K setting out the MD&A requirements is very detailed. A summary of the main requirements is set out in Exhibit 15.4. The section dealing with 'off-balance-sheet finance' reflects concerns arising from Enron (see section 3.2). The Sarbanes—Oxley Act of 2002 instructed the SEC to add rules for disclosing off-balance-sheet arrangements.[4]

In December 2003 the SEC issued interpretive guidance on the MD&A, intended to encourage more meaningful disclosures in the MD&A in a number of areas, with general emphasis on the discussion and analysis of known trends, demands, commitments, events and uncertainties, and specific guidance on disclosures about liquidity, capital resources and accounting estimates.[5] It gave some general guidance on good presentation, including starting with an executive-level overview and making the most important information the most prominent. It pointed to a focus on:

- key indicators of financial condition and operating performance,
- materiality,
- material trends and uncertainties,
- analysis.

It also gave specific guidance on reporting liquidity and capital resources, as being essential to the survival of a business, and on disclosing critical accounting estimates or assumptions (see Exhibit 8.20).

15.3.2 Market risk disclosure

There is a further disclosure requirement of Regulation S-K that extends the contents of the MD&A. Item 305 requires quantitative and qualitative disclosures about market risk (see Exhibit 15.5). Some companies incorporate this disclosure within the MD&A report, while others have a separate section in the Form 10-K. It is an example of the way in which the SEC adds disclosure detail, both quantitative and qualitative, beyond the requirements of financial reporting standards.

15.3.3 Forward-looking information

Those who use narrative information are looking for indications of the future prospects of the company. Financial statements are mainly concerned with stewardship and are backward-looking. The narrative reports provide an opportunity for looking forward. However, those managing companies face a risk in making projections or forecasts because legal action may be taken by investors if the projections or forecasts are not met.

---

[4] Release No. 33–8182 'Disclosure in Management's Discussion and Analysis about off-balance-sheet arrangements and aggregate contractual obligations' www.sec.gov/rules/final/33-8182.htm.

[5] Release No. 33–8350 'Interpretation: Commission guidance regarding management's discussion and analysis of financial condition and results of operations' www.sec.gov/rules/interp/33–8350.htm.

| Exhibit 15.4 | Summary of contents of the MD&A report |

(a) *Full fiscal years. For each of the three years covered by the annual report*, discuss registrant's financial condition, changes in financial condition and results of operations.

(1) *Liquidity*

Describe known trends or events that are likely to increase or decrease liquidity materially; course of action taken or proposed to remedy any deficiency; internal and external sources of liquidity, and any material unused sources of liquid assets.

(2) *Capital resources*

    (i) material commitments for capital expenditures

    (ii) any known material trends, favorable or unfavorable, in the registrant's capital resources; changes between equity, debt and any off-balance-sheet financing arrangements.

(3) *Results of operations*

Discuss:

    (i) unusual or infrequent events or transactions or any significant economic changes that materially affected the amount of reported income from continuing operations; the extent to which income was affected; any other significant components of revenues or expenses.

    (ii) known trends or uncertainties that have had or will have a material favorable or unfavorable impact on net sales or revenues or income from continuing operations known events that will cause a material change in the relationship between costs and revenues.

    (iii) narrative discussion of the extent to which material increases in net sales or revenues are attributable to increases in prices or to increases in the volume or amount of goods or services being sold or to the introduction of new products or services.

    (iv) impact of inflation and changing prices on the registrant's net sales and revenues and on income from continuing operations for the three most recent fiscal years.

(4) *Off-balance sheet arrangements*

    (i) In a separately-captioned section, discuss

        (A) nature and business purpose of off-balance sheet arrangements

        (B) importance to the registrant of such off-balance sheet arrangements in respect of its liquidity, capital resources, market risk support, credit risk support or other benefits

        (C) amounts of revenues, expenses and cash flows of the registrant arising from such arrangements; nature and amounts of any interests retained; nature and amounts of any other obligations or liabilities (including contingent obligations or liabilities

        (D) likely termination of off-balance-sheet arrangements

    (ii) This section defines the term 'off-balance-sheet arrangement'.

(5) *Tabular disclosure of contractual obligations*

This section sets out a table for disclosing contractual obligations payments due by period, separated as: less than one year, 1–3 years, 3–5 years, and more than five years.

The contractual obligations listed are: long-term debt obligations, capital (finance) lease obligations, operating lease obligations, purchase obligations, and other long-term liabilities reflected on the company's balance sheet.

Source: The above summary is based on Regulation S-K, §229.303. Item 303, December 2003.

Exhibit 15.5 Quantitative and qualitative disclosures about market risk

(a) *Quantitative information about market risk*

Give quantitative information for each category of market risk exposure (i.e., interest rate risk, foreign currency exchange rate risk, commodity price risk, and other relevant market risks, such as equity price risk). Use one of three alternatives:

(i) Tabular presentation of information related to market risk sensitive instruments, including fair values, contract terms that indicate future cash flows, and expected maturity dates.

(ii) Sensitivity analysis disclosures that express the potential loss in future earnings, fair values, or cash flows of market risk sensitive instruments resulting from one or more selected hypothetical changes in interest rates, foreign currency exchange rates, commodity prices, and other relevant market rates or prices over a selected period of time.

(iii) Value at risk disclosures that express the potential loss in future earnings, fair values, or cash flows of market risk sensitive instruments over a selected period of time, with a selected likelihood of occurrence, from changes in interest rates, foreign currency exchange rates, commodity prices, and other relevant market rates or prices;

Explain any limitations in the information, make comparisons with preceding year and explain any changes in models or assumptions used.

(b) *Qualitative information about market risk*

(i) Primary market risk exposures
(ii) How those exposures are managed
(iii) Changes in either of the above

Source: Summarized from Regulation S-K. §229.305 (Item 305).

This risk of legal action is particularly high in the US, where shareholders may decide to bring 'class actions' in which all shareholders of the same class take action together against the management.

To protect management, the Private Securities Litigation Reform Act of 1995 extended the basic legislation of the Securities Act of 1933 and the Securities Exchange Act of 1934, allowing the SEC to clarify what is called a 'safe harbor' of protection against legal action in respect of forward-looking statements. To benefit from this protection the forward-looking statements must be made outside the financial statements and notes. Companies must state the factors that could affect the financial performance or cause actual results to differ from any estimates made in forward-looking statements. Because this statement provides warnings, it is given the title 'Cautionary statement'. It must be a meaningful cautionary statement with relevance to the company. Companies give the cautionary statement in the Form 10-K. They usually repeat it in the published annual report. Exhibit 15.6 shows an example of forward-looking information and a cautionary statement from Kellogg Company.

15.3.4 Pro-forma ('non-GAAP') financial statements

In 2001 the SEC expressed concern about the growing frequency of presenting earnings information using accounting methods that were not based on Generally Accepted Accounting Principles ('GAAP').[6] This type of presentation is often referred to as 'pro-forma'

---

[6] Release No. 33–8039 'Cautionary advice regarding the use of "pro-forma" financial information in earnings releases', www.sec.gov/rules/other/33–8039.htm.

Exhibit 15.6 Outlook and Cautionary Statement, Kellogg Company

FUTURE OUTLOOK

Our long-term annual growth targets are low single-digit for internal net sales, mid single-digit for operating profit, and high single-digit for net earnings per share. In general, we expect 2004 results to be consistent with these targets, despite several important challenges continuing from 2003:

- higher employee benefits expense;
- significant increases in the prices of certain grains, cocoa, other ingredients, packaging, and energy;
- increased cost and reduced availability of certain types of insurance; and
- economic volatility in Latin America.

In addition to the continuing challenges listed above, the following important trends and uncertainties particular to 2004 should be noted:

- Our 2004 fiscal year will include a 53rd week, which could add approximately one percentage point of extra growth to our sales results.
- We expect another year of sales decline for the cookie portion of our U.S. snacks business, due principally to category factors, aggressive SKU eliminations, and discontinuance of a custom manufacturing business during 2003.
- We expect to continue to incur asset write-offs and exit costs associated with productivity initiatives throughout 2004.
- We expect full-year growth in brand-building expenditures to exceed the rate of sales growth.
- We expect our 2004 consolidated effective income tax rate to be approximately 35% versus less than 33% in 2003.

FORWARD-LOOKING STATEMENTS

Our Management's Discussion and Analysis and other parts of this Annual Report contain "forward-looking statements" with projections concerning, among other things, our srategy, financial principles, and plans; initiatives, improvements, and growth; sales, gross margins, advertising, promotion, merchandising, brand-building expenditures, operating profit, and earnings per share; innovation opportunities; exit plans and costs related to productivity initiatives; the impact of accounting changes and FASB authoritative guidance to be issued; our ability to meet interest and debt principal repayment obligations; common stock repurchases or debt reduction; effective income tax rate; cash flow and core working capital; capital expenditures; interest expense; commodity and energy prices; and employee benefit plan costs and funding. Forward-looking statements include predictions of future results or activities and may contain the words "expect," "believe," "will," "will deliver," "anticipate," "project," "should," or words or phrases of similar meaning. Our actual results or acivites may differ materially from these predictions. In particular, future results or acivities could be affected by factors related to the Keebler acquisition, such as the substantial amount of debt incurred to finance the acquisition, which could, among other things, hinder our ability to adjust rapidly to changing market conditions, make us more vulnerable in the event of a downturn, and place us at a competitive disadvantage relative to less-leveraged competitors. In addition, our future results could be affected by a variety of other factors, including:

▶

- the impact of competitive conditions;
- the effectiveness of pricing, advertising, and promotional programs;
- the success of innovation and new product introductions;
- the recoverability of the carrying value of goodwill and other intangibles;
- the success of productivity improvements and business transitions;
- commodity and energy prices, and labor costs;
- the availability of and interest rates on short-term financing;
- actual market performance of benefit plan trust investments;
- the levels of spending on systems initiatives, properties, business opportunities, integration of acquired businesses, and other general and administrative costs;
- changes in consumer behavior and preferences;
- the effect of U.S. and foreign economic conditions on items such as interest rates, statutory tax rates, currency conversion and availability;
- legal and regulatory factors; and,
- business disruption or other losses from war, terrorist acts, or political unrest.
- Forward-looking statements speak only as of the date they were made, and we undertake no obligation to publicly update them.

Source: Kellogg Company, Annual Report, 2003, p. 30.

information. The SEC explained that some 'pro-forma' financial information serves useful purposes. Companies may wish to focus the attention of investors on some particular aspect of the interim or annual results to give comparisons or to emphasize particular activities. One purpose of the MD&A is to focus attention in this way, so it seems reasonable to use pro-forma figures to achieve the same outcome. However it could also be the case that pro-forma information confuses investors, who do not realize that it fails to comply with official GAAP. The SEC was therefore warning investors to be cautious in reading pro-forma information.

The concern expressed in 2001 increased after the collapse of Enron. The Sarbanes–Oxley Act of 2002 (see section 3.2.3) required the SEC to adopt new rules to address public companies' disclosure of financial information that is calculated and presented on the basis of methodologies other than GAAP.[7] As a result of this concern a new disclosure regulation, Regulation G, was introduced and also Regulation S-K was amended to set rules for such pro-forma information.[8] The detail is extensive but the essence of the requirements is as follows:

- Present, with equal or greater prominence, the most directly comparable financial measure or measures calculated and presented in accordance with GAAP, together with a reconciliation of the non-GAAP measure to the GAAP measure.
- Explain why the registrant's management believes that presentation of the non-GAAP financial measure provides useful information to investors regarding the registrant's financial condition and results of operations.

---

[7] Release No 33–8176 'Final Rule: Conditions for use of non-GAAP financial measures' www.sec.gov/rules/final/33–8176.htm.

[8] Reg. §229.10 (e) Use of non-GAAP financial measures in Commission filings.

Exhibit 15.7 Pro-forma financial statement, Motorola

NON-GAAP MEASUREMENTS: RESULTS OF OPERATIONS EXCLUDING SPECIAL ITEMS AND CERTAIN EXITED BUSINESSES

The tabular presentation below and as found on pages 28–30 reflects non-GAAP measurements of Motorola's results of operations presented on a basis excluding special items and certain exited businesses. The non-GAAP measurements used throughout this report do not replace the presentation of Motorola's GAAP financial results. These measurements provide supplemental information to assist the reader in analyzing the Company's financial condition and results of operations. Items that the Company considers to be special items generally relate to restructuring activities and asset revaluations.

The Company is providing this information to enable comparisons of current operating results to prior years and show the results of core ongoing operations. These ongoing results of operations are used by investors and management to measure the Company's current and future performance.

CONSOLIDATED STATEMENTS OF OPERATIONS EXCLUDING SPECIAL ITEMS

(In million, except per share amounts) Year Ended December 31, 2002	GAAP Results	Special Items Inc/(Exp)	Excluding Special Items
Net sales	$ 26,679	$ –	$ 26,679
Costs of sales	17,938	(56)	17,882
Gross margin	8,741	(56)	8,797
Selling, general and administrative expenses	4,203	(44)	4,159
Research and development expenditures	3,754	–	3,754
Reorganization of businesses	1,764	(1,764)	–
Other charges	883	(833)	–
Operating earnings (loss)	(1,813)	(2,697)	884
Other income (expense):			
Interest expense, net	(356)	–	(356)
Gains on sales of investments and businesses, net	96	96	–
Other	(1,373)	(1,351)	(22)
Total other income (expense)	(1,633)	(1,255)	(378)
Earnings (loss) before income taxes	(3,446)	(3,952)	(506)
Income tax provision	(961)	1,153	192
Net earnings (loss)	$ (2,485)	$ (2,799)	$ 314
Earnings (loss) per common share			
Basic	$ (1.09)		$ 0.14
Diluted	$ (1.09)		$ 0.14

Source: Motorola annual report (2002), p. 27. www.motorola.com

Motorola (Exhibit 15.7) provides an example of a pro-forma statement that meets the new conditions. It has an introductory paragraph of explanation and columns that compare GAAP and non-GAAP results.

15.3.5 Internal control over financial reporting

The Sarbanes–Oxley Act of 2002 required the SEC to write new rules requiring companies to include in their annual reports a report of management on the company's internal control over financial reporting.[9] The report must include:

- a statement of management's responsibility for establishing and maintaining adequate internal control over financial reporting for the company;
- management's assessment of the effectiveness of the company's internal control over financial reporting at the end of the most recent fiscal year;
- a statement identifying the framework used by management to evaluate the effectiveness of the company's internal control over financial reporting;
- a statement that the registered public accounting firm that audited the company's financial statements has issued an attestation report on management's assessment of the company's internal control over financial reporting.

The new items 307 and 308 in Regulation S-K reflect this requirement for reporting on internal control. The wording is relatively narrow, confining attention to internal control over financial reporting. Internal control has a much wider remit in many countries, covering organisational and operational controls as well as financial controls.

15.4 Management reports in other countries

15.4.1 The EU Modernisation Directive[10]

In June 2003 the EU adopted the Accounts Modernisation Directive (see section 9.6.4). For company financial years starting on or after 1 January 2005, large and medium-sized companies are required by this Directive to provide a balanced and comprehensive analysis of the development and performance of the company's business. This analysis shall include both financial and non-financial key performance indicators, including information relating to environmental and employee matters. The requirements of the Directive are very general, so that member states have the opportunity to add more specific requirements to match national circumstances.

15.4.2 France[11]

By law, commercial companies must publish each year a management report on the group. It may be combined with the management report on the parent company. For a *société anonyme* the content of the management report is based on brief legal requirements augmented by advice from the *Autorité des marchés financiers* (AMF) (see section 10.4.3.1). Information that might be found in a management report includes: the structure of the

---

[9] Release No. 33–8238 Final Rule: Management's report on internal control over financial reporting and certification of disclosure in Exchange Act periodic reports, www.sec.gov/rules/final/33-8238.htm.

[10] EC (2003).

[11] Richard, J., 'France: Group Accounts' in Ordelheide and KPMG (2001): Vol. 2: 1197–1204.

group and its evolution, identities of major shareholders, employees and their training, the situation of the entity (without defining 'situation') important events following the balance sheet date, research and development, probable evolution of the situation, the activity of the company and its subsidiaries and information on branches.

Richard (2001)[12] commented that French companies did not yet appear to give high importance to this report. Its location in the annual report may vary, even to the extent of being spread across different sections. There appeared to be deficiencies in matters of provisions, events after the balance sheet date, research and development and segmental information.

Under the *loi de sécurité financière* (LSF), issuers of securities are subject to new disclosure requirements for corporate governance and internal control. From 2003, the chairmen of the board of directors or the supervisory board of limited-liability companies (*sociétés anonymes*) are required to report to shareholders annually, in a document appended to the Management Report issued by the board of directors, regarding the way in which the board prepares and organizes its work ('corporate governance'), as well as on the internal control procedures implemented by the company. For limited companies with a board of directors, the report must also specify whether the powers of the chief executive have been restricted in any way. Statutory auditors are required to submit their observations concerning the section of the chairman's report dealing with the internal control procedures for preparing and handling financial and accounting information. These observations are contained in a special report appended to the auditors' report.

Companies that have more than 300 employees and that are required to establish a staff committee are required by French employment law to produce a social report (*bilan social*).[13] The social report contains seven sections covering: employment policy, remuneration and social security costs, health and safety at work, other working conditions, training policy, professional relations, and facilities available to employees and their families. The social report is given to the staff committee and the trade union representatives, who make comments prior to publication. It is then sent to the Employment Inspectorate and is made available to employees and to shareholders, together with any comments from the staff committee.

15.4.3 Germany[14]

Corporations that are of medium or large size are required by the HGB to present an annual management report. The management report must be audited and published. The nature of the report is defined in law (the HGB). It must include a description of the development of the business and the situation of the business, so as to give a true and fair view. The risks of future developments must be mentioned. The report must also comment on post-balance-sheet events of special importance, anticipated development of the company, and research and development. The words 'development' and 'situation' are equivalent to 'past' and 'present' respectively.

In describing the present situation the report will give information about factors affecting employees and structural changes in the business. The discussion of research and development requires description of the activities but there is no necessity to quantify details. Important post-balance-sheet events might include changes in capacity, closure

---

[12] Richard, J. 'France: Group Accounts' in Ordelheide and KPMG (2001): Vol. 2: 1203.

[13] Gelard, G. 'France: Individual Accounts' in Ordelheide and KPMG (2001) Vol. 2: 1110.

[14] Ballwieser, W. 'Germany: Individual Accounts' in Ordelheide and KPMG (2001) Vol. 2: 1331–1332.

or start-up of new plant, new agreements, or significant changes in ownership. The requirement to provide information about risks was added in 1998 but there is no clear agreement on how such information should be conveyed in the public domain.

15.4.4 Japan[15]

The Commercial Code (law) in Japan requires a business report to be filed with the balance sheet and income statement for reporting to shareholders. The business report must be audited. The financial statements issued under the Securities and Exchange Law do not contain a business report. However similar information is provided in a Registration statement filed with the Stock Exchange.[16] The information that must be reported includes: a description of the principal business activities, location of factories and offices, description of the capital of the business, operating results by division, relationship with the parent company and status of significant subsidiaries, results of operations and financial position for the past three years, significant problems facing the corporation, name of directors and statutory auditors, the top seven shareholders and their holdings, major lenders with the amount of borrowings and the number of shares owned by these major lenders, treasury stocks acquired or disposed of in the period, and post-balance-sheet events.

15.4.5 Sweden[17]

The law requires a management report that provides sufficient information on facts not available in the financial statements, to allow the user to form an opinion on the profitability and financial position of the company. There should also be information on: important transactions or events that occurred during the year or since the balance sheet date; expectations for future years; ongoing research and development work; and foreign branches. Rundfelt indicates that in practice the management report has become a formal document with little information value. Most companies publish a overview based on the US MD&A, but it is not a mandatory part of the annual report.

Some companies are required to report on how their operations affect the environment. These are companies who operate under a special licence because their activities may be harmful to the environment. The report only covers their activities in Sweden. An example is Holmen, a forest industry group (Exhibit 15.8).

15.4.6 UK

Narrative reporting in the annual reports of UK companies consists of all the information within the annual report but outside the statutory financial statements. Typically the narrative reporting includes the Chairman's statement, the directors' report, the statement on corporate governance, the remuneration and environmental reports, and the Operating and Financial Review.

For UK companies the closest equivalent of the MD&A is the Operating and Financial Review (OFR).[18] This was developed by the UK Accounting Standards Board (ASB) in 1993

---

[15] Sakurai, H. 'Japan: Individual Accounts' in Ordelheide and KPMG (2001) Vol. 2: 1778.

[16] Sakurai, H. 'Japan: Individual Accounts' in Ordelheide and KPMG (2001) Vol. 2: 1796–1797.

[17] Rundfelt, R. 'Sweden: Individual Accounts' in Ordelheide and KPMG (2001) Vol. 3: 2408–2411.

[18] ASB (1993, 2003).

| Exhibit 15.8 | Environmental disclosure, Holmen AB |

Extract from 'Holmen and the Environment', pp. 18–19

Permits

Hallsta. New permit granted in 2000 on basis of the Environmental Protection Act.

Braviken and Wargon have permits under the terms of the Environmental Code since 2002.

Papelera Peninsular. The mill's existing and planned activities (installation of an additional newsprint machine) were reviewed in 2003 in accordance with the EU's IPPC directive. The decision is expected early in 2004.

Iggesunds Bruk. In March, the Environmental Court handed down a decision pursuant to the Environmental Protection Act on the mill's application for a permit for its ac'tivities. The Swedish Environmental Protection Agency appealed against the point in the decision that related to emissions into water and demanded that certain specific emission levels should be satisfied. The Supreme Environmental Court decided in favour of this claim. To satisfy the demands that now apply, even more extensive investments will be required, probably in the form of an entirely new biological treatment plant. The company considers there is a sound scientific basis for believing that its own proposed combination of internal and external measures is adequate for creating a sustainable, healthy environment in the recipient Iggesund Paperboard has therefore applied to the Supreme Court for a judicial review of the case, which will be decided in 2004.

Workington. The mill has a permit under the terms of the EU's IPPC directive since 2002. Stroms Bruk. The unit was built in 1980 and was registered in on the basis of the environmental legislation in effect at the time. When the Environmental Code came into effect, the mill was classed as a "B facility", for which a permit is required. New rules are introduced at the beginning of 2004, which will probably mean that Stroms Bruk will be reclassified as a "C facility" with a registration obligation.

....

Iggesund Sawmill. A permit under the terms of the Environmental Protection Act was obtained in 1994.

Holmen Kraft. The permit under the terms of the Water Act, that all power stations with associated water regulation systems must have, includes environmental conditions.

Exceeded limits and complaints

The applicable threshold limits for emissions were met. A few limits were exceeded and incidents occurred at Holmen's businesses in 2003. There were a small number of complaints. Deviations were dealt with in accordance with the procedures laid down in the environmental management systems. The actions taken were accepted by the environmental authorities in all cases.

Environmental management and certification

All of Holmen's mills are certificated in accordance with ISO 14001. Holmen's forestry is certificated in accordance with ISO 14001 and the international FSC (1998) and PEFC (2003) forestry standards.

Joint action groups

In order to improve efficiency and develop competence in key environmental areas, Holmen has set up joint action groups for policy and strategy, management systems, water treatment, waste processing, transportation and energy and the climate. These groups are run by Group Technology.

Holmen – Facts about the Environment 2003

One effect of the tight electricity supply situation in Sweden in 2003 was that several mills stepped up their own production of back pressure power, as a result of which their consumption of fossil fuels rose slightly.

In relation to the situation in 2002, total emissions into air and water increased as a result of higher production in 2003. However, specific emissions (per tonne of end product) remained at the same level as in 2002.

Much of the waste that Holmen's activities generate is used for different purposes, and the volume sent to land-fill has declined further.

For further information see Holmen Environmental Report 2003.

Environmental protection costs
Holmen states environmental protection costs in accordance with Statistics Sweden (SCB) guidelines.[1]

Environmental investments, MSEK

	2003	2002
Direct (treatment)	20	21
Integrated (prevention)	26	19
Total	46	40

Environmental costs, MSEK

	2003	2002
Internal and external	158	158
Capital (depreciations)	79	82
Environmental taxes and charges	63	74
Total	300	314

[1]Source: SCB, Environmental protection expenditure in industry (2001).

Source: Holmen AB annual report (2003) pp. 18–19. www.hdmen.com

as a voluntary statement to be prepared by listed companies. The ASB provided non-mandatory Guidance on the OFR, updating this in 2003. The ASB preferred not to have a compulsory accounting standard because it might lead to 'boiler-plating' where companies would develop standard forms of wording to satisfy the rules, rather than try to follow the spirit of the disclosures proposed. The contents of OFR (2003) are summarized in Exhibit 15.9. The opening section of 'principles' reinforces the idea that applying the principles is more important than following precise rules. This is followed by 'guidance' giving general guidance on the main areas to be covered, but encouraging the company to adapt the guidance to its particular circumstances. The major change in the 2003 revision, compared to the 1993 original version, was to add a requirement to describe the business, its objectives and strategy. The ASB places strong emphasis on providing forward-looking information that will be useful to users in assessing future performance.

A survey of the contents of annual reports in 2003[19] found that, in a sample of 100 companies across the full range of UK listed companies, only 61 per cent produced a formal OFR or clearly adopted the recommendations on the OFR. In comparison with previous surveys, the level of narrative reporting had increased more slowly between 2000 and 2003, compared to the period 1996 to 2000.

A survey of users' needs[20] asked expert users, private shareholders, audit partners and finance directors to rank the relative importance of 130 items of information that might appear in a narrative report. Financial information, objectives and strategy ranked highly, followed by management discussion and analysis, background, innovation value drivers, risks and opportunities, customer, process and employee value drivers, and intellectual capital. Environmental, social and community information trailed behind.

---

[19] *From carrots to sticks: A survey of narrative reporting in annual reports*, Deloitte & Touche LLP www.deloitte.co.uk.
[20] Beattie and Pratt (2002).

Exhibit 15.9 Summary of ASB's Operating and Financial Review (2003)

Principles

(i) Purpose: *assist users' assessment of future performance*

(ii) Audience: *presume a wide range of users, but focus on matters relevant to investors*

(iii) Time-frame: *performance of the period and trends and factors relevant to assessment of future performance*

(iv) Reliability: *neutral, free from bias, complete, even-handed with good and bad aspects*

(v) Comparability: *allow comparability with previous periods, highlight accounting policies that are key to understanding performance and financial position*

(vi) Measures: *include financial and non-financial measures, comment on key performance indicators*

Guidance

The business, its objectives and strategy

● Description of the business as a context for the directors' discussion and analysis of performance and financial position

● Objectives of the business and management's strategy for achieving those objectives

● Measures used by management to assess the achievement of objectives

Operating review

● Performance in the period: *profits and losses, focus on business segments, factors affecting current and future performance*

● Returns to shareholders: *distributions (dividends) and share repurchases*

● Dynamics of the business: *factors and influences affecting future performance*

● Investment for the future: *expenditure for the long term such as employee training, product marketing, planned capital expenditure*

Financial review

● Capital structure and treasury policy: *maturity profile of debt, type of capital instruments used, currency, interest rate structure*

● Cash flows: *discuss inflows and outflows, principal sources and destinations*

● Current liquidity: *liquidity, borrowings, seasonality and peak of borrowings, maturity profile*

● Going concern: *OFR could include the directors' statement on going concern required by the Combined Code* [see section 11.4.3.2].

Source: Operating and Financial Review, Accounting Standards Board, January 2003.

The UK government carried out a major review of company law in the early 2000s. One of the recommendations of the company law review was that an OFR should become a compulsory requirement for all quoted[21] companies. Companies that are not quoted but are large or medium-sized are required to follow the Modernisation Directive in providing an enhanced review of the company's business.

In 2004 the Department of Trade and Industry (DTI) published draft regulations for an OFR and Directors' report. Exhibit 15.10 summarizes the main points of the draft regulations. The government sees the OFR as a major element in improving transparency

---

[21] A quoted company is one whose equity share capital has been included in the official list in accordance with the Securities and Markets Act 2000, or is officially listed in an EEA state, or is admitted to dealing on the New York Stock Exchange or NASDAQ (s. 262 CA 1985).

Exhibit 15.10 Summary of draft regulations for the OFR

An operating and financial review shall be a balanced and comprehensive analysis of:

● Development and performance of the business and position at the end of the year,
● The main trends and developments (i) underlying the development, performance and position of the current year and (ii) likely to affect future development, performance and position.

It shall include

● A statement of the business, objectives and strategies of the group
● Resources available to the group
● Principal risks and uncertainties facing the group
● Capital structure, treasury policies and objectives and liquidity of the group

To the extent necessary to meet the general requirements, set out above, the review shall include:

● Information about the employees, environmental matters and social and community matters
● Information about related persons
● Receipts from, and returns to, shareholders
● Analysis using financial and other key performance indicators
● Additional explanations of amounts included in the financial statements

The review must state whether it has been prepared in accordance with the relevant reporting standards, and explain reasons for departure from those standards.

Source: Draft regulations on the operating and financial review and directors' report: A consultative document, DTI, May 2004.

and accountability. It is intended to encourage shareholders to exercise effective control by having meaningful information. The government has asked the ASB to prepare reporting standards for the OFR, building on the framework set in the regulation. Directors are required to state that they have complied with the OFR requirements or explain departures. The auditors are required to state in their report whether in their opinion the directors have prepared the review after due and careful enquiry. They must also state whether, in their opinion, the information in the OFR is consistent with the financial statements and whether any matters have come to their attention that are inconsistent with the OFR. The focus of the audit is on the process of preparing the OFR; auditors do not give an opinion on the content of the OFR.

15.5 Corporate social responsibility (CSR) reports

Section 3.5 explains the sources of encouragement and pressure on companies to produce CSR reports, either with the annual financial report or as a separate document. Look back at that section which describes how those activities have led to action in various countries.

15.5.1 The European Commission

In July 2001 the Commission presented a Green Paper (a discussion document) 'Promoting a European Framework for Corporate Social Responsibility'. The aims of that document were to launch a debate on the concept of CSR and to build a partnership for promoting CSR in a European framework. The Green Paper defined CSR as 'a concept whereby companies integrate social and environmental concerns in their business operations and in their interactions with their shareholders on a voluntary basis'. In July 2002 the Commission presented a EU strategy to promote CSR.[22] The strategy document was wide-ranging over the possible contributions that business might make in relation to CSR. In relation to developing accounting, auditing and reporting, the Commission established a EU Multi-Stakeholder Forum on CSR (the CSR EMS Forum) to help promote transparency and convergence of CSR practices and instruments.

We have already noted in Chapter 3 (see Exhibit 3.12) that the German company BASF has redesigned its entire annual report to comply with the GRI Guidelines. In Exhibit 15.11 we set out a section from the Operating and Financial Review of a UK company, BT, which deals with CSR reporting partly in the OFR and partly in a separate social and environmental report. This extract from the OFR may also give an indication of the direction being encouraged by the draft regulations for a statutory OFR (see Exhibit 15.10). It gives

---

Exhibit 15.11 CSR report, BT

Our commitment to society

Corporate social responsibility (CSR)
Our challenge is to manage social, ethical and environmental issues in ways that grow shareholder value and help make sustainable development happen.

The Dow Jones Sustainability Indexes rank companies for their success in meeting this challenge. During the 2004 financial year, BT was ranked as the top telecommunications company in the Dow Jones Sustainability Index for the third year running.

We also hold the Queen's Award for Enterprise in recognition of our contribution to sustainable development.

This section of the report, together with the broad statement on social, environmental and ethical matters included in the section on Corporate governance, provides information in response to the Association of British Insurers' disclosure guidelines on social responsibility.

More detailed disclosures on BT's implementation of social, ethical and environmental policies and procedures are available online in our independently verified social and environmental report, which has been prepared in accordance with the 2002 Global Reporting Initiative (GRI) sustainability reporting guidelines.

CSR governance
The Board is kept informed of BT's main CSR risks and opportunities and any new developments which may impact on its duties and reviews annually our CSR strategy. In addition, social, ethical and environmental matters have been incorporated into the directors' induction programme.

A Board committee – the Community Support Committee – oversees community, charitable and arts expenditure and establishes the strategy for maximising our contribution to society. The committee, chaired by Sir Christopher Bland, consists of representatives from BT businesses, two nonexecutive directors and two external independent members, who have a reputation for excellence in this field.

An executive committee, the Corporate Social Responsibility Steering Group (CSRSG), oversees the implementation of our CSR programme. This includes risk assessment, target and objective setting, ISO14001 certification – the international standard for environmental management systems – and public accountability.

▶

---

[22] COM (2002) 347 final. Communication from the Commission concerning Corporate Social Responsibility: A business contribution to Sustainable Development. www.europa.eu.int/comm/employment_social/soc-dial/csr_index.htm.

The CSRSG consists of CSR champions nominated by the lines of business and six support functions (human resources, corporate governance, health and safety, finance, communications and procurement).

The CSRSG is chaired by BT's overall CSR champion, Alison Ritchie, Chief Broadband Officer and a member of the Operating Committee. It is supported by advice from an independent panel of CSR experts.

To ensure that CSR is embedded into BT's commercial operations, we undertake CSR "health checks" of our main commercial initiatives.

These health checks identify specific social, economic and environmental impacts (both positive and negative) and particular CSR risks and opportunities. A report is then compiled, including recommended actions.

We have important relationships with a wide range of stakeholders, including employees, customers and suppliers. We engage with these stakeholders in a number of ways, including consumer liaison panels, an annual employee survey and a supplier relationship management programme.

We also employ a number of CSR experts who investigate long-term societal trends, identify potential issues that might affect the business and support BT's commercial activities.

We have identified 11 non-financial KPIs (key performance indicators) in this context to provide a quick overview of BT's social and environmental performance.

These KPIs have also been used to establish ten strategic social and environmental targets and are published in our social and environmental report.

Social, environmental and ethical risks
During the 2004 financial year, we developed a separate CSR risk register that sets out our important social, ethical and environmental risks. It identifies the following risks as the most significant in the context of CSR:

- supply chain working conditions
- health and safety
- climate change
- diversity
- geography of jobs ("offshoring")
- breach of the code of business ethics.

Each of these CSR risks has a risk owner and mitigation strategy in place (more detail can be found in our social and environmental report).

CSR business opportunities
Following a detailed statistical analysis of customer opinion data going back up to 80 months and based on tens of thousands of interviews, we have been able to show that a 1 per cent improvement in the public's perception of our CSR activities results in a 0.1 per cent increase in our retail customer satisfaction figures.

This is a critical correlation and shows how important it is not only to protect our reputation through appropriate risk management activities, but also to enhance it through our community activities.

Long-term sustainability trends are creating market opportunities for us, such as the use of teleconferencing and flexible working to reduce the need to travel and provide more flexible lifestyles.

Increasingly, BT has to address social and environmental matters when bidding for business. In the 2004 financial year, bids to the value of almost £900 million required us to demonstrate expertise in managing these issues.

Environment
BT is one of the largest consumers of industrial and commercial electricity in the UK, and the growth of broadband is likely to increase our electricity use. However, during the 2004 financial year, a £675,000 investment in our energy conservation programme enabled us to reduce our electricity consumption by 1.5 per cent.

Exhibit 15.11 *(Continued)*

The use of renewable energy and combined heat and power – together with energy and transport efficiency measures – has enabled us to reduce our global-warming CO_2 emissions by 42 per cent since 1996. We have set a target to cap our 2010 CO_2 emissions at 25 per cent below those of 1996.

CO_2 emissions

Financial year	2004	2003	2002
Total (UK only; million tonnes)	0.92	0.96	1.03
% below 1996	42%	40%	36%
Tonnes per £1m turnover	50	51	56

During the 2004 financial year, we received an income of £4 million from our recycling activities, offset against the £10 million we spent managing our waste contracts, recycling our waste and sending waste to landfill.

Waste

Financial year	2004	2003	2002
Total waste (tonnes)	107,303	117,688	114,999
Total waste recycled (tonnes)	27,626	27,809	24,099
% Recycled	26%	24%	21%

Also during the 2004 financial year we reduced both our commercial fleet – still one of the largest in the UK – and our fuel consumption by 4 per cent.

Transport

Financial year	2004	2003	2002
Number of vehicles (UK only)	32,663	33,979	37,509
Fuel consumption (million litres)	53.85	56.12	62.76

Digital inclusion
Digital inclusion is a key public policy issue and we are working with the UK Government and the voluntary sector to find effective ways to use communications technology to tackle social exclusion.

In particular, we launched a digital inclusion campaign to support the Government's aim to give all citizens online access within the next few years and demonstrate how communications can help improve society.

A key element of the campaign is the "Everybodyonline" programme, established in partnership with charity campaign group, Citizens Online. The campaign is currently focused on eight deprived communities and aims to increase skills and access to communications technology in underprivileged areas and to deepen the understanding of the causes and effects of the digital divide and how they may be addressed nationally.

Disability services
Our Age and Disability Action team promotes equal access to a wide range of products and services. We work directly with older and disabled people and their representatives to raise awareness of BT's inclusive approach.

For people with hearing or speech impairments, for example, our textphone offers easy access to BT TextDirect – the service that enables users to dial direct to other text or voice users. Customers with visual or mobility impairments benefit from products with large clear keypads and cordless or hands-free options. A variety of new products and network services with mixed-ability appeal will be launched during the 2005 financial year.

We continue to offer services to protect the telephone lines of people who need support. This includes free directory enquiries for those unable to use the printed directory and billing, service and product information in a variety of formats, such as Braille and large print.

We are committed to increasing the accessibility of our internet pages. In the 2004 financial year, our Age and Disability Action website (www.btplc.com/age_disability) was awarded the RNIB See it Right logo.

Community
We commit a minimum of 0.5 per cent of our UK pre-tax profits to direct activities in support of society. This has ranged from £10 million in 1987, peaking at £16 million in 2001 and was £5.6 million (including £1.2 million to charities) in the 2004 financial year. BT operations also provided a further £12.4 million in funding and support in kind over the past financial year.

The focus of our community programmes is on big issues where better communication can make a real difference to society.

For example, more than 9,500 schools and over two million young people have taken part in the BT Education Programme – a drama-based campaign helping children to improve their communication skills. This activity is supported by our volunteering programme which, at 31 March 2004, had 3,000 registered volunteers working with schools.

We are working with ChildLine on a major new campaign to raise funds to ensure that every one of the 4,000 children who call ChildLine every day has his/her call answered.

In addition, BT people gave £2 million directly to charities during the 2004 financial year through Give as you Earn, to which BT added a direct contribution of £1 million.

Source: BT annual report and Form 20-F 2004, Operating and financial review (2003), pp. 47–48. www.bt.com

information about risks and uncertainties, key performance indicators and information about the employees, environmental matters and social and community matters.

We have explained in section 10.7.5.1 the Law on New Economic Regulations which requires a social and environmental report. In its 2003 annual report, Michelin provides six pages of detail on social and environmental information, with the majority relating to employment issues. An example of the detail available is shown in Exhibit 15.12 which compares the training expense in various geographic regions.

Exhibit 15.12 Training expense, CSR report, Michelin

6. Training
Breakdown of training expenses by region and type, as a percentage of payroll costs.

Geographical zone	Training budget	For management training	For general training	For core know-how training
Europe*	3.99%	7.60%	12.50%	79.90%
North America	2.44%	5.70%	1.80%	92.50%
South America**	2.52%	11.07%	30.15%	58.78%
Asia***	2.50%	17.69%	33.36%	48.95%

*Excluding Euromaster.
**Excluding plantations.
***Japan, Thailand, Singapore, China.

The bulk of the Group's training policy is concentrated on core know-how and is designed with a long-term view aimed at building staff qualification and development.

Source: Michelin annual report (2003), p. 125. www.michelin.com

15.5.2 Comparative research studies

Bebbington *et al.* (2000) point out that although there have been developments in social and enviromental reporting across Europe, the English language research literature says relatively little about activities outside English-speaking countries. An attempt was made to address this defect by devoting an entire issue of *The European Accounting Review* (2000, Vol. 9(1)) to environmental and social accounting in Europe. One concern for the editors was the lack of pan-European and nation-specific studies across the range of European countries that emerged from their call for papers. The largest number of submissions came from Spain and the UK. The journal issue gives a range of perspectives on environmental and social issues across Europe but there is no single article giving a comprehensive comparative evaluation.

15.5.3 Questioning CSR[23]

Goyder (2003) comments on the growing enthusiasm for CSR in all quarters and asks whether it is a victory to celebrate. He distinguishes two types of CSR. In the first type, CSR expresses a company's purpose and values in all its relationships. Some companies will have higher levels of commitments to society, others will have less, but in all cases the CSR report will faithfully reflect the values and commitment of the company. Goyder calls this 'conviction' or 'values-led' CSR. In the second type, companies are required by social pressures to comply with a widening range of social expectations. CSR becomes a kind of fashion parade in which companies are applauded for saying the right things in their annual report, without anyone questioning whether they actually mean what they say. He calls this 'compliance' CSR. He is concerned that the CSR which is emerging from the current intensive activity around the world looks more like compliance CSR than conviction CSR. His concern is that communications from companies should reinforce the unique personality of the company, rather than bury it in meaningless forms of words.

15.6 Remuneration reports

The discussion of corporate governance codes in previous sections of this chapter and also in Chapter 3 has shown the emphasis that is placed on remuneration reports. The managers of the company must be accountable for their actions in the accounting information they present, but they must also be transparent in the rewards that they are taking for their actions as managers. Remuneration reports now cover many pages in the annual reports of some companies and provide a useful starting point for research into the agency relationship between managers and shareholders. For US companies the detailed information about management compensation arrangements is often found in the proxy statement published in preparation for the annual general meeting. For UK companies the information is found in the report of the remuneration committee. Exhibit 15.13 shows the contents table of the remuneration report of GlaxoSmithKline, a UK company having a US listing, while Exhibit 15.14 presents an extract from the remuneration report stating the remuneration policy for rewarding performance. The full report contains a great deal of detail, covering several pages, with information about each director separately. In contrast, Fiat (Exhibit 15.15) explains remuneration policy in its report on operations but gives only one further page of details in the notes, listing each director and broad details of compensation received by each.

---

[23] Goyder (2003).

| Exhibit 15.13 | Remuneration report, contents, GlaxoSmithKline |

Remuneration Report

The Remuneration Report sets out the remuneration policies operated by GlaxoSmithKline in respect of the Directors and Corporate Executive Team (CET) members, together with disclosures on Directors' remuneration including those required by The Directors' Remuneration Report Regulations 2002 (the Regulations). In accordance with the Regulations, the following sections of the Remuneration Report are subject to audit: Annual remuneration; Non-Executive Directors' remuneration; Share options; Incentive plan, and Pensions. The remaining sections are not subject to audit, neither are the pages referred to from within the auditable sections.

This Report is submitted to shareholders by the Board for approval at the Annual General Meeting, as referenced in the Chairman's letter and notice of Annual General Meeting, which has been sent to all shareholders

Throughout the Remuneration Report the Executive Directors and CET members are referred to as the 'Executives'.

References to GlaxoSmithKline shares and ADSs mean, respectively, Ordinary Shares of GlaxoSmithKline plc of 25p and American Depositary Shares of GlaxoSmithKline plc. Each ADS represents two GlaxoSmithKline shares.

Contents

Source: GlaxoSmithKline annual report (2003), p. 43. www.gsk.com

| Exhibit 15.14 | Remuneration report, policy, GlaxoSmithKline |

Remuneration policy

Principles
The Committee considered the findings and established three core principles which underpin the new remuneration policy for GlaxoSmithKline. These are

● pay for performance and only for performance

● robust and transparent governance structures

● a commitment to be a leader of good remuneration practice in the pharmaceutical industry

▶

Exhibit 15.14 *(Continued)*

In formulating the policy, the Committee also decided that

- the remuneration structure must support the business by securing, retaining and motivating key talent in a very competitive market place
- UK shareholder guidelines would be followed to the maximum extent consistent with the needs of the business and the company would maintain a regular dialogue with shareholders
- global pharmaceutical companies are the primary pay comparator group
- performance conditions would be based on the measurable delivery of strong financial performance and the delivery of superior returns to shareholders as compared with other pharmaceutical companies
- a high proportion of the total remuneration opportunity would be based on performance-related remuneration which will be delivered over the medium to long-term
- remuneration would be determined using the projected value method (see explanation below)
- one remuneration structure for Executive Directors and the CET, in particular, the same performance conditions will apply equally to their long-term incentive awards
- no ex-gratia payments would be made
- pay structures would be as simple as is consistent with the business needs.

Overall the policy is intended to provide median total remuneration for median performance. Poor performance will result in total remuneration significantly below the pay comparator group median, with the opportunity to earn upper quartile total remuneration for exceptional performance.

Source: GlaxoSmithKline annual report (2003), p. 45. www.gsk.com

Exhibit 15.15 Executive remuneration, Fiat

Nominating and Compensation Committee
(*extract from Corporate Governance section of Report on Operations*)

The Board of Directors established an internal Nominating and Compensation Committee that is comprised of the following five directors, three of whom are non-executive directors, with two of these in turn being independent directors: Umberto Agnelli (Chairman), Flavio Cotti, Franzo Grande Stevens, Hermann Josef Lamberti, and Giuseppe Morchio. The basic rules governing the composition, duties, and functioning of the Committee are envisaged in the Charter of the Nominating and Compensation Committee.

The Committee expresses its opinions on proposals regarding the general compensation policies applicable to senior management and appointment of the executive directors at the principal subsidiaries. It participates in the definition and elaboration of stock option plans to be submitted for approval by the Board of Directors and makes proposals to the Board, in the absence of the interested parties, on the individual compensation of the Chairman, Chief Executive Officer, and the other directors with particular duties.

In 2003, the Nominating and Compensation Committee met five times to discuss the submission to the Board of Directors of motions concerning the definition of compensation and stock option plans for the Group's senior managers and new appointments at the Group's Parent Company and for corporate posts at the lead companies of the various Sectors.

The compensation of directors, as decided by the Stockholders' Meeting of May 13, 2003, consists of a fixed fee of 50,000 euros annually, attendance compensation of 3,000 euros for every board or committee meeting

▶

attended, and the proportional amount of the premium of the insurance policy covering civil liability resulting from legal and contractual obligations inherent in the office of director.

The Board of Directors, with the approval of the Board of Statutory Auditors, granted the Chairman and Chief Executive Officer a fixed compensation pursuant to Article 2389 of the Italian Civil Code. Furthermore, as compensation that varies according to performance, the Chief Executive Officer was granted stock options whose exercise is partially subject to satisfaction of predetermined profitability targets by specific dates.

Detailed information on the compensation of directors and the stock options is provided in the Notes to the Financial Statements of Fiat S.p.A.

Source: Fiat annual report (2003), pp. 38–39; parent company annual report (2003), p. 187. www.fiatgroup.com

15.7 Comparative research into disclosure

Much of the research into disclosure is based on single country studies. A comprehensive review of research methods and issues in disclosure studies is provided by Healy and Palepu (2001) with discussion by Core (2001). The review is confined to US studies and calls for extension to other countries. Any research into narrative disclosures runs into two significant problems. The first problem is obtaining the data and the second is the time required to analyze it manually. This section gives examples of comparative studies and in each case explains how the authors dealt with the problems of obtaining and analyzing data.

One feature to note is that in many papers the year of publication is several years later than the period of the data under investigation. This means that considerable caution is needed before drawing any conclusions about the relevance of the findings to current-day practice. For researchers the interest lies in the method of research and the potential to replicate the research with more recent data.

15.7.1 Making use of surveys

One way of avoiding the time taken to measure disclosure in annual reports is to use scores created for some other purpose.

15.7.1.1 CIFAR database

A source that has been used repeatedly in comparative studies is the CIFAR database, created by CIFAR, the Center for International Financial Analysis and Research at Princeton, New Jersey. The data provides to scores for disclosures measured for companies in 42 countries in the first half of the 1990s. Researchers use this database as their source of information and test hypotheses about the factors that are associated with different types and amounts of disclosure.

Hope (2003) uses legal origin (common law or code law) to represent institutional differences between countries. It uses Hofstede's culture measures to represent country cultures. Using regression analysis the paper finds that both culture and legal system are significant in explaining the CIFAR disclosure scores. It is not possible to say which of these is dominant. Companies in common law countries have significantly higher disclosure scores than companies in code law countries. However the number of stock exchange listings and the number of analysts following the company's performance are also positively related to disclosure, so Hope suggests an explanation that companies in common law countries are more active in capital markets. Of the culture variables, individualism is significantly positively associated with disclosure and masculinity (low nurture) is significantly negatively associated with disclosure. The author concludes that 'it may be prudent to consider cultural variations when attempting to change a country's accounting infrastructure'.

Archambault and Archambault (2003) used the CIFAR scores to test a model of cultural, national and corporate factors that influence the financial disclosure of companies. They found that each factor contributed significantly to the disclosure model and concluded that disclosure is a complex process influenced by a broad set of factors. As the signs and significance of some relationships changed with the model used they were not able to draw firmer conclusions but felt that nevertheless they had extended the literature by simultaneous testing of a range of factors.

Bushman et al. (2004) investigated corporate transparency by specifying their own perception of transparency and then quantifying it. We explained in section 15.2 that they offered a definition of transparency as 'the availability of firm-specific information to those outside publicly traded firms'. They then collected a range of measures from the CIFAR database that captured the information environments of different countries. Using the analytical technique of factor analysis, which applies statistical analysis to group the measures that seem to relate closely to each other, they identified two main factors, each representing a group of measures. One was 'financial transparency', describing the intensity and timeliness of financial disclosures, and their interpretation and dissemination by analysts and the media. The other was 'governance transparency', describing the intensity of governance disclosures used by outside investors to hold officers and directors accountable. They found that the governance transparency factor was primarily related to a country's legal/judicial regime, whereas the financial transparency factor was primarily related to political economy. The legal/judicial regime was represented by protection of investor rights and efficiency of the judicial system, both evaluated in La Porta et al. (1998) and patent protection levels taken from an economic survey. Political economy was represented by autocracy, state-owned enterprises, cost of entry (all from political and economic data sources) and state-owned banks and risk of expropriation (both from La Porta et al., 1998).

Bushman et al. (2004) is interesting for its use of a wide range of date sets. Reporting conference discussion and comments on the paper Miller (2004) focus on the lack of theory and therefore lack of expectations against which to judge the empirical findings. Bushman et al. would say that their paper is an example of 'let the data speak'. There are also comments on the detail of the statistical analysis and the problems of using data sets relating to different periods of time. However the most interesting comment from the perspective of comparative study is Miller's concern (p.265) that we run the risk of creating a standard that is accepted without being critically examined. The classification of regimes as code law or common law is quite crucial and Miller points out that other research papers have used different classifications. This may not affect the results in a broadly-based paper such as Bushman et al. but could become significant if applied uncritically in a different combination of countries.

Using a data set such as the CIFAR survey has the benefit of speed of working and provides a relatively large amount of data for comparison but it has the limitation of freezing research at a point in time. Salter and Niswander (1995) (see section 5.4.4) used the CIFAR data. Thus a range of research papers spanning almost 10 years of publication dates are all based on the same data collection from the early 1990s. Also these papers tend to use the common law/code law distinction as a representation of institutional differences. The distinction is convenient as a variable for regression analysis but tells us little about disclosure differences within those broad categories. The papers that use the distinction do not add a discussion of limitations such as that found in Ball *et al.* (2000) (see section 7.7.3).

15.7.1.2 Standard & Poor's ratings

Section 15.2.1 explains Standard & Poor's major initiative to measure transparency through identifying and scoring 98 disclosure items covering accounting and corporate governance information.

Khanna *et al.* (2004) used the transparency and disclosure scores developed by Standard & Poor's. The data in their investigation covered 794 companies in 24 countries from the 2002 S&P survey. Country representation is uneven (e.g. Japan 150, UK 127, down to Portugal seven and Denmark six). The researchers found a positive association between the disclosure scores and a variety of market interaction measures, including US listing, US investment flows, exports to, and operations, in the US. They acknowledge that correlation evidence does not allow conclusions about the direction of causes. It does not show whether interacting with US markets causes the sample companies to adopt US practices, or whether adopting US practices allows the companies to become more active in US markets.

15.7.1.3 World Federation of Exchanges (WFE) 2003[24]

The 2003 WFE Disclosure Survey, carried out by Carol Ann Frost, examines systems for disclosure of information about listed companies at 52 members of the WFE. It has three aims:

- to describe noteworthy features of the disclosure systems;
- to identify recent changes in these disclosure systems;
- to identify and interpret recent trends and emerging issues relevant to the regulated financial exchanges industry.

The reported results of the survey are based on evidence from a questionnaire to WFE members. The value of the survey to researchers lies in helping them to plan comparative disclosure studies by being aware of the potential range of disclosures available and the possible restrictions on availability.

15.7.2 Using a disclosure checklist

We have explained in Chapter 7 the general principles of measuring disclosure practices and we have given examples of disclosure checklists from research papers that have been applied widely in subsequent research. This section expands in more detail on the developments that have taken place in various aspects of disclosure studies.

15.7.2.1 Scoring to an independent checklist

One method of carrying out comparative research is to find a suitable checklist and then apply it to a range of company reports. Robb *et al.* (2001) studied non-financial

---

[24] Frost (2003).

disclosures as recommended by US financial analysts to the Jenkins Committee in 1994 (see section 8.7.1.6). They compared corporate annual reports of companies in Australia, Canada and the US, sampled in 1995. In comparisons of the disclosure scores the US companies scored highest on average, both in forward-looking disclosures and in historical disclosures. However the Canadian and Australian companies were not significantly different from the US in historical disclosures. The Australian companies were significantly lower in forward-looking scores than the US companies, with the Canadian companies in between. The authors concluded that similar cultures provide similar levels of historical disclosures, but dissimilar levels of forward-looking disclosures that are non-financial in nature. In regression analysis the authors found that the disclosure scores were positively related with size of company and with listing on foreign stock exchanges.

The benefit of creating a checklist from an independent source, such as the Jenkins Report, lies in avoiding researcher bias in creating the list. The disadvantage is that it biases the research towards the US as the country in which Jenkins reported. It is perhaps not surprising that the US companies had more feeling for what US analysts are expecting in corporate reports. In its conclusions on cultural influence, the paper assumes that Australia, Canada and the US share an 'Ango-Saxon' or 'Anglo-American' culture, an assumption that has been questioned by Alexander and Archer (2000) (see section 11.5.1).

15.7.2.2 Comparing disclosure scores to analysts' forecasts

Researchers may try to link disclosure studies to the uses of disclosed information. Vanstraelen *et al.* (2003) asked whether there was an association between non-financial disclosures, as recommended by the Jenkins Committee, and the accuracy of financial analysts' earnings forecasts. They used the same checklist as did Robb *et al.* (2001), applied to annual reports in Belgium, Germany and The Netherlands. The analysis was based on the manual analysis of the contents of the annual reports of 120 companies across these three countries in 1999. The disclosure scores were compared with accuracy of analysts' forecasts as reported by IBES, the International Brokers' Estimate System. The research found that voluntary disclosure of forward-looking non-financial information was significantly associated with higher levels of accuracy in analysts' earnings forecasts. The paper concludes that increased disclosure of non-financial information may help to level the playing field for analysts and investors. There could be another explanation, which is that companies providing more information in their annual reports are also more open in their discussions with analysts, in helping them to understand the information provided.

15.7.2.3 Creating a checklist tailored to the project

Creating a tailored checklist has the benefit of matching the research design to the purpose of the investigation. It has the limitation that the checklist is less readily verifiable as independent and so is open to suggestions of researcher bias. It also lacks comparability with previous work. One approach to providing a degree of comparability is to build on previous work. We explained in section 7.6.2 that the work of Meek *et al.* (1995) and Gray, Meek and Roberts (1995) has been widely cited and built upon in subsequent research, including some of the papers summarized in Appendix 7.2. One example is Chau and Gray (2002) who found a significant positive relationship between the extent of voluntary disclosure and the proportion of outsiders' interests in Hong Kong and Singapore listed company annual reports. They defined 'outside owners' by the total proportion of shares not held by directors and dominant shareholders (treating both of these groups as 'insiders'). They explain their choice of checklist in terms of the advantages of benchmarking against previous work.

Researchers who design their own checklist have to explain carefully how they have used prior literature to give some basis of validity and comparability, and must justify the modifications they make. Newson and Deegan (2002) used this approach in comparing social disclosure practices in Australia, Singapore and South Korea. They examined the annual reports of the 50 largest companies by market capitalization in each country. The size of each disclosure was measured to the nearest hundredth of a page using a transparent plastic A4 sheet. This is an alternative to counting sentences. The findings were compared to 'global expectations' derived from previous surveys in other research works. Australian companies had higher mean disclosure (in number of pages) than Singaporean or South Korean companies. Detailed analysis of the nature of disclosures showed variations in country differences – Singaporean companies gave the most disclosure about training and empowering employees.

15.7.3 Choosing a specific aspect of disclosure

Some researchers choose a specific aspect of disclosure and make comparisons over a range of countries.

15.7.3.1 Going concern uncertainties

Narrative disclosures cover a wide area of subject matter. One way of making comparisons more manageable is to focus on a specific aspect of disclosure. Martin (2000) chose going-concern uncertainty disclosures in French, German and US practices. The sample size was not large. It compared 61 French and German companies with 61 US companies in the period 1987–91. The research found that going concern uncertainty disclosures, whether in the audit report or the management discussion, occurred more frequently in the US companies than in the French and German companies. It also analyzed the different causes of going concern qualifications in these countries. The data were taken from annual reports in electronic form, paper form on request to the companies, or purchased from CIFAR.

15.7.3.2 Financial graphs

Financial graphs appear in many corporate annual reports. They are placed in a prominent position and are intended to create an impression on the reader. If the scale of the graphs is distorted (measurement distortion) or the graph shows only the good news (selectivity distortion) the financial graphs may mislead the readers. This is called 'impression management'. Beattie and Jones (2000) compared financial graphs in the corporate annual reports of 300 companies in Australia, France, Germany, The Netherlands, the UK and the US. They found evidence of selectivity, particularly in the US and Australia, and of measurement distortion, particularly in the US and The Netherlands and concluded that there was some evidence that impression management was greater in the countries with strong capital markets.

The data for the paper was taken from the largest companies in each country having only a domestic listing. Annual reports for 1992 were obtained from the companies, in the English language where possible. Analyzing the data required a manual exercise, finding and evaluating financial graphs for sales, earnings and earnings per share.

15.7.3.3 Ethical issues

A comparative study of corporate reporting on ethical issues by UK and German chemical and pharmaceutical companies was reported by Adams and Kuasirikun (2000). They analyzed the annual reports of UK and German companies in the *Times 1000* companies in 1995. This method of sampling has the benefit of selecting the largest, and so probably the most influential, companies in the stock market for those industries. It has the limitation that the German companies in particular would be looking towards reaching international investors and therefore might be expected to be willing to give disclosures to reassure English-speaking investors who were unfamiliar with the German market. The checklist used for scoring is one developed by Adams in previous research, which gives the benefit of comparability. The results show that the German companies scored higher than the UK companies in reporting environmental information and in reporting on other ethical issues. The higher level of environmental reporting is explained by the authors in terms of the greater amount of environmental legislation in Germany at the time of the study. They also pointed out that the German companies did not show the secrecy that might be expected from Gray (1988) as outlined in Chapter 5.

15.7.3.4 Environmental disclosures

A comparative study of environmental reporting in the UK and US (Holland and Boon Foo, 2003) analysed the annual reports of 37 companies across five environmentally sensitive industries at the end of 2000. They found that the most frequently occurring disclosures by the UK companies in the sample were the environmental policy and environmental awards. The most frequently occurring disclosures by the US companies were environmental expenditure and a discussion of environmental issues or risks. In general the US reporting appeared to reflect the requirements of legislation while the UK dicslosure appeared to be driven by management and reporting initiatives. The authors concluded that the voluntary approach in the UK was preferable to the stronger regulatory hand in the US.

Summary and conclusions

Corporate financial reporting no longer stops with the financial statements and notes to the accounts. The need to be assured about the reliability and quality of the financial statements has created a framework of assurance (see Chapter 3) which in turn has led to an explosion of disclosures, outlined in Chapter 3 and expanded upon in this chapter. Some are mandatory regulation under law and accounting standards; others are voluntary but with strong guidance. The new disclosures also reflect the need for accountability regarding the non-financial aspects of business operations. Under the broad heading of corporate social responsibility (CSR) there are sources of guidance on disclosure that are increasingly being endorsed by market regulators and are being applied by companies who seek to maintain the best standards of communication with stakeholders. Information on the remuneration of those managing a company, and the conditions applied to their rewards, is seen as an essential element of corporate governance in which those who own the company can see how their agents (the directors) are rewarded for their stewardship of the business.

Research into transparency of disclosures is mainly of the kind that explains which types of company show high scores and which type show low scores. It is an area of comparative international research that seems likely to continue while independent bodies are measuring disclosure scores across countries to evaluate the success of new regulations and recommendations.

Key points from the chapter:

● Transparency is a criterion applied in many commentaries on the quality of accounting disclosure, but there is no agreement on how it is defined or evaluated.

● Narrative reporting in the US is highly regulated through SEC requirements but this sets a benchmark against which other countries are evaluated.

● Management reports have an established tradition in some countries; in other they are recent additions to the disclosure package. Regulation varies from statutory control, with flexible interpretation, to voluntary disclosure under guidance or codes.

● Corporate social responsibility reports have become increasingly common sections within the annual report, rather than being stand-alone documents available to interested parties. At the extreme, companies are beginning to restructure the entire annual report in the framework of CSR reporting.

● Remuneration reports, as part of corporate governance reporting, provide information that allows users to evaluate the effectiveness of company managers. They also provided researchers with information on management compensation that can be used in investigations linking accounting information to managerial performance (and vice versa).

● Comparative research into disclosure continues to be an active area of investigation, with more emphasis on the narrative disclosures. Some papers focus on using transparency scores created by organizations monitoring corporate reports, while others apply or create tailored scores to meet specific research aims.

Questions

The following questions test your understanding of the material contained in the chapter and allow you to relate your understanding to the learning outcomes specified at the start of this chapter. The learning outcomes are repeated here. Each question is cross-referenced to the relevant section of the chapter.

Explain the problems of defining 'transparency' in disclosure

1 What does 'transparency' mean? (section 15.2)

2 Why might a regulator's definition of 'transparency' differ from that of (a) a preparer of accounts; (b) an academic researcher? (section 15.2)

Explain the requirements of narrative reporting in the US

3 What is the purpose of the MD&A in US annual reporting? (section 15.3.1)

4 What are the main contents of the MD&A? (section 15.3.1)

5 Why is market risk disclosure regarded as important by the SEC? (section 15.3.2)

6 What are the problems for companies in reporting forward looking information? (section 15.3.3)

7 What are the benefits and problems of 'non-GAAP' pro-forma financial statements? (section 15.3.4)

8 How is internal control over financial reporting achieved and described to shareholders? (section 15.3.5)

Explain how management reports are produced outside the US

9 What does the EU Modernisation Directive recommend about management reports? (section 15.4.1)

10 What is the evidence from specific countries that suggests diversity in reporting will continue to be seen in management reports? (sections 15.4.2 to 15.4.6)

Explain and evaluate the initiatives being taken on developing CSR reports

11 What actions are recommended by the European Commission in the development of CSR reports? (section 15.5.1)

12 What has been shown by comparative research studies of economic and social disclosures? (section 15.5.2)

13 Is CSR reporting likely to be effective in achieving the aim of improving CSR? (section 15.5.3)

Explain the nature and evaluate the usefulness of remuneration reports

14 Why are remuneration reports seen as an important item for inclusion in corporate annual reports? (section 15.6)

15 What kind of information is contained in remuneration reports? (section 15.6)

Explain and contrast methods used to carry out research into disclosure

16 How do published surveys help in the design of academic research into transparency and disclosure? (section 15.7.1)

17 What are the limitations of using published surveys in academic research? (section 15.7.1)

18 What are the benefits and limitations of using a purpose-designed disclosure checklist in academic research? (section 15.7.3)

19 What are the benefits and limitations of selecting a specific item of disclosure for comparative study in academic research? (section 15.7.3)

References and further reading

Adams, C.A.A. and Kuasirikun, N. (2000) 'A comparative analysis of corporate reporting on ethical issues by UK and German chemical and pharmaceutical companies', *The European Accounting Review*, 9(1): 53–79.

Alexander, D. and Archer, S. (2000) 'On the myth of Anglo-Saxon financial accounting', *International Journal of Accounting*, 33(4): 539–557.

Archambault, J.J. and Archambault, M.E. (2003) 'A multinational test of determinants of corporate disclosure', *The International Journal of Accounting*, 38: 173–194.

ASB (1993) *Operating and Financial Review*, Statement issued by the Accounting Standards Board.

ASB (2003) *Operating and Financial Review*, Statement issued by the Accounting Standards Board.

Ball, R., Kothari, S.P. and Robin, A. (2000) 'The effect of international institutional factors on properties of accounting earnings', *Journal of Accounting and Economics*, 29: 1–52.

Beattie, V.A. and Jones, M.J. (2000) 'Impression management: the case of inter-country financial graphs', *Journal of International Accounting, Auditing and Taxation*, 9(2): 159–183.

Beattie, V. and Pratt, K. (2002) *Voluntary annual report disclosures: what users want*. The Institute of Chartered Accountants of Scotland, 107 pp. www.icas.org.uk

Bebbington, J., Gray, R. and Larrinaga, C. (2000) 'Editorial: environmental and social accounting in Europe', *The European Accounting Review*, 9(1): 3–6.

Bushman, R.M., Piotroski, J.D. and Smith, A.J. (2004) 'What determines corporate transparency?' *Journal of Accounting Research*, 42(2): 207–251.

Chau, G.K. and Gray, S.J. (2002) 'Ownership structure and corporate voluntary disclosure in Hong Kong and Singapore', *The International Journal of Accounting*, 37: 247–265.

Core, J.E. (2001) 'A review of the empirical disclosure literature: discussion', *Journal of Accounting and Economics*, 31: 441–56.

EC (2003) Directive 2003/51/EC of the European Parliament and of the Council of 18 June 2003.

Frost, C.A. (2003) *Disclosure Survey 2003*, World Federation of Exchanges, www.world-exchanges.org

Goyder, M. (2003) *Redefining CSR: From the rhetoric of accountability to the reality of earning trust*, Tomorrow's Company, www.tomorrowscompany.com

Gray, S.J. (1988) 'Towards a theory of cultural influence on the development of accounting systems internationally', *Abacus*, 24(1): 1–15.

Gray, S.J., Meek, G.K. and Roberts, C.B. (1995) 'International capital market pressures and voluntary annual report disclosures by US and UK multinationals', *Journal of International Financial Management and Accounting*, 6(1): 43–68.

Healy, P.M. and Palepu, K.G. (2001) 'Information asymmetry, corporate disclosure, and the capital markets: A review of the empirical disclosure literature', *Journal of Accounting and Economics*, 31: 405–440.

Holland, L. and Boon Foo, Y. (2003) 'Differences in environmental reporting practices in the UK and the US: the legal and regulatory context', *The British Accounting Review*, 35(1): 1–18.

Hope, O.-K. (2003) 'Firm-level disclosures and the relative roles of culture and legal origin', *Journal of International Financial Management and Accounting*, 14(3): 218–248.

Khanna, T., Palepu, K.G. and Srinivasan, S. (2004) 'Disclosure practices of foreign companies interacting with US markets', *Journal of Accounting Research*, 42(2): 475–508.

La Porta, R., Lopez-de-Silanes, F. and Shleifer, A. (1998) 'Law and finance', *Journal of Political Economy*, 106(6): 1113–1155.

Martin, R.D. (2000) 'Going-concern uncertainty disclosures and conditions: a comparison of French, German and US practices', *Journal of International Accounting, Auditing and Taxation*, 9(2): 137–158.

Meek, G.K., Roberts, C.B. and Gray, S.J. (1995) 'Factors influencing voluntary annual report disclosures by US, UK and continental European multinational corporations', *Journal of International Business Studies*, Third Quarter: 555–572.

Miller, G.S. (2004) 'Discussion of "What determines corporate transparency?"', *Journal of Accounting Research*, 42(2): 253–268.

Newson, M. and Deegan, C. (2002) 'Global expectations and their association with corporate social disclosure practices in Australia, Singapore and South Korea', *The International Journal of Accounting*, 37: 183–213.

Ordelheide, D. and KPMG (eds) (2001) *Transnational Accounting* (2nd edn). Basingstoke, UK: Palgrave Publishers.

Parker, R.H. (2001) 'European languages of account', *The European Accounting Review*, 10(1): 133–147.

Robb, S.W.G., Single, L.E. and Zarzeski, M.T. (2001) 'Nonfinancial disclosures across Anglo-American countries', *Journal of International Accounting, Auditing and Taxation*, 10: 71–83.

Rutherford, B.A. (2003) *Half the Story: Progress and Prospects for the Operating and Financial Review*. ACCA Research Report No. 80, Association of Chartered Certified Accountants www.accaglobal.com

Salter, S.B. and Niswander, F. (1995) 'Cultural influence on the development of accounting systems internationally: A test of Gray's [1988] theory', *Journal of International Business Studies*, 26(2): 379–398.

Vanstraelen, A., Zarzeski, M. and Robb, S.W.G. (2003) 'Corporate nonfinancial disclosure practices and financial analyst forecast abilities across three European countries', *Journal of International Management and Accounting*, 14(3): 249–278.

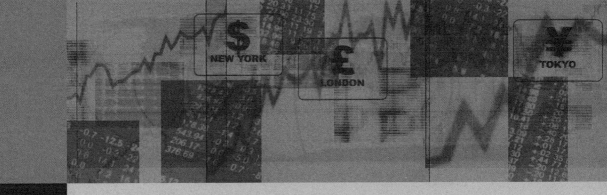

Issues in multinational accounting

▶

Learning outcomes

After reading this chapter you should be able to discuss the problems, explain the IFRS treatment and compare differences in the US, Japan and the EU in each of the following topics:

● defining a group,

● acquisitions and uniting of interests,

● goodwill on acquisition,

● associates and joint ventures,

● segmental reporting,

● foreign currency translation.

16.1   Introduction

This chapter considers issues that offer particular challenges to multinational groups of companies in harmonization because of the underlying differences in institutional characteristics and accounting cultures. They are areas where the imposition of a standard approach – either IFRS or US GAAP – could seem an attractive proposition in eliminating a wide range of national variations. However it could also be that, in these controversial areas of accounting, the apparent standardization of the accounting rules may give a false sense of comparability when the underlying economic stories are different. Multinational means 'many countries', reflecting the wide geographical spread of companies within a group entity. The basis of accounting used in the consolidated financial statements will be a single accounting system, which may be IFRS, US GAAP or the national accounting system of the parent company. When reading consolidated financial statements it is important to be aware of the benefits and limitations of this apparent harmonization of accounting information.

We discuss first some of the particular problems in business combinations – the definition of a group (section 16.2), acquisitions and uniting of interests (section 16.3), goodwill on acquisition (section 16.4) and associates and joint ventures (section 16.5). Segmental reporting follows (section 16.6) and we conclude with foreign currency translation (section 16.7).

16.2 Defining a group

16.2.1 Issues of definition

An economic entity is formed when a group of companies are brought together under arrangements involving ownership and control, in order to provide future benefits to the owners of the group. The arrangements usually mean that risks that are shared across all or parts of the group and are ultimately borne by the owners of the group. Defining the membership of such an economic entity is not an easy task and so accounting resorts to identifying the economic entity through legal relationships. These legal relationships may define ownership, or they may establish contractual control. Further problems follow where the law defines some of the relationships within an economic entity but is not designed to match the economic relationships precisely. The result is that some entities that ought to be included within the economic group are excluded by legal definitions, while some entities that are included by legal definition are not part of the economic substance and should possibly be excluded from the accounting procedures. Accounting standard-setters then step in to propose a solution to such problems in order to establish comparability of treatment. The accounting standards seek to represent the economic entity but also want to maintain the objectivity that comes from using definitions based in law. Accounting standard-setters are also aware of the problems that have arisen where company managers have used the precise wording legal definitions to create or eliminate relationships in order to avoid reporting some part of the economic entity, perhaps because it would portray 'bad news' to investors or lenders.

16.2.2 IFRS

16.2.2.1 Parent and subsidiaries

A group of companies usually has a parent and subsidiaries. IFRS definitions of 'parent' and 'subsidiary' are given in Exhibit 16.1 which also defines the relationship of control that links the parent to the subsidiary. The definitions of control are built on a combination of 'power' and 'benefit'.

16.2.2.2 Special Purpose Entitites

The 'Special Purpose Entity' (SPE) is a particularly important aspect of defining a group because these special purpose entities have in previous times been created in some countries in order to avoid consolidation (sometimes referred to as 'off-balance-sheet finance', OBSF). Managerial motives for avoiding consolidation include concealing borrowing from shareholders and intending investors in order to give a better impression of gearing (leverage); concealing losses in order to give a better impression of performance; concealing non-performing assets in order to give a better impression of performance; and avoiding reporting expenditure such as research and development in the group profit or loss. The benefits claimed by managers who create SPEs are that they package risks and rewards in a way that meets the requirements of particular investors or lenders and so reduce the cost of capital for the activity within the SPE. The essential message of SIC-12 is that if the parent obtains the benefits and carries the risks of the SPE, then the SPE should be consolidated.

| Exhibit 16.1 | Defining a group in IFRS |

A *group* is a parent and all its subsidiaries.[1]

Control is the power to govern the financial and operating policies of an entity so as to obtain benefits from its activities.[2]

A *parent* is an entity that has one or more subsidiaries.[3]

A *subsidiary* is an entity, including an unincorporated entity such as a partnership, that is controlled by another entity (known as the parent).[4]

Consolidated financial statements shall include *all subsidiaries* of the parent.[5]

Control is presumed to exist when the parent owns, directly or indirectly, more than half of the voting power of an entity.

Control also exists where the parent owns half or less than half of the voting power of an entity where there is:[6]

(a) power over more than half of the voting rights by virtue of an agreement with other investors;
(b) power to govern the financial and operating policies of the entity under a statute or an agreement;
(c) power to appoint or remove the majority of the members of the board of directors or equivalent governing body;
(d) power to cast the majority of votes at a meeting of the board of directors or equivalent governing body.

In addition to the situations described in IAS 27 (paragraph 13) the following circumstances may indicate a relationship in which an entity controls an *SPE* (*special purpose entity*):[7]

(a) in substance, the activities of the SPE are being conducted on behalf of the entity according to its specific business needs so that the entity obtains benefits from the SPE's operations; or
(b) in substance, the entity has the decision-making powers to obtain the majority of the benefits of the activities of the SPE; or
(c) in substance, the entity has the right to obtain the majority of the benefits of the SPE and therefore may be exposed to risks of the activities of the entity; or
(d) in substance, the entity retains the majority of the residual or ownership risks relating to the SPE.

---

[1] IAS 27 (2004) paragraph 4.

[2] Ibid.

[3] Ibid.

[4] Ibid.

[5] IAS 27 (2004) paragraph 12. A scope exclusion for temporary control, retained in the first 2003 version, was removed by IFRS 5 issued in March 2004, see BC 14.

[6] IAS 27 (2004) paragraph 13.

[7] SIC 12 (1998) paragraph 10.

16.2.2.3 Exclusions and exemptions

'Exclusion' means that some subsidiaries are omitted from the consolidated financial statements. 'Exemption' means that under specific conditions the parent company does not produce consolidated financial statements.

Exclusion from consolidation is a subject of debate in situations where the legal entity appears not to be a good representation of the economic entity. Managers tend to want to omit loss-making subsidiaries, or any subsidiary that reflects poorly on economic performance. That distorts the reported performance and position of the group. The IASB has gradually tightened up on exclusions, with its decision in March 2004 to remove from IAS 27 the previously permitted exclusion for temporary control. In most countries the law has allowed exclusions from consolidation on grounds such as:

- the activities of the subsidiary are sufficiently different from those of the rest of the group;
- there are severe long-term restrictions over the parent's rights;
- the subsidiary is held with a view to subsequent resale;
- obtaining the information required would involve disproportionate expense or undue delay;
- the subsidiaries are immaterial (separately or in aggregate).

When you read the accounting policies in consolidated financial statements you should look for the definition of the group to be sure that it is fully represented. If there are exclusions, look for the reasons given and consider the implications for the full accounting picture of performance and position.

Exemption is allowed by IFRS where the parent is wholly owned by another company or else the owners of the minority interest have been informed and do not object to the parent not presenting consolidated financial statements and the securities are not publicly traded. In all cases the exemption only applies if the ultimate parent publishes consolidated financial statements that comply with IFRS.[8]

16.2.2.4 Disclosures

IFRS 3 substantially increased the disclosures required about a business combination. The full list (paragraphs 66 to 77) is too long to reproduce here but the principles provide a useful starting point. An acquirer must disclose information that enables users of its financial statements to evaluate the nature and financial effect of business combinations that took place during the period, or after the balance sheet date but before the financial statements were authorized for issue.[9] The acquirer must disclose information that enables users of is financial statements to evaluate the financial effects of gains, losses, error corrections and other adjustments recognized in the current period that relate to business combinations put in place in previous periods.[10] An entity must disclose information that enables users of its financial statements to evaluate changes in the carrying amount of goodwill during the period.[11]

IAS 27 (paragraphs 40–42) set out disclosure requirements for consolidated financial statements. These are primarily concerned with explaining the exceptions,

---

[8] IAS 27 (2004) paragraph 10.
[9] IFRS 3 (2004) paragraph 66.
[10] IFRS 3 (2004) paragraph 72.
[11] IFRS 3 (2004) paragraph 74.

such as reasons for not consolidating a subsidiary, and exclusions, such as the information expected when the parent elects not to prepare consolidated financial statements.

16.2.3 US

We have described in Chapter 8 the history and current state of US definitions of a group. The approach to definition of a subsidiary differs from that of IFRS. In the US a dual decision model is applied. All consolidation decisions should be evaluated under traditional consolidation models, focusing on majority voting interests, and under the relatively new 'variable interest' model. Variable interest entities are those in which the parent does not have a controlling voting interest but the parent absorbs the majority of the VIE's expected losses or returns. Special Purpose Entities (SPEs) are tested for consolidation using the VIE tests. This idea of identifying VIEs emerged in the Sarbanes–Oxley Act, following the collapse of Enron, as explained in Chapter 8. However, even with the variable interest entities percentage-based tests of ownership continue to be applied to establish 'at risk' equity. An example is seen in Sara Lee (Exhibit 16.2).

A different story about FIN 46 is shown by The Walt Disney Company in its annual report for 2003 (Exhibit 16.3). The company indicates that FIN 46 will change the balance sheet by fully consolidating two companies for which equity accounting was previously applied. It explains the change and gives a proforma balance sheet in the 'as adjusted' column.

Exhibit 16.2 Variable interest entities, Sara Lee

Issued But Not Yet Effective Accounting Standards
Following is a discussion of recently issued accounting standards that the corporation will be required to adopt in a future period.

Consolidation of Variable Interest Entities
In January 2003, the FASB issued Interpretation No. 46, "Consolidation of Variable Interest Entities, an Interpretation of Accounting Research Bulletin No. 51" (FIN 46). Prior to the effective date of FIN 46, an entity was generally included in the Consolidated Financial Statements if it was controlled through ownership of a majority voting interest. In FIN 46, the FASB concluded that the voting interest approach is not always effective in identifying controlling financial interest. In some arrangements, equity investors may not bear the residual economic risks, and in others, control is not exercised through voting shares.

FIN 46 provides guidance for determining whether an entity lacks sufficient equity or its equity holders lack adequate decision-making ability. These entities – variable interest entities (VIEs) – are evaluated for consolidation. Variable interests are ownership, contractual or other interests in a VIE that change with changes in the VIE's net assets. The party with the majority of the variability in gains or losses of the VIE is the VIE's primary beneficiary, and is required to consolidate the VIE.

The corporation was required to apply the provisions of FIN 46 to variable interests in VIEs created after January 31, 2003. Beginning in 2004, the corporation will be required to apply the provisions of FIN 46 to variable interests in VIEs created before February 1, 2003. The corporation does not believe that the provisions of FIN 46, when fully adopted in 2004, will have a material impact on its financial statements.

Source: Sara Lee annual report (2003), pp. 45–46. www.saralee.com

Effect of FIN 46, Walt Disney Company

Impact of FIN 46 on Equity Investments   As discussed in Note 2, the implementation of FIN 46 will likely require the Company to consolidate both Euro Disney and Hong Kong Disneyland for financial reporting purposes in the first quarter of fiscal 2004. The following tables present consolidated results of operations and financial position for the Company as of and for the year ended September 30, 2003 as if Euro Disney and Hong Kong Disneyland had been consolidated based on our current analysis and understanding of FIN 46.

(all in million dollars)	As Reported	Euro Disney	Hong Kong Disneyland	Adjustments	As Adjusted
Results of Operations:					
Revenues	$ 27,061	$ 1,077	$ 5	$ (10)	$ 28,133
Cost and expenses	(24,330)	(1,032)	(7)	9	(25,360)
Amortization of intangibles assets	(18)	–	–	–	(18)
Gain on sale of business	16	–	–	–	16
Net interest expense	(793)	(101)	–	–	(894)
Equity in the income of investees	334	–	–	24	358
Restructuring and impairment charges	(16)	–	–	–	(16)
Income before income taxes, minority interest and the cumulative effect of accounting change	2,254	(56)	(2)	23	2,219
Income taxes	(789)	–	–	13	(776)
Minority interests	(127)	–	–	22	(105)
Cumulative effect of accounting change	(71)	–	–	–	(71)
Net income/(loss)	$ 1,267	$ (56)	$ (2)	$ 58	$ 1,267
Balance Sheet:					
Cash and cash equivalents	$ 1,583	$ 103	$ 76	$ –	$ 1,762
Other current assets	6,731	191	9	(9)	6,922
Total current assets	8,314	294	85	(9)	8,684
Investments	1,849	–	–	(623)	1,226
Fixed assets	12,678	2,951	524	–	16,153
Intangible assets	2,786	–	–	–	2,786
Goodwill	16,966	–	–	–	16,966
Other assets	7,395	128	9	–	7,532
Total assets	$49,988	$ 3,373	$618	$(632)	$ 53,347
Current portion of borrowings[1]	$ 2,457	$ 2,528	$ –	$(388)	$ 4,597
Other current liabilities	6,212	487	61	(35)	6,675
Total current liabilities	8,669	3,015	61	(473)	11,272
Borrowings	10,643	–	237	–	10,880
Deferred income taxes	2,712	–	–	–	2,712
Other long-term liabilities	3,745	289	–	(71)	3,963
Minority interests	428	–	–	301	729
Shareholders' equity	23,791	69	320	(389)	23,791
Total liabilities and shareholders' equity	$49,988	$3,373	$618	$(632)	$53,347

[1]All of Euro Disney's borrowings are classified as current as they are subject to acceleration if a long-term solution to Euro Disney's financing needs is not achieved by March 31, 2004.

Source: Walt Disney annual report (2003). www.disney.com/investors

16.2.4 Japan

Section 12.3.6 explains that a standard issued in 1997 changed the definition of a subsidiary from being based purely on percentage ownership to include control, bringing it closer to IAS 27 at that time. SMFG (Exhibit 16.4) shows exclusions for reasons of materiality and 'silent partnerships' .

16.2.5 EU

The approach to consolidation is described in section 9.8.3. The Seventh Directive allowed flexibility for member states through use of options. Section 9.8.3 explains the definition in terms of control by dominant influence established by contract. The origins of group accounting in Germany date back to 1965 with the Stock Corporation Act. One of the important elements of that Act was the economic concept of the group. It was intially limited to the German part of the group; overseas subsidiaries did not have to be consolidated.[12] However, large groups were including foreign-resident subsidiaries voluntarily.[13] The Disclosure Act of 1969 regulated holding companies existing in a legal form other than that of a stock corporation. It required group accounts to be prepared by such holding companies above a specified size.

The concept of the group in The Netherlands was similarly based on a tradition of an economic entity, using a definition based on dominant influence.[14] When Dutch accounting rules were revised in 1984 they included a requirement for group accounts; previously consolidation had been voluntary but with a tradition from as far back as the 1930s.[15] This focus on the economic concept of the group explains the options in the Seventh Directive that focus on control.

Groups were not a strong feature of accounting in France prior to the implementation of the Seventh Directive in the 1983 Act, because of their lack of legal identity. The 1983 Act introduced a control-based approach to definition.[16]

In contrast to the German, Dutch and French focus on the economic entity and control, the UK, until 1989, applied a definition of the group that focused on majority

Exhibit 16.4	Exclusions from consolidation SMFG

(ii) Nonconsolidated subsidiaries
Principal company:
SBCS Co., Ltd.

One hundred and eleven subsidiaries including S.B.L. Mercury Co., Ltd. are silent partnerships for lease transactions and their assets and profits/losses do not belong to them substantially. Therefore, pursuant to Article 5 Paragraph 1 Item 2 of Consolidated Financial Statements Regulation, they were excluded from consolidation.

Other nonconsolidated subsidiaries' total assets, ordinary income, net income and retained earnings have no material impact on the consolidated financial statements.

Source: Sumitomo Mitsui Financial Group Inc (2004), p. 69. www.smfg.co.jp

---

[12] Ordelheide (2001) p. 1360.
[13] We are obliged to Prof Dr Wolfgang Ballwieser for this observation.
[14] Klaassen (2001) p. 2023.
[15] Klaassen (2001) p. 2019.
[16] Richard (2001) pp. 1148,1154.

voting control. It was only concerns about special purpose entities and off-balance-sheet finance in the late 1980s that encouraged the UK regulators to adopt a control-based definition of a subsidiary in the 1989 Companies Act.

In the UK the accounting standard FRS 5 *Reporting the substance of transactions* defines a *quasi-subsidiary* as any entity which, although not fulfilling the definition of a subsidiary, is directly or indirectly controlled by the reporting entity and gives rise to benefits which are in substance no different from those that would arise from a subsidiary.[17] ('Quasi subsidiary' means 'as if it were a subsidiary'.) At the time of the collapse of Enron it was suggested that the non-consolidation of SPEs could not have occurred in the UK because FRS 5 would have brought them onto the group balance sheet.

Exclusion from consolidation has been permitted in Germany for reasons of long-term restrictions hindering parent company rights, or the information cannot be obtained without disproportionate cost or unreasonable delay.[18] Exclusion is required where the subsidiary's activities are so divergent from the activities of the rest of the group that it would conflict with the requirement for a 'true and fair view'. Exclusion from consolidation has been permitted in the Netherlands for reasons of very different activities.[19] Mandatory exclusions have been in place in France for reasons of severe long-term restrictions and different structures of subsidiaries' accounts, with optional exclusions available for temporary holding, excess cost and delay and non-materiality.[20] UK company law allows exclusions for reasons of sufficiently different activities, severe long-term restrictions, held with a view to subsequent resale, disproportionate expense or delay and immaterial in aggregate. The UK accounting standard FRS 2 *Subsidiary undertakings* only permits the first three of these reasons.

BNP Paribas (Exhibit 16.5) gives an example of the complexity of definition in terms of control. Particular features are the focus on *de facto* control and the acceptance of 40 per cent voting rights as sufficiently high, when coupled with *de facto* control, to allow consolidation. Although this variant is not permitted after 2005 for listed companies, the note indicates the diversity that could continue in non-listed groups operating under the Directive.

Exhibit 16.5 **Scope of consolidation, BNP Paribas**

SCOPE OF CONSOLIDATION

The consolidated financial statements include the financial statements of BNP Paribas and of all subsidiaries whose financial statements are material in relation to the consolidated financial statements of the Group as a whole. Subsidiaries are considered as being material if they contribute over EUR 8 million to consolidated net banking income, EUR 4 million to gross operating income or income before tax and amortisation of goodwill or EUR 40 million to total consolidated assets. Companies that hold shares in consolidated companies are also consolidated. Entities over which a Group company exercises de facto control, by virtue of contractual provisions or provisions of the entity's bylaws, are consolidated even in cases where the Group does not hold an interest in their capital. However, entities in which powers are not exercised in the sole interests of a Group company but in a fiduciary capacity on behalf of third parties and in the interests of all of the parties involved, none of which exercises exclusive control over the entity, are not consolidated.

▶

---

[17] FRS 5 (1994) paragraph 7.
[18] Ordelheide (2001) p. 1386.
[19] Klaassen (2001) p. 2027.
[20] Richard (2001) p. 1156.

Exhibit 16.5 *(Continued)*

De facto control is considered as being exercised when more than one of the following three criteria are met:

- The Group has decision-making and management powers over the routine operations or the assets of the entity, as evidenced in particular by the power to wind up the business, amend its articles of association or formally oppose any such amendments;
- The Group is entitled to all or the majority of the entity's profits, whether distributed or appropriated to reserves, and has the right to sell one or several assets and to benefit from any assets remaining after the entity has been liquidated;
- The Group is exposed to the majority of the risks relating to the entity. This is the case if a Group company gives a guarantee to external investors, in order to significantly reduce those investors' risk.

The first of the above three criteria is critical to assessing whether *de facto* control is exercised over entities set up in connection with the sale of proprietary loan portfolios, including fonds communs de créances (securitization funds) governed by French law and foreign entities offering equivalent guarantees to those existing in France.

Entities whose shares have been acquired exclusively with a view to their subsequent disposal are not consolidated. This is the case of shares which are intended to be sold in connection with the active management of the portfolio held by BNP Paribas Capital. Additionally, if the Group's ability to control the operating policies and assets of a subsidiary or affiliate is severely and permanently restricted, the subsidiary or affiliate is not consolidated. Shares in these companies are recorded in the consolidated balance sheet under "Investments in non-consolidated undertakings and other participating interests".

CONSOLIDATION METHODS
Fully-consolidated Companies
Subsidiaries over which the Group exercises exclusive control are fully consolidated, including subsidiaries whose financial statements are presented in a different format and which are engaged in a business that represents an extension of the Group's banking and financial services businesses or a related business, including insurance, real estate investment, real estate development and data processing services.

Exclusive control is considered as being exercised in cases where the Group is in a position to manage the subsidiary's financial and operating policies with a view to benefiting from its business, as a result of:

- direct or indirect ownership of the majority of voting rights of the subsidiary;
- the designation in two successive years of the majority of the members of the Board of Directors, Supervisory Board or equivalent. This is considered to be the case if a Group company holds over 40 per cent of the voting rights during the two-year period and no other shareholder holds a larger percentage, directly or indirectly;
- the right to exercise dominant influence over the subsidiary by virtue of contractual provisions or provisions of the bylaws, provided that the Group company exercising the dominant influence is a shareholder or partner of the subsidiary. Dominant influence is considered as being exercised in cases where the Group company is in a position to use or decide on the utilisation of the subsidiary's assets, liabilities or off balance sheet items as if they were its own. In the absence of contractual provisions or provisions of the bylaws, a Group company is considered as exercising dominant influence over a credit institution in cases where it holds at least 20 per cent of the voting rights and no other shareholder or group of shareholders holds a larger percentage.

Source: BNP Paribas annual report (2003), p. 183. www.bnpparibas.com

16.3 Acquisition and uniting of interests

The general term *business combination* may be applied to any transaction whereby one company becomes a subsidiary of another. The most common form of business combination is an *acquisition* (also called a *purchase*) where one of the combining entities obtains control over the other, enabling an acquirer to be identified. A *uniting of interests* occurs where it is not possible to identify an acquirer; instead the shareholders of the combining entities join in substantially equal arrangements to share control. A uniting of interests is called 'pooling of interests' in some countries, and 'merger' in others.

The identification of a 'uniting of interests' has in the past allowed special accounting treatment. In particular the profit of both parties for the full year of a merger may be added together in the consolidated financial statements despite the merger taking place part way through the year. This special treatment has led groups to claim a uniting of interests when in reality there has been an acquisition. In some countries the accounting rules have allowed this ambiguity of treatment. Recent trends have been moving towards tightening the accounting rules for uniting of interests or else eliminating them entirely. However there has been a longer debate over the treatment of 'entities under common control'.

16.3.1 Comparing acquisition with uniting of interests

This section gives a simplified comparison of the purchase (acquisition) method of accounting and uniting of interests accounting in order to bring out the key differences. A specialist text book or manual should be consulted for further detail.

The examples are based on two companies, A and B, consolidating their separate balance sheets at the date of acquisition. Both cases involve an acquisition of A by B where the shareholders in B accept shares of A in exchange for their shares in B on a one-for-one basis. The share price of A is $2 and the share price of B is $2. The directors of A examine the fixed assets of B at the date of acquisition and decide that the fair value of these fixed assets is $10m greater than their recorded book value.

The acquisition method is shown in Exhibit 16.6. Column 1 records the cost of the investment to A as $120m, consisting of $60m nominal value and $60m share premium. Column 2 shows the recorded balance sheet of B. Column 3 shows the fair value adjustment increasing the fixed assets of B and the reserves of B. Column 4 shows the adjusted balance sheet of B. Column 5 shows the consolidation adjustment where the goodwill is calculated as the excess of the fair value of the consideration given, $120m, over the fair value of the net assets acquired, $100m. Column 6 shows the consolidated balance sheet of the group.

The consolidation worksheet for the uniting of interests method is shown in Exhibit 16.7. The principle applied in this approach is to create a balance sheet as it would appear if these two companies had always been united. In column A the cost of the investment to A is shown as $60m which is the nominal value of the shares issued. The share premium is not recorded because there would not be a share premium if they had always been united. Column 2 shows the recorded balance sheet of B. There is no fair value adjustment, again because there would not be such an adjustment if they had always been united. The consolidated balance sheet is

Exhibit 16.6 Illustrating the purchase (acquisition) method

	A $m	B $m	Fair value adjusted $m	B adjusted $m	Consol adjusted $m	Consolidated $m
	(1)	(2)	(3)	(4)	(5)	(6)
Goodwill					+20	20
Fixed assets	100	60	+10	70		170
Investment in B	120				−120	–
Net current assets	20	30		30		50
Net assets	240	90	10	100	−100	240
Ordinary share capital	140	60		60	−60	140
Share premium	60					60
Fair value adjustment	–		+10	+10	−10	
Reserves of retained profit	40	30		30	−30	40
	240	90	10	100	−100	240

therefore a direct addition of the two separate balance sheets, as if they had always been united.

Comparing Exhibit 16.6 and Exhibit 16.7 allows us to draw the following conclusions about acquisition accounting and uniting of interests accounting.

If the purchase method (acquisition accounting) has been used:

- There will probably be goodwill on consolidation which is recorded as an asset and subsequently amortized through profit and loss account or subjected to an impairment test.
- There may be negative goodwill on consolidation which is immediately or subsequently released to profit and loss account.
- Assets and liabilities of the subsidiary will be consolidated at their fair value at the date of acquisition.

Exhibit 16.7 Illustrating the uniting of interests method

	A £m	B £m	Consol adjusted £m	Consolidated £m
Fixed assets	100	60		160
Investment in B	60		−60	–
Net current assets	20	30	–	50
Net assets	180	90	−60	210
Ordinary share capital	140	60	−60	140
Reserves of retained profit	40	30	–	70
	180	90	−60	210

- Where the acquisition takes place part-way through an accounting period, a proportion of the subsidiary's profit or loss for the period will be included in the profit and loss account, representing only the period after the date of acquisition.

If uniting of interests accounting has been used:

- There will be no goodwill or negative goodwill, and no subsequent impact on profit and loss account.
- The assets and liabilities of the merging companies will be combined at recorded book value, not fair value.
- Where the acquisition takes place part-way through an accounting period, the full amount of the subsidiary's profit or loss for the period will be included in the profit and loss account, regardless of the date of acquisition.

This comparison shows why some companies try to create the circumstances that allow uniting of interests accounting. It tends to produce higher profit and lower net assets in the year of acquisition, giving an apparently higher return on capital employed. In the longer term there is no amortization of goodwill, which continues the appearance of better performance.

16.3.2 IFRS

The IASB made significant changes to its previous standards when it issued IFRS 3 *Business Combinations* in March 2004.

16.3.2.1 Prohibiting 'uniting of interests' accounting

Previously IAS 22 had permitted both the purchase method and the pooling of interests method. Although it restricted the pooling of interests method to combinations that met the test of 'uniting of interests' there was a lack of comparability because transactions were deliberately structured to match the accounting rules and the methods produced quite different results. Once the US and Canada had changed their rules to prohibit pooling of interests accounting, joining Australia which already prohibited it, the IASB decided to converge with the standards in these countries.[21]

Basic definitions from IFRS 3 are set out in Exhibit 16.8.

16.3.2.2 Provisions for restructuring

In allocating the cost of the combination, the acquirer recognizes only the identifiable assets, liabilities and contingent liabilities of the acquiree that existed at the date of acquisition. If the acquiree has a liability for restructuring which already exists at the date of acquisition, that is recognized in allocating the cost of acquisition. The acquirer must not recognize liabilities for future losses or other costs expected to be incurred as a result of the business combination.

This was a significant change in IFRS 3, compared to previous international accounting standards. It is discussed in the 'Basis of Conclusions' to IFRS 3, paragraphs BC 74–87. In particular, paragraph BC 80 notes that the price paid by the acquirer will take account of future costs arising from the acquisition. To make a provision for such

---

[21] IFRS 3 (2004) IN3.

| Exhibit 16.8 | Business combination definitions[22] |

- *Business combination*. Bringing together separate entities or businesses into one reporting entity.

- *Acquisition date*. The date on which an acquirer effectively obtains control of the acquiree.

- *Fair value*. The amount for which an asset could be exchanged, or a liability settled, between knowledgeable, willing parties in an arm's length transaction.

- *Goodwill*. Future economic benefits arising from assets that are not capable of being individually identified and separately recognized.

- Where shares are issued as '*consideration*' (the price paid) for the acquisition, they are recorded at their fair value at the date of the exchange. In an active market the published price of a share at the date of exchange is the best evidence of fair value.[23]

costs at the date of acquisition would be double counting. Paragraph BC 87 confirms that there was majority support for this change among the respondents to the exposure draft ED3.

The scenario set out in Exhibit 16.9 shows the potential for creative accounting and income smoothing by the use of provisions at the date of acquisition where these provisions take 'the acquirer's perspective. This type of flexibility has been curtailed by IFRS 3. In this particular case the acquirer, Over, would not be permitted under IFRS 3 to make the provision because it was not a liability of the acquiree at the date of the acquisition. We will refer to the same scenario later in this section to explain how other standard-setters would treat the same situation.

16.3.2.3 Minority interests on acquisition

Because the acquirer recognizes the acquiree's identifiable assets, liabilities and contingent liabilities at their fair values at the date of acquisition, any minority interest in the acquiree is stated at the minority's portion of the net fair value of those items.[24] Exhibit 16.10 shows how a South African company, SAB Miller, reports the acquisition of 60 per cent of an Italian subsidiary, reporting the minority interest at 40 per cent of fair value.

16.3.2.4 Businesses under common control

The IASB decided to defer the treatment of businesses under common control to Phase 2 of the Business Combinations project, along with mutual entities and entities brought together by contract alone. These appear to be the kinds of organization for which 'uniting of interests' would be an appropriate treatment. However the IASB felt that if this were allowed there would be cases where acquisitions would be restructured

---

[22] IFRS 3 (2004) Appendix A.
[23] IFRS 3 (2004) paragraph 24.
[24] IFRS 3 (2004) paragraph 40.

Exhibit 16.9 Provision for restructuring

Provision for restructuring

At the start of Year 1 the entire share capital of Under Inc was acquired by Over Inc. The recorded net assets of Under were £260m and the price paid for the acquisition was £320m.

The directors of Over were satisfied that the recorded book values of fixed and current assets were equivalent to fair values, but they decided, prior to acquisition, that restructuring would probably be necessary. On the date of acquisition they held a board meeting to confirm their plans. During the following week they signed contracts for building work and issued the necessary warnings to staff where relocation would take place. There was no doubt about the commitment of Over to carry out the reorganization but there was a long debate about the likely cost. The finance director asked for a conservative approach and estimated a total cost of £30m over three years. The personnel director was optimistic about staff flexibility and suggested that £21m over three years would be sufficient. The board decided to take the advice of the finance director on grounds of prudence.

At the date of acquisition the goodwill was calculated as follows:

	£m	£m
Price paid for subsidiary		320
Recorded net assets acquired, at fair value	260	
Less provision for reorganization	(30)	
Net fair value		230
Consolidation adjustment: goodwill		90

Note that the provision caused the goodwill figure to be higher than it would have been based on recorded net assets alone.

If the finance director has estimated correctly, then in each of the three subsequent years there will be a cost of £10m for reorganization. This can be matched against the provision of £30m which will reduce to £20m at the end of Year 1, £10m at the end of Year 2 and nil at the end of Year 3. The profit and loss account in those years will not be encumbered by costs of reorganization.

However, supposing the personnel director estimated correctly. Each year there will be a cost of £7m rather than the expected cost of £10m. This means that each year there is an unused provision of £3m which could be returned to enhance the appearance of the profit and loss account. IFRS 3 does not permit this creative accounting.

---

to appear to be combinations under common control to avoid purchase method accounting. There is an argument for applying 'fresh start' accounting to such 'true mergers'. Fresh start requires the revaluation of all the assets of the combining entities at the date of the combination. It has also been called the 'new entity method' in the debate leading to IFRS 3. In a dissenting view on IFRS 3 one member of the Board felt that the 'fresh start' method should have been available for some of the former 'uniting of interests' cases rather than forcing the identification of an acquirer.[25]

---

[25] IFRS 3 (2004) BC 24–8, DO 1–6.

Exhibit 16.10	Fair value and minority interest, SAB Miller

29. Acquisitions and disposals
Birra Peroni SpA

The acquisition of a 60 per cent interest in Birra Peroni SpA (Peroni), the number two brewer in Italy, with options to increase the holding in the future, was completed on 4 June 2003, although control passed to SAB Miller on 21 May 2003 when the SAB Miller appointed directors assumed control of the business. Consequently, the business has been accounted for from 21 May 2003. The acquisition was funded in cash from existing resources.

Put and call option arrangement exist between the group and the remaining Birra Peroni minority shareholders which, if exercised, will result in the group's interest increasing to 99.36 per cent over a three to six-year period. The price payable in relation to these options is based on the equity value of Birra Peroni together with earn-out arrangements dependent on the future domestic and international performance of Birra Peroni.

The fair values of the assets and liabilities acquired, which are considered to be provisional as a number of matters are still under consideration, were as follows:

	Book value US$m	Fair value adjustments US$m	Provisional fiar value US$m
Tangible fixed assets	224	(10)[1]	214
Intangible assets	33	(33)[2]	–
Investments in associates	2	(2)[3]	–
Other fixed asset investments	17	(1)[4]	16
Stock	71	(4)[6]	67
Debtors	217	(25)[6]	192
Cash and cash equivalents	14	–	14
Creditors – amount falling due within one year	(348)	(3)[7]	(351)
Creditors – amounts falling due after one year	(95)	–	(95)
Provisions for liabilities and charges	(22)	(6)[8]	(28)
	113	(84)	29
Equity minority interests	(49)	36[9]	(13)
Net assets acquired	6	(48)	16
Goodwill			283
Consideration – all cash			299

In accordance with the group's accounting policy, the goodwill of US$283 million arising on consolidation has been stated in the group's balance sheet as an intangible asset.

Source: SAB Miller annual report (2004) p. 95. www.sabmiller.com

16.3.3 US

The US is in agreement with IFRS on prohibiting 'uniting of interests' accounting but differs in the treatment of provisions for restructuring and in the method of measuring and reporting minority interests.

16.3.3.1 Prohibiting 'uniting of interests' accounting

We have explained in section 8.3.4 the controversy in the US that surrounded the FASB's decision to prohibit the 'pooling of interests' method of accounting (called 'uniting of interests' in IFRS). SFAS 141 *Business combinations* allows only the purchase method of accounting. One aspect of the objections lay in the concern that the purchase method involves applying fair values to the acquiree's assets and liabilities and then charging amortization of the asset of goodwill. Fair values and goodwill do not appear in uniting of interests. The parallel development of SFAS 142 allowed companies to use an impairment test on goodwill rather than amortize for up to 40 years. This softened the blow to the profit and loss of implementing SFAS 141.

16.3.3.2 Provisions for restructuring

At the date of the acquisition, management must begin to assess and formulate a plan to close down or reorganize a part of the acquired entity. The plan must be completed as soon as possible, but no longer than 12 months from the date of the acquisition. Management must then communicate the termination or relocation plans to the employees of the acquired company. The restructuring provision can then be recorded in fair value at the date of acquisition, if it meets the definition of a liability. In the case study of Exhibit 16.9, the provision would probably be allowed. The guidance would not necessarily help in choosing between the two different proposals for the amount of the provision. We explained in section 16.3.2.2 that the IASB considered the US approach in preparing IFRS 3 but rejected it for the reasons explained in the standard.

16.3.3.3 Minority interest

The US treatment of minority interest is not prescribed in the standards but the usual treatment is to calculate the minority's percentage of share capital and reserves at the book value of the acquiree, without including any fair value adjustment. There is no clear position in the balance sheet for reporting minority interest. Some companies do not regard it as part of the equity interest and report it between the liability section and the stockholders' equity section. This is described as the *parent company theory*. Other companies report minority interest as part of the stockholders' equity section. This is described as the *entity theory*. The treatment of minority interests is a topic for phase II of the Business Combinations project for convergence between IFRS and FASB on purchase accounting.

16.3.4 Japan

Group accounting in Japan is a relatively recent development as described in Chapter 12. It does not yet match the approach taken in IFRS.

16.3.4.1 Uniting of interests

Under the BAC Statement of Opinion issued in October 2003, pooling of interests must be applied if certain strict conditions are met. Otherwise purchase accounting is applied. The conditions for applying pooling of interests are:

- the consideration is in shares with voting rights;
- the ratio of ownership by voting rights after combination must be close to 50/50;
- there is no fact that indicates relationships of control other than by means of voting rights.

16.3.4.2 Provisions for restructuring

There is no specific detail to match the strong rules of IFRS 3.

16.3.4.3 Minority interest[26]

The minority interest can be calculated as the minority's percentage of share capital and reserves at the book value of the acquiree, without including any fair value adjustment, or it can be calculated with the inclusion of the minority's proportion of the fair value adjustment. This reflects the flexibility of US GAAP. Before 1999 the minority interest was reported under a separate main subsection 'minority interest' at the end of the liability section of the consolidated balance sheet. Effectively this treated the minority interest as a liability. The amended BADC consolidation standard, which took effect in 1999, provides that a separate section be provided between the liabilities and the equity sections of the annual report. That change reflected the US influence of the 'parent company theory' (see section 16.3.3.3).

16.3.5 EU

16.3.5.1 Uniting of interests

German and French laws allow pooling of interests on the basis allowed by the Seventh Directive.[27] UK allows pooling of interests (called merger accounting) under strict rules set out in FRS 6 *Acquisitions and mergers*, and the ASB has argued for continuation of pooling of interests under specific conditions in IFRS. Pooling of interests is allowed in The Netherlands but rarely used.[28]

16.3.5.2 Restructuring costs

The UK took a strict line in FRS 7 *Fair values in acquisition accounting* that the acquiring company could not make provisions at the balance sheet date for expenditure to be incurred in restructuring after the date of acquisition. In Germany GAS 4 *Acquisition accounting in consolidated financial statements* contains explicit rules on the treatment of restructuring costs.[29] In France there is considerable flexibility under the revised 'methodology' of the 1999 Plan Comptable[30] (see section 10.7.3.1). In The Netherlands there should not be a provision against future costs.[31]

16.3.5.3 Minority interests

The Seventh Directive is broad in its coverage and so we have to look to national laws for the specific applications. The central principle underlying German accounting practice is the entity principle. Minority interests in subsidiary companies are treated as shareholders of the group. Their share of equity is reported under the heading of 'capital' in the group balance sheet, reported as a separate line item. In The Netherlands minority interest is part of the group shareholders' equity as a separate line item. UK companies are required to show the minority interest as a separate line item, usually seen at the end of the shareholders' equity section.

For the amount reported, there is flexibility in France and Germany either restricting the measurement to a percentage of net book value or adding in a percentage of fair value.[32] In both the UK and The Netherlands the calculation is based on the full fair value at the date of acquisition.[33]

---

[26] Kuroda (2001) p. 1851.
[27] Ordelheide (2001) p. 1407, Richard (2001) p. 1169.
[28] Klaassen (2001) p. 2033.
[29] Ordelheide (2001) p. 1407.
[30] Richard (2001) p. 1170.
[31] Klaassen (2001) p. 2035.
[32] Richard (2001) pp. 1172, Ordelheide (2001) pp. 1400–1402.
[33] Klaassen (2001) p. 2034.

16.4 Goodwill

16.4.1 Questions about goodwill

Goodwill arising on acquisition is essentially an arithmetic difference. It is the description given to the difference between the fair value of the payment for a subsidiary and the fair value of the net assets acquired. The directors of an acquirer which offers more than the fair value of the net assets acquired must be seeing some value in the target in terms of future earnings potential and growth. It is described in IFRS 3 as 'future economic benefits arising from assets that are not capable of being individually identified and separately recognized'. Goodwill has the characteristic of an asset in the expectation of future benefit but it is different from any other asset because it is not separable from the business. The term 'goodwill' has been applied in Anglo-American terminology. In some countries it is described as a 'difference on consolidation'. Questions about the measurement of goodwill include the following:

- How is the goodwill measured at the date of acquisition?
- How is goodwill measured subsequent to the date of acquisition?
- How is negative goodwill treated?

We will answer these questions from the viewpoint of IFRS and then compare the IFRS with other treatments.

16.4.2 IFRS

The answers to the three questions about goodwill measurement are given in Exhibit 16.11.

Exhibit 16.11 Treatment of goodwill and negative goodwill, IFRS

How is goodwill measured at the date of acquisition?
The acquirer initially measures goodwill at its cost, being the excess of the cost of the business combination over the acquirer's interest in the net fair value of the identifiable assets, liabilities and contingent liabilities recognized according to the procedures set out in IFRS 3.[34]

How is goodwill measured subsequent to the date of acquisition?
After initial recognition the acquirer shall measure goodwill acquired in a business combination at cost less any accumulated losses.[35] Goodwill acquired in a business combination is not amortized. It is tested annually for impairment in accordance with IAS 36 *Impairment of Assets*.[36]

How is negative goodwill treated?
If the goodwill is negative then the acquirer shall:

(a) reassess the identification and measurement of the acquiree's identifiable assets, liabilities and contingent liabilities and the measurement of the cost of the combination; and

(b) recognize immediately in profit or loss any excess remaining after that assessment.[37]

---

[34] IFRS 3 (2004) paragraph 51.
[35] IFRS 3 (2004) paragraph 54.
[36] IFRS 3 (2004) paragraph 55.
[37] IFRS 3 (2004) paragraph 56.

16.4.3 US

The initial measurement of goodwill and the subsequent annual impairment test are applied in the US under FAS 141 and 142 in a manner consistent with that required by IFRS 3.

Negative goodwill is initially allocated on a 'pro rata' basis against the carrying amounts of certain acquired non-financial assets. If, after reducing these assets to zero, an excess of negative goodwill remains, the excess is recognized as an extraordinary gain.[38] Under the convergence project, FASB is considering whether to move to the IASB model for negative goodwill.

16.4.4 Japan

The calculation of goodwill is based on fair values. At the date of acquisition there is a choice between the partial revaluation method and the overall revaluation method. Under partial revaluation, the portion of the subsidiary's net assets corresponding to the parent's equity is measured at fair value. The overall revaluation method measures all net assets at fair value. The term 'capital consolidation' is applied to the usual consolidation adjustments.

Prior to 2003 the MOF consolidation regulations required amortization over a period up to 20 years. Under the BAC Statement of Opinion issued in October 2003, goodwill is to be amortized over 20 years or less and is also subject to an impairment test. The effective date of this statement is fiscal years beginning on or after 1 April 2006.

The 1999 standard did not explain in detail how to treat negative goodwill. It was possible to set off negative goodwill against positive goodwill. Under the 2003 Opinion, the amortization period of up to 20 years will also apply to negative goodwill from April 2006.

16.4.5 EU

16.4.5.1 Amortization of goodwill

German law allows a range of treatments of goodwill. It may be amortized over four years of at least 25 per cent per year, or amortized over its useful economic life (in practice up to 20 years) or may be set against reserves at acquisition (Ordelheide, p. 1403). Ordelheide explains that setting goodwill against reserves was contrary to the German approach to profit but was introduced to allow German companies comparable treatment to those in other member states.

In The Netherlands goodwill may be charged in full to profit and loss in the year of acquisition, or charged against equity reserves in the year of acquisition, or capitalized and amortized over its expected useful life.[39]

In France the consolidation goodwill is called 'positive acquisition variance'. Under the 1999 Plan immediate write-off is not permitted; systematic amortization is expected but with a conservative approach of first minimizing the acquisition variance.[40]

---

[38] Williams & Carcello (2004) p. 4.10.
[39] Klaassen (2001) p. 1965.
[40] Richard (2001) p. 1171.

In the UK there is a requirement in FRS 10 *Goodwill and intangible assets* for either amortization of goodwill over its useful life in a period up to 20 years or an annual impairment test. This requirement was introduced in 1998 to replace a previous policy that allowed goodwill to be set against reserves at the date of acquisition. The change was not retrospective and so the balance sheets of UK companies contain a mixture of treatments depending on the date of the acquisition.

16.4.5.2 Negative goodwill

Negative goodwill in The Netherlands is given flexible treatment, depending on whether it arises as a result of low profit expectations or as a bargain purchase. If it is due to low expectations the negative goodwill can be set against positive goodwill reserves or can be taken to income. If it results from a bargain purchase it must be taken to a special reserve from which it may be transferred to other reserves or taken through profit and loss account. If an unexpected need for reorganization arises, the new loss can be charged to the reserve created from negative goodwill.[41] In France the negative goodwill is released to profit or loss on a systematic basis.[42] In Germany the difference may be released to profit and loss account only where stringent criteria are met. More frequently it remains in the equity section of the balance sheet but may be set against positive goodwill.[43] In the UK one approach is to release to profit or loss on the basis of the period of depreciation of the fixed assets acquired. The other is to set it against non-monetary assets acquired and then release any remaining amount to the period expected to benefit (without defining that period).[44]

16.5 Associates and joint ventures

The issues of interest here are the definition of associates and joint ventures, and the arguments for and against equity accounting, proportionate consolidation and full consolidation. This section first compares equity accounting and proportionate consolidation before moving to the IFRS definitions and some international comparisons. (Some national legislation uses the term 'proportional consolidation'; we use 'proportionate' throughout for consistency.)

16.5.1 Comparing equity accounting and proportionate consolidation

This section presents a simple example to show the difference between equity accounting and proportionate consolidation of the balance sheet. For more information it is necessary to consult a specialist text.

In the following example, P Co owns 25 per cent of the ordinary share capital of Q Ltd. The investment cost $5m some years ago when the retained profits of Q Ltd were zero. Three other companies each own 25 per cent of Q Ltd. This is effectively a partnership of the four shareholders in owning Q Ltd. Exhibit 16.12 shows the balance sheet of P Co reporting its investment in Q Ltd as a trade investment (i.e. applying the cost method). The balance sheet of Q Ltd is shown alongside.

---

[41] Klaassen (2001) p. 1966.
[42] Richard (2001) p. 1172.
[43] Ordelheide (2001) p. 1403–1404.
[44] FRS 10 paragraphs 49 and 50.

Exhibit 16.12 Balance sheets (Q Ltd treated as a trade investment)

	P Co $m	Q Ltd $m
Assets less current liabilities	45	120
Investment in Q Ltd	5	
Long-term loan	(20)	(80)
	30	40
Share capital	10	20
Retained profits (all post acquisition)	20	20
	30	40

We now compare the balance sheet of P Co using equity accounting with its balance sheet using proportionate consolidation. Both are set out in Exhibit 16.13.

For the equity method of accounting the investment in Q is reported at the cost of the equity investment ($5m) plus the parent's share of reserves of retained profit accumulated since the date of acquisition (25 per cent of $20m). This is the reason for the description 'equity accounting'; in one line it shows the amount of the equity investment for the 25 per cent holding. The group reserves are increased by the same amount, to balance the accounting equation, but all other items remain unchanged compared to the individual balance sheet of P Co in Exhibit 16.12.

Proportionate consolidation takes a totally different approach. It consolidates the parent's proportionate interest on each line of assets and liabilities on each. The usual consolidation adjustments are made to set the cost of the investment against the equity interest acquired.

It may be seen from the calculation of gearing (leverage) that proportionate consolidation reports a higher ratio and therefore gives a higher perception of financial risk. Equity accounting produces a single-line figure for net investment that sets assets against liabilities.

Equity accounting might be viewed as a means of keeping liabilities off the balance sheet. Imagine the situation where a group has a highly geared subsidiary. The group

Exhibit 16.13 Group Accounts, P Co

	Equity method Calculation	$m	$m	Proportionate consolidation Calculation
Assets less current liabilities		45	75	45 + (0.25% × 120)
Investment in Q Ltd	5 + 5	10		
Long-term loan		(20)	(40)	20 + (0.25% × 80)
		35	35	
Share capital		10	10	
Retained profits	(20 + 5)	25	25	
		35	35	
Debt/equity ratio		20/35	40/35	
		57%	114%	

| Exhibit 16.14 | Definitions of associate and joint venture |

- An *associate* is an entity, including an unincorporated entity such as a partnership, over which the investor has significant influence and that is neither a subsidiary nor an interest in a joint venture.[45]

- *Significant influence* is the power to participate in the financial and operating policy decisions of the investee but is not control or joint control over those policies.[46]

- The *equity method* is a method of accounting whereby the investment is initially recognized at cost and adjusted thereafter for the post-acquisition change in the investor's share of the net assets of the investee. The profit or loss of the investor includes the investor's share of the profit or loss of the investee.[47]

- A *joint venture* is a contractual arrangement whereby two or more parties undertake an economic activity that is subject to joint control.[48]

- *Joint control* is the contractually agreed sharing of control over an economic activity, and exists only when the strategic financial and operating decisions relating to the activity require the unanimous consent of the parties sharing control (the venturers).[49]

- A *venturer* is a party to a joint venture and has joint control over that joint venture.[50]

might reduce its reported gearing by setting up a company that avoids the legal definition of a subsidiary, while retaining significant influence. It could then move the trading activity of the former subsidiary to this new company. Application of equity accounting would allow the benefit of reporting a share of profit without the disadvantage of reporting the full extent of gearing.

16.5.2 IFRS

The relevant standards are IAS 28 Investments in Associates and IAS 31 Interests in Joint Ventures. Basic definitions are set out in Exhibit 16.14.

An investment in an associate must be accounted for using the equity method except where the investment is held for sale (see IFRS 5), or special conditions apply where the investing company has an ultimate parent company that is publishing financial statements that comply with IFRS.[51]

Joint control may apply to operations, assets or entities. In respect of its interests in jointly controlled operations, a venturer shall recognize in its financial statements the assets it controls and the liabilities that it incurs, the expenses that it incurs and its share of the income that it earns.[52] Similar treatment is applied to jointly controlled assets.[53]

---

[45] IAS 28 (2004) paragraph 2.

[46] IAS 28 (2004) paragraph 2.

[47] IAS 28 (2004) paragraph 2.

[48] IAS 31 (2004) paragraph 3.

[49] IAS 31 (2004) paragraph 3.

[50] IAS 31 (2004) paragraph 3.

[51] IAS 28 (2004) paragraph 13.

[52] IAS 31 (2004) paragraph 15.

[53] IAS 31 (2004) paragraph 21.

For a jointly controlled entity the venturer shall use proportionate consolidation[54] or the equity method.[55] Where proportionate consolidation is used the venturer may either combine the items line-by-line or have separate lines under each category of asset and liability.[56] It must not offset assets and liabilities.[57]

16.5.3 US

The US does not permit proportionate consolidation. Equity accounting is applied to associates and joint ventures.

16.5.4 Japan

Accounting rules in Japan do not permit proportionate consolidation. Equity accounting first became compulsory in 1983 and is applied to unconsolidated subsidiaries and associates. The concept of 'shared control' is not recognized in Japanese accounting.

16.5.5 EU

Proportionate consolidation for joint ventures and equity accounting for associates did not exist in Germany prior to 1985 (the Accounting Directives Act implementing the Seventh Directive). Subsequently joint ventures have been given the choice of either approach, with proportionate consolidation being widely used.[58] In France proportionate consolidation is compulsory for joint ventures.[59] The Netherlands allows joint ventures the choice but most use proportionate consolidation.[60]

The UK did not take up the proportionate consolidation option in the Seventh Directive and so equity accounting is required for associates and joint ventures. If the joint ventures are quasi-subsidiaries then they are consolidated as full subsidiaries under FRS 5. Where equity accounting is applied to joint ventures, it is the 'gross equity method' set out in FRS 9 *Associates and joint ventures*. This gives the same profit as the normal equity method but gives more detail about assets and liabilities of the joint venture.

16.6 Segment reporting

Consolidated accounts are often the only sets of financial statements presented to users. The financial statements of the individual companies within a group may be available through a registration system but they are not readily accessible and are not publicized by companies. Consolidated financial statements have the benefit of bringing a large group down to a manageable size for reporting as a single entity. They have the disadvantage that they lose the detail of the separate component parts of the group. The enthusiastic investor might decide to seek out and read the financial statements of all

---

[54] IAS 31 (2004) paragraph 30.
[55] IAS 31 (2004) paragraph 38.
[56] IAS 31 (2004) paragraph 34.
[57] IAS 31 (2004) paragraph 35.
[58] Ordelheide (2001) pp. 1383, 1409.
[59] Richard (2001) p. 1176.
[60] Klaassen (2001) pp. 2036–2037.

the companies in a group. However that would be time consuming and there could be problems of gaining access to information about subsidiaries overseas from the parent. Segmental reporting is a half-way house in restoring the detail available in the separate financial statements, but with a selective approach that focuses on what users need.

16.6.1 What to look for in segment reporting

16.6.1.1 Evaluating performance

Obviously, there is no point in making companies disclose additional information if it does not tell users something new and of interest. One question therefore is to ask: Does segment information tell the user something that is not obvious from the group accounts? The answer will depend upon the degree of diversification of the company. There would be little benefit in making a company report line of industry data if it operated only in one industry or report geographical data if it operated in only one country. But there would also be little point if it operates in several industries or countries that are very similar to each other so each segment resembles the other, or if it was so diversified that it resembled the entire world, so that it could not reduce its risk by changing its mix of operations. However, most companies fall somewhere between these two extremes, operating in a relatively small number of industries or countries with each industry or country varying in some important way(s) from the others. Different industries and countries are usually expected to perform differently. They have different profit potentials, growth opportunities and degrees of and types of risk, different rates of return on investment and different capital needs. For example, a company that operates in a fairly stable market with well-understood and relatively simple technology, such as food processing, would face relatively little risk and so should have lower but more stable profits than, for example, a biotechnology company which is dependent upon high levels of risky research and constantly changing, extremely complex and expensive technology. Therefore, the past performance of a company and its future prospects can usually only be understood in the context of information on the importance of each class of business and geographical area that the company operates in.

16.6.1.2 Relevance to stakeholders

The second question is: Is this extra information of use? Many users of financial accounts will be interested in the performance and prospects of one particular part of the company. For example, employees' security of employment, pay and conditions will generally be more directly dependent upon the performance of the specific division they work for than the performance of the whole group. Similarly, host governments will be primarily interested in the performance of that part of the group that is located in their countries. Customers, suppliers and creditors will be most interested in the subsidiary that they have contracted with. All of these users will therefore want disaggregated information. Segment information, while far from perfect, goes some way towards meeting these needs. Such information will be especially important for users such as trade unions and developing country host governments, who lack the power to demand the information they want.

Shareholders, in contrast, invest in the company as a whole and it is therefore the performance and prospects of the entire company that they are interested in. Investing in a diversified company is similar to investing in a unit trust which in turns invests in a number of individual companies. Here, the investor is directly affected by the returns of the portfolio as a whole. However, knowledge of the individual stocks is important as it helps the investor assess the risks and likely returns of the portfolio as a whole and helps them judge whether or not that particular portfolio is for them. Similarly, a single company may be thought of as a portfolio of segments. While the shareholder cannot invest in the individual segments, knowledge of the performance and prospects of the constituent parts helps the shareholder to understand the risk and returns of the group.

An investor will want to know many things about a company. One obvious question of interest to all investors should be the question of whether or not its past performance is satisfactory. There are many ways of tackling this question, but one place to start is to compare the company's performance with that of similar companies. Segment data may allow the user to compare the performance of individual segments with non-diversified companies or with segments of other diversified companies. An idea of the success of the entire company can then be built-up from these individual segment assessments. Users may also be able to combine company specific information with external information. This should help them to assess the future prospects of the company. For example, knowledge regarding the geographical sales of a company can be combined with know-ledge of the growth prospects of particular countries or regions to aid in the more accu-rate prediction of future sales.[61]

16.6.1.3 Defining segments

To create segment reports, a company can break down its operations in any number of ways, although there should be some logical reason for the choices made. The two most common categories are segmentation by industry or type of business (often called line of business or LoB) and by geographical area (either in terms of location of operations or location of customers). If both categories are used then either two separate tables are required or a large table is used (a 'matrix') with one category running vertically and the other running horizontally. This requires very small print and soon overflows a page and so most groups have separate tables for each category of segmentation.

16.6.2 IFRS

This section describes the development of IAS 14 from an encouraging but somewhat flexible original version to a more precisely defined and extensive revision issued in 1997.

16.6.2.1 History of IAS 14[62]

The original version of IAS 14, issued in 1981, used geographical segments and industry segments but called for relatively little information on each. It required only segment sales (with internal and external sales shown separately), operating results and identifi-able assets. This was supplemented by a reconciliation statement explaining the differ-ence between the group results reported and the sum of the segment results when these differed, plus information on the composition of each segment and the basis for deter-mining the value of any inter-segment transfers.

The original IAS 14 received increasing amounts of criticisms over the years for three rea-sons. First, the number of items of information disclosed was thought to be inadequate. Secondly, and, more importantly, it contained relatively little guidance on either identify-ing a segment or measuring the items reported. In consequence, identical companies could have used discretion to produce very difference segments and very different numbers of

---

[61] See for example Hermann (1996), Roberts (1989).
[62] See Introduction to IAS 14 (1997), IN1 to IN 14.

segments.[63] Finally, it also ignored the internal structure of an enterprise. If the internal structure is not organized along a geographical and a line-of-business basis, it can sometimes be very expensive to produce the required information. Companies may even have to redesign information systems to the extent that the costs may outweigh the benefits. Indeed, it is not even clear that in all cases line-of-business and geographical segment information is going to be particularly useful. It might be that the enterprise is organized in a different way for very good and logical reasons and that reporting on this basis would also be more logical and useful.

These types of consideration led the IASC, in consultation with North American standard-setters, to review its standard. The revised IAS 14 was issued in 1997. While it did not go as far as those of either the US or Canada, it involved some substantial changes which changed both the method of identification of segments and the disclosure requirements. In particular it focused on the internal reporting system and the relative risks and returns as being the key features that distinguish segments.

16.6.2.2 Main requirements of IAS 14 (1997)

A *reportable segment* is a business segment or a geographical segment.[64] One of these is the *primary segment* and the other is the *secondary segment*. The dominant source and nature of an entity's *risks and rewards* determines which is primary and which is secondary.[65] The internal organization and management structure and the system of reporting to the board of directors and the chief executive officer is normally the basis for identifying the dominant source and nature of risks and rewards.[66] If the company's risks and returns are strongly affected by differences in both geographical areas and industries, then both types of segments will be regarded as primary segments.[67]

A *business segment* is a distinguishable component of an entity that is engaged in providing an individual product or service or a group of related products or services. A *geographical segment* is a distinguishable component of an entity that is engaged in providing products or services within a particular economic environment. In both cases the segment is distinguished by risks and returns that are different from those of other business segments.[68]

For each *primary segment*, companies must disclose:[69]

- revenue from sales to external customers,
- revenue from sales to other segments,
- operating result from continuing operations,
- operating result from discontinued operations,
- total carrying amount of segment assets,
- total segment liabilities,
- capital expenditure (on an accrual basis, not a cash basis),
- depreciation and amortization of segment assets,
- total amount of significant non-cash expenses, other than depreciation and amortization,
- aggregate of the entity's share of profit or losses of associates, joint ventures and investments if these are within the segment.

---

[63] See for example Gray and Radebaugh (1984), Street *et al.* (2000).
[64] IAS 14 (1997) paragraph 9.
[65] IAS 14 (1997) paragraph 26.
[66] IAS 14 (1997) paragraph 26.
[67] IAS 14 (1997) paragraph 29.
[68] IAS 14 (1997) paragraph 9.
[69] IAS 14 (1997) paragraphs 58–67.

For each *secondary segment* the disclosures are specified as:[70]

- revenue from external customers,
- carrying amounts of segment assets,
- capital expenditure.

The *accounting policies* used for all items should be the same across all segments and should be the same as those used for external reporting.[71]

16.6.2.3 Problems of segment identification

If the operating divisions of a company are not suitable for segment reporting purposes it can often be difficult to decide exactly what the segments should be. Although IAS 14 lays out fairly unambiguous disclosure rules, this is of little use if the company is left free to decide for itself if it has any reportable segments, and if so, how many and of what type. This problem may be compounded by the unwillingness of companies to disclose segment information for a variety of reasons. If the segments reported do not reflect the operating structure of the company and the information is not collected for internal purposes, it may be expensive to collect, collate, audit and disseminate. Alternatively, segment data may highlight particularly poor or good performance. Indeed, this question of the competitive disadvantage of reporting segment information has in the past been claimed to be major problem by a significant number of companies.[72]

IAS 14 gives detailed guidance on the identification of segments.

A *business segment* is a distinguishable component of an enterprise that is engaged in providing an individual product or service or a related group of products or services and that is subject to risks and returns that are different from those of other business segments. Factors that should be considered in determining whether products and services are related include:

- the nature of the products or services;
- the nature of the production processes;
- the types or class of customer for the products or services;
- the methods used to distribute the products or provide the services; and
- if applicable, the nature of the regulatory environment, for example, banking, insurance, or public utilities.[73]

A *geographical segment* is a distinguishable component of an enterprise that is engaged in providing products or services within a particular economic environment and that is subject to risks and returns that are different from those of components operating in other economic environments. Factors that should be considered in identifying geographical segments include:

- similarity of economic and political conditions;
- relationships between operations in different geographical areas;
- proximity of operations;
- special risks associated with operations in a particular area;
- exchange control regulations; and
- the underlying currency risks.[74]

---

[70] IAS 14 (1997) paragraphs 68–72.

[71] IAS 14 (1997) paragraph 44.

[72] Edwards and Smith (1996).

[73] IAS 14 (1997) paragraph 9.

[74] Ibid.

While IAS 14 provides what appears to be quite specific guidance it is clear that segment identification is still very much left to the discretion of companies and the guidance offered is simply that – guidance and not rules. This means that, perhaps inevitably, the company which wishes to provide minimal disclosures, or 'good news' only, may manipulate its segment disclosures to achieve these objectives. However, the scope to manipulate disclosure has been reduced as the standard also requires the disclosure of the changes made. If the company changes the policies adopted, it must disclose the nature of the changes, the reasons for them and their effect.[75] If it changes the segments disclosed, the comparative figures should be restated to reflect the changes.[76]

While the guidance regarding the identification of segments will often be difficult to apply in practice, the rules subsequently used to decide whether or not an identified segment should be separately reported are very specific.[77]

A segment should be reported if

- its total revenue is at least 10 per cent of the group's total revenues (ie both internal and external revenues); or
- its result (profit or loss) is at least 10 per cent of the total of all segments in profit or loss, whichever is the greater; or
- its assets are at least 10 per cent of total segment assets.

The sum of the reportable segments must exceed 75 per cent of consolidated revenue. If the total is not 75 per cent then further segments must be identified, even if they fail the 10 per cent test, until 75 per cent is reached. The remaining small segments can then be combined into an 'other' segment (which could therefore be as large as 25 per cent in total).

16.6.3 US

While the US standard FAS 131 is similar to IAS 14, there are two important differences. First, while FAS 131 also uses the 'management structure' approach for determining the primary segments, it allows more flexibility in the design of the management structure. The primary segments may be defined by a combination of both geographical spread and line-of-business, or they may be defined on any other basis employed by the enterprise. Secondly, FAS 131 does not require consistent earnings or assets definitions or accounting methods across the primary segments. Instead, they must be based upon the accounting rules and definitions used for internal management purposes. However, the problem of lack of comparability within any one enterprise is reduced by the additional requirements to explain both differences in the measurement of segments and total profits or losses and assets, and differences in the allocations across segments. Companies must also disclose, where relevant, a reconciliation statement explaining the differences between segment and consolidated figures.

Nestlé (Exhibit 16.15) provides an example of segments following the US approach, with the primary segments being based upon a combination of line-of-business and geographical segments.

---

[75] IAS 14 (1997) paragraphs 77–78.

[76] IAS 14 (1997) paragraph 79.

[77] IAS 14 (1997) paragraphs 34–43.

Exhibit 16.15 Segment disclosures, Nestlé

Segmental information

Segmental information disclosure is based upon two segment formats: the primary format reflects the Group's management structure, whereas the secondary format is product oriented. The primary segment format – by management responsibility and geographic area – represents the Group's management structure. The principal activity of the Group is the food business, which is managed through three geographic zones. Nestlé Waters, managed on a worldwide basis, is disclosed separately. The other activities encompass mainly pharmaceutical products as well as other food businesses, which are generally managed on a worldwide basis. The secondary segment format representing products is divided into six categories (segments).

NOTES

1. Segmental information
By management responsibility and geographic area

In millions of CHF	2003	2002	2003	2002
	Sales		EBITA	
Zone Europe[a]	28 574	28 068	3 561	3 442
Zone Americas	27 655	29 293	4 150	4 189
Zone Asia, Oceania and Africa	14 432	14 880	2 508	2 564
Nestlé Waters	8 066	7 720	782	696
Other activities[a],[b]	9 252	9 199	1 537	1 517
	87 979	89 160	12 538	12 408
Unallocated items[c]			(1 532)	(1 468)
EBITA			11 006	10 940

The analysis of sales by geographic area is stated by customer location. Inter-segment sales are not significant.

[a] Eismann, a frozen food distributor, has been reclassified from Zone Europe to Other activities because it is under a new management following the December 2003 announcement that this business, or at least a majority stake, has been put up for sale. 2002 comparative figures have been restated.
[b] Mainly Pharmaceutical products, Joint Ventures and "Trinks" (Germany).
[c] Mainly corporate expenses as well as research and development costs.

In millions of CHF	2003	2002	2003	2002
	Assets		Liabilities	
Zone Europe[a]	12 154	11 541	5 503	5 171
Zone Americas	9 643	9 567	3 205	3 500
Zone Asia, Oceania and Africa	6 071	6 139	1 829	2 271
Nestlé Waters	5 116	4 751	2 137	1 863
Other activities[a],[b]	3 730	3 585	1 539	1 497
	36 714	35 583	14 213	14 302
Unallocated items[d]	30 507	29 335	364	365
Eliminations	(1 026)	(841)	(1 026)	(841)
	66 195	64 077	13 551	13 826

[d] Corporate and research and development assets/liabilities, including goodwill.

In millions of CHF	2003	2002	2003	2002
	Capital expenditure		Depreciation of property, plant and equipment	
Zone Europe[a]	925	868	642	738
Zone Americas	739	904	674	732
Zone Asia, Oceania and Africa	541	584	364	398
Nestlé Waters	647	769	391	374
Other activities[a],[b]	375	322	215	196
	3 227	3 447	2 286	2 438
Unallocated items[e]	110	130	122	104
	3 337	3 577	2 408	2 542

[e] Corporate and research and development property, plant and equipment.

In millions of CHF	2003	2002	2003	2002
	Impairment of assets		Restructuring costs	
Zone Europe[a]	42	1 460	253	719
Zone Americas	43	228	98	302
Zone Asia, Oceania and Africa	81	355	56	27
Nestlé Waters	55	151	182	33
Other activities	1	2	9	24
	222	2 196	598	1 105
Unallocated items[c]			5	25
			603	1 130

[a] Eismann, a frozen food distributor, has been reclassified from Zone Europe to Other activities because it is under a new management following the December 2003 announcement that this business, or at least a majority stake, has been put for sale. 2002 comparative figures have been restated.
[b] Mainly Pharmaceutical products, Joint Ventures and "Trinks" (Germany).
[c] Corporate and research and development.

By product group

In millions of CHF	2003	2002	2003	2002
	Sales		EBITA	
Beverages	23 520	23 325	4 038	4 075
Milk products, nutrition and ice cream	23 283	23 376	2 796	2 756
Prepared dishes and cooking aids	16 068	15 834	1 884	1 712
Petcare	9 816	10 719	1 444	1 418
Chocolate, confectionery and biscuits	10 240	10 774	1 047	1 180
Pharmaceutical products	5 052	5 132	1 329	1 267
	87 979	89 160	12 538	12 408
Unallocated items[a]			(1 532)	(1 468)
EBITA			11 006	10 940

[a] Mainly corporate expenses as well as research and development costs.

Exhibit 16.15 *(Continued)*

In millions of CHF	2003	2002
	\multicolumn{2}{Assets}	
Beverages	11 237	11 283
Milk products, nutrition and ice cream	10 303	10 972
Prepared dishes and cooking aids	5 787	6 291
Petcare	3 481	3 790
Chocolate, confectionery and biscuits	5 208	5 403
Pharmaceutical products	2 708	2 847
	38 724	40 586

In millions of CHF	2003	2002
	Capital expenditure	
Beverages	936	1 004
Milk products, nutrition and ice cream	421	495
Prepared dishes and cooking aids	251	304
Petcare	254	284
Chocolate, confectionery and biscuits	208	285
Pharmaceutical products	86	101
	2 156	2 473
Administration, distribution, research and development	1 181	1 104
	3 337	3 577

In millions of CHF	2003	2002	2003	2002
	Impairment of assets		Restructuring costs	
Beverages	121	350	248	117
Milk products, nutrition and ice cream	63	612	128	388
Prepared dishes and cooking aids	14	275	60	104
Petcare	19	740	26	313
Chocolate, confectionery and biscuits	5	209	133	134
Pharmaceutical products	–	–	4	1
	222	2 186	599	1 057
Administration, distribution, research and development	–	10	4	73
	222	2 196	603	1130

Source: Nestlé annual report (2003), pp.19–22. www.ir.nestle.com

16.6.4 Japan

Some Japanese multinationals follow US GAAP and therefore apply the approach of FAS 131. Those which follow Japanese accounting rules have historically shown greater flexibility. Regulations applying from 1999 require industry segments, geographical segments and overseas sales, as part of the MOF Consolidation Regulation. A survey carried out in 1996/7 showed that the most frequently occurring disclosure was for two segments, with the highest number reported being five.[78] It may be that if you are reading the annual report of a Japanese company in English you will be seeing a US approach rather than the effect of the MOF Consolidation Regulation.

Examples of Japanese companies applying the US approach in 2004 were:

- Honda
- Nippon Telegraph and Telephone Corporation
- Nomura Holdings
- Toyota

16.6.5 EU

The Seventh Directive contained very little about segment reporting. Article 34(8) required turnover by activity and by geographical market. The information could be omitted if it was thought to be seriously prejudicial the company. It was therefore left to the standard-setters of member states to define the amount of detail expected. Generally the regulators in most member states did little more than repeat Article 34(8) in their rules. In the UK, SSAP 25 (1990) provided guidance on identifying segments and making disclosures but was very flexible on the definition of segments and the freedom to change definitions. It also allowed the 'seriously prejudicial' exclusion of the Seventh Directive. The ASB tried on more than one occasion to bring SSAP 25 to the level of IAS 14 but encountered lack of enthusiasm and did not pursue the matter.[79]

Disclosure of segment information was left largely to the discretion of the multinational groups themselves. As they moved into international capital markets they realized that segmental disclosure was important and responded to market demands by moving closer to, or even exceeding, IAS 14 and FAS 131.

Some of the most remarkable transformations have taken place in German companies. From a long-standing reputation for high secrecy, many German multinationals have moved to high transparency in segmental reporting. An example which brings out very detailed segment disclosure may be seen in the 2003 annual report (pp. 108–109) of the German company Bayer (www.bayer.com), reporting under IFRS. It is a broad matrix extending over a double page, containing segments and sub-segments across the page, and a mixture of data items and ratios down the page. This gives a very detailed table. It has the same level of detail for line-of-business and geographical segments (i.e. two sets of primary segments).

16.6.6 Research into segment reporting

Segmental data has provided an interesting motivation for research projects over many years. The main research interest lies in the identification of segments and the disclosures relating to segments. An example of this research is provided in Emmanuel and Garrod (2002) using data from UK companies in 1995. They linked their investigation of segment data to the concepts of 'relevance' and 'comparability' used in conceptual frameworks. They suggested that segmental data is relevant if it confirms the consolidated results. It is comparable if it provides data that are comparable within industry norms. They then calculated return on assets for the industry, the group, and the segments. They found that for a significant portion of the sample the levels of

---

[78] Kuroda (2001) p. 1880–1884.
[79] Wilson *et al.* (2001) p. 1443.

both relevance and comparability were low because of the choices made in identifying segments. They suggested that this might indicate a problem in allowing the management of companies to have discretion in identifying segments.

Illustration. Exhibit 16.16 sets out an illustrative analysis based on Unilever.

Exhibit 16.16 Extract from segment data, Unilever, analysed

	Savoury & dressings	Spreads	Health & beverages	Ice cream & frozen food	Home care	Personal care	Other
2003 Turnover (Euro million)							
At 2002 exch rate	9482	5419	4052	7517	8034	12784	412
At 2003 exch rate	8609	5028	3569	6994	7230	11153	359
2003 Trading results							
At 2002 exch rate	1500	910	595	1105	973	2179	95
At 2003 exch rate	1369	861	517	1035	896	1888	77
2002 Turnover							
At 2002 exch rate	9503	6216	4215	7456	8579	12245	546
2002 Trading results							
At 2002 exch rate	1381	849	510	706	854	1998	30
2003 Profit margin %							
At 2002 exch rate	15.8	16.8	14.7	14.7	12.1	17.0	23.1
At 2003 exch rate	15.9	17.1	14.5	14.8	12.4	16.9	21.4
Growth in sales %							
At 2002 exch rate	−0.2	−12.8	−3.9	0.8	−6.4	4.4	−24.5
At 2003 exch rate	−9.4	−19.1	−15.3	−6.2	−15.7	−8.9	−34.2

	Europe	North America	Africa, M.E. & Turkey	Asia & Pacific	Latin America
2003 Turnover	18208	9774	3276	7063	4372
2002 Turnover	19573	12446	3139	7679	5433
2003 Operating profit	2576	1101	422	1072	358
Profit margin %	14.1	11.3	12.9	15.1	8.1
Sales growth %	−7.0	−24.1	4.4	−8.05	−19.5

Source: www.unilever.com

Comment:
This company is far less industrially diversified than many large companies, with four of the seven LoB segments being food related and two being home and personal care. Despite this, some quite large differences can be seen in the profit margin and sales growth between the segments, while even larger differences are seen across the five geographical areas. It is also interesting to see the impact of multinationality as reflected in the impact of exchange rate changes. Unilever reports, for its industry segments, the figures used for internal management purposes, namely this year's figures adjusted to remove the impact of exchange rate changes since the prior year. Using these adjusted figures to calculate profit margins and sales changes results in even larger differences across the various segments.

Source: www.unilever.com

16.7 Foreign currency translation

Most companies will be affected in some way by changes in exchange rates. If they import goods or services, their costs will change because the prices paid in domestic currency will change. If they export goods or services, their revenues will change in one of two ways. If companies price goods in their domestic currency, the volume of sales will decrease if the domestic currency strengthens (becomes more expensive). If companies price goods in foreign currency then the amount received in domestic currency will fluctuate. Companies may face risk through borrowing or lending money in other currencies. They may have foreign currency investments or may trade in foreign currency contracts. The parent company must then decide how to use those figures for internal or management purposes and how to incorporate them in group accounts for external reporting purposes.

16.7.1 Issues in translation

The financial statements of overseas subsidiaries need to be restated in terms of the currency of the parent company before they can be consolidated as part of the group. Two questions arise:

- What rate of exchange should be used when translating accounting statement?
- How do we report gains and losses resulting from the process of translation?

16.7.1.1 Relationship between parent and subsidiary

One factor relevant to answering both questions is the nature of the relationship between the parent and its foreign subsidiary. In some cases the subsidiary is quite independent in its day-to-day operations, having a local management structure in which operating decisions are taken. The subsidiary raises finance on its own initiative and retains profit for reinvestment after paying a dividend to the parent. Such a subsidiary is seen by the parent company as an investment in equity, with the emphasis on growth of the ownership interest through generation of profit. In other cases the subsidiary is closely controlled from the parent, having a local management which operates under direction from the parent company. Such a subsidiary is seen by the parent company as a branch activity where monetary resources (cash and loans) are provided to the subsidiary as needed and surplus monetary resources are returned to the parent on a regular basis.

Both of these types of relationship leave the parent exposed to fluctuations in foreign exchange rates but there is a different type of exposure. In the first case the parent has regard for the investment in equity and whether it is increasing or decreasing in terms of the home currency. It may also arrange the timing of dividend payments to avoid temporary weaknesses in the home currency. In the second case there is a constant flow of monetary resources to and from the parent and so there is exposure in terms of the balance of monetary assets and monetary liabilities held in the subsidiary at any point in time. These different views of exposure to foreign currency fluctuations have led to different views of the process of translation, as explained in the rest of this section.

The parent company's view of the translation process is also affected by the relative strength of the currency of the parent company compared with that of the subsidiary. Parent companies do not like to report losses, particularly where they feel that the losses are caused by factors beyond their control. If choice exists they may prefer to use a method of translation which avoids giving an impression of loss. Recognizing this characteristic of multinationals helps us to understand the positions taken by them when an accounting standard is in the course of preparation.

In the absence of a standard, companies could in practice choose between two exchange rates, the *historic rate*, being the rate of exchange when the transaction took place, and the *closing rate*, being the rate of exchange at the balance sheet date. In theory, it might be reasonable to consider *future exchange rates*, defined as the expected rate of exchange when the obligation will be met. In practice the high degree of uncertainty about *future exchange rates* is regarded as too great for these to be used, so that the choice lies between the historic rate and the closing rate method.

16.7.1.2 Translating the balance sheet

Before accounting standards were developed, various systems were developed and applied at different times and in different countries. Two which caused particularly intensive debate about their relative merits and limitations were:

- the temporal method,
- the closing rate (net investment) method.

Each one makes a different assumption about exposure to the risk of a movement in exchange rates. This section explain the assumption made under each system, and the rate of exchange to be applied.

Temporal method

There are cases in which the affairs of a foreign enterprise are so closely interlinked with those of the investing company that its results may be regarded as being more dependent on the economic environment of the investing company's currency than on that of its own reporting currency. In such a case the financial statements of the foreign enterprise should be included in the consolidated financial statements as if all its transactions had been entered into by the investing company itself in its own currency. For this purpose the temporal method of translation should be used; the mechanics of this method are identical with those used in preparing the accounts of an individual company.

All the available evidence should be considered in determining whether the currency of the investing company is the dominant currency in the economic environment in which the foreign enterprise operates. Amongst the factors to be taken into account will be:

- the extent to which the cash flows of the enterprise have a direct impact upon those of the investigating company;
- the extent to which the functioning of the enterprise is dependent directly upon the investing company;
- the currency in which the majority of the trading transactions are denominated;
- the major currency to which the operation is exposed in its financing structure.

Examples of situations where the temporal method may be appropriate are where the foreign enterprise:

- acts as a selling agency receiving stocks of goods from the investing company and remitting the proceeds back to the company; or
- produces a raw material or manufactures parts of sub-assemblies which are then shipped to the investing company for inclusion in its own products; or
- is located overseas for tax, exchange control or similar reasons to act as a means of raising finance for other companies in the group.

Rate of exchange to be applied

The rate of exchange to be used will be the one that is appropriate with regards to when the transaction was undertaken or when the valuation process being used in the financial reports took place.

- Cash, short-term debtors and short-term creditors are translated at the closing rate.
- Other assets and liabilities may be translated at current or historic rates depending on how the item has been valued in the original financial statements. If they are valued at historic cost then the historic rate will be used. If they are valued at current (or expected future) market price the closing rate of exchange will be used. The rate of exchange is sensitive to the underlying basis of valuation of non-monetary items.

Closing rate/net investment method

The closing rate method recognizes that the investment of a company is in the net worth of its foreign enterprise rather than a direct investment in the individual assets and liabilities of that enterprise. The foreign enterprise will normally have net current assets and fixed assets which may be financed partly by local currency borrowings. In its day-to-day operations the foreign enterprise is not normally dependent on the reporting currency of the parent company. The parent company may look forward to a stream of dividends but the net investment will remain until the business is liquidated or the investment is sold.

Rate of exchange to be applied

All assets and liabilities are translated at the closing rate of exchange. Exchange differences will arise if this rate differs from that ruling at the previous balance sheet date or at the date of any subsequent capital injection (or reduction).

Exhibit 16.17 compares the temporal and closing rate methods of translating the balance sheet of a subsidiary into the currency of the parent company.

The example ends with a gain or loss on translation shown in the reserves of shareholders' equity as a balancing figure in the balance sheet. The key accounting question arising at this point is: 'Should this gain or loss on exchange be treated as part of current year's profit or as a movement on reserve?' The argument in favour of using the profit and loss account is that the gain or loss relates to the current period and so should be reported as part of the profit. The argument against using the profit and loss account is that the foreign exchange effects can distort the underlying trends of business activity. The treatment of the translation gain or loss depends on other assumptions about the business and so varies according to the model chosen. In the previous version of IAS 21, and in US and UK standards, the gain or loss on translation has been reported as a movement on reserves under the closing rate method and as part of the

Exhibit 16.17 Temporal and Closing rate compared

Hill plc ('Hill'), a company based in Home country, set up a wholly-owned subsidiary, Valley Inc ('Valley'), in Away country on 1 January Year 1. The share capital of Valley Inc is A$3,000,000. Initial information about Hill and Valley is provided in Step 1.

Step 1   Initial information about Hill and Valley on 1 January Year 1

The rate of exchange on 1 January Year 1 was H$1 = A$12. Hill plc subscribed H$250,000 for the share capital of Valley Inc.

On 1 January Year 1, Valley carried out two transactions:

(a) raised a long term loan amounting to A$1,000,000;
(b) bought plant and machinery costing A$3,500,000 and having a useful life of ten years, to be depreciated on a straight-line basis.

The balance sheet of Valley on 1 January Year 1 is translated as shown in Step 2. The rate of exchange used is the same for both systems of translation because the historical rate equals the current rate at the date on which the transaction takes place.

Step 2   Valley: Balance sheet at 1 January Year 1

	A$000s	Conversion factor	H$000s
Plant and machinery	3,500	1/12	292
Cash	500	1/12	42
	4,000		334
Long-term loan	(1,000)	1/12	(84)
	3,000		250
Share capital	3,000	1/12	250

The investment in share capital of Valley is included in the balance sheet of Hill at the amount of H$250,000m.

The business of Valley operates during Year 1. The rates of exchange between the H$ and the A$ vary during the year as shown in Step 3.

Step 3   Rates of exchange rate between the H$ and the A$ during Year 1

Date	Exchange rate	Comment
1 January Year 1	H$1 = A$12	This is the historic rate (hr) for fixed assets and the long-term loan.
Purchase of goods held as closing stock	H$1 = A$10.5	This is the historic rate (hr) for the closing stock.
31 December Year 1	H$1 = A$10	This is the closing rate.

The balance sheet of Valley in A$ is shown in the first column of Step 4. It is then translated into H$ using each of the two systems of translation described earlier.

Step 4   Balance sheet of Valley at 31 December Year 1 in its own currency and translated using closing rate and temporal systems of translation

Balance sheet at 31 December Year 1	Own currency A$000s	Calculation	Translations to parent's currency Closing rate H$000s	Calculation	Temporal H$000s
Fixed assets	3,150	/10	315	/12	263
Stock	1,050	/10	105	/10.5	100
Cash and net current monetary items (creditors and debtors)	200	/10	20	/10	20
Long-term loan	(1,000)		(100)		(100)
	3,400		340		283

▶

Share capital at					
1 Jan Year 1	3,000	/12	250	/12	250
Reserves (Profit for year		Balancing		Balancing	
to 31 December Year 1)	400	figure	90	figure	33
	3,400		340		283

Each system of translation uses a different combination of rate of exchange for various elements of financial statements.

Both these translation methods will leave the resulting financial statement out of balance. This creates a need for a 'balancing figure' to be given a suitable description. It is normally reported in reserves and described as *Reserves at the balance sheet date*.

The rates of exchange used in each method are summarized in Step 5.

Step 5   Translation rates of exchange and treatment of gain or loss on exchange

Balance sheet item	Translation methods	
	Closing rate	Temporal
Cash and net current monetary items (creditors and debtors)	cr	cr
Stock and work in progress	cr	hr or cr*
Fixed assets	cr	hr or cr*
Long-term monetary items (creditors and debtors)	cr	cr
Ownership equity (share capital and reserves) when subsidiary acquired	hr	hr
Increase in reserves since acquisition	Balancing figure	Balancing figure

*In the temporal method when stocks and fixed assets are valued on historic cost terms the historic rate (hr) will be used. When current market value is used (replacement/current cost/net realizable value) the closing rate (cr) will be applied.

Key: hr = historical rate; cr = closing rate

If the sum of opening reserves plus profit for the year does not equal this balancing figure an adjustment is needed in the form of a *gain on exchange* or *loss on exchange*.

current year's profit or loss under the temporal method. This increased the non-comparability of the outcome of foreign currency translations and gave further opportunities for earnings management.

16.7.2 IAS 21

IAS 21 *The effects of changes in foreign exchange rates* was first issued in 1983. For many years IAS 21 allowed both the temporal method and the closing rate method of translation of the financial statements of foreign subsidiaries, reflecting the diversity of national practices. It tried to achieve comparability by setting conditions on the circumstances in which each could be applied. This reflected the US and UK standards, both of which set circumstances in which the temporal method should be used, and circumstances in which the closing rate method should be used. However in the US in particular the SEC was aware that companies tended to change their use of accounting method whenever exchange rates strengthened or weakened, and there appeared to be a great deal of flexibility in the choices available to each company.

16.7.2.1 Definitions

The revision of IAS 21 in 2003 (to be applied to annual periods beginning on or after 1 January 2005) cuts through all the problems of flexibility and makes the process of translation much more straightforward, without destroying the underlying concepts of the previous versions.

One key to the simplicity of the standard lies in the ideas of 'functional currency' and 'presentation currency' which replace the previous idea of 'reporting currency'. The other key to simplicity lies in the focus on the underlying economy that determines the pricing of transactions. IAS 21 now takes the view that an 'integral' foreign subsidiary could not have a functional currency that differs from that of the parent. This eliminates another source of variability in translation of the results of foreign subsidiaries for consolidation with the parent's financial statements. It allows the basic principle of the temporal method to be preserved without allowing companies the scope for creative accounting through redefining the functional currency of a subsidiary. The economic facts drive the accounting.

The *functional currency* is the currency of the primary economic environment in which the entity operates.[80]

The *presentation currency* is the currency in which the financial statements are presented. The company is allowed to choose whatever presentation currency it wishes.[81]

Exhibit 16.18 illustrates these definitions by way of examples.

Exhibit 16.18 **Illustration of definitions**

Functional currency of a dependent subsidiary

A multinational parent company based in the US sets up a manufacturing subsidiary in an export-zone in Malaysia. The parent company supplies the capital, debt, management expertise and the raw materials and then exports the goods out of the country when manufacture is completed. The subsidiary controls neither its inputs nor its outputs. In this case, any exchange rate changes between Malaysian currency and the US dollar will have an immediate effect upon the subsidiary's cash flows and will also affect the subsidiary's monetary assets and liabilities (cash, accounts receivable and payable, and loans). In this case the functional currency would be the currency of the parent, which is the US dollar.

Functional currency and economic market

A parent company based in France sets up a subsidiary in India to produce oil from an oil field and then supply the amount demanded by the parent at current market prices. Given that world oil prices are stated in US dollars this subsidiary may be more dependent upon US dollar exchange rates than it is on the Indian rupee . Any change in the value of the dollar would have an immediate effect upon the subsidiary's cash flows and the US dollar is the functional currency of the subsidiary even if neither it nor its parent company is in the US.

Presentation currency

Gamma is based in Italy. Gamma has a US parent and is dependent on the US parent. Gamma buys and sells goods using US dollars and regards the US dollar as its *functional currency*. The day-to-day accounting records are maintained in dollars. However Gamma reports to its own shareholders in euro. In the terminology of IAS 21, the euro is the *presentation currency* for the financial statements of Gamma. The US dollar is the currency of the economic environment in which Gamma operates. The parent can not choose to change the definition of Gamma's *functional currency* to the euro. This eliminates one possibility for 'earnings management' that some parent companies have used previously.

---

[80] IAS 21 (2003) paragraph 8.
[81] Ibid.

IAS 21 sets procedures for reporting foreign currency transactions in the functional currency. It also sets procedures for translating the financial statements of a foreign operation for inclusion in the financial statements of the reporting entity. The same procedures must be used for translating the results and financial position from the entity's functional currency to its presentation currency.

16.7.2.2 Transactions

The accounting treatment for transactions under IAS 21 is relatively straightforward. This section gives three examples of transactions:

- a foreign currency monetary item (Exhibit 16.19);
- a non-monetary item measured in historical cost (Exhibit 16.20); and
- a long-term loan made to a foreign subsidiary (Exhibit 16.21).

The explanation of the treatment of the unrealized gain or loss in the consolidated financial statements, as in Exhibit 16.21, is based on the special relationships within a group.

Exhibit 16.19	Foreign currency, monetary item

AB Inc is based in the US and its functional currency is the dollar. The company borrowed €2m on a three-year loan from a bank in a European country on 1 July Year 1. The rate of exchange on that date was $1.22 = €1. At the balance sheet date, 31 December Year 1, the rate of exchange is $1.20 = €1.

On initial recognition the liability is recorded by AB Inc using the spot rate at the date of the transaction. The loan is recorded at $2.44m.

At the balance sheet date the liability is translated using the closing rate of $1.20 = €1.[82] It is shown in the balance sheet as $2.40m. This means that AB Inc has benefited from the stronger dollar at the end of the year. It would require fewer dollars to repay the loan which is fixed in euros. However the loan has not actually been repaid. There is an unrealized gain of $40,000. This is reported in the profit or loss of AB Inc.

Exhibit 16.20	Foreign currency, non-monetary item at historical cost

AB Inc is based in the US and its functional currency is the dollar. The company purchased a fixed asset from a European country on 1 July Year 1. The price is €2m. The rate of exchange on the date of purchase is $1.22 = €1. At the balance sheet date, 31 December Year 1, the rate of exchange is $1.20 = €1.

On initial recognition the transaction is recorded by AB Inc using the spot exchange rate at the date of the transaction. The asset is recorded at $2.44m. This is the cost base that is used for depreciation calculations.[83]

At each balance sheet date the fixed asset is translated using the exchange rate at the date of the transaction, which is $1.22 = €1 in our example. The rate of exchange at the balance sheet date has no relevance.[84]

---

[82] IAS 21 (2003) paragraph 23(a).
[83] IAS 21 (2003) paragraph 21.
[84] IAS 21 (2003) paragraphs 23(c) and 24.

Exhibit 16.21 Long-term loan to a foreign subsidiary

AB Inc is based in the US and its functional currency is the dollar. The company has a subsidiary, MN SA, located in a European country. MN SA owes €2m to AB Inc for management advice on capital projects. AB Inc has allowed MN SA to regard this as a long-term loan which will not be repaid until MN SA ceases to be a subsidiary of AB Inc. The rate of exchange on 1 July Year 1, when the long-term loan agreement started, was $1.22 = €1. At the balance sheet date, 31 December Year 1, the rate of exchange is $1.20 = €1.

On initial recognition the long-term asset is recorded by AB Inc using the spot exchange rate at the date of the transaction. The amount of the asset is $2.44m. At the balance sheet date the asset is measured at the closing rate $1.20 = €1. The amount of the asset is now $2.40m. There is an unrealized loss of $40,000. It is recorded as a loss in the separate profit and loss statement of AB Inc but is recorded as a separate component of equity in the consolidated financial statements of the AB Group. It is recognized in profit or loss of the group when the subsidiary is disposed of.[85]

Exhibits 16.19 and 16.20 show that there is different treatment for a monetary item and a non-monetary item. A gain or loss on a monetary item is recognized but no loss or gain on a non-monetary item is recognized. This unsymmetrical treatment of monetary and non-monetary transactions can have a significant and potentially misleading effect on the group's reported figures if the monetary item is being used to fund part of the net investment in a foreign entity. For example, a group will often purchase a foreign subsidiary with a combination of equity and locally raised long-term debt, raised by the parent company. The interest on the long-term debt and the repayment of the debt is all based on the foreign subsidiary's local currency cash flows. No monies are ever transferred to or from the parent from the initial loan or to pay interest or repay the loan. As such, the loan is effectively cushioned from and unaffected by subsequent exchange rate changes. Yet, if the monetary item was treated using the approach in Exhibit 16.19, the group would report a profit or loss in the consolidated account. This would be misleading as a loss implies a fall in the wealth of the group's shareholders and a profit implies an increase in their wealth while, in this case, the group's shareholders are unaffected by the change in the reported value of the foreign debt. Therefore IAS 21 requires that, in this situation, any gain or loss on the long-term monetary item should be recognized as a separate component of equity in the balance sheet rather than as income or expense in the income statement.

It is important to note that these three examples are discussed separately. If the transactions were combined in some way, perhaps to hedge against the risks of foreign currency fluctuations, they would come within the scope of IAS 39. There would then be a series of tests to examine whether the transactions could be matched as hedges rather than being accounted for separately.

16.7.2.3 Translation of a foreign operation[86]

When a group contains individual entities with different functional currencies, the results and financial position of each entity are expressed in common currency so that consolidated financial statements may be presented.[87] This process is called *translation*.

---

[85] IAS 21 (2003) paragraph 32.
[86] IAS 21 paragraphs 44–47.
[87] IAS 21 paragraph 38.

The results and financial position of the foreign operation are translated as follows:[88]

- assets and liabilities in each balance sheet presented shall be translated at the closing rate at the date of that balance sheet;
- income and expenses for each income statement presented shall be translated at exchange rates ruling at the date of the transaction (the average rate for the period may be used as a practical approximation provided the exchange rates do not fluctuate significantly[89]);
- all resulting exchange differences shall be recognised as a separate component of equity.

These exchange differences will result from:[90]

- translating income and expenses at the exchange rates at the date of the transactions, while translating assets and liabilities at the closing rate;
- translating the opening net assets at a closing rate that differs from the previous closing rate.

16.7.2.4 Hyperinflation

IAS 21 (2003) was used to clarify ambiguity between IAS 21 and IAS 29 on the treatment of hyperinflation where translation is also required.

The term *hyperinflation* is used to describe a situation of very high rates of inflation where the purchasing power of money is diminishing rapidly during an accounting period. Because exchange rates tend to reflect the relative inflation of different countries, the exchange rate of the hyperinflationary country will weaken in relation to low-inflation countries.

There is no ready definition of hyperinflation but some characteristics of hyperinflationary economies are set out in IAS 29:[91]

- The general population prefers to hold its wealth in the form of non-monetary assets or in a more stable foreign currency.
- Sales and purchases on credit take place on terms that allow for an expected loss of purchasing power in the short term.
- Interest rates, wages and prices are linked to a price index.
- The cumulative inflation rate over three years is approaching, or exceeds, 100 per cent.

IAS 29 requires adjustment for inflation. It has been interpreted flexibly by companies so that some have adjusted for inflation and then translated, while others have translated and then adjusted for inflation. This has led to some earnings management and non-comparable results. IAS 21 gives the clarification that when an entity's functional currency is the currency of a hyperinflationary economy, the entity shall restate its financial statements in accordance with IAS 29 before applying the translation process.[92] IAS 21 explains the process of translation to be used.[93] The results and financial position of an

---

[88] IAS 21 paragraph 39.
[89] IAS 21 paragraph 40.
[90] IAS 21 paragraph 41.
[91] IAS 29 *Financial Reporting in Hyper-inflationary Economies.*
[92] IAS 21 paragraph 43.
[93] IAS 21 paragraphs 42–43.

entity whose functional currency is the currency of a hyperinflationary economy shall be translated into a different presentation currency using the following procedures:

- all amounts shall be translated at the closing rate at the date of the most recent balance sheet, except that
- when amounts are translated into the currency of a non-hyperinflationary economy, comparative amounts shall be those that were presented as current year amounts in the relevant prior year statements (i.e. not adjusted for subsequent changes in the price level or subsequent changes in exchange rates).

16.7.3 US

The US standard on foreign currency translation is FAS 52. It is substantially similar in approach to IAS 21 although the detailed terminology and guidance differ. The creation of FAS 52 in the US, SSAP 20 in the UK and the original version of IAS 21 in the 1980s could be seen as an early example of the convergence process at work,[94] or it could be taken as an example of Anglo-American dominance of IFRS.

16.7.4 Japan

A standard issued in 1979 created a 'modified temporal' approach at a time when the US was still using the temporal method under FAS 8 (predecessor of FAS 52), giving an example of US influence modified to Japanese views. One of the modifications was to adjust assets and liabilities for the translation difference, rather than adjust shareholders' equity. In 1995 a new Foreign Currency Standard was issued, based essentially on the closing rate method. The translation adjustment was reported through a 'translation adjustment account' in either the asset or liability section of the balance sheet (see Exhibit 16.22). In 1999 the BADC Foreign Currency Standards were further amended to show the translation adjustment account in the shareholders' equity section of the balance sheet. This, and other changes in detail, removed significant conflicts between Japanese accounting standards and IFRS.[95]

| Exhibit 16.22 | Translation adjustment account, KDDI |

e. Foreign currency translation

All monetary assets and liabilities denominated in foreign currencies, whether long-term or short-term, are translated into Japanese yen at the exchange rates prevailing at the balance sheet date. Resulting gains and losses are included in net profit or loss for the period. Then, all assets and liabilities of foreign subsidiaries and affiliates are translated into Japanese yen at the exchange rates prevailing at the balance sheet date. Shareholders' equity at the beginning of the year is translated into Japanese yen at the historical rates. Profit and loss accounts for the year are translated into Japanese yen using the average exchange rate during the year. The resulting differences in yen amounts are presented as minority interests and foreign currency translation adjustments in shareholders' equity.

Source: KDDI annual report (2004), pp. 40–41. www.kddi.com

---

[94] Wilson *et al.* (2001) p. 556.
[95] Ordelheide (2001) pp. 1848–1849.

16.7.5 EU

Foreign currency translation is not covered in the Seventh Directive, leaving flexibility for national regulators and for multinational companies in making choices and in varying approaches from one year to the next. In France under the 'second methodology' of 1999, the closing rate is used for independent subsidiaries but the monetary/non-monetary method (similar to the temporal method under historical cost accounting) is used for dependent subsidiaries.[96] Prior to the 'second methodology' the approach in France was highly flexible. In Germany, prior to GAS 14 (which is similar to IAS 21, see also section 10.3.3) there was considerable flexibility in the choice of the translation method used and the location of the translation gains and losses. Despite the legislative flexibility, most companies used the closing rate method.[97] In the UK the standard SSAP 20 *Foreign currency translation*, issued in 1983, is compatible with the approach taken in IAS 21. In The Netherlands the guidance from the RJ (see section 10.3.4) largely follows IAS 21.[98] The terminology and detailed guidance in each vary but the accounting outcomes are comparable. In the UK the Statement of Total Recognised Gains and Losses (STRGL) highlights the effects of exchange rate changes in a primary financial statement without these figures affecting the reported profit or loss.

Summary and conclusions

The application of IFRS will bring greater harmonization of accounting practices to multinational groups in the areas of business combinations, segmental reporting and foreign currency translation. This will be particularly true of groups based in Europe where these areas of accounting have been flexible through the choices offered by the Seventh Directive and the silences of the Seventh Directive. US multinationals, and those based in other countries that have followed US GAAP, have applied the standards of one regulatory body, the FASB, but within those standards there has again been flexibility of choice. The FASB has removed some of the flexibility surrounding business combinations and is working with the IASB on the convergence of accounting for business combinations. In the area of segment reporting IAS 14 offers a leading example to many countries and is of comparable standard to US GAAP, if not identical in detail. On foreign currency IAS 21 brings greater harmonization, particularly across Europe where the Directives did not address the issue and so left considerable flexibility.

In all these accounting matters it is important to be aware that flexibility of choice still exists within the IFRS. It is necessary to read the accounting policies and notes to the accounts to understand how particular companies have used that flexibility of choice and to consider its relevance to the company. A fundamental concern is that this harmonization of accounting rules may create underlying disharmony if the economic situation of a particular group of companies is not well represented by the accounting practices applied. This leads to the question of whether accounting reports reality or creates reality.[99]

---

[96] Richard (2001) p. 1166.
[97] Ordelheide (2001) pp. 1397–1399.
[98] Klaassen (2001) p. 2031.
[99] Hines (1988).

Key points from the chapter:

In reading the annual report of a multinational group and considering its comparability with other groups, ask the following questions, each of which may potentially affect the reported profit or loss and net assets:

● How is the group defined, and are there any exclusions?

● Has the group applied the purchase method of accounting or pooling of interests?

● How has the group calculated goodwill on acquisition and how is it amortized or tested for impairment

● How does the group identity associates and joint ventures and how are these reported – equity method or proportionate consolidation?

● What is the basis of defining segments and what does the segment information reveal about segment performance?

● How has the group chosen its functional currency and presentation currency? How have changes in rates of exchange affected the shareholders' equity?

Questions

The following questions test your understanding of the material contained in the chapter and allow you to relate your understanding to the learning outcomes specified at the start of this chapter. The learning outcomes are repeated here. Each question is cross-referenced to the relevant section of the chapter.

Defining a group

1 What are the main problems in defining a group for consolidated financial statements?

2 How does IFRS define a group? (section 16.2.2)

3 What are the similarities and differences of US, Japan and EU countries when compared to each other and to IFRS? (sections 16.2.3, 16.2.4, 16.2.5)

4 How will IFRS improve harmonization of definition of a group? (section 16.2)

5 Are there any problems with global harmonization based on the IFRS definition of a group? (section 16.2)

Acquisitions and uniting of interests

6 What are the main problems in defining an acquisition and a uniting of interests? (section 16.3.1)

7 How does IFRS deal with the problem of defining an acquisition and a uniting of interests? (section 16.3.2)

8 What are the similarities and differences of US, Japan and EU countries when compared to each other and to IFRS? (sections 16.3.3, 16.3.4, 16.3.5)

9 How will IFRS improve the accounting treatment of acquisitions and uniting of interests? (section 16.3)

10 Are there any problems with the IFRS approach to acquisitions and uniting of interests? (section 16.3)

Goodwill on acquisition

11 What are the main problems in defining and measuring goodwill? (section 16.4)

12 How does IFRS deal with the problem of defining and measuring goodwill? (section 16.4)

13 What are the similarities and differences of US, Japan and EU countries when compared to each other and to IFRS? (sections 16.4.3, 16.4.4, 16.4.5)

14 How will IFRS improve the accounting treatment of goodwill? (section 16.4)

15 Are there any problems with the IFRS approach to accounting for goodwill? (section 16.4)

Associates and joint ventures

16 What are the main problems in defining and reporting associates and joint ventures? (section 16.5.1)

17 How does IFRS deal with the problem of defining and reporting associates and joint ventures? (section 16.5.2)

18 What are the similarities and differences of US, Japan and EU countries when compared to each other and to IFRS? (sections 16.5.3, 16.5.4, 16.5.5)

19 How will IFRS improve the accounting treatment of associates and joint ventures? (section 16.5)

20 Are there any problems with the IFRS approach to associates and joint ventures? (section 16.5)

Segmental reporting

21 What are the main problems in defining and reporting segments? (section 16.6.1)

22 How does IFRS deal with the problem of defining and reporting segments? (section 16.6.2)

23 What are the similarities and differences of US, Japan and EU countries when compared to each other and to IFRS? (sections 16.6.3, 16.6.4, 16.6.5)

24 How will IFRS improve the accounting treatment of segment reporting? (section 16.6)

25 Are there any problems with the IFRS approach to segment reporting? (section 16.6)

Foreign currency translation

26 What are the main problems in foreign currency translation? (section 16.7.1)

27 How does IFRS deal with the problem of foreign currency translation? (section 16.7.2)

28 What are the similarities and differences of US, Japan and EU countries when compared to each other and to IFRS? (sections 16.7.3, 16.7.4, 16.7.5)

29 How will IFRS improve the accounting treatment of foreign currency translation? (section 16.7)

30 Are there any problems with the IFRS approach to foreign currency translation? (section 16.7)

References and further reading

Edwards, P. and Smith, R.A. (1996) 'Competitive disadvantage and voluntary disclosures', *British Accounting Review*, 28(2): 155–172.

Emmanuel, C.R. and Garrod, N. (2002) 'On the relevance and comparability of segmental data', *Abacus*, 38(2): 215–234.

FASB (1997) *Statement of Financial Accounting Standards 131: Reporting Disaggregated Information About a Business Enterprise*. Financial Accounting Standards Board.

Gray, S.J. and Radebaugh, L. (1984) 'International segment disclosures by US and UK multinational enterprises: a descriptive study', *Journal of Accounting Research*: 351–360.

Herrmann, D. (1996) 'The predictive ability of geographic segment information at the country, continent and consolidated levels', *Journal of International Financial Management and Accounting*, 7(1): 50–73.

Hines, R. (1988) 'In communicating reality, we construct reality', *Accounting, Organizations and Society*, (13)3: 251–261.

International Accounting Standards Committee (1997) *IAS 14 Revised: Segment Reporting*.

Klaassen, J. (2001) 'The Netherlands – Group accounts', in Ordelheide, D. and KPMG (eds), *Transnational Accounting TRANSACC*. Basingstoke and New York: Palgrave.

Kuroda, M. (2001) 'Japan – Group accounts', in Ordelheide, D. and KPMG (eds), *Transnational Accounting TRANSACC*. Basingstoke and New York: Palgrave.

Ordelheide, D. (2001) 'Germany – Group accounts', in Ordelheide, D. and KPMG (eds), *Transnational Accounting TRANSACC*. Basingstoke and New York: Palgrave.

Richard, J. (2001) 'France – Group accounts', in Ordelheide, D. and KPMG (eds), *Transnational Accounting TRANSACC*. Basingstoke and New York: Palgrave.

Roberts, C.B. (1989) 'Forecasting earnings using geographic segment data: some UK evidence', *Journal of International Financial Management and Accounting*, 1(2): 130–151.

Street, D.L. Nichols, N.B. and Gray, S.J. (2000) 'Segment disclosures under SFAS131: has business segment reporting improved?', *Accounting Horizons*, 14(3): 259–286.

Williams, J.R. and Carcello, J.V. (2004) *Miller GAAP Guide 2004*, New York: Aspen

Wilson, A., Davies, M., Curtis, M. and Wilkinson-Riddle, G., *UK and International GAAP*. London: Butterworths Tolley with Ernst & Young.

Index

CAREERS OFF THE FIELD

Sports Marketing

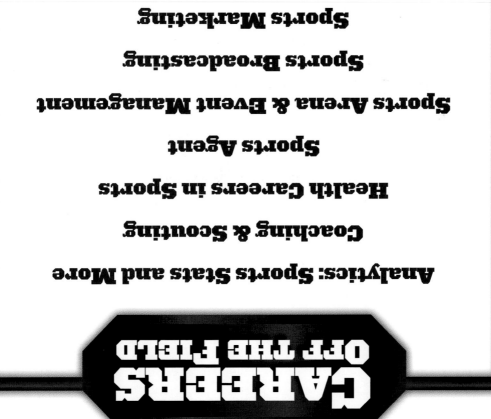

CAREERS OFF THE FIELD

Analytics: Sports Stats and More

Coaching & Scouting

Health Careers in Sports

Sports Agent

Sports Arena & Event Management

Sports Broadcasting

Sports Marketing

Sports Media Relations

Sportswriting and Sports Photography

Working in College Sports

Sports Marketing

By Brian C. Peterson

CAREERS OFF THE FIELD

Mason Crest

450 Parkway Drive, Suite D
Broomall, PA 19008
www.masoncrest.com

Printed and bound in the United States of America.

Series ISBN: 978-1-4222-3264-4
Hardback ISBN: 978-1-4222-3272-9
EBook ISBN: 978-1-4222-8530-5

First printing
1 3 5 7 9 8 6 4 2

Produced by Shoreline Publishing Group LLC
Santa Barbara, California
Editorial Director: James Buckley Jr.
Designer: Bill Madrid
Production: Sandy Gordon
www.shorelinepublishing.com
Cover photo: Imdan/Dreamstime.com

Library of Congress Cataloging-in-Publication Data
Peterson, Brian C.
    Sports marketing : careers off the field / by Brian C. Peterson.
    pages cm
    Includes index.
ISBN 978-1-4222-3272-9 (hardback) -- ISBN 978-1-4222-3264-4 (series) -- ISBN 978-1-4222-8530-5 (ebook) 1. Sports administration--Juvenile literature. 2. Sports--Marketing--Juvenile literature. 3. Sports journalism--Juvenile literature. 4. Sports medicine--Juvenile literature. I. Title.
GV713.P47 2016
796.06'9--dc23
                               2015006712

CONTENTS

Key Icons to Look For

Words to Understand: These words with their easy-to-understand definitions will increase the reader's understanding of the text, while building vocabulary skills.

Sidebars: This boxed material within the main text allows readers to build knowledge, gain insights, explore possibilities, and broaden their perspectives by weaving together additional information to provide realistic and holistic perspectives.

Research Projects: Readers are pointed toward areas of further inquiry connected to each chapter. Suggestions are provided for projects that encourage deeper research and analysis.

Text-Dependent Questions: These questions send the reader back to the text for more careful attention to the evidence presented here.

Series Glossary of Key Terms: This back-of-the-book glossary contains terminology used throughout this series. Words found here increase the reader's ability to read and comprehend higher-level books and articles in this field.

Foreword

By Al Ferrer

So you want to work in sports? Good luck! You've taken a great first step by picking up this volume of CAREERS OFF THE FIELD. I've been around sports professionally—on and off the field, in the front office, and in the classroom—for more than 35 years. My students have gone on to work in all the major sports leagues and for university athletic programs. They've become agents, writers, coaches, and broadcasters. They were just where you are now, and the lessons they learned can help you succeed.

One of the most important things to remember when looking for a job in sports is that being a sports fan is not enough. If you get an interview with a team, and your first sentence is "I'm your biggest fan," that's a kiss of death. They don't want fans, they want pros. Show your experience, show what you know, show how you can contribute.

Another big no-no is to say, "I'll do anything." That makes you a non-professional or a wanna-be. You have to do the research and find out what area is best for your personality and your skills. This book series will be a vital tool for you to do that research, to find out what areas in sports are out there, what kind of people work in them, and where you would best fit in.

That leads to my third point: Know yourself. Look carefully at your interests and skills. You need to understand what you're good at and how you like to work. If you get energy from being around people, then you don't want to be in a room with a computer because you'll go nuts. You want to be in the action, around people, so you might look at sales or marketing or media relations or being an agent. If you're more comfortable being by yourself, then you look at analysis, research, perhaps the numbers side of scouting or recruiting. You have to know yourself.

You also have to manage your expectations. There is a lot of money in sports, but unless you are a star athlete, you probably won't be making much in your early years. I'm not trying to be negative, but I want to be realistic. I've loved every minute of my life in sports. If you have a passion for sports and you can bring professionalism and quality work—and you understand your expectations—you can have a great career. Just like the athletes we admire, though, you have to prepare, you have to work hard, and you have to never, ever quit.

Series consultant Al Ferrer founded the sports management program at the University of California, Santa Barbara, after an award-winning career as a Division I baseball coach. Along with his work as a professor, Ferrer is an advisor to pro and college teams, athletes, and sports businesses.

Introduction

Words to Understand

brainstorming: the act of thinking of ideas with a group of people

campaigns: series of promotional events and activities used to support a marketing theme, usually conducted during a set period of time

intern: a person, usually a student, who works for free to learn a new job or career

licensee: a company that pays a fee, or license, to gain the right to use a sports or company logo

Sports marketing happens on a daily basis all over the world, from the largest cities, such as New York, Tokyo, and Paris, to smaller towns, such as Green Bay, Manchester, England; and Ottawa, Canada. Teams being marketed to fans include those with names such as the Pelicans, Wild, Sand Gnats, Salukis, Anteaters, Horned Frogs, and Banana Slugs. Companies use every sport imaginable to sell products used daily by billions of people. The people who do the work of selling those teams or using sports to sell to others are sports marketing professionals.

Sports marketers do everything from getting coffee for star athletes to stuffing envelopes with thank you letters. They fill hot tubs with water, speak to youth groups, count thousands of promotional fliers, verify the number of bobbleheads being given away on game day, or write and approve scripts for advertising campaigns. They work for teams to help promote the organization to fans and sponsors. They also work with companies wanting to use sports as a way to sell their products or services. They arrange events attended by a few dozen people, and manage campaigns that will be seen by billions.

The average day of a sports marketer can start at the first ray of sunlight in a large empty stadium with sprinklers showering freshly mowed grass. It can also begin with a group of people **brainstorming** ideas in an air-conditioned conference room. Many times the day ends well past midnight, when the last car leaves the stadium parking lot.

There is no such thing as an average day in sports marketing. There is also no such thing as a typical type of sports marketing, which includes team, league, college, television, **licensee**, sponsorship, youth, extreme, and club.

Sports marketing is part of the overall practice of marketing, which involves helping individuals and organizations easily exchange goods and services. In sports marketing, organizations or teams work hard to satisfy the needs and wants of fans, which usually revolve around winning championships. Fans want value, and successful sports marketers are masters at delivering superior value to fans.

Meg Patten studied at New York University at the Tisch Institute for Sports Management, Media, and Business. In the summer of 2014, she worked as an **intern** in the sports marketing department of Fox Sports San Diego, the television network

of Major League Baseball's San Diego Padres. Her day began before she even got to her office.

"I was constantly checking scores, staying up to date with all sports news, and posting to social media outlets before, during, and after work," she said. "While I was in the office, the marketing team would meet to discuss weekly events, games, and goals."

Her marketing group was tasked with promoting everything from the game itself to a volunteer opportunity to a surfing contest. "Every day was different and allowed me to do a bunch of different things that relate to the business of sports broadcasting," she said.

Companies put their messages in front of huge audiences at sports events, such as on this scoreboard at San Diego's Petco Park.

Patrick Klinger is one of America's most influential sports marketers. Klinger is the chief executive officer (CEO) of Patrick Klinger & Company, a leading sports marketing agency. Before starting his own firm, he served as the vice president of marketing for the Minnesota Twins for 14 years. While he was working there, the baseball team was named "Sports Organization of the Year" in 2002 by Horizon Awards, and Klinger was the Horizon "Sports Person of the Year" in 2006.

While with the Twins, Klinger managed all areas of advertising, promotion, broadcasting, game presentation, special events, and emerging markets. He was a leader in the design of the Twins' new ballpark, Target Field, which often is considered among the best in baseball. He also has been widely credited for the bobblehead doll craze that has swept sports.

"A typical day is dependent upon where we are in the season," said Klinger. "The off-season is a time of planning and preparation, including development of the advertising campaign, creation of collateral materials, coordination of promotions and special events, and determining pricing. We also have off-season events to keep the team in the public eye. During the season, everything is adjusted based on the team's win-loss record, trades, player acquisitions, etcetera."

Bill Robertson serves as commissioner of the Western Collegiate Hockey Association (WCHA), where he oversees all the business operations. The historic conference has ten teams competing at the Division I level in collegiate hockey in five different time zones across the United States. Before leading the WCHA, Robertson was vice president of communications and broadcasting for the NHL's Minnesota Wild from 1999 to 2011. During that time, he helped establish the then-new franchise and the events it hosted. The experienced sports executive has also worked for the Los Angeles Angels baseball team, the Minnesota Timberwolves of the NBA, and the NHL's Anaheim Ducks, while also

Bill Robertson had a marketing challenge introducing a new team to the NHL when the Minnesota Wild joined the league in 2000.

working for the U.S. Olympic hockey teams. Like many sports marketers, his skills transfer fairly easily among different sports. "I think the thing that's most typical is that there is not a typical day in sports marketing or communications," said Robertson. "The biggest thing is that you enter each day with a detailed game plan of what you want to accomplish. At a moment's notice in sports, you can get thrown off by a trade, a

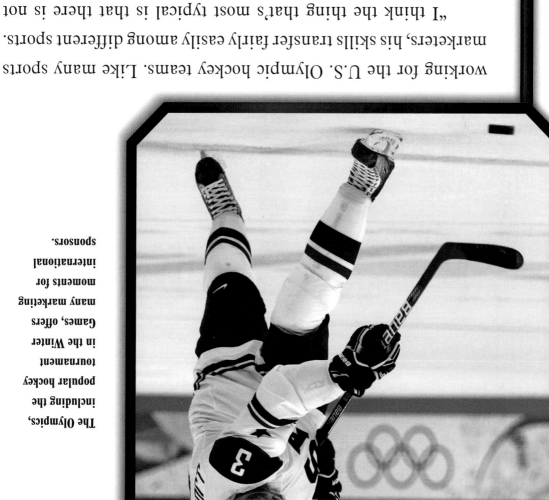

The Olympics, including the popular hockey tournament in the Winter Games, offers many marketing moments for international sponsors.

new business hire, or a new sponsorship that comes in the door.

"You have to be able to react quickly to the changing landscape. This is one of the biggest challenges that marketing people face. You may only get to pieces of your detailed plan, but at least you keep the ball moving forward. Organization and attention to detail are really key to being a successful sports marketer."

———

Sports marketing can be consuming, and no matter the sport, there is no rest or "regular" season to it. If you love the game, though, the hard work is all worth it. Part of your working day might include the roar of a jet airplane flyover before kickoff, the crack of the bat, the squeak of shoes on hardwood, or the quiet claps when the ball lands two inches from the cup. Read on to see what it takes to be part of the game.

Words to Understand

brand: the name or image of a team, and the value associated with the name and image

focus group: a random set of people brought together to test products, ads, or marketing plans

imperative: the most important; vital; key

perseverance: the ability to stick to a task with focus and determination for a long period of time

vision statement: a short and direct written description of what an individual or organization aspires to be

Getting Started

CHAPTER 1

Just as there are many different sports marketing opportunities (that's NASCAR star Jimmie Johnson covered with logos at left), there is no set way to get an education in this field. There are, however, some general guidelines to follow.

The first step is to set a vision for yourself. A **vision statement** is usually very short, but direct, with a focus that can be measured. It might read like this: "I want to become a creative sports marketing wizard for a professional sports team in a small-market city." The vision statement attempts to describe where you want to go in your sports career, what area of sports you want to aim at (youth, college, pro?), and what area you want to work in.

Creating a vision statement is how a successful business launches its marketing campaigns. Everything the campaigns do ties back to a bigger goal.

Education

A doctor or a lawyer zeroes in on one particular career and educational path. People aiming at sports marketing need knowledge in many areas.

just one project at a time."

have the luxury of focusing on success. Sports marketers don't projects at once is critical to And the ability to juggle many skill that isn't taught in school. opportunities is an important create, and take advantage of Having creativity to identify, customer is also **imperative.** the wants and needs of your Klinger, the former Twins' executive. "The ability to understand that requires excellent communication skills," said Patrick colleagues, sponsors, vendors, media, players, and fans, and "A sports marketing professional is always dealing with

Picking a School

According to *U.S. News and World Report,* the top 10 universities for marketing in 2014 are the following:

- **University of Michigan–Ann Arbor**
- **University of Pennsylvania**
- **University of Texas–Austin**
- **Indiana University**
- **University of California–Berkeley**
- **University of North Carolina–Chapel Hill**
- **New York University**
- **University of Virginia**
- **University of Wisconsin–Madison**
- **University of Southern California**

Other top sports marketing programs are at Oregon, Syracuse, Ohio, Florida, and North Carolina State.

They might have any of a wide range of college degrees, and in many cases more than one.

The most common college major for sports marketing is marketing. However, because sports marketing requires the ability to tell stories, understand the preferences and mentality of sports fans, plan events, and think of creative ideas, it's just as useful to get degrees in advertising, journalism, writing, psychology, sociology, business, economics, or design.

"In college, I would recommend speech and business communications, public relations, marketing, and advertising," said Bill Robertson, the longtime hockey marketing executive. "For electives, if you're targeting sports marketing, coaching and sports theory classes can be helpful. You need to find ways to better understand sports in general."

"Marketing, advertising, and public relations are all big parts of sports marketing, so I'd recommend taking those, too."

Taking a class in which you have to make presentations to a group can be a big asset.

added Lauren Dunn, who worked at the major advertising company Saatchi & Saatchi on many pro motor sports campaigns. "Also, if specific course offerings in the sports management and/or sports marketing areas are available, I'd recommend those, too."

On the other hand, some experts feel that students don't need to specialize to make it in sports marketing. "I don't believe a sports marketing degree is essential," said Klinger. "Any well-rounded education combined with a strong work ethic and **perseverance** can lead to success."

Internships

A college degree is very important, though there are many options to choose from. However, experts also agree that hands-on experience is the best way to learn this business.

Undergraduate and graduate degrees in advertising (from Michigan State) helped Lauren Dunn launch a long and successful sports marketing career.

"There's no better training ground nor road to a career in sports management than an internship with a prominent organization," said Klinger.

From the author: As a high school senior who was going to play college football on a scholarship, I still felt the necessity to begin searching for internships if I wanted a career in sports. Early in the process, my high school principal mentioned to me that he had a close friend who worked for the NFL and would be glad to make an introduction if I wanted.

In my haste, I forgot about the offer and proceeded to send out hundreds of applications and letters for an internship to minor league, college, and professional sports teams. I didn't receive a single positive reply. Not even a nibble. The hundreds of rejection notices tested my resolve. Fortunately, I ran into my principal again, and he reminded me of the offer. This time, I welcomed the help, but also doubted whether it would work. I had been rejected by too many sports organizations to count. Why would the NFL want me?

My principal reached out to his friend, and I sent in my application and résumé. Less than a week after sending my information, I received a call from the NFL. My principal's friend said that the league didn't normally need interns, but they

liked my previous work and wanted to give me a shot. I would have worked for free, but gladly accepted the offer of a small hourly wage. Most of my job consisted of working on projects that helped market the NFL teams and the league's sponsorships.

It turned out to be a break of a lifetime. Not only did I complete two internships with the NFL and gain an opportunity to work with the U.S. Olympic Committee because of that work, but I also ultimately received a full-time work offer from the NFL after graduating from college.

That experience is typical of thousands of people working in sports. The internships—with teams, leagues, schools, companies, or media outlets—can be challenging to obtain. They are worth the effort, however, providing contacts that will pay off down the road.

Traits

The list of traits necessary for sports marketing work is long. It starts with a passion for the game, creativity, and the ability to do research.

A person needs knowledge of the fans, must be a consumer of information, and must have a strong work ethic. All of those things are essential to make it as a sports marketer.

"Personal traits include flexibility, being a bridge-builder, being someone who not only listens but understands, and being someone who is solution-oriented," said Dunn. "Necessary professional skills include having a keen eye when it comes to evaluating sponsorship proposals."

Dunn added that creativity and kindness are important. People who know how to lead and motivate a team will have far more success in the long run than people who dictate and demand.

Can you sell your ideas to a group of people? Can you create a winning proposal? Sports marketing pros can do both.

"Public-speaking skills are important," added Robertson. "You'll need writing and editing skills. People skills are important in situations from large boardrooms to small meetings. You need to know how to resolve conflict, quickly and efficiently. We need people that are detail oriented with a sense of humor that can adapt and be flexible. Most importantly, marketing professionals need common sense."

Jane Brown Grimes often has taken to the podium during her long career in the tennis industry. She was chief executive officer and, later, chairman of the board of the United States Tennis Association, with marketing as one of her key duties.

Growth Market

"I feel sports marketing is growing as an element of the overall marketing mix," said Dunn. "Sports marketing is not just about slapping signs on a stadium, track, or arena—it's also about having frequent access to your customers; it's like a

International marketing is a key part of many sports organizations, such as this display in China for the NBA.

giant **focus group** waiting to be tapped. Any type of marketing requires creativity, problem solving, and having an eye for the big picture. Being able to use the loyal fan base at your fingertips for the good of your team is invaluable to both a **brand**'s growth and a marketer's career."

"I think it's growing, but people need to be creative in how they look at it," said Robertson. "There are only a limited number of teams in professional sports, and jobs are limited. But if people open up their minds to look at minor-league sports, events, arenas, and venues, there are a lot more opportunities than people know about. If they are creative and are persistent and network, there is the ability to find these jobs."

"Sports marketing is a growing, yet changing, career," said Klinger. "There's much more focus on social media, statistics,

Show Them the Money

According to salary information on the job search Web site Indeed.com, the entry-level salary for a sports marketing project manager is $45,000 to $60,000 per year. Salary increases to $70,000 to $110,000 after ten years in the field. A marketing brand manager earns from $35,000 to $60,000 to start and $70,000 to $140,000 after ten years. These jobs pay well, but they also have a lot of stress and need a lot of hours worked to be successful.

trends, research, segmentation and psychographics than when I first entered the field. There are many more tools at a marketer's disposal. Figuring out which ones to use and which ones to avoid is an on-going challenge. What's hot today can be gone tomorrow."

Text-Dependent Questions

1. What are three traits the experts say are needed to be a successful sports marketer?

2. Along with a college degree, what is the best way to get your foot in the door in sports marketing?

3. List three different college degrees that can be useful for marketing.

Research Project

Write a cover letter to a sports organization, college, or company that you would send to apply for an internship. You can find actual internships listed on the organization's Web site in the careers section.

Words to Understand

embed: in journalism, to place a journalist or camera crew into combat operations with a military unit for the purpose of reporting

programming: in this case, all the television productions surrounding a sports team, including live game coverage and other special shows

target audience: the specific group of fans that you want to purchase your goods or services

Hard at Work

CHAPTER 2

What does an award-winning sports marketing campaign look like? It's a big idea, theme, or concept that ultimately becomes a way for a sports organization or organizations to deepen their relationships and connections with fans, customers, viewers, or communities.

In 2006, the Minnesota Twins and their official television partner, Fox Sports North, wanted to show their appreciation and commitment to their fans. At that time, there were thousands of military members from the region serving in Iraq.

The Twins and Fox Sports joined with the Minnesota National Guard and came up with the idea of "Freedom Week" and "Operation Home Base" (pictured at left). They wanted to connect local troops serving in Iraq with their families in the week leading up to the Fourth of July holiday. To show viewers the accomplishments of—and challenges facing—the troops

overseas, they would use **programming** created by a sports reporting crew in Iraq. They wanted to create a lasting impression that Fox Sports North and the Minnesota Twins were willing to support local communities throughout the region. They wanted to do something that no cable sports network had ever done.

The results were incredible. Fox Sports and the Twins won television Emmy Awards, national programming awards, and community-relations awards. Television ratings and stadium attendance both went up. The biggest success was the lasting reaction they received from the community at which these efforts were targeted. From across the state of Minnesota and the surrounding region, thousands of emails and letters of support and thanks were sent to the Twins and Fox.

Having the ability to come up with big ideas like this one, ideas that are easy to understand and that connect on a personal level with your **target audience,** is one of the most important traits of a great sports marketer.

Step-by-Step

Here's how that award-winning campaign came together. In the fall of 2005, meetings were held with the Minnesota National Guard, Fox Sports, and the Twins. The groups

During the Twins' Freedom Week, members of the military spoke about their service to stadium crowds.

brainstormed ideas and ultimately decided to create a special "Freedom Week" of programming. The shows would be part of the Twins' pregame and postgame shows around live games on June 26, 27, 28, and 30 in 2006. "Freedom Week" would wrap up with "Operation Home Base," a commercial-free telecast of the Twins and Milwaukee Brewers game on July 1, 2006.

Sports-watching soldiers like these enjoyed connecting to the Freedom Week celebrations.

To make the campaign unique, Fox Sports decided to become the first sports network ever to **embed** a reporting team overseas. That crew would transmit live features and interviews from Iraq. To do that, they had to obtain body armor and security clearances for the reporting team.

The entire campaign was coordinated closely with the National Guard in Minnesota and in Iraq to secure satellite time

and develop a plan that featured soldiers and their families. The production equipment had to be protected so that it could withstand the intense environment in Iraq, which had sandstorms and temperatures as high at 130°F (55°C).

Fox Sports North worked with all of its team partners (the Twins, Minnesota Wild of the NHL, Minnesota Timberwolves of

Servicemen even picked up their instruments to serenade Twins' fans waiting for the first pitch.

the NBA, Minnesota Vikings of the NFL, and the University of Minnesota) and the Major League Baseball Players Association to send care packages to the troops in Iraq. The packages included items such as Xbox games, T-shirts, hats, and reading material.

Fox Sports had arranged for U.S. troops around the globe to watch the "Operation Home Base" game live on July 1. The June

After the festivities and the marketing was over, it was time for Twins baseball!

26 and 27 Twins-Dodgers telecasts were also put on American Forces Network, seen by more than one million U.S. Armed Forces personnel in 176 countries and aboard 200 ships at sea.

Special logos and television graphics were created for the effort, and a "Freedom Week" and "Operation Home Base" banner even hung across the main drive of the 20th Century Fox Movie lot in Los Angeles during the week. Fox Sports televised live shows from four military locations around Minnesota. The network turned the live shows into large community events.

The reporters who were in Iraq filmed "shout-out" video greetings from U.S. troops around the country. They were shown to more than a dozen other states on the Fox Sports regional networks.

"Operation Home Base" was a commercial-free telecast of the MLB game between the Twins and Brewers. Instead of ads between innings, the network showed visits between troops and family members at the Metrodome (which was then the home ballpark of the Twins). Fans also could see interviews with Twins players and coaches, taped greetings from soldiers, and short features about Minnesotans serving in Iraq. Yes, it cost the Twins some money, but the payoff in good feelings of the fans was worth it.

The game's first pitch, the national anthem, and a rendition of "Take Me Out to the Ball Game" were performed by U.S. soldiers in Iraq. Minnesota Governor Tim Pawlenty provided an in-game taped greeting to the troops, as did a variety of local sports celebrities and personalities from Minnesota. Both teams wore baseball caps during the game that honored all branches of the U.S. military forces.

A great sports marketing campaign involves a wide range of people and ways to get the message out. It helps the team by creating something that brings a positive message. It is targeted to a specific event or, in this case, a series of events

Demolition Marketing

Bill Veeck owned three Major League Baseball teams at different times of his life. He is one of the greatest marketers in sports history. He played a role in the integration of baseball, started the tradition of singing "Take Me Out to the Ball Game" during the seventh-inning stretch, and pioneered the names of players on the backs of jerseys. He once even hired a "little person" to take an official at-bat as a publicity stunt.

Not all of Veeck's stunts were a success. One blunder is considered one of the biggest promotional failures ever. In 1979, he was the owner of the Chicago White Sox, who staged Disco Demolition Night. If fans brought a vinyl disco record to the game, they could get a ticket for 98 cents. The records would then be blown up on the field. Fans poured into the park, and began throwing the discs onto the field. After the explosion before the game, fans rushed the field to dance in the debris. Police had to restore order, and the game against the Detroit Tigers had to be forfeited.

that took place around the world. Everything around those events ties back to the key themes.

The Twins' Freedom Week hit a home run with fans and with the community, thanks to a great plan by a team of sports marketing pros.

Text-Dependent Questions

1. Who was the target audience of "Operation Home Base"?

2. What awards did Fox Sports North and the Minnesota Twins win?

3. Which Fox Sports regional networks received taped greetings from the troops?

Research Project

Choose your favorite team and collect examples of its advertising, news stories, Web site, mobile apps, etc. Once you have all of this, write a short paper about what is positive or negative about the promotion item and offer a couple of personal ideas of what you think would work for the team.

Companies love the PGA Tour because they can target their high-dollar products at fans of the sport.

Words to Understand

liaison: a person who helps communicate between different groups or organizations

CHAPTER 3

Realities of the Workplace

You might get good seats to a game. You might meet a star athlete or get to attend a star-studded pregame party. You might enjoy travel to watch your team play. Those are the fun bonuses for working in sports marketing. Young people aiming for a career in sports marketing need to remember, however, that it is work first. Jobs in this field demand dedication and an ability to work long hours. There are rewards, of course, but there are also costs.

Sports Marketing: 24/7

Some of the best games, matches, or competitions end in overtime or extra innings. For people who choose sports marketing as a career, overtime and extra innings have become just a normal day at work.

A big event such as a Super Bowl creates many opportunities for sports-themed products.

There used to be a time when marketing sports matched the season in which the sport or games were played. For example, the NFL season would begin with preseason in late July and August and end with the Super Bowl in the last week of January.

That is no longer the case. As fan interest has increased to the highest levels ever—and sports marketing played a big role in that growth—sports leagues and teams have become "top of mind" year round. There is no time off, and, because of that,

sports marketers need to be on their game all the time.

Bill Robertson managed the 2004 NHL All-Star Weekend and the World Cup of hockey. He also was the **liaison** between the Minnesota Wild and the NHL for the 2011 NHL Draft. The skills he learned during these "offseason" events

Part of a marketing job when working with a sports league is to help put on major events, such as a league's annual draft, its championship game, or an all-star weekend.

helped prepare him for his job as commissioner of the WACHL.

"The hardest parts of these jobs are the time commitment and the so-called news cycles that are twenty-four hours a day, seven days a week in nature," said Robertson. "The job has changed dramatically. In the past five to seven years, with social media becoming such a dominant factor in everything we do, you can't go to sleep anymore and know that everything has been put to bed for the night.

"I've received calls at midnight. I've received calls at six A.M. wanting a reaction from me on stuff that is either online or tweeted. That's where you learn the balance of how to react to those situations. People think that you just work the games, but that's not the only thing you do. The time that's committed to it is unbelievable."

Because the work seems to never end, Robertson considers it a positive thing that you don't have time to get caught up in the wins and losses because there are so many of both. You can't go up and down with your emotions when working in sports.

Is it worth it? According to Robertson and others who have a passion for sports, you better believe it.

"One of the most satisfying moments of my career came after the 2004 NHL All-Star Game ended," said Robertson. "I was

driving home late at night, and I heard NHL Commissioner Gary Bettman talking on local radio about how this was the most successful All-Star Game ever presented by the NHL.

"Everything turned out extremely well, and I was so pleased by that. I couldn't get over how excited I was. I was overwhelmed. I got letters from all over the country saying what a great experience it was, even though it was extremely cold weather [in Minnesota]."

Patrick Klinger agrees with Robertson's comments about time, and adds that sports marketers also have to develop a thick skin. Fans are very eager to share their opinions—both good and bad—about the teams they love.

"I worked for a very high profile organization with a passionate following," he said of his time with the Twins. "The

Robertson got a thrill when his hard work on the 2004 NHL All-Star Game paid off. A few lucky fans even caught pucks tossed by superstar Jeremy Roenick.

media and fans rarely hesitated to share their opinions. It's also a business that requires a huge time commitment. When the team is playing at home, a sports marketer is expected to be at the game no matter what—if it's during the evening, on a weekend or holiday, or even one of your kids' birthdays. I've missed many family events because they conflicted with a game.

"What often surprises people is the offseason is busier than the season. It's an intense time of planning, selling, and developing new programs. The hardest part is the inability to control what happens on the field. The best marketing can't disguise a bad product on the field.

"Ultimately, fans want to see wins. If the team doesn't win, the beer is flat, and the hot dogs cold, they go home disappointed. That can be frustrating."

Information Is King!

You never know where a great marketing idea or brand design may come from. Carolyn Davidson was a student at Portland State when she had a chance meeting with Nike cofounders Phil Knight and Bill Bowerman, who were both working at the university at the time. Knight originally offered her an opportunity to letter some signs for him. She ended up creating

the legendary Nike Swoosh logo and was paid a "whopping" $35 for her work. Don't feel too bad for her. She also received some stock in the company, which is now worth quite a bit more than what she was originally paid.

Coming up with great marketing ideas is a combination of inspiration and dedication. In order to become a great sports

Sports marketers know the power of branding, and few brands are as instantly well-known as Nike.

marketer, you need to be an eager consumer of information. Read about sports, pop culture, politics, economics, business, entertainment, philosophy, and psychology wherever and whenever you can. There is no shortage of great books, magazine, and online materials to enjoy. From the list on page 47 or other sources, find out all you can about pop culture and sports culture.

The Playing Field

There are more than 146 billion reasons why sports marketing is an excellent place to find a career. According to Statista, a leading statistic portal, total global sports revenue topped $146 billion in 2014. North American sports were the biggest contributors with more than $50 billion generated from ticket revenues, media rights, sponsorships, and merchandising.

The amount of money being spent on professional, college, Olympic, extreme, youth, minor-league, and club sports around the world shows no signs of slowing down. In fact, the numbers are growing at a staggering pace. Headlined by the NFL, U.S. professional sports leagues combined to generate more than $23 billion dollars in profit in 2014.

The average value of an NFL team (there are 32 in the league) tops $1 billion. Super Bowl XLIX in February 2015

American professional sports have become wildly popular on social media. The NBA has more than 20 million Facebook fans, while the NFL has more than 9 million and the NHL, more than 3.9 million. The NBA's Lakers have more the 3.6 million Twitter followers. The New York Yankees lead all MLB teams with 1.25 million, and the NFL's New England Patriots top their league at more than 800,000.

Pro sports are not the only place where sports marketing money—and jobs—can be found. The Summer Olympics in London in 2012 was watched by 114.4 million people, the most ever to tune in to any U.S. broadcast ever.

Reading Up

The American sports business community has some media gathering places. By staying in tune with these publications and sites, you'll help gather information that will help your sports marketing career. Some of these publications offer discounts for students; you can find most of them at the library or online, too.

Newspapers
Wall Street Journal
Investor's Business Daily
The New York Times

Magazines
Sports Illustrated
Sports Business Journal
ESPN the Magazine
Baseball Digest
GOLF
Forbes
Fortune
Bloomberg Businessweek

Web sites
www.sportsbusinessdaily.com
www.espn.com
www.foxsports.com
www.adweek.com
www.gameops.com

generated more than $2.5 billion in television revenue, $950 million in major sponsorships, and millions more in ticket revenue. According to Statista, in 2014 the National Collegiate Athletic Association (NCAA) earned $797 million in revenue, with more than $700 million of that coming from television rights agreements. Look at the more than 75 million people who watched NCAA football games on television, and you have a lot of folks investing a lot of time watching kids play games.

Action-sports events are drawing big crowds of young fans, which marketers are eager to reach.

Don't forget about action sports, such as skateboarding, mountain biking, motocross, snowmobile racing, surfing, freestyle biking, wakeboarding, and others, which currently count more than six million people among a growing number of avid fans. More than 170,000 fans have attended ESPN's X Games since 1995. All those sports have become big parts of many companies' efforts to sell their products.

The numbers tell the story. More than ever, sports marketers are needed to connect fans with their favorite teams, players, sports, and leagues.

Text-Dependent Questions

1. Who created the Nike "Swoosh" logo?

2. When is the best time to create a marketing plan?

3. What new media have revolutionized sports marketing?

Research Project

Set a goal of reading at least five sports article per week. Print them out and save them in a file for future reference.

Words to Understand

marketing mix: the product, price, place, and promotion of the goods and services that are being sold

The Nitty-Gritty

CHAPTER 4

Knowing some of the basic principles of the discipline of marketing is essential to really understanding sports marketing. The earlier chapters shared the definition of marketing and how important it is to set a vision for yourself and whatever you are marketing. We also looked at parts of the sports world and how a campaign comes together.

Now it's time to reveal the secret formula for success. If you learn this formula—and what it means—you'll have the key to succeeding in this field. The following sections break down each part to find the answer. (Hint: The answer is not "26.") Here is the formula:

$$6 + 4 + 5 + 4 + 7 = X$$

6

The number six in the equation stand for the six Ws that have been taught since children entered kindergarten. The first step to marketing is to make sure you answer the six key questions: Who? What? Why? Where? When? How? (Of course, for "how" we count the last letter, not the first.)

Who is the target audience for the marketing campaign that will be executed? What product or service is being communicated, or what outcome is expected? Why is it necessary to include marketing? Where is the area that will best receive your messages? When do you want to start? How is everything going to come together?

Just like a great story, a great marketing plan needs to answer all those questions.

4

The number four represents the four Ps—Product, Price, Place, and Promotion. Those are the four building-block categories for marketing. The elements are fully controlled by your team. How the audience or fans react to your marketing can't be controlled, but the four Ps make up what is commonly called the "**marketing mix.**"

For sports, the product may be the team, a piece of equipment, the stadium experience, or the television programming. Does the product have a good brand name? Is it high quality? What makes it different from the other products in its category?

How much will it cost? That's the price. The price of a product needs to cover the costs of making it, but can't be at more than the customers value it. For example, the New York Yankees have a high payroll, and their fans are accustomed to winning. Therefore, they can charge a higher ticket price than smaller market teams such as the Oakland A's or Arizona Diamondbacks.

In what place will the product be sold? Fans need a convenient place to buy products of their favorite teams. Many new stadiums being built have easy access for the fans from

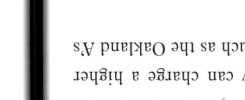

Part of sports marketing is making sure fans enjoy a great experience every time they attend a game.

public transportation, as well as good roads, and lots of parking. Sporting goods stores are located in areas where fans usually shop for other things as well.

Once you know what it is, how much it will be, and where you'll sell, it's time to promote. How are you going to get fans to notice the product? The most common types of promotion are advertising, sales promotion, public relations, and new media. Teams do a lot of advertising, especially on television, billboards, and newspapers. Their ticket sellers include people who sell sponsorships to large companies. The public relations department produces information about the team and works to get stories placed in media. New media include the team's Web sites, its mobile apps, and online advertising.

How do you make sure everyone knows about the event? Use every method you can, from quick tweets to massive billboards.

5

The number five in our formula is a bit less obvious. Harvard University's Michael E. Porter created what is known as Porter's Five Forces. They are often taught in beginning marketing classes. The five forces determine what competition a business might face.

Porter's Five Competitive Forces include Industry Rivalry, Threat of New Entrants, Bargaining Power of Suppliers, Bargaining Power of Buyers, and Threat of Substitutes. College classes will explain these in more detail, but using the NFL as an example, here's a quick look.

There is a lot of rivalry among NFL teams, and that causes each of them to market to their fans. The threat of new entrants is not big, but the league is always considering adding new teams. Companies that supply teams with equipment and stadium goods don't have a lot of bargaining power because there are only 32 teams. The fans have solid buying power because if the price for NFL products gets too high, they don't have to spend their money. Sports are usually a luxury item. The NFL remains very strong because the threat of new entrants is very low. It costs a lot of money to run a professional sports league.

4

The second four in the equation stands for the 4 Cs—Company, Context, Customers, and Competitors. A good marketing mix needs to consider all of these areas. Teams need to constantly evaluate how good their "company" is. That is, how good are the players, how effective are their coaches, and are they all meeting the needs of their fans? Context refers to the environment around them. In 2014, NFL teams began to take a more serious look at their equipment because players were getting a lot of head injuries. This is part of the context of the time; the customers/fans were becoming alarmed at the damage to players. The NFL had to respond to that.

Customers in sports are fans. Teams constantly need to do their best to satisfy the needs, wants, and aspirations of their fans. Finally, teams are always watching their competitors, on and off the field. In sports, the final score is both on the scoreboard and at the bank.

7

The last number in the formula for success is seven, which represents seven areas that marketers need to consider when promoting their products. College marketing and general

business classes will cover these environments in depth, but following is a short sample of how sports marketers might see them.

A sports marketing team worked with NASCAR, Jimmie Johnson's team, and a major hardware store to create this rolling gift store.

Teams need to know as much about their fans as possible. *Demographics* tells teams things about their fans, such as how much money they make, what types of careers they have, how old they are, and a lot more. The *sociocultural* environment describes the general attitudes, values, and

Marketers know how to tailor their ads to the fans they will reach. Tennis fans are often higher-income, so a fancy watch company and an international airline are perfect fits.

behaviors of their fans. The way teams play can reflect the sociocultural environment of their fans, such as the Chicago Blackhawks play like the tough people of Chicago.

The *economic* environment has been very important. When the United States entered a recession in 2008, it was tougher on sports teams to make money because fans had less to spend. Sports teams are equally concerned about the *regulatory* (player safety), *natural* (weather conditions), and *micro* (analysis of individuals in the market

such as players, fans, etc.) environments.

The seventh environment is *technological*, and it has undergone the biggest change of all in recent years. Video games, fantasy sports, and mobile television streaming, among many other developments, have brought the games and sports organizations closer to the fans. Marketers have to be aware of how to use those developments to sell.

X

So what does all this mean? The answer to the equation will always be X. Sports marketers can put all these things together perfectly, but they'll never be 100 percent sure of the outcome. Fans are fickle. One minute they love their teams, and the next minute they are screaming to "throw out the bums." Keeping the basics in mind is essential. After all, it's a matter of winning and losing.

Text-Dependent Questions

1. What are the 4 Cs?"

2. What are the 6 Ws?

3. What are the 4 Ps?

 **Special Research Project**

"The Brand Is Me"

If you are considering becoming a sports marketer or a marketer in general, start first by looking at yourself. You are a brand, just like the Dallas Cowboys, New York Yankees, or Los Angeles Lakers.

In order to market a brand effectively, you need to know as much about the brand as possible. You know more about your brand than anyone else. You exist in a competitive environment. That is, you are looking for a job or a place in a school at the same time many other students are doing the same. How well you do in this search depends on how you are perceived and your ability to develop relationships. When someone thinks of your brand, what do they think?

The following exercise was designed by award-winning marketer Robert Liljenwall, a teacher at UCLA and president of the Liljenwall Group. He is the editor and coauthor of *Marketing at Retail*, the core textbook for the retail marketing industry.

The exercise will help you discover a lot about yourself, and put your future on a solid path. Remember: Any brand resides in the minds of its customers or people with which it interacts.

Answer each of the four major sections below. Once you have answers, create a PowerPoint presentation that you can share with those close to you.

Who are you? List your achievements, key skills and attributes, education, and where you are right now.

How are you perceived? Ask your friends and family how they perceive you. Ask them what they like or don't like about your work or attitude. Get a "fix" on how you measure up to your own self-perception.

What do you need to do to improve the perception of your brand and skills? List things you can do to get where you want to go. Reading this book is a good first step to making an improvement.

If you were a car, what brand/model would you be? Our individual brand choices reflect our self-perception. A car is usually one of the most important "brand statements" we make about who we are. You may also answer: What kind of car would you be today? What kind of car would be you in the future? Identify which choice you make and why.

Have fun! Once you're on your way in college or a career in sports marketing, complete this exercise again. It's always good to evaluate what shape your brand is in.

Find Out More

Books

Spoelstra, Jon. *Ice to the Eskimos: How to Market a Product Nobody Wants*. New York: HarperBusiness, 1997.

Sweeney, Joe. *Networking Is a Contact Sport*. Dallas: BenBella Books, 2011.

Vaynerchuck, Gary. *Jab, Jab, Jab, Right Hook: How to Tell Your Story in a Noisy Social World*. New York: HarperBusiness, 2013.

Wooden, John. *They Call Me Coach*. New York: McGraw-Hill, 2003.

Note: Former UCLA men's basketball coach John Wooden also wrote other books about leadership, management, and coaching that are very popular with sports business leaders.

Web Sites

http://www.theproduct.com/marketing/index.htm

http://www.marketingprofs.com/

Series Glossary of Key Terms

academic: relating to classes and studies

alumni: people who graduate from a particular college

boilerplate: a standard set of text and information that an organization puts at the end of every press release

compliance: the action of following rules

conferences: groups of schools that play each other frequently in sports

constituencies: a specific group of people related by their connection to an organization or demographic group

credential: a document that gives the holder permission to take part in an event in a way not open to the public

eligibility: a student's ability to compete in sports, based on grades or other school or NCAA requirements

entrepreneurs: people who start their own companies

freelance: a person who does not work full-time for a company, but is paid for each piece of work

gamer: in sports journalism, a write-up of a game

intercollegiate: something that takes places between two schools, such as a sporting event

internships: positions that rarely offer pay but provide on-the-job experience

objective: material written based solely on the facts of a situation

orthopedics: the branch of medicine that specializes in preventing and correcting problems with bones and muscles

recruiting: the process of finding the best athletes to play for a team

revenue: money earned from a business or event

spreadsheets: computer programs that calculate numbers and organize information in rows and columns

subjective: material written from a particular point of view, choosing facts to suit the opinion

Index

Credits

About the Author

A former college football player, **Brian C. Peterson** has enjoyed an extensive, award-winning career as a sports communicator and marketer with Fox Sports, the NFL, and the U.S. Olympic Committee. He is the chief media relations officer with Esri, a mapping technology company. He teaches marketing management at the University of Redlands and has taught brand management at UCLA Extension. Peterson earned a bachelor's degree in journalism from the University of Missouri–Columbia, and an MBA from Pepperdine University.

ARMONK YOUTH
JANUARY
2016